Profiles in Contemporary Social Theory

Profiles in Contemporary Social Theory

Edited by

ANTHONY ELLIOTT and BRYAN S. TURNER

SAGE Publications
London • Thousand Oaks • New Delhi

First published 2001

SAGE Publications Ltd
6 Bonhill Street
London EC2A 4PU

SAGE Publications Inc
2455 Teller Road
Thousand Oaks, California 91320

SAGE Publications India Pvt Ltd
32, M-Block Market
Greater Kailash-I
New Delhi 110 048

British Library Cataloguing in Publication data

A catalogue record for this book is
available from the British Library

ISBN 0 7619 6588 2
ISBN 0 7619 6589 0 (pbk)

Library of Congress Control Number 00 136384

Typeset by Keyword Publishing Services
Printed in Great Britain by The Cromwell Press, Trowbridge, Wiltshire

Contents

Acknowledgments

Discussions regarding the scope of this book took place over a lengthy period of time and in various contexts: we carried out the initial planning at cafés in Lygon Street, Carlton; negotiations commenced at the 1998 ASA meetings in San Francisco; and the bulk of editorial work was conducted through daily emails between Melbourne and Cambridge. Many people have helped us in the preparation of the book. Anthony Moran deserves special mention for assisting us with initial editing of the contributions. We are grateful to Chris Rojek and to Jackie Griffin at Sage. We would also like to thank the contributors for their commitment to this project, and for responding to our various queries about earlier drafts. Others who contributed to the book, and whom we would like to thank, are Nicola Geraghty, Caoimhe Elliott, and Eileen Richardson.

Anthony Elliott
Bryan S. Turner

Contributors

Marcos Ancelovici is a PhD candidate in Political Science at Massachusetts Institute of Technology, USA. He is co-author of *L'Archipel identitaire* (1997) and a contributor to *The Encyclopedia of Nationalism*. His work has also appeared in *Citizenship Studies*.

John Armitage is Principal Lecturer in Politics and Media Studies at the University of Northumbria, UK. Among his edited works are *Paul Virilio: From Modernism to Hypermodernism and Beyond* and *Machinic Modulations: New Cultural Theory and Technopolitics*. His most recent editorships are *Economies of Excess* and *Virilio Live: Selected Interviews*.

Jakob Arnoldi is a doctoral student at Goldsmiths College, London University, where he is working on a dissertation on the complexification of sense (of matter, time and others). He is currently editing a special section of *Theory Culture & Society* on Niklas Luhmann (forthcoming).

Patrick Baert is currently Fellow at New Hall, Cambridge, and Director of Studies in Social and Political Sciences at King's College, University of Cambridge. He studied at the Vrije Universiteit Brussel and Oxford University, where he obtained his D.Phil. He was a researcher at the Institut de Sociologie of the Université Libre de Bruxelles before taking up his current post at Cambridge. He is the author of *Time, Self and Social Being* (1992) and *Social Theory in the Twentieth Century* (1998), and editor of *Time in Contemporary Intellectual Thought* (2000).

Caroline Bainbridge lectures in film studies at Buckinghamshire Chilterns University College. She recently completed a PhD on Luce Irigaray and Film at the University of Sheffield. She has published articles on Luce Irigaray and sexual difference and feminist theories of spectatorship as University of Sheffield teaching materials and is currently working on a range of publications related to her research.

Kathleen Blamey writes on modern European philosophy, and has translated into English various works of Paul Ricoeur.

Andrew Bowie is Professor of German at Royal Holloway, University of London. His books include *Aesthetics and Subjectivity: from Kant to Nietzsche* (1990), *Schelling and Modern European Philosophy* (1993), *F.W.J. von Schelling. 'On the History of Modern Philosophy'* (1994), *From Romanticism to Critical Theory. The Philosophy of German Literary Theory* (1997), *Manfred Frank, The Subject and the Text* (editor, 1997), and *F.D.E Schleiermacher. 'Hermeneutics and Criticism' and Other Texts on Language and Interpretation* (1998).

Ann Branaman is an Assistant Professor of Sociology at Florida Atlantic University. Her recent publications include *The Self and Society Reader* (2001) and *The Goffman Reader* (1997).

Patricia Ticineto Clough is Professor of Sociology, Women's Studies, and Intercultural Studies at the Graduate Center, City University of New York. Her books include *Autoaffection: Unconscious Thought in the Age of Teletechnology* (2000), *The End(s) of Ethnography: From Realism to Social Criticism* (1998), and *Feminist Thought: Desire, Power, and Academic Discourse* (1994). Her essays have appeared in *Sociological Quarterly* and *Sociological Theory.*

Nick Crossley is Lecturer in Sociology at the University of Manchester, UK. He has published two books, *The Politics of Subjectivity: Between Foucault and Merleau-Ponty* (1994) and *Intersubjectivity; the Fabric of Social Becoming* (1996), and is currently working on two further books, *Embodied Sociology: Habit, Identity and Desire* and *Making Sense of Social Movements*.

Francis Dupuis-Déri teaches Political Science at Sainte-Marcelline College, Montreal, Canada, and is affiliated to the Research Group in International Security (based at the universities of Montreal and McGill). He is co-author of *L'Archipel identitaire* (1997), and has published in several journals, including *Citizenship Studies, Agone*, and *Études Internationales*. He is currently working on a book on Jewish identity.

Anthony Elliott is Professor of Social and Political Theory at the University of the West of England, where he is Research Director of the Faculty of Economics and Social Science and Director of the Centre for Critical Theory. He was an Australian Research Council Fellow between 1992 and 2000. His recent books include *Subject To Ourselves* (1996), *Freud 2000* (editor, 1998), *Social Theory and Psychoanalysis in Transition* (2nd edn, 1999), *The Mourning of John Lennon* (1999), *The Blackwell Reader in*

Contemporary Social Theory (editor, 1999), and *Psychoanalysis at its Limits* (co-editor, 2000).

Bridget Fowler is Lecturer in Sociology at the University of Glasgow. She is author of *The Alienated Reader: Women and Popular Romantic Literature* (1991) and *Pierre Bourdieu and Cultural Theory* (1997).

Mike Gane is Reader in Sociology in the Department of Social Sciences, Loughborough University. He has written widely on social theory, specializing in the French tradition, and his most recent book is *Jean Baudrillard: in Radical Uncertainty* (2000). He is working on a book titled *French Social Theory: From Positivism to Postmodernism.*

Geoffrey Gershenson is in the Department of Political Science at the University of California, Berkeley. He is writing a dissertation on Rousseau's political thought.

Graeme Gilloch is author of *Myth and Metropolis: Walter Benjamin and the City* (1996) and *Walter Benjamin* (forthcoming).

Sean Homer is Lecturer in Psychoanalytic Studies at the University of Sheffield. He is the author of *Fredric Jameson: Marxism, Hermeneutics, Postmodernism* (1998). He is co-editing *Fredric Jameson: A Critical Reader,* and writing a book on psychoanalysis and cultural theory.

Christina Howells is Professor of French at the University of Oxford and Fellow of Wadham College. She is author of *Sartre's Theory of Literature* and *Sartre: the Necessity of Freedom,* and editor of *The Cambridge Companion to Sartre* and a collection of essays on Sartre's literature. Her most recent publication is *Derrida: Deconstruction from Phenomenology to Ethics* and she is currently working on contemporary French women philosophers. Her research interests centre on Continental philosophy, literary theory, and modern French literature and thought.

Stephen Katz is Associate Professor of Sociology at Trent University, Ontario. He is the author of *Disciplining Old Age: the Formation of Gerontological Knowledge* (1996), and several articles and book chapters on critical aging studies and the sociology of the body.

Douglas Kellner is George Kneller Chair in the Philosophy of Education at UCLA and is author of many books on social theory, politics, history, and culture, including *Herbert Marcuse and the Crisis of Marxism, Critical Theory, Marxism, and Modernity, Jean Baudrillard: From Marxism to Postmodernism and Beyond, Postmodern Theory: Critical Interrogations* (co-author), *Television and the Crisis of Democracy, The Persian Gulf TV War, Media Culture,* and *The Postmodern Turn* (co-author).

Kelly Oliver is Associate Professor of Philosophy and Women's Studies at SUNY Stony Brook. She is the author of *Beyond Recognition: Witnessing Subjectivity* (2000), *Subjectivity Without Subjects: From Abject Fathers to Desiring Mothers* (1998), *Family Values: Subjects Between Nature and Culture* (1997), *Womanizing Nietzsche: Philosophy's Relation to 'the Feminine'* (1995), and *Reading Kristeva: Unraveling the Double-Bind* (1993). She has edited several books, including *Ethics, Politics and Difference in Kristeva's Writings* (1993), and *The Portable Kristeva* (1998).

Paul Patton is Associate Professor of Philosophy at The University of Sydney. He translated Deleuze's *Difference and Repetition* (1994), edited *Deleuze: A Critical Reader* (1996), and is the author of *Deleuze and the Political* (2000). He has published articles on post-structuralism, social and political theory in a number of journals including *Substance, Man and World, Political Studies, Theory and Event,* and *Parallax.*

Richard Polt is Professor of Philosophy at Xavier University, Cincinnati. He is the author of *Heidegger: An Introduction,* and has translated Heidegger's *Introduction to Metaphysics* in collaboration with Gregory Fried.

Michael Richardson is author of *Georges Bataille* (1994), and editor of *Georges Bataille: Essential Writings* (1998).

Chris Rojek is Professor of Sociology and Culture at the Theory, Culture and Society Centre, Nottingham Trent University. He is the author of several books on leisure, culture, and social theory, including *Ways of Escape* (1993) and *Leisure and Culture* (2000).

Joseph Schneider is Professor of Sociology at Drake University. He is co-author of *Giving Care, Writing Self: A 'New' Ethnography* (2000) and *Deviance and Medicalization: From Badness to Sickness* (1990).

Victor Jeleniewski Seidler is Professor of Social Theory in the Department of Sociology, Goldsmiths College, University of London. He has written widely in the areas of social theory, philosophy, ethics, and gender studies. His most recent work includes *Unreasonable Men: Masculinity and Social Theory* (1994), *Recovering the Self: Morality and Social Theory* (1995), *Man Enough: Embodying Masculinities* (1997), and *Shadows of the Shoah: Jewish Identity and Belonging* (2000).

Rob Shields is Associate Professor of Sociology and Anthropology, and a member of the Institute for Interdisciplinary Studies, at Carleton University, Ottowa. He is the author of *Places on the Margin: Alternative Geographies of Modernity* (1989) and *Henri Lefebvre: A Critical Introduction* (1999). He is editor of *Lifestyle Shopping: The Subject of*

Consumption (1991), *Cultures of Internet* (1996), and co-editor of *Social Engineering* (1996).

Barry Smart is Professor of Sociology at the University of Portsmouth. He is author of *Modern Conditions, Postmodern Controversies* (1992), *Postmodernity* (1993), and *Facing Modernity: Ambivalence, Reflexivity and Morality* (1999). He is editor of *Resisting McDonaldization* (1999) and co-editor of *Handbook of Social Theory* (2000).

Nick Stevenson is Lecturer in Sociology at the University of Sheffield. His books include *Culture, Ideology and Socialism: Raymond Williams and E.P. Thompson* (1995), *Understanding Media Cultures* (1995), and *The Transformation of the Media: Globalization, Morality and Ethics* (1999).

Bryan S. Turner is Professor of Sociology at the University of Cambridge. He has held professorial positions at Flinders University (1982–8), University of Utrecht (1988-90), University of Essex (1990–3), and Deakin University (1993-8). His research interests include the sociology of citizenship, medical sociology, and social theory. He is the editor of the journal of *Citizenship Studies*, co-editor of *Body & Society*, and co-editor of the *Journal of Classical Sociology*. He recently edited *Max Weber: Critical Responses* (three volumes) and *Orientalism: Early Sources* (12 volumes). His most recent publication was *Classical Sociology* (1999). He is currently working on two projects: a study of civil society and social capital in the United Kingdom, and the culture and politics of postwar generations.

Michelle Williams is in the Department of Sociology at the University of California, Berkeley. She is writing a dissertation on the Communist Party in South Africa and Kerala, India.

Sarah Wright is Lecturer in the Department of Hispanic Studies at the University of Hull. Her research interests include film studies, modern Spanish literature, psychoanalysis, and literature. She is the author of *The Trickster-Function in the Theatre of García Lorca* (2000).

Editors' Introduction

ANTHONY ELLIOTT AND BRYAN S. TURNER

Profiles in Contemporary Social Theory provides a comprehensive guide to the leading intellectuals and theorists in social theory today. The volume comprises critical discussion of a variety of thinkers that have dominated social and political debate in recent decades. In disciplinary sweep, these figures include sociologists, historians, philosophers, psychoanalysts, and political theorists. Yet the contributions of these individual figures to contemporary social theory consistently illuminate the dangers to knowledge and freedom of limiting reflection on society and the social to any particular discipline. The leading figures in contemporary intellectual life – Jürgen Habermas, Jacques Derrida, Julia Kristeva, Fredric Jameson, Richard Rorty, Luce Irigaray, and Michel Foucault – propose interdisciplinary studies on the self, society, and history.

The motivation leading us to put together this book has been a growing awareness of crucial conceptual and institutional transformations taking place in recent years. During the last two decades in particular, many dominant perspectives in Anglo-American philosophy and social theory have been subjected to sustained critique, dismantling and reconstruction. Structuralist and post-structuralist theory has been energetically deconstructed and appraised, with new constellations of knowledge, including deconstruction, postmodernism, and postfeminism, evolving. Traditions of thought that previously had been marginal or ignored, such as psychoanalysis and hermeneutics, have come to exert a powerful influence across the social sciences. There has also been a proliferation of new discourses and social theories, including structuration theory, postcolonialism, Queer theory, postfeminism, as well as suggestive research programmes such as the theory of world risk society associated in particular with Ulrich Beck (see Seidman, 1998; Delanty, 1999; Elliott, 1999a; Turner, 2000).

Undoubtedly these developments in social thought have been for many people at once daunting and exhilarating: daunting, since the major traditions of classical social theory appear profoundly strained in the face of core institutional transitions now sweeping the globe; exhilarating, since their implications and consequences are not only intellectually important, but point to new possibilities for radical social and political change. Of key significance here are dramatic changes to the contemporary global order. Among these changes are to be counted the intensification of globalization; transnational corporations advancing economic interdependence by communication technology; the techno-industrialization of war; the rapid explosion of new information technologies; the proliferation of identity-politics; and the rise of issues relating to lifestyle, intimacy, sexuality and the body.

In view of these intellectual and institutional changes, there is a pressing need for sustained critical discussion of both the coherence and dispersion of contemporary social theory in the hands of its leading practitioners. *Profiles in Contemporary Social Theory* represents an attempt to meet this need. The authors contributing to this volume are highly distinguished international social theorists, sociologists, and philosophers; all of the *Profiles* are published here for the first time. To facilitate the reader-friendly design of the book, each chapter provides a biographical overview and situates the work of social thinkers in relation to various schools of thought; and each presents both a detailed exposition and critique of the individual figures. Each chapter concludes with a comprehensive bibliography of the thinker's major works, along with details of secondary references. As a result, *Profiles in Contemporary Social Theory* is a state-of-the-art account of the field.

In this introduction we shall sketch a backcloth for the critical discussion of individual thinkers that follow. Our aim is limited. In summarizing some of the major trends in contemporary social theory, we shall chart key themes and traditions that animate the work of leading theorists, of intellectual movements, and of interpretative approaches. We shall divide our commentary around three areas, or sets of debates, in contemporary theory: subjectivity, psychoanalysis, and feminism; modernity, postmodernization, globalism; and Marxism, neo-Marxism, and post-Marxism.

SUBJECTIVITY, PSYCHOANALYSIS, AND FEMINISM

Amid the proliferating topics that preoccupy social theorists today, one question stands out as of core importance: that is, the question of the constitution of the human subject. The issues at stake in the contemporary deconstruction and reconstruction of subjectivity are profound. Some of the key concerns that have crystallized in recent years include the following: the psychological, social, and cultural forms through which individuals are constructed as subjects; the complex, contradictory ways in which individuals define themselves as autonomous, self-legislating, and rational; the emotional investments that individuals come to have in their identities and communities; and the impact that self-constitution carries for understanding the reproduction, disruption, and transformation of society and culture.

It was not until the 1970s, among social scientists of various persuasions, that human subjectivity fell within a space of more considered reflection and critical practice. While the project of the decentring of the subject had been at the heart of structuralist theory for several decades, the emergence of new discursive orientations concerned with the process of subjectivization began where structuralists left off. Following in the wake of Freud, Nietzsche, and Heidegger, a number of leading figures in contemporary intellectual life reconsidered afresh the intersection of psyche and culture. Here the post-structuralist positions of Lacan, Foucault, Derrida, Deleuze, Guattari, and Lyotard are central. These theorists, in various ways, promote interest in the character of human subjectivity, in the crisis of representation, in the relational nature of human experience, and in the unconscious pattern of oppositions (norm/pathology, masculine/feminine, majority/minority) that fuse to connect an identity of reason and reality. Psychoanalytic theory, and especially Lacan's 'return to Freud', has been central to the post-structuralist task of decentring and deconstructing the subject, since Freudian thought profoundly reconfigures the relation of self and Other. Psychoanalysis has of course also been deployed by post-structuralists to question the positioning of the theorist, particularly the male theorist; to debunk – via notions of projection and transference – the link between the One who sees All and programmes of liberation; and to warn of the idealizations and illusions governing modernist dreams of rationality, objectivity, and certitude.

If psychoanalysis has loomed large in the language of post-structuralism, it has played an equally central role in disciplines from sociology to political science to cultural studies. Why this impact? What can psychoanalysis offer social theory? In the writings of Herbert Marcuse, Theodor Adorno, Anthony Giddens, Paul Ricoeur, and Cornelius Castoriadis, to name only a few, psychoanalysis is engaged with critically to analyse afresh the symbolic forms through which individuals represent the social world internally. Through psychoanalysis, social theorists are able to explore, question and critique the rich, imaginary organization of psychic reality and ultimately of selfhood (Elliott, 1999b). Of key importance here is the clash or gap between consciousness, rationality, and agency on the one hand, and unconscious desire, fantasy, and emotion on the other. The notion that conscious awareness is sometimes subsumed within, or swamped by, unconscious forces of the mind has been central to the study of the self and social organization alike. Here the debate over repression is particularly important, as is current concern with the ways in which globalization, postmodernization, and privatization may be adding another repressive layer to subjective experience in the late modern world (Whitebook, 1995; Castoriadis, 1997).

Perhaps more than anywhere else, psychoanalysis has made its biggest impact in feminist theory and gender studies. In broad terms, psychoanalysis has been adopted by feminists not as a supplement to, or displacement of, the history of sexuality and gender studies, but as questioning them, as containing the possibility of a different way of understanding gender oppression. In this area of debate as in others, psychoanalysis means different things to different people. In Anglo-American object-relations theory, and particularly in the work of feminists such as Juliet Mitchell and Nancy Chodorow, feminism engages with Freudian and post-Freudian thought to trace the gender framing of interpersonal relationships – with particular emphasis on the pre-Oedipal mother/child bond. French post-structuralist feminists, including Julia Kristeva and Luce Irigaray, take their cue more from Lacanian psychoanalysis. More specifically in this psychoanalytic context, masculinity and femininity are viewed as subjective, sexual positions; the power of the symbolic order is to fix gender positions so securely that it becomes almost impossible to notice the emotional investment that individuals have in the patriarchal regulation of sexual difference. What has come to be called post-Lacanian feminist theory plays with new ways of figuring sexual difference and with alternative possibilities for reimagining gender. The path-breaking contributions to these debates in feminism and psychoanalysis are discussed and debated in several contributions to this book.

MODERNITY, POSTMODERNIZATION, GLOBALISM

Bewitched by the discourse of the modernity/postmodernity debate, social theory throughout the 1990s became obsessed with the idea that we are living in new times, by thoughts of an alternative and distinct form of social organization from modernity. The one thing that emerged from this debate – throughout a series of controversies in which ambivalence, ambiguity, and indeterminancy reigned supreme – is that a number of core distinctions operate from within the languages of the modern and the postmodern. Postmodernism is distinguished from modernism, above all, as an aesthetic style or cultural movement – principally in the plastic arts and architecture, but in painting, literature and cinema also. In this reading, postmodernism represents an aesthetic reflection upon modernism, its ambitions and limits.

Postmodernity, by contrast, designates a change of mood at the level of interpersonal relationships, social practices, and modern institutions (see Kellner, 1988). A baffling variety of critical terms – 'postmodern condition', 'postindustrial society', 'global age', 'consumer society', 'postmodern scene' – have been deployed to denote a break with modernity, to announce the end of history and the social, and to welcome the collapse of European or Western global hegemony. Various authors in this book sketch out the complex, contradictory ways in which the postmodern impulse has been distinguished from social and cultural forms characteristic of modernism. For some, an inadequate level of specification has dogged the deployment of these terms, while for others the discourse of modernity and postmodernism has produced illumination. What is of interest for us in the present context are the lines of intersection between modern and postmodern social theory; there are, as Bauman (1990, 1997) has argued, high levels of envelopment, containment, translation, and incorporation in the interacting forms of the modern and the postmodern. The organizing frame for this debate is, following Bauman's formulation, postmodernity as modernity without illusions. The postmodern order recognizes the fragile and contested nature of modern living, and directly embraces plurality, ambiguity, contingency, and ambivalence. Yet the postmodern does not eclipse the modern. Modern and postmodern orders cross and tangle – sometimes across different forms of life, and often within identities and communities.

A similar ambiguity is traceable at the level of postmodern theory itself. On the one hand, a wide range of social theorists from Foucault to Baudrillard to Derrida came to be designated as 'postmodern', as having broken with the oppressive hierarchies of classical social theory, as having inaugurated new theoretical constructs designed to assault elitist culture. On the other hand, many of these same theorists came to reject the postmodern label as relevant to their own conceptual and political endeavours. *Profiles in Contemporary Social Theory* provides new sources of insight into both the distinctiveness of, and interconnections between, postmodern social theorists. While it is indeed clear that there is no one approach to postmodern theory, there are nevertheless a number of core themes that run through the writings of radical analysts of the postmodern cultural condition. The interrogation of traditional conceptions of reality, truth, and justice; the ongoing decentring and deconstruction of human subjectivity; the reflexive subversion of epistemological closure; the levelling of low and high culture; the raising of passion, affect, desire, sensation, bodies, erotic flow, difference, and power as sites for radical critique: these themes are central to the postmodernist political project. The distinctive inflections these themes are given in the work of authors including Jean-François Lyotard, Donna Haraway, Luce Irigaray, Paul Virilio, Fredric Jameson, Zygmunt Bauman, and Richard Rorty are discussed in the contributions that follow.

The conditions of this widening of postmodernization are primarily historical, and relate principally to globalization. It has often been argued that globalization does not mark a critical break between the epochs of modernity and postmodernity; this line of commentary tends to stress that global interconnections had their origins centuries ago in the expansion of the world economy and the rise of the modern state (see Wallerstein, 1974). However there are now strong indications that there has been a sudden institutional and cultural enlargement of the process of globalization, involving transnational economic relations and instantaneous electronic communications; the freeing of financial markets and capital transfers; dense webs of regional, national, and international political processes which reach beyond the control of any nation state; the development of a world-wide military order, and the techno-industrialization of war. One can detect such an emphasis upon the deepening and stretching of social relations and institutions across the world market in some recent approaches within sociology, politics, philosophy, and cultural studies. Anthony Giddens, for example, has stressed the organizational predominance of global processes in everything from self-identity and intimacy to class relationships and business cycles. Ulrich Beck also suggests that social, cultural, economic, and political activity has become world-wide in scope, connecting these developments to risks, uncertainties, and hazards of the modernization process in advanced industrial countries. In this framework, globalization is a double-edged phenomenon, producing risk, uncertainty, and fragmentation on the one side, and interdependence, co-operation, and dialogue on the other.

In the postmodern cultural context within which self and social activity evolves, one of the salient features of globalization is that it commands the social imaginary and imagination as never before. For Baudrillard, the global condition of postmodern experience is that of simulation; people are now caught up in an endless play of media images and spectacles, mesmerized by the encircling signs of multinational capital, transfixed by the obliteration of 'reality' and the growing allure of 'hyperreality'. The debate over the impact of postmodernization and globalism upon our psychic landscape has established a plurality of alternative positions, as many of the contributions to this book make clear. For some social theorists, including Baudrillard, Jameson, Deleuze, and Guattari, the postmodern global system outstrips the capacities of any self-understanding, perception, reflexivity. The result is a new fragmentation of experience, erosion of core distinctions between mind and world or self and society, and a schizophrenic shattering of the self. Here personal and cultural life becomes disarmingly episodic, fracturing, inconsequential, and fleeting. Having set out the psychic stakes of postmodernity in this way, such theorists tend to argue for a new politics, described variously as schizoanalysis, cognitive mapping, and the like. Though controversial, many commentators have argued that it is very difficult to derive a coherent political critique from such versions of social theory. For other social theorists, however, postmodernity does not threaten such discontinuity; the postmodern, on the contrary, promotes sensitivity to experience, difference, otherness, and everyday needs and concerns.

MARXISM, NEO-MARXISM, AND POST-MARXISM

Social theory was, and remains, sensitive to the external social and political environment within which it operates. It would be remarkable if this were not the case, in the sense that social theory must be a reflection on the period in which it is set, reflecting the major political and economic transformations of the epoch. Marxism has been a profound and persistent influence on twentieth-century social theory. In putting together *Profiles*, we have attempted to illustrate and explore some of these influences through the work of Theodor Adorno, Jean Baudrillard, Walter Benjamin, Fredric Jameson, Stuart Hall, Henri Lefebvre, Jean-François Lyotard, and Herbert Marcuse. Indeed probably every social theorist in this collection has been, at some stage, influenced by either Marx or Marxism.

The twentieth century saw major changes in the character of Marxist social theory. The critical theorists of the

Franfurt School (represented here in particular by Marcuse and Adorno) attempted to develop Marxism as a general critical theory of modern society through an examination of the relationships between psychoanalysis (especially Freud) and critical theory; the changing character of culture in capitalism (for instance through Adorno's studies of jazz); and the social causes of fascism. They also developed a more sophisticated view of epistemology and the sociology of knowledge. These re-evaluations of Marxism produced a complex and far-reaching body of social theory that, for example, continues in the work of Habermas.

Marxist social theory was also influenced by the discovery of the Paris Manuscripts of the young Marx, which led anthropologists and sociologists to reconsider the humanism of Marx, his philosophical anthropology, and his understanding of alienation. This revival of interest in the early Marx was also stimulated in France by a brilliant interpretation of Hegel by Alexandre Kojéve that drew attention to the importance of Hegel for Marx, and the significance of Hegel's view of community in relation to the state. The revival of interest in the themes of alienation and reification was also dependent on the work of the young Hungarian scholar Georg Lukács whose *History and Class Consciousness* came to have an enduring relevance to the understanding of reification, ideology, and critical theory. The discovery of the young Marx provided some of the philosophical framework for the development of neo-Marxism in Europe. The phenomenology of the young Marx who was influential in the development, for example, of the sociology of Peter Berger and Thomas Luckmann, was eventually challenged by the growth of structuralism which, in the case of Marxism, was developed by Louis Althusser who seriously questioned whether Marxist humanism was scientific, and attempted to develop Marxism as a structuralist theory of the economy, especially the capitalist mode of production. Althusserian Marxism came to have a significant impact on the structuralism of Foucault, on the psychoanalytical work of Lacan, and on Lyotard, as well as feminist social theorists.

These developments in Marxist theory were particularly important in France where Lyotard and Baudrillard developed their perspectives on contemporary society through the framework of Marx's critique of capitalism. The events of 1968 were an important turning point in social theory, and many young radical scholars became disillusioned with the platform of the French Communist Party. This disillusionment with communism came to influence their views of Marxism as a theory, and Baudrillard for example in his analysis of consumerism came to reject Marxism. The crisis of the Soviet Union in the late 1980s reinforced the sense of alienation from organized communism that began with an earlier generation's response to the Soviet invasion of Hungary , the Solidarity movement in Poland, and the Afghan war. As communism did not appear to offer any solutions to capitalism, the validity of Marxism as a social theory became a major issue. With the final collapse of the Soviet Union in 1989–92, there was a widespread sense of the failure of both communism and Marxism, and the sense of failure brought many social theorists to consider the idea of post-Marxism (alongside post-modernism, posthistory and postfeminism). There was a general sense that the fin de siècle had created an environment of general re-appraisal and re-evaluation of the legacy of the twentieth century that expressed itself through the notion of 'post'.

This burial of Marxism will undoubtedly turn out to be premature, if not adolescent. Marxism still provides an important general theory of society that combines economics, politics, and sociology, and offers a critical reflection on basic dimensions of society – equality, justice and ideology being obvious illustrations (see, for example, Eagleton, 1990 and Jameson, 1990). As *Profiles* demonstrates, it is impossible to understand twentieth-century philosophy, economics, politics, and sociology without a thorough grounding in Marxist theory. Marxism has also had an important contribution to make to the evolution of feminism, psychoanalysis, and cultural studies. Marxism will continue to be important because it provides at least one possibility of combining moral analysis with social science, and because it profoundly questions the division between facts and values. It has as a result made a significant contribution to postcolonialism and to the critique of Orientalism. As it becomes clear that the market is not a solution to all of the problems of the twenty-first century, one can feel very confident that there will be a general revival of interest in, as well as further development of, Marxist social theory.

AN EMBARRASSMENT OF RICHES

In attempting to select social theorists for inclusion in *Profiles in Contemporary Social Theory*, we have been faced with an embarrassment of riches. Our difficulty has been the question: who can we leave out? Our main aim has been to secure some balance in our representation of social theory. In our commentary on Marxism, for example, it is clear that generally speaking Marxism has been far more influential in Europe than in North America – a difference that reflects the different history of socialism in Europe and the United States. We have attempted to give some representation of both American and European social theorists, recognizing that the empirical traditions of American sociology and political science have not favoured social theory as such.

We have also attempted to achieve some balance in our selection from various disciplines, especially sociology, anthropology, philosophy, and psychoanalysis. We have also sought to recognize that social theory as such is essentially interdisciplinary, and the theorists whom we have included have made extensive contributions across many fields.

Our principle criterion of selection has, however, been that the social theorist must be relevant to *contemporary* theory. We have attempted to explore those social theories that are currently making a major impact on the analysis of modern culture, society, and politics. We have attempted to avoid being simply fashionable, while still attempting to represent contemporary developments. The theorists included in *Profiles* are generally people who have been active and influential in the second half of the twentieth century, and whom we anticipate will continue to be influential in the twenty-first century.

CONCLUSION

The chapters that follow underscore that a fluid diversification of research agendas is productive for contemporary social theory. Such diversification, emerging from traditions of thought ranging from feminism and psychoanalysis to post-structuralism and postmodernism, engenders new modes for conceptualizing a bewildering array of social phenomena, cultural artifacts, and theoretical discourses in the contemporary epoch. It follows that a critical social theory responsive to these interdisciplinary positions and topics should regard the demand for difference (psychological, social, cultural, political, and historical) as a promising starting point for mapping the terrain of postmodern culture and society. In our view, the primacy of concern for cultural diversity and social divergence in much current social theory emerges not simply from epistemological discontinuities, but from a new social context of globalization, transnational corporations, virtualized communication interaction, individualization, democratization, and the like. However, a critical social theory alert to the changing nature of self and society must be based as much on identity or identification as on difference and otherness, and this necessarily requires a radical engagement in political debate and moral concerns. It is our hope that the reader will find *Profiles in Contemporary Social Theory* a useful and instructive guide to both the parameters of social-theoretical trends and of the nature of social critique.

REFERENCES

Bauman, Z. (1990) *Modernity and Ambivalence.* Cambridge: Polity Press.

Bauman, Z. (1997) *Postmodernity and Its Discontents.* Cambridge: Polity Press.

Castoriadis, C. (1997) *World in Fragments.* Stanford, CA: Stanford University Press.

Delanty, G. (1999) *Social Theory in a Changing World.* Cambridge: Polity Press.

Eagleton, T. (1990) *The Ideology of the Aesthetic.* Oxford: Blackwell.

Elliott, A. (1999a) *The Blackwell Reader in Contemporary Social Theory.* Oxford: Blackwell.

Elliott, A. (1999b) *Social Theory and Psychoanalysis in Transition: Self and Society from Freud to Kristeva.* London: Free Association Books.

Jameson, F. (1990) *Late Marxism.* London: Verso.

Kellner, D. (1988) 'Postmodernism as social theory: some challenges and problems', *Theory, Culture and Society,* 5 (2-3): 239–70.

Seidman, S. (1998) *Contested Knowledge.* Oxford: Blackwell.

Turner, B.S. (2000) *The Blackwell Companion to Social Theory.* Oxford: Blackwell.

Wallerstein, I. (1974) *The Modern World-System.* New York: Academic Press.

Whitebook, J. (1995) *Perversion and Utopia.* Cambridge, MA: MIT Press.

1

Martin Heidegger

RICHARD POLT

BIOGRAPHICAL DETAILS AND THEORETICAL CONTEXT

Martin Heidegger, one of the most significant philosophers of the twentieth century, lived the life of a provincial German academic, interrupted by an unsuccessful foray into political action at the beginning of the Nazi regime. Heidegger was born on 26 September 1889 to a modest family in the Swabian town of Messkirch (his father was the sexton of St Martin's Catholic Church). After brief experiences as a Jesuit seminarian in 1909 and a student of theology, he devoted himself to philosophy, finishing his graduate studies at the University of Freiburg in 1915. He was married in 1917, and served in the military as a noncombatant in 1918. From 1919 to 1923 he was the primary assistant to Edmund Husserl, the leader of the phenomenological movement, at the University of Freiburg. Heidegger taught philosophy at the University of Marburg from 1923 to 1928, and at Freiburg from 1928 to 1945. His first and greatest book, *Being and Time*, appeared in 1927 and quickly made him famous.

Under the National Socialist regime, Heidegger rose to the position of rector of the University of Freiburg in April 1933 and joined the Nazi party in May 1933. He stepped down from the rectorship in April 1934 after administrative conflicts with faculty and students, but maintained his party membership. Refusing an invitation to teach in Berlin (Heidegger, 1981), he remained in Freiburg. After the Second World War, a 'denazification' programme forced him to retire; however, in 1950 he regained the right to teach as an emeritus, and he delivered some lecture courses during the subsequent decade. Heidegger died on 26 May 1976 in Freiburg and was buried in the family plot in Messkirch.

Despite the great volume and range of Heidegger's work, it is best understood as a response to a single question, the question of 'Being' (*das Sein*, not to be confused with *das Seiende* – 'that which is', 'entities', or 'beings'). The question of Being has two dimensions. First, what does it mean (for any entity) to *be*? Although this is a classic metaphysical question, Heidegger argues that metaphysics and all its scientific offshoots have long taken the answer to the question for granted: Being is assumed to be equivalent to *presence*. (Interpreters of Heidegger thus often use the expression 'metaphysics of presence', referring to metaphysical systems that are built on the traditional assumption that to be is to be present.) Second, the question of what it means to be presupposes a prior question: how is it that we human beings understand what it means to be? What enables Being to have meaning for us, or be given to us, at all? This problem involves an investigation of human beings as *Dasein* ('Being-there') – that is, the entity that is distinguished by its ability to understand Being.

Heidegger's main account of *Dasein* is presented in *Being and Time* (Heidegger, 1962, 1996a; for closely related lecture courses, see Heidegger, 1982, 1985). *Being and Time* is a work of hermeneutical, phenomenological ontology. That is, it describes major phenomena that form part of both everyday life and extraordinary experiences; these phenomena are subjected to an ever-deepening interpretation in regard to their fundamental modes of Being. Heidegger interprets *Dasein* as a radically temporal and historical entity, whose way of Being involves essential ties to the past, the future, and the present. First, we essentially have a past, or are 'thrown': we find ourselves in the position of already having an identity and being in a particular situation. (This 'facticity' is made manifest to us in various ways through our moods.) We are unable to remake ourselves and gain complete control over the basis of our existence; instead, we must take up the task of existing on the basis of who we already are. Second, we are essentially 'projecting' future possibilities – not necessarily through explicit planning, but simply by pursuing options for behaviour. In terms of these possibilities, we understand ourselves and our surroundings. Third, thanks to these dimensions of past and future, we are able to inhabit a present, a 'there' or 'world' within which entities can become accessible or 'unconcealed' for us as having various sorts of significance. *Dasein* is essentially 'Being-in-the-world' – that is, we are not isolated minds, but engaged participants in a realm of meaning within which we encounter all sorts of beings.

Being and Time is incomplete. As it stands, it consists of an interpretation of *Dasein* as temporal Being-in-the-world. Heidegger had also hoped to show, however, that time is the 'horizon' for Being – that is, our essential temporality enables us to understand what it means to be. This would undercut the traditional assumption that Being is equivalent to presence, or more precisely 'presence-at-hand' (*Vorhandenheit*). Presence-at-hand is only one mode of Being, which is made available by only one dimension of temporality (the present). Other modes of Being include 'readiness-to-hand' (*Zuhandenheit*, the Being of 'equipment' or useful things) and Being-in-the-world (the Being of *Dasein*). Heidegger planned to use this analysis in a 'destruction' (*Destruktion*) or 'deconstruction' (*Abbau*) of traditional metaphysics, in order to prepare for a new and richer interpretation of Being in general.

However, Heidegger abandoned the project of *Being and Time*, because he decided that it was itself excessively indebted to the tradition. His later work (from around 1930) turns to more fluid and poetic evocations of the happening in which Being comes to have meaning for *Dasein*. From the mid-1930s Heidegger dubs this happening *das Ereignis*, 'the event of appropriation' or 'enowning' (Heidegger, 1999). In enowning, both Being and *Dasein* come into their own within a unique historical 'site for the moment'. The task of human beings is to found this site and enter properly into the condition of *Dasein* by 'sheltering the truth of Being' within entities.

Starting in the late 1930s, Heidegger increasingly de-emphasizes will and subjectivity, stressing that we must wait for the granting of Being and respond gratefully if it is granted to us. In the 1940s he adopts a word from the mystic Meister Eckhart, *Gelassenheit* or 'releasement', to name this attitude (Heidegger, 1966; Zimmerman, 1986). Parallels between this notion and some Taoist and

Buddhist notions, as well as Heidegger's talk of 'the nothing' ('What is Metaphysics?' in Heidegger, 1993a), have led to speculation that he borrowed extensively from East Asian traditions (Parkes, 1987; May, 1996). However, his relation toward the East is perhaps better characterized as one of respect and curiosity.

Heidegger's late thought does not present a systematic doctrine, but circles around several topics of enduring concern. He explores many facets of the 'history of Being', or the story of its manifestations and concealments in the West; he understands Being itself as happening historically, in a dynamic of granting and withdrawal. He names our contemporary understanding of Being *Technik* ('technology' or 'technicity'), and tries to show that this understanding is only one, limited historical 'sending' of Being (Heidegger, 1977). His search for an alternative relation to beings leads him to investigate the work of art as a locus of the strife between 'world and earth' – roughly, a culture's interpretation of beings and the obscure precultural ground of this interpretation ('The Origin of the Work of Art' in Heidegger, 1993a). He also explores language as the 'house of Being' ('Letter on Humanism' in Heidegger, 1993a). Many of his late essays and lectures are devoted to poetry (Heidegger, 1971), especially that of the Romantic poet Friedrich Hölderlin, whom he came to see as a prophet of German destiny (Heidegger, 1996b).

SOCIAL THEORY AND CONTRIBUTIONS

Heidegger claims that he is not interested in human beings in general, but only insofar as they are *Dasein* – that is, only insofar as they are open to Being. This accounts for a certain sketchiness in *Being and Time*'s interpretation of some aspects of our existence: he does not intend to produce a complete anthropology, but only a description of our existence that is sufficiently rich to make manifest our temporality as the horizon for our understanding of Being. Nevertheless, at least five aspects of *Dasein* as presented in *Being and Time* have important implications for understanding society.

The first aspect is *the priority of engaged involvement over theory and assertion*. One of Heidegger's main goals in *Being and Time* is to show that we are primarily in the world by means of *doing* things, in a broad sense, rather than by means of beliefs, theories, concepts, or propositions. (He shows this by way of a detailed interpretation of the everyday 'environment' in which we make and use 'equipment'.) Our relation to other entities is one of 'concern' (*Besorgen*), and our whole way of Being can be called 'care' (*Sorge*); these words are meant to indicate that we relate to things and people primarily by letting them matter to us in engaged involvement, and only secondarily by forming propositional beliefs about them. Theoretical assertions thus always depend on a pretheoretical dwelling in the world; the truths of theory presuppose a primordial truth, in the sense of 'unconcealment', that always accompanies our Being-in-the-world. For social theory, this would imply that interpersonal relations and social structures should primarily be understood not in terms of our opinions, values, or other 'mental' contents, but in terms of how we reveal ourselves to each other in and through practical dealings.

The second aspect concerns *'Being-with'* (*Mitsein*). When Heidegger turns to the question of 'who' is engaged in the world, he tries to show that *Dasein*'s Being is 'Being-with'; in other words, we are essentially social beings (*Being and Time*, sec. 26). Phenomena such as loneliness, withdrawal, and hostility do not show that *Dasein* is fundamentally an atomic individual; instead, they are merely 'deficient modes' of Being-with. Heidegger shows this initially by demonstrating that even when an individual *Dasein* is alone, its everyday environment intrinsically involves 'references' to other *Dasein* who are fellow users and producers of 'equipment'. Thus each *Dasein* necessarily interprets itself in relation to others, and constantly has a sense of 'distantiality' – that is, its status in relation to other *Dasein*. Here Heidegger's analysis undercuts the solitary, first-person perspective of much modern philosophy, as inaugurated by Descartes's 'I think, therefore I am'.

The third aspect relates to *the 'they'* (*das Man*). As essentially social beings, we share a basic repertoire of practices and self-interpretations with the other members of our community. Since this repertoire is fundamentally anonymous rather than individualized, I am not primarily 'I myself', but rather anyone or 'they' (sec. 27). With this expression, Heidegger points to the interchangeability of everyday roles: my practices could, in principle, be performed by anyone else.

The fourth aspect concerns the ideas of *authenticity and inauthenticity*. The anonymity of the 'they' both enables and encourages an 'inauthentic' mode of existence, in which one exists as a 'they-self'. Instead of making our own choices, we usually simply allow ourselves to act and judge as 'one' does – even when we take ourselves to be individual or original (we *all* shrink back from 'the great mass'). We are normally 'falling' into the present world, and we ignore the task of choosing explicitly what we are to make of ourselves. Authenticity, in contrast, is a mode of existing in which one truly behaves as a self: one makes 'resolute' choices and takes responsibility for them. One can be awakened to the need for authenticity by disturbing experiences, such as the mood of anxiety (*Angst*) and the call of conscience, that force one to confront one's own 'Being-towards-death' (the constant possibility of the impossibility of existing) and 'guilt' (indebtedness to the past plus responsibility for the future). One can then recognize that existence is not *completely* anonymous and interchangeable: no one but I can do the job of choosing who I am to be, in the face of my own mortality. However, authenticity does not simply disengage one from the 'they'; this would be impossible, since all one's options grow from one's community and heritage. Authenticity is a responsible and lucid appropriation of one's sociality, rather than a solitary withdrawal from sociality in which one would try to create oneself anew. Heidegger also briefly sketches the difference between some authentic and some inauthentic ways of relating to others. For example, inauthentic 'leaping in' for someone relieves the other of the need to do something, whereas authentic 'leaping ahead' opens up new possibilities for the other. Heidegger claims that this is not a moral distinction, but simply an indication of two different modes of Being-in-the-world.

The final aspect of *Dasein* is *historicality*. Heidegger's most dramatic descriptions of authenticity and of *Dasein*'s temporality are reserved for his account of 'historicality' (sec. 74). An entire community or 'people' (*Volk*) has a shared past (a 'heritage') and a shared range of future possibilities (a 'destiny'); a people 'happens' historically by stretching from a heritage into a destiny. Heidegger proposes that each generation is faced with the task of authentically appropriating its heritage and discovering its destiny, through a process of 'communication and struggle'. A heritage can serve as a source of heroes – role models whose existence can be 'retrieved' creatively and adapted to the unique exigencies of the present situation. There are no ahistorical standards for human existence – only past examples that can be resurrected and transformed into future possibilities.

Around the time of his own abortive attempt at authentically historical action, Heidegger draws some connections between the very general analyses of *Being and Time* and the particular situation of Germany. He asserts that 'historicity' and 'care' imply the desirability of a certain social structure, a regime dedicated to preserving the destiny of the *Volk* through a strong state (Heidegger, 1993b, 1998; Löwith, 1994). This is clearly how he interprets National Socialism during this period.

In the later 1930s, however, Heidegger became increasingly discontented with the Nazi regime. Nazi political measures may have some justification, he thought, but they fail to address the basic issue: the status of the German people's relation to Being. As the people at the centre of the West, the Germans are entrusted with the destiny of reawakening the question of Being (Heidegger, 2000). It is in these terms, and not on the basis of race, that national identity is to be understood (Heidegger, 1999). The Being of a *Volk* is essentially contested and questionable, rather than definable like the Being of an object ('Who are we?', Heidegger likes to ask). By the end of the decade, he was looking not to Hitler, but to the poet Hölderlin as the spokesman for national destiny. He was thoroughly disillusioned with Nazi propaganda and its quasi-Nietzschean metaphysics. However, he condemns liberalism and Communism as equally nihilistic manifestations of the modern worldview (Zimmerman, 1990; Polt, 1997; Fried, 2000).

Heidegger's readings of Nietzsche (Heidegger, 1979–87) parallel this shift in his politics. His lectures on Nietzsche from the mid-1930s are sympathetic explorations of Nietzsche's attempts to escape the constraints of traditional metaphysics, particularly through a revaluation of art. By the 1940s, however, Heidegger has developed an almost dismissive reading of Nietzsche as 'the last metaphysician'. According to this interpretation, Nietzsche understands the Being of beings as the eternally recurring will to power – but like all metaphysicians, Nietzsche fails to ask how it is that we are able to understand Being in the first place. Nietzsche's attempt to combat nihilism falls prey to the deepest sort of nihilism – the oblivion of Being. In the end, he offers nothing but an exaltation of the subject as pure will, or a 'will to will' that imposes representations and values on objects.

The Nietzschean overman is only the final form of 'humanism'; Heidegger's postwar thought continues his thoroughgoing critique of this phenomenon ('Letter on Humanism,' in Heidegger, 1993a). Humanism, in the Heideggerian sense, is any way of thinking that glorifies human beings yet fails to ask about Being itself. Humanism represents all beings in terms of some concept of their Being and gives humanity a central position among beings as a whole; however, humanism takes the meaning of Being for granted and does not grasp the human being as the one who is called to engage in a respectful, creative response to Being. Thus, humanism inappropriately raises humanity above Being; at the same time, humanism misses the real dignity of humans by failing to understand our true calling. On the political level, Heidegger's antihumanism translates into a sweeping rejection of all existing regimes. All modern political alternatives are surface phenomena, variants of the same underlying humanism. They all celebrate the human subject (as an individual, a nation, a class or a species) at the expense of Being.

Technology (or technicity) is a closely related sign of the 'oblivion of Being'. By *Technik*, Heidegger means not just sophisticated machinery, but a way of dealing with and conceiving of beings in general. The technological world view experiences beings as 'standing reserve', or sources of energy that can be represented and manipulated by subjects (Heidegger, 1977). Modern natural science is essentially 'technological', quite apart from its application to the construction of machinery, because it proceeds by forcing a mathematical means of representation upon beings; when approached in this way, beings are reduced to a supply of manageable information.

Heidegger sees technicity at work in the political realm as well as in all other spheres of the modern world. For instance, in one of the most controversial of his rare postwar references to Nazism, he declares, 'Agriculture is now a motorized food industry, essentially the same as the manufacture of corpses in gas chambers and extermination camps, the same as the blockade and starvation of countries, the same as the manufacture of hydrogen bombs' ('Das Ge-Stell' in Heidegger, 1994). In other words, all these phenomena are manifestations of a manipulative, exploitative relation to beings – including human beings. For some readers, this thought offers a deep insight into the roots of fascism; for others, it is a reductive view that tries to minimize the distinctive evil of Nazism.

The most original aspect of Heidegger's account of technology is his understanding of it in relation to the 'history of Being'. Technicity is not simply a mistake or a careless interpretation of the world; it is our destiny. The technological relation to beings is the way in which a meaning of Being has been 'sent' to us. We must learn to experience this meaning of Being as a gift, and realize that it stems from a mysterious historical granting that cannot itself be understood in technological terms.

For these reasons, Heidegger offers no sweeping plan of action to combat humanism and technology. He limits himself to suggesting that we may be able to make small changes in our practices; perhaps we can use technical devices without succumbing completely to a technological understanding of the world (Heidegger, 1966). Such changes may hold open the possibility of a future 'poetic dwelling' that would gather us into a new proximity to Being. To suppose that we can solve all our problems through reason and will is merely to continue along the path of technicity – thus there is little we can do but wait attentively for a new destiny. To put it most dramatically, 'only a god can save us' (Heidegger, 1990).

APPRAISAL OF KEY ADVANCES AND CONTROVERSIES

Influence

Heidegger's influence on contemporary thought is multiform. His writings have become almost inevitable points of reference for Continental philosophers and cultural theorists, especially in France; they have also affected disciplines such as theology and literary theory. Here we can do no more than sketch some of the most important appropriations of Heidegger's thought, particularly as they relate to social theory.

Being and Time, along with some essays such as 'What is Metaphysics?', had an impact on existentialists during the 1940s – notably on Jean-Paul Sartre, who drew on Heidegger's vocabulary in his phenomenology of freedom and consciousness (Sartre, 1966). Like 'existential' thinkers such as Kierkegaard, Karl Jaspers, and Sartre, the early Heidegger attempts to understand the dynamics of human existence in terms of decision and individuality, and stresses that human beings cannot be understood as if they were objects. However, he differs from highly individualistic existentialists in that he rejects the notion of absolute freedom and stresses that human identity is possible only within a group and a tradition. For the later Heidegger, Sartre's position falls prey to all the problems of humanism. For these reasons, Heidegger himself rejected the label 'existentialist'.

The 1950s saw the flourishing of the thought of Hannah Arendt, who had been Heidegger's student in the 1920s. The influence of Heidegger's earlier thought is clear in Arendt's emphasis on action over contemplation and in her opposition to notions of the subject as an internal, private realm (Arendt, 1959; Villa, 1996). Arendt develops these insights into a philosophy centred on the practice of political debate within a deliberative democracy, whereas Heidegger never seemed to appreciate politics as a deliberative sphere, and in his later years withdrew completely from the political world.

Another pupil of Heidegger, Hans-Georg Gadamer, has developed Heidegger's account of the appropriation of tradition as a fundamental mode of understanding (Gadamer, 1997). This ontology of understanding makes Heidegger a major figure in hermeneutics, the theory of interpretation. His influence is clear in the work of Gadamer as well as in that of other hermeneutic thinkers, such as Paul Ricoeur (Ricoeur, 1974).

Gadamer's emphasis on tradition has given him a perhaps undeserved reputation as a conservative thinker. However, Heidegger's thought has also appealed to some thinkers on the left. As early as 1928, his student Herbert Marcuse proposed that Heidegger's interpretation of practical Being-in-the-world could round out the Marxist view of human nature (Marcuse, 1969). After Heidegger's own political misadventures, his philosophy was off-limits to orthodox Marxists. However, his thought has continued to attract leftist theorists because (at least in *Being and Time*) he stresses the importance of engaged action in the material world, and because his thought undermines the standard liberal theory of society as a collection of independent individuals. For these reasons, and because of his influence on Marcuse, Heidegger may be understood as an indirect source of the politics of 'authenticity' and the revolt against conformism by the New Left of the 1960s. As a narrative purporting to reveal a deep, repressed truth, Heidegger's later 'history of Being' can also function as a powerful tool for criticism of established ideologies; in this respect, his thought functions somewhat like that of Marx, Nietzsche, or Freud. The Heideggerian notions of humanism and technology can then serve the purposes of a radical critique of capitalism, fascism, and existing socialism in the name of a possible post-humanist alternative. (For a history and criticism of the appropriation of Heidegger by the 'antihumanist' French left, see Ferry and Renaut, 1990a, 1990b.)

The thought of Jacques Derrida is one of the most original of the radical appropriations of Heidegger that began in the France of the 1960s. For Derrida, Heidegger's main importance lies in his critique of the 'metaphysics of presence'. Derrida argues that this critique implies that it is impossible to set up a system in which one entity is successfully represented as supreme, or in which one means of representation is established as totally transparent – that is, perfectly unambiguous and perfectly adapted to the representation of its objects. The centre of a representational system is always dependent on the margins, despite its attempt to establish hegemony over them (e.g. Derrida, 1982). Derrida applies this critique to politics: by deconstructing the various metaphysical systems that prop up political regimes (the theory of *apartheid*, for example), we can make room for the liberation of their marginalized 'others'. Thus, justice can never be deconstructed – for deconstruction *is* justice (Derrida, 1992).

Michel Foucault's work has often been seen as having similar liberating potential, although he disclaimed such an intent. His thought can be seen as a creative combination of Nietzsche and Heidegger. From Nietzsche, Foucault adopts the project of a 'genealogical' study of concrete systems of power relations. From Heidegger's history of Being, he adopts the idea that these power relations are indissociable from 'epistemes', or systems of representations of beings, and that no such system can establish its own necessity. Foucault also borrows from Heidegger's critique of humanism, although in Foucault's analysis, 'man' has a very specific sense: 'man' is the being who is both an empirical object that can be represented, and the subject whose modes of representation are transcendental conditions of possibility for all objects. 'Man' in this sense is a relatively recent, post-Kantian 'invention' (Foucault, 1970). This analysis is inspired by Heidegger inasmuch as it highlights the tensions within modern 'representational' thinking, which according to Heidegger presupposes the metaphysics of presence.

More recently, Heidegger's subordination of theory to engaged dwelling has been taken up by American thinkers in search of a revived pragmatism (e.g. Okrent, 1988). For Hubert Dreyfus, *Being and Time* teaches us that representations and concepts stem from a more basic competence or 'coping' (Dreyfus, 1991). For

Dreyfus this implies, among other things, that artificial intelligence is impossible as it is currently conceived, and that ethical insight should be understood as a kind of practical expertise. According to Richard Rorty, Heidegger (along with Dewey and Wittgenstein) deflates the traditional ambition of philosophy to serve as the 'mirror of nature'. Rorty's appropriation of Heidegger is not unlike Derrida's, in that he seeks to undermine the claims to absoluteness of any system of representation. Rorty holds that the role of philosophers is not to construct dominant theories, but to foster conversation in their culture; this translates into a politics of liberal tolerance (Rorty, 1991).

Points of Controversy

The debates concerning Heidegger's social thinking are inevitably coloured by the highly controversial topic of his affiliation with the Nazi regime. There is a wide variety of opinion on whether his philosophical thought has fascist political implications. (For a range of views, see Neske and Kettering, 1990; Rockmore and Margolis, 1992; Wolin, 1993; Harries and Jamme, 1994.)

At one extreme, we find total condemnation: Heidegger's thinking is simply the philosophical codification of a reactionary political position (Adorno, 1986; Bourdieu, 1991). Bourdieu provides a rhetorical analysis of Heidegger's texts as covert, euphemistic political statements. His intent is not only to expose Heidegger, but to challenge the supposed autonomy of philosophical discourse; the philosophical 'field' must be reintegrated into the social field at large. Even the most exalted ontology is a manoeuvre conducted within an established 'game', a set of possible social stances. For instance, Bourdieu reads the distinction between authenticity and inauthenticity as a way of obscuring 'objective' differences of class.

A similar, more detailed reading of *Being and Time* is provided by Johannes Fritsche (1999). Fritsche points out, for example, that Heidegger's account of *Dasein* parallels the language of many of his antiliberal contemporaries, who criticized atomized 'society' (*Gesellschaft*) in the name of a deeper 'community' (*Gemeinschaft*) (cf. Sluga, 1993). For Fritsche, the account of historicity in *Being and Time* is nothing short of a call for a National Socialist revolution.

On the other extreme, one can argue that despite Heidegger's personal failings, his philosophical thought rises above them completely. The ontology of *Dasein* provided in *Being and Time* is in part too general to be associated exclusively with a fascist politics, and in part actually inconsistent with fascism. Fascism treats human beings as objects to be manipulated and used, but *Being and Time* implies that such behaviour is a misunderstanding of *Dasein*'s way of Being. A strong example of this type of argument is provided by Young (1997).

Perhaps the most interesting readings of Heidegger's Nazi connection are those that fall between these two extremes (e.g. Derrida, 1989; Lacoue-Labarthe, 1990; Caputo, 1993; Thiele, 1995; de Beistegui, 1998). These interpretations neither use Heidegger's politics to reject his philosophy, nor dismiss his politics as irrelevant; they seek to find food for independent thought both in Heidegger's philosophy and in the implications of his Nazi sympathies. One common suggestion is that these sympathies demonstrate the continuing, insidious power of the metaphysics of presence; Heidegger's attraction to fascism shows that it was difficult for him to escape the metaphysical thinking that his own thought renders unworkable. This view is essentially in agreement with Heidegger's own final interpretation of Nazism as a form of 'humanism'. A more original interpretation is that of Gregory Fried (2000), who argues that, regardless of the depth or length of Heidegger's commitment to National Socialism, his thought involves an enduring commitment to a 'polemical' understanding of *Dasein* and Being. For Heidegger, genuine unconcealment demands an ongoing confrontation with the limits of one's understanding of Being; this vision presents a serious challenge to conventional understandings of politics as a means to ensure peace, rights, and equality.

Heidegger's social thinking is equally controversial on the level of his analysis of person-to-person relationships. In the influential reading of Emmanuel Levinas (1969), Heidegger's preoccupation with the question of Being crowds out the question of 'the other', leaving no room for a genuine understanding of the face-to-face encounter and of the ethical demand for justice. (Here one should consider Heidegger's argument in a 1929 lecture course: the 'I–thou' relationship is not primary, but is only one particular mode of *Dasein*'s Being, Heidegger, 1984.)

In contrast, others (Olafson, 1998; Hatab, 2000) hold that Heidegger's early work actually makes it possible to conceive of interpersonal relations in a way that is freed from many traditional prejudices; he thus suggests the ontological groundwork for an ethics, even if he does not provide an ethics in his own writings. Hatab makes a strong case that Heidegger's interpretation of *Dasein* as situated and finite can alert us both to the need for ethical responsibility and to the difficult, questionable character of ethical decisions.

Assessment

One way of considering Heidegger's significance for philosophy in general is to view him as dealing the death blow to the typical modern picture of the human condition, according to which human beings are fundamentally private minds, atomic subjects who relate to external objects by means of representations and judgments. Heidegger describes us, instead, as social beings who interpret themselves and their surroundings primarily through engaged action. This could be read as a return to Aristotle's insights into the human being as a 'political animal' and into the irreducibility of practical knowledge to theoretical knowledge.

At the same time, however, at least in *Being and Time*, Heidegger satisfies certain aspirations of modernity. He makes room for the modern demand for individual autonomy and the modern view of humanity as free and self-interpreting, rather than constrained by a fixed essence. His concept of authenticity manages to combine sociality with responsibility by developing an account of situated, finite freedom.

For these reasons, Heidegger's early work holds promise for our understanding of society. His provocative descriptions of everydayness and authenticity have the potential to enrich and transform the standard concepts of sociology – just as they transformed psychological concepts when they were adopted by the existential psychotherapy movement in the 1950s.

When Heidegger turns away from everydayness in the 1930s, he stops describing actual social life and instead focuses on its supposed deep causes – the historically unfolding understanding of Being, including the presumed dominance of the 'metaphysics of presence' in Western thought. This analysis is more useful as a reading of the history of philosophy than as a guide to history at large. Heidegger never tries to support his view that all human history is grounded in the history of Being by carrying out detailed cultural and historical analyses. His late opinions on social life are too abstract and reductive to provide genuine insight into how society works and into the varieties of possible human regimes and cultures. It can be argued that cultural theorists such as Foucault have gone some distance towards applying Heideggerian ideas to actual history. However, like standard Marxist and Freudian theories, Heidegger's late thought tends to function as an unfalsifiable framework rather than as a hypothesis that can be confirmed or countered by empirical studies. As such, it should be treated as a suggestive tool for social interpretation, but not as the last word.

The disturbing political overtones of some of Heidegger's thought should not be forgotten, but one must beware of readings such as those of Bourdieu and Fritsche, which are sophisticated versions of what is traditionally called an *ad hominem* argument. They locate Heidegger's discourse in its contemporary milieu; this in itself is unobjectionable, and is even quite consistent with Heidegger's own view that human beings are situated and historical. Such efforts are also helpful in alerting us to possible blind spots in Heidegger's thinking. However, when a rhetorical and political analysis is presented as the *final* analysis, it becomes reductive; it rules out the possibility that Heidegger's thoughts, situated though they are, may also have relevance and truth for us. For example, it is possible that his view of human existence as essentially 'Being-with' simply is truer than the concept of society as a collection of wholly independent individuals. Even if this insight has sometimes been invoked in support of fascism, there is certainly more than one way to try to convert it into a political programme; the concept of community has often been used by non-fascist thinkers, including contemporary democratic 'communitarians' (e.g. Walzer, 1983; Taylor, 1989; Sandel, 1998). We should also recognize that sociological, political, and rhetorical interpretations presuppose an understanding of the 'Being' of society, polity, language, and human beings in general. Whether or not one agrees with Heidegger's account of *Dasein*, it deserves to be taken seriously as an attempt to enrich our understanding of ourselves.

HEIDEGGER'S MAJOR WORKS

Heidegger, M. (1962) *Being and Time*. (Trans. J. Macquarrie and E. Robinson.) New York: Harper & Row.

Heidegger, M. (1966) *Discourse on Thinking*. New York: Harper & Row.

Heidegger, M. (1971) *Poetry, Language, Thought*. New York: Harper & Row.

Heidegger, M. (1977) *The Question Concerning Technology and Other Essays*. New York: Harper & Row.

Heidegger, M. (1979–87) *Nietzsche*. New York: Harper & Row.

Heidegger, M. (1981) 'Why do I stay in the provinces?', in T. Sheehan (ed.), *Heidegger: The Man and the Thinker*. Chicago: Precedent.

Heidegger, M. (1982) *The Basic Problems of Phenomenology*. Bloomington: Indiana University Press.

Heidegger, M. (1984) *The Metaphysical Foundations of Logic*. Bloomington: Indiana University Press.

Heidegger, M. (1985) *History of the Concept of Time: Prolegomena*. Bloomington: Indiana University Press.

Heidegger, M. (1990) 'Only a god can save us', in G. Neske and E. Kettering (eds), *Martin Heidegger and National Socialism: Questions and Answers*. New York: Paragon House.

Heidegger, M. (1993a) *Basic Writings*, 2nd edn. San Francisco, CA: HarperSanFrancisco.

Heidegger, M. (1993b) 'The self-assertion of the German university', in R. Wolin (ed.), *The Heidegger Controversy: A Critical Reader*. Cambridge, MA: MIT Press.

Heidegger, M. (1994) *Bremer und Freiburger Vorträge. Gesamtausgabe*, vol. 79. Frankfurt am Main: Vittorio Klostermann.

Heidegger, M. (1995) *The Fundamental Concepts of Metaphysics: World, Finitude, Solitude*. Bloomington: Indiana University Press.

Heidegger, M. (1996a) *Being and Time*. (Trans. J. Stambaugh.) Albany: State University of New York Press.

Heidegger, M. (1996b) *Hölderlin's Hymn 'The Ister'*. Bloomington: Indiana University Press.

Heidegger, M. (1998a) *Logik als die Frage nach dem Wesen der Sprache. Gesamtausgabe*, vol. 38. Frankfurt am Main: Vittorio Klostermann.

Heidegger, M. (1998b) *Pathmarks*. Cambridge: Cambridge University Press.

Heidegger, M. (1999) *Contributions to Philosophy (From Enowning)*. Bloomington: Indiana University Press.

Heidegger, M. (2000) *Introduction to Metaphysics*. New Haven, CT: Yale University Press.

SECONDARY WORKS

Adorno, T. (1986) *The Jargon of Authenticity*. London: Routledge & Kegan Paul.

Arendt, H. (1959) *The Human Condition*. Garden City, NY: Doubleday.

Bernstein, R.J. (1992) *The New Constellation: The Ethical-Political Horizons of Modernity/ Postmodernity*. Cambridge, Mass.: MIT Press.

Bourdieu, P. (1991) *The Political Ontology of Martin Heidegger*. Stanford: Stanford University Press.

Caputo, J.D. (1993) *Demythologizing Heidegger*. Bloomington: Indiana University Press.

de Beistegui, M. (1998) *Heidegger and the Political: Dystopias*. London: Routledge.

Derrida, J. (1982) *Margins of Philosophy*. Chicago: University of Chicago Press.

Derrida, J. (1989) *Of Spirit: Heidegger and the Question*. Chicago: University of Chicago Press.

Derrida, J. (1992) 'Force of Law: The "Mystical Foundation of Authority"'. In D. Cornell et al. (eds), *Deconstruction and the Possibility of Justice*. New York: Routledge.

Dreyfus, H.L. (1991) *Being-in-the-World: A Commentary on Heidegger's Being and Time, Division I*. Cambridge, MA: MIT Press.

Ferry, L. and Renaut, A. (1990a) *French Philosophy of the Sixties: An Essay on Anti-Humanism*. Amherst: University of Massachusetts Press.

Ferry, L. and Renaut, A. (1990b) *Heidegger and Modern Philosophy*. Chicago: University of Chicago Press.

Foucault, M. (1970) *The Order of Things: An Archaeology of the Human Sciences*. New York: Vintage.

Fried, G. (2000) *Heidegger's Polemos: From Being to Politics*. New Haven, CT: Yale University Press.

Fried, G. and Polt, R. (eds) (2000) *A Companion to Heidegger's Introduction to Metaphysics*. New Haven, CT: Yale University Press.

Fritsche, J. (1999) *Historical Destiny and National Socialism in Heidegger's Being and Time*. Berkeley: University of California Press.

Gadamer, H.-G. (1997) *Truth and Method*. New York: Continuum.

Guignon, C.B. (ed.) (1993) *The Cambridge Companion to Heidegger*. Cambridge: Cambridge University Press.

Harries, K. and Jamme, C. (eds) (1994) *Martin Heidegger: Politics, Art, and Technology*. New York/ London: Holmes & Meier.

Hatab, L. (2000) *Ethics and Finitude: Heideggerian Contributions to Moral Philosophy*. Lanham, MD: Rowman & Littlefield.

Lacoue-Labarthe, P. (1990) *Heidegger, Art and Politics*. Oxford: Basil Blackwell.

Levinas, E. (1969) *Totality and Infinity: An Essay on Exteriority*. Pittsburgh, PA: Duquesne University Press.

Löwith, K. (1994) *My Life in Germany Before and After 1933: A Report*. Urbana: University of Illinois Press.

Marcuse, H. (1969) 'Contribution to a phenomenology of historical materialism', *Telos*, 4.

May, R. (1996) *Heidegger's Hidden Sources: East Asian Influences on his Work*. London: Routledge.

Neske, G. and Kettering, E. (eds) (1990) *Martin Heidegger and National Socialism: Questions and Answers*. New York: Paragon House.

Okrent, M. (1988) *Heidegger's Pragmatism: Understanding, Being, and the Critique of Metaphysics*. Ithaca, NY: Cornell University Press.

Olafson, F. (1998) *Heidegger and the Ground of Ethics: A Study of Mitsein*. Cambridge: Cambridge University Press.

Ott, H. (1993) *Heidegger: A Political Life*. New York: Basic Books.

Parkes, G. (ed.) (1987) *Heidegger and Asian Thought*. Honolulu: University of Hawaii Press.

Polt, R. (1997) 'Metaphysical Liberalism in Heidegger's *Beiträge zur Philosophie*', *Political Theory*, 25: 5.

Polt, R. (1999) *Heidegger: An Introduction*. London: UCL Press.

Ricoeur, P. (1974) *The Conflict of Interpretations: Essays in Hermeneutics*. Evanston, IL: Northwestern University Press.

Rockmore, T. and Margolis, J. (eds) (1992) *The Heidegger Case: On Philosophy and Politics*. Philadelphia, PA: Temple University Press.

Rorty, R. (1991) *Essays on Heidegger and Others*. Cambridge: Cambridge University Press.

Safranski, R. (1998) *Martin Heidegger: Between Good and Evil*. Cambridge, MA: Harvard University Press.

Sandel, M. (1998) *Liberalism and the Limits of Justice*. Cambridge: Cambridge University Press.

Sartre, J.-P. (1966) *Being and Nothingness*. New York: Washington Square Press.

Sheehan, T. (ed.) (1981) *Heidegger: the Man and the Thinker*. Chicago: Precedent.

Sluga, H. (1993) *Heidegger's Crisis. Philosophy and Politics in Nazi Germany*. Cambridge, MA: Harvard University Press.

Taylor, C. (1989) *Sources of the Self: The Making of the Modern Identity*. Cambridge, MA: Harvard University Press.

Thiele, L. (1995) *Timely Meditations: Martin Heidegger and Postmodern Politics*. Princeton, NJ: Princeton University Press.

Villa, D.R. (1996) *Heidegger and Arendt: The Fate of the Political*. Princeton, NJ: Princeton University Press.

Walzer, M. (1983) *Spheres of Justice: A Defense of Pluralism and Equality*. New York: Basic Books.

Wolin, R. (ed.) (1993) *The Heidegger Controversy: A Critical Reader*. Cambridge, MA: MIT Press.

Young, J. (1997) *Heidegger, Philosophy, Nazism*. Cambridge: Cambridge University Press.

Zimmerman, M.E. (1986) *Eclipse of the Self: The Development of Heidegger's Concept of Authenticity*, 2nd edn. Athens, OH: Ohio University Press.

Zimmerman, M.E. (1990) *Heidegger's Confrontation with Modernity: Technology, Politics and Art*. Bloomington: Indiana University Press.

2

Georges Bataille

MICHAEL RICHARDSON

BIOGRAPHICAL DETAILS AND THEORETICAL CONTEXT

As a writer whose identity was partly created through his writing, the facts of Bataille's life should be treated with caution. Born on 10 September 1897 at Billom, Puy-de-Dôme, Bataille later regarded his childhood in traumatic terms. His father was blind and syphilitic and suffered a general paralysis when Bataille was three. Having been brought up by atheist parents who had no interest in religion, in adolescence he became a Catholic. Even though he was soon to reject Christianity (having enrolled for the priesthood, by 1920 he had lost his faith), the impulse that drew him towards it still provided a focus for an essential underlying aspect of his work: what moral necessity justifies our existence in the modern world? His conversion to Catholicism coincided with declaration of war in 1914, two events that seem linked in the evolution of his thinking. Even though he did not see combat (he was called up but soon demobilized after a bout of tuberculosis), Bataille's personality was still marked by the experience of the war. Having studied to become a medievalist at the Ecole des Chartes in 1922 he was given a grant to study in Spain where he witnessed the death in the ring of the bullfighter Manuelo Granero. This was to have a powerful impact on him, uniting eroticism and death in his mind and making a link that would fascinate him for the rest of his life.

Upon return to Paris, he obtained work at the Bibliothèque Nationale, a position he held for the next 20 years (he was a librarian for most of his life). At the same time, he began serious study of philosophy. As a student of the exiled Russian philosopher Leon Chestov, he gained a deep understanding of Nietzsche, who was to be the great influence on his social thinking. Chestov's teaching offered a powerful lesson to Bataille: it showed him that thought was valuable only when related to experience, and that cultivation of sensory perception was as important as cultivation of the mind. In this, Nietzsche's rehabilitation of the body was crucial. A period of great instability in Bataille's personal life followed, in which he lived a dissolute night life and came into contact with the surrealists, whose sensibility he shared, even if he found the atmosphere around the Surrealist Group stifling.

He started to write seriously in about 1927 and his experience of extreme states of mind is apparent in his early work, as can be seen in such articles as 'The solar anus' and 'The pineal eye', and in the clandestinely published novel, *The Story of the Eye*. In the same year he was asked to assist in the production of the journal *Documents*, which was published regularly until 1931, and for which he wrote numerous articles and soon became its de-facto co-editor.

During the next few years, Bataille's interests expanded into the fields of anthropology and sociology and he attended the lectures of Marcel Mauss. He also became politically involved, participating in Boris Souvarine's *Cercle Communiste Démocratique* and contributing key essays to its journal *La Critique sociale*, in which he explored for the first time in extended form his ideas about expenditure and loss and on the dangers represented by the emergence of fascism. He also took part in an abortive attempt to create a 'popular university' and in 1935 founded, with André Breton, the anti-Popular Front group Contre-Attaque.

In 1934, he began attending Alexandre Kojève's lectures on Hegel's phenomenology, which were crucial in giving him a new perspective on the possibilities of Hegel's philosophy. Further turmoil in his personal life led to the break-up of his first marriage and the start of an intense relationship with Colette Peignot, whose death in 1938 was to have a devastating effect on him.

In 1936, he created the College of Sociology, an attempt at an 'activist sociology', as well as Acéphale, a secret society intent on a 'voyage out of this world', which also had the practical purpose of rescuing Nietzsche from the distortions promulgated about him by the Nazis.

A decade of intense public activity came to an end with the coming of a new war which caused Bataille to withdraw into himself. He began writing his most introspective books, *Le Coupable* and *L'Expérience intérieure*, as well as the intense erotic tales *Madame Edwarda* and *The Dead Man*. Having been forced by sickness to leave the Bibliothèque Nationale, he retired to the French countryside and, in 1943, published his first substantial work of social theory, *L'Expérience intérieure*, which explored the existential problems of existing in the modern world. During the next few years he immersed himself in a range of projects. He published various works, including the volume of poems *L'Archangélique* (1944), the reflective philosophical texts *Sur Nietzsche* (1945) and *Méthode de méditation* (1947), the theoretical work, *Théorie de religion* (1948) and the economic analysis of *La Part maudite* (1949). In 1946 he founded *Critique*, a journal devoted to substantial reviews of recently published books in a wide range of subjects. He was to be its editor until his death and published numerous articles in it. In 1947 he gave some lectures at the Collège philosophique, but had no regular employment and experienced severe financial difficulties until 1949, when he became a librarian in Charpentras.

During the 1950s, he struggled with illness but was still productive. He published the novels *L'Abbé C.* (1950) and *Le Bleu du ciel* (1957), a collection of essays on literature, *La Litérature et le mal* (1957), three books on art (on Manet and prehistoric art, both in 1955, and *Les Larmes d'Eros*, on eroticism in art, 1961), as well as his most important study, *L'Erotisme* (1957). He died in Paris in 1962.

Bataille had wide-ranging interests and published books in the realms of philosophy, economic theory, art history, literature, and fiction. All of this work is dominated by a concern with social themes. It has to be seen against the background of his times. Traumatized as Bataille was by childhood experiences and the impact of the First World War, his work is an attempt to engage with the moral issue of whether it is possible to exist in society or whether the modern consciousness has reached such a state of infirmity that social being is impossible. In this sense he is firmly within the framework of surrealist revolt and was repelled by a civilization that had been responsible for the horrors of the trenches. He felt that the tradition of French rationalist thought was implicated in this débâcle and, again like the surrealists, he was ready to 'hold out a hand to the enemy', looking to the German tradition, precisely to Nietzsche and later Hegel, as thinkers who had a depth that was able to address the moral crisis of contemporary consciousness.

SOCIAL THEORY AND CONTRIBUTIONS

At the core of Bataille's preoccupations is the nature of humanity's collective existence and how we respond to it as individuals. How do we live in society and in the world? How do we co-exist with our fellow beings? These were the questions that haunted him. He had little interest in being itself, nor was he concerned about the nature of individual identity. Existence was only of interest to him in its social dimension. In this respect, humanist ideas were alien to his way of thinking, for human beings exist only in relation with others. Human life is unable to tolerate isolated being: we are formed as humans only through social interaction. Equally, we can exist only within the frame established by social limits and this defines our reality. It means that any idea of transcendence is a delusion. Bataille considered that it is essential to face social and existential reality as squarely as one can and not strive to elude the inevitability of one's fate. Looking for the reasons for existence has little meaning. The most important focus for social investigation is to understand how we are able to live within the limits that life imposes on us.

Yet, unlike most thinkers interested in understanding social existence, Bataille had little interest in taking the observed world as an object of study. Rather, he began with his own life. He did not analyse given data with a view to drawing a theory from it. His social theory emerges from within himself and projected outwards. It is for this reason that philosophical reflection, novels, and poetic texts all become the means to explore the nature of what he called 'inner experience'.

In using his own experience as the basis of his social theory, however, Bataille was not succumbing to subjectivism. There is nothing narcissistic about his method. He explored his inner experience only in order to grasp the relation of his being with that of others. The data of his own life was of value only to the extent that it was the most reliable available source open to him.

Bataille's understanding of what constituted a social fact emerged from Durkheim's sociology. He agreed with Durkheim that societies are organic wholes whose essential characteristics differ from the sum of their parts. At the same time, though, social and personal being are not to be seen as different things. Collective consciousness is not abstract but has a concrete reality as distinctive as that of a particular individual existing within it. The individual is related to the collective in the same way as cells in a body to an individual. In order to understand the social body, therefore, we also need to understand the relation an individual has to it.

Bataille's debt to Durkheim is most clearly seen in his analysis of the sacred. Accepting the distinction Durkheim made between sacred and profane, Bataille considered that the balance between them had been broken in modern society, in which the sacred struggles to survive in a world dominated by the profane.

The sacred is communication and Bataille saw the possibilities of communication today being broken down by the dominance of exchange values. This has an impact at every level of society. The existence of the sacred implies an inherent contract between human society and the cosmos. This is given expression in such practices as ritual sacrifice. Sacrifice maintained the balance between sacred and profane by allowing an outlet to the surplus effusion generated by human activity. It was a transgressive act serving to maintain the taboo that protected the world of work from contagious violence. As societies develop, though, this complex interrelation is ruptured and the homogeneity of modern societies is instituted by means of a fundamental profanation.

The nature of this profanation can be explored through what Bataille calls the 'restricted economy'. This is characteristic of modern societies and is based on the need to reduce scarcity. It encourages the accumulation of wealth at the expense of the social communication that is the basic quality of the sacred. Bataille saw this as a delusion. He regarded life in its essentials as being energy striving to expend itself uselessly. Humanity has increasingly tried to regulate this basic effusion by means of work, to the extent that, in modern society, work provides the parameter by which all activity is judged. It is this that represents the triumph of the profane and establishes the frame within which the restricted economy is able to dominate all activity. Against this process, Bataille posits the idea of the 'general economy', which would restore the principle of generosity into human relations.

The general economy, as Bataille understands it, is determined not by the accumulation of wealth through work but by expenditure: the joyful consumption of excess wealth by means of the festival, laughter, and play. In modern societies the latter activities are accursed, being given to us only as recompense for our devotion to the principle of work. As such it is no longer possible to experience pure effusion. Transgression, as the secret of the sacred, is tamed and reduced to a means of social control. It can be manifested only in regulated pleasure (perhaps symbolized most clearly by the package holiday), or in destructive activities such as war.

For Bataille, then, the essential social problem facing humankind is not, as generally assumed, poverty. On the contrary, we are, as he says, 'sick with wealth'. And this sickness is the result not of wealth itself but of the fact that we have individualized it. We have convinced ourselves that wealth is something we can own, that accrues to us as individuals rather than belonging to humanity in its generality. This is the lie that irrevocably ruptures any sense of harmony we can achieve with the cosmos and which, in the past, was encapsulated by the idea of the sacred.

The consequence is that distinction becomes the only measure of social prestige. And servility in turn is established as the gauge against which distinction gains its value. Class distinction is institutionalized and so status comes to determine being. This results in servility pervading each aspect of society, so that even power itself comes to be applied in servility instead of in sovereignty.

Sovereignty is a principle of life that takes a moral shape in human interaction. Sovereignty is simultaneously present in the consecration of the immediate and the human will to realize itself. It represents the essence of becoming: acceptance of the immediacy offered by life, rather than a striving to transcend its limits, combined with a refusal to accept a debased existence. But this is paradoxical, because the very flow of human life works against the possibility of a sovereign existence. In order to survive in society we are forced to make an accommodation both with our fellow beings and with the world. This establishes a fundamental breach which can never be entirely surmounted. The fact of this gap means that we are incomplete beings whose existence is discontinuous, that is, separated from all other beings.

It is the existence of death that reveals this gap. Knowing we shall die, we recognize that we are limited beings. The principle of work and building for the future are attempts to deny this, to try to convince ourselves that we shall not die. However, we are also marked with a longing for the continuity we have lost by the fact of being born. This is at the basis of what Freud called the death instinct. Death perpetrates violence against us but in so doing it reunites us with the continuity of the world. It is in the realization of death that communication between humans is founded. And it is for this reason that sexual activity – especially nonproductive sexual activity, in other words eroticism – assumes such importance. The sexual act unites life and death, providing the link between them, but also suggesting the possibility of reconciling the disjunction between them, even if only for a moment. In eroticism, life momentarily overflows its limits and gives us the promise of a devastating profusion. But this promise takes shape due to the awareness we have of death, which immediately negates it. This is why Bataille says that eroticism is an affirmation of life up to the point of, and even in, death.

The sex act is thus not simply instinctive, an activity we need for the propagation of the species. Rather it is necessary for us in our psychic depths: it is a mental act that arises as a will to experience an elemental communication with the lover. It represents the body wishing to surpass the limits imposed on it by life and the will to unite with another being even with the recognition that this clash is a threat to its own integral sensibility. The erotic act, then, is a form of communication with death; it is life asserting the essential link it has with death. And this also entails an encounter with the loss of identity that death entails. The tension at the centre of this clash is what founds the anguish of human existence.

Like eroticism, the impulse to write is also founded in the need for communication. Bataille considered writing to be fundamentally a moral act, but one that is evil or sinful. This is because the very condition of existence is guilt, a guilt that is manifested through anguish and is an inherent part of our nature that is created simply by the fact that we have been born. Coming into being, we recognize ourselves as an absence or lack and the genuine writer is the one who recognizes this. Like the ancient sacrificer, the writer is engaged in a necessary task of seeking to establish a sense – always provisional – of harmony between human existence and the cosmos. And indeed, in its highest form, that is in poetry, writing has something of the same momentous quality that was once the condition of sacrifice. Poetry is, in fact, perhaps the only possibility we have in today's world for an authentic experience of the sacred. The acts of writing and reading are thus, for Bataille, discreet and intimately tied in with silence. This silence is at once the gap between human experience and the cosmos, and that between what is written and what is read. It offers an alternative to pursuing the utilitarian needs of self-interest that dominate modern society. But this is still a paradox for, if the impulse to write is to establish an immediate communication with the reader, the very fact of writing precludes this immediacy since the reader can only encounter the text in conditions the writer has not chosen: the experience is always mediated in one way or another. For this reason, writing is a less authentic means of expression than that found in sacrifice.

This realization also conditions Bataille's understanding of truth. Like Nietzsche, he had a profound distrust of Enlightenment claims for truth as a criterion for absolute understanding. For Bataille knowledge itself had an intrinsic ability to undermine itself. He characterized this by his concept of 'nonknowledge'. This was a direct challenge to evolutionary views of knowledge as necessarily leading to a greater knowledge. Bataille argued, on the contrary, that knowledge can also lead both to ignorance and to the collapse of knowledge. On the other hand, there is also a state of being in which lack of knowledge may itself contain wisdom: we may 'understand' not through the accumulation of knowledge but by the calm contentment of vacancy. This has a lot in common with meditative techniques and is also linked with Bataille's idea of silence as a desirable condition of life. However, this is not to deny either knowledge or truth. If truth exists it is to be found not in knowledge itself but in the margins between knowledge and nonknowledge.

This idea also affects the practice of writing. Bataille had no wish to convince. He wanted a to establish a relation of intimacy and complicity with the reader. At times his writing is provocative, it seeks to jolt the reader out of complacency. Rather than providing an argument, he lays down a challenge.

The condition of life, as Bataille saw it, is paradoxical, based on an impossible combination of different states of being. This paradox lies at the heart of our nature as human beings. Living with the awareness that we are impermanent beings who will one day die, we recoil from this awareness in terror. And yet, just as we flee this realization and build for a future that will never come, we also have an urge to shatter the works by which we strive to achieve a transcendence of death. This is the basis of the transgression that is central to the very structure of human society. The tension between the will towards order and the pull of disorder is the reality that Bataille sought to explore through an examination of how awareness of death affects human experience.

It was from this point of view that he denied the very possibility of ultimate knowledge. We can never fully understand the world because life's condition is necessarily incomplete. In this respect, the labyrinth provides a metaphor for human existence: we are led inexorably along a path by a mystery we can never fully unravel but which we are destined to pursue to the end.

APPRAISAL OF KEY ADVANCES AND CONTROVERSIES

During his life, Bataille was a marginal figure whose influence on French intellectual life was discreet but significant. Through editing the journals *Documents* and *Critique* and as the motivating figure in the groups Acéphale and College of Sociology, he came into contact with many of the leading figures of the interwar period, making firm friends with writers and artists of the surrealist circles, such as Michel Leiris, Roger Caillois, René Char, and André Masson. Friendship, indeed, was a crucial element in Bataille's make-up, which meant far more to him that any impersonal 'influence', whether with his contemporaries or with ancestors – most notably Nietzsche and Hegel – as he was drawn by the community founded in a fundamental refusal of the poison of servility. This was the 'journey to the end of the night' of which he spoke at the time of Acéphale.

The community of which Bataille dreamed in the 1930s was continued in the friendships he later formed, especially with Maurice Blanchot and Michel Fardoulis-Lagrange, who responded most firmly to what Blanchot would call the 'unconfessable community'. In no sense were they his 'disciples'. Rather they engaged in a conversation in which Bataille is – as interlocutor or confidant – ever present. Blanchot was the more explicit in making clear the nature of this friendship that had, by its very nature, to be unacknowledged. It was founded, as Blanchot put it, in 'thought's profound grief'. The idea of this community is ultimately transgressive, which is why it cannot be 'confessed'.

Blanchot's relation with Bataille has been widely recognized. It lies in a concern with social being, the problem of the consciousness of death, and the moral responsibility that transgression entails. A similar interest in human existence as resulting from an act that is essentially transgressive is central to the less well-known work of Fardoulis-Lagrange, who is similarly intrigued by the limits of existence and the pull of death.

Friendship is often also marked by the quality of one's enemies and Bataille did not lack for the latter. An early tiff between him and André Breton is well known, reflecting an ambivalent relation between the two men which was the result of a clash of different temperaments rather than any substantial differences of opinion.

A less ambivalent antagonist was Jean-Paul Sartre. Sartre criticized Bataille in an early (1943) essay, 'Un nouveau mystique'. Sartre's critique reads oddly today, as it has little relation to the issues now associated with Bataille. Yet it remains important. Based on the idea of self-creation by assuming responsibility and commitment, Sartre's philosophy is fundamentally at odds with Bataille's undermining of individual becoming. Bataille's ideas about the nature of existence are a threat to the way Sartre conceives of both the self and the responsibility it must assume in order to realize itself. For Sartre, Bataille's ideas revealed a return to a dangerous form of mysticism, which had to be combated through philosophical analysis. Bataille responded in an essay included in *On Nietzsche*. In it he refused to reduce his argument to the frame of reference Sartre would impose. Instead he brought attention to Sartre's fundamental bad faith in seeking to reduce the problem of communication to an issue of philosophical coherence.

If Sartre's critique now seems anachronistic and even off-beam, it has still served to mark out the way Bataille has been received by later writers – both by his detractors and by his admirers – as an antirationalist precursor of the post-structuralist project of deconstruction. And it is in relation to the latter that Bataille has generally been judged.

Whatever their orientation, all of the early encounters with Bataille's thought were marked by a sense of passion. While he lived, Bataille was outside the mainstream of French thought. He was respected within a narrow circle and his thought tended to provoke some extreme reactions. In contrast, since his death, he has become almost an icon of a particular type of social criticism. His importance is now recognized in fields as diverse as philosophy, literature, theology, sociology, anthropology, and even political economy. Yet a very different Bataille has emerged with the appearance of the post-structuralist criticism which has been responsible for establishing Bataille's reputation. Derrida, Sollers, Barthes, Kristeva, Baudrillard, and Foucault have all written about him and it is these texts that have served to mark Bataille as a key figure in contemporary thought.

What unites all of these writers, beyond the very real differences that exist between them, is the will to unravel – in one way or another – the power relations that frame Western ideas. Bataille is undoubtedly an important figure in opening the way into such a project. Through the critique he made of the coherence of thought and the integrity of the subject, Bataille provided ammunition for the deconstructive impulse that characterizes post-structuralism. Yet in many other ways, his thought is intrinsically alien to its discourse. As much was at times apparent even to Derrida who stated that it is necessary to read Bataille against himself. Similar doubts have also been voiced by Baudrillard and Foucault. Yet this has not prevented Bataille's thought from being appropriated as part of the post-structuralist discourse.

It is true that Bataille gave both Baudrillard and Foucault some points of departure. Baudrillard drew upon Bataille in his critique of Marxist ideas of consumerism, and his idea of seduction has a provocative quality that recalls Bataille. Yet there is a cynical side to Baudrillard that leads him to vulgarize his argument by reducing it to a level of derision in which the only thing that is real is the reproduction of signs.

Foucault's attraction to Bataille was founded in the idea of transgression. In this respect, Bataille opened up a fertile path for Foucault to follow. Yet Foucault conceived transgression in quite a different way to Bataille. He saw it as a subversive subtext within modern society. It refers to whatever has the effect of dissolving categories and resisting essentializing processes. As such, it provided a key to understanding how discourse had taken the shape it has and so provides a means by which to resist the universalizing processes that lie at the root of humanist tenets. This provides the background to Foucault's concept of power, which is seen as diffuse, arising from an ungraspable, abstract play of contingencies. It upholds a pluralistic view that denies dialectical resolution (indeed, in his text on Bataille, he sees transgression as providing almost an antidote to dialectical thinking). This could hardly be further from Bataille, who saw transgression as being irrevocably and dialectically tied to an initial interdiction. In this respect, Bataille's understanding of social relationships is in line with the complicity that Hegel saw as central to the master and slave relation which for Foucault was fundamentally erroneous. In Bataille's view transgression was a communal dynamic that, far from being realized in modern society, was fast vanishing. It was part of the sacred which the forward thrust of capitalism must shatter if it is to realize itself and which it is unable to contain. This is because, for Bataille, transgression does not subvert the taboo but completes and reinforces it. This does mean that it is a simple bolster for the taboo: Bataille's thinking is not a roundabout way of legitimating authority and the law. Quite the contrary: the purpose of transgression is to challenge the taboo, to ensure that it retains a dynamic force and is not reduced to the level of fixed laws. The taming of the sacred and of transgression in modern society is thus a triumph of a law that is inexorable rather than subject to transgressive forces.

Plurality of being is what matters above all to Foucault and this represents a crucial difference with Bataille, whose analysis is founded in an assumption of universality and a will towards totality. This is precisely what Foucault sees as being the core component of the false analysis of power relations, especially that which is founded on the Hegelian dialectic. Crucially, Foucault believed that power relations could be unpicked. He seems to have conceived himself as a safebreaker able to crack the combination that maintains the existing state of things. Bataille, on the other hand, saw social relations as founded in a movement that is unknowable (as it stands outside the concept of understanding) and there could never be any possibility of their being 'remade'. It was thus the complicity at the heart of the master–slave dialectic that provided the key for an understanding of power relations, not a breaking down of their structures. And it was transformation, not deconstruction, that was the focus for change as Bataille saw it.

From this point of view, too, the idea that Bataille was in some way concerned with a critique of reason is also a misconception. This is the opinion of Jürgen Habermas. Yet if Bataille's thought is rooted in a suspicion of the Western tradition of rational thought, this does not mean that he was concerned to undermine reason itself. He was more interested in revealing the limitations of Western, and especially French, traditions of rationality.

There exists a considerable gulf between Bataille and the ideas about the nature of reality that are associated with post-structuralism and its concern with discursive structures and signs. This distrust of meta-narrative leads to a refusal to engage with the moral centre that founds any idea of human society. Life is perceived as a top that spins endlessly on itself and offers no escape from its gyratory motion. It may be true that in Bataille too there is no escape from its paradox, but this does not mean that life is simply a plurality of endless possibilities turning on themselves. If there is no prospect of transcendence or salvation, this is because we are beings who are confined to a limited frame that defines our humanness. But as humans we are only a small part of the potentiality of existence. The continuity of existence remains present all around us. We may not be able to conceive of its heterogeneous possibilities, but we do gain glimpses of them in moments of dissolution. And we have a duty as humans to follow up such glimpses, wherever they might lead.

What one fails to detect in almost all of the writings about Bataille emerging from the post-structuralist and postmodernist stable is any tone of intimacy or discretion. Most of these texts are raucous; they bring attention to themselves and proclaim their transgressions in a way that Bataille would without much doubt have found vulgar.

In many ways, Bataille is a modest thinker. He made no claim to be able to explain the world, or even the small part of it of which he had experience. This makes him difficult to place as a social theorist. Yet even if, by bringing attention to the idea of nonknowledge, he undermined the path of pure knowledge that Western thought has tended to see as the route to enlightenment, he still upheld the significance of the quest for understanding in the widest sense. In this respect, his method has a good deal in common with Adorno's call for a negative dialectic.

In bringing attention to the way that all knowledge is, in the end, delusory, Bataille shows how it is ultimately impossible to grasp the essence of any person's thought. Any account that aims to reduce someone's life to a few words is therefore to be treated with caution. Including, no doubt, this one.

BATAILLE'S MAJOR WORKS

Bataille's writings are available in the 12 volumes of his *Oeuvres Complètes* (1971–88) Paris: Gallimard. The contents are as follows:

Volume I: *Early Writings, 1922–40, Histoire de l'oeil, L'Anus solaire, Sacrifices, Articles.*

Volume II: *Posthumously Published Writings, 1922–40.*

Volume III: *Literary Works, Madame Edwarda, Le Petit, L'Archangélique, L'Impossible, La Scissiparité, L'Abbé C, L'Etre indifférencié n'est rien, Le Bleu du ciel.*

Volume IV: *Posthumously Published Literary Works, Poems, Le Mort, Julie, La Maison brûlée, La Tombe de Louis XXX, Divinus Deus, Ebauches.*

Volume V: *La Somme Athéologique 1, L'Expérience intérieure, Méthode de Méditation, Le Coupable, L'Alleluiah.*

Volume VI: *La Somme Athéologique 2, Sur Nietzsche, Mémorandum.*

Volume VII: *L'Économie à la mesure de l'univers, La Part maudite, La Limite de l'utile, Théorie de la religion, Conférences 1947–48.*

Volume VIII: *L'Histoire de l'érotisme, Le Surréalisme au jour le jour, Conférences 1951–53, La Souveraineté.*

Volume IX: *Lascaux ou la naissance de l'art, Manet, La Littérature et le Mal.*

Volume X: *L'Erotisme, Le Procès de Gilles de Rais, Les Larmes d'Eros.*

Volume XI: *Articles, 1944–49.*

Volume XII: *Articles, 1950–61.*

In addition, his letters to Roger Caillois are available in:

Bataille, G. (1987) *Lettres à Roger Caillois.* Rennes: Editions Folle Avoine.

He is the subject of an excellent biography: Michel Surya (1987) *Georges Bataille: la mort à l'oeuvre* Paris: Garamont. Jean-Paul Sartre's essay, 'Un nouveau mystique' is to be found in the journal *Cahiers du Sud* (1943) and is reprinted in *Situations 1* Paris: Gallimard, 1947.

English Translations

Bataille, G. (1955a) *Manet* (Trans. Austryn Wainhouse & James Emmons). Geneva: Skira; London: Macmillan.

Bataille, G. (1955b) *Prehistoric Painting: Lascaux or the Birth of Art.* (Trans Austryn Wainhouse). Geneva: Skira; London: Macmillan.

Bataille, G. (1956) *The Beast At Heaven's Gate* (Madame Edwarda) (Trans. Austryn Wainhouse). Paris: Olympia Press.

Bataille, G. (1962) *Eroticism.* (Trans Mary Dalwood). London: Calder & Boyars; (1986) San Fransisco: City Lights; (1987) London: Marion Boyars.

Bataille, G. (1972) *My Mother.* (Trans. Austryn Wainhouse). London: Jonathan Cape.

Bataille, G. (1973) *Literature and Evil* (Trans. Alastair Hamilton). London: Calder & Boyars.

Bataille, G. (1977) *The Story of the Eye.* (Trans. Joachim Neugroschel). New York: Urizen Books; (1979) London: Marion Boyars; (1982) Harmondsworth: Penguin.

Bataille, G. (1979) *Blue of Noon* (Trans. Harry Matthews). London: Marion Boyars.

Bataille, G. (1983) *L'Abbé C.* (Trans. Philip A. Facey). London: Marion Boyars.

Bataille, G. (1985) *Visions of Excess: Selected Writings 1927–1939.* (Trans. Allan Stoekl). Manchester: Manchester University Press.

Bataille, G. (1986) 'Writings on laughter, sacrifice, Nietzsche, un-knowing. (Trans. Annette Michelson), *October*, 36, Spring.

Bataille, G. (1988a) *Inner Experience* (Trans. Leslie Anne Boldt). Albany: State University of New York.

Bataille, G. (1988b) *Guilty.* (Trans Bruce Boone). Venice, CA: Lapis Press.

Bataille, G. (1988c) *The Accursed Share.* (Trans Robert Hurley). New York: Zone Books.

Bataille, G. (1988d) *Theory of Religion.* (Trans Robert Hurley). New York: Zone Books.

Bataille, G. (1989b). *The Tears of Eros.* (Trans. John Connor). San Fransisco, CA: City Lights.

Bataille, G. (1989b) *My Mother, Madame Edwarda, The Dead Man.* (Trans. Austryn Wainhouse). London: Marion Boyars.

Bataille, G. (1991a) *The Impossible*. (Trans. Robert Hurley). San Fransisco, CA: City Lights.

Bataille, G. (1991b) *The Trial of Gilles de Rais*. (Trans Robert Robinson). Los Angeles, CA: Amok.

Bataille, G. (1992) *On Nietzsche* (Trans. Bruce Boone). London: The Athlone Press.

Bataille, G. (1994) *The Absence of Myth*. (Trans. Michael Richardson). London: Verso.

Bataille, G. (1997) *The Bataille Reader* (ed. Fred Botting and Scott Wilson). Oxford: Blackwell.

Bataille, G. (1998) *Georges Bataille: Essential Writings* (ed. Michael Richardson). London: Sage.

SECONDARY REFERENCES

Blanchot, Maurice (1997) 'Friendship', in *Friendship*. (Trans. Elizabeth Rottenberg). Stanford, CA: Stanford University Press.

Bois, Yve-Alain and Krauss, Rosalind (1997) *Formless: A User's Guide*. New York: Zone Books.

Boldt-Irons, Leslie Anne (ed.) (1995) *On Bataille: Critical Essays*. Albany, NY: SUNY.

Botting, Fred and Wilson Scott (eds) (1998) *Bataille: A Critical Reader*. Oxford: Blackwell.

Brotchie, A. (ed) (1995) *Encyclopaedia Acéphalica*. (Trans. Iain White). London: The Atlas Press.

Brown, Norman O. (1991) 'Dionysus in 1990' in *Apocalypse And/Or Metamorphosis*. Berkeley, CA: University of California Press.

Buck, P. (ed,) (1984) *Violent Silence*. London.

Calas, Nicolas (1945) 'Acephalic mysticism', *Hemispheres II*, 6. Reprinted in (1985) *Transfigurations: Art Critical Essays in the Modern Period*. Ann Arbor, MI: UMI Research Press.

Dean, Carolyn J. (1992) *The Self and its Pleasures: Bataille, Lacan and the History of the Decentered Subject*. Ithaca, NY: Cornell University Press.

Derrida, Jacques (1978) 'From restricted to general economy: a Hegelianism without reserve', in *Writing and Difference*. (Trans. Alan Bass). Chicago: University of Chicago Press.

Foucault, Michel (1977) 'Preface to transgression', in his *Language, Counter-Memory, Practice: Selected Essays and Interviews*. (ed. and trans. Donald Bouchard and Sherry Simon). Ithaca, NY: Cornell Univerisity Press.

Gill, Carolyn Bailey (ed.) (1995) *Bataille: Writing the Sacred*. London: Routledge.

Hollier, Denis (1990) *Beyond Architecture*. (Trans. Betsy Wing). Cambridge, MA: MIT Press.

Habermas, Jürgen (1987) 'Between eroticism and general economics: Georges Bataille,' in *The Philosophical Discourse of Modernity*. (Trans. Frederick Lawrence). Oxford: Polity Press.

Hollier, D. (ed.) (1988) *The College de Sociologie (1937–39)*. (Trans. Betsy Wing). Minneapolis: University of Minnesota Press.

Laure (1995) *The Collected Writings* (Trans. Jeanine Herman). San Fransisco, CA: City Lights.

Leiris, Michel (1989) 'From the impossible Bataille to the impossible *Documents*', in *Brisées: Broken Branches* (Trans. Lydia Davis). San Fransisco, CA: North Point Press.

Libertson Joseph (1982) *Proximity: Levinas, Blanchot, Bataille and Communication*. The Hague: Martinus Nihoff.

Michelson, Annette (1986) 'Heterology and the critique of instrumental reason', *October*, 36: 111–28.

Pefanis, Julian (1991) *Heterology and the Postmodern: Bataille, Baudrillard, Lyotard*. Durham, NC & London: Duke University Press.

Richardson, Michael (1994) *Georges Bataille*. London: Routledge.

Richman, Michèle (1982) *Beyond the Gift: Reading Georges Bataille*. Baltimore, MD: Johns Hopkins University Press.

Shaviro, Steven (1990) *Passion and Excess: Blanchot, Bataille, and Literary Theory*. Tallahassee: Florida State University Press.

Sollers, Philippe (1983) 'The roof', in *Writing and the Experience of Limits*. New York: Columbia University Press.

Sontag, Susan (1967) 'The pornographic imagination', in *Styles of Radical Will*. London: Secker & Warburg.

Stoekl, Allan (ed.) (1990) On Bataille, Special issue of *Yale French Studies*, 78.

Suleiman, Susan Rubin (1986) 'Pornography, transgression and the avant-garde: Bataille's *Story of the Eye*', in Nancy K. Miller (ed.) *The Poetics of Gender*. New York: Columbia University Press.

Weiss, Allen S. (1986) 'Impossible sovereignty: Between the will to power and the will to chance', *October*, 36: 129–46.

3

Maurice Merleau-Ponty

NICK CROSSLEY

> I belong to a generation of people for whom the horizon of reflection was defined by Husserl in general, Sartre more precisely, and Merleau-Ponty even more precisely.
>
> (Foucault 1988a: 141).

BIOGRAPHICAL DETAILS AND THEORETICAL CONTEXT

Though overshadowed in the public eye by his colleague and intellectual sparring partner, Sartre, Merleau-Ponty was very much at the centre of French intellectual life in the 1940s and 1950s. Eribon (1991), for example, writes of the great enthusiasm for his work amongst Parisian students, including a young Foucault and other fledgling intellectuals. Furthermore, it is notable that central structuralist writers, who condemned the work of Sartre, exempted Merleau-Ponty from their critiques and even spoke of what they had learned from him. Althusser (1994) is one example and Lévi-Strauss, who dedicated *The Savage Mind* to Merleau-Ponty, is another.

Born in 1908, Merleau-Ponty graduated from the Ecole Normale Supérieure in 1930, subsequently taking a lecturing post there, before moving on to the Sorbonne and, later, the Collège de France. He was, for a short time, the political editor of *Les Temps Modernes* and, like many of the key French thinkers of his day, attended and was greatly influenced by Kojéve's famous lectures on Hegel. He died, somewhat prematurely and unexpectedly, in May 1961.

If his work is to be pigeon-holed then 'existential phenomenology' is the most appropriate slot. *The Phenomenology of Perception*, which is his most famous and arguably his best work, is a study in existential phenomenology par excellence. As I show in this chapter, however, his work draws upon a much wider range of sources than this label might suggest, addressing issues and contributing to debates far removed from the conventional phenomenological paradigm. Moreover, even at his most technical, philosophical moments, Merleau-Ponty was always alive to the events in his own historical milieu, and always keen to bring his philosophy to bear upon these events. In particular he, like many of the French existentialists, was profoundly influenced by the impact of the Nazi occupation of France during the Second World War, and the related problem of collaboration which the French public began to address in the immediate aftermath of the liberation.

Along with many other intellectuals Merleau-Ponty had actively resisted occupation. His postwar reflections on the issue and on the role of the collaborators are notably less bold than those of many others, however. What the French learned from collaboration was 'history', he argued. That is, they learned of the interconnectedness of their own lives with those of others and the ways in which this shapes both their ways of making sense of the world, their opportunities, and the constraints they must circumnavigate. They learned that the meaning and morality of their actions are derived not from the action itself but from the place it assumes in a constantly shifting and sometimes unpredictable social whole. It is this sense of 'history' which he attempts to convey in so many of his best philosophical works.

Sociological interest in Merleau-Ponty's work has grown recently, largely as a consequence of a developing concern with issues of embodiment and the body – issues about which Merleau-Ponty says a great deal. There is clear evidence of a Merleau-Ponty influence within sociology and social theory before this time, however, specifically in the broadly 'phenomenological' traditions. Much of the early reception of Merleau-Ponty's work in the English speaking world was shaped by the seminal contributions of the sociologist and social theorist John O'Neill. O'Neill both translated a number of Merleau-Ponty's texts and offered his own critical exegesis and development of them in many central works, including *Perception, Expression and History*, *Sociology as a Skin Trade*, and *The Communicative Body* (O'Neill, 1970, 1972, 1989).

SOCIAL THEORY AND CONTRIBUTIONS

Merleau-Ponty's first major work, *The Structure of Behaviour*, is best regarded as a contribution to the philosophy of biology and psychology. It is informed by the work of Hegel and Husserl, both of whom would remain central reference points in all of his writing, but the influence of the gestalt psychologists is even more evident. Though problematic in some respects, in his view, their theories and findings, not least their commitment to a structural-holistic position, have important philosophical implications. The key achievement of *The Structure of Behaviour* is to posit a strong critique of mechanistic and reductionist accounts of human behaviour and to develop a clear conception of 'the human order' as a distinct and irreducible level of reality.

Next came *The Phenomenology of Perception*. This text is more obviously 'phenomenological' and picks up on the three central themes that had emerged in the later writings of Husserl: habitus, embodiment, and history. In *The Crisis of the European Sciences*, Husserl (1970) had argued that we need to examine the world of immediate experience, the world as we experience it prior to scientific objectification. This is what Merleau-Ponty does, establishing in particular the corporeal nature of that experience. Science encourages us to think of 'the body' as an object, he argues, but we discover a very different body in our experience. Our bodies are not given to us as objects. Rather, we are our bodies. They are our very way of being-in-the-world and they thereby 'give' us a world. Reinterpreting the Husserlian conception of intentionality, he then considers the multiple ways in which the world appears for us by way of our corporeal dispositions and activities. Moreover, he argues that this same embodied experience underlies and makes possible the work of the scientist, whatever they might say about 'the body' as a physical object.

Even as he does this, however, Merleau-Ponty adds a curious twist to the Husserlian project, by incorporating the findings of the human sciences, particularly psychology, in his discussion. Husserl had warned against any such incorporation, arguing that it would reduce knowledge claims to their alleged psychological 'causes', displacing questions of their validity and, at the same time, undermining its own claim to truth. The practice of the human sciences for Husserl raises epistemological questions whose answers must be resolved without recourse to the claims of those sciences if circularity is to be avoided. In addition, he claims that the human sciences cannot find solutions to these epistemological questions as they reduce human subjects to the status of empirical objects. Merleau-Ponty takes a different view, however. He believed that 'modern' psychology, which for him meant gestalt psychology, was arriving at many of the same conclusions as phenomenology and, in essence, accorded a similar degree of respect to the structure of (embodied) 'consciousness'. This paved the way, in his view, for a dialogue between the two. Moreover, he argued that one could not ignore the findings of science, as more abstract and intellectualist philosophies tended to do. Experiments, he believed, were no less valuable sources for philosophical reflection than introspection and could, in fact, teach us things that we could not discover by way of introspection.

Substantively, Merleau-Ponty's investigation of embodiment stresses two key points. On the one hand, he seeks to emphasize that our body is our 'point of view on the world'. All experience is necessarily perspectival, he maintains, and our bodies are our perspective. The other side of this claim is that our embodiment necessarily entails worldliness; our bodies involve us in the world and we are always already engaged in it, so much so that body and world should be deemed elements of a single system. Secondly, following on from this, Merleau-Ponty's conception of the body is profoundly holistic. Whether discussing sexuality, perception, or motor behaviour, he is always concerned to reveal their interrelatedness within the body–world whole.

Logocentrism and the Lived World

For Merleau-Ponty, the world as it is revealed through lived bodily experience is not the objective world of the scientist. It is preobjective and prereflective; a practical world which we have a grasp upon, literally as well as metaphorically, but which we do not, in the first instance, 'know' in a conceptual or intellectual manner. The 'space' that we live in and through is not that described by geometry, for example. It is an oriented and practical space centred around our own corporeal agency, with its capacities and projects; a space of 'ups', 'downs', 'highs', and 'lows' which we 'know' in the form of a feel we have for it and a capacity to move within it. Following Husserl's *Crisis*, Merleau-Ponty identifies this 'lifeworld' as fundamental, suggesting that the objective world of science rests upon it. Geometrical space, for example, is an idealization erected upon the foundation of lived space. Like Husserl, however, Merleau-Ponty also believes that we live in a logocentric era (not a word he actually uses) in which the derivative idealizations of science are taken to be more real than the fuzzy realities of the lifeworld. Thus, his investigations of the lived world are not simply descriptions of a primordial level of experience but equally critiques of logocentrism and the excesses of scientific objectivism. From a sociological point of view this clearly anticipates Bourdieu's (1977, 1992) notion of the 'fuzzy logic' of practice, offering a somewhat more extensive exploration of the matter than one finds in Bourdieu.

Habit, Freedom, and Structuration

The Phenomenology of Perception also builds upon and takes issue with the work of Sartre (1969), whose *Being and Nothingness* blended Husserlian and Hegelian phenomenologies in a very distinctive way. Sartre had posited a peculiarly radical conception of freedom in his work, which effectively suggested that everything human beings are and do, qua humans, can be explained in these terms. Merleau-Ponty finds this problematic. It renders the notion of freedom unintelligible, he argues. In the first instance, any meaningful conception of freedom necessitates a notion of choice, but choice presupposes a prior engagement with and belongingness to the world. To choose we must always already experience our position within the world as a meaningful site of predelineated possible actions, we must have preferences upon which to base our choice, and we must have taken-for-granted means of deliberation and decision making at our disposal. None of these preconditions can themselves be chosen, however, at least not in the final instance, precisely because they are prerequisites. They must be pregiven and our choices are therefore necessarily rooted in and shaped by them. Secondly, our choices must not simply be rooted in the world; they must take root in the world if we are to speak meaningfully of freedom. An individual who approaches each day or each hour anew has no freedom as none of their projects would ever come to fruition. Each momentary burst of free will would undo the achievements of the one preceding it. True freedom entails that by acting we commit ourselves, transforming both ourselves and our circumstances in relatively durable ways which cannot be simply erased or undone.

The Husserlian notion of habitus (Husserl, 1972, 1989, 1991), which Merleau-Ponty renders as 'habit', is used to add weight to both of these arguments, at the same time building in a third argument, that human subjects necessarily belong to a social-historical world which they share in with others and which shapes their ways of perceiving, thinking, and acting. Habits, which in their collective form we know as culture or custom, root us in the world, providing the necessary background of meaning and preference which makes choice possible. Furthermore, it is our tendency towards habituation which makes choices meaningful by affording them durability. This does not imply, as in many psychological renderings of 'habit', a conditioned reflex; nor is it necessarily restricted to simple behaviours or 'bad habits'. Restoring the more traditional sense of habit (see Camic, 1986) and at the same time anticipating Bourdieu (1977, 1992), Merleau-Ponty views habitual action as purposive, meaningful, and 'competent'. And he applies it to a range of higher intellectual and moral activities. Our disposition to talk and think in the language of our society is one clear example of habit for Merleau-Ponty, for example. Notwithstanding this, however, habit implies a certain prereflective and even prepersonal disposition towards predictable but at the same time arbitrary patterns of actions. It is the realm of the taken-for-granted. The process by which our thoughts take shape in language is not one to which we are privy, for example. Our thoughts just occur to us in linguistic form. Furthermore, as the language example also illustrates, many of our habits are collective constructions, passed on through generations, which function to reproduce both a shared social world and, of necessity, the agents who embody that world. The agent, for Merleau-Ponty as for Husserl (1991), is a product of habit; and habituation is an incorporation of social practices into the subject's 'bodily schema', where they effectively become structures of subjective being.

None of this seeks to challenge the notion that human beings are, in a sense, free. But it suggests a 'situated' rather than an absolute freedom. Human beings transcend the given by way of their projects, for Merleau-Ponty. They are capable of both creative action and choice. But they are always situated within the world, anchored by their habits, and are never 'suspended in nothingness'. This renders their actions predictable and more or less probable and, as such, is far truer to our sense of history than Sartre's model. Sartre's philosophy points to an absurd situation, in Merleau-Ponty's view, in which any event is equally likely at any time and we have no reason to suppose that states of affairs might not be transformed into their opposite at any moment; dictators might become democrats and stable social orders might explode in revolutionary fervour. The notion of habit and its cognates, custom and institution, do not preclude change, of course. Indeed, they are very much consistent with a processual view of social life. But they do suggest that changes are never absolute; that some continuity is necessary and inevitable. Moreover, they suggest that radical changes, whether at the personal or the public level, generally have a history which allows us to understand and perhaps even sometimes predict them. The durability provided by habit makes history a process rather than a series of discontinuous events, in Merleau-Ponty's view, allowing us to speak of direction and patterns therein. It gives history meaning, in the sense of which Husserl speaks in *The Crisis* (1970).

It is important to emphasize here that 'situatedness' does not imply causation or some unholy alliance of causation and free will. It points to a completely different way of thinking about agency which refuses to structure the debate around these polarities, tracing out a third term between them which does more justice to the evidence of reason, experience, and social science. Causal accounts require reference to 'external' forces, Merleau-Ponty notes, but the notion of 'situation' implies no such thing. I am not determined by 'my body' for the very simple reason that I am my body and 'it' enjoys no independent existence from me. Similarly with language, thought, and speech; language does not determine my thought or speech any more than they determine it, for the simple reason that thought, speech, and language are different aspects of a single form of embodied action.

This point has an interesting implication that Merleau-Ponty develops in both early and later essays; namely, that social structures, such as language, do not exist independently of the interactions which embody them. In effect this amounts to an anticipation of the 'structurationist' theories of Giddens (1984) and, more particularly, Bourdieu (1977, 1992). Action is said to be rooted in acquired habits or 'institutions'. Indeed, one of the key themes of Merleau-Ponty's lectures at the Collège de France was that the phenomenological notion of the 'constituting subject' should be replaced with the notion of the 'instituting subject'; that is, of the subject who bestows meaning upon the world by way of the institutionalized repertoires they have acquired from their society (Merleau-Ponty, 1979b). But these institutions, in turn, have no existence independently of the activities of embodied agents. Though social institutions predate individuals and outlive them, it is a mistake to infer from this that they are, in any meaningful sense, 'external' to the human populations who embody them at any one time.

The issues of embodied subjectivity and habituation are central here. The social world is effectively reproduced by way of its incorporation within the body, its sedimentation in the form of habit, and its subsequent and consequent enactment. The social is incorporated in and constantly regenerated by the prereflective corporeal schema of the agent. It is in this sense that Merleau-Ponty was to claim that:

> Our relationship to the social is like our relationship to the world, deeper than any express perception or judgment. It is as false to place ourselves in society as an object amongst objects as it is to place society in ourselves as an object of thought, and in both cases the mistake lies in treating the social as an object. We must return to the social with which we are in contact by the mere fact of existing, and which we carry around inseparably with us before any objectification. (Merleau-Ponty, 1962: 362)

The social, in other words, is no more separate from us than our bodies. It is what we 'do'. Integral to this, moreover, is the notion of the social as an interworld or intersubjective structure. The social world is not just what we do but what we do collectively in the context of social relations, and our habits are the collective habits of a shared culture or subculture. Social relations, as embodied in interactions, constitute the occasion and the mechanism for the construction, modification, and reproduction of our habits and, at the same time, it is these relations and the orientations they rest upon that are reproduced by way of our habits.

The key social relations identified in *The Phenomenology of Perception* are class relations and, in his brief discussion of them, Merleau-Ponty again emphasizes the sense in which they are embodied in habitual ways of being. Such ways of being are formed in the context of conflictual class relations which they then help to perpetuate. Merleau-Ponty writes:

> What makes me a proletarian is not the economic system or society considered as systems of impersonal forces but these institutions as I carry them within me and experience them [as habits -NC]; nor is it an intellectual operation devoid of motive, but my way of being in the world within this institutional framework.
>
> Let us suppose that I have a certain style of living, being at the mercy of booms and slumps, not being free to do as I like, receiving a weekly wage, having no control over either the conditions or the products of my work, and consequently feeling a stranger in my factory, my nation and my life. I have acquired the habit of reckoning with a fatum, or appointed order, which I do not respect but which I have to humour. (Merleau-Ponty, 1962: 443-4)

Empiricism and Intellectualism

At a more general level *The Phenomenology of Perception* is structured around a dialectical critique of 'empiricism' and 'intellectualism'. Almost every issue tackled in the book is approached by way of a critique of these two traditions. The empiricism to which Merleau-Ponty refers in this context comprises both the philosophical tradition of British empiricism and the behaviourist tradition in psychology. It understands human beings to be objects within a world which, itself, is an object. Intellectualism, by contrast, formulates a conception of the human subject who bestows sense upon the world through constituting acts of consciousness. Kant, and to some extent Husserl, are the candidates for this school. The latter of these schools is the most preferable of the two, for Merleau-Ponty, but it is nevertheless flawed. The relation of human beings to the world is not, in the first instance, that of a subject to an object. It consists, as we have said, in practical and embodied engagement. We have a practical 'grasp' upon the world, an embodied know-how, before we have explicit discursive knowledge of it and the latter, insofar as it does arise, necessarily forms upon the basis of the former. Furthermore, the intellectualist view is flawed insofar as it fails to properly consider our aforementioned 'situatedness': we are situated in a body which is vulnerable to the physical forces which may act upon it, a world of habit and cultural institutions which structure our perceptions, thoughts, and actions; and we are always bound up in various relations of interconnectedness with others, subject to the dynamics of intersubjective life and social relations. Finally, intellectualism is flawed insofar as it focuses exclusively upon the reflective level of consciousness. Following Sartre's (1957) argument in *The Transcendence of the Ego*, Merleau-Ponty argues that consciousness does not necessarily entail self-consciousness and that, for much of the time, we are absorbed in what we are doing and have no real sense of ourselves at the reflective level.

Existential Marxism

At the same time as he wrote *The Phenomenology of Perception*, Merleau-Ponty was writing a number of political articles. Some of these articles, collected in *Humanism and Terror*, addressed the moral questions raised by the Moscow Trials, the fictional representation of those trials in Koestler's *Darkness at Noon*, and the problems of collaboration during the Nazi occupation of France. Merleau-Ponty was particularly concerned, in this book, with the manner in which actions acquire meaning through history. We cannot determine or know the meaning of our actions when we act, he argues, since that meaning will depend upon the place which our actions assume in a wider schema of history. A well-intentioned act may transpire as the gravest form of treachery if subsequent events so dictate, and individuals must be prepared to face the music if this is so.

The broader context of these reflections on history is influenced by Husserl's *Crisis*. Marx is the more immediate and obvious interlocuter, however, and this dialogue is even more direct in some of the essays in *Sense and Non-Sense*. Here Merleau-Ponty reads Marx in an existential light, even claiming that '... the concrete thinking which Marx calls "critique" to distinguish it from speculative philosophy, is what others propound under the name "existential philosophy"' (Merleau-Ponty, 1971: 133). Marx's battle with idealism and materialism, he argues, mirrors his own battle with intellectualism and empiricism. And he, like Marx, identifies a philosophy of praxis as the only reasonable way past this unhelpful dualism. Interestingly, as I have spelled out in more detail elsewhere (Crossley, 1994), much that he says in this connection prefigures key Althusserian concepts, such as 'relative autonomy' and 'structure in dominance'. Without dismissing the possibility that economic relations and dynamics may prove, in fact, to be the primary driving force of history, shaping ideological and political practices to a far greater extent than vice versa, Merleau-Ponty was determined to rescue Marxism from the deterministic, reductionist, and mechanistic interpretations espoused by the French communist party. He aspired to a philosophy of history and the social world that gave due consideration to the 'relative autonomy' of specific arenas of practice, particularly art and literature, whilst at the same time being both praxiological and holistic.

Post-Marxism

In this early writing Merleau-Ponty adopted what he called a 'wait and see' attitude towards the big questions of Marxism: that is, actual and potential revolutions. In his later writing, however, he clearly did not like what he saw and refused to wait any longer. In particular the Korean war and Kruschev's denunciation of Stalin in 1956 persuaded him of the need to renounce Marxism, which he did in a number of articles (collectively published in *Signs*) and, most famously, in *Adventures of the Dialectic*. This latter text reflects upon the work of Weber, Trotsky, Lukàcs, Lenin, and Sartre (who had not yet published the *Critique of Dialectical Reason* but whose *Communists and Peace* had just been published). Ironically Sartre was shifting towards Marxism at this time, when Merleau-Ponty, who had always been the more political and leftist of the two, was abandoning it. And *Adventures of the Dialectic* involves a strong, uncompromising, and very long critique of Sartre's 'ultrabolshevism'. Indeed, this critique occupies almost half of the book. Sartre's Marxism is just one in a long line of attempts ('Adventures') to sustain the Marxist vision in the face of historical adversity, for Merleau-Ponty, however. As the tides of history have turned, so too has the theory been altered or reinterpreted. This is theoretically problematic; whilst revisions may be necessary there reaches a point where one has to consider whether the theory ought not simply to be abandoned. Over and above this, however, he argued that the continual resurrection and revision of the theory had allowed it to serve an ideological function within a regime of political terror. Deterministic and voluntaristic versions of Marxism alike served to fuel the illusion and to justify the forcing of individuals into a historical system that was not working and was quite literally killing many of them.

In *Humanism and Terror* Merleau-Ponty had shocked many by seemingly supporting the Moscow Trials and observing that all major social transitions involve bloodshed. By the mid-1950s, however, he had decided that the USSR (as it was) could no longer be considered a society in transition. Its violence was institutionalized, necessary to its own perpetuation and without any hope of ever becoming any other than what it was. He thus condemned it.

Structuralism

The Adventures of the Dialectic and some related essays appear to identify the work of Weber as a possible starting point for Merleau-Ponty's post-Marxist reconstruction of social theory. What comes through more strongly, however, is his move in a more structuralist and even post-structuralist direction. As Foucault (1998b: 21) recalled, Merleau-Ponty was the first of the French philosophers to lecture on the work of Saussure and to reflect upon its philosophical significance. Indeed, in his inaugural lecture at the Collège de France, in 1953, Merleau-Ponty went as far as to suggest that the philosophy of history might be reconstructed using Saussure's framework. This tendency was doubtless reinforced by his friendship with both Lévi-Strauss and Lacan and his interest in their work. He wrote an essay on Lévi-Strauss, and he explored Lacan's early formulation of 'the mirror stage', tying it back to some of the notions from gestalt psychology upon which it is based, in his lectures on child development.

There can be no doubt that Merleau-Ponty's engagement with these ideas was enthusiastic and this should perhaps be less surprising than it sounds with hindsight. Not only had he been fascinated with the concept of structure from his very earliest exploration of it in *The Structure of Behaviour*, but the dividing line between structuralism and phenomenology was by no means as sharply drawn in the Parisian philosophical circles of the 1950s as they subsequently became in structuralist social theory. Notwithstanding this, however, Merleau-Ponty's appropriation of structuralist ideas was both critical and idiosyncratic. He identified an equal role for *langue/parole* or structure/action, for example, and certainly refused to 'dissolve man'. I noted earlier that he anticipated the structurationist move in social theory and this is evident in his reading of structuralism. In his essay on Lévi-Strauss, for example, he writes:

> For the philosopher, the presence of structure outside us in natural and social systems and within us as a symbolic function points to a way beyond the subject–object correlation which has dominated philosophy from Descartes to Hegel. By showing us that man is eccentric to himself and that the social finds its centre only in man, structure particularly enables us to understand how we are in a sort of circuit with the socio-historical world. (Merleau-Ponty, 1964: 123)

This passage concedes that the meaning of human action lies outside of the sphere of agents themselves; 'man', Merleau-Ponty writes, is 'eccentric to himself'. One obvious example of this would be that the human speaker must conform to the law of their language if they are to make sense either to themselves or to others. Sense depends upon the structure of language. But the structure of language is not external to human beings for Merleau-Ponty. It is an intersubjective structure; an interworld rooted in shared habits or conventions and modified across time by way of 'coherent deformations'. In this sense, as he says, 'the social finds its centre only in man'. It is for this reason that Merleau-Ponty resists the notion that structures 'dissolve man' and maintains, instead, that they reveal us to be 'in a sort of circuit with the socio-historical world'.

Integral to this is a reservation about both the theoreticism of structuralism and its totalizing aspirations. In *Adventures of the Dialectic* Merleau-Ponty criticized the totalizing aspirations of Marxism as both a theoretical and a political project. Totalizing projects often become terrorizing projects in the view of the later Merleau-Ponty. In his discussion of Lévi-Strauss and more particularly Saussure, these reservations re-emerge in a different, more philosophical form. Saussure's '*langue*' is a theoretical model, he notes, based upon abstraction from linguistic praxis. There is a danger within structuralism that this becomes forgotten, however, such that the model is taken to be more real than the praxis and is afforded primacy over it. It is assumed that structure somehow 'determines' practice, which is clearly absurd given that the only reality the structure has is its partial realization in practice. Or alternatively, it is assumed that linguistic agents in some sense follow the 'rules' of language, which is again absurd as the rules are quite insufficient to specify action and, in any case, could not be followed as they are not known. What Merleau-Ponty appears to be arriving at here is a critique of structuralism similar to that of Bourdieu (1977, 1992). It is interesting, however, that he also anticipates one of Derrida's central critiques of Saussure, albeit taking it in a different direction. In a diacritical system of the sort posited by the structuralists, he notes, the meaning of every word is dependent upon every other and thus ultimately upon the totality. This is problematic from two points of view. First, languages are historical structures, constantly changing, and are thus never totalized. If meaning was dependent upon the totality then we could literally never make sense. Secondly, the notion of totality is problematic if we consider the users of language. How could they ever learn to make and understand meaning in language if meaning is dependent upon the totality of language? One learns first to use a few words, with no sense of the whole, and yet one can make and communicate sense. Furthermore, one never acquires the 'whole' of language, not least for the aforementioned reason that the whole is in a constant flux and cannot ever be said to be bounded. Merleau-Ponty's solution to these problems, seemingly, is to call for a focus on linguistic praxis, the uses of language. It is in use that the sense of language is determined and it is therefore to use that we, as philosophers and social scientists, must look for an understanding of language and meaning.

APPRAISAL OF KEY ADVANCES AND CONTROVERSIES

In terms of social theory, Merleau-Ponty is perhaps best remembered for his analysis of human embodiment and the notions of habit and the lived world which emerge out of it. This analysis has received much praise but it has equally been subject to a range of criticisms. On the one hand, for example, Habermas (1987: 317) dismisses Merleau-Ponty in a sentence, with the claim that he reduces rationality to the body. On the other, the phenomenology of the body has been juxtaposed to post-structuralist accounts which, firstly, focus upon the effects of power on the body and, secondly, emphasize change and instability in relation to the body. Merleau-Ponty's 'body' is deemed too stable and rational. I have criticized both of these critiques elsewhere (Crossley, 1996b, 1997). Habermas misinterprets Merleau-Ponty, in my view. His own intersubjective conception of rationality (Habermas, 1991) was actually prefigured in phenomenology. Husserl's (1991) concern to account for intersubjectivity was precisely based on a recognition that rationality presupposes intersubjectivity (see Crossley, 1996a) and Merleau-Ponty takes this notion on board even more strongly. Rationality emerges in the intersubjective interworld for Merleau-Ponty, and is in no way reducible to individual bodies. Furthermore, Habermas is too quick to dismiss the body. Intersubjective encounters are necessarily embodied and if they are to be rational too, this necessitates that our embodied state lends itself to 'communicative rationality'. If what Merleau-Ponty establishes is that our bodies do lend themselves in this way, and to some extent I believe this is so, then Merleau-Ponty may be required reading for any critical theorist who wishes to rescue the theory of communicative action from the overly abstract and disembodied clutches of the universal pragmatist.

In reply to the post-structuralist critics it is important to point out, first, that Merleau-Ponty quite clearly appreciated that our bodies are 'targets' of power, even if his understanding of power and of the ways in which it regulates the body was insufficient:

> ... consciousness can do nothing without its body and can only act upon others by acting upon their bodies. It can only reduce them to slavery by making nature an appendix of its body, by appropriating nature to itself and establishing in nature its instruments of power. (Merleau-Ponty, 1969: 102)

Moreover, if we want to go beyond the basic claim that our bodies are targets of power, to suggest that our bodies are indeed 'disciplined' by power, that is, to suggest that power is effective to some degree, then the 'stable' body that Merleau-Ponty posits is necessary on three counts. First, the application of techniques of power in real contexts of struggle presupposes competent agents who are sufficiently 'stable' and co-ordinated to manage the task. Secondly, discipline could only get a foothold on the body if the actions of the body were regular in some way. A truly unstable body would be beyond the bounds of discipline or, indeed, social life. Thirdly, a body that is disciplined is stable; discipline implies stability. If we add to this that 'body-power' can only really be an issue of serious moral concern if we assume that 'bodies', in some respects, embody agents who might act differently were they not 'invested' by power, then Merleau-Ponty's phenomenology of the embodied subject seems to have a strong reply to post-structuralism. It should be added that Merleau-Ponty's commitment to a conception of stable bodily habits which root our being-in-the-world does not preclude the possibility that bodily ways of being vary across historical epochs or cultures. Indeed, Merleau-Ponty very much believes in such variation and, as such, would doubtless agree with much of what has been argued with respect to historical variation within post-structuralist circles. The stability which he identifies in the body is very much that of short-term, day-to-day continuity.

Notwithstanding this, however, issues of difference which have been raised within post-structuralist theories of embodiment do pose more of a problem. His understanding of the situation of the subject and of power is very much focused upon a notion of class (and, to a lesser extent imperialism), to the detriment of any other forms of social differentiation and inequality. Even in his fascinating discussion of sexuality in *The Phenomenology of Perception*, for example, issues pertaining to gender and sexual identity are not discussed. This is not to say that these issues could not be developed from his perspective. In her essay, 'Throwing Like a Girl', for example, Young (1980) uses Merleau-Ponty's framework, combined with elements of Beauvoir, to develop a preliminary investigation of female subjectivity and its subjection. Similarly, the work of Fanon (1986), with its considerable debt to Sartre, might be taken as a possible starting point for a phenomenological investigation of racialized subjectivity and subjection. These are not issues which Merleau-Ponty himself pursued, however, and they clearly transcend his framework as he himself developed it.

In addition, it has been argued by Kruks (1981) that Merleau-Ponty's later social theory ran aground. While his early reflections on Marxism were both cogent and instructive, she argues, his later critique of Marxism was weak and he was able to develop no realistic alternative. Furthermore, she suggests that the drafts he was working on at the time of his death, published posthumously as *The Visible and the Invisible*, suggest no way out of this. Other commentators, particularly those who believe that Merleau-Ponty anticipated many key themes of postmodern and post-structuralist thought, tend to take a different view (see Dillon, 1988, 1991; Busch and Gallagher, 1992; Johnson and Smith, 1990). His unfinished notes have become a central focus for them. I am more in agreement with Kruks, however. *The Visible and the Invisible* presents a vague outline of ideas that could have been developed into a convincing position, but were not, and which are as problematic exegetically as they are incomplete. They may well have been models which Merleau-Ponty, in his predictable dialectical style, was going to knock down in any case.

Furthermore, though I am more persuaded than Kruks is by Merleau-Ponty's critique of Marxism, I agree that it is not clear where it leads him. Combined with the fact that Merleau-Ponty's social and political writings were very much a reflection upon his own time, this considerably limits the direct value that his broader social and political writings may have for today.

Notwithstanding this, however, we can abstract important philosophical points from his work which have a contemporary salience. Kruks (1990) herself, for example, in a different work, argues that the theory of 'situated subjectivity' provides a clear and viable path for social and political theory, between the equally problematic treatments of subjectivity that one finds in the work of liberals, such as Rawls (1971), and the post-structuralists (see also Whiteside, 1988). While Rawls ab-stracts subjects from their situations, she argues, creating a hopelessly unrealistic model of the moral agent, the post-structuralists dissolve subjects into their situations to a point where moral and political discourse becomes redundant. Merleau-Ponty, by contrast, maintains a sense of the genuine tension of a being who is, to cite an earlier quotation, 'in a sort of circuit with the socio-historical world'.

The sociological value of this notion, as I have suggested in this chapter, is an anticipation and exploration of the themes of 'structuration' theories, particularly that of Bourdieu. Bourdieu (1986) himself acknowledges the importance of Merleau-Ponty's work for the transcendence of sociological dualisms and his indebtedness to Merleau-Ponty is spelled out in some detail by Bourdieu and Wacquant in Bourdieu and Wacquant (1992). Though I do not agree entirely with Wacquant's account of Merleau-Ponty, I do agree that much of Bourdieu's work has a Merleau-Pontyan feel and that the sophistication of Bourdieu's own position is only fully appreciated when this is recognized. I do not agree with the apparent implication of Wacquant's view, however, which is that all that is useful in Merleau-Ponty is absorbed into Bourdieu. There can be no doubt that Bourdieu's concepts of power, capital, and field could lend considerable sophistication to Merleau-Ponty's attempts to make sense of the social world qua 'interworld', providing a possible escape route from the impasse of his later work; or that his account of the social shaping of the habitus develops Merleau-Ponty's own reflections on that matter in an important and substantial fashion. Merleau-Ponty's own work still retains an important phenomenological aspect that is neither contained, critiqued, nor contradicted by these developments, however, and which remains of considerable importance. He argued himself, for example, that:

> ... the social, like man himself, has two poles or facets: it is significant, capable of being understood from within, and at the same time personal intentions within it are generalized, toned down, and tend towards processes, being (as the famous [Marxist] expression has it) mediated by things. (Merleau-Ponty, 1964: 114)

What his work has to offer structuration theory, even today, is a range of insights from 'within' and an account of the 'within' which recognizes and embraces the notion that there is equally a 'without' and that, as Bourdieu (1992) argues, subjectivity can and should be 'objectified' if a full picture of our being-in-the world is to be striven for. Like Bourdieu, Merleau-Ponty identifies our habitual ways of being, our habitus, as a hinge between subjectivity and an objective social world. If Bourdieu advances our understanding of the 'outside' of that hinge, then Merleau-Ponty can still advance our grasp of the inside, and in a way which complements, rather than contradicts, Bourdieu. It goes without saying that his thesis of embodiment is central to this potential.

MERLEAU-PONTY'S MAJOR WORKS

Main English Translations of Merleau-Ponty's Work

Merleau-Ponty, M. ([1945] 1962) *The Phenomenology of Perception*. London: Routledge and Kegan Paul.

Merleau-Ponty, M. ([1960] 1964) *Signs*. Evanston, IL: Northwestern University Press.

Merleau-Ponty, M. ([1942] 1965) *The Structure of Behaviour*. Northampton: Methuen.

Merleau-Ponty, M. ([1964] 1968a) *The Visible and the Invisible*. Evanston, IL: Northwestern University Press, Evanston.

Merleau-Ponty, M. (1968b) *The Primacy of Perception and Other Essays*. Evanston, IL: Northwestern University Press.

Merleau-Ponty, M. ([1947] 1969) *Humanism and Terror*. Boston: Beacon.

Merleau-Ponty, M. ([1948] 1971) *Sense and Non-Sense*. Evanston, IL: Northwestern University Press.

Merleau-Ponty, M. ([1955] 1973) *Adventures of the Dialectic*. Evanston, IL: Northwestern University Press.

Merleau-Ponty, M. ([1970] 1974a) *The Prose of the World*. London: Heinemann.

Merleau-Ponty, M. (1974b) *Phenomenology, Language and Sociology: Selected Essays of Maurice Merleau-Ponty*. (ed. John O'Neill). London: Heinemann.

Merleau-Ponty, M. ([1964] 1979a) *Consciousness and the Acquisition of Language*. Evanston, IL: Northwestern University Press.

Merleau-Ponty, M. ([1964] 1979b) *Themes From the Lectures at the College de France*. Evanston, IL: Northwestern University Press.

Merleau-Ponty, M. ([1953] 1988) *In Praise of Philosophy*. Evanston, IL: Northwestern University Press.

Merleau-Ponty, M. (1972) *Texts and Dialogues*. New Jersey: Humanities Press.

SECONDARY REFERENCES

Althusser, L. (1994) *The Future Lasts a Long Time*. London: Vintage.

Bannan, J. (1967) *The Philosophy of Merleau-Ponty*. New York: Harcourt, Brace and World.

Bourdieu, P. (1977) *Outline of a Theory of Practice*. Cambridge: Cambridge University Press.

Bourdieu, P. (1986) 'The struggle over symbolic order', *Theory, Culture and Society*, 3(3): 35–55.

Bourdieu, P. (1992) *The Logic of Practice*. Cambridge: Polity.

Bourdieu, P. and Wacquant, L. (1992) *Invitation to Reflexive Sociology*. Cambridge: Polity.

Busch, T. and Gallagher, S. (eds) (1992) *Merleau-Ponty: Hermeneutics and Postmodernism*. New York: SUNY.

Camic, C. (1986) 'The matter of habit', *American Journal of Sociology*, 91: 1039–87.

Crossley, N. (1994) *The Politics of Subjectivity*. Avebury: Ashgate.

Crossley, N. (1995) 'Merleau-Ponty, the elusive body and carnal sociology', *Body and Society*, 1(1), 43–63.

Crossley, N. (1996a) *Intersubjectivity: the Fabric of Social Becoming*. London: Sage.

Crossley, N. (1996b) 'Body–subject/body–power: Agency, power and inscription in Foucault and Merleau-Ponty', *Body and Society*, 2(1): 99–116.

Crossley, N. (1997) 'Corporeality and communicative action', *Body and Society*, 3(1): 17–46.

Dillon, M. (1988) *Merleau-Ponty's Ontology*. Evanston, IL: Northwestern University Press.

Dillon, M. (ed.) (1991) *Merleau-Ponty Vivant*. New York: SUNY.

Edie, J. (1987) *Merleau-Ponty's Philosophy of Language: Structuralism and Dialectics*. Washington: Centre for Advanced Research In Phenomenology and University Press of America.

Eribon, D. (1991) *Michel Foucault*. Cambridge, MA: Harvard University Press.

Fanon, F. (1986) *Black Skin, White Masks*. London: Pluto.

Foucault, M. (1988a) *Foucault Live*. New York: Semiotext(e).

Foucault, M. (1988b) *Politics, Philosophy, Culture*. London: Routledge.

Froman, W. (1982) *Merleau-Ponty: Language and the Act of Speech*. London: Associated University Presses.

Giddens, A. (1984) *The Constitution of Society*. Cambridge: Polity.

Habermas, J. (1987) *The Philosophical Discourse of Modernity*. Cambridge: Polity.

Habermas, J. (1991) *The Theory of Communicative Action Vol 1: Reason and the Rationalisation of Society*. Cambridge: Polity.

Husserl, E. (1970) *The Crisis of the European Sciences and Transcendental Phenomenology*. Evanston, IL: Northwestern University Press.

Husserl, E. (1972) *Experience and Judgement*. Evanston, IL: Northwestern University Press.

Husserl, E. (1989) *Ideas Pertaining to a Pure Phenomenology: Book Two*. Dordrecht: Kluwer.

Husserl, E. (1991) *Cartesian Meditations*. Dordrecht: Kluwer.

Johnson, G. and Smith, M. (eds.) (1990) *Ontology and Alterity in Merleau-Ponty*. Evanston, IL: Northwestern University Press.

Koestler, A. (1940) *Darkness at Noon*. Harmondsworth: Penguin.

Kruks, S. (1981) *The Political Philosophy of Merleau-Ponty*. Brighton: Harvester.

Kruks, S. (1990) *Situation and Human Existence*. London: Unwin Hyman.

Kwant, R. (1963) *The Phenomenological Philosophy of Merleau-Ponty*. Pittsburgh, PA: Duquesne.

Kwant, R. (1966) *From Phenomenology to Metaphysics*. Pittsburgh, PA: Duquesne.

Langer, M. (1989) *Merleau-Ponty's Phenomenology of Perception*. London: Macmillan.

Low, D. (1987) *The Existential Dialectic of Marx and Merleau-Ponty*. New York: Peter Lang.

O'Neill, J. (1970) *Perception, Expression and History*. Evanston, IL: Northwestern University Press.

O'Neill, J. (1972) *Sociology as a Skin Trade*. London: Heinemann.

O'Neill, J. (1989) *The Communicative Body.* Evanston, IL: Northwestern University Press.

Rawls, J. (1971) *A Theory of Justice.* Cambridge, MA: MIT.

Rosenthal, S. and Bourgeois, P. (1991) *Mead and Merleau-Ponty: Towards a Common Vision.* New York: SUNY.

Sallis, J. (ed.) (1981) *Merleau-Ponty: Perception, Structure, Language.* New Jersey: Humanities Press.

Sartre, J-P. (1957) *The Transcendence of the Ego.* New York: Noonday Press.

Sartre, J-P. (1969) *Being and Nothingness.* London: Routledge.

Schmidt, J. (1985) *Maurice Merleau-Ponty: Between Phenomenology and Structuralism.* London: Macmillan.

Spurling, L. (1977) *Phenomenology and the Social World; the Philosophy of Merleau-Ponty and its Relation to the Social Sciences.* London: RKP.

Whiteside, K. (1988) *Merleau-Ponty and the Foundations of an Existential Politics.* Princeton: Princeton University Press.

Young, I. (1980) 'Throwing like a girl: A phenomenology of feminine bodily comportment, motility and spatiality', *Human Studies,* 3: 137–56.

4

Herbert Marcuse

DOUGLAS KELLNER

BIOGRAPHICAL DETAILS AND THEORETICAL CONTEXT

Herbert Marcuse was born 19 July 1898 in Berlin, Germany. The son of Carl Marcuse, a prosperous Jewish merchant and Gertrud Kreslawsky, daughter of a wealthy German factory owner, Marcuse had a typical upper-middle class Jewish life during the first two decades of the twentieth century, in which Anti-semitism was not overt in Germany. Marcuse studied in the Mommsen Gymnasium in Berlin prior to the Second World War and served with the German army in the war. Transferred to Berlin early in 1918, he participated in the German Revolution that drove Kaiser Wilhelm II out of Germany and established a Social Democratic government.

After demobilization, Marcuse went to Freiburg to pursue his studies and received a PhD in literature in 1922 for a dissertation on *The German Artist-Novel*. After a short career as a bookseller in Berlin, Marcuse returned to Freiburg and in 1928 began studying philosophy with Martin Heidegger, then one of the most significant thinkers in Germany.

In his first published articles, written from 1928–33 when he was studying with Heidegger in Freiburg, Marcuse developed a synthesis of phenomenology, existentialism, and Marxism, anticipating a project which decades later would be carried out by various 'existential' and 'phenomenological' Marxists, such as Jean-Paul Sartre and Maurice Merleau-Ponty, as well as others in Eastern Europe and the United States in the post-war period. Marcuse contended that Marxist thought had deteriorated into a rigid orthodoxy and needed concrete 'phenomenological' experience of contemporary social conditions to update and enliven the Marxian theory, which had neglected social, cultural, and psychological analysis in favour of focus on economic and political conditions. He also believed that Marxism neglected the problem of the individual, and throughout his life was concerned with personal liberation and happiness, in addition to social transformation.

Marcuse published the first major review in 1932 of Marx's recently printed *Economic and Philosophical Manuscripts of 1844*, anticipating the later tendency to revise interpretations of Marxism from the standpoint of the works of the early Marx. Marcuse was thus one of the first to see the importance of the philosophical perspectives of the early Marx on labour, human nature, and alienation which he thought were necessary to give concrete substance to Marxism. At the same time that he was writing essays synthesizing Marxism and phenomenology, Marcuse completed a study of *Hegel's Ontology and Theory of Historicity* (1932), which he intended as a *Habilitation* dissertation that would gain him university employment. The text stressed the importance of the categories of life and history in Hegel and contributed to the revival of interest in Hegel that was taking place in Europe.

In 1933, Marcuse joined the *Institut für Sozialforschung* (Institute for Social Research) in Frankfurt and became one of the most active participants in their interdisciplinary projects (see Kellner, 1989; Wiggershaus, 1994). Marcuse deeply identified with the work of the Institute, and throughout his life was close to Max Horkheimer, T.W. Adorno, Leo Lowenthal, Franz Neumann, and its other members. In 1934, Marcuse – a Jew and radical – fled from Nazism and emigrated to the United States where he lived for the rest of his life. The Institute was granted offices and an academic affiliation with Columbia University, where Marcuse worked during the 1930s and early 1940s. His first major work in English, *Reason and Revolution* (1941), introduced the ideas of Hegel, Marx, and German social theory to an English-speaking audience. Marcuse demonstrated the similarities between Hegel and Marx, and argued for discontinuities between Hegel's philosophy of the state and German Fascism, placing Hegel instead in a liberal constitutional tradition political and theoretically as a precursor of critical social theory.

In December 1942, Marcuse joined the Office of War Information as a senior analyst in the Bureau of Intelligence. He prepared a report that proposed ways that the mass media of the allied countries could present images of German Fascism. In March 1943, Marcuse transferred to the Office of Strategic Services (OSS), working until the end of the war in the Research and Analysis Division of the Central European Branch. Marcuse and his colleagues wrote reports attempting to identify Nazi and anti-Nazi groups and individuals in Germany and drafted a 'Civil Affairs Handbook' that dealt with denazification (see the texts collected in Marcuse, 1998). In September 1945, he moved over to the State Department after the dissolution of the OSS, becoming head of the Central European bureau, and remained until 1951 when he left Government service, following the death of his first wife Sophie Wertheim Marcuse; they had married in 1923 and had one child, Peter Marcuse.

After working for the US government for almost 10 years, Marcuse returned to university life. He received a Rockefeller Foundation grant to study Soviet Marxism, lecturing on the topic at Columbia during 1952–53 and Harvard from 1954–55. At the same time, he was intensely studying Freud and published in 1955 *Eros and Civilization*, a philosophical synthesis of Marx and Freud which used Freud's categories to provide a critique of bourgeois society and to sketch the outlines of a nonrepressive society. The book was well-received and anticipated many of the values of the 1960s counterculture, helping to make Marcuse a major intellectual and political force during that turbulent decade.

In 1955, Marcuse married his second wife, Inge Werner Marcuse, the widow of his friend Franz Neumann who had died in a car crash the year before. In 1958, Marcuse received a tenured position at Brandeis University, and the same year published a critical study of the Soviet Union (*Soviet Marxism*) which broke the taboo in his circles against speaking critically of the USSR and Soviet communism. Stressing the differences between the Marxian theory and the Soviet version of Marxism, Marcuse provided a sharp critique of Soviet bureaucracy, culture, values, and system. Yet he also distanced himself from those who believed Soviet communism to be incapable of reform and democratization, and pointed to potential 'liberalizing trends', which countered the Stalinist bureaucracy and that indeed eventually materialized, leading, however, to the collapse of the Soviet Union in the 1980s.

In 1964, Marcuse published *One-Dimensional Man*, which is perhaps his most important work. In 1965, Brandeis refused to renew his teaching contract and Marcuse soon after received a position at the University of California at La Jolla where he remained until his retirement in the 1970s. Throughout the 1960s, Marcuse supported demands for revolutionary change and defended the new, emerging forces of radical opposition, thus winning him the hatred of mainstream academics and conservatives and the respect of the new radicals. In a series of pivotal books and articles, Marcuse articulated New Left politics and critiques of capitalist societies, including 'Repressive Tolerance' (1965), *An Essay on Liberation* (1969a), *Five Lectures* (1970), and *Counterrevolution and Revolt* (1972). During this time, Marcuse achieved world renown as 'the guru of the New Left', giving lectures and advice to student radicals all over the world. His work was often discussed in the mass media and he became one of the few American intellectuals to gain such attention. Marcuse was a charismatic teacher, and his students began to gain academic positions and further promoted his ideas, thus contributing to his authority and importance.

After the death of his second wife, Inge Werner Marcuse in 1974, he married his third wife, Erica Sherover Marcuse, on 21 June 1976. Following the collapse of the New Left, Marcuse dedicated much of his later work to aesthetics and his final book, *The Aesthetic Dimension* (1978), contains a defence of the emancipatory potential of aesthetic form. Marcuse undertook one last trip to Germany where he lectured on topics including the Holocaust, ecology, and the fate of the Left; he suffered a severe heart attack and died in Starnberg on 29 July 1979. Since his death, Marcuse's influence has waned, surpassed, perhaps, by his Institute colleagues Adorno and Benjamin and the emergence of new modes of thinking, such as those found in post-structuralist and postmodern theory. World renowned during the 1960s as a theorist of revolution, it is perhaps as a philosopher and social theorist that Marcuse remains an important intellectual figure. Accordingly, in this chapter I will present Marcuse as a theorist who attempted to develop a synthesis of philosophy, critical social theory, and political activism in specific historical conjunctures, and will focus on delineating what I take to be his contributions, limitations, and enduring legacy.

SOCIAL THEORY AND CONTRIBUTIONS

Marcuse's thought was intimately shaped by his work with the Institute for Social Research (1933–42). The Institute was founded in Frankfurt, Germany, during the 1920s as the first Marxist-oriented research institute in Europe. Under the directorship of Max Horkheimer, who assumed his position in 1930, the Institute developed a conception of critical social theory which they contrasted with 'traditional theory'. 'Critical theory' combined philosophy, social theory, economics, cultural criticism, psychology, and other disciplines in an attempt to develop a theory of the present age. This project involved developing analyses of the new stage of state and monopoly capitalism, of the role of mass communication and culture, of the decline of the individual, and of the institutions and effects of German Fascism. Marcuse participated in all of these projects and was one of the central and most productive participants in the Institute.

In addition, the Institute for Social Research developed critiques of dominant theories and concepts of bourgeois ideology, philosophy, and social science, culminating in a critique of positivism for which it became distinguished. In his work in the 1930s and 1940s, Marcuse was one of the first critical theorists of the new forms of technological and political domination in the advanced industrial societies. Marcuse published a series of studies of German Fascism which argued that it was characterized by tensions between lawlessness and disorder contrasted with extreme rationalization and order, thus seeing it both as an anarchic gangster state that violated systematically both internal and international law and a highly rationalized system of social organization and domination. Marcuse also saw National Socialism as a new kind of state in which it was difficult to say whether economic or political factors were primary, combining economic, political, and technological domination (see Marcuse, 1998).

In a 1941 article, 'Some Social Implications of Modern Technology' (published in Marcuse, 1998) Marcuse distinguishes between 'technology' (defined 'as a mode of production, as the totality of instruments, devices and contrivances which characterize the machine age') and 'technics' (taken as the instruments and practices 'of industry, transportation, communication'). This distinction demarcates the system of technological domination from specific technical devices and their uses (see Marcuse, 1998: 41). Marcuse thus contrasts *technology* as an entire 'mode of organizing and perpetuating (or changing) social relationships, a manifestation of prevalent thought and behavior patterns, an instrument for control and domination', to *technics* which refer to techniques of production and such instruments as aeroplanes or computers. Whereas the former constitutes for Marcuse a system of technological domination, he claims that the latter can themselves 'promote authoritarianism as well as liberty, scarcity as well as abundance, the extension as well as the abolition of toil' (1998: 41).

Marcuse's critique focuses on technology as a system of domination and he presents National Socialism as an example in which technology and a rationalized society and economy can serve as instruments of totalitarian domination. But after documenting in detail the ways that technology and technological rationality promote conformity and erode individuality, Marcuse concludes his study with a vision of how technics might produce abundance for all, eliminate the necessity for excessive toil and alienated labour, and increase the realm of freedom. Building on Marx's sketch on automation in the *Grundrisse*, Marcuse writes:

> Technics hampers individual development only insofar as they are tied to a social apparatus which perpetuates scarcity, and this same apparatus has released forces which may shatter the special historical form in which technics is utilized. For this reason, all programs of an antitechnological character, all propaganda for an anti-industrial revolution serve only those who regard human needs as a by-product of the utilization of technics. The enemies of technics readily join forces with a terroristic technocracy. (Marcuse, 1998: 63)

The latter reference is to those German theorists like Heidegger (1977) who sharply criticized technology, yet embraced National Socialism, which in Marcuse's vision combined a terrorist technocracy with irrationalist ideology. Unlike the wholly negative critics of technology, with whom he is sometimes identified, Marcuse sketches out a dialectical theory that avoids both its technocratic celebration as inherently an instrument of liberation and progress, as well as its technophobic denunciation as solely an instrument of domination. In the concluding pages, he points to the 'possible democratization of functions which technics may promote and which may facilitate complete human development in all branches of work and administration'. In addition, 'mechanization and standardization may one day help to shift the center of gravity from the necessities of material production to the arena of free human realization' (1998: 63).

This dialectical model is important for studying specific technologies and the technological society of the present era since contemporary discourses on technology tend to dichotomize into either technophilic celebrations of the arrival of new technologies upon which they predicate a golden future, or technophobic discourses which demonize technology as an instrument of destruction and domination. Marcuse's critical theory of technics/technology, by contrast, differentiates negative features with positive potentials that could be used to democratize and enhance human life. Following Marx's classical positions, Marcuse envisages the possibility that new technologies could significantly reduce the working day and increase the realm of freedom: 'The less time and energy man has to expend in maintaining his life and that of society, the greater the possibility that he can "individualize" the sphere of his human realization' (1998: 64). The essay thus concludes with Marcusean utopian speculations on how a new technological society of abundance and wealth could allow the full realization of individual potentials and generate a realm of freedom and happiness.

Marcuse thus emerges as an important theorist of technology, Fascism, and the vicissitudes of industrial society – themes that he would develop in his post-Second World War writings. It is perhaps as a theorist of liberation and domination that Marcuse is most significant. His work *Eros and Civilization* (1955) attempted an audacious synthesis of Marx and Freud and sketched the outlines of a nonrepressive society. While Freud argued in *Civilization and its Discontents* that civilization inevitably involved repression and suffering, Marcuse maintained that other elements in Freud's theory suggested that the unconscious contained evidence of an instinctual drive toward happiness and freedom. This material is articulated, Marcuse suggests, in daydreams, works of art, philosophy, and other cultural products. Based on this reading of Freud and study of an emancipatory tradition of philosophy and culture, Marcuse sketched the outlines of a nonrepressive civilization which would involve libidinal and nonalienated labour, play, free and open sexuality, and production of a society and culture which would further freedom and happiness. His vision of liberation anticipated many of the values of the 1960s counterculture and helped Marcuse to become a major intellectual and political figure during that decade.

Marcuse contended that the current organization of society generated 'surplus repression' by imposing socially unnecessary labour, excessive restrictions on sexuality, and a social system organized around profit and exploitation. In light of the diminution of scarcity and prospects for increased abundance, Marcuse called for the end of repression and creation of a new society. His radical critique of existing society and its values, and his call for a nonrepressive civilization, elicited a dispute with his former colleague Erich Fromm (1955) who accused him of 'nihilism' (toward existing values and society) and irresponsible hedonism. Marcuse (1955) criticized Fromm for excessive 'conformity' and 'idealism', and repeated these charges in the polemical debates over his work following the publication of *Eros and Civilization* which heatedly discussed Marcuse's use of Freud, his critique of existing civilization, and his proposals for an alternative organization of society and culture.

While *Eros* provides the most detailed depiction of his vision of liberation, *One-Dimensional Man* (1964) provides Marcuse's most systematic analysis of forces of domination. In this book, he analysed the development of new forms of social control which were producing a 'one-dimensional man' and 'society without opposition'. Citing trends toward conformity, Marcuse described the forms of culture and society that created 'false' consumer needs that integrated individuals into the existing system of production and consumption via mass media, advertising, industrial management, and uncritical modes of thought. To 'one-dimensional society', Marcuse counterpoised critical and dialectical thinking, which perceived a freer and happier form of culture and society, and advocated a 'great refusal' of all modes of repression and domination.

This book theorized the decline of revolutionary potential in capitalist societies and the development of new forms of social control. Marcuse claimed that 'advanced industrial society' created false needs which integrated individuals into the existing system of production and consumption. Mass media and culture, advertising, industrial management, and contemporary modes of thought all reproduced the existing system and attempted to eliminate negativity, critique, and opposition. The result was a 'one-dimensional' universe of thought and behaviour in which the very aptitude and ability for critical thinking and oppositional behaviour was withering away.

Not only had capitalism integrated the working class, the source of potential revolutionary opposition, but they had developed new techniques of stabilization through state policies and the development of new forms of social control. Thus Marcuse questioned two of the fundamental postulates of orthodox Marxism: the revolutionary proletariat and inevitability of capitalist crisis. In contrast with the more extravagant demands of orthodox Marxism, Marcuse championed nonintegrated forces of minorities, outsiders, and radical intelligentsia and attempted to nourish oppositional thought and behaviour through promoting radical thinking and opposition.

For Marcuse, domination combined economics, politics, technology and social organization. While for orthodox Marxists domination is inscribed in capitalist relations of production and the logic of commodification, for Heideggerians, Weberians, and others it is technology, technological rationality, and/or political institutions that are the major force of societal domination. Marcuse, by contrast, has a multicausal analysis that ferrets out aspects of domination and resistance throughout the social order. Moreover, Marcuse insisted that contradictions of the system, theorized by classical Marxism as the antagonism of capital and labour, continued to exist, albeit in altered form. Marcuse constantly cited the unity of production and destruction, the ways that creation of wealth produced systematic poverty, war, and violence. Hence, for Marcuse there was an 'objective ambiguity' to even the seeming achievements of advanced industrial society which had the wealth, science, technology, and industry to alleviate poverty and suffering, but used the instruments of production to enhance domination, violence, aggression, and injustice.

In contrast to his Institute colleagues, however, Marcuse constantly attempted to politicize critical theory and to detect forces of resistance and transformation to counterpose to forces of domination and repression. After a period of pessimism during the period of *One-Dimensional Man*, Marcuse was encouraged by the global forces of revolt, centred around the student and antiwar movement, the counterculture, national liberation movements, and what became known as 'new social movements'. Marcuse sought in these forces the instruments of radical social change that classical Marxism found in the proletariat.

But just as radical working class movements were defeated in the course of the twentieth century and the working class, in Marcuse's view, was integrated into contemporary capitalism, so too were the radical movements of the 1960s defeated or integrated into the triumphant system of global capitalism. Up until his death, however, Marcuse continued to seek agents of social change in new social movements and in currents of art and philosophy. As in previous times of political quiescence during his life, Marcuse turned to aesthetics for consolation, publishing a series of studies that resulted in his last published work, *The Aesthetic Dimension* (1978). His defence of 'authentic art' was accompanied by criticisms of both Marxist aesthetics that celebrated 'proletarian culture', and contemporary advocacy of 'antiart' which renounced the exigencies of aesthetic form. For decades, Marcuse had held that there was a critical tradition of bourgeois art which contained powerful indictments of the society from which it emerged and emancipatory visions of a better society – accomplishments preserved in aesthetic form. Throughout his life, Marcuse defended the importance of 'authentic art' for the project of emancipation and revolution, and believed that 'the aesthetic dimension' was a crucial component of an emancipated life.

APPRAISAL OF KEY ADVANCES AND CONTROVERSIES

Marcuse's work in philosophy and social theory generated fierce controversy and polemics, and most studies of his work are highly tendentious and frequently sectarian. *One-Dimensional Man* was severely criticized by orthodox Marxists and theorists of various political and theoretical commitments. Despite its pessimism, it influenced many in the New Left as it articulated their growing dissatisfaction with both capitalist societies and Soviet communist societies. Moreover, Marcuse himself continued to foster demands for revolutionary change and defended the new, emerging forces of radical opposition.

During the 1960s, when he gained world renown as 'guru of the New Left', Marcuse was probably the most controversial public intellectual of the day, as students painted 'Marx, Mao, and Marcuse' on walls, the media debated his work, and intellectuals of every tendency criticized his views. Identifying Marcuse with the politics of the 1960s, however, does him a disservice, as it covers over his important contributions to philosophy and social theory, by reducing his thought to his political positions of the day.

Reconstructions of Subjectivity

In retrospect, Marcuse carried through a radical critique of philosophy and social theory, while developing his own unique blend of critical theory, which contains many important contributions. The past decades have witnessed a relentless philosophical assault on the concept of the subject, once the alpha and omega of modern philosophy. For traditional philosophy, the subject was unitary, ideal, universal, self-grounded, asexual and the centre of the human being and foundation for knowledge and philosophy, while for the post-structuralist and postmodern critique the human being is corporeal, gendered, social, fractured, and historical with the subject radically decentred as an effect of language, society, culture, and history. Yet if the construction of the subject in language, the social, and nature is the key mark of a post-structuralist or postmodern conception, then Marcuse and the Frankfurt School are not that antithetical to such perspectives. The entire tradition of critical theory – which draws on Hegel, Marx, Nietzsche, Freud, and Weber – posits the social construction of the individual, and Hegel, Nietzsche, and Freud can be read as providing aspects of theorizing the social construction of the subject in language. Habermas in particular has followed this motif and has attacked the philosophy of the subject while proposing replacing its subject–object model with an ego–alter model that is based upon the ideal of communicative reason (1984, 1987).

In his major philosophical works, Marcuse undertakes sharp critiques of the rationalist subject of modern philosophy which he counterposes to notions of libidinal rationality, eros, and the aesthetic-erotic dimensions of an embodied subjectivity. Marcuse is part of a historicist tradition of critical theory which rejects essentialism and sees subjectivity developing in history, evolving and mutating, in interaction with specific sociopolitical conditions. Following Adorno and Horkheimer and the earlier Frankfurt School tradition, Marcuse also sees dominant forms of subjectivity as oppressive and constraining while challenging us to reconstruct subjectivity and to develop a new sensibility, qualitatively different from the normalized subjectivity of contemporary industrial societies. In particular, Marcuse was engaged in a lifelong search for a revolutionary subjectivity, for a sensibility that would revolt against the existing society and attempt to create a new one.

Against the notion of the rational, domineering subject of modern theory, Marcuse posits a subjectivity that is evolving, developing, striving for happiness, gratification, and harmony. Such subjectivity is always in process, is never fixed or static, and is thus a creation, an achievement, and a goal, and not an absolute metaphysical entity. Marcusean subjectivity is also embodied, gendered, oppositional, and struggles against domination, repression, and oppression, and for freedom and happiness. There is thus nothing essentialist, idealist, or metaphysical here. Instead, Marcuse's conception of subjectivity is corporeal, cultivates the aesthetic and erotic dimensions of experience, and strives for gratification and harmonious relations with others and nature. Marcuse's radical subjectivity is also political, refusing domination and oppression, struggling against conditions that block freedom and happiness.

Hence, Marcuse contributes important perspectives for criticizing the traditional concept of the subject and for rethinking subjectivity to develop conceptions potent enough to meet post-structuralist, postmodern, materialist, feminist, and other forms of critique. Crucially, the assault on the subject has had serious consequences, for without a robust notion of subjectivity and agency there is no refuge for individual freedom and liberation, no locus of struggle and opposition, and no agency for progressive political transformation. For these reasons, theorists from diverse camps, including feminists, multiculturalists, and post-structuralists who have had second thoughts about the all-too-hasty dissolution of the subject, have attempted to rehabilitate the subject, to reconstruct the discourse of subjectivity and agency, in the light of contemporary critique.

Marcuse therefore anticipates the post-structuralist critique of the subject and provides a reconstructed notion of subjectivity. In drawing on Nietzsche, Freud, and aesthetic modernism, Marcuse posits a bodily, erotic, gendered, social, and aestheticized subjectivity that overcomes mind–body dualism, avoids idealist and rationalist essentialism, and is constructed in a specific social milieu and is challenged to reconstruct itself and emancipate itself. Contrasting Habermasian perspectives on subjectivity with Marcusean ones help indicate the specific contributions and strengths, and limitations, of Marcuse's position. While Marcuse offers a notion of a corporeal subjectivity with an emphasis on its aesthetic and erotic dimensions, Habermas's communicative reason lacks a body, grounding in nature and materiality, and the aesthetic and erotic components. That is, while Habermas's conception of subjectivity contains a grounding in sociality and ego–alter relations, he does not offer a notion of aesthetic, erotic, and embodied and sensual subjectivity as in Marcuse's conception. There is also not as strong a critique of the tendencies toward conformity and normalization as in Marcuse's conception, nor is there as forceful a notion of transformation and emancipation. Nor does Habermas offer a notion of revolutionary subjectivity.

There are, on the other hand, problems with Marcuse's conceptions of subjectivity. I have downplayed the extent of Marcuse's dependence on questionable aspects of Freud's instinct theory because I believe that a Marcusean conception of subjectivity can be constructed without dependence on Freud's conception of the political economy of the instincts, the death instinct, and the somewhat biologistic notion of Eros that Marcuse draws from Freud. Yet while Marcuse's focus on the corporeal, aesthetic, erotic, and political dimensions of subjectivity constitutes a positive legacy, there are omissions and deficiencies in his account. Crucially, he underemphasizes the ethical dimension and in addition does not adequately develop notions of justice and democracy. Since notions of ethical, just, and democratic subjectivity and social relations are not cultivated in Marcuse's writings, Habermas's analyses provide a necessary complement. Habermas's primary focus on the ego–alter relation and his subsequent treatises on morals and moral development, democracy and law, and the social obligations and constraints on subjectivity offer an important correction to Marcuse's analyses. Hence, both perspectives on subjectivity by themselves are one-sided and require supplementation by the other.

The New Sensibility and Radical Subjectivity

Marcuse's conception of radical subjectivity involves developing a synthesis of what he calls 'the new sensibility' and the 'new rationality'. Throughout his later writings, Marcuse was vitally concerned to discover and theorize a 'new sensibility', with needs, values, and aspirations that would be qualitatively different from subjectivity in one-dimensional society. To create a new subjectivity, there must be 'the emergence and education of a new type of human being free from the aggressive and repressive needs and aspirations and attitudes of class society, human beings created, in solidarity and on their own initiative, their own environment, their own *Lebenswelt*, their own "property"' (Marcuse, 1969b: 24). Such a revolution in needs and values would help overcome a central dilemma in Marcuse's theory – sharply formulated in *One-Dimensional Man* (hereafter *ODM*) – that continued to haunt him: 'How can the administered individuals – who have made their mutilation into their own liberties and satisfactions... liberate themselves from themselves as well as from their masters? How is it even thinkable that the vicious circle be broken?' (1964: 250–1).

In order to break through this vicious circle, individuals must transform their present needs, sensibility, consciousness, values, and behaviour while developing a new radical subjectivity, so as to create the necessary conditions for social transformation (Marcuse, 1970: 67). Radical subjectivity for Marcuse practices the 'great refusal' valorized in both *Eros and Civilization* (hereafter *E&C*) and *ODM*. In *E&C* (pp. 149ff), the 'Great Refusal is the protest against unnecessary repression, the struggle for the ultimate form of freedom – "to live without anxiety"'. In *ODM* (pp. 256ff), however, the Great Refusal is fundamentally political, a refusal of repression and injustice, a saying no, an elemental oppositional to a system of oppression, a noncompliance with the rules of a rigged game, a form of radical resistance and struggle. In both cases, the Great Refusal is based on a subjectivity that is not able to tolerate injustice and that engages in resistance and opposition to all forms of domination, instinctual and political.

In the late 1960s, Marcuse argued that emancipatory needs and a 'new sensibility' were developing within contemporary society. He believed that in the New Left and counterculture there were the beginnings of 'a political practice of methodical disengagement and the refusal of the Establishment aiming at a radical transvaluation of values' (1969a: 6) that was generating a new type of human being and subject. The new sensibility 'expresses the ascent of the life instincts over aggressiveness and guilt' (1969a: 23) and contains a 'negation of the needs that sustain the present system of domination and the negation of the values on which they are based' (1970: 67). Underlying the theory of the new sensibility is a concept of the active role of the senses in the constitution of experience which rejects the Kantian and other philosophical devaluation of the senses as passive, merely receptive. For Marcuse, our senses are shaped and moulded by society, yet constitute in turn our primary experience of the world and provide both imagination and reason with its material. He believes that the senses are currently socially constrained and mutilated and argues that only an emancipation of the senses and a new sensibility can produce liberating social change (1969a: 24ff, 1972: 62ff; in Marcuse, 1972: 63ff., he connects his notion of the new sensibility with the analysis of the early Marx on the liberation of the senses; his conception is also influenced by Schiller's conception of aesthetic education.)

Instead of the need for repressive performance and competition, the new sensibility posits the need for meaningful work, gratification and community; instead of the need for aggression and destructive productivity, it affirms love and the preservation of the environment; and against the demands of industrialization, it affirms the need for beauty, sensuousness, and play, affirming the aesthetic and erotic components of experience. The 'new sensibility' translates these values and needs into 'a practice that involves a break with the familiar, the routine ways of seeing, hearing, feeling, understanding things so that the organism may become receptive to the potential forms of a nonaggressive, nonexploitative world' (1969a: 6). This total refusal of the dominant societal needs, values, and institutions represents a radical break with the entirety of the society's institutions, culture and lifestyle, and supplies prefigurations of a new culture and society.

The new sensibility required aesthetic education, which cultivated the senses, with a 'new rationality' that reconstructed reason and sought a harmony between mind and body, humans and nature, man and woman. Art and the aesthetic dimension thus played a crucial role in the Marcusean conception of a new sensibility, since art cultivates the senses and provides reason with images of a better world, remembrances of past gratification, and projection of future freedom and happiness. Both art and eros contained a 'promise of happiness', both were unifying, overcoming oppositions between mind and body, self and other. Both refuse repression and are thus potentially oppositional.

For Marcuse, memory contains images of gratification and can play a cognitive and therapeutic role in mental life: 'Its truth value lies in the specific function of memory to preserve promises and potentialities which are betrayed and even outlawed by the mature, civilized individual, but which had once been fulfilled in the dim past and which are never entirely forgotten' (*E&C*: 18–19). In his reconstruction of Freud, Marcuse suggests that remembrance of past experiences of freedom and happiness could put into question the painful performances of alienated labour and manifold oppressions of everyday life.

Memory for Marcuse remembers, reconstructs, experience, going to the past to construct future images of freedom and happiness. Whereas romanticism is past-oriented, remembering the joys of nature and the past in the face of the onslaught of industrialization, Marcuse is future-oriented, looking to the past to construct a better future. (This conception might be contrasted with Walter Benjamin who in his 'Theses on the Philosophy of History' claims that 'images of enslaved ancestors rather than that of liberated grandchildren' drive the oppressed to struggle against their oppressors (1969: 260). Benjamin's conception is similar to Freud's who holds that past traumas enslave individuals, and argues, in a different register to Benjamin's, that working through the source of trauma can free individuals from past blockages and suffering. A dialectical conception of memory merging Marcuse and Benjamin might argue that both remembrances of past joys and suffering, happiness and oppression, can motivate construction of a better future if oriented toward changing rather than just remembering the world.) Marcuse's analysis implies that society trains the individual for the systematic repression of those emancipatory memories, and devalues experiences guided solely by the pleasure principle. Following Nietzsche in the *Genealogy of Morals*, Marcuse criticizes 'the one-sidedness of memory-training in civilization: the faculty was chiefly directed towards remembering duties rather than pleasures; memory was linked with bad conscience, guilt and sin. Unhappiness and the threat of punishment, not happiness and the promise of freedom, linger in the memory' (*E&C*: 232).

Along with memory, Marcuse suggests that fantasy generates images of a better life by speaking the language of the pleasure principle and its demands for gratification. He stresses the importance of great art for liberation because it embodies the emancipatory contents of fantasy and the imagination through producing images of happiness and a life without anxiety. In Marcuse's view, the fantasies in our daydreams and hopes anticipate a better life and embody the eruption of desires for increased freedom and gratification. The unconscious on this account contains the memory of integral gratification experienced in the womb, in childhood, and in peak experiences during one's life. Marcuse holds that the 'psychoanalytic liberation of memory' and 'restoration of phantasy' provide access to experiences of happiness and freedom which are subversive of the present life. He suggests that Freud's theory of human nature, far from refuting the possibility of a nonrepressive civilization, indicates that there are aspects of human nature that are striving for happiness and freedom.

Aesthetic education would thus cultivate imagination, fantasy, the senses, and memory to construct a new sensibility. The new sensibility would combine the senses and reason, producing a 'new rationality' in which reason would be bodily, erotic, and political. Far from being an irrationalist, Marcuse always argued that the senses and reason needed to be mediated, that reason needed to be reconstructed, and that critical and dialectical thinking were an important core of the new sensibility. Marcuse always argued that aesthetic education constituted a cultivation of the senses and that theory and education were essential components of transformative social change.

In the writings of the late 1960s, Marcuse believed that the new sensibility was embodied in the liberation movements of the day, the counterculture, and revolutionary movements (see Marcuse, 1969a). Of course, he was disappointed that the new sensibility did not become the agent of revolution that he sought to replace the proletariat; he was also dismayed that the New Left and counterculture fell prey to the seductions of the consumer society or were repressed and disintegrated. In the 1970s, however, he sought precisely the same values and subjectivity in new social movements, in particular feminism, the environmental movement, peace movement, and various forms of grass-roots activism which were eventually described as 'new social movements'. In a 1974 lecture on 'Marxism and Feminism', Marcuse notes for the first time the constitutive role of gender, and theorizes the differences between men and women in terms of his categories in *Eros and Civilization* in which the conception of the feminine is associated with the traits he ascribes to the new sensibility while the masculine is associated with the traits of the Western ego and rationality of domination which Marcuse long criticized, thus anticipating 'difference feminism', which would also valorize the feminine and maternal against the masculine. (For an argument parallel to mine developed through an engagement with French feminism and post-structuralism, see Kelly Oliver (1998). Oliver provides an extended argument that we can talk about subjectivity (and agency) without presupposing or needing a subject, claiming that subjectivity does not necessarily imply a 'subject' and that we are better off without such a concept. She develops notions of subjectivity as relational and intersubjective at its 'centre' and contrasts varying discourses and forms of masculine and feminine subjectivity. This project is parallel, I suggest, to Marcuse and the Frankfurt School, disclosing a surprising affinity between critical theory, French feminism, and post-structuralism.)

In this article, which generated significant debate, Marcuse argues that 'feminine' values and qualities represent a determinate negation of the values of capitalism, patriarchy, and the performance principle. In his view, 'socialism, as a qualitatively different society, must embody the antithesis, the definite negation of aggressive and repressive needs and values of capitalism as a form of male-dominated culture' (1974: 285). Furthermore:

> Formulated as the antithesis of the dominating masculine qualities, such feminine qualities would be receptivity, sensitivity, nonviolence, tenderness and so on. These characteristics appear indeed as opposite of domination and exploitation. On the primary psychological level, they would pertain to the domain of Eros, they would express the energy of the life instincts, against the death instinct and destructive energy. (Marcuse, 1974: 285–286)

Marcuse was, however, criticized by women within the feminist movement and others for essentializing gender difference, although he insisted the distinction was a historical product of Western society and not an essential gender difference. Women, he argued, possess a 'feminine' nature qualitatively different from men because they have been frequently freed from repression in the workplace, brutality in the military, and competition in the public sphere. Hence, they developed characteristics that for Marcuse are the marks of an emancipated humanity. He summarizes the difference between aggressive masculine and capitalist values as against feminist values as the contrast between 'repressive productivity' and 'creative receptivity', suggesting that increased emancipation of feminine qualities in the established society will subvert the dominant masculine values and the capitalist performance principle.

During the same decade, Marcuse also worked with Rudolf Bahro's conception of 'surplus consciousness', maintaining that just as Bahro argued that in the socialist countries a new consciousness was developing which could see the discrepancy between 'what is' and 'what could be' and was not satisfied with its way of life, so too was such oppositional consciousness developing in the advanced capitalist countries. The argument is that:

> through the increasing mechanization and intellectualization of labour, [there] accumulates an increasing quantity of general ability, skills, knowledge, a human potential which cannot be developed within the established apparatus of production, because it would conflict with the need for full-time de-humanized labour. A large part of it is channelled into unnecessary work, unnecessary in that it is not required for the construction and preservation of a better society but is necessitated only by the requirements of a capitalist production.
>
> Under these circumstances, a 'counterconsciousness' emerges among the dependent population (today about 90% of the total?), an awareness of the ever more blatant obsolescence of the established social division and organization of work. Rudolf Bahro, the militant East German dissident (he was immediately jailed after the publication, in West Germany, of his book *The Alternative*) uses the term *surplus-consciousness* to designate this (still largely vague and diffused) awareness. He defines it as 'the growing quantity of free mental energy which is no longer tied up in necessary labor and hierarchical knowledge'. (Marcuse, 1979: 21; see also Marcuse, 1980)

'Surplus consciousness' in the Bahro–Marcuse conception is a product of expanding education, scientific and technical development, and refinement of the forces of production and labour process that at once produce a higher form of consciousness and yet do not satisfy in the labour process or everyday life the needs and ideals produced by contemporary society itself. In effect, Bahro and Marcuse are arguing that critical consciousness is produced by the very social processes of the technological society and that this subjectivity comes into conflict with existing hierarchy, waste, repression, and domination, generating the need for social change. This position maintains that existing social processes themselves are helping to produce a subjectivity that demands participation and fulfilment in the labour process and sociopolitical life, as well as increased freedom, equality, opportunities for advancement and development. If these needs are not satisfied, Bahro and

Marcuse suggest, rebellion and social transformation will be generated.

Marcuse's Legacy

While there are problems with aspects of Marcuse's theory of revolution (see Kellner, 1984), he is to be lauded for his many provocative critiques of the Marxian theory and for his sustained attempts to develop new revolutionary perspectives adequate to the social conditions of contemporary capitalism. Of all the Marxists of his generation, Marcuse perhaps went furthest in trying to discover and theorize the subjective conditions of revolution and to develop a theory of radical subjectivity, while seeking new forces of radical change in the contemporary situation. In so doing, he developed a powerful critique of the philosophical concept of the subject and an alternative conception of subjectivity. While some of his formulations were too closely interwoven with Freud's instinct theory and the Marxian problematic of the revolutionary subject, I have argued that there are other aspects of Marcuse's thought that avoid such formulations and that he provides many important contributions to our understanding of subjectivity and agency while challenging us to further rethink the problematics of subjectivity in relation to the socioeconomic developments and political struggles of our own turbulent period. In this way, the contemporary critiques of the subject challenge us to come up with better conceptions and to develop new resources for critical theory and practice.

Although much of the controversy around Marcuse involved his critiques of contemporary capitalist societies and defence of radical social change, in retrospect, Marcuse left behind a complex and many-sided body of work comparable to the legacies of Ernst Bloch, Georg Lukács, T.W. Adorno, and Walter Benjamin. His social theory is characterized by broad critical perspectives that attempt to capture the major sociohistorical, political, and cultural features of the day. Such attempts to get at the Big Picture, to theorize the fundamental changes, developments, contradictions, and struggles of the day are more necessary than ever in an era of globalization in which the restructuring of capital and technological revolution are changing all aspects of life. Marcuse's thought thus continues to be relevant because he provides a mode of global theoretical analysis and addresses issues that continue to be of relevance to contemporary theory and politics. His unpublished manuscripts contain much material pertinent to contemporary concerns which could provide the basis for a rebirth of interest in Marcuse's thought (for examples of the contemporary relevance of Marcuse, see the studies in Bokina and Lukes, 1994).

Secondly, Marcuse provides comprehensive philosophical perspectives on domination and liberation, a powerful method and framework for analysing contemporary society, and a vision of liberation that is richer than classical Marxism, other versions of critical theory, and current versions of postmodern theory. Indeed, Marcuse presents critical philosophical perspectives on human beings and their relationship to nature and society, as well as substantive social theory and radical politics. In retrospect, Marcuse's vision of liberation – of the full development of the individual in a non-repressive society – distinguishes his work, along with sharp critique of existing forms of domination and oppression, and he emerges in this narrative as a theorist of forces of domination and liberation. Deeply rooted in philosophy and the conception of social theory developed by the Institute for Social Research, Marcuse's work lacked the sustained empirical analysis of some versions of Marxist theory and the detailed conceptual analysis found in many versions of political theory. Yet he constantly showed how science, technology, and theory itself had a political dimension and produced a solid body of ideological and political analysis of many of the dominant forms of society, culture, and thought during the turbulent era in which he lived and struggled for a better world.

Thus, I believe that Marcuse overcomes the limitations of many current varieties of philosophy and social theory and that his writings provide a viable starting-point for theoretical and political concerns of the present age. In particular, his articulations of philosophy with social theory, cultural criticism, and radical politics constitute an enduring legacy. While mainstream academic divisions of labour isolate social theory from philosophy and other disciplines, Marcuse provides a robust philosophical dimension and cultural criticism to social theory, while developing his theoretical perspectives in interaction with concrete analyses of society, politics, and culture in the present age. This dialectical approach thus assigns philosophy an important role within social theory, providing critical theory with strong normative and philosophical perspectives.

In addition, Marcuse emerges as a sharp, even prescient, social analyst. He was one of the first on the left who both developed a sharp critique of Soviet Marxism and yet foresaw the liberalizing trends in the Soviet Union (see Marcuse, 1958). After the uprisings in Poland and Hungary in 1956 were ruthlessly suppressed, many speculated that Khrushchev would have to roll back his programme of de-Stalinization and crack down further. Marcuse, however, differed:

> The Eastern European events were likely to slow down and perhaps even reverse de-Stalinization in some fields; particularly in international strategy, a considerable 'hardening' has been apparent. However, if our analysis is correct, the fundamental trend will continue and reassert itself throughout such reversals. With respect to internal Soviet developments, this means at present continuation of 'collective leadership', decline in the power of the secret police, decentralization, legal reforms, relaxation in censorship, liberalization in cultural life. (Marcuse, 1958: 174)

In part as a response to the collapse of communism and in part as a result of new technological and economic conditions, the capitalist system has been undergoing disorganization and reorganization. Marcuse's loyalty to Marxism always led him to analyse new conditions within capitalist societies that had emerged since Marx. Social theory today can thus build on this Marcusean tradition in developing critical theories of contemporary society grounded in analyses of the transformations of capitalism and emergence of a new global economic world system. For Marcuse, social theory was integrally historical and must conceptualize the salient phenomena of the present age and changes from previous social formations. While the postmodern theories of Baudrillard and Lyotard claim to postulate a rupture in history, they fail to analyse the key constituents of the changes going on, with Baudrillard even declaring the 'end of political economy'. Marcuse, by contrast, always attempted to analyse the changing configurations of capitalism and to relate social and cultural changes to transformations in the economy.

Moreover, Marcuse always paid special attention to the important role of technology in organizing contemporary societies and with the emergence of new technologies in our time the Marcusean emphasis on the relationship between technology, the economy, culture, and everyday life is especially important. Marcuse also paid attention to new forms of culture and the ways that culture provided both instruments of manipulation and liberation. The proliferation of new media technologies and cultural forms in recent years also demands a Marcusean perspective to capture both their potentialities for progressive social change and the possibilities of more streamlined forms of social domination. While postmodern theories also describe new technologies, Marcuse always related the economy to culture and technology, seeing both emancipatory and dominating potentials, while theorists like Baudrillard are one-dimensional, often falling prey to technological determinism and views of society and culture that fail to see positive and emancipatory potentials.

Finally, while versions of postmodern theory, like Baudrillard's, have renounced radical politics, Marcuse always attempted to link his critical theory with the most radical political movements of the day, and thus to politicize his philosophy and social theory. Thus, I am suggesting that Marcuse's thought continues to provide important resources and stimulus for critical theory and radical politics in the present age. Marcuse himself was open to new theoretical and political currents, yet remained loyal to those theories which he believed provided inspiration and substance for the tasks of the present age. Consequently, as we confront the theoretical and political problems of the day, I believe that the works of Herbert Marcuse provide important resources for our current situation and that a Marcusean renaissance could help inspire new theories and politics for the contemporary era, providing critical social theory with new impulses and tasks.

MARCUSE'S MAJOR WORKS

Marcuse's unpublished papers are collected in the Stadtsbibliothek in Frankfurt Germany. Suhrkamp published a 10-volume German-language edition *Schriften* in the 1980s. Routledge has begun publishing in 1997 six volumes of unpublished material under the general editorship of Douglas Kellner, and a German edition of the unpublished material is being published under the editorship of Peter-Erwin Jansen for zu Klampen Verlag. Marcuse's major works in English include:

Marcuse, H. (1941) *Reason and Revolution*. New York: Oxford University Press; reprinted Boston: Beacon Press, 1960.

Marcuse, H. (1955) *Eros and Civilization*. Boston: Beacon Press.

Marcuse, H. (1958) *Soviet Marxism*. New York: Columbia University Press; 2nd edn. 1988).

Marcuse, H. (1964) *One-Dimensional Man*. Boston: Beacon Press; 2nd edn. 1991.

Marcuse, H. (1965) 'Repressive tolerance', in *A Critique of Pure Tolerance*. Boston: Beacon Press.

Marcuse, H. (1968) *Negations*. Boston: Beacon Press.

Marcuse, H. (1969a) *An Essay on Liberation*. Boston: Beacon Press.

Marcuse, H. (1969b) 'The realm of freedom and the realm of necessity: A reconsideration', *Praxis*, 5(1): 20–5.

Marcuse, H. (1970) *Five Lectures*. Boston: Beacon Press.

Marcuse, H. (1972) *Counterrevolution and Revolt*. Boston: Beacon Press.

Marcuse, H. (1973) *Studies in Critical Philosophy*. Boston: Beacon Press.

Marcuse, H. (1974) 'Marxism and feminism', *Women's Studies*, 2(3): 279–88.

Marcuse, H. (1978) *The Aesthetic Dimension*. Boston: Beacon Press.

Marcuse, H. (1979) 'The reification of the proletariat', *Canadian Journal of Philosophy and Social Theory*, 3(1): 24–28.

Marcuse, H. (1980) 'Protosocialism and late capitalism: Toward a theoretical synthesis based on Bahro's analysis', in O Wolter (ed.) *Rudolf Bahro: Critical Responses*. White Plains, NY: M.E. Sharpe.

Marcuse, H. (1998) *Technology, War and Fascism*. (ed. Douglas Kellner.) London and New York: Routledge.

SECONDARY REFERENCES

Alford, C. Fred (1985) *Science and the Revenge of Nature: Marcuse and Habermas*. Gainesville: University of Florida Press.

Bokina, John and Lukes, Timothy J. (eds) (1994) *Marcuse: New Perspectives*. Lawrence: University of Kansas Press.

Benjamin, W. (1969) *Illuminations*. New York: Schocken Press.

Fromm, Erich (1955) 'The political implications of instinctual radicalism', *Dissent*, II(4): 342–9.

Habermas, Jurgen (1984, 1987) *Theory of Communicative Action, Vols. 1 and 2*. Boston: Beacon Press.

Heidegger, Martin (1977) *The Question Concerning Technology*. New York: Harper and Row.

Institut für Sozialforschung (1992): *Kritik und Utopie im Werk von Herbert Marcuse*. Frankfurt: Suhrkamp.

Kellner, Douglas (1984) *Herbert Marcuse and the Crisis of Marxism*. London and Berkeley: Macmillan and University of California Press.

Kellner, Douglas (1989) *Critical Theory, Marxism, and Modernity*. Cambridge and Baltimore, MD: Polity and John Hopkins University Press.

Lukàcs, Georg (1971) *History and Class Consciousness*. Cambridge, MA: MIT Press.

Marx, Karl (1973) *Grundrisse*. London: Penguin Books.

Oliver, Kelly (1998) *Subjectivity without Subjects*. New York: Rowman and Littlefield.

Pippin, Robert, Feenberg, A. and Webel, C. (1988) *Marcuse. Critical Theory and the Promise of Utopia*. South Hadley, MA: Bergin and Garvey.

Schoolman, Morton (1980) *The Imaginary Witness*. New York: Free Press.

Wiggershaus, Rolf (1994) *The Frankfurt School*. Cambridge: Polity Press.

5

Theodor Adorno

ANDREW BOWIE

BIOGRAPHICAL DETAILS AND THEORETICAL CONTEXT

Theodor Wiesengrund Adorno was born in Frankfurt am Main in 1903. After showing early talent as a musician he began lessons in composition at the age of 16, and by the age of 18 was studying philosophy, music, and psychology at university, and publishing music criticism. Having completed a largely derivative PhD on the phenomenology of Edmund Husserl in 1924 under the supervision of Hans Cornelius, he moved to Vienna in 1925 to study composition with Alban Berg. After returning to Frankfurt he withdrew, on the advice of Cornelius, a *Habilitation* dissertation on 'The Concept of the Unconscious in the Transcendental Doctrine of the Soul', the last part of which manifests a new Marx-influenced concern, of the kind that he would retain throughout his career, with the relationship between the emergence and adoption of philosophical theories and socioeconomic developments. At the end of the 1920s, while editing the musical journal 'Anbruch' ('Dawn'), Adorno encountered Georg Lukács's *History and Class-Consciousness* and developed a more intensive contact with Walter Benjamin, whom he had got to know in 1923. In 1931 he completed his *Habilitation* on 'Kierkegaard: Construction of the Aesthetic', which bears many of the traits of his mature work and is influenced, like his other work at this time, by Benjamin.

Adorno initially regarded the seizure of power by the Nazis as a merely passing phenomenon, and continued to visit Germany until 1937, while working as an 'advanced student' at Merton College, Oxford. In 1938 he moved to the United States to work with Max Horkheimer as a member of the Institute for Social Research, living in New York until he moved to Los Angeles for the years 1941–9. During this time he wrote *Dialectic of Enlightenment* with Horkheimer, completed *Minima Moralia*, a collection of short pieces which bears the subtitle 'Reflections from Damaged Life', and *Philosophy of New Music*, which deals mainly with the work of Schönberg and Stravinsky and which influenced Thomas Mann's novel *Doktor Faustus*, and he was a member of the group that wrote *The Authoritarian Personality* as part of the Berkeley 'Project on the Nature and Extent of Anti-Semitism'. Adorno returned to Frankfurt in 1949, where he finally gained his first (and only) tenured professorship, at the re-established Institute for Social Research, in 1956. In the early 1960s he was involved, along with, among others, his academic assistant Jürgen Habermas, in the 'Positivism Dispute in German Sociology', in which his main opponents were Karl Popper and Hans Albert. Throughout the 1960s he was engaged in writing major works, such as *Negative Dialectics*, *Aesthetic Theory*, and a host of other projects, some of which remained incomplete. He died on holiday in Switzerland in 1969, at the time of disturbances associated with the student Movement.

Even such a brief biographical summary suggests the remarkable diversity of Adorno's work, which has to be considered in the contexts of aesthetics, cultural studies, musicology, philosophy, psychology, sociology, and social theory. His work is perhaps best understood as a series of critical approaches to the major questions of a post-theological modernity. However, finding a common denominator in these approaches and locating Adorno in relation to the issues of contemporary social theory is made difficult by the fact that his work derives from traditions of thought which remain too little known in the English-speaking world. His early philosophical work is, for example, concerned with questions deriving from Kant's philosophy, which are seen through the filter of the neo-Kantianism and phenomenology that dominate German philosophy in the first quarter of the twentieth century. The main question in that philosophy is how to establish a basis for claims to truth about the natural and social world in the wake of Kant's claim that one can no longer assume that the world has an inherent 'ready-made' structure which exists independently of the ways in which it is apprehended. In common with other influential thinkers in the 1920s, like Martin Heidegger, Adorno came to believe that a philosophy concerned with establishing timeless principles – even principles of the kind proposed by Kant in his account of the 'transcendental' conditions of possibility of knowledge – is no longer viable in the modern world. This means that philosophy and sociology move into a new relationship, in which 'the absolute division between the question of the social origin, the social history of [philosophical] thought, and its truth content' (Adorno, 1998b: 73) can no longer be sustained. At the same time Adorno rejected a relativistic sociology of knowledge of the kind developed by Karl Mannheim. By the beginning of the 1930s he was, then, already convinced that a farewell to the idea of philosophical principles which transcend those in any other discipline should result in the eventual abolition of philosophy as a foundational discipline, and in a relocation of philosophy in relation to social theory.

This leaves open the precise nature of the role of both philosophy and social theory, and Adorno tried throughout his career to negotiate a course between the adoption of a Hegel- and Marx-influenced contextualization and historicization of philosophy, and attention to ideas about language and philosophy informed by Jewish mysticism which were developed in the pre-Marxist work of his friend Walter Benjamin. In doing so he addresses issues concerning the potentially repressive nature of totalizing forms of thinking that have come to play a role in the debates around the nature of 'postmetaphysical thinking' (Habermas) in the work of, for example, Foucault, Derrida, and Lyotard, and in various forms of recent cultural theory. The advantage of Adorno's work over some of these approaches lies both in its concern to anchor theoretical reflections in a critical awareness of the specificity of modern social life, and in its refusal to abandon the notion of rationality, even as it analyses the destructive effects of certain aspects of 'Enlightenment' thinking on modern societies. This brings Adorno close at times – even though he himself did not see it in these terms, because he mistakenly equated pragmatism with positivism – to the tradition of American pragmatism derived from John Dewey, which is represented today by Hilary Putnam, Richard Rorty and others. Adorno's concern that truth should be seen in terms of 'giving a voice to suffering' (Adorno, 1975: 29), rather than of adequacy of thought to a 'ready-made' reality, is echoed, for instance, in Rorty's conviction that philosophy should now be interested in helping to avoid the infliction of pain and in augmenting the sources of post-theological hope, rather than in grounding epistemology.

SOCIAL THEORY AND CONTRIBUTIONS

Despite its still disputed status in relation to mainstream social theory, Adorno's work can be approached as part of the debate concerning the relationship between scientific explanation and the understanding of human action and culture which develops towards the end of the nineteenth century via the work of Wilhelm Dilthey, Max Weber, and others. Adorno attempts to elaborate ways of thinking which come to terms with the massive advances in the explanatory power of the natural sciences and yet also take account of the fact that these advances take place within sociohistorical contexts which often render them a threat both to human well-being and to non-human nature. He questions the idea that the methods of the natural sciences are appropriate to social inquiry, highlighting the resistance of social existence to analysis in terms of definitive methodological principles. The main conceptual resources for his ideas are, like those of many critical social theorists, drawn from the work of Hegel, Marx, Nietzsche, Weber, and Freud, but Adorno often understands these resources in the light of the work of Benjamin, which relies both on Jewish theology and on early German Romantic thought from the end of the eighteenth century, particularly that of Novalis and Friedrich Schlegel (see Bowie, 1997).

The essential conviction of the early Romantics is, much as it is for Adorno, that the project of grounding a complete philosophical system which could encompass thought's relation to reality is doomed to failure. Novalis and Schlegel are led by this conviction to a concern with fragmentariness and incompleteness, and to the idea, which becomes central to Adorno's thought, that art may in some respects tell us more about the nature of modern existence than philosophy. For the Romantics this is because art's resistance to definitive interpretation reminds us of the inherently temporal nature of our capacity to grasp the world, and they are led by such ideas, as Adorno will be, to a new evaluation of the significance of music. Works of art are also significant for Adorno because they are irreducibly particular and cannot be reduced to general explanatory concepts, though they may, for that very reason, give access to insights into society not available to approaches based on general concepts. Adorno developed the implications of such ideas throughout his career.

Adorno does not offer a social theory in the sense that his pupil Habermas does in the *Theorie des kommunikativen Handelns (Theory of Communicative Action)* (1981), which attempts to map out a methodological framework for understanding the workings of modern societies. Adorno's relation to social theory is more indirect and must be established in relation to works as diverse as, for instance, his book on Richard Wagner, the study of the 'authoritarian personality', his texts on the sociology of music, the critiques of positivism in sociology, or his more immediately philosophical works, like *Against Epistemology, Dialectic of Enlightenment, Negative Dialectics,* and *Aesthetic Theory.* Adorno's earlier work on music, for example, such as the essay 'On the Social Situation of Music' of 1932, is a rather clumsy attempt to use aspects of Marx's theory of the commodity to show how the commodity world has deprived all but the most radical and difficult music – that of Schönberg and his followers, whose abandonment of the conventions of tonality makes it resistant to immediate aesthetic enjoyment – of its ability to bring about a critical stance towards existing social reality. On the other hand, although his philosophical work of the same period retains a Marx-oriented concern with the historical location of philosophical problems, Adorno also relies in some respects upon Benjamin's theologically inspired idea that language in the modern world has lost its essential connection to things and has become a merely arbitrary subjective imposition on reality. Despite the differences between these approaches, they both involve a conceptual structure which takes one to the heart of Adorno's social thought.

In his work from the 1920s until the end of his life Adorno often refers to 'idealism' as the target of his theories. By idealism he means both the broadly conceived 'Platonic' tradition which gives primacy to the universal 'idea' or 'form' of things before their particular existence, and the tradition of German idealism which emerges as a response to Kant and culminates in Hegel's system. His objection to 'idealism' stems in particular from his belief that systematic philosophical thinking obscures the irreducible particularity of both people and things. The crucial link which Adorno makes in this respect is between the principle of much modern systematic thinking and Marx's analysis of the commodity form's subordination of use-value to exchange-value. In the German philosophical tradition the conceptual basis of this link develops as a consequence of the rediscovery of Spinoza in the 1780s by F.H. Jacobi, which influenced nearly every major German thinker from the Romantics to Hegel, Nietzsche, and beyond (see Bowie, 1997). Spinoza's systematic principle of 'all determination is negation' entails that every individual element of a system can only gain an identity via the relations it has to the other things which it is not – the same principle will later be employed by Saussure in his assertion that there are no positive terms in language (and is also the principle of digital technology). Jacobi argued that Spinoza's principle led to what he came to term 'nihilism', because nothing was of value or significance in itself, its significance depending rather on chains of relations to other things with no necessary end. Analogously, in Marx's theory of the commodity the value of an object in capitalism is not its intrinsic use-value, but rather its exchange-value, which is determined by its relation to other exchange-values.

Adorno regards Marx's claims about the nature of capitalism as the key to understanding the historical significance of Hegel's idealist system, which is for him perhaps the central expression of the essential nature of modernity. It is, though, at the same time important to remember that Adorno's criticisms of Hegel are directed against the systematic completeness at which Hegel aims, not at those parts of Hegel's dialectical method that seek to avoid fixed concepts, which Adorno appropriates for his own thinking. Hegel's system is based on the idea that the truth of things emerges precisely via insight into their inherent 'negativity', which results from their dependence on other things. This leads Hegel to the claim that everything can only be adequately determined in terms of its place within the whole – hence his dictum that 'The true is the whole'. The awareness of the negativity of everything particular does not, for Hegel, lead to nihilism, but instead ultimately leads to 'absolute knowledge', in which the negative is subsumed at the end of the system into the positive totality articulated by philosophy. In the light both of Weber's account of rationalization in modernity, which functions in terms of the destruction of the particularity of tradition-based values, and of Lukács' account in *History and Class-Consciousness* of how capitalism creates a totality which obscures the qualitative features of the world via the 'reifying' principle of exchange-value, Adorno connects the systematic aspect of Hegel with real totalizing processes which occur in the spread of the commodity form across the globe. Rather than assuming that the true is the whole, Adorno argues that these processes obscure the underlying truth about modern societies, rendering judgments about the whole inappropriate, whence his inversion of Hegel in *Negative Dialectics* in 1966: 'The whole is the untrue'. However, this leaves Adorno with a paradoxical position, in which he both renounces totalizing claims and yet relies as the basis of his renunciation upon a totalizing characterization of the 'universal context of delusion' that results from the dominance of the commodity principle. This problematic dialectic between totalization and the critique of totalization recurs throughout his mature work.

Adorno is already concerned from the end of the 1920s onwards, and will remain so throughout his life, with how it is possible to articulate truth in modernity if thought must renounce claims to grasp the totality of the processes which determine social phenomena. This concern is the source of his interest in Benjamin's theory of language. Benjamin claims modernity is characterized by an arbitrariness of signification which he illustrates by the role of allegory in early modern German baroque drama, where 'Every person, every thing, every relationship can arbitrarily mean something else' (Benjamin, 1980: 350). In his later, Marx-influenced work on Baudelaire, Benjamin suggests how the conception of allegory can apply to ideas like those of Adorno, thereby revealing the reasons for Adorno's link between Benjamin's conception of language and the critique of commodity form: 'The specific devaluation of the world of things which is present in the commodity is the foundation of the allegorical intention in Baudelaire' (Benjamin, 1980: 1151). Benjamin's response to the idea of the devaluation of the particular is to propose the idea of a language of 'names', which would have an essential, rather than an arbitrary relation to what they designate. Although Adorno, much like Benjamin, thinks 'the contingency of the significative attribution of language and things becomes radically problematic' (Adorno, 1973c: 366) in the modern era, he does not adopt all of Benjamin's position, which he later critically characterizes as 'metaphysical' in *Negative Dialectics*.

Significant parts of Adorno's work are, though, devoted to the idea of a conception of language which would be adequate to the situation where there no longer seems to be a way of definitively grounding the truth. Many of Adorno's key ideas about literature and about the importance of music for understanding modernity derive from his interpretation of this situation. He claims in 1957, for example, that 'As language, music moves towards the pure name, the absolute unity of thing and sign, which is lost in its immediacy to all human knowledge' (Adorno, 1984: 154). Ideas like this about language are also the source of his notion of the 'constellation', in which a unique configuration of words is intended to articulate a particular issue without claiming to found a methodology with a universal application, something he also sees in terms of creating 'thought-models' which are adequate to the specificity of their object. The notions of the constellation and of the thought-model can be used to explain – if not always to justify – the often dense, exploratory nature of Adorno's own writing, which prevents it being easily reduced to a series of essential precepts.

Adorno initially employed notions of the kind just outlined in a framework which associates the critical intent of his thinking with the idea of proletarian revolution as the means of breaking the socially destructive dominance of the exchange principle. However, in light of events in the Soviet Union and Germany in the mid-1930s, he ceases to believe in the possibility of radical social transformation by revolutionary means. This does not mean that he becomes uncritical of the repressive manifestations of modern capitalism, or that his essential conception changes – the ideas outlined above remain remarkably constant in most of his work –

but he focuses more on what makes rationality in modern societies often incapable of eliminating suffering and injustice, even when the means for doing so are already in existence.

The most extreme manifestation of Adorno's questioning of modern rationality is *Dialectic of Enlightenment* (hereafter *DoE*), which, although written in the 1940s, only began to have a significant influence on social theory some 20 years later, in relation to the breakdown of the illusory revolutionary hopes of the student movement and to the emergence of ecological concerns. The bleak tone of the book is hardly surprising, given the time of its genesis, but the degree of negativity it evinces with regard to modern forms of rationality is greater than in Adorno's previous – and much of his subsequent – work. *DoE* relies on a Nietzschean conception of knowledge as power over the 'other', be it nature or other people, and this has been the source of its appeal to other Nietzsche-influenced directions in modern thought, such as post-structuralism. Horkheimer and Adorno present 'Enlightenment' as the 'mythical fear' of nature which 'has become radical'. Reason in modernity is therefore characterized almost exclusively as mathematically based 'instrumental' reason – which takes the systematic form described above in relation to Spinoza, Hegel and Marx – whose aim is to subdue the threat posed to self-preservation by external nature. The authors regard even premodern myth as a form of reason, because it is an attempt to subordinate nature to forms which will control and manipulate it, by reducing the inherent difference of things to restrictive forms of identity. The basis of their argument is a conception of subjectivity derived from Nietzsche and Freud, which they connect directly to their conception of instrumental reason. What happens in capitalism is 'already perceptible in the primal history of subjectivity' (Horkheimer and Adorno, 1971: 51, my translation). In this history the stable identity of the self is established via the internal repression of drives, in the name of the self-discipline required for self-preservation. However, this obviates the point of existing as an individual subject, because of the violence done by the subject to its own nature. The process of 'primal history' is seen as the source even of the inhumanity of the system of the fulfilment of needs in 'late capitalism', which distorts the subject's needs into destructive forms which are appropriate for the functioning of the system but not for those within it. The only way beyond such a situation involves an appeal to the idea of a 'reconciliation' of the subject with the nature of which it is a part: how this could take place is, though, left open. Adorno suggests elsewhere that a 'mimetic' relation to nature, which exemplifies such a reconciliation, is somehow present in the way significant works of modern art have a 'nonconceptual affinity' to what they present.

Perhaps the most influential part of *DoE* is its critique of the 'culture industry', in which the commodity form, like the other forms of 'Enlightenment', is seen as making culture, which was formerly in some measure the expression of human freedom and individuality, into a mere schematic repetition of pregiven forms. This repetition is epitomized by Hollywood film and jazz, which supposedly accord with what market research shows people want who have been subjected to the consciousness-forming effects of the commodity world – the argument now seems more relevant to much that goes on in the rock music industry than to its original target, especially in the case of jazz. Although Horkheimer and Adorno's aim in *DoE* is to provide resources for establishing models of reason which avoid the results of the 'dialectic of enlightenment', it is not clear whether the theoretical model they employ can lead to anything but the consequence that reason is inherently based on repression, rather than also being potentially enabling and emancipatory. Adorno's approaches in the rest of his work to the dilemmas evident in *DoE* are decisive in assessing his contribution to social theory.

APPRAISAL OF KEY ADVANCES AND CONTROVERSIES

DoE itself is highly speculative, and its incorporation of the whole history of the West into the story just described is at odds with Adorno's desire elsewhere to avoid the Procrustean effects of abstraction. One of the central – thoroughly rational – claims of *Negative Dialectics* is that the 'utopia of cognition would be to open up the conceptless with concepts, without reducing it to them' (Adorno, 1975: 21, my translation). The concepts employed in *DoE* are, though, all too crudely imposed on their subject matter. *DoE* also points to another potential weakness in Adorno: it bases its account of the history of subjectivity on an interpretation of myth via Nietzsche, Freud, and others, but uses very little empirical research to confirm that myth can indeed be interpreted in this manner. During his work for the Princeton Radio Research Project with Paul Lazarsfeld in 1938, his work on *The Authoritarian Personality*, and, after his return to Frankfurt, on a study of attitudes in the German population to the Nazi period and to the occupying forces, Adorno tried – in some cases, such as the anti-Semitism project, quite successfully – to develop means for adequately carrying out empirical social research, using resources from social psychology and psychoanalysis. Even in 1938, though, this aim was marked by considerable tensions in relation to his philosophical claims, and in his later work he sometimes regards empirical social research as inherently questionable.

The problem faced by Adorno with regard to empirical research is evident in the analysis of the culture industry. If the consciousness of people is indeed constituted by commodity-determined forms of culture, the task of the theorist is to reveal the damaging implications of such culture. Adorno claims that this is best accomplished by analysing the production and nature of commodified culture, such as the factors determining commercialized radio's transmission of music, and the structure and the content of the music transmitted. In the essay 'On the Fetish-Character of Music' of 1938, he therefore argued that asking listeners about their reactions would merely reproduce information about the surface manifestation of this production, and thus fail to grasp its essence: 'in a completely blinded reality the truth that reveals is moved easily enough into compromising proximity to the system of delusion' (Adorno, 1938: 339, my translation). Just how debatable this rejection of empirical research is becomes apparent in Adorno's later reflections in 1968 on his own admitted failure in the Radio Project: 'It is an open question, which can indeed only be answered empirically, whether, to what extent, in what dimensions the social implications revealed in musical content analysis are also grasped by the listeners' (cited in Dahms, 1994: 252–3). The paradigmatic divergence of these approaches results from tensions in Adorno's conception of the role of method in social inquiry and in his related reflections on the question of subjectivity.

Adorno's suspicion of empirical research, for example into the reactions of listeners to the 'stimuli' of radio music, can be justified insofar as the research fails to carry out any investigation into what is being listened to. Such investigation requires detailed analysis of the relationship between musical and social forms of the kind that can be found in Adorno's best work on music and society, like the book on Mahler or his uncompleted work on Beethoven. This sort of research is necessarily resistant to an empiricist approach, because its object cannot be specified as, for example, the musical score: it is only when the score is located in a specific constellation of contexts and practices that it can give rise to insights into society. The hermeneutic holism involved in research like this has proved to be a vital aspect of postempiricist methodology in the social (and in some cases the natural) sciences. However, Adorno also adheres to the much more problematic holism we have already encountered, which regards modernity as dominated and constituted by the forms of identity produced by the exchange principle.

During the dispute with Popper and Albert concerning the methodology of the social sciences in the early 1960s, Adorno claims that 'The abstractness of exchange-value is connected a priori with the domination of the general over the particular, of society over its compulsory members' (Adorno, 1972: 21), and this domination seems sometimes to include any sort of identification in such a society, from the simple predicative sentence which subsumes a particular phenomenon under a general term, to empirical claims about social phenomena. There is, though, a vital ambiguity in Adorno's conception of identity. The idea that there is a source of repressive identification common to the sphere of commodity exchange and to conceptual thinking relies on two different senses of identity, which Adorno sometimes (but not always) conflates. The identification of any commodity *with* all other commodities, as an exchange-value independent of its use-value, does involve the danger of devaluing the particular thing (whilst also facilitating the – unjustly distributed – availability of otherwise inaccessible goods). However, things in the social world, including those bought as commodities, can also be identified *as* a whole (potentially unlimited) number of things, which may be completely particular and which can only be assessed in particular terms in particular contexts. If the two senses of identity are indeed different, then the *inherent* link of the commodity structure to all forms of identity and their possibly damaging consequences cannot be upheld, and the totalizing aspect of Adorno's conception is no longer defensible in this respect (on this see Schnädelbach, 1987; Thyen, 1989). This does not mean, though, that the second sense of identity, which can include the aim of doing justice to things that is one of Adorno's main goals, cannot be used for critical purposes, for instance when the particular way something is identified precludes the realization of its most significant possibilities.

Adorno's suggestion, both in the dispute with Popper and Albert and elsewhere, that 'positivism' involves a necessary link between identifying social facts and legitimating the existence of those facts is evidently implausible. Furthermore, much of the so-called 'positivism dispute' was itself actually based on a series of misunderstandings and misinterpretations by both sides. One of Adorno's essential targets is, for example, scientism, but Popper is equally concerned to attack what he sees as the scientism of some of the members of the Vienna Circle, which only allows knowledge claims on the basis of observation sentences and inductive generalizations (see Dahms, 1994; Bowie, 2000). Adorno's linking of identification and legitimation could only be sustained if the very gathering of facts about society were, as he seems to suggest, itself subjected to the logic of identity inherent in the commodity structure which produces the consciousness of the people in that society, and therefore precluded the adoption of a critical perspective. However, this situation would render the position of the critical theorist who makes such claims about the effects of commodification itself problematic, because of their lack of a location from which to judge those effects without also being subjected to them.

Valid as they may be, criticisms of this kind can unfairly obscure the fact that Adorno's primary aim in his postwar work is not methodological, but practical. He wishes to make what he sees as the new 'categorical imperative' forced upon us by Hitler into the focus of reflection on human thought and action. This is the imperative that Auschwitz could never be repeated, an aim recently echoed in Zygmunt Bauman's demand to make the lessons of the Holocaust the centre of theories of modernity. Looked at in this perspective the manner of the industrialized mass murder of the victims of the Holocaust does seem, despite the problem of how this is to be established, to be connected in some respects to the processes Adorno associates with 'identity thinking'. Adorno claims that 'Auschwitz confirms the philosopheme of pure identity as death' (Adorno, 1975: 355) because of its absolute lack of concern for the individuality of its victims. The fact that the crimes of the Holocaust were perpetrated in a developed industrial society with a cultural tradition regarded by many – including Adorno himself – as second to none is a further reason to take Adorno's theory very seriously. Even if one rejects Adorno's assertion that 'Auschwitz has irrefutably proved the failure of culture' (Adorno, 1975: 359), the challenge it poses to social theory and to the rest of the humanities cannot be ignored. The decisive question is whether Adorno's model linking the structures of reason to the dominance of the exchange principle and the concomitant domination of people is adequate for interpreting modernity as a whole. Is Auschwitz the key to the essential nature of modern societies that is merely disguised by the forms of modern culture?

The most sustained attempt to move beyond this view has been the work of Adorno's pupil Habermas, who claims that Adorno reduces reason, which can be both instrumental and communicative, solely to the former. This reduction, which echoes the later Heidegger's interpretation of modern thought and its application in modern technology as the 'subjectification of being', relies, Habermas maintains, upon a questionable founding conception of subjectivity as self-preservation, which leads to the equation of reason with dominance over the 'other'. In contrast, Habermas seeks to replace the centrality of the notion of 'purposive rationality', which underlies Adorno's conception of 'instrumental reason', with 'communicative action'. This change of orientation precludes complete domination of the other because the 'telos of agreement' in validity-oriented communication can always keep open the possibility that the other may be in possession of the truth. It is therefore possible to see that advances in rationality need not be reducible to advances in technical control of nature, as ethical and legal developments in democratic societies can suggest. Habermas associates his view with the need for a wholesale replacement of the 'paradigm of subject philosophy' by the paradigm of intersubjectivity based on the 'linguistic turn', in which 'world-constituting capacities are transferred from transcendental subjectivity to grammatical structures' (Habermas, 1988: 15).

This alternative has itself been criticized for its failure to acknowledge those conceptions of subjectivity in the Western tradition which do not see it as being reducible either to self-preservation or to its language (see e.g. Henrich, 1987; Frank, 1991; Dews, 1995; Bowie, 1999b). Adorno's own claim in this regard, in *Minima Moralia*, that the individual subject is perhaps the only remaining locus of emancipatory possibilities in advanced capitalist societies, therefore suggests a crucial ambiguity in his work. On the one hand, Adorno insists, with a radicality he himself sometimes characterizes as exaggeration, on the overwhelming pressure of the consciousness-forming objective conditions that led to Fascism, which he believes (with some justification) still characterize advanced capitalist societies; on the other, he can also suggest in the same context that 'Critical incorporation (*Aufarbeitung*) of the past as enlightenment is essentially... a turn to the subject, a reinforcement of its self-awareness/self-confidence (*Selbstbewusstsein*) and thus also of its self' (Adorno, 1970: 27). Adorno's work on the dynamic between the overwhelming pressures exerted by modern societies on their members and the cultural and philosophical responses to those pressures suffers, then, from an unnecessarily metaphysical conception of the effects of the commodity principle.

A conception of modern subjectivity that retains even a diminished role for the subject's autonomous individuality can, while still taking account of the undoubted effects of the pressures for conformity in modern societies, make Adorno's work a more useful resource for social theory. Such a conception allows one to draw on the insights offered by the best of his specific explorations of modern culture and his criticisms of the Western philosophical tradition without falling prey to his exaggerations.

ADORNO'S MAJOR WORKS

Works in English

Adorno, T.W. (1972) *Aspects of Sociology.* Boston: Beacon.

Adorno, T.W. (1973a) *Negative Dialectics.* London: Routledge.

Adorno, T.W. (1973b) *The Philosophy of Modern Music.* New York: Seabury.

Adorno, T.W. (1974) *Minima Moralia.* London: New Left Books.

Adorno, T.W. (1976a) *Introduction to the Sociology of Music.* New York: Seabury.

Adorno, T.W. (1976b) *The Positivist Dispute in German Sociology.* London: Heinemann.

Adorno, T.W. (1981a) *Prisms.* Cambridge, MA: MIT Press.

Adorno, T.W. (1981b) *In Search of Wagner.* London: Verso.

Adorno, T.W. (1982) *Against Epistemology.* Oxford: Blackwell.

Adorno, T.W. (1989) *Kierkegaard: Construction of the Aesthetic.* Minneapolis: Minnesota University Press.

Adorno, T.W. (1991) *The Culture Industry.* London: Routledge.

Adorno, T.W. (1991–2) *Notes to Literature.* (2 Vols.). New York: Columbia University Press.

Adorno, T.W. (1992) *Mahler: A Musical Physiognomy.* Chicago: University of Chicago Press.

Adorno, T.W. (1993) *Hegel: Three Studies.* Cambridge, MA: MIT Press.

Adorno, T.W. (1998a) *Beethoven.* Cambridge: Polity Press.

Adorno, T.W. (1997) *Aesthetic Theory.* London: Athlone.

Adorno, T.W., Frenkel-Brunswick, E., Levinson, D.J. and Sanford, R.N. (1950) *The Authoritarian Personality.* New York: Harper.

Adorno, T.W. and Horkheimer, M. (1972) *Dialectic of Enlightenment.* New York: Seabury.

Works in German

Adorno, T.W. (1938) 'Über den Fetischcharakter in Musik', *Zeitschrift für Sozialforschung,* 7: 321–56.

Adorno, T.W. (1970) *Erziehung zur Mündigkeit.* Frankfurt: Suhrkamp.

Adorno, T.W. (1973c) *Philosophische Frühschriften,* in *Gesammelte Schriften.* Vol. 1. Frankfurt: Suhrkamp.

Adorno, T.W. (1975) *Negative Dialektik.* Frankfurt: Suhrkamp.

Adorno, T.W. (1984) *Musikalische Schriften V,* in *Gesammelte Schriften,* Vol. 18. Frankfurt: Suhrkamp.

Adorno, T.W. (1998b) *Metaphysik. Begriff und Probleme.* Frankfurt: Suhrkamp.

Adorno, T.W., Dahrendorf, R., Albert, H., Habermas, J. and Popper, K.R. (1972) *Der Positivismusstreit in der deutschen Soziologie.* Darmstadt and Neuwied: Luchterhand.

Horkheimer, M., and Adorno, T.W. (1971) *Dialektik der Aufklärung.* Frankfurt: Fischer.

SECONDARY REFERENCES

Arato, A. and Gebhardt, E. (1978) *The Essential Frankfurt School Reader.* New York: Urizen.

Benhabib, Seyla (1986) *Critique, Norm and Utopia: A Study of the Foundations of Critical Theory.* New York: Columbia University Press.

Benjamin, A. (ed.) (1989) *The Problems of Modernity. Adorno and Benjamin.* London: Routledge.

Benjamin, W. (1980) *Gesammelte Schriften.* Frankfurt: Suhrkamp.

Bernstein, J. (1991) *The Fate of Art.* Cambridge: Polity Press.

Bowie, A. (1997) *From Romanticism to Critical Theory. The Philosophy of German Literary Theory.* London: Routledge.

Bowie, A. (1999a) 'Adorno, Heidegger and the meaning of music', *Thesis,* 11: 56.

Bowie, A. (1999b) 'German philosophy today: between idealism, romanticism and pragmatism', in ed. A. O'Hear (ed.), *German Philosophy Since Kant.* Cambridge: Cambridge University Press.

Bowie, A. (2000) 'The romantic connection: Neurath, the Frankfurt School, and Heidegger', Part 1, *British Journal for the History of Philosophy,* 8(2): 275–98.

Bowie, A. (in press) 'The romantic connection: Neurath, the Frankfurt School, and Heidegger, Part 2, *British Journal for the History of Philosophy,* 8(3).

Buck-Morss, S. (1977) *The Origin of Negative Dialectics.* Hassocks: Harvester.

Connerton, P. (1980) *The Tragedy of Enlightenment: An Essay on the Frankfurt School.* Cambridge: Cambridge University Press.

Dahms, H.-J. (1994) *Positivismusstreit: die Auseinandersetzung der Frankfurter Schule mit dem logischen*

Positivismus, dem amerikanischen Pragmatismus, und dem kritischen Rationalismus. Frankfurt: Suhrkamp.
Dews, P. (1995) *The Limits of Disenchantment*. London: Verso.
Frank, Manfred (1991) *Selbstbewußtsein und Selbsterkenntnis*. Stuttgart: Reclam.
Geuss, R. (1981) *The Idea of a Critical Theory*. Cambridge: Cambridge University Press.
Habermas, J. (1981) *Theorie des kommunikativen Handelns*. Frankfurt: Suhrkamp.
Habermas, J. (1987) *The Philosophical Discourse of Modernity*. Cambridge: Polity Press.
Habermas, J. (1988) *Nachmetaphysisches Denken*. Frankfurt: Suhrkamp.
Held, D. (1980) *Introduction to Critical Theory. From Horkheimer to Habermas*. London: Hutchinson.
Henrich, D. (1987) *Konzepte*. Frankfurt: Suhrkamp.
Jameson, F. (1970) *Marxism and Form*. Princeton, NJ: Princeton University Press.
Jameson, F. (1990) *Late Marxism. Adorno, or the Persistence of the Dialectic*. London: Verso.
Jarvis, S. (1998) *Adorno*. Cambridge: Polity Press.
Jay, M. (1984) *Adorno*. London: Fontana.
Paddison, M. (1993) *Adorno's Aesthetics of Music*. Cambridge: Cambridge University Press.
Rose, G. (1978) *The Melancholy Science*. London: Macmillan.
Schnädelbach, Herbert (1987) *Vernunft und Geschichte*. Frankfurt: Suhrkamp.
Thyen, Anke (1989) *Negative Dialektik und Erfahrung. Zur Rationalität des Nichtidentischen bei Adorno*. Frankfurt: Suhrkamp.
Wellmer, A. (1991) *The Persistence of Modernity*. Cambridge: Polity Press.
Wiggershaus, R. (1993) *The Frankfurt School*. Cambridge: Polity Press.
Zuidervaart, L. (1991) *Adorno's Aesthetic Theory*. Cambridge, MA: MIT Press.

6

Walter Benjamin

GRAEME GILLOCH

BIOGRAPHICAL DETAILS AND THEORETICAL CONTEXT

After a substantial period of neglect, Walter Benjamin (1892–1940) is now widely recognized as one of the most original and insightful thinkers of his generation and as perhaps the most important German literary theorist of the twentieth century. Like several of the other figures profiled in this book, Benjamin would not have thought of himself as a social theorist as such. Nevertheless, his idiosyncratic and frequently enigmatic writings on literature, aesthetics, philosophy, and historiography are increasingly seen to have a special resonance with, and relevance for, contemporary social and cultural analysis. A close friend of the Judaic scholar Gershom Scholem, the Marxist playwright Bertolt Brecht, and the philosopher Theodor Adorno, Benjamin became an associate of the Frankfurt Institute for Social Research and his ideas exist in an intricate interplay with the critical theory of the so-called 'Frankfurt School'. Although Benjamin's texts often differ radically in terms of their evaluation of phenomena, they also frequently prefigure key concerns and concepts for critical theory and are, above all, marked by the same catastrophic historical experiences of war, economic ruin, revolution, and totalitarianism.

In stark contrast to such traumas, Benjamin's childhood was a time of material comfort and tedious tranquility. Born on 15 July 1892, the son of an auctioneer and eldest of three children, Walter Benedix Schönflies Benjamin grew up in the desirable west end districts of Berlin in an affluent, assimilated German-Jewish family. As has often been observed, his 1932 semiautobiographical reflections on his formative years, 'A Berlin Childhood Around 1900' (in Benjamin, 1991, Vol. VI) and 'Berlin Chronicle' (in Benjamin, 1985b), are more disquisitions on the promises, possibilities, and prohibitions attending a middle-class, urban childhood in general than an intimate portrait of the intellectual as a young man. His reminiscences speak of a solitary and sickly childhood cloistered in the desperately 'cosy', cluttered, bourgeois interior of the time, of the dull round of visits to ageing relations, and of the strictures of school life. They tell of a child whose primary consolations for this dry, disciplined existence were in the daydreams stimulated by reading, by visits to the enchanting Tiergarten and

Berlin zoo, and, on one memorable occasion, by a wholly unexpected and unsanctioned foray into an alluring and thoroughly disreputable quarter of the city.

On health grounds Benjamin spent two years of his schooling (1905–6) at a relatively progressive boarding school at Haubinda in Thuringia, studying there under Gustav Wyneken, a key advocate of the radical wing of the youth movement and its mission of German cultural regeneration. Benjamin returned to complete his school studies in Berlin but remained in regular contact with Wyneken. After enrolling to study philosophy at Freiburg University in 1912, Benjamin's commitment to the cultural and educational politics of youth intensified and he published a number of poetic and idealistic polemics espousing radical reform in Wyneken's journal *Der Anfang* ('The Beginning') around 1913. Benjamin returned to Berlin to pursue his university studies in 1913 and was elected to the committee, and then to the chair, of the Free Students Movement there. The days of his involvement with the Youth Movement and student politics were numbered, however. The outbreak of the Great War in August 1914 split the movement into those who, like Wyneken, viewed the conflict as the very defence and renewal of German culture, and those who saw only catastrophe ahead. Two of Benjamin's closest friends, Fritz Heinle and Rika Seligson, committed suicide as a desperate protest against the hostilities. Deeply moved, Benjamin broke completely with Wyneken in March 1915. Three months later Benjamin met an 18-year-old student of mathematics, Gershom Scholem, an acquaintance who would prove a lifelong friend and a figure who would profoundly and enduringly influence Benjamin's work in the direction of Judaic thought, mysticism, and the Kabbala. Benjamin's concern with the critical and redemptive task of youth gave way to a preoccupation with redirecting philosophical enquiry away from the impoverished Enlightenment conception of experience, cognition, and knowledge exemplified by Kant, and towards an understanding of the linguistic grounding of truth in revelation. In his enigmatic fragments from 1916-17 Benjamin identifies the task of philosophy, to call things by their proper name, as the recovery of the perfect language with which Adam named Creation at God's behest.

Deemed unfit for military service on account of his poor eyesight, Benjamin moved to study in Munich in the autumn of 1915. He managed to avoid subsequent call-ups by feigning sciatica and, in 1917, relocated to neutral Switzerland and Berne University with Dora Kellner, whom he had married in April 1917. Benjamin spent the remaining war years in self-imposed Swiss exile and finally completed his doctorate on 'The Concept of Criticism in German Romanticism' in 1919. This study sought to develop a notion of immanent criticism which unfolded the inherent tendencies of the work of art, its 'truth-content', through the activity of critical reflection. Back in Germany, Benjamin subsequently undertook to provide an exemplary instance of such an approach in an extended essay on Goethe's famous novella 'Elective Affinities'. Eschewing conventional readings of the story as a cautionary moral tale of tragic, illicit love, Benjamin foregrounds the contrast between human subjection to fate and characterful, decisive action, a comparison which serves as an instructive lesson in the need to contest mythic forces. Above all, for Benjamin, the protracted death of one of the miscreant lovers, Ottilie, presents the demise of beauty, its mortification, for a higher purpose, truth, and thus serves as an allegory of the task of criticism itself.

In the early 1920s Benjamin hoped to make his mark in literary criticism through editing his own journal, *Angelus Novus*, the 'New Angel'. In Judaic thought, the Angelus Novus appears fleetingly before God to sing his praises before vanishing once more. Benjamin's angel never made even this brief appearance: uneasy that the erudite material would prove financially unviable, the publisher pulled out before the first edition was even finalized. This disappointment prompted Benjamin's return to the academic sphere and he embarked upon his *Habilitationsschrift* (a piece of research above and beyond the doctoral dissertation which, once completed, would entitle him to an academic post). Benjamin studied at the University of Frankfurt, taking as his theme the seventeenth-century German play of mourning, the *Trauerspiel*. Dismissed as bastardized tragedies, these baroque dramas with their preposterous plots and lurid language had long been consigned to the dusty attic of literary failures. Benjamin's immanent critique of these scorned and neglected works fundamentally distinguished them from the classical tragic form and reinterpreted and redeemed them as the quintessential expression of the frailties and vanities of God-forsaken human existence and the 'natural history' of the human *physis* as decay. In so doing, Benjamin argued for the importance of allegory as a trope which precisely renders and represents the world as fragmentation, ruination, and mortification. Now justly celebrated as a critical masterpiece, Benjamin's (1985c) *Origin of German Tragic Drama* (*Ursprung des deutschen Trauerspiels*), with its arcane subject matter and esoteric methodological preamble, baffled and bemused its inept examiners and Benjamin was advised and obliged to withdraw his study rather than face the ultimate humiliation of an outright rejection. By late summer 1925, Benjamin's ambitions for an academic career lay in ruins.

Benjamin was thus to spend the rest of his life eking out a precarious living as a freelance writer earning money through contributions to newspapers, literary reviews, magazines, journals, and even, in the early 1930s, through writing and presenting a series of radio broadcasts for children. Benjamin's growing association with Adorno, whom he met while in Frankfurt in 1923, and with the Institute for Social Research also led to a small stipend, but, as his correspondence continually indicates, his was an insecure and impecunious condition. As an intellectual outsider, Benjamin was able to lambast and lampoon scholarly conventions and the 'fat books' spawned by the overfed and underachieving bourgeois academy; at the same time, he was utterly dependent on the good offices of publishers, the press, commissioning editors and others who, like Ernst Schoen at Südwestdeutsche Rundfunk and Siegfried Kracauer at the *Frankfurter Zeitung*, offered what work and remuneration they could. It is this work of necessity which gives Benjamin's oeuvre its distinctive sense of fragmentation and astonishing diversity. Benjamin translated and wrote on Marcel Proust; he produced eloquent essays on such key literary figures as Franz Kafka, Bertolt Brecht, Karl Kraus, the Surrealists, and Charles Baudelaire; and also penned a radio piece entitled 'True Stories of Dogs', a set of reflections on Russian peasant toys, and a review of Charlie Chaplin. Only this can be said of such enforced eclecticism: whatever attracted his attention, Benjamin always discovered the most telling insights in the least likely and most trivial of things.

Benjamin was never to write another book in the, for him compromised, 'scholarly' style of his *Trauerspiel* book, which was eventually published in 1928. Instead, the aphorism, the illuminating aside, the quotation, the imagistic fragment became his preferred, indeed essential, mode of expression. In presenting and representing the everyday in a new light, observing it from an unexpected angle, such miniatures were intended to catch the reader off-guard (like a series of blows decisively dealt, Benjamin once observed, left-handed). Starting with his pen-portraits of cities he visited ('Naples', 'Marseilles', 'Moscow') and his 1926 montage of urban images *One-Way Street* (1985b), Benjamin's writings began to take on a new, contemporary inflection and radical political colouring. While working on the *Trauerspiel* study on Capri in the summer of 1924, Benjamin had read Georg Lukács's *History and Class Consciousness* and been introduced to a Latvian theatre director, Asja Lacis. His enthusiasm for the former, and his troubled love affair with the latter, drew Benjamin to Marxist ideas. In the winter of 1926–7 Benjamin visited Moscow to see the new Soviet system for himself. Benjamin's initial enthusiasm was tempered by the indifference of the Soviet authorities, the impossibility of the language, and, above all, by his unease at the incipient artistic impoverishment and intellectual compromises already discernible. Benjamin returned to Berlin where, through Lacis, he met and became friends with the playwright Bertolt Brecht. Much to the dismay of Adorno and Scholem, who saw Benjamin's always unorthodox and unconvincing espousal of Marxist ideas as a foolhardy flirtation, he became an advocate of Brecht's 'epic theatre' and the bald political messages of these didactic dramas. While Benjamin himself refrained from 'crude thinking', its traces and imperatives are evident in many of his key writings in the 1930s on the situation and task of the contemporary artist ('The Author as Producer', [1934] 1983b), and the character and consequences of new media forms for the work of art and aesthetic discourse (especially 'The Work of Art in the Age of Mechanical Reproduction', [1935] 1973).

Benjamin's concern with the fate of art within capitalist modernity, with the Marxist critique of commodity culture, and with the character and experience of the urban environment were to combine in a project which was to preoccupy him for the rest of his life. Inspired by the Parisian perambulations of the Surrealist writer Louis Aragon ([1926] 1987), Benjamin embarked in 1927 upon a study of the then ruinous and derelict Parisian shopping arcades built in the first half of the nineteenth century. Initially modest in scope, Benjamin's *Passagenarbeit* or *Passagen-Werk* (*The Arcades Project*, Benjamin, 1999b) was eventually to comprise over a thousand pages of notes, quotations, sketches and drafts, and today remains as an unfinished, indeed never written, 'prehistory' of nineteenth-century Paris as the original site of modern consumer capitalism, as a plethora of fragments providing for a panoramic and kaleidoscopic exploration of the city's fashions and phantasmagoria, architecture and boulevards, literature and politics.

It was to Paris, rather than Moscow or Palestine (where Scholem had emigrated), that Benjamin fled in 1933 to escape the Nazi tyranny and terror. There he pursued his researches for the 'Arcades Project' in the Bibliothèque Nationale, work which led to a proposed book on Baudelaire and a series of historiographical reflections and principles intended to form a methodological introduction. Like the wider *Passagenarbeit*, these too were never to be completed. Despite the advice and efforts of Adorno and Horkheimer, now in exile in New York, Benjamin lingered too long in Paris and was trapped in 1940 by the German invasion. He fled to the south of the country, was temporarily interned and, once released, desperately sought an escape route. It was not to be. Benjamin attempted to cross into the relative safety of Spain but was turned back at the border because of inadequate documentation resulting from last-minute changes to visa regulations. Wearied by his exertions, facing certain arrest on his return to France, Benjamin committed suicide on 26 September 1940. He is buried at Port Bou.

SOCIAL THEORY AND CONTRIBUTIONS

Benjamin's fragmentary oeuvre presents a highly eclectic and provocative combination of concepts, themes, and motifs drawn from a distinctive and diverse set of sources: Judaic mysticism and messianism; early German Romanticism; modernism, and in particular Surrealism; and a distinctive, highly unorthodox Marxism. Moreover, Benjamin was particularly attentive to, and appreciative of, objects and ideas that had been neglected, disregarded, and passed by. He had a keen eye for the manner in which the minutiae of mundane life, the inconspicuous instances of everyday experiences, could possess and provide the most profound insights and profane illumination of modern existence. Long-forgotten dramas, obsolete objects and outmoded fashions, children's books and toys, postage stamps – from such curios and collectibles Benjamin sought to unfold, critique and redeem the innermost tendencies and potentialities of contemporary cultural forms and practices.

How can one do justice to such an intriguing figure and rich body of work within the necessary limits of an overview such as this? Benjamin's own playful attempts to map out his life and work on paper produced only that ultimate figure of complexity and confusion: the labyrinth. Attempts to conceptualize Benjamin's work by distinguishing between his early and late writings, dividing his texts into an initial messianic phase influenced by Judaic motifs and themes, and a subsequent materialist period characterized by Brechtian elements and Marxist orientations, have been rightly criticized for their failure to perceive the complex continuity of his thought. From mysticism to Marxism – such a simplification obscures more than it illuminates and suggests a linearity of development which is thoroughly alien to Benjamin's own work. I wish to suggest another way of mapping Benjamin's work, one which draws on another of his key figures: not the labyrinth, but the constellation, a figure constituted by a plethora of points which together compose an intelligible, legible, though contingent, pattern. Benjamin's work might usefully be seen in terms of two textual constellations: first, that of the *Trauerspiel* study (comprising his reflections on language and translation, his doctoral dissertation and the essay on Goethe (both in 1996–9, Vol. 1), his plans for *Angelus Novus* (ibid.), various fragments on fate, history, tragedy, *Trauerspiel* and allegory, in 1985b); and, secondly, that of the 'Arcades Project' – including his urban *Denkbilder, One-Way Street*, the essays on Proust ([1929] 1973), Surrealism ([1929] 1985b) and Baudelaire ([1937–8 and 1939] 1983a), the texts on Brecht ([1930 and 1931] 1983b), photography ([1931] 1985b) and film ([1935] 1973), his childhood reminiscences ([1932] 1991) and historiographical theses ([1940] 1973).

Benjamin's dense and enigmatic early texts on language, truth, and history – 'On Language as Such and the Language of Man ([1916] 1985b), 'The Task of the Coming Philosophy' ([1918] 1996–9, Vol. 1), 'The Task of the Translator' ([1921] 1973) and the 'Theologico-Political Fragment' ([1920–1] 1985b) – combine to articulate what is, at first sight, an obtuse and obscure set of ideas. They are of key significance, however. Indeed, though there have been recent views to the contrary (Caygill, 1997), an understanding of Benjamin's linguistic theory is essential for his work as a whole (see Menninghaus, 1980). These texts elaborate a fragmentary critique of Enlightenment and rationalist thought as involving an impoverished and mechanistic conception of human experience; as a vain privileging of 'progress' based on the rabid pursuit and accumulation of scientific knowledge; as the development of a cold, calculating instrumentality in human relations with nature; and as the source of a debased understanding of human language. Benjamin's critique is not an articulation of or invitation to irrationalism, but rather seeks to foster an alternative understanding grounded not in the mediocrity of scientific knowledge but in the theological truth of the Judaic tradition. This should be understood less as a set of dogmatic principles than as a mode of gaining critical purchase on the contemporary human condition.

For Benjamin, the starting point is language. According to scripture, language in the form of the divine word of God is the origin of things. Adam is called by God to name Creation, to give things their proper names, that is, to translate the divine and creative word of God into human language. The blissful, paradisiacal language of Adamic naming comes to an end with the Fall and shatters into the multiplicity of historical human languages. Unlike Adam's perfect language, these are arbitrary in terms of the relation between word and thing and, in their plethora of terms for the same phenomenon, overname nature. Human history is this continuing life amidst a Babel of prattling languages which reduce nature to a state of mournful silence. Benjamin thus counterpoises a history of suffering and catastrophe against the idea of continual progress; a mystical vision of a sorrowful nature burdened by human folly against a view of nature as inert material for human exploitation; an understanding of the arbitrariness of language as an index of its fallen condition rather than as its essential characteristic, as Saussure (1966) famously contends. For Benjamin, the task of philosophy as the love of truth is a redemptive one: to call things once more by their proper name, to recall the perfect language of Adamic naming.

Two activities become important here: translation and criticism. In the work of translating one language into another, one discovers a pointer to the shared origin of language. It is, however, the task of the critic which becomes Benjamin's central focus. In his 1919 doctoral dissertation, Benjamin draws upon the writings of Schlegel and Novalis, themselves no strangers to the mystical tradition, to articulate a notion of immanent critique which emphasizes the unfolding of truth from within the work of art itself. Fichte's idea of the human individual coming to self-consciousness and self-understanding through a never-ending process of self-reflection is transposed onto the work of art. For the Romantics, criticism provides the successive mirrors for the work of art, through which it comes to reflect upon itself and thereby disclose its meaning and truth. Truth does not reside in the intentions of the author, but is perpetually constituted anew through the work of critique until, recognizing its relationship with other works of art, the artwork takes its rightful place within the pantheon of art, dissolves into the Idea of art. The self-disclosure of the meaning and the self-discovery of truth of the work of art occur during its 'afterlife', conceived as on-going criticism and final dissolution.

Like the essay on the 'Elective Affinities', Benjamin's *Trauerspiel* study sought to provide an exemplary instance of immanent critique in which the work of art was subjected not so much to a process of reflection, as one of ruination or mortification for the sake of its truth content. Benjamin's intention was to correct two fundamental misunderstandings of the *Trauerspiel* form. First, it should be distinguished from tragedy. The baroque plays were not failed attempts to produce classical dramas, but had a completely different grounding and purpose: instead of a concern with myth and the fate of the tragic hero, the *Trauerspiel* presented the dismal events of history as they conspired to ruin the sorrowful sovereign. It is not ennobling heroic action but human indecision which leads to catastrophe and melancholy. The *Trauerspiel* involves the articulation and illumination of a mournful and utterly profane realm of creaturely compulsion and human misery in a God-forsaken world. This finds expression in allegory. In recovering the *Trauerspiel* as a distinctive and legitimate aesthetic form, Benjamin also redeems allegory. Benjamin rejects the usual privileging of the symbol as the aesthetic figure *par excellence*, and instead argues for the importance of the much derided allegorical form. The dramatists of the baroque relied on this trope and, drawing on medieval emblematics, extended the range of allegorical referents such that dramatic objects came to take on manifold significance. In this overdetermination, objects and words, because they can refer to so many contradictory things, lose any precise sense. Allegory hollows out meaning, ruins it, reduces language to verbose prattle.

Allegory, like criticism, thus becomes a form of mortification which discloses a truth: the postlapsarian condition of language as arbitrary overnaming.

Benjamin understood his *Passagenarbeit* as a clear counterpart to his *Trauerspiel* study. The arcade and the play of mourning were both monadological and ruinous entities from which to unfold fragmentary insights into, and illuminations of, the past and its relationship with the present: of the nineteenth century as the prehistory of modernity, and of the seventeenth century as the origin of the baroque imagination. If the *Trauerspiel* study brought together immanent critique, ruinous history, and mournful, mute nature, the 'Arcades Project' and its constellation of texts combined 'strategic critique', redemptive history and the melancholy, mnemonic cityscape.

'Strategic critique' (Caygill, 1997), or polytechnical aesthetic engineering (Gilloch, forthcoming) involves a political understanding of the writer within the capitalist production process (of the 'author as producer') and of the meltdown of conventional bourgeois aesthetic forms and categories. Benjamin argues that the progressive critic/artist must pioneer and embrace new cultural forms (epic theatre), practices (interruption, montage, distraction) and media (radio, photography, film) to explode/implode the traditional work of art itself. 'Aura' is the fundamental concept here. In his 'Small History of Photography' (1931) and his 'Work of Art in the Age of Mechanical Reproduction' (1935), Benjamin famously argues that 'aura', the sense of awe, reverence, and distance experienced in the presence and contemplation of the work of art, a function of its cultic origins, authenticity and embeddedness in tradition, is dissolved by the advent of new media. Film and photography replace the unique painting with the multiplicity of the negative and print in which there is no distinction between original and copy. In these media, distance gives way to proximity, concentrated contemplation to distracted appropriation, cultic worship to political engagement and pedagogical practice.

The construction of the 'Arcades Project' was to be based on the imperatives of polytechnical aesthetic engineering and was to develop historiographic principles which radically contested bourgeois 'historicist' understandings of the past and the duty of the historian. The *Passagenarbeit* was to be imagistic in character, juxtaposing fragmentary insights into a mosaic or, in Benjamin's new terminology, a montage of elements. It was conceived not as a simple narration of the past but as a critical intervention into its afterlife. Arcades, fashions, commodities – these phantasmagorical and fetishized forms were indices not of historical progress but of new forms of mythic domination and human subservience. Inspired by the Surrealists, Benjamin's gaze focused on the 'afterlife' of these fantastical 'dream' forms – the ruined arcade, the obsolete object, the outmoded artefact – so as to disenchant them and redeem their utopian promise. As they are ruined, ridiculed, and demolished, the enslaving forms of yesteryear yield their critical potential, their revolutionary energy, their truth. History is not a bald and bland recounting of events, but a political engagement with, and actualization of, the past. The past is not given, but is continually reconfigured according to the interests of the present. This intersection and interplay of the 'then' and the 'now' was conceptualized by Benjamin within a visual register: as the 'dialectical image', the key methodological category of the *Passagenarbeit*.

The 'dialectical image' was inspired both by the instantaneousness of the photographic snapshot (Konersmann, 1991) and by the transformation of experience and memory in the modern metropolis. For Benjamin, the cityscape is a site of shock, amnesia, and remembrance. Baudelaire's allegorical poetics constitute a melancholy language with which to give expression to the hollowed-out commodity form and the collapse of coherent, communicable experience (*Erfahrung*) amid the swarming metropolitan crowd. The figures of the flaneur, the gambler, the prostitute, and the ragpicker serve as allegories of the modern poet who endures the shock collisions and fleeting encounters of the cityscape. Forgetfulness might seem the obvious corollary of such trauma, but the city is also the setting and stimulus for a particular mode of remembering: Proust's *mémoire involontaire*. Memories are not recoverable at will, but rather, return unexpectedly and unbidden. An occurrence or accident in the present fleetingly recalls former and forgotten impressions and experiences. Past and present momentarily intersect and mutually illuminate one another. The dialectical image is the transposition of the *mémoire involontaire* into a historiographic method which recognizes those whom conventional history has consigned to the oblivion of forgetting.

Intentionless knowing and the fleeting and fragmentary disclosure of truth; melancholy silence and the sorrowful condition of human existence; history as ruination and redemption; criticism as mortification and construction: such themes underpin the *Passagenarbeit*, the *Trauerspiel* study, and indeed Benjamin's work as a whole. Hence, and this is fundamental, the conceptualization of Benjamin's oeuvre as two constellations should not be thought of as reproducing the facile dichotomy of messianism versus materialism. These constellations are not to be envisaged as distinct chronological phases, rather they must be imagined as superimposed, one upon the other so that now this one, now the other, takes precedence, appears closest to us. The notion of constellations captures both the potential duplicity of any scheme – points that seem nearest to one another may prove those furthest apart – and, most importantly, their contingency. Each constellation is recognized as only one permutation among an infinite number of possible configurations, conjunctions, and correspondences. Such is the intricacy, such the interplay, such the ingenuity of Benjamin's writings.

APPRAISAL OF KEY ADVANCES AND CONTROVERSIES

In his notions of the dialectical image and afterlife of the work of art, Benjamin is precisely concerned with the resonance and relevance of the past in the present. Meaning is continually being reconstituted and reconfigured, actualized, in the present through critical mortification and appropriation. The work of art becomes legible in specific ways at particular historical junctures. In this manner, Benjamin presents a way of understanding the interpretation and reassessment of his own texts by subsequent commentators as a critically transformative and open endeavour. Indeed, Benjamin's transformation from neglected outsider to key theoretical innovator perhaps has much to do with the way in which his work is seen to prefigure and chime with contemporary (postmodern) cultural thought, while maintaining a keen and critical political edge. Prefiguring the 'cultural turn' in social theory, his texts are preoccupied with developing a complex and sophisticated understanding of the relationship between cultural products/texts and the socioeconomic, ideological, and historical conditions which give rise to them, which they express, and which they transform. There are a number of aspects here which give Benjamin's writings a particular pertinence today: the centrality of the fragment, the afterlife of the text, the legibility of the city, the reproducibility of the image, the reclamation of the past.

The Fragment

The world is broken into fragments, is legible in fragments and is representable through fragments – these are axiomatic for Benjamin. His interest in the *Trauerspiel* in particular was encouraged by the recognition that the baroque – an era scarred by the experiences of war and economic chaos; fascinated with the pathetic, profane condition of humanity bereft of transcendence; and characterized by an aesthetic of ostentation, excess, and waste – might have a special significance for, an 'elective affinity' with, his own time, itself convulsed by the carnage of the Great War, the financial turmoil and inflation of the Weimar years, and a sense of cultural crisis. Ruins and remnants are all that survive such calamitous events and the shattering of ontological certainties and existential consolations (Baudrillard, 1997: 9). They perhaps also have an acute relevance for the postmodern condition, defined in terms of the collapse of venerable 'grand narratives' (Lyotard, 1984), a radical scepticism with respect to the claims of science, humanism, and 'progress', and a privileging instead of eclecticism, alterity, and irony. As totalizing explanatory systems with their universal claims and teleological promises become ever less tenable, we are left to play scornfully but ruefully with their pieces, to survey their foundations now reconceptualized as vainglorious ruins. The apposite aphorism, the quotation out of context, the shocking juxtaposition of heterogeneous elements – these textual tactics are neither unique to, nor instigated by, Benjamin, but they do have a particular prominence in his work and pertinence today. 'Baroque reason' (Buci-Glucksmann, 1994) and Benjamin's 'charmed circle of fragments' may have a special attraction for the social theorist in the era of late capitalism.

The Text

Benjamin's notion of immanent criticism as a process of unfolding the work of art, as the continual constitution and reconstitution of its meaning in its afterlife, is extremely suggestive and prefigures some key postmodern insights. Such criticism seeks neither to (re)discover some original authorial intention nor to impose the canonical aesthetic judgments of self-appointed literary experts. The meaning of a text is determined by the manner of its apprehension and comprehension in the present. The decentring of the author is accompanied by the elevation of reading and interpretation. Indeed, textual meaning is never fixed and finalized but always contingent, open to 'endless interpolations', infinitely deferred. Moreover, as Benjamin both observes and exemplifies in his *Trauerspiel* study, genuine criticism radically contests the traditional evaluation of texts. Neglected and disdained forms are to be recovered and restored, and 'lesser works' are to be subject to the same careful scrutiny as supposed greater ones because, Benjamin observes, the architecture of the genre is more apparent in their design.

If the texts of Benjamin's *Trauerspiel* constellation disturb traditional cultural and aesthetic hierarchies, those associated with the 'Arcades Project' purposefully explode them. The critic as aesthetic engineer sabotages bourgeois aesthetic categories and the pretensions of the artistic genius to locate texts in sociohistorical matrices and material conditions and reposition the author as producer. Read against the grain, texts, such as Baudelaire's poetry, do not crudely reflect, but intricately express and critically articulate prevailing circumstances and tendencies. Whether canonical works of art or banal and popular forms, texts are hieroglyphs demanding patient translation and interpretation. Such an understanding has a particular appeal for those who argue for textual deconstruction and relish the postmodern implosion of high and popular cultural forms.

The City

In identifying the modern metropolis as the principal locus of commodity culture, Benjamin's various writings on urban space and experience have become key points of departure for contemporary theorists of consumption and the city (cf. Baudrillard, 1998). Benjamin's contribution is of fundamental significance. He not only recognizes commodity consumption as *the* hallmark of metropolitan modernity, but also seeks to locate consumer practices within wider cultural patterns: fashion, advertising, and display; architecture, design, and lighting; notions of progress and technological change; and, fantasy, fetishism, and sexuality. Indeed, the Parisian arcades, with their phantasmagorical construction and inversion of space, are readily recognizable as the precursors of contemporary shopping malls with their street simulations and themed interiors. Benjamin's work is a necessary starting point for scholars concerned with the proliferation of the commodity form and the spectacular superabundance of images, signs, and things in the contemporary city. Importantly Benjamin's physiognomy of the cityscape is concerned with deciphering urban objects and structures, with making them legible as signs and rebuses. Under his gaze, the city is transformed into a 'semiotic universe', a text to be read. In so doing, Benjamin not only prefigures concerns with the legibility of urban space (Lynch, 1960; de Certeau, 1984), but also introduces one of the most suggestive and frequently invoked figures in discussions of urban culture and experience, the flaneur (Tester, 1994; Gilloch, 1999).

The dawdling dandy has been reconfigured (and regendered) as a trope to elucidate and explore a plethora of urban (and virtual) experiences and activities: the prototypical sociologist (see Frisby, 1981, and in Tester, 1994); the privileged male gaze and the absence/presence of woman in the nineteenth-century city (Wolff, 1990; Wilson, 1991; Walkowitz, 1992); shoppers, tourists, and travellers; streetwise radicals and subversives (see Jenks, 1995; de Certeau, 1984); channel-hoppers and samplers; and internet browsers and cybersurfers (see Hartmann, forthcoming). On the one hand, the flaneur is understood as the quintessential postmodern pedestrian: the banal seeker of distraction amid the malls, theme-parks and other pseudo-public spaces of the postmodern city (Bauman, in Tester, 1994). On the other, the flaneur returns as an intrepid expert in the knowing and nonchalant use of public space (Jenks, 1995). The flaneur has been transformed from the snobbish spectator into an ideal, intellectual exponent of the cityscape, the utopian urbanite (Morawski, in Tester, 1994).

The flaneur has a particular relevance for postmodern theory beyond such identifications and debates. He is the ultimate figure of fragmentation and limitation. As a wanderer in the city, it is the flaneur who lacks an overview of the metropolitan whole, who is afforded no panoramic or bird's-eye perspective. The flaneur is not a privileged spectator in this sense, but, granted only an ant's eye-view, a limited witness of a complexity which eludes his vision and understanding, a melancholy, 'heroic' actor buffeted by forces but dimly perceived. Indeed, the flaneur is a part of that which he observes – he watches the crowd and is a member (however reluctantly) of that crowd. Spectator and spectacle are one and the same. As a result, the flaneur is a figure in perpetual motion – there is no safe and stable vantage point from which to behold events, but only a series of briefly held positions offering glimpses of a world itself in flux. Collapsing subject and object, partial in scope, situated yet shifting, the vision of the flaneur provocatively prefigures that of the postmodern social theorist.

The Image

Benjamin's interest in the political potential of new media and his positive evaluation of film, radio, and photography provide a welcome counterpoint and corrective to the indiscriminate and undifferentiated tirade against the 'culture industry' produced by Horkheimer and Adorno. For example, Benjamin's rejection of contemplation as a mode of aesthetic appreciation in favour of the 'distraction' experienced by the cinema-goer radically contests critical theory's vision of the stultified, infantalized, media audience. Indeed, only Kracauer and Benjamin among the 'Frankfurt School' writers genuinely recognize and explore the complexities of new visual cultural forms. Benjamin's understanding of the photographic image as containing a 'spark of contingency', an unexpected element captured by the photographer which disturbs the intended meaning of the picture and which produces a shock of recognition in its reader, prefigures Barthes's (1993) attempt to comprehend the power of certain photographs through the concept of the *punctum* (see Krauss, 1998; Price, 1994).

Most important, perhaps, is Benjamin's prescient recognition of the fundamental transformation of the work of art occasioned by the advent of new technologies of reproducibility and the move from the dichotomy of original/fake to an endless series of identical items without an original. For Baudrillard (1994), Benjamin here identifies a key stage in the history of representation, one which has now given way to an era characterized by the precession of simulacra, of the model, the 'fake'. Benjamin's arguments in the 'Work of Art' essay are radicalized by Baudrillard in his vision of the pre-eminence of the simulation and the constitution of the more real than real, the hyperreal.

The Past

Benjamin is not only important for the history of the image, but also for the image of history. His historiographic 'Theses' present a perceptive and timely critique of scientific and social 'progress' as the human domination of nature and continuing barbarism. Writing against both Enlightenment and orthodox Marxist thinking, Benjamin's argument that human emancipation does not reside in the mere overcoming of scarcity through the instrumental exploitation of nature but rather only in the development of a harmonious relationship with nature prefigures one of the principal themes of subsequent critical theory (Adorno and Horkheimer, 1986; Horkheimer, 1974a, 1974b; Marcuse, 1964) and contemporary ecological thought.

In addition, the 'Theses' point to the construction and fabrication of history. History is made in the image and interests of those who have been victorious in the past and are powerful in the present. Benjamin demands that the critical historian 'brush history against the grain' to reveal those who have been unsuccessful, silenced and silent, the past of those who are powerless in the present. To remember the sufferings of the forgotten dead and redeem their traces for the sake of the living – this call for a counterhistory of modernity is an inspiration to those engaged in the struggle to rethink the past so as to refashion the present and future: the poor, the oppressed, the downtrodden.

And, of course, Benjamin's writings themselves are objects to be redeemed, reconfigured, and reinterpreted as part of a vital critical tradition. To read, recognize and remember Benjamin as a key figure for contemporary social theory is the undertaking to which this profile has sought to contribute, however modestly, however imperfectly. If the present reader is encouraged to pursue such an enterprise, this text will have fulfilled its purpose.

BENJAMIN'S MAJOR WORKS

Benjamin, W. (1991) *Gesammelte Schriften*, Vols I-VII. (Eds. Rolf Tiedemann and Herman Schweppenhäuser, with the collaboration of Theodor Adorno and Gershom Scholem.) Frankfurt am Main: Suhrkamp Verlag; Taschenbuch Ausgabe.

Benjamin, W. (1995–9) *Gesammelte Briefe*, Vols I-V. (Eds. The Theodor W. Adorno Archive). Frankfurt am Main: Suhrkamp Verlag.

English Language Translations of Benjamin's Works

Benjamin, W. (1973) *Illuminations*. (Ed. and 'Introduction' by Hannah Arendt. Trans. Harry Zohn). London: Fontana.

Benjamin, W. (1978) *Reflections: Aphorisms, Essays and Autobiographical Writings*. (Ed. Peter Demetz. Trans. Edmund Jephcott). New York: Harcourt, Brace, Jovanovitch.

Benjamin, W. (1980) *Aesthetics and Politics: Debates between Bloch, Lukács, Brecht, Benjamin, Adorno*. (Trans. and ed. Ronald Taylor. 'Afterword' by Frederic Jameson). London: Verso.

Benjamin, W. (1983a) *Charles Baudelaire: A Lyric Poet in the Era of High Capitalism*. (Trans. Harry Zohn). London: Verso.

Benjamin, W. (1983b) *Understanding Brecht*. (Trans. Anna Bostock. 'Introduction' by Stanley Mitchell). London: Verso.

Benjamin, W. (1985a) 'Central Park'. (Trans. Lloyd Spencer), *New German Critique*, 34: 28–58

Benjamin, W. (1985b) *One-Way Street and Other Writings*. (Trans. Edmund Jephcott and Kingsley Shorter. 'Introduction' by Susan Sontag). London: Verso.

Benjamin, W. (1985c) *The Origin of German Tragic Drama*. (Trans. John Osbourne, 'Introduction' by George Steiner). London: Verso.

Benjamin, W. (1986) *Moscow Diary*. (Ed. Gary Smith. Trans. Richard Sieburth. 'Preface' by Gershom Scholem). Cambridge, MA and London: Harvard University Press.

Benjamin, W. (1989) 'N. (Re the theory of knowledge, theory of progress' (Trans. Leigh Hafrey and Richard Sieburth), in Gary Smith (ed.) *Benjamin: Philosophy, Aesthetics, History*. Chicago: University of Chicago Press.

Benjamin, W. (1994) *The Correspondence of Walter Benjamin*. (Ed. and annotated by Gershom Scholem and Theodor Adorno. Trans. Manfred Jacobson and Evelyn Jacobson, 'Foreword' by Gershom Scholem). Chicago and London: University of Chicago Press.

Benjamin, W. (1992) *The Correspondence of Walter Benjamin and Gershom Scholem 1932–1940*. (Ed. Gershom Scholem. Trans. Gary Smith and Andre Lefevre, 'Introduction' by Anson Rabinbach). Cambridge, MA: Harvard University Press.

Benjamin, W. (1996–9) *Selected Writings. Vols 1 and 2*. (Eds Marcus Bullock and Michael Jennings et al.) Cambridge, MA: Harvard University Press.

Benjamin, W. (1999a) *Theodor W. Adorno – Walter Benjamin: The Complete Correspondence 1928–1940*. Cambridge: Polity Press.

Benjamin, W. (1999b) *The Arcades Project*. Trans. Howard Eiland and Kevin McLaughlin. Cambridge, MA: Harvard University Press.

SECONDARY REFERENCES

Adorno, Theodor (1990) *Über Walter Benjamin*. (Ed. Rolf Tiedemann). Frankfurt am Main: Suhrkamp Verlag.

Adorno, Theodor and Horkheimer, Max (1986) *Dialectic of Enlightenment*. London: Verso.

Aragon, Louis (1987) *Paris Peasant*. London: Picador.

Barthes, Roland (1993) *Camera Lucida*. London: Vintage.

Baudrillard, Jean (1994) *Simulacra and Simulation*. Ann Arbor: University of Michigan Press.

Baudrillard, Jean (1997) *Fragments. Cool Memories III, 1991–5*. London: Verso.

Baudrillard, Jean (1998) *The Consumer Society: Myths and Structures*. London: Sage.

Benjamin, Andrew and Osborne, Peter (eds) (1994) *Walter Benjamin's Philosophy: Destruction and Experience*. London: Routledge.

Bolz, Norbert and van Reijen, Willem (1996) *Walter Benjamin*. New Jersey: Humanities Press.

Brodersen, Momme (1996) *Walter Benjamin: A Biography*. London: Verso.

Buci-Glucksmann, Christine (1994) *Baroque Reason: The Aesthetics of Modernity*. London: Sage.

Buck-Morss, Susan (1977) *The Origin of Negative Dialectics: Theodor Adorno, Walter Benjamin and the Frankfurt Institute*. Hassocks, Sussex: Harvester Press.

Buck-Morss, Susan (1983) 'Benjamin's *Passagenwerk*: Redeeming mass culture for the revolution', *New German Critique*, 29: 211–40.

Buck-Morss, Susan (1989) *The Dialectics of Seeing: Walter Benjamin and the Arcades Project*. Cambridge, MA: MIT Press.

Caygill, Howard (1997) *Walter Benjamin: The Colour of Experience*. London: Routledge.

Cohen, Margaret (1993) *Profane Illumination: Walter Benjamin and the Paris of Surrealist Revolution*. Berkeley, Los Angeles and London: University of California Press.

De Certeau, Michel (1984) *The Practice of Everyday Life*. Berkeley: University of California Press.

Doderer, Klaus (ed.) (1988) *Walter Benjamin und die Kinderliteratur*. Weinheim and Munich: Juventa Verlag.

Eagleton, Terry (1981) *Walter Benjamin: Or Towards a Revolutionary Criticism*. London: Verso.

Ferris, David (ed.) (1996) *Walter Benjamin: Theoretical Questions*. Stanford CA: Stanford University Press.

Fischer, Gerhard (ed.) (1996) *With the Sharpened Axe of Reason. Approaches to Walter Benjamin*. Oxford: Berg.

Frisby, David (1981) *Sociological Impressionism: A Reassessment of Georg Simmel's Social Theory*. London: Heinemann.

Frisby, David (1988) *Fragments of Modernity: Theories of Modernity in the Work of Simmel, Kracauer and Benjamin*. Cambridge, MA: MIT Press.

Fuld, Werner (1990) *Walter Benjamin: Eine Biographie*. Reinbeck bei Hamburg: Rowohlt Taschenbuch Verlag.

Geuss, Raymond (1981) *The Idea of a Critical Theory: Habermas and the Frankfurt School*. Cambridge: Cambridge University Press.

Gilloch, Graeme (1996) *Myth and Metropolis: Walter Benjamin and the City*. Polity Press: Cambridge.

Gilloch, Graeme (1999): 'The return of the flaneur: the afterlife of an allegory', *New Formations*, 38: 101–9.

Gilloch, Graeme (forthcoming) *Walter Benjamin: Critical Constellations*. Polity Press: Cambridge.

Habermas, Jürgen (1983) 'Walter Benjamin: consciousness-raising or rescuing critique', in *Philosophical-Political Profiles*. London: Heinemann.

Handelman, Susan (1991) *Fragments of Redemption: Jewish Thought and Literary Theory in Benjamin, Scholem and Levinas*. Bloomington: Indiana University Press.

Hartmann, Maren (forthcoming) 'The cyberflaneuse — strolling freely through the virtual worlds?', in *On/Off + Across: Language, Identity and New Technologies*. London: The Cutting Edge Research Group in conjunction with I. B. Tauris.

Held, David (1980) *Introduction to Critical Theory*. London: Hutchinson Press.

Horkheimer, Max (1974a) *Critique of Instrumental Reason*. New York: Seabury.

Horkheimer, Max (1974b) *Eclipse of Reason*. New York: Seabury.

Jäger, Lorenz and Reghely, Thomas (eds) (1992) *'Was nie geschrieben wurde, lesen'. Frankfurter Benjamin-Vortrage*. Bielefeld: Aisthesis Verlag.

Jameson, Frederic (1971) *Marxism and Form*. Princeton, NJ: Princeton University Press.

Jay, Martin (1974) *The Dialectical Imagination: a History of the Frankfurt School and the Institute of Social Research 1923–1950*. London: Heinemann.

Jenks, Chris (ed.) (1995) *Visual Culture*. London: Routledge.

Jennings, Michael (1987) *Dialectical Images: Walter Benjamin's Theory of Literary Criticism*. Ithaca, NY: Cornell University Press.

Konersmann, Ralf (1991) *Erstarrte Unruhe: Walter Benjamins Begriff der Geschichte*. Frankfurt am Main: Fischer Verlag.

Krauss, Rolf (1998) *Walter Benjamin und der neue Blick auf die Photographie*. Ostfildern/Stuttgart: Cantz Verlag.

Lindner, Burkhardt (ed.) (1978) *Walter Benjamin im Kontext*. Konigstein/Ts: Athenaum Verlag.

Lunn, Eugene (1985) *Marxism and Modernism: An Historical Study of Lukács, Brecht, Benjamin and Adorno*. London: Verso.

Lynch, Kevin (1960) *The Image of the City*. Cambridge, MA: MIT.

Lyotard, Jean-François (1984) *The Postmodern Condition: A Report on Knowledge*. Manchester: Manchester University Press.

Marcus, Laura and Nead, Lynda (eds) (1998) *The Actuality of Walter Benjamin*. London: Lawrence and Wishart.

Marcuse, Herbert (1964) *One-Dimensional Man*. London: Routledge.

Markner, Reinhard and Weber, Thomas (eds) (1993) *Literatur über Walter Benjamin: Kommentierte Bibliographie 1983–92*. Hamburg: Argument Verlag.

McCole, John (1993): *Walter Benjamin and the Antinomies of Tradition*. Ithaca, NY: Cornell University Press.

Mehlman, Jeffrey (1993) *Walter Benjamin for Children: An Essay on His Radio Years*. Chicago and London: University of Chicago Press.

Menninghaus, Winfried (1980) *Walter Benjamins Theorie der Sprachmagie*. Frankfurt am Main: Suhrkamp Verlag.

Menninghaus, Winfried (1986) *Schwellenkunde: Walter Benjamins Passage des Mythos*. Frankfurt am Main: Suhrkamp Verlag.

Missac, Pierre (1995) *Walter Benjamin's Passages*. Cambridge, MA: MIT Press.

Nägele, Rainer (1988) *Benjamin's Ground: New Readings of Walter Benjamin*. Detroit, MI: Wayne State University Press.

Nägele, Rainer (1991) *Theatre, Theory and Speculation: Walter Benjamin and the Scenes of Modernity*. Baltimore and London: Johns Hopkins University Press.

Pensky, Max (1993) *Melancholy Dialectics: Walter Benjamin and the Play of Mourning*. Amherst: University of Massachusetts Press.

Price, Mary (1994) *The Photograph: A Strange Confined Space*. Stanford, CA: Stanford University Press.

Puttnies, Hans and Smith, Gary (eds). (1991) *Benjaminiana: Eine Biografische Recherche*. Giessen: Anabas Verlag.

Roberts, Julian (1982) *Walter Benjamin*. London: Macmillan Press.

Rochlitz, Rainer (1996) *The Disenchantment of Art. The Philosophy of Walter Benjamin*. New York: Guilford Press.

Saussure, Ferdinand de (1966) *A Course in General Linguistics*. New York: McGraw-Hill.

Schiller-Lerg, Sabine (1984) *Walter Benjamin und der Rundfunk*. Munich: K. G. Verlag.

Scholem, Gershom (1982) *Walter Benjamin: The Story of a Friendship*. London: Faber and Faber.

Scholem, Gershom (1983) *Walter Benjamin und Sein Engel*. Frankfurt am Main: Suhrkamp Verlag.

Smith, Gary (ed.) (1988) *On Walter Benjamin: Critical Essays and Recollections*. Cambridge, Mass.: MIT Press.

Smith, Gary (ed.) (1989) *Benjamin: Philosophy, Aesthetics, History*. Chicago: University of Chicago Press.

Steinberg, Michael (ed.) (1996) *Walter Benjamin and the Demands of History*. Ithaca, NY: Cornell University Press.

Stüssi, Anna (1977) 'Erinnerung an die Zukunft: Walter Benjamins *Berliner Kindheit um Neunzehnhundert*', *Paelaestra*, 266.

Tester, Keith (ed.) (1994) *The Flaneur*. London and New York: Routledge.

Tiedemann, Rolf (1973) *Studien zur Philosophie Walter Benjamins*. Frankfurt am Main: Suhrkamp Verlag.

Tiedemann, Rolf (1983) *Dialektik im Stillstand: Versuche zum Spätwerk Walter Benjamin*. Frankfurt am Main: Suhrkamp Verlag.

Walkowitz, Judith (1992) *City of Dreadful Delight*. London: Virago.

Weigel, Sigrid (1996) *Body- and Image-Space: Rereading Walter Benjamin*. London: Routledge.

Weigel, Sigrid (1997) *Entstellte Ähnlichkeit: Walter Benjamins Schreibweise*. Frankfurt am Main: Fischer Verlag.

Wiggershaus, Rolf (1993) *The Frankfurt School*. Cambridge: Polity.

Wilson, Elizabeth (1991) *The Sphinx in the City*. London: Virago.

Wolff, Janet (1990) *Feminine Sentences: Essays on Women and Culture*. Cambridge: Polity.

Wolin, Richard (1982) *Walter Benjamin: An Aesthetics of Redemption*. New York: Columbia University Press.

7

Jürgen Habermas

PATRICK BAERT

BIOGRAPHICAL DETAILS AND THEORETICAL CONTEXT

Born in 1929, Jürgen Habermas grew up in Gummersbach, Germany. Between 1949 and 1954, he studied at the Universities of Göttingen, Zurich, and Bonn. After a short spell as a journalist, he became Theodor Adorno's assistant at the Institute for Social Research at Frankfurt. The early Frankfurt School clearly influenced the young Habermas but he soon developed his own research programme. He initially taught at the University of Heidelberg and at the Max Planck Institute; for the latter part of his teaching career he was at the Johann Wolfgang Goethe University in Frankfurt. Since the early 1970s Habermas has become one of the leading critical theorists in the world.

The term 'critical theory' may need some explanation. Critical theorists do not simply describe or explain the social; they aim at evaluating it. In particular, critical theorists attempt to demonstrate the potential and deficiencies of contemporary society. The early Frankfurt School aimed to develop such a critical theory as opposed to what Adorno and Horkheimer dismissively coined as 'traditional theory'. In this respect some commentators have been tempted to see Habermas's critical theory as a revamped version of the project of the early Frankfurt School. Furthermore, like the interdisciplinary nature of the early Frankfurt School, Habermas draws upon a wide range of disciplines which include linguistics, sociology, philosophy, and psychology. Finally, like Adorno and Horkheimer, Habermas pays attention to the problematic nature of the project of modernity, in particular the spread of means–ends rationality.

But this is only part of the story. Although some of Habermas's views are indebted to his old mentor, to treat his oeuvre simply as the extension of Adorno or Horkheimer's concerns would be a gross misrepresentation. First, Habermas's writings are indicative of a (post-1945) generation of German social theorists who clearly transcend their national roots. Whereas Adorno and Horkheimer draw extensively upon German authors like Marx, Nietzsche, Weber, and Freud, Habermas's work appears far less embedded in the German intellectual tradition. Habermas is influenced by a wide variety of intellectual traditions that include, for instance,

Parsons's system theory (obviously American), pragmatic philosophy (also a truly American project), 'ordinary language philosophy' (initiated by Wittgenstein and developed by Oxford philosophers), and ethnomethodology (initially a Californian product). Second, whereas Adorno and Horkheimer deplore the increasing means–ends rationality in the West, Habermas's appraisal of modernity is more subtle. For him rationalization is a twofold and selective process: it not only entails the spread of instrumental rationality but also communicative rationality. As communicative rationality refers to procedures of open discussion and criticism, rationalization is not to be rejected in toto. As a matter of fact, communicative rationality becomes the base for Habermas's critical theory. By contrast with Adorno, for whom the aesthetic domain provides a defence against instrumental rationality, Habermas's solution resides in the dialogical notion of reason. Finally, whereas the early Frankfurt School provides a comprehensive critique of bourgeois society, Habermas argues that liberal democracy presupposes his notion of communicative rationality. As such, it is possible to develop a critique of bourgeois society from within.

This brings me to the core of Habermas's thinking. Habermas's leitmotif, one may say, is the notion of unconstrained, open debate amongst equals. His 1962 *Habilitationschrift* (advanced doctoral dissertation) 'Structural Transformation in the Public Sphere' already expressed this idea. With the advent of bourgeois society, so Habermas contends, there was some potential for realizing the ideal of a 'discursive will-formation'. Unfortunately our society today is far from such an 'open' society, not in the least because the media have contributed to the trivialization of politics. But the ideal of a 'public sphere' is still worth pursuing. Society ought to be organized such that procedures are in place that allow for open discussion and criticism. The social philosopher ought to instruct people not upon what they decide but how they come to those decisions. Habermas's *The Theory of Communicative Action*, probably his most well-known work to date, elaborates further on this idea, and locates communicative rationality in linguistically mediated interaction. This highly abstract work, originally published in 1981, aims at defining the concept of rationality whilst avoiding a Cartesian philosophy of consciousness. The very same notion of open unconstrained debate underscores his recent work on law and ethics, *Moral Consciousness and Communicative Action* and *Justification and Application: Remarks on Discourse Ethics*.

Another of Habermas's chief concerns is the epistemological foundation of the social sciences. *Theory and Practice*, *Knowledge and Human Interests*, and *On the Logic of the Social Sciences* (all first published between the late 1960s and early 1970s) deal with this issue. Habermas attempts to define critical theory in relationship to two rival traditions in the philosophy of the social sciences: hermeneutics and positivism. He also reflects upon the deficiencies and fruitfulness of structural-functionalism and system theory – then prominent sociological theories. Here again, Habermas's position is moderate compared to say Adorno's. Whereas Adorno unambiguously rejects positivist epistemology and traditional theory, Habermas is careful not to pour the baby out with the bathwater and is willing to take on board some empiricist, functionalist, and system-theoretic notions.

Habermas's writings often reflect upon real changes in society, and engage with contemporary intellectual debates. For example, *Towards a Rational Society: Student Protest, Science and Politics* (a collection of articles from the 1960s) reflects upon the student uprisings in Germany and the then current political climate in the Western world. Habermas's concern is mainly with the loss of 'substantive rationality'; politics is no longer directed towards obtaining ultimate values, but towards avoiding technical problems that endanger the smooth functioning of the social and economic system. In *Legitimation Crisis* Habermas contends that this shift towards technical politics plus the in-built economic instability of capitalism leads to recurrent political crises. Indeed, political legitimacy nowadays depends heavily upon the state of the economy, but perpetual economic crises are intrinsic to the current capitalist mode of production. In this atmosphere, authority in the political sphere has become highly unstable.

Not only does Habermas comment on contemporary sociopolitical phenomena, he also engages with the work of other intellectuals. His well-known *The Philosophical Discourse of Modernity* defends the Enlightenment project against antimodernist, post-structuralist and postmodern assaults such as those by Nietzsche, Derrida, and Foucault. Maybe less well-known are Habermas's exchanges with Niklas Luhmann vis-à-vis the use and disuse of system theory in their co-authored *Theorie der Gesellschaft oder Sozialtechnologie*. More contentiously, Habermas has also entered a debate concerning the historical writings about Nazi Germany. The edited volume *The New Conservatism* addresses that which is known in Germany as the *Aufarbeitung der Vergangenheit* – the coming to terms with the past.

A comparison with Karl Popper is appropriate in the context of Habermas's involvement in public debates. Popper also advocated the principles of open dialogue and criticism, both in science and politics. The irony is that Popper himself showed no patience for different views, let alone for critics of his works. Contrary to the spirit of his own doctrine, Popper remained remarkably reluctant to learn from dialogue with others. Habermas, on the other hand, genuinely engages with others and shows willingness to be persuaded by what he himself calls the 'force of the better argument'. In short, considering Habermas's notion of communicative rationality, he practises what he preaches.

SOCIAL THEORY AND CONTRIBUTIONS

Critical Theory

Habermas's earlier work deals with the epistemological foundations of the social sciences, in particular critical theory. Partly by using Peirce's pragmatism, Habermas develops a typology of different forms of knowledge: empirical-analytical knowledge, hermeneutics, and critical theory. Habermas claims that these types of knowledge are linked to three forms of a priori interests. These interests are 'basic orientations' tied to essential conditions of reproduction and self-constitution of the human species. Empirical-analytical knowledge aims at control and prediction, whereas hermeneutics aims at understanding. Critical theory attempts to emancipate, and it relies upon a combination of empirical-analytical and hermeneutic knowledge. To emancipate is to question presuppositions that previously were taken for granted, and to eliminate sociopsychological constraints. In Habermas's systemic terms, empirical-analytical knowledge operates at the level of 'instrumental action' or 'work', hermeneutics at the level of 'language' and 'interaction', and critical theory deals with 'asymmetrical relations' or 'power'.

This threefold typology allows Habermas to locate his epistemological position. Habermas criticizes positivism for regarding empirical-analytical knowledge as the only valid knowledge. Habermas's point is not that empirical-analytical knowledge is flawed as such, but that it is only one type of knowledge amongst many – and one that is appropriate for obtaining control and prediction only. It would be a mistake, Habermas continues, to regard empirical-analytical types of knowledge as sufficient for gaining understanding or emancipation. After all, different aims call for different types of knowledge.

In his assault on positivism, Habermas also borrows from Gadamer's hermeneutics. Like Gadamer, Habermas appears sceptical of the early positivist notion of value-free and theory-independent knowledge. Any knowledge acquisition relies upon theoretical presuppositions; the latter is not an impediment for the former but its precondition. This is not to say that Habermas follows Gadamer blindly. Habermas is highly critical of Gadamer for not taking seriously the notion of critique. Gadamer is of course right when he asserts that people's knowledge relies upon assumptions that form part of a tradition, but he ignores the fact that not all assumptions (or traditions) are equally defensible. For Habermas, Gadamer's insights need to be supplemented by 'depth hermeneutics'. As such, Habermas develops a yardstick that allows one to compare, contrast, and evaluate various traditions, and so identify ideological distortions.

This brings me to the third type of knowledge: critical theory. For Habermas, critical theory draws upon the two other forms of knowledge but it differs from both in that it aims at self-emancipation. Psychoanalysis is Habermas's prime example of critical theory. The psychoanalyst employs interpretative techniques so as to help the patient re-enact hitherto repressed memories and wishes. In this context, Habermas talks about 'depth hermeneutics'. Whereas 'hermeneutics' refers to the interpretative techniques involved, the notion of 'depth' alludes to the fact that the psychoanalyst tries to go beyond the surface level and gain access to repressed experiences and desires. Depth hermeneutics then enables the psychoanalyst to obtain empirical-analytical knowledge in that he or she gains access to those causal mechanisms that have hitherto inhibited the personal growth of the patient. But the ultimate aim of psychoanalysis is to uplift these restrictions.

Psychoanalysis is one example of critical theory; historical materialism is another. What psychoanalysis manages at an individual level, historical materialism accomplishes in the social realm. Like psychoanalysis, historical materialism uncovers previously latent structures and is ultimately aimed at enhancing reflection and critical awareness.

Theory of Communicative Action

I mentioned earlier that Habermas's account of the Enlightenment project is not altogether negative. As a matter of fact, the political institutions of liberal democracy already imply the notion of open debate, and it is precisely this vision of communicative rationality which underlies the theory of 'universal pragmatics' as spelled out in the two volumes of *Theory of Communicative Action*. As such Habermas appeals for a communicative notion of reason as opposed to subject-centred notions of rationality. Habermas's main point is to show that a radical potential is implied in language.

There are two important building blocks to Habermas's theory of universal pragmatics. First he assumes that people are able to make distinctions, in particular between three realms: external nature, society, and internal nature. External nature deals with correct representation of things, society with the moral rightness of social rules, and internal nature refers to issues of intentions and sincerity. Second, Habermas's notion of rationality presupposes communication, and he elaborates on this by drawing upon speech act theory, in particular Austin's distinction between locutionary and illocutionary speech acts. This is a distinction between saying something on the one hand, and doing something by saying something on the other. In Habermasian parlance, every speech act can be divided up into a propositional and an illocutionary level.

These two ideas lead to Habermas's notion of 'validity claim'. Whilst communicating, people implicitly presuppose four culturally invariant 'validity claims': 'intelligibility', 'truth', 'moral rightness', and 'sincerity'. Implicit in the act of speaking is that what is said makes sense (intelligibility), that its factual content is correct (truth, linked to the external world), that the speaker is justified in saying this (moral rightness, related to the social world), and that he or she is not attempting to deceive anybody (sincerity, which ties in with the internal realm). Take, for example, a university teacher who describes a student's essay as 'unfinished but promising'. Habermas's point would be that, by making that assertion, much more has been said than meets the eye. Implicit in making the statement is the presupposition by the teacher that the statement is intelligible and factually correct, and that the teacher is perfectly justified in expressing the view in that way. Also implicit is that the teacher is not trying to deceive the student or anybody else by saying this: for instance, the teacher is not saying it to distract attention from other issues.

Habermas wants to promote 'undistorted communication' which allows people to openly defend and criticize all validity claims. He introduces the 'ideal speech situation' as a yardstick to compare between and judge real situations. The ideal speech situation is an ideal type of open debate for all; no constraints are put onto the debate except for the 'force of the better argument'. All individuals can enter the dicussion on an equal footing, and no repressed motives or self-deceit affect the outcome.

Let us examine the example of the teacher and student once again. In an ideal speech situation, the student would be able to challenge the teacher. The student might claim that the teacher's comment is vague ('what does "promising" mean exactly?') or wrong ('several passages are very insightful indeed'). The student might also argue that it is not acceptable for a teacher to take such a stance ('how dare you patronize me like that?'), or that, regardless of whether the comment is true or false, the intention was to deceive ('you are trying to distract attention from your poor lecture reports').

In an ideal speech situation the teacher would also be able to present a defence without constraints. The initial comment may be clarified ('"promising" as "having potential"') or shown to be correct ('although nicely put together, the essay is too much of a cut and paste work based on secondary sources'). The teacher may also argue that he or she is perfectly justified in saying this ('what else am I, as your teacher, to say than the plain truth about your essay?') or that there was no attempt to deceive ('this is a time slot devoted to assessing your essay, not my lectures'). Note that in the ideal speech situation all constraints, external (sociological) and internal (psychological), are to be lifted. For example, neither teacher nor student can appeal to power to impose their view ('I will have to fail you if you keep on challenging what I say'). Nor would they be intimidated by the other or exhibit fear of retaliation.

Habermas is anxious to emphasize that not all validity claims can be redeemed through discourse. Intelligibility and sincerity cannot be reclaimed in that way; the former can only be demonstrated by rephrasing the original assertion, the latter merely through action. But truth and moral rightness can be redeemed in ideal speech situations. Hence Habermas introduces a procedural notion of rationality and truth: rather than suggesting absolute foundations of knowledge, he suggests particular procedures for arriving at knowledge. In particular Habermas's consensus theory of truth refers to agreements reached by equal participants in an open debate. It follows that knowledge is always temporary – held until these participants arrive at a different conclusion.

Habermas describes societal and individual development in terms of increasing rationalization. In this respect he sees a homology between the two types of development. With regard to psychological development, Habermas draws upon the writings of Piaget and Kohlberg. Each phase leads to a 'decentring' of an egocentric view of the world. Children gradually learn to distinguish between different realms of reality (the subjective, the objective, and the social). Eventually children learn to reflect critically upon their actions and values by taking on board other perspectives. As for societal development, Habermas argues that mythical world views conflated nature, culture, and the external world. Only gradually did people manage to distinguish the different realms and, mutatis mutandis, to develop the ability for a rational *Lebensführung*.

Habermas has spent the last two decades expanding on the theory of communicative action, refining some of its central notions, and applying it to various realms. In particular, Habermas elaborates on ethics, and on issues regarding law and the state. Take Habermas and Apel's discourse ethic, which is a direct application of the theory of universal pragmatics to the realm of ethics. The notion of an open discussion, aimed at agreement, does not simply relate to matters of fact, but also to moral issues. Their discourse-based ethical theory starts from two assumptions. First, discourse ethics treats normative validity claims like truth claims; they are regarded as having a cognitive meaning. Second, Habermas and Apel believe that the grounding of norms and prescriptions requires a dialogue. As such, discourse ethics attempts to transcend the opposition between 'formal' and 'communitarian' perspectives on ethics. Moral judgments are not simply the conclusions reached by isolated individuals, nor do they simply reflect social codes.

The same discourse-based approach is applied to law and the state. Habermas rejects Luhmann's view that legal and political decisions are so complex that they should be left in the hands of experts. For Habermas, these issues ought to be subject to public discussion, and attempts should be made to inform as many people as possible and to include them in the debate. More generally, Habermas's appeal for 'discursive democracy' attempts to conceive of law in terms of 'discursively achieved understanding'. In a discursive democracy, norms are valid when they are accepted by the individuals who are potentially affected by these norms, and if this acceptance is based upon rational discourse. Discursive democracy is especially relevant today. After all, a multicultural society cannot be founded any longer on universal values or a social contract. For Habermas, contemporary society should be based on universal procedures of discursively achieved understanding.

APPRAISAL OF KEY ADVANCES AND CONTROVERSIES

There is no doubt that Habermas is one of the most influential social theorists of his generation although his writings have been controversial and provoked many criticisms. In what follows I will first discuss the legacy of Habermas, and then discuss some of its deficiencies.

The Legacy

Habermas's writings are significant for many reasons. Two are especially worth mentioning: his relationship to the Enlightenment and to critical theory.

Habermas is one of the most coherent and persuasive defenders of the project of Enlightenment. Enlightenment thinking has come under severe attack in the latter part of the twentieth century, especially in the writings of post-structuralist and postmodern authors like Foucault, Derrida, and Lyotard. Of course, the first assaults on the project of modernity preceded the work of these French intellectuals, but the critical comments of, say, Nietzsche, Adorno, and Horkheimer became influential only when the postmodern bandwagon was well on its way. Whilst the Enlightenment project was gradually regarded as *vieux jeu*, Habermas has remained one of its staunch defenders, and a very persuasive one. In the midst of these assaults on the Enlightenment, Habermas has consistently tried to underscore and promote its dialogical nature – not an entirely original idea, but one easily overlooked by its French critics. The solution, Habermas argues, is to divorce Enlightenment thinking from a

Cartesian philosophy of consciousness (*Bewußtseinsfilosofie*). Once the separation is completed, the French objections seem to lose their grip.

Second, the contemporary status of critical theory would not be the same without Habermas's contributions. Here again Habermas is not afraid to go against the Zeitgeist. In the 1960s there was a growing interest in critical theory but little epistemological groundwork had been done. Habermas filled the gap. He managed to define critical theory in opposition to rival forms of knowledge (positivism and hermeneutics), and made a serious epistemological case for critical theory. During the 1970s and early 1980s several sociologists and philosophers regarded the idea of critical theory as intellectually flawed, and it is precisely during this period that Habermas developed his theory of universal pragmatics – the basics behind his critical theory. On a related theme, Habermas's lifelong preoccupation with the 'public sphere' spurred a huge interest in sociology, politics, and philosophy, and remains one of the empirical cornerstones of contemporary critical theory (see, for instance, Calhoun, 1992).

Critique of Habermas

It is important to distinguish between how Habermas's writings have been received on the one hand, and my own assessment on the other. I will therefore first spell out a number of criticisms that can regularly be found in the secondary literature, and then move on to what I personally see as his main deficiencies.

This is not the place to provide an exhaustive list of the various criticisms of Habermas's writings. The list is simply too long, and Habermas has incorporated some of these criticisms into his own work anyway. I will briefly elaborate on one recurrent, and not unimportant, criticism. That is, Habermas has often been criticized for failing to provide a solid empirical base for his theorizing. Take his first major book, *The Structural Transformation of the Public Sphere*. Some commentators argue that the empirical evidence is at best flimsy. Habermas may have overstated the prominence of a public sphere at the beginning of the nineteenth century. Other than some privileged members of the bourgeoisie, few appeared to have had access to the public sphere (Negt and Kluge, 1993; Landes, 1988; Ryan, 1990). The critics certainly have a point in that, given his liberal political agenda, Habermas pays remarkably little attention to the extent to which women or minorities tended to be excluded from the sociopolitical debates of the time. Habermas now agrees with this, and furthermore concedes the feminist point that the exclusion of women (and their allocation to a private sphere) was probably constitutive of the emergence of the bourgeois public sphere (see his 'Further Reflections on the Public Sphere' in Calhoun, 1992). In Habermas's defence, however, it needs to be added that he actually never asserted that the public sphere embraced all sections of society. What he did write is that there was more scope for these debates than there is now, and that this juxtaposition allows one to infer a yardstick in order to judge and compare between present institutions. As Habermas commented, 30 years after *The Transformation of the Public Sphere* was published:

> What I meant to do was to take the liberal limitations of public opinion, publicity, the public sphere, and so on, at their worst, and then try to confront these ideas of publicness with their selective embodiments and even the change of their very meaning during the process of transformation from liberal to organized capitalism, as I described it at that time. (Calhoun, 1992: 463)

Not only has his earlier work been subject to the criticism that his empirical evidence is flawed; his theory of communicative action has been also. Habermas draws upon what he calls 'reconstructive sciences' to support his case, and amongst these are, for instance, Piaget and Kohlberg's account of personal development. Recently, however, a significant amount of empirical counterevidence has been mounted against these theories.

For example, although Kohlberg's theory might be applicable to men, women's development appears to be very different (e.g. Gilligan, 1982). Habermas also draws upon Lévi-Strauss's studies of primitive societies – again a highly contentious set of analyses. Although these criticisms are justified, they actually indicate a deeper lacuna in Habermas's writings. That is, Habermas tends to implicate the work of other theoreticians to support his case. Whether he elaborates on, say, the theory of communicative action or his theory of societal evolution, Habermas shows how other theoreticians have adumbrated his own theory. This may serve well to illustrate the theory but it is not particularly persuasive as a proof of its validity.

I will now move on to what I personally see as the main weaknesses of his theory. For the sake of brevity, I will focus on his theory of communicative action, which is after all his most important contribution to social theory.

First, the notion of *Verständigung* has a double meaning. Note that Habermas asserts that communicative rationality is directed towards *Verständigung*. But *Verständigung* means both understanding and consensus. It may well be the case that an unconstrained, open debate between equals leads to a situation in which each has a better grasp of the other's position, but to understand better somebody's viewpoint is by no means to acquiesce. I agree that the debate might be an opportunity for each participant to learn about the exact nature of the others' position. Each may clarify under which adjustments the other's position is acceptable. Each may clarify what he or she means by the concepts involved, and so on. There is indeed a lot to be said for clarifying these ambiguities. But it is also true that there are few cases in which individuals, who had very different opinions to start off with, end up converging. This shows that both his theory of communicative action and its attendant discourse ethics have a limited range.

Second, his notion of the 'force of the better argument' is problematic. Underlying Habermas's communicative notion of reason is the belief that there is a neutral algorithm that will enable individuals to decide between competing perspectives. Habermas's algorithm can be found in the vision of an open, unconstrained debate between equals. In this ideal-type, only the force of the better argument counts. The problem with this Habermasian position is that it stands or falls with the assumption that people necessarily agree on what counts as a superior or inferior argument. One does not have to be a sophisticated sociological observer to realize that there are remarkably few cases in which people disagree about significant topics whilst agreeing on what counts as a proper way of arguing about these issues. This qualification seriously limits the scope of Habermas's research programme. Moreover, there is often a lack of disagreement about how to argue properly if the participants in the debate occupy different cultures, 'forms of life', or paradigms: for instance, whether people consider it legitimate to refer to religious texts, scientific findings, or popular myths will depend on a number of culturally embedded assumptions. It could of course be counterargued that what counts as the force of a better argument can be decided by another open debate and so on. But this is only to postpone and highlight the severity of the problem as one enters a regression ad infinitum.

Lastly, the problem with the ideal speech situation is not that it is unreal in itself (it is after all a yardstick that allows one to judge real settings), but that it is devoid of real people. Remember that Habermas's ideal speech situation not only excludes external constraints such as power; it also rules out internal constraints. An internal constraint is any psychological feature that may inhibit people from openly criticizing others and defending themselves. For instance, being impressed by authority figures or to be embarrassed about expressing oneself in public are examples of how internal constraints may interfere with unconstrained communication. The problem for Habermas is that these psychological characteristics are so tied in with our everyday notion of what it is to be an individual that it becomes difficult to eradicate them without succumbing to remarkably impoverished notions of self and personhood. Even leaving aside this point, the individuals in the counterfactual have such different psychological compositions that they ought probably to be treated as different entities. Again, this seems to put into doubt the practical value of the yardstick.

HABERMAS'S MAJOR WORKS

Habermas, J. (1971) *Towards a Rational Society: Student Protest, Science and Politics*. London: Heinemann.

Habermas, J. (1974) *Theory and Practice*. London: Heinemann.

Habermas, J. (1976) *Legitimation Crisis*. London: Heinemann.

Habermas, J. (1979) *Communication and the Evolution of Society*. Boston: Beacon Press.

Habermas, J. (1983) *Philosophical-Political Profiles*. London: Heinemann.

Habermas, J. (1987a) *Knowledge and Human Interests*. Cambridge: Polity Press.

Habermas, J. (1987b) *The Philosophical Discourse of Modernity*. Cambridge: Polity Press.

Habermas, J. (1988) *On the Logic of the Social Sciences*. Cambridge: Polity Press.

Habermas, J. (1989a) *The Structural Transformation of the Public Sphere: An Inquiry into a Category of Bourgeois Society*. Cambridge: Polity Press.

Habermas, J. (1989b) *The New Conservatism: Cultural Criticism and the Historian's Debate*. Cambridge: Polity Press.

Habermas, J. (1990) *Moral Consciousness and Communicative Action*. Cambridge, MA: MIT Press.

Habermas, J. (1991a) *The Theory of Communicative Action, Volume 1: Reason and the Rationalization of Society*. Cambridge: Polity Press.

Habermas, J. (1991b) *The Theory of Communicative Action, Volume 2: Lifeworld and System: A Critique of Functionalist Reason*. Cambridge: Polity Press.

Habermas, J. (1993) *Justification and Application: Remarks on Discourse Ethics*. Cambridge: Polity Press.

Habermas, J. (1998) *On the Pragmatics of Communication*. Cambridge, MA: MIT Press.

Habermas, J. and Luhmann, N. (1971) *Theorie der Gesellschaft oder Sozialtechnologie*. Frankfurt: Suhrkamp.

SECONDARY REFERENCES

Alway, J. (1995) *Critical Theory and Political Possibilities: Conceptions of Emancipatory Politics in the Works of Horkheimer, Adorno, Marcuse and Habermas*. London: Greenwood Press.

Baynes, K. (1992) *The Normative Grounds of Social Criticism: Kant, Rawls, and Habermas*. Albany: State University of New York.

Bernstein, R.J. (1985) *Habermas and Modernity*. Cambridge: Polity Press.

Brand, A. (1990) *The Force of Reason: An Introduction to Habermas's Theory of Communicative Action*. London: Allen Unwin.

Calhoun, C. (ed.) (1992) *Habermas and the Public Sphere*. Cambridge, MA: MIT Press.

Chambers, S. (1996) *Reasonable Democracy, Jürgen Habermas and the Politics of Discourse*. Ithaca, NY: Cornell University Press.

Cooke, M. (1994) *Language and Reason: A Study of Habermas's Pragmatics*. Cambridge, MA: MIT Press.

Deflem, M. (ed.) (1996) *Habermas, Modernity and Law*. London: Sage.

Dews, P. (ed.) (1986) *Autonomy and Solidarity: Interviews with Jürgen Habermas*. London: Verso.

Geuss, R. (1981) *The Idea of a Critical Theory: Habermas and the Frankfurt School*. Cambridge: Cambridge University Press.

Gilligan, C. (1982) *In a Different Voice: Psychological Theory and Women's Development*. Cambridge, MA: Harvard University Press.

Held, D. (1980) *Introduction to Critical Theory: Horkheimer to Habermas*. London: Hutchinson.

Holub, R.C. (1985) *Jürgen Habermas: Critic in the Public Sphere*. London: Routledge.

Honneth, A. and Joas, H. (1991) *Communicative Action: Essays on Jürgen Habermas's Theory of Communicative Action*. Cambridge: Polity Press.

Ingram, D. (1987) *Habermas and the Dialectic of Reason*. New Haven, CT: Yale University Press.

Keat, R. (1981) *The Politics of Social Theory: Habermas, Freud and the Critique of Positivism*. Chicago: University of Chicago Press.

Kelly, M. (1994) *Critique and Power: Recasting the Foucault/Habermas Debate*. Cambridge, MA: MIT Press.

Landes, J. (1988) *Women and the Public Sphere in the Age of the French Revolution*. Ithaca, NY: Cornell University Press.

McCarthy, T. (1978) *The Critical Theory of Jürgen Habermas*. Cambridge, MA: MIT Press.

Negt, O. and Kluge, O. (1993) *The Public Sphere and Experience*. Minneapolis: University of Minnesota Press.

Outhwaite, W. (1994) *Jürgen Habermas*. Cambridge: Polity Press.

Passerin d'Entreves, M. and S. Benhabib (ed.) (1996) *Habermas and the Unfinished Project of Modernity: Critical Essays on The Philosophical Discourse of Modernity*. Cambridge: Polity Press.

Pusey, M. (1987) *Jürgen Habermas*. New York: Tavistock.

Rehg, W. (1994) *Insight and Solidarity: A Study in the Discourse Ethics of Jürgen Habermas*. Berkeley: University of California Press.

Raffel, S. (1992) *Habermas, Lyotard and the Concept of Justice*. Basingstoke: Macmillan.

Rasmussen, D.M. (1990) *Reading Habermas*. Oxford: Basil Blackwell.

Rockmore, T. (1989) *Habermas on Historical Materialism*. Indianapolis: Indiana University Press.

Roderick, R. (1986) *Habermas and the Foundations of Critical Theory*. London: Macmillan.

Ryan, M.P. (1990) *Women in Public: Between Banners and Ballots, 1825–1880*. Baltimore: John Hopkins University Press.

Thompson, J. (1981) *Critical Hermeneutics: A Study in the Thought of Paul Ricoeur and Jürgen Habermas*. Cambridge: Cambridge University Press.

Thompson, J. and D. Held (1982) *Habermas: Critical Debates*. London: Macmillan.

Trey, G. (1998) *Solidarity and Difference: The Politics in the Aftermath of Modernity*. Albany, NY: State University of Albany Press.

Wallulis, J. (1990) *The Hermeneutics of Life History, Personal Achievement and History in Gadamer, Habermas and Erikson*. Evanston, IL: Northwestern University Press.

White, S. (1988) *The Recent Work of Jürgen Habermas. Reason, Justice and Modernity*. Cambridge: Cambridge University Press.

White, S. (1995) *The Cambridge Companion to Habermas*. Cambridge: Cambridge University Press.

8

Erving Goffman

ANN BRANAMAN

BIOGRAPHICAL DETAILS AND THEORETICAL CONTEXT

Erving Goffman was born in Canada in 1922. He completed a BA in sociology and anthropology at the University of Toronto in 1945 and a PhD in sociology at the University of Chicago in 1953. For his doctoral thesis ('Communication Conduct in an Island Community'), Goffman spent a year living and observing social interaction on a small island community off the coast of Scotland. Goffman wrote his doctoral dissertation in Paris where he became familiar with existentialism. Drawing on his research in the Shetland Isles, Goffman published his first major work *The Presentation of Self in Everyday Life* in 1956. The reissued version of this book in 1959 would become Goffman's most popular and widely read work. From 1954 to 1957, Goffman studied the behaviour of staff and patients in psychiatric hospitals – first, in the National Institutes of Health Clinical Center in Bethesda, Maryland and then at St Elizabeth's Hospital in Washington, D.C. His research in these two settings formed the basis of his book *Asylums* (1961a), a collection of essays that examined the subjective experience of inmates in 'total institutions'.

At the invitation of Herbert Blumer, Goffman joined the sociology faculty at the University of California at Berkeley in 1957. Quickly rising to the status of full professor in 1962, Goffman remained at Berkeley until 1968. During his years in California, he conducted fieldwork in Las Vegas casinos. Though never fully developed and reported, this work contributed to his formulation of a game perspective in social life. Implicit in much of his work, the game metaphor is explicitly utilized in *Encounters* (1961b), 'Where the Action Is' (Published in Goffman, 1967), and *Strategic Interaction* (1970). In 1968, Goffman took a position at the University of Pennsylvania where he remained until his death. Here, Goffman became involved with the university's prominent sociolinguistics school. His encounter with sociolinguistics, begun during his years of doctoral study but intensified in his years at Pennsylvania, formed the basis for much of his later work, particularly *Forms of Talk* (1981) and 'Felicity's Condition' (1983a). Prior to his death in 1982, Goffman was President of the American Sociological Association. His ASA presidential address 'The Interaction Order'

(1983b), undelivered due to his fatal illness, articulates the guiding premise of more than two decades of his work: that there is an order to face-to-face interaction that is worthy of sociological study in its own right.

Goffman cannot easily be placed into any particular theoretical school, nor has his own work generated a 'Goffman School'. Goffman's graduate training at Chicago, one of the two leading schools of sociology in the United States at the time, was probably the greatest influence on his approach. At Chicago, Goffman was supervised by both sociologists and social anthropologists, including Lloyd Warner, Robert Park, Ernest Burgess, and Everett Hughes. The Chicago School at the time drew no clear boundary between social anthropology and sociology, emphasizing 'participant observation' as the favoured method of empirical research.

Goffman rejected the label 'symbolic interactionism', a term coined by Herbert Blumer and derived from George Herbert Mead's social psychology, because he believed it was too vague to be useful. Although Goffman found Mead's and Blumer's ideas congenial, he was committed in his own work to empirical study and attention to the structure of the social world that he believed was missing in Mead's and Blumer's work. Including Georg Simmel as a foundational figure in the development of symbolic interactionism, Goffman's work could even more comfortably be included in this tradition. Goffman learned Simmel's ideas in graduate school at Chicago and took Simmel's charge for sociologists to study the otherwise unnoticed and seemingly trivial actions and interactions in everyday life as a basis for his own sociological approach. Furthermore, if symbolic interactionism is defined loosely as a sociological approach that focuses on understanding the meaning rather than the causation of social behaviour – an approach advocated by Max Weber and by the social phenomenologist Alfred Schutz – Goffman fits squarely within this tradition. Though ultimately critical of phenomenology and ethnomethodology, Goffman credits Schutz's paper 'On Multiple Realities' as a source of influence on *Frame Analysis* (1974).

Goffman also considered himself a structural-functionalist of sorts. Like the functionalists Talcott Parsons and Robert Merton and unlike social constructionists, Goffman believed that individuals come into a world largely premade and do very little of the constructing themselves. Goffman's basic concern with the question of what makes sustained social interaction possible, furthermore, parallels the central question of the functionalist tradition, namely, 'what makes society possible?' (Lofland, 1980: 37–8). Goffman included Emile Durkheim as one of the most influential figures in his intellectual development. The 'interaction rituals' that Goffman describes, rituals focused especially on affirming the dignity and worth of the self, parallel the religious rituals in Durkheim's analysis whereby social solidarity is produced. In *The Division of Labor in Society* and in the short essay 'Individualism and the Intellectuals', Durkheim had argued that individualism is the only common morality of modern society and that regard for the dignity, freedom, and worth of the individual must therefore replace traditional forms of religious worship. Goffman's analysis portrays a social world in which such reverence for the self has indeed become the basis of social order. Compatible with Durkheim's view that society rests on a basis of morality, the social world described by Goffman is one in which moral norms, sentiments, emotions, and feelings – much more than thoughts and interests – drive human behaviour.

Though Goffman was influenced by diverse and prominent figures in the history of sociological thought, he vehemently opposed canons and the studying of social theorists as an end in itself. Goffman's approach was to take whatever insight can be gained from sociological forerunners and get on with the business of studying social life. Was Goffman a social theorist? He would say not, though he might also say that he was as much of a social theorist as anyone else. He did not believe sociology had advanced to the stage of constructing theories and hypotheses and thus did not think there was such a thing as a social theory at all. Furthermore, no sharp distinctions can be made in his work between the empirical and the theoretical. Reported observations (his own and others') make up the majority of his written work. Yet, these observations are interwoven into conceptual frameworks insightfully crafted by Goffman. And this is how Goffman defined the current task of sociology: 'We are just trying to get reasonable classifications, one or two useful concepts, ways of touching on and describing processes and practices . . .' (Verhoeven, 1993: 340. Verhoeven (1993), Burns (1992), and Manning (1992) are primary sources of biographical information on Goffman. In particular, I relied heavily on Verhoeven's interview with Goffman for information on Goffman's intellectual background.

SOCIAL THEORY AND CONTRIBUTIONS

Certainly, it is Goffman's conceptual frameworks much more than any particular observations of social life that have drawn enduring attention. In addition to Goffman's extraordinary gift for 'touching on and describing processes and practices' (Verhoeven, 1993: 340) of everyday life, an important contribution to social theory in its own right, Goffman's analyses develop a number of core social theoretical themes – including the social production of self, the ritual basis of social life, the interaction order, and the organization of experience.

The Social Production of Self

One of the most central themes in Goffman's work is his analysis of the social production of the self. Although the idea that the self is a product of social life was earlier developed by George Herbert Mead, Goffman's idea is less abstract and more radical than Mead's. Mead's idea was that the self arises in social experience, that development of the ability to view oneself from the perspective of the 'generalized other' precedes the development of self. Goffman's idea is that the self does not merely *arise* in social experience, but it is a *product* of the social scene or a dramatic effect of performances in social life.

In *The Presentation of Self in Everyday Life*, Goffman distinguishes between the self-as-performer and the self-as-character. The self-as-performer refers to the human being as a psychobiological organism with impulses, moods, energies, and feelings who is driven to be regarded favourably by others. The self-as-performer, according to Goffman, is 'universal human nature' and is an essential basis of motivation for social participation and conformity to the rules of social life. Though the self-as-performer could accurately be thought of as something 'inner', Goffman argues that it is not the self-as-performer but rather the self-as-character, or the character performed, that most in our society have in mind when they speak of the self. The self-as-character is a product of performances in social life. Goffman quotes Park, who says that the 'mask is the truer self' (Goffman, [1956] 1959: 19). Goffman admits that we have a sense of self as separate from the performance, but that this sense of self is a product of the performance and not the cause of it (Goffman [1956] 1959: 252–3.) Essential to any performance is the support and reception it receives from others, and this is why the self cannot be understood to be a property of the individual to whom it is attributed.

Perhaps the greatest part of Goffman's work can be viewed as an analysis of the contingencies involved in sustaining a self. *The Presentation of Self* is an analysis of the techniques used in everyday life to build and sustain images of self. Noting that we do distinguish between theatre and real life, Goffman uses drama as a metaphor for analysing the performances of everyday life to demonstrate that both 'real' and 'contrived' images of self and reality require successful staging for their realization in social life. In *Asylums* (1961a), Goffman looks at what happens to the self when the usual supports for staging a self – such as autonomy, privacy, control of material resources, an occupational identity – are lacking. By analysing how the self is mortified in 'total institutions', institutions such as prisons and psychiatric hospitals which control every aspect of the inmate's life, Goffman's aim is to 'help us to see the arrangements that ordinary establishments must guarantee if members are to preserve their civilian selves' (1961a: 14). *Stigma* (1963b) deals with another source of difficulty in the staging of the self: the potential discrediting to which selves are subject. 'Normal' identity, Goffman says, is defined in terms of culturally-valued attributes which few of us fully possess or achieve. *Stigma* analyses the variety of ways in which discreditable persons manage discrediting information in order to maintain a semblance of normality, as well as the ways in which discredited persons, that is, persons known to possess a stigmatizing attribute, manage the implications of their stigma. Though Goffman outlines a number of strategies stigmatized persons have for dealing with stigma, he suggests that 'normal' society calls for the stigmatized to minimize any interactional disruption that might result from the stigma and to accept treatment as 'not quite human'.

The Ritual Basis of Social Life

Although Goffman uses the metaphors of drama and the game, the predominant image of social life that runs through his work is that of a ritual order. The central focus of his work, particularly his work of the 1950s and 1960s, is an examination of how the social routines, the face-saving practices, and the traffic rules of everyday social interaction are used to maintain social order. Much of his work – especially *Interaction Ritual* (1967), *Behavior in Public Places* (1963a), and *Relations in Public* (1971) – is a fine-grained analysis of the seemingly trivial rules of conduct of social life and of the mechanisms that lend stability to social order. 'On Face-Work' ([1955] 1967) is an analysis of the face-saving practices that social actors routinely employ in social interaction and of how these practices enhance social order. 'The Nature of Deference and Demeanor' ([1956] 1967) analyses the deferential behaviours individuals are expected to use to build the images of others and the proper demeanour that individuals must exhibit to maintain their own images. Both, he argues, are essential not only to the individual's image of self but also to the social order. 'Embarassment and Social Organization' ([1956] 1967) examines embarrassment as an aspect of orderly behaviour. When an individual projects an image of self that cannot be sustained in social interaction, a show of embarrassment demonstrates recognition of this fact and thereby communicates regard for the obligations that were breached. 'Alienation from Interaction' ([1957] 1967) examines the obligations of individuals to be ready for spoken interaction and how such readiness is necessary 'if society's work is to be done' (1967: 135–6). In *Behavior in Public Places* (1963a), Goffman outlines the 'situational proprieties' of social interaction and argues that, though seemingly trivial, these 'give body to the joint social life' (1963: 196). Similarly, *Relations in Public* (1971) examines a variety of social routines and practices that are used to affirm social relationships, social rank, and social order.

According to Goffman, face-saving and the traffic rules of social interaction go hand in hand. The primary motivation of individuals, Goffman assumes, is to be regarded favourably by others. This motivation draws them to social life and motivates them to demonstrate approved attributes and abide by rules of conduct in social interaction. Face-saving (of self and others) is the most fundamental traffic rule of social interaction and is essential to the maintenance of social order ([1955] 1967: 12). Drawing on Durkheim's analysis of ritual as a basis of social solidarity, Goffman argues that the self has become a sacred object in modern life. 'Many gods have been done away with, but the individual himself stubbornly remains as a deity of considerable importance' (1956: 55). According to Durkheim's theory, such respect for the individual would be essential to the social solidarity of modern society. As the increasing complexity of society dissolved the common beliefs, norms, and shared ways of living characteristic of earlier societal forms, Durkheim believed that individualism could be the only common basis of morality and was therefore essential as a basis of social solidarity. According to Goffman, the obligation that members of social life feel to cooperate in affirming the dignity of self and others in everyday social interaction attests to the supreme value of the individual in modern society. Also as Durkheim had suggested, Goffman argues that this felt obligation to provide such supportive worship is a primary basis of social order. Unlike Durkheim, who promoted individualism in the context of defending the right of intellectuals to think freely and criticize existing social institutions, Goffman implies that the accommodative approach that individuals take towards one another's faces is a somewhat more conservative dynamic. As Goffman says in *Interaction Ritual*: 'Approved attributes and their relation to face make of every man his own jailer; this is a fundamental social constraint even though each man may like his cell' ([1955] 1967: 10).

The Interaction Order

Typically, Goffman was not one to enter into meta-theoretical debates about such issues as the relationship between interaction and social structure. Implicitly, social class was apparent in many of Goffman's works as a variable affecting the dynamics of social interaction. But rarely was Goffman concerned to specify the relative primacy of interaction and social structure. In the introduction to *Frame Analysis* he did state offhandedly that he considered social organization and social structure to be primary relative to the organization of experience in social encounters (1974: 13). Only in 'The Interaction Order' (1983b), however, did Goffman explicitly address the relationship between social interaction and social structure. Here he argues that the interaction order should be considered 'a substantive domain in its own right' (1983b: 2). Though he emphasizes that considering the interaction order a substantive domain in its own right does not imply the viewpoint that interaction is prior to or constitutive of society and macro-level social organization, it does imply that there is an order to social interaction that does not entirely derive from larger social structures. In some respects, he argues, the interaction order is autonomous relative to social structure. Although he admits differences in resources and advantages within the interaction order that derive from structures of inequality in the larger society, he argues that the forms and processes of the interaction order are independent of these inequalities – 'the central theme remains of a traffic of use, and of arrangements which allow a great diversity of projects and intents to be realized through unthinking recourse to procedural forms' (1983b: 6).

Not only is the interaction order relatively autonomous from society and social organization, but Goffman suggests that the interaction order can have a direct impact on larger social structures. An implicit theme throughout Goffman's work is that the norms of social interaction – for example, deference and demeanour, distribution of personal territories according to social rank, protective and defensive facework – contribute significantly to consolidating social hierarchies that otherwise might be quite tenuous. Organizational life, Goffman points out, depends on 'people-processing encounters. . . . It is in these processing encounters

... that the quiet sorting can occur which, as Bourdieu might have it, reproduces the social structure' (1983b: 8). Though the interaction order typically plays a conservative role, Goffman suggests that the processing that occurs in social interaction 'may consolidate or loosen structural arrangements' (1983b: 8).

The Social Construction of Experience

A central theme that runs through Goffman's work – from *The Presentation of Self in Everyday Life* (1956) to *Frame Analysis* (1974) – is that human experience is socially constructed. Goffman disagreed with the hyperrelativism of social constructionism, a perspective that he believed accorded an undue amount of power to individual actors to define situations that are constructed prior to their arrival in particular situations. Adopting a Durkheimian line, Goffman argues that society is external to and prior to the individual, that social situations have a structure to them, and that individual participants usually arrive at rather than construct definitions of situations (Collins, 1988: 58). As Goffman puts it in the introduction to *Frame Analysis*, W.I. Thomas's statement that definitions of situations are real in their consequences is 'true as it reads but false as it is taken' (1974: 1). Arguably, a major portion of Goffman's work could be accurately understood as an elaboration on Thomas's statement.

To answer such basic questions of social life as 'what is going on here?' or 'who is this person really?', Goffman suggests that we must discern the frames – or principles of interpretation – that provide meaning to any spate of activity. In other words, a person or an event rarely 'speaks for itself'. An act of caring for a child, for instance, could be understood as 'parenting', 'babysitting', or 'kidnapping'. Though the physical motion involved in the act might be identical in each instance, the meaning of the act varies according to the frame that governs it. Goffman suggests that there is a certain 'objective reality' to the frames that govern our experience, in the sense that frames are usually anchored in layers of other frames and in societal and situational structures that we as individuals do not control. In the sense that he believed there was a reality to the social world to be discovered, Goffman considered himself a positivist. But, as positivists go, he heavily emphasized that the 'objective reality' of the social world was built out of a myriad of framing devices and interactional techniques by which human beings give meaning to their experience. That there is no 'original' beneath the layers of frames and no 'real self' beneath the performances of social life is a common theme that connects *The Presentation of Self* with *Frame Analysis*.

APPRAISAL OF KEY ADVANCES AND CONTROVERSIES

Goffman's work has held wide appeal and has generated a variety of interpretations, often contradictory ones, by social theorists. Due at least in part to Goffman's evasion of placement within any theoretical school, it could almost be said that Goffman has been everything to everybody! Goffman is considered a symbolic interactionist and a critic of symbolic interactionism. His theory of the self is applauded by postmodernist social theorists, while others interpret his view of the self as a counter to postmodernism. Goffman's work has been criticized by some existentialists for its portrayal of the inauthenticity of human actors and applauded by others for its portrayal of the human struggle to maintain authenticity in the face of attack. Goffman has been criticized for presenting a cynical view of social life, while others see him as a moralist of sorts who is concerned with the maintenance of trust, morality, and order in social life. Goffman has been interpreted as a conservative functionalist and a radical social critic. In this section, I shall elaborate on each of these interpretations.

Goffman and Symbolic Interactionism

Goffman's analytic focus on the self, social interaction, and the interpretive frames that give meaning to human experience has earned him inclusion in the symbolic interactionist camp, and he has accordingly received criticism commonly directed at symbolic interactionists for inattention to social structure, social inequality, and social-historical context and for failure to formulate ways in which larger social processes constrain microsocial interaction. In *The Coming Crisis in Western Sociology,* Alvin Gouldner argued that Goffman's

> is a sociology of co-presence, of what happens when people are in one another's presence. It is a social theory that dwells upon the episodic and sees life only as it is lived in a narrow interpersonal circumference, ahistorical and noninstitutional, an existence beyond history and society .... Goffman's image of social life is not of firm, well-bounded social structures, but rather of a loosely stranded, criss-crossing, swaying catwalk along which men dart precariously. In this view, people are acrobatic actors and gamesmen who have, somehow, become disengaged from social structures and are growing detached even from culturally standardized roles. (Gouldner, 1970: 379)

Similarly, Allan Dawe argues that Goffman's work portrays a social world lacking in power, class conflict, and political domination (Dawe, 1973: 247–8). Countering the view of Goffman as neglectful of structural inequalities of power, Rogers (1977, 1980) argues that Goffman offers insight into the nature of power as a pervasive fact of people's everyday lives (1977: 88). According to Rogers, Goffman is 'clearly sensitive to the unequal distribution of opportunities for face-maintenance as well as the ways in which social-structural factors render problematic the sense of self-determination through pressures toward conformity' (Rogers, 1980: 115).

Though Goffman's inclusion in the interactionist camp is merited by his micro-analytical focus, he is also accurately understood as a critic of symbolic interactionism – a structuralist of sorts who emphasizes that social situations are socially structured prior to any individual's arrival at them (Collins, 1988; Gonos, 1980; Katovich and Reese, 1993). As Randall Collins (1988) puts it: 'Symbolic interactionists focus on the ability of individuals to transform meaning in social situations; Goffman stresses that situations have a structure to them that is external and prior to the individual' (Collins, 1988: 58). Similarly, George Gonos (1980) argues that Goffman 'inverts' symbolic interactionism by eliminating the view of the 'self' as a free subject and creator of the world and replacing this view with an institutional view of the self (Gonos, 1980: 158). Katovich and Reese (1993) include Goffman among late modern interactionists who went beyond the early interactionists conception of a natural harmony between the self and society to a conception of selves 'pitted against an obdurate reality which included overpowering and often hostile societal responses' (Katovich and Reese, 1993: 404).

Existentialist and Postmodern Interpretations of Goffman's Analysis of Self

Goffman has been criticized by existentialists and humanists for portraying the inauthenticity of the human self and endowing inauthenticity with an equal claim to reality as 'authentic' experience (MacIntyre, 1969; Gouldner, 1970; Dawe, 1973). Gouldner argues that Goffman 'declares a moratorium on the conventional distinction between make-believe and reality, or between cynical and the sincere' (Gouldner, 1970: 380). MacIntyre (1969) argues that Goffman 'dissolves the individual into his role-playing performances', losing from view human agency and morality (MacIntyre, 1969: 447). Dawe argues that personal identity, if there is even such a thing in Goffman's analysis, can survive only by concealment (Dawe, 1973: 248).

In contradiction to this interpretation, other existentialists and humanists have read Goffman's work as a depiction of the self's struggle to maintain integrity in the face of dehumanizing social constraints (Friedson, 1983; Creelan, 1984; Lofland, 1980). Friedson characterizes Goffman as a 'celebrant and defender of the self against society' (Friedson, 1983: 362) and points out 'Goffman's deep moral sensibility, the compassion he displays for those whose selves are attacked, whose identities are spoiled' (Friedson 1983: 361). Creelan (1984) likens Goffman's moral perspective to the moral struggle depicted in the Book of Job. Lofland (1980) points out an affinity between existentialism and the Goffmanian portrayal of the self as a 'stance-taking entity' who acts to promote dignity and freedom. Goffman's work, Lofland argues, can be viewed as a 'search for the conditions under which people can be persons' (Lofland, 1980: 48).

An alternative and more recent interpretation has been to identify Goffman's analysis of the self with postmodernist social theory, insofar as both challenge the notion that the 'self' is a stable, inner reality (Tseelon, 1992; Dowd, 1996; Battershill, 1990). Tseelon argues that the Goffmanesque self is postmodern, consisting of surfaces or performances, a transient self which is situationally or interactively defined. Goffman himself, Tseelon argues, did not take issue with the question 'when is performance more sincere?' because in true postmodern spirit he regarded even sincere performance as nonetheless constructed and was more concerned with the mechanics of creating an appearance and less with the relationship between appearance and reality (Tseelon, 1992: 124). Also characterizing Goffman's view of the self as a precursor to postmodernist views, Dowd (1996) argues that Goffman's view of the self contradicted not only the conventional wisdom of a 'true self' but also the social psychological notions that the self is stabilized either through cognitive balancing or the internalization of role requirements (Dowd, 1996: 244). Dowd argues that 'any strong conception of human agency or autonomy must be reassessed in the wake of postmodernism's emergence' (Dowd, 1996: 256), and he suggests that Goffman's work provides material for such a reassessment.

Against this postmodern interpretation, Schwalbe (1993) interprets Goffman as demonstrating the reality of the self. Like the existentialists who view the self portrayed in Goffman's work as a 'stance-taking entity', Schwalbe argues that the self is expressed in moments of decision about what face to present in a social encounter and in moments of resistance where we assert ourselves against social expectations (Schwalbe, 1993: 337). The reality of the self as a psychobiological process, the basic human need to maintain the coherence of the self, Schwalbe argues, is the basis of the interaction order (Schwalbe, 1993: 338).

Goffman as Cynic or Moralist?

Goffman has been criticized for holding a cynical view of the self and social life, particularly by the existentialist and humanist critics discussed above. According to some interpretations, Goffman's cynical depiction is a description of the life of the new middle class in late modern American society. One of the first to draw connections between Goffman's work and its social-historical context, Gouldner (1970) argues that Goffman's dramaturgy 'marks the transition from an older economy centred on production to a new one centred on mass marketing and promotion, including the marketing of the self' (1970: 381). Goffman's sociology, he argues, expresses the experience of the educated middle class, a class that lives in a world in which 'utility and morality are less and less viable' and in which 'getting ahead' depends less on talents and skills and more on the manipulation of impressions (Gouldner, 1970: 387). A couple of variations on a similar theme include Young (1971) and Gonos (1980). Young agrees with the connections Gouldner makes, but sees Goffman's work as an indictment of the 'inauthentic self' and of the social and institutional factors that create it (Young, 1971: 278). Gonos (1980) takes issue with Gouldner's view of Goffman's work as a sociology of the new middle class, and rather considers it a critique of the values of this class from the perspective of the 'old middle class'. He points out that Goffman's sociology showed the *necessity* of impression management, that the requirement of 'dramatising one's work' is built into the structure of unproductive labour (Gonos, 1980: 145). However, he argues that Goffman's sociology *depicts* the new middle class but does not resonate with their conceptions of themselves as authentic beings (1980: 154). On the contrary, he argues, Goffman's sociology takes the perspective of the 'underlife' figures who have a 'keen realistic understanding of the new corporatism' and who understand the relationship between 'what is outwardly communicated and the reality of the game' (1980: 151).

In contrast to the cynical interpretation and/or the interpretation of Goffman as an unacknowledged analyst of the life of a specific social class at a specific point in history, other social theorists see in Goffman's work an analysis of the interactional processes whereby humans, in all times and places, build social and moral order (Collins, 1980, 1988; Giddens, 1988; Hall, 1977). Collins (1980) believes that Goffman's core contribution is his analysis of the way that interactional rituals directed towards the self facilitate moral order among members of a social group (Collins, 1980: 46–7). According to Giddens, Goffman's sociology is an analysis of a 'highly moralized world of social relationships. ... Trust and tact are more fundamental and binding features of social interaction than is the cynical manipulation of appearances' (Giddens, 1988: 113). Hall (1977) argues that Goffman's portrayal of human actors and social life is 'less of a competitive set of liars, and much more of a rather altruistic mutual aid society helping each other over difficult moments' (Hall, 1977: 539). Like Collins, Hall (1977) views Goffman's work as a continuation of the Durkheimian tradition, going beyond Durkheim in recognizing how important for the ordering and integration of society are the interaction rituals that affirm the sacred quality of the individual (Hall, 1977: 540).

While Goffman does emphasize moral obligations as a basis of social order, the cynical interpretation understandably derives from his view that actors are more concerned with putting on a show of morality than they are with living up to moral standards themselves (Collins, 1980; Bovone, 1993). As Goffman puts it in an often-quoted passage: 'The individuals who are performers dwell more than we might think in a moral world. But, *qua* performers, individuals are concerned not with the moral issue of realizing these standards, but with the amoral issue of engineering a convincing impression that these standards are being realized' ([1956] 1959: 251). But it is not because they are 'sinister manipulators', as some critics have argued, that actors manipulate appearances to convey their morality. Rather, management of appearance is itself a moral obligation. As Goffman says: '... the very obligation and profitability of appearing always in a steady light, of being a socialized character, forces one to be the sort of person who is practiced in the ways of the stage' ([1956] 1959: 251). Unlike Parsons, Collins (1980) points out, Goffman 'does not find social order to be founded on *internalization* of moral obligations; the obligations, rather, come because of the way we encounter pressures from each other in specific situations to help each other construct a consistent definition of reality' (Collins, 1980: 182).

Goffman as Conservative Functionalist or Social Critic?

Finally, Goffman has been viewed as a functionalist and a social critic. The interpretation of Goffman as a functionalist derives from Goffman's fundamental concern with the interactional mechanisms by which social order is maintained. Taking Goffman at his word, the functionalist interpretation is, as Collins (1988) has argued, probably the more accurate of the two interpretations. Goffman stated that he regarded himself as a functionalist and as an objective analyst and not a critic of the social world. Yet several interpreters have viewed Goffman as an implicit social critic, an analyst of the interaction dynamics that perpetuate social hierarchies and a critic of the structures that dehumanize all but the most privileged of social actors (Rogers, 1980; Gamson, 1985; Branaman, 1997). While perhaps not an interpretation Goffman intended, there is nonetheless an abundance of material in Goffman's work that is amenable to a *reading* of him as a social critic. A central theme in *The Presentation of Self* and *Asylums* is that the self depends on a variety of props (e.g. territories of the self, team-mate support) to maintain human dignity, and that access to these props is unequally distributed according to social rank (Goffman, 1971). While *Interaction Ritual* (1967) can be read as a functionalist analysis of the interactional maintenance of social order, it can also be read as a critical analysis of the way that interactional norms conserve existing social orders and hierarchies independently of their merits. His statement in *Stigma* (1963b: 128) that 'there is only one completely unblushing male in America' can similarly be read as an indictment of the exclusiveness of the social requisites of full-fledged humanity (Branaman, 1997). In addition to the view of Goffman as a critical analyst of the interactional dynamics of inequality, Goffman's work has also been viewed as an analysis of the self's resistance to mortifying social constraints (Friedson, 1983; Creelan, 1984; Lofland, 1980) and of the potential for the interaction order to subvert larger social structures (Rawls, 1984).

Conclusion

Who or what is Goffman really? Symbolic interactionist or structuralist, existentialist or postmodernist, cynic or moralist, functionalist or social critic? Goffman is amenable to such a variety of interpretations, I would argue, because he imports no clear-cut meta-theoretical, moral, or political agenda into his writings. As he claims, he is an observer and analyst of social life – not a meta-theoretician, moralist, or politician. Yet, because his subject matter is the nature of the self and social interaction and the morality and politics of everyday social life, he draws the attention of meta-theorists, moralists, and politicians. My own interpretation is that each of the major interpretations capture an important piece of Goffman, and that one of Goffman's most important contributions is to break down the dichotomies implicit in these seemingly competing interpretations.

Clearly, Goffman's analytical focus is on everyday social interaction, and it goes without saying that he thinks that what goes on here has significant implications for the larger social order. At the same time, his work illustrates that the dynamics of social interaction are powerfully constrained by social structures that transcend the everyday realm. Compatible with existentialist readings, there is in Goffman's writings a depiction of a moral and emotional core to the self that struggles to maintain dignity and to avoid dehumanization. Yet, as the postmodern interpreters say, the self is not a stable inner reality but rather a precarious accomplishment of social life. The view of Goffman as a cynic is warranted by his exposure of the dramatic techniques and the seemingly manipulative practices that people use in social life to sustain desired definitions of self and social reality. Goffman certainly offends readers who take themselves and their realities too seriously and are unwilling to admit their dependence on dramatic props and social support. At the same time, the major aim of such practices in Goffman's view is to foster dignity, morality, and trust. Certainly, Goffman's primary focus on the (interactional) ritual basis of social order places him in the Durkheimian tradition and warrants viewing him as a functionalist of sorts. At the same time, his dissection of the conservative nature of interactional norms, of the divergence between social placement and merit, of the exclusiveness and arbitrariness of the standards of 'normality', and his analysis of the unequal distribution of the props and social support necessary to generate positive regard in social life certainly provides material for social critics.

Even though Goffman did not allow himself to be pinned down into any theoretical school, it could be argued that the diversity of interpretations attest to what may be his greatest contribution – his ability to describe the social world in such a way as to invite the application of larger social theoretical questions to the everyday world of social interaction.

GOFFMAN'S MAJOR WORKS

Goffman, E. (1956) *The Presentation of Self in Everyday Life*. Edinburgh: University of Edinburgh Social Sciences Research Centre; Harmondsworth: Penguin, 1959.

Goffman, E. (1961a) *Asylums*. Garden City, NY: Doubleday, Anchor Books.

Goffman, E. (1961b) *Encounters: Two Studies in the Sociology of Interaction*. Indianapolis, IN: Bobbs-Merrill.

Goffman, E. (1963a) *Behavior in Public Places: Notes on the Social Organization of Gatherings*. New York: The Free Press.

Goffman, E. (1963b) *Stigma: Notes on the Management of Spoiled Identity*. Englewood Cliffs, NJ: Prentice Hall and New York: Touchstone Books, Simon and Schuster, 1986.

Goffman, E. (1967) *Interaction Ritual: Essays on Face-to-Face Behavior*. Garden City, NY: Doubleday, Anchor Books; Chicago, IL: Aldine.

Goffman, E. (1969) *Strategic Interaction*. Philadelphia: University of Pennsylvania; New York: Ballantine Books, 1972; Oxford: Basil Blackwell, 1970.

Goffman, E. (1971) *Relations in Public: Microstudies of the Public Order*. New York: Basic Books; New York: Harper and Row, 1972; London, Allen Lane, 1971.

Goffman, E. (1974) *Frame Analysis: An Essay on the Organization of Experience*. Cambridge, MA: Harvard University Press; New York: Harper and Row; Harmondsworth: Penguin, 1975.

Goffman, E. (1979) *Gender Advertisements*. Cambridge, MA: Harvard University Press; New York: Harper and Row (Introduction by Vivian Gornick), and London: Macmillan (Introduction by Richard Hoggart).

Goffman, E. (1981). *Forms of Talk*. Philadelphia: University of Pennsylvania, and Oxford: Basil Blackwell.

Goffman, E. (1983a) 'Felicity's condition', *American Journal of Sociology*, 89 (1): 1–53.

Goffman, E. (1983b) 'The interaction order', *American Sociological Review*, 48: 1–17.

SECONDARY REFERENCES

Battershill, C. D. (1990) 'Goffman as a precursor to post-modern sociology', in *Beyond Goffman: Studies on Communication, Institution, and Social Interaction*. Berlin and New York: Mouton de Gruyter.

Bourdieu, Pierre (1983) 'Erving Goffman, discoverer of the infinitely small', *Theory, Culture, and Society*, 2 (1): 112–13.

Bovone, Laura (1993) 'Ethics as etiquette: the emblematic contribution of Erving Goffman', *Theory, Culture, and Society*, 10 (4): 25–39.

Branaman, Ann (1997) 'Goffman's social theory', in C. Lemert and A. Branaman (eds), *The Goffman Reader*. Cambridge, MA: Blackwell.

Burns, Tom (1992) *Erving Goffman*. London and New York: Routledge.

Chriss, James J. (1993) 'Durkheim's cult of the individual as civil religion: its appropriation by Erving Goffman', *Sociological Spectrum*, 13 (2): 251–75.

Chriss, James J. (1995) Habermas, Goffman, and communicative action: implications for professional practice', *American Sociological Review*, 60 (4): 545–65.

Collins, Randall (1980). 'Erving Goffman and the development of modern social theory'. in J. Ditton (ed.), *The View from Goffman*. London: Macmillan.

Collins, Randall (1986) 'The passing of intellectual generations: Reflections on the death of Erving Goffman', *Sociological Theory*, 4 (1): 106–13.

Collins, Randall (1988) 'Theoretical continuities in Goffman's work', in P. Drew and A. Wooten (eds), *Erving Goffman: Exploring the Interaction Order*. Cambridge: Polity Press.

Creelan, Paul (1984) 'Vicissitudes of the sacred: Erving Goffman and the Book of Job', *Theory and Society*, 13: 649–62.

Creelan, Paul (1987) 'The degradation of the sacred: Approaches of Cooley and Goffman', *Symbolic Interaction*, 10 (1): 29–56.

Davis, Murray S. (1997) 'Georg Simmel and Erving Goffman: Legitimators of the sociological investigation of human experience', *Qualitative Sociology*, 20 (3): 369–88.

Dawe, Alan (1973) 'The underworld view of Erving Goffman', *British Journal of Sociology*, 24: 246–53.

Denzin, N. and Keller, C. (1981) *Frame Analysis* reconsidered', *Contemporary Sociology* 10: 52–60.

Ditton, Jason (ed.) (1980) *The View from Goffman*. London: Macmillan.

Dowd, James J. (1996) 'An act made perfect in habit: the self in the postmodern age'. *Current Perspectives in Social Theory*, 16: 237–263.

Drew, Paul and Anthony Wooton (eds.) (1988) *Erving Goffman: Exploring the Interaction Order*. Cambridge: Polity Press.

Friedson, Eliot (1983) 'Celebrating Erving Goffman', *Contemporary Sociology*, 12: 359–62.

Gamson, William A. (1985) 'Goffman's legacy to political sociology', *Theory and Society*, 14: 605–22.

Giddens, Anthony (1988) 'Goffman as a systematic social theorist', in P. Drew and A. Wooten (eds), *Erving Goffman: Exploring the Interaction Order*. Cambridge: Polity Press.

Gonos, George (1977) '"Situation" versus "frame": the "interactionist" and the "structuralist" analyses of everyday life', *American Sociological Review*, 42: 854–67.

Gonos, George (1980) 'The class position of Goffman's sociology: Social origins of an American structuralism', in J. Ditton (ed.), *The View from Goffman*. London: Macmillan.

Gouldner, Alvin W. (1970). 'Other symptoms of the crisis: Goffman's dramaturgy and other new theories', in *The Coming Crisis of Western Sociology*. London: Heinemann.

Hall, J.A. (1977) 'Sincerity and politics: "Existentialists" vs. Goffman and Proust', *Sociological Review*, 25 (3): 535–50.

Jaworski, Gary D. (1996) 'Park, Doyle, and Hughes: Neglected antecedents of Goffman's theory of ceremony', *Sociological Inquiry*, 66 (2): 160–74.

Katovich, Michael and Reese, William (1993) 'Postmodern thought in light of late-modern concerns', *Sociological Quarterly*, 34 (3): 391–411.

Kuzmics, H. (1991) 'Embarrassment and civilization: On some similarities and differences in the work of Goffman and Elias', *Theory, Culture, and Society*, 8 (2): 1–30.

Lemert, Charles and Branaman, Ann (1997) *The Goffman Reader*. Malden, MA: Blackwell.

Lofland, John (1980) 'Early Goffman: Style, structure, substance, soul', in J. Ditton (ed.), *The View from Goffman*. London: Macmillan.

Lofland, John (1984) 'Erving Goffman's sociological legacies', *Urban Life*, 13: 7–34.

MacIntyre, Alasdair (1969) 'The self as a work of art', *New Statesman*, 177: 447–8.

Manning, Peter K (1993) 'Drama=life?', *Symbolic Interaction*, 16 (1): 85–89.

Manning, Philip (1991) 'Drama as life: the significance of Goffman's changing use of the dramaturgical metaphor', *Sociological Theory*, 9 (1): 70–86.

Manning, Philip (1992) *Erving Goffman and Modern Sociology*. Stanford, CA: Stanford University Press.

Miller, T. (1984) 'Goffman, social acting and moral behavior', *Journal for the Theory of Social Behavior*, 14 (2): 141–63.

Miller, T. (1987) 'Goffman, positivism and the self', *Philosophy of the Social Sciences*, 16: 177–195.

Rawls, Anne (1984) 'Interaction as a resource for epistemological critique: a comparison of Goffman and Sartre', *Sociological Theory*, 2: 222–52.

Rawls, Anne (1987) 'The interaction order *sui generis*: Goffman's contribution to social theory', *Sociological Theory*, 5 (2): 136–49.

Rawls, Anne (1989) 'Language, self and social order: A reformulation of Goffman and Sacks', *Human Studies*, 12 (1-2): 147–72.

Riggins, Stephen Harold (ed.) (1990) *Beyond Goffman: Studies on Communication, Institution, and Social Interaction*. Berlin and New York: Mouton de Gruyter.

Rogers, Mary (1977) 'Goffman on power', *American Sociologist*, 12 (2): 88–95.

Rogers, Mary (1980) 'Goffman on power, hierarchy, and status', in J. Ditton (ed.), *The View from Goffman*. London: Macmillan.

Schudson, Michael (1984) 'Embarrassment and Erving Goffman's idea of human nature', *Theory and Society*, 13: 633–48.

Schwalbe, Michael L. (1993) 'Goffman against postmodernism: Emotion and the reality of the self', *Symbolic Interaction*, 16 (4): 333–350.

Smith, Gregory (1989) 'Snapshots "sub specie aeternitatis": Simmel, Goffman and formal sociology', *Human Studies*, 12: 19–57.

Smith, Gregory (1999) *Goffman and Social Organization: Studies in a Sociological Legacy*. London: New York.

Travers, Andrew (1992a) 'The conversion of self in everyday life', *Human Studies*, 15: 169–238.

Travers, Andrew (1992b) 'Strangers to themselves: How interactants are other than they are', *British Journal of Sociology*, 43 (4): 601–37.

Travers, Andrew (1994) 'Destigmatizing the stigma of self in Garfinkel's and Goffman's accounts of normal appearances', *Philosophy of the Social Sciences*, 24: 5–40.

Tseelon, Efrat (1992) 'Is the presented self sincere? Goffman, impression management and the postmodern self', *Theory, Culture, and Society*, 9: 115–28.

Verhoeven, J. (1985) 'Goffman's frame analysis and modern micro-sociological paradigms', in H.J. Helle and S. Eisenstadt (eds), *Micro Sociological Theory*. New York: Sage.

Verhoeven, J.C. (1993) 'An interview with Erving Goffman, 1980', *Research on Language and Social Interaction*, 26 (3): 317–48.

Vester, Heinz-Guenter (1989) 'Erving Goffman's sociology as a semiotics of postmodern culture', *Semiotica*, 76 (3-4): 191–203.

Waksler, Frances Chaput (1989) 'Erving Goffman's sociology: An introductory essay', *Human Studies* 12: 1–18.

Welsh, John F. (1984) The presentation of self in capitalist society: Bureacratic visibility as a social source of impression management', *Humanity and Society,* 8 (3): 253–71.

Winkin, Y. (1988) *Erving Goffman: Les Moments et Leurs Hommes*. Paris: Minuit.

Young, T.R. (1971) 'The politics of sociology: Gouldner, Goffman and Garfinkel', *American Sociologist*, 6: 276–81.

9

Peter Berger

BRYAN S. TURNER

BIOGRAPHICAL DETAILS AND THEORETICAL CONTEXT

Born in Vienna in 1929, Peter Ludwig Berger has lived in the United States since 1946. After completing his BA in philosophy at Wagner College, he went on to take his MA and PhD in sociology at the New School for Social Research. From 1954 to 1955 he was a lecturer at the University of Georgia. He was an associate professor in 1963 and then Professor of Sociology in 1966 in the Graduate Faculty of the New School for Social Research. An editor of the quarterly *Social Research* and president of the Society for the Scientific Study of Religion, he is University Professor and Director of the Institute for the Study of Economic Culture at Boston University.

Peter Berger has made a number of important and influential contributions to various branches of twentieth-century sociology. He has, for example, written one of the most elegant and witty introductions to sociology in his *Invitation to Sociology* (1963). The notion of sociology as a vocation was further explored with Hansfried Kellner in *Sociology Reinterpreted* (1981). He has made decisive contributions to the sociology of religion in *The Noise of Solemn Assemblies* (1961a), *The Precarious Vision* (1961b), *The Sacred Canopy* (1967; published in England as *The Social Reality of Religion* in 1969) and *The Heretical Imperative* (1979). He has made controversial contributions to the study of the family in *The War Over the Family* (Berger and Berger, 1983). Throughout his career he has been a close student of modernity and modernization processes, which he has considered with Brigitte Berger and Hansfried Kellner in *The Homeless Mind* (1973), *Pyramids of Sacrifice* (1975), *Facing up to Modernity* (1977) and *The Capitalist Revolution* (1987). More recently his work has addressed issues relating to human rights and political participation in *To Empower People* (Berger and Neuhaus, 1977) and *Movement and Revolution* (Berger and Neuhaus, 1970). Finally, he has addressed the humanistic and emancipatory aspects of humour in *Redeeming Laughter* (1997).

Although he has covered a wide range of institutions in his sociological research, his perspective is remarkably consistent and its central focus has been the sociology of knowledge. In this discussion of Berger, it should be recognized that his work is closley connected with the sociology of Thomas Luckmann with whom he wrote his most influential and important study, namely *The Social Construction of Reality* (Berger and Luckmann, 1966). Although this profile is exclusively about Berger, it is in reality difficult to identify discretely the separate contributions of Berger and Luckmann. Both sociologists have significantly developed the sociology of knowledge and the sociology of religion, where for instance Luckmann's *The Invisible Religion* (1967) has been highly regarded.

SOCIAL THEORY AND CONTRIBUTIONS

This discussion of Berger's general sociology demonstrates that he has had a major influence over twentieth-century sociology in both Europe and North America. It is surprising, therefore, that, apart from specific studies of his sociology of knowledge (Abercrombie, 1980), his sociology of religion (Milbank, 1990), and his contribution to cultural analysis (Wuthnow et al., 1984), there have not been more comprehensive and critical evaluations of his work as a whole (Ainlay and Hunter, 1986).

Sociology of Knowledge: Meaning and Order

Berger's sociology of knowledge is overtly and self-consciously based on the traditions of classical sociology, especially Karl Marx, Max Weber, and Emile Durkheim. This classical tradition is seen through the framework of European phenomenology. The work of Alfred Schutz has, for example, been important in understanding the everyday world for both Berger and Luckmann (Thomason, 1982: 29–61). However, the principal interpretative claim of this profile is that Berger's general sociology has been dominated by the philosophical anthropology of Arnold Gehlen. To achieve clarity in our understanding of Berger's sociology, we need to study his introduction to Gehlen's *Man in the Age of Technology* (Gehlen, 1980). Berger has been completely explicit about the importance of Gehlen's philosophical anthropology in the development of his own work (Berger and Kellner, 1965). In various interpretations of Berger's sociology of knowledge (Ainlay and Hunter, 1986) his dependence on Gehlen has been either ignored or neglected. In particular, Gehlen's conservatism with respect to the role of institutionalization was carried over into Berger's work; it is the tension between the conservative impulse of Gehlen and the radical agenda of the early (Mannheimian) sociology of knowledge that makes Berger's sociology both interesting and problematic. Berger's sociology, especially in the *Invitation to Sociology,* has a critical dimension that deconstructs everyday reality by uncovering its taken-for-granted assumptions. This humanistic sociology promises to expose the disguises that cloak our social worlds (O'Neill, 1972: 17), but paradoxically he also demonstrates that we need these disguises to make our world orderly.

In general terms Gehlen argued, following Nietzsche, that human beings are not yet finished animals. By this notion, Gehlen meant that human beings are biologically ill equipped to deal with the world into which they are involuntarily inserted; they have no finite instinctual basis that is specific to a given environment, and depend upon a long period of socialization in order to adapt themselves to the world. Gehlen argued that in order to cope with this world openness, human beings have to create a cultural world to replace or to supplement their instinctual world. It is this ontological incompleteness that provides an anthropological explanation for the origins of human social instititutions. Berger and Luckmann adopted this position to argue that, since human beings are biologically underdeveloped, they have to construct a social canopy around themselves in order to complete or supplement their biology. This argument by extension suggested that human societies need to ensure the stability of their cultural world in order to protect individuals from the threat of anomie. It is interesting therefore that one of the most important contributions to the debate about social constructionism was in fact based upon a foundationalist ontology. This theoretical combination may explain why the reception of Berger and Luckmann's approach was characterized by a profound ambiguity. Ontological foundationalism often appeared to point to a rather conservative theory of institutions, while the social constructionist position in the sociology of knowledge implied a thorough criticism of the taken-for-granted nature of social institutions.

The core of Gehlen's work is a theory of institutions. Human beings are characterized by their 'instinctual deprivation' and therefore humans do not have a stable structure within which to operate. Humans are defined by their 'world openness' because they are not equipped instinctively for a specific environment, and as a result they have to build or construct their own environment, a construction that requires the building of institutions. Social institutions are the bridges between humans and their physical environment and it is through these institutions that human life becomes coherent, meaningful, and continuous. In filling the gap created by instinctual deprivation, institutions provide humans with relief from the tensions generated by undirected instinctual drives. Over time, these institutions are taken for granted and become part of the background of social action. The foreground is occupied by reflexive, practical, and conscious activities. With modernization, there is a process of deinstitutionalization with the result that the background becomes less reliable, more open to negotiation, culturally thinner and increasingly an object of reflection. Accordingly the foreground expands, and life is seen to be risky and reflexive. The objective and sacred institutions of the past recede, and modern life becomes subjective, contingent, and uncertain. In fact we live in a world of secondary or quasi-institutions. There are profound psychological consequences associated with these changes. Archaic human beings had character, that is, a firm and definite psychological structure that corresponded with the reliable background institutions. In modern societies, people have personalities that are fluid and flexible, like the institutions in which they live. The existential pressures on human beings are very profound and to some extent contemporary people are confronted with the uncertainties of a 'homeless mind' (Berger et al., 1973).

Berger and Luckmann's sociologies of knowledge and religion can be interpreted as applications of Gehlenic principles to specific fields of sociological thinking and to specific domains of modern society. Berger's reflections on identity (Berger, 1966), marriage (Berger and Kellner, 1964), and honour (Berger, 1970) have a characteristic line of argumentation. Institutions that we take for granted and regard as natural are shown to be socially constructed and precarious. We become disillusioned with these 'social facts', because we can see that they are human products. However, Berger then shows that, while they are constructed, they are socially necessary, and indeed collective life would be intolerable without them. Indeed, the implication of Berger's deconstructive critique is to suggest by implication that we would be wise to discard our sociological awareness that identity, marriage, and honour are socially constructed, because their legitimacy and effectiveness depend on their taken-for-granted facticity.

Having briefly discussed Gehlen's theory of institutions, we can now turn more directly to Berger's account of the construction of knowledge. Berger approaches the question of knowledge in society through a dialectical method that specifies three 'moments' in the construction and production of knowledge: externalization, objectivation, and internalization. The first concept is closely related to Marx's account of 'praxis' in the Paris Manuscripts where the human world is built by human beings in terms of ceaseless activity (or 'labour' as Marx calls it). Objectivation is the process by which the humanly created world comes to have an objective reality of its own as it confronts its makers. Finally, this external world is reappropriated by human beings as they transform this external and objective world back into a subjective consciousness. This whole process is parallel to the early discussion of religion in the critical philosophy of Feuerbach, Engels, and Marx (Turner, 1991), The gods and spiritual beings that populate the heavenly world are in fact constructs or projections of the human world, but often in an inverted form, whereby the powers of human beings are transferred and elevated to the world of the gods. Religion is both a form of inverted consciousness and an alienation of human powers. For Marx, critical criticism was the first line of attack on this fantastic world. For Berger, reification is ironically necessary for social order.

Contemporary sociological theories of knowledge occupy positions on a philosophical continuum between foundationalism and constructionism. For example, radical constructionism denies that there are given or fixed ontological foundations and asserts that knowledge of social reality is socially constructed by the languages we have available to us. By contrast, positivism asserts the existence of ontological foundationalism, while remaining hostile to the proposition that reality is constructed through categories of understanding and perception. In contemporary social theory, the most commonly held position is that of radical constructionism. This radical tradition has been significantly influenced by a variety of sources: pragmatism, the social constructionism of Michel Foucault, and the postmodern relativism of Richard Rorty. The interesting dimension of Berger's relativism is that it combines foundationalism with constructionism. Human beings have to construct the world, because their biology does not provide them with specific instincts. Institutions replace instincts through socialization and internalization. Berger's version of social constructionism has become unfashionable, because it is not easily reconciled with the radical deconstruction of sexual categories by feminism or with the attack on racialized identities by decolonization theory or with the rejection of determinate homosexual identities by queer theory. In short, popular forms of social constructionism are basically anti-essentialist, whereas Berger's sociology is rooted in a foundationalist epistemology that recognizes the need for social order and cultural stability if the world is to have any meaning. Because Berger deconstructs identity from an interpretation of the essential biological characteristics of human beings (namely their instinctual incompleteness), one could imagine that Berger could be categorized as an essentialist. My point is not necessarily to criticize essentialism, but to note that constructionism and essentialism are not typically combined.

This foundationalist epistemology in the work of Berger and Luckmann should help us to identify the political nature of constructionist theories. One could argue historically that radical social constructionism has emerged for the very reasons outlined by Gehlen, namely that our background assumptions can no longer be taken for granted, and as a result they are in the foreground, where their legitimacy is constantly challenged. The world has become postmodern, because there is scepticism about the legitimacy of our grand narratives. In the social theory of Richard Rorty (1989: 73), there are no 'final vocabularies' in a postmodern world, because there are no secure, objective, background assumptions. To return to the issue of the relationships between sex, gender, and sexuality, the notion that sexual positions are socially constructed rather than biologically given appears in social and political contexts, wherein basic categories of behaviour have been challenged and questioned. It is because we cannot rely on our background institutions and characters that sexual identity is seen to be historically and socially contingent. Sexuality is no longer a regular aspect of character; it is a negotiated feature of personality.

Religion and Relativism

Berger's work has been influential, partly because it has been challenging. His introduction to sociology in *Invitation to Sociology* presents a 'humanistic perspective' of sociology, the aim of which is to reconcile humanism with a sociological perspective on how institutions shape social life. In fact, as we have seen, his view of the relationship between agency and structure is dialectical. This theme is expressed through the contrast between 'man in society' and 'society in man'. Individuals create meaning in order to shape the world they inhabit; these meanings become institutionalized over time; and in turn these institutions become social structures that causally determine social life. The classic illustration in *Invitation to Sociology* is the story of the young couple in the moonlight in a process of courtship. At some stage the young man in the story is confronted with the imperative: Marry! Marry! Marry! This imperative is not an instinct that the young man shares with animals. Berger argues that 'marriage is not an instinct but an institution. Yet the way it leads behaviour into predetermined channels is very similar to what the instincts do where they hold sway' (Berger, 1963: 105). Berger's sociology of knowledge is complex, because it is both a radical view of the possibilities of deconstruction and a counsel of conservatism that not too much can be transformed within the institutional arrangements of society. We can deconstruct the imperatives of marriage and recognize that what masquerades as an inevitable fact about human arrangements is precisely human made, not God-given. However, the imperative is necessary if human beings are to get on with the disciplines and routines that make life possible and tolerable. In short, marry – or else.

The dialectic of meaning and structure is intended to recognize both human agency and objective constraints, and yet the general mood of Berger's sociology is melancholic (Lepenies, 1992). Human beings renounce their capacity for action in the interests of securing a meaningful social structure. As Berger and Luckmann argue in *The Social Construction of Reality*, human actors prefer reification to anomie, because the former offers comfort through amnesia. As Berger argues in *The Sacred Canopy*, human beings require the security of their plausibility structures to be maintained, if their world is to have any sense of legitimacy. We need the traumatic disappointments of our lives to be explained and justified by theodicy. I have argued in this profile that this renunciation is prefigured in the work of Gehlen, upon whose philosophical anthropology the Bergerian life-world is constructed. The trend of these arguments about the necessity of order to secure meaning is necessarily conservative, but to recognize this outcome is simply an interpretation rather than a value judgment. In the development of Berger's understanding of man as a figure of discomfort, Helmut Schelsky's question ('Can continuous questioning and reflection be fully institutionalised?') proved especially influential in Berger's conservative sociology of knowledge (Schelsky, 1965). Schelsky's conclusion was that a process of continuous reflexivity was not possible if enduring social relationship were to survive; Berger's dialectical sociology of order and meaningfulness contributed further support to the melancholic view that the human consciousness could not tolerate such a burden – a conclusion that raises interesting questions for the somewhat optimistic views on 'detraditionalization' and 'reflexive modernization' of Ulrich Beck, Anthony Giddens and Scott Lash (1994). The burden of the homeless mind cannot be easily endured.

The implications of this melancholic sociology of knowledge appear to be highly relativistic. The social world produces a range of systems of knowledge and meaning in response to the need for a sacred canopy. These social realities are all valid insofar as they satisfy the necessities of meaning and protect the individual from despair. It is difficult then to make value judgments across cultures, given their specificity. The problem of relativism has been a specific issue for Berger, especially in his sociology of religion, and he is perfectly aware of the intellectual damage the sociology of knowledge can cause for Christian theology. For example, he rejects one solution to relativism that has been developed in Christian theology between 'profane history' and 'sacred history'. While the former charts the secular history of the church over time, salvational history is the record of divine intervention in the world. Sacred history is a record of human faith; profane history, a narrative of the church in the world. Berger rejects this explanation as meaningless on the grounds that 'faith' is just another manifestation of 'religion' (Berger, 1969a: 51). There are no neat theological answers to the relativistic problems raised by history and sociology.

Berger's sociology of religion has to confront a basic and difficult problem. The problem of a meaningful order is solved in Berger's sociology of knowledge by claiming that religion is a necessary condition of social existence. Without a sacred canopy, social life would be impossible. But would any sacred canopy (religion) do? His position reminds one of the arguments embraced by Leo Strauss, for whom liberal and secular society had led to nihilism and meaninglessness. A vibrant social order requires a social world that is legitimized by religion, and that is also hierarchical and unequal. Strauss believed that almost any religion would be appropriate to give society coherence and cohesiveness. Religion is a noble lie, because, while its beliefs are not rational, it has a necessary function in society. Religion is fundamental to the deception that is required for devotion and loyalty to the state. The work of philosophers must be secretive, because their ideas can never be shared by the masses (Strauss, 1952). Berger is certainly not a conservative in the tradition of Strauss, but his sociology cannot easily escape from the conclusion that people need a sacred canopy, because a deinstitutionalized social existence, based on continuous reflexivity, would be a psychological nightmare or a homeless mind. His sociology struggles with a dialectic of critical reflection and anthropological nostalgia.

Such a negative position towards values in a pluralistic world is troublesome, as Berger recognizes. Although Berger cannot present a general answer to the relativistic difficulties created by the sociology of knowledge, he attempts to sketch out the conditions for a response in *A Rumor of Angels*. First, theology can perhaps start more productively with anthropology than with sociology, since the anthropological tradition is not unlike theology – it is an attempt to spell out the human condition in all its messy detail. An anthropology of man – Berger's language follows Gehlen's by employing 'man' as a generic term for 'humanity' – can produce what he calls an 'indicative faith', that is a vision of man's anthropological condition that is derived from experience rather than deductively from abstract principles. Secondly, he argues that through this methodology we can inductively identify some signs of transcendence in the everyday world. Berger identifies five arguments (from order, play, hope, damnation, and humour). These arguments point to a realm of experience and value that stand beyond or outside the everyday. Let us take the argument from damnation. Some acts and events in history are thought to go beyond the realm of ordinary human experience. Events like the Holocaust and the trial of Eichmann appear to challenge the adequacy of our routine sense of justice. Such events 'cry out to heaven. These deeds are not only an outrage to our moral sense, they seem to violate a fundamental awareness of the constitution of our humanity' (Berger, 1969b: 82). This sense of human outrage and moral puzzlement is also indicative of the limitations of relativism. To argue that Eichmann was a social product of his time and place may be sociologically correct, but it is hardly appropriate or convincing. Because we have no means of punishment appropriate to people convicted of terrible war crimes, we experience a need for a higher order of values and justice. We feel compelled to describe gross or monstrous behaviour within a paradigm that allows for the existence of evil. Berger treats these situations as indications of the possibility of transcendence in the everyday world. A similar line of argument has been developed by Berger in *Redeeming Laughter* (1997). Humour depends for its effects on a sense of incongruity; laughter as a result can take us out of our situation, indeed out of ourselves. Humour is bound up with the experience of ecstasy in everyday life, and ecstasy (*ek-stasis*) is the experience of being outside or beside ourselves. These experiences provide a window on a world that is beyond or outside relativization, an overview of a larger whole. In a world of evil, there is always the possibility of the rumour of angels.

Such an alternative to relativism is obviously appealing and Berger writes about this need (for transcendence) and about the possibilities of ecstasy with conviction and charm. The argument for the importance of humanistic values to give meaning to the problems of modernity is certainly compelling. One difficulty with this argument is that in modern society the media often appear to stand between us (as an audience) and the possibility of experiences of reality. In a literal sense, the media are those cultural institutions that process and co-ordinate cultural messages from our environment. It is only in retrospect that the Holocaust has assumed a definite quality of evil, because its significance has been shaped by half a century of debate. The slaughter of gypsies and other communities in the same period has not yet been mediated by the global media to such an extent. If we turn to the collapse of socialist Yugoslavia and the ethnic cleansing of Serbia, we are retrospectively conscious of the fact that the media constructed the pillage of Kosovo as unambiguously a case of evil. However, as the response of NATO unfolded, it became clear that the situation on the ground was far more complex. The revenge attacks of the Kosovo Liberation Army on civilian Serbs revealed a long history of interethnic violence. Furthermore, had NATO bombing destroyed more Kosovan Albanians than Serb police attacks? Had NATO bombing inflicted any damage on the Serbian army? Because it is difficult to allocate blame to either Serbs or Albanians, it became easier to regard Slobodan Milosevic as the evil figure behind the ethnic cleansing. In this case, I am less concerned to make an empirical judgment about Kosovo and more concerned to use this event as an illustration of how the media construct and simulate reality. In a postmodern world of global information, it is difficult to act spontaneously or to think naively towards events in our social world, because they have been heavily mediated by the media. In this sense, we live in a postemotional world, where our emotive response to politics is constructed for us (Mestrovic, 1997). The rumour of angels becomes more distant and polyphonic as the media noise obscures immediate and heartfelt emotional responses by the cultural construction of everyday life.

The problem of relativism in social science is a well-established problem. There is an important argument that ironically it had its origins in the biblical criticism of Protestant theology in the early nineteenth century. The issue of the historical relativism of the biblical texts became a general problem of historicism that influenced Weber and the origins of sociology (Antoni, 1998). This legacy was further compounded by anthropological relativism when the fieldwork discoveries of anthropologists in Australia, New Guinea, south-eastern Asia, and the Pacific began to have a distinct impact on philosophy, theology, and literature in mid-century. These traditional problems of relativism have now taken a new direction under the impact of postmodernism. To the traditional arguments of anthropological relativism, postmodern theory has recognized the complex processes by which 'reality' is constructed by a consumer materialism that is dominated by information technologies, communication systems, and global cultures. With what Fredric Jameson calls the cultural logic age of late capitalism, we are living in 'a period in which, with the extinction of the sacred and the "spiritual", the deep underlying materiality of all things has finally risen dripping and convulsive into the light of day' (Jameson, 1991: 67). 'Primitive cultures' are incorporated into the global world of tourism as objects of anthropological experience, and cannibalism is elaborated and reinvented as an exotic component of tourism in Fiji. The challenge to Berger's 'rumour of angels' is to what extent naive anthropological experiences are possible upon which an indicative faith could be successfully created and preserved. In short, the postmodern challenge to the plausibility structures of religion may be more profound than traditional forms of relativism. One can argue that Berger's notion of relativism has been more concerned with the first two stages of the debate – what we might call textual relativism and anthropological relativism – and less engaged with postmodern relativism which takes account of the mediation of reality by the cultural media.

APPRAISAL OF KEY ADVANCES AND CONTROVERSIES

Berger's social theory has achieved a remarkable coherence in direction and a considerable range of applications as a comprehensive approach to sociology. First, the basis of his humanistic sociology has been his approach to the sociology of knowledge. Whereas the tradition of Mannheim had been to examine articulate and literate systems of belief such as conservatism or Christianity, Berger has examined the constitution and maintenance of everyday understanding of the mundane world. Berger has also departed from the Marxist and Frankfurt traditions, because he makes no clear distinction between knowledge and ideology. He has not been concerned with the truth or falsity of beliefs, but only with their role in constructing and sustaining a meaningful world. Berger's notions of legitimacy and plausibility have not been grounded in a critical notion of rationality or truth, because his principal question is: what passes for 'knowledge' in social interaction?

Secondly, we should note Berger's interest in the centrality of religious institutions to human society. Generally speaking, from Weber's death in 1920 to the publication of *The Sacred Canopy* in 1967, the sociology of religion had become marginal to mainstream sociology, and there had been no attempt to provide a general or synthetic contribution to the sociological study of religious institutions. Berger brought religious phenomena back to the centre of sociological attention by showing how religion was fundamental to the processes of constructing symbolic worlds. In the 1950s and 1960s, industrialization and modernization theories paid little attention to religion, which was seen to be largely irrelevant to the problems of society. Secularization was seen to be an inevitable consequence of modernization. The principal exception to this neglect of religion was to be found in the work of Talcott Parsons who saw American individualism and activism as a fulfilment rather than a negation of Christianity. Pluralism and activism in American values were an institutionalization of Protestant denominationalism (Robertson and Turner, 1991). Although the roots of the sociology of religion in Parsons and Berger were very different, their approach to religious institutions represented a synthesis of Weber and Durkheim (Milbank, 1990: 106). Both sociologists have challenged conventional perspectives on secularization by suggesting that all forms of institutionalization have a sacred dimension.

Thirdly, it is possible to suggest therefore that Berger brought about a (re)integration of sociology and theology. From the perspective of the late twentieth century, it is difficult to realize that classical sociology was grounded in a debate with, and adaptations from, theology. Classical sociology was critically concerned with the possible demise of Christianity in the face of capitalist industrialization. Weber's views on charisma, the Protestant ethic, and social change were profoundly influenced by the theologian and historian Ernst Troeltsch (Drescher, 1992). Emile Durkheim's understanding on the ritualistic roots of social solidarity would not have developed without the contributions of the Protestant theologian William Robertson Smith (Turner, 1997). Berger's analysis of transcendence in everyday life represents an effort to understand the roots of religious experience through the lens of the sociology of knowledge.

Finally, Berger's work is a synthesis of sociology and theology in the sense that he has been committed to understanding the relevance of sociology to the human condition and the dilemmas of modern society. Within this synthesis of ethical and sociological perspectives, the concept of theodicy has played a central role. Within theological discourse, it is concerned with the problem of explaining the contradiction between the existence of evil and the nature of divinity. If God is all powerful and merciful, how can evil exist? Berger has transformed this theological question into a powerful sociology of knowledge that is concerned with how the social world can be justified or legitimated. The discussion of plausibility structures is one facet of this larger project, which is to understand how the social world is made and how it appears as natural and comprehensible.

BERGER'S MAJOR WORKS

Berger, P.L. (1961a) *The Noise of Solemn Assemblies*. Garden City, NY: Doubleday.

Berger, P.L. (1961b) *The Precarious Vision*. Garden City, NY: Doubleday.

Berger, P.L. (1963) *Invitation to Sociology*. Garden City, NY: Doubleday.

Berger, P.L. (1966) 'Identity as a problem in the sociology of knowledge', *European Journal of Sociology*, 7 (1): 105–15.

Berger, P.L. (1967) *The Sacred Canopy*. Garden City, NY: Doubleday.

Berger, P.L. (1969a) *The Social Reality of Religion*. London: Faber and Faber.

Berger, P.L. (1969b) *A Rumor of Angels*. New York: Doubleday.

Berger, P.L. (1970) 'On the obsolescence of the concept of honour', *European Journal of Sociology*, 11: 339–47.

Berger, P.L. (1979) *The Heretical Imperative. Contemporary Possibilities of Religious Affirmation*. Garden City, NY: Anchor Press.

Berger, P.L. (1980) 'Foreword', in Gehlen, A. *Man in an Age of Technology*. New York: Columbia University Press.

Berger, P.L. (1987) *The Capitalist Revolution. Fifty Propositions about Prosperity, Equality and Liberty*. Aldershot: Wildwood House.

Berger, P.L. (1997) *Redeeming Laughter. The Comic Dimension of Human Experience*. Berlin and New York: Walter de Gruyter.

Berger, P.L. (1975) *Pyramids of Sacrifice: Political Ethics and Social Change*. New York: Basic Books.

Berger, P.L. (1977) *Facing up to Modernity Excursions in Society, Politics and Religous*. New York: Basic Books.

Berger, P.L. and Berger, B. (1983) *The War Over the Family: Capturing the Middle Ground*. Garden City, NY: Doubleday.

Berger, P.L., Berger, B. and Kellner, H. (1973) *The Homeless Mind*. New York: Random House.

Berger, P.L. and Kellner, H. (1964) 'Marriage and the construction of reality', *Diogenes*, 46: 1–21.

Berger, P.L. and Kellner, H. (1965) 'Arnold Gehlen and the theory of institutions', *Social Research*, 32 (1): 110–13.

Berger, P.L. and Kellner, H. (1981) *Sociology Reinterpreted*. Garden City, NY: Doubleday Books.

Berger, P.L. and Luckmann, T. (1966) *The Social Construction of Reality. A Treatise in the Sociology of Knowledge*. Garden City, NY: Doubleday.

Berger, P.L. and Neuhaus, R.J. (1970) *Movement and Revolution*. Garden City, NY: Doubleday.

Berger, P.L. and Neuhaus, R.J. (1977) *To Empower People. The Role of Mediating Structures in Public Policy*. Washington, DC: American Enterprise Institute for Public Policy Research.

SECONDARY REFERENCES

Abercrombie, N. (1980) *Class, Structure and Knowledge*. Oxford: Basil Blackwell.

Ainlay, S.C. and Hunter, D.J. (1986) *Making Sense of Modern Times. Peter L. Berger and the Vision of*

Interpretative Sociology. London: Routledge and Kegan Paul.

Antoni, C. (1998) *From History to Sociology*. London: Routledge.

Beck, U., Giddens, A. and Lash, S. (1994) *Reflexive Modernization. Politics, Tradition and Aesthetics in the Modern Social Order*. Cambridge: Polity Press.

Drescher, H-G. (1992) *Ernst Troeltsch. His Life and Work*. London: SCM Press.

Gehlen, A. (1980) *Man in the Age of Technology*. New York: Columbia University Press.

Jameson, F. (1991) *Postmodernism or the Cultural Logic of Late Capitalism*. London: Verso.

Lepenies, W. (1992) *Melancholy and Society*. Cambridge, MA: Harvard University Press.

Luckmann, T. (1967) *The Invisible Religion, The Transformation of Symbols in Industrial Society*. New York: Macmillan.

Mestrovic, S.G. (1997) *Postemotional Society*. London: Sage.

Milbank, J. (1990) *Theology and Social Theory. Beyond Secular Reason*. Oxford: Blackwell.

O'Neill, J. (1972) *Sociology as a Skin Trade. Essays Towards a Reflexive Sociology*. London: Heinemann.

Robertson, R. and Turner, B.S. (eds) (1991) *Talcott Parsons, Theorist of Modernity*. London: Sage.

Rorty, R. (1989) *Contingency, Irony and Solidarity*. Cambridge: Cambridge University Press.

Schelsky, H. (1965) 'Ist die Dauerreflexion institutionalisierbar? Zum Thema einer modernen Religionssoziologie', in *Auf der Suche nach Wirklichkeit. Gesammelte Aufsatze*. Dusseldorf-Koln: Eugen Diederichs Verlag.

Strauss, L. (1952) *Persecution and the Art of Writing*. Chicago: University of Chicago Press.

Thomason, B.C. (1982) *Making Sense of Reification. Alfred Schutz and Constructionist Theory*. London: Macmillan.

Turner, B.S. (1991) *Religion and Social Theory*. London: Sage.

Turner, B.S. (1997) 'Introduction: the study of religion', in B.S. Turner (ed.) *The Early Sociology of Religion*. London: Routledge/Thoemmes Press.

Wuthnow, R. (1984) *Cultural Analysis: the work of Peter L. Berger, Mary Douglas, Michel Foucault, and Jürgen Habermas*. London: Routledge.

10

Michel Foucault

STEPHEN KATZ

> The key thing, as Nietzsche said, is that thinkers are always, so to speak, shooting arrows into the air, and other thinkers pick them up and shoot them in another direction. That's what happens with Foucault.
>
> (Gilles Deleuze)

BIOGRAPHICAL DETAILS AND THEORETICAL CONTEXT

Michel Foucault was born on 15 October 1926 in Poitiers, France and died on 25 June 1984 from complications resulting from AIDS. He is regarded as one of the most important and popular thinkers of the twentieth century. While his ascetic, shaven-headed image has become an icon of postmodern theory, Foucault should most appropriately be remembered for his imaginative pursuit of thought outside the given truths and resigned scepticism of our time, and for his distinctive accomplishments in four areas. First, he mapped out the material practices and power relations that underlie the rise of Western philosophy, history, politics, and literary studies. Second, his work has renewed professional fields such as urban planning, medicine, criminology, mental health, education, managerial studies, architecture, public policy, and social work. (Some examples amongst many others are: Garland, 1997; McKinlay and Starkey, 1998; Chambon et al., 1999). Third, Foucault challenged the major critical traditions, such as structuralism, Marxism and humanism, and provided vital critiques of their limitations. Finally, Foucault became a public intellectual who defied dominant culture through his political affiliations, lectures, interviews, and gay activism.

These accomplishments create a challenge for those seeking to chart his career, as David Macey reveals in his 1993 biography, *The Lives of Michel Foucault*, and in his depiction of Foucault's creative juggling of his intellectual, political, and public personae. Further complicating the task is the fact that Foucault's prodigious writings display no unified theoretical model or political orientation, and no single text tidily represents his scholarship. James Miller, another biographer, states that 'Foucault left behind no synoptic critique of society, no system of ethics, no comprehensive theory of power, not even (current impressions to the contrary) a generally useful historical method ... What value, then, does his work really have? What can it mean for us? How should it be used?' (1993: 19).

Foucault, the product of a middle-class family, revealed his enthusiasm for interdisciplinary scholarship from his earliest university studies. He graduated from the prestigious Ecole Normale Supérieure in Paris with *licences* in philosophy and psychology in 1948 and 1949 respectively. The heated intellectual atmosphere of the Ecole Normale also reflected the postwar enthusiasm in France for ideas coming from Marxism, structural linguistics, and Hegelian phenomenology, and it was here that Foucault met influential contemporaries such as science historian Georges Canguilhem and Marxist theorist Louis Althusser. In 1951 Foucault received his *agrégation* in philosophy from the Ecole Normale (a very demanding set of examinations which he initially failed), and in 1952 he completed a diploma course in psychopathology. From 1952–5 he taught psychology in the philosophy department at the university in the northern city of Lille. During this time he also worked as a researcher and an 'unofficial intern' (Miller 1993: 63) at the Saint-Anne Hospital in Paris, gaining valuable clinical experience that would later figure in his books on psychology, medicine, and asylums. Foucault wrote his first book, *Maladie mentale et personnalité* (*Mental Illness and Psychology*) in 1954. (The English translation by Alan Sheridan appeared in 1976, based on the revised French version in 1962 entitled *Maladie mentale et psychologie*. While this text prefigured *Madness and Civilization*, it was also overshadowed by it and has been largely ignored in the scholarly literature on Foucault.) In the following five years he pursued a career combining teaching and cultural diplomacy, taking up positions in Uppsala, Warsaw, and Hamburg. These postings offered significant intellectual opportunities, however. The library at the university in Uppsala provided him with the materials to write *Folie et déraison: histoire de la folie à l'âge classique* (*Madness and Civilization: A History of Insanity in the Age of Reason*), and his work in Warsaw and Hamburg allowed him to complete the text by 1960. In that year Foucault submitted *Folie et déraison* for his doctoral thesis in Paris, which was passed and praised by Georges Canguilhem (1995). From 1960 to 1966, while Foucault commuted from Paris to a teaching position at the University of Clermont-Ferrand, his book on the history of madness gained its first round of scholarly acclaim. It had all the markings of what would later be recognized as Foucault's brilliant style, ingenious methodology, and tireless erudition, a blend of talents rarely applied to such a prosaic topic by a social theorist.

Folie et déraison is ostensibly about the medicalization of madness during the eighteenth and nineteenth centuries and the development of the asylum and the psy-sciences. But it is also a critique of the Enlightenment's liberal traditions and philosophies of reason, and as such launches Foucault's wider project to lay bare the ontological means by which truth, knowledge and power have become intertwined. A second international round of acclaim followed the book's 1965 publication in English under the title *Madness and Civilization*. Praise for the book was accompanied, however, by criticisms accusing Foucault of discourse determinism, shoddy historical research, and failure to acknowledge the genuinely curative functions of modern therapeutics. Such criticisms would resurface throughout Foucault's career, but this early round was provoked unfairly by the truncated 1965 translation of the original that excised important sections and references (see Gordon, 1990; Still and Velody, 1992). Despite the criticisms, *Madness and Civilization* continued to expand its influence. In the late 1960s inside France it was linked to the social upheavals of 1968, while outside of France it was embraced by the highly politicized 'antipsychiatry' movement spearheaded by Thomas

Szasz, Ronald D. Laing, Ivan Illich, and David Cooper. As Robert Castel points out, Foucault's first major work thus had a dual importance: in the early 1960s it emerged as a key contribution to the 'epistemology of the human sciences' (Castel, 1990: 27); and in the late 1960s it became an analytic tool for 'political activism and a generalized anti-repressive sensibility' (Castel, 1990: 29).

Foucault's second major work, *Naissance de la clinique: une archéologie du regard médical* (1963), translated as *The Birth of the Clinic: An Archaeology of Medical Perception* (1973), marked two developments in his career. First, it indicated his experimentation with (though not adherence to) structuralism and semiology, through its focus on linguistic systems of signification and spatialized discourses of perception. In this, Foucault was joining an intellectual vogue shared by fellow French thinkers Claude Lévi-Strauss, Roland Barthes, Jacques Lacan, and Louis Althusser. Second, *The Birth of the Clinic* advanced 'archaeology' as a new historical methodology. Influenced by Gaston Bachelard and Georges Canguilhem's ideas on historical discontinuity and critiques of progressivism and presentism in the history of science (see Gutting, 1989), 'archaeology', as Foucault applies it in *The Birth of the Clinic*, is a way of rendering visible the discursive strata embedded within modern formations of medical authority. On the surface the book is about the changes in medical practices in France from the late eighteenth century to the early nineteenth century. Beneath its canonical trappings, Foucault reveals layered within modern medicine the new linguistic, technological, epistemological and political constituents of human life.

Foucault expanded his archaeological approach in two subsequent texts, *Les Mots et les choses: une archéologie des sciences humaines (The Order of Things: An Archaeology of the Human Sciences)* in 1966 and *L'Archéologie du savoir (The Archaeology of Knowledge)* in 1969. (During this period Foucault also wrote a number of books and essays on art, literature and philosophy, such as *Death and the Labyrinth: The World of Raymond Roussel* ([1963] 1986), and on the work of George Bataille, Maurice Blanchot, and René Margritte. Since Foucault did not return to these areas after the 1960s, nor have these works been influential in literary studies, they are not considered part of his major corpus. See Foucault, 1998 for some of these writings.) In *The Archaeology of knowledge*, Foucault sharpened his archaeological methodology and outlined the formalities underlying the discursive formations in the human sciences he sought to understand. But *The Archaeology of Knowledge* has remained obscure for many readers compared to *The Order of Things*, which became a best-seller, with wide popular as well as scholarly appeal. In it, Foucault traces the discontinuities in the human sciences from their emergence in the Renaissance through the development of their core fields – economics, biology and linguistics – in the nineteenth century. The book's controversial exploration of the 'death' of the figure of 'man' in contemporary thought triggered a critical reaction by Jean-Paul Sartre (1971), amongst others, that was symptomatic of the growing humanist and Marxist opposition to Foucault's ideas. Foucault was away from France teaching in Tunisia during the critical period between 1966 to 1968, however. Upon returning to Paris, he distanced himself from his popular image as a structuralist. 'In France, certain half-witted "commentators" persist in labelling me a "structuralist". I have been unable to get it into their tiny minds that I have used none of the methods, concepts, or key terms that characterize structural analysis', wrote Foucault in his Foreword to the English edition of *The Order of Things* (1971: xiv).

Foucault's appointment as professor of philosophy at the new experimental University of Vincennes in 1968 marked the different intellectual direction he was to pursue during the 1970s. While his radical character fit well in the alternative interdisciplinary environment of

Vincennes, he soon was elected to the pre-eminent Collège de France, to take up a new Chair in the History of Systems of Thought. He occupied this post for the rest of his life. The Collège de France requires its Chairs to conceive yearly courses relevant to the theme of their chairships. Foucault's course summaries are fascinating chronicles of his initial ventures into areas that would inspire the latter half of his career: criminology, sexuality, governmentality, and ethics (see Foucault, 1997).

Between 1969 and 1975 Foucault became politically involved with groups such as the Prison Information Group in France and travelled to Poland and Iran to write about repression and revolution. During these years Foucault wrote essays, gave interviews and edited texts such as the memoir of nineteenth-century murderer Pierre Rivière (Foucault, 1975). While he produced no major texts, he was working towards his next methodological breakthrough inspired by the ideas of Friedrich Nietzsche, in particular his work *On The Genealogy of Morals*. In an essay entitled 'Nietzsche, Genealogy, History' ([1971] 1977c), Foucault clearly outlines the strengths of what he sees as a Nietzschean genealogical method: a multidisciplinary technique for discovering the contingent historical trends that underpin contemporary discourses and practices of power. 'Genealogy is gray, meticulous, and patiently documentary. It operates on a field of entangled and confused parchments' (1977c: 139), and thus opposes the search for traditional origins and the erection of foundations in favour of disturbing 'what was previously considered immobile' and fragmenting 'what was thought unified' (1977c: 147). Ideally, the aim of genealogy is to understand 'the history of the present' separate from the familiar historical narratives and political ideologies which have represented the past. Prado provides a clear introduction to Foucault's 'genealogical analytics' (1995). Other writers have traced or contested Foucault's connection to Nietzsche (Mahon, 1992; Owen, 1996; Nilson, 1998).

Foucault's methodological turn to genealogy, and to a new range of topical interests, found expression in the dramatic book that emerged after his publishing hiatus, *Surveiller et punir: naissance de la prison (Discipline and Punish: The Birth of the Prison)* in 1975. Forcefully articulating both the political and intellectual concerns that preoccupied him in the preceding seven years, the book set forth a genealogical revamping of the criminological history of the prison system. It also became the most famous of Foucault's books because it artfully recast modernity as a 'disciplinary society' shaped by the new forms of power that followed the decline of European sovereign regimes. Interest in genealogical histories of the present animated Foucault's subsequent series on the history of sexuality: *Histoire de la sexualité I: La Volonté de savoir (The History of Sexuality Volume I: An Introduction)* (1976); *L'Usage des plaisirs (The Use of Pleasure)* (1984); *Le Souci de soi (The Care of the Self)* (1984). Despite their differences, these texts consistently employ a Nietzschean deconstruction of the lineages of the Western soul and the abiding regimes of truth, ethics, and identity. The books also share a more comprehensible language than Foucault's earlier works: thus they have become indispensable to any university course on crime, sexuality, and related topics dealing with regulation and social control.

In a touching irony Foucault's last days in June 1984 were spent at the Salpêtrière, the famous hospital he frequently excoriated in his work for its historical role in establishing the 'bio-power' of the French government: lying in his bed at the hospital, he was pleased to read the first reviews of his last books, volumes 2 and 3 of *The History of Sexuality*.

SOCIAL THEORY AND CONTRIBUTIONS

Much of the literature commenting on Foucault's contributions to social theory has sought to compartmentalize his work in relation to (and sometimes as derivative of) other theorists or schools of thought, such as Marxism (Poster, 1984), critical theory (Ransom, 1997), Durkheim studies (Cladis, 1999), and the sociology of Max Weber (Turner, 1992; Szakolczai, 1998), the latter in particular because of Weber's emphasis on bureaucratic expertise and the disciplinary aesthetics of the government of the self. Further writings link Foucault to Nietzsche, Jacques Derrida (Boyne, 1990), Gilles Deleuze (Braidotti, 1991), Thomas Kuhn (Dreyfus & Rabinow, 1983), Maurice Merleau-Ponty (Crossley, 1994) and Jurgen Habermas (Kelly, 1994; Ashenden & Owen, 1999). Feminist critics have been particularly important to this exercise (discussed further below).

Foucault strove his last years to establish a unique theoretical standing for his life's work independent of his commentators, however.

> My objective ... has been to create a history of the different modes by which, in our culture, human beings are made subjects. My work has dealt with three modes of objectification which transform human beings into subjects. The first is the modes of inquiry which try to give themselves the status of sciences ... In the second part of my work, I have studied the objectivizing of the subject in what I shall call 'dividing practices'. The subject is either divided inside himself or divided from others. Finally, I have sought to study ... the way a human being turns him- or herself into a subject. (Foucault, 1983a: 208)

Elsewhere Foucault repeats this tripartite organization of his corpus (1983b: 237; 1985: 3–13; 1988b). Thus, we should follow Foucault's own assessment of his work to understand further the problems his theoretical ideas made intelligible. Rabinow's commentary (1984: 7–11) is one that does indeed stay true to Foucault's purpose by delineating his work in terms of *classification practices, dividing practices,* and *self-subjectification practices,* and hence provides a useful formulation. In addition, Foucault elaborated how this series of practices operated most evidently across three fields of subjectivity: the body, the population and the individual. By creating a history of the modes by which 'human beings are made subjects', Foucault reconceptualized modern politics as a subjectifying grid of practices and fields. In so doing, he added a vibrant critical dimension to contemporary social theory, as the following discussion illustrates.

Practices of Subjectification

Classification practices

Throughout his writings, Foucault emphasized that the professional status of a knowledge derives from the fields in which it is deployed, rather than from the authority of the professionals themselves. Thus, he sharpened our understanding of how knowledge production in the human sciences, such as psychiatry, medicine, sexology, and criminology, has transformed people into types of subjects by classifying them according to the dualistic logics that pervade Western thinking: reason/unreason, normal/pathological, and living/dying. For example, in *The Order of Things* Foucault argues that economics constructed the producing subject accountable to economic rules and laws; biology constructed the living subject governed by biological laws of nature that condition it as an organism; and linguistics constructed the speaking subject characterized by structures of signification. Economics, biology, and linguistics are linked as well because their classification schemes were grounded in the study of 'man', the definitive figure around which the makers of modern knowledge shaped their discourses and justified their interventions into all domains of human existence.

Dividing practices

In Foucault's work dividing practices are political strategies that separate, normalize, and institutionalize populations for the sake of social stability. In his texts *Madness and Civilization, The Birth of the Clinic,* and *Discipline and Punish,* Foucault illustrates how modern European states marked vagabond and supposedly 'unproductive' people as political problems, and regrouped them into the mad, the poor, and the delinquent. This disciplinary ordering of society coincided with the development of powerful institutions – asylums, hospitals, prisons, and schools. Most importantly, Foucault highlighted how dividing practices historically drew their power from both mercantile state agencies and the Enlightenment's political philosophies of individual rights and human freedom. For example, in *Discipline and Punish* Foucault describes how, since the late eighteenth and nineteenth centuries, regulatory techniques based on examinations, training, record-keeping, and surveillance were also connected to new corrective programmes aimed at individual rehabilitation. Hence, it was the ironic convergence of disciplinarity with liberal humanism that became the defining characteristic of what Foucault calls the 'birth of the prison' (the subtitle of *Discipline and Punish*).

Self-subjectification practices

Self-subjectification practices constitute a more elusive mode of subjectification because, as Foucault explains, they entail the deployment of *technologies of the self*: 'Techniques that permit individuals to affect, by their own means, a certain number of operations on their own bodies, their own souls, their own thoughts, their own conduct, and this in a manner so as to transform themselves, modify themselves, and attain a certain state of perfection, happiness, purity, supernatural power' (Foucault and Sennett, 1982: 10). In *The History of Sexuality*, Foucault identifies the confession as the exemplary technology of the self, one that originated with Christianity and later featured in modern medicine and psychiatry. Social scientists, therapeutic experts, and associated moral engineers exercise technologies of the self in a variety of ways (see Martin et al., 1988). In Foucault's work, self-subjectification practices proliferate in the domain of sexuality, however, because the sexological sciences have historically characterized sex as secretive, hidden, and dangerous, thus obligating subjects to speak about it in intensely self-reflexive terms. Consequently, these sciences continue to enhance their own expertise by forging sexual truth at the core of human identity. This is why, according to Foucault, our most long-standing ideas about the self should be scrutinized in terms of the self-subjectifying practices that sustain them.

Fields of Subjectivity

The body

While Foucault is not alone in focusing on the political rule of the body, he is unique for detailing the multifarious ways in which 'bio-power' played a role in establishing modern regimes of power. Indeed, Foucault's work on the body has encouraged an expansive sociology of the body spanning several fields (e.g. Sawicki, 1991; Jones and Porter, 1994; Terry and Urla, 1995). *Discipline and Punish* and *The History of Sexuality* are the two key texts in which Foucault develops his analysis of the body as a field of subjectivity. In the former, he says that penal practices actually produce the 'soul' of the delinquent by disciplining the body and corporealizing prison environments. Hence, the body's most intimate needs – food, space, exercise, sleep, sex, privacy, light, and heat – become the materials upon which prison schedules, curfews, check-ups, timetables, and micro-penalties are enacted. The body-discipline developed in prisons has parallels throughout the broader disciplinary society. Indeed, the success of modernity's dominion over efficient bodies in industry, docile bodies in prisons, and regimented bodies in schools attests to Foucault's thesis that the human body is a highly adaptable terminus for the circulation of power.

Similarly, in *The History of Sexuality* Foucault depicts the frightening mastery with which nineteenth-century experts constructed a hierarchy of sexualized bodies and segmented the population into groups of normal, deviant, and perverted individuals. Furthermore, Victorian sexual discourse idealized a particularly bourgeois male body, distinguished by its health and longevity, endurance and productivity, and descent and race. The bourgeois male body was used then to mark as inferior the bodies of women, lower classes, non-Western peoples, and the elderly. For Foucault, the connection between the individual body and the social body, or population, was thus vital to the formation of modern politics.

The population

Foucault radically historicized the notion of *population* by extracting it from traditional demographic conceptions and tracing its discursive and political origins to the power/knowledge networks that grew out of the Enlightenment's concerns with health and wealth. Population emerged as a field of subjectivity where administrative power over people became exercised through the identification, standardization, and regulation of public behaviour and risks. For example, *The Birth of the Clinic* examines how the medical crises around urban hygiene and epidemics in the eighteenth and nineteenth centuries empowered a centralized medical government to monitor the health of the population and the social spaces of its activities. In later studies Foucault expands the medical focus and outlines how the modern state enhanced its power by intervening in the *life* of the population, or what Foucault calls the 'bio-politics of the population' (1978).

Foucault's concept of bio-politics leads to his overall view of politics, or *governmentality*, 'the art of government' (1991: 90) and his essays on the genealogy of liberal rule (1981, 1988a). Beginning in the seventeenth century, Western administrations rationalized their management of social problems with novel governmental techniques such as statistics, surveys, police, health regulations, and centralized welfare. Nikolas Rose, in his inventive case study of British social psychology, explains that 'with the entry of the population into political thought, rule takes as its object such phenomena as the numbers of subjects, their ages, their longevity, their sicknesses and types of death, their habits and vices, their rates of reproduction'. Hence 'the birth and history of the knowledges of subjectivity and intersubjectivity are intrinsically bound up with programmes which, in order to govern subjects, have found that they need to know them' (Rose, 1990: 5).

The arguments of Foucault, Rose, and others about governmentality and the population-as-subject pose a fresh critical slant on the politics of demographic knowledge, and have led to an exciting subfield of governmentality studies (Burchell et al., 1991; Barry et al., 1996; Dean, 1999; Rose, 1999). Such studies elaborate Foucault's perspective on the governmentalization of power to critique neoliberal regimes, insurential and risk-management programmes, and the utilization of data-technology and market rationalities in state enterprises. The governmentality literature also emphasizes how personal conduct, freedom, choice, and responsibility are refigured as political resources and enfolded into the fabric of 'the social' (see Petersen & Bunton, 1997; Cruikshank, 1999). In this sense Mitchell Dean's definition is apposite: Governmentality 'defines a novel thought-space across the domains of ethics and politics, of what might be called "practices of the self" and "practices of government", that weaves them together without a reduction of one to the other' (Dean, 1994: 174). While more Marxist critics have accused governmentality studies of abandoning radical politics (e.g. Frankel, 1997), governmentality researchers are also not uncritical of the subfield's drawbacks (see Hindess, 1997; O'Malley et al., 1997).

The individual

Despite Foucault's radical social constructivism, his work accentuates two important aspects of individual agency. First, Foucault's work and that of his adherents indicate that the subjects of modernity's disciplinary matrix – soldiers, prisoners, sexual deviants, patients and children – can and do subvert the conditions of their subjectivity. For example, in his history of nineteenth-century sexology Jeffrey Weeks notes that while sexologists 'sought to regulate through naming; it also provided the springboard for self-definition and individual and collective resistance' (1987: 38). This made it possible in the twentieth century for the gay movement to reverse medical 'naming' practices around restrictive homosexual categories, and mobilize itself as a collective agent of social change. Second, Foucault's individual is not the traditional subject caught in an ontological tug-of-war between liberation and domination. This is an image created by traditional philosophical and social science discourses limited by rigid theoretical models and political ideologies. Rather, the individual for Foucault is the personal space where both active and passive, and regulated and resistant possibilities for human agency surface in the context of material practices.

These ideas about individual subjectivity figure largely in Foucault's later work on pre-Christian ethics and sexuality (1985, 1986, 1993). Here his innovative research on the 'self' and subjective 'games of truth' incorporates a highly active dimension of individual subjectivity, one less confined to relations of power and scientific discourse and more geared to the social imperatives of a self-stylized autonomy. Most significantly, in thinking through the ethical configurations of ancient society, Foucault began to consider how self-knowledge can be separate from practices of subjectification. His remarks in one of his last interviews suggest the directions in which his future work may have been heading: 'I would call subjectivization the process through which results the constitution of a subject, or more exactly, of a subjectivity which is obviously only one of the given possibilities of organizing a consciousness of self' (1989: 330). Individual subjectivity is thus contingent and unstable because there are other 'possibilities of organizing a consciousness of self'. Foucault's commentators generally agree that had he lived he would have refined this aspect of his work and created a new set of questions on refashioning the arts of life. In this regard, historian and friend Paul Veyne comments that during the last eight months of Foucault's life the writing of his two final books on the history of sexuality 'played the role for him that philosophical writing and the personal journal played in ancient philosophy: that of a work of the self on the self, a self-stylization' (1993: 8). And with Foucault's demise in mind, Veyne concludes that, 'Foucault's originality among the great thinkers of our century lay in his refusal to convert our finitude into the basis for new certainties' (1993: 5).

APPRAISAL OF KEY ADVANCES AND CONTROVERSIES

Foucault's contestations of the human sciences and the legacy of the Enlightenment have inspired an industry of vigorous controversy, in particular around his historical method and political theories. Critics concerned with historical method have taken Foucault to task for forefronting his antipositivist archaeological and genealogical strategies at the expense of proper scholarly explication. The result, to the critics, has been the popularization of inaccurate accounts of the past often based on indiscriminate and poorly researched documentation. For example, when Foucault refers to the period spanning the seventeenth to eighteenth centuries as the 'classical age' in *The Order of Things* and *Madness and Civilization*, he provides no clear account of how this 'age' transmuted into the 'modern age' in the nineteenth century. Further, historians have complained about Foucault's assumption that the historical discontinuities and reversals he discovered apply cross-nationally, when in fact large differences exist between nations and localities. For instance, the history of asylums and hospitals in England and other countries is quite distinctive from that of France (see Porter, 1987; Bynum, 1994). Other critiques of Foucault's historical method can be found in the excellent collection *Foucault and the Writing of History* (Goldstein, 1994).

In an interview relevant to the critique of historical method, Foucault claimed he was 'well aware' that he had never 'written anything but fictions', although fictions do not mean 'that truth is therefore absent' (1980: 193). And in a sense Foucault does invent quasi-historical formations such as a 'disciplinary society' and a 'classical age'. His case studies of the clinic, prison, asylum, sexuality, and ancient ethics are not factually comprehensive histories; rather, they illustrate how specific problems arose in particular historical conjunctures. Nevertheless, Foucault's critics have been challenged to examine their own methodological assumptions, even if they are right about his historical oversights.

More widespread have been the debates over Foucault's political theories, especially his sweeping notion of power, which, it is claimed, denies the political field of human agency and resistance. It is true that Foucault's work often traces the historical classification and division of bodies and populations by way of their domination, despite his insistence that power is 'productive' as well as repressive. Foucault's later investigations into the ethics of the individual self partially resolved the place of the active subject in political life (as the discussion above indicates). Still, readers who expected Foucault to align himself with a particular political agenda or outline a theory of resistance are left hanging. Feminist scholars and activists have presented the most extensive critique of Foucault's political theories, developing a sophisticated Foucault-feminist literature in the process (Bell, 1993; McNay 1993; Ramazanoglu 1993; Deveaux, 1994; Hekman, 1996). They have either castigated Foucault for his lack of attention to gender inequality, women's history, and sexual violence, or only provisionally accepted his theoretical interventions, substantially reworking them in order to overcome their limitations. Feminists have stressed in particular that the body is both a site of regulation, where gendered identities are maintained, and a site of resistance, where they are undone. For example, Lois McNay agrees with Foucault that 'sexuality is produced in the body in such a manner as to facilitate the regulation of social relations' (1993: 32). She adds that not all aspects of sexuality, corporeality, and desire are products of power relations, however. In a similar vein, Judith Butler writes that ritualized body performances that bind women to fictional feminine identities can also become deconstructive performances that expose the arbitrariness of such identities (1990: 140–41). Feminist writers, through their critique of Foucault based on body politics and gendered relations of power and resistance, have indeed advanced Foucaultian social theory in the most innovative directions.

It is precisely because Foucault eschewed political alliance and theoretical affiliation that his readers have been able to inscribe their own politics and scholarship on his intentions, and to create a lively critical exchange around his ideas. But Foucault also inspired controversy because he was passionate about ideas. He says in one of his most interesting interviews that he dreams 'of a new age of curiosity' (1989: 199). To Foucault, curiosity 'evokes the care one takes for what exists and could exist; a readiness to find strange and singular what surrounds us' and 'a fervour to grasp what is happening and what passes' (1989: 198–9). If care, readiness, fervour and curiosity are the dreams and guidelines that inspired Foucault's career, then perhaps these are the true keys to understanding his place in contemporary social theory.

FOUCAULT'S MAJOR WORKS

Foucault, M. ([1954] 1976) *Mental Illness and Psychology*. New York: Harper & Row.

Foucault, M. (1986) *Death and the Labyrinth: The World of Raymond Roussel*. Garden City, NJ: Doubleday.

Foucault, M. ([1961] 1965) *Madness and Civilization: A History of Insanity in the Age of Reason*. New York: Pantheon Books.

Foucault, M. ([1963] 1973) *The Birth of the Clinic: An Archaeology of Medical Perception*. New York: Pantheon Books.

Foucault. M. ([1966] 1971) *The Order of Things: An Archaeology of the Human Sciences*. New York: Pantheon Books.

Foucault, M. ([1969] 1972) *The Archaeology of Knowledge*. New York: Pantheon Books.

Foucault, M. ([1975] 1977a) *Discipline and Punish: The Birth of the Prison*. New York: Pantheon Books.

Foucault, M. ([1976] 1978) *The History of Sexuality Volume I: An Introduction*. New York: Pantheon Books.

Foucault, M. ([1984] 1985) *The Use of Pleasure: The History of Sexuality Volume Two*. New York: Pantheon Books.

Foucault, M. ([1984] 1986). *The Care of the Self: The History of Sexuality Volume Three*. New York: Pantheon Books.

Essays and Interviews

Foucault, M. (1977b) *Language, Counter-Memory, Practice: Selected Essays and Interviews by Michel Foucault*. (Ed. D.F. Bouchard.) Ithaca, NY: Cornell University Press.

Foucault, M. (1980) *Power/Knowledge: Selected Interviews & Other Writings 1972–1977*. (Ed. C. Gordon.) New York: Pantheon Books.

Foucault, M. (1989) *Foucault Live (Interviews, 1966–84)*. (Ed. S. Lotringer.) New York: Semiotext(e).

Foucault, M. (1997) *Essential Works of Foucault: 1954–1984, Vol. 1. Ethics, Subjectivity and Truth*. (Ed. P. Rabinow.) New York: The New Press.

Foucault, M. (1998) *Essential Works of Foucault 1954–1984, Vol. 2. Aesthetics, Method, and Epistemology*. (Ed. P. Rabinow.) New York: The New Press.

Foucault, M. (2000) *Essential Works of Foucault 1954–1984, Vol. 3. Power*. (Ed. P. Rabinow.) New York: The Free Press.

Other Foucault References

Foucault, M. (ed.) (1975) *I, Pierre Rivière, Having Slaughtered My Mother, My Sister and My Brother: A Case of Parricide in the 19th Century*. New York: Pantheon Books.

Foucault, M. ([1971] 1977c) 'Nietzsche, Genealogy, History', in D. F. Bouchard (ed.), *Language, Counter-Memory, Practice: Selected Essays and Interviews by Michel Foucault*. Ithaca, NY: Cornell University Press.

Foucault, M. (1981) 'Omnes et singulatim: Towards a criticism of "Political Reason", in S. McMurrin (ed.), *The Tanner Lectures on Human Values*, vol. 2. Salt Lake City: University of Utah Press.

Foucault, M. (1983a) 'The subject and power', in H.L. Dreyfus and P. Rabinow (eds), *Michel Foucault: Beyond Structuralism and Hermeneutics*. Chicago: University of Chicago Press.

Foucault, M. (1983b) 'On the genealogy of ethics: an overview of work in progress', in H.L. Dreyfus and P. Rabinow (eds), *Michel Foucault: Beyond Structuralism and Hermeneutics*. Chicago: University of Chicago Press.

Foucault, M. (1988a) 'The political technology of individuals', in L.H. Martin, H. Gutman and P.H. Hutton (eds), *Technologies of the Self: A Seminar with Michel Foucault*. London: Tavistock.

Foucault, M. (1988b) 'The ethic of care for the self as a practice of freedom: an interview with Michel Foucault on January 20, 1984', In J. Bernauer and D. Rasmussen (eds), *The Final Foucault*, Cambridge, MA: MIT Press.

Foucault, M. (1991) 'Governmentality', in G. Burchell, C. Gordon, and P. Miller (eds) *The Foucault Effect: Studies in Governmentality*. Chicago: University of Chicago Press.

Foucault, M. (1993) 'About the beginnings of the hermeneutics of the self', *Political Theory*, 21(2): 198–227.

Foucault, M. and Sennett, R. (1982) 'Sexuality and solitude', *Humanities in Review*, 1: 3–21.

SECONDARY REFERENCES

Ashenden, S. and Owen, D. (eds) (1999) *Foucault Contra Habermas: Recasting the Debate between Genealogy and Critical Theory*. London: Sage.

Barry, A., Osborne, T. and Rose, N. (eds) (1996) *Foucault and Political Reason: Liberalism, Neo-Liberalism and Rationalities of Government*. London: UCL Press.

Bell, V. (1993) *Interrogating Incest: Feminism, Foucault and the Law*. London and New York: Routledge.

Boyne, R. (1990) *Foucault and Derrida: The Other Side of Reason*. London and New York: Routledge.

Braidotti, R. (1991) *Patterns of Dissonance*. New York: Routledge.

Burchell, G., Gordon, C. and Miller, P. (eds) (1991) *The Foucault Effect: Studies in Governmentality*. Chicago: University of Chicago Press.

Butler, J. (1990) *Gender Trouble: Feminism and the Subversion of Identity*. London and New York: Routledge.

Bynum, W. F. (1994) *Science and the Practice of Medicine in the Nineteenth Century*. Cambridge: Cambridge University Press.

Canguilhem, G. (1995) 'Georges Canguilhem on Michel Foucault's *Histoire de la folie*', *Critical Inquiry*, 21(2): 275–89.

Castel, R. (1990) 'The Two Readings of *Histoire de la folie* in France', *History of the Human Sciences*, 3(1): 27–30.

Chambon, A., Irving, A. and Epstein, L. (eds) (1999) *Reading Foucault for Social Work*. New York: Columbia University Press.

Cladis, M. S. (ed.) (1999) *Durkheim and Foucault: Perspectives on Education and Punishment*. Oxford: Durkheim Press.

Crossley, N. (1994) *The Politics of Subjectivity: Between Foucault and Merleau-Ponty*. Aldershot: Avebury.

Cruikshank, B. (1999) *The Will to Empower: Democratic Citizens and Other Subjects*. Ithaca, NY: Cornell University Press.

Dean, M. (1994) *Critical and Effective Histories: Foucault's Methods and Historical Sociology*. London and New York: Routledge.

Dean, M. (1999) *Governmentality: Power and Rule in Modern Society*. London: Sage.

Deveaux, M. (1994) 'Feminism and Empowerment: A Critical Reading of Foucault', *Feminist Studies*, 20 (2): 223–47.

Dreyfus, H.L. and Rabinow, P. (1983) *Michel Foucault: Beyond Structuralism and Hermeneutics*. Chicago: University of Chicago Press.

Frankel, B. (1997) 'Confronting neoliberal regimes: the post-Marxist embrace of popularism and realpolitik', *New Left Review*, 226: 57-92.

Garland, D. (1997) '"Governmentality" and the Problem of Crime: Foucault, Criminology, Sociology', *Theoretical Criminology*, 1(2): 173–214.

Goldstein, J. (ed.) (1994) *Foucault and the Writing of History*. Oxford: Blackwell.

Gordon C. (1990) '*Histoire de la folie*: an unknown book by Michel Foucault', *History of the Human Sciences*, 3 (1): 3–26.

Gutting, G. (1989) *Michel Foucault's Archaeology of Scientific Reason*. Cambridge: Cambridge University Press.

Hekman, S. (ed.) (1996) *Feminist Interpretations of Michel Foucault*. University Park: Pennsylvania State University Press.

Hindess, B. (1997) 'Politics and governmentality', *Economy and Society*, 26 (2): 257–72.

Jones, C. and R. Porter (eds) (1994) *Reassessing Foucault: Power, Medicine and the Body*. London: Routledge.

Kelly, M. (ed.) (1994) *Critique and Power: Recasting the Foucault/Habermas Debate*. Cambridge, MA: MIT Press.

Macey, D. (1993) *The Lives of Michel Foucault*. London: Hutchinson.

Mahon, M. (1992) *Foucault's Nietzschean Genealogy: Truth, Power, and the Subject*. Albany: State University of New York Press.

Martin, L. H, Gutman, H. and Hutton, P. H. (eds) (1988) *Technologies of the Self: A Seminar with Michel Foucault*. London: Tavistock.

McKinlay, A. and Starkey, K. (eds) (1998) *Foucault, Management, and Organization Theory*. Thousand Oaks, CA: Sage.

McNay, L. (1993) *Foucault and Feminism*. Boston: Northeastern University Press.

Miller, J. (1993) *The Passion of Michel Foucault*. New York: Simon & Shuster.

Nilson, H. (1998) *Michel Foucault and the Games of Truth*. London: Macmillan.

O'Malley, P., Weir, L. and Shearing, C. (1997) 'Governmentality, criticism, politics', *Economy and Society*, 26 (4): 501–17.

Owen, D. (1996). *Maturity and Modernity: Nietzsche, Weber, Foucault and the Ambivalence of Reason*. London and New York: Routledge.

Peterson, A. and Bunton, R. (eds) (1997) *Foucault, Health and Medicine*. London and New York: Routledge.

Porter, R. (1987) *Mind-Forg'd Manacles: A History of Madness in England from the Restoration to the Regency*. London: Athlone.

Poster, M. (1984) *Foucault, Marxism and History: Mode of Production versus Mode of Information*. Cambridge: Polity Press.

Prado, C. G. (1995) *Starting with Foucault: An Introduction to Genealogy*. Boulder, CO: Westview Press.

Rabinow, P. (1984) 'Introduction', in P. Rabinow (ed.), *The Foucault Reader*. New York: Pantheon Books.

Ramazanoglu, C. (ed.) (1993) *Up Against Foucault: Explorations of Some Tensions Between Foucault and Feminism*. London and New York: Routledge.

Ransom, J. S. (1997) *Foucault's Discipline: The Politics of Subjectivity*. Durham, NC: Duke University Press.

Rose, N. (1990) *Governing the Soul: The Shaping of the Private Self*. London: Routledge.

Rose, N. (1999) *Powers of Freedom: Reframing Political Thought*. Cambridge: Cambridge University Press.

Sartre, J-P. (1971) 'Replies to structuralism: an interview with Jean-Paul Sartre', *Telos*, 9: 110–16.

Sawicki, J. (1991) *Disciplining Foucault: Feminism, Power and the Body*. London and New York: Routledge.

Still, A. and Velody, I. (eds) (1992) *Rewriting the History of Madness: Studies in Foucault's Histoire de la Folie*. London and New York: Routledge.

Szakolczai, A. (1998) *Max Weber and Michel Foucault: Parallel Life-Works*. London: Routledge.

Terry, J. and Urla, J. (eds) (1995) *Deviant Bodies*. Bloomington and Indianapolis: Indiana University Press.

Turner, B. S. (1992) *Regulating Bodies: Essays in Medical Sociology*. London and New York: Routledge.

Veyne, P. (1993) 'The final Foucault and his ethics', *Critical Inquiry*, 20 (1): 1–9.

Weeks, J. (1987) 'Questions of identity', in P. Caplan (ed.), *The Cultural Construction of Sexuality*. London: Tavistock.

11

Jean-François Lyotard

VICTOR J. SEIDLER

BIOGRAPHICAL DETAILS AND THEORETICAL CONTEXT

Though Jean-François Lyotard (1924–98) is known within the terms of social theory for his writing *The Postmodern Condition: A Report on Knowledge*, which helped define the terms for the discussion around post-modernity, this was a text which he was to feel very ambivalent about. In different ways he felt estranged from the manner in which the contrast between modernity and postmodernity was being drawn. He was much less concerned with making a temporal distinction and in different ways distanced himself in his later writings which had much to do with aesthetics, from the discussion that he helped open up around the postmodern. He was still concerned to question the grand narratives of history, freedom, and progress which had shaped classical forms of social theory. In different ways he was critical of Marxism as well as liberalism as grand narratives which were at least partly trapped within the terms of an Enlightenment vision of modernity.

But Lyotard's questioning of grand narratives and the forms of social theory which would flow from them should not be understood as an abandonment of politics. Rather he sought a different kind of politics which could engage with the ways the world had changed since the 1960s. He makes this clear in his own reflections on his early political writings on Algeria and his intense involvement over many years from the 1950s with the journal *Socialism or Barbarism*. Writing in June 1989, less than a decade before his death in a piece 'The Name of Algeria', he pays homage to the education he received from the group and the support they gave to his writings. He also remembers how he lived in Constantine in Algeria between 1950 and 1952 when he arrived from the Sorbonne to teach in its high school. 'But with what colours should I paint what astonished me, that is the immensity of the injustice? An entire people, from a great civilisation, wronged, humiliated, denied their identity' (Lyotard, 1993b: 170).

As a young teacher coming from France he owed a debt to Constantine. 'The French Republic contrived to burden a few young Algerians with a borrowed culture while their own culture, that of their people – it language, its space, its time – had been and continued to be devastated by a century of French occupation'

(Lyotard, 1993b: 170) When the group *Socialism or Barbarism* gave Lyotard responsibility for the Algerian section in 1955, it allowed him to honour a debt.

> I owed and I owe my awakening, tout court, to Constantine. The differend showed itself with such a sharpness that the consolations then common among my peers (vague reformism, pious Stalinism, futile leftism) were denied to me. This humiliated people, once risen up, would not compromise. But at the same time, they did not have the means of achieving what is called liberty. (Lyotard, 1993b: 170)

It was through lending practical 'support' to the militants of the FLN (National Liberation Front), whilst at the same time making theoretical criticisms of the organization in the journal, that Lyotard learnt his politics. It was indispensable to criticize the class nature of the independent society that their struggle was preparing to bring about. There could be no easy reconciliation. As far as he was concerned 'This intimate differend *should* remain unresolved, unless we wish to lend credence to the false and dangerous idea that history marches at the same pace everywhere . . .' (Lyotard, 1993b: 168).

Socialism or Barbarism had broken with the Fourth International founded by Trotsky in 1937, which had been unable to define the class nature of 'communist' societies and the formation of a new exploitative ruling class. Trapped by an economism, Trotskyism had failed to profoundly rethink the desire for autonomy – or disalienation – which animates workers' struggles in developed capitalist societies. In contrast to democratic centralism, *Socialism or Barbarism* was concerned to learn from forms of organization that workers spontaneously invent in their struggles and daily resistance. Drawing on a variety of sources – including Pannekoek's Workers Council movement – they were concerned to also analyse changes which capitalism undergoes by virtue of its own development. This remained crucial to Lyotard who was constantly attempting to engage with the transformations in capitalist societies. The inventiveness which he saw in workers' struggles is *already* emancipation. It was not a matter of providing a 'correct' analysis, rather: 'Such a description perpetuates the forgetting of what was actually at stake (this is a common idiocy of historical and sociological studies)' (Lyotard, 1993b: 166).

Reflecting back, long after the influence of *The Postmodern Condition*, Lyotard was concerned not to forget

> what is and remains absolutely true about what was at stake. True even today, when the principle of a radical alternative to capitalist domination (workers power) *must* be abandoned (something that allows many people, innocent or guilty, to relinquish all resistance and surrender unconditionally to the state of things). This stake, which motivates the carrying on of resistance by other means, on other terrains, and perhaps without goals that can be clearly defined, has always been, and remains, the intractable [*intraitable*]. (Lyotard, 1993b: 166)

We might think for a moment of the road protesters in Britain and the recent movements against the export of livestock and GM crops that had not been anticipated.

Lyotard still thinks that the ideas that guided *Socialism or Barbarism*, even if it was expressed in other terms, is 'the idea that there is something within that system that it cannot, in principle, *deal with [traitor]*. Something that a system must, by virtue of its nature, overlook' (Lyotard, 1993b: 166). By helping to show the motive of their resistance in capitalist as well as in 'postcapitalist' societies which can remain 'inexpressible' to those who resist you can support them in their resistance and so prevent them from being 'robbed of it under the pretext that it is necessary to organize oneself in order to resist.' (p. 167) Lyotard still appreciated the value of this work and its continuing relevance especially when it 'was directed by an open attention, a free-floating attention, to living contemporary struggle, in which the intractable continued to show itself.' (p. 167) For a long time the group practised self-effacement in order to give the workers the opportunity to speak. It was only much later in 1968 that the group appeared on what is called the political stage when the student movement took up its vision.

SOCIAL THEORY AND CONTRIBUTIONS

Grand Narratives and the 'Postmodern'

Writing in 1989, recalling the education he had received in *Socialism or Barbarism* and by placing their work under the sign of the intractable, Lyotard was concerned

> that the 'work' we did can and must be continued, even when everything indicates that Marxism is finished with as a revolutionary perspective (and doubtless every truly revolutionary perspective is finished with), when the intractable voice or the voice of the intractable is no longer heard in Western societies on the social and political wavelengths. (Lyotard, 1993b: 168)

Lyotard recognizes as a reality we have to face that

> the intractable has fallen silent in the realm in which it has spoken for over a century, that is in the realm of social and political struggles. I am not claiming that one should cease to take an interest in that realm. Rather, those struggles no longer demand 'work,' this work of spirit, of body and soul, that was required in order to hear them and take part in them only thirty years ago. It seems to me that they do not demand anything more than intellectual, ethical and civic probity. (Lyotard, 1993b: 169)

We might question where this judgment comes from and what the somewhat enigmatic conclusion means. But it might be that he is just trying to remind us of a suspicion that was already felt by some in the group in 1960 'that the political was ceasing or would cease to be the privileged site in which the intractable appeared. We spoke of a "depoliticization". It was on account of this that the group split up' (Lyotard, 1993b: 169). Lyotard seemed to learn that we should be ready to listen from wherever the cry of resistance would come. He concludes though that it would be 'intellectually dishonest' just to look round for another revolutionary subject to fill the vacated place of the industrial proletariat. Rather than looking to the freely spontaneous activities of such as young people, immigrants, women, homosexuals, prisoners, or the people of the Third World, as far as Lyotard concludes 'thought must yield to the evidence that the grand narratives of emancipation, beginning (or ending) with "ours", that of radical Marxism, have lost their intelligibility and their substance' (Lyotard, 1993b: 169).

Reflecting back to the days of political activity with the benefit of hindsight, Lyotard seeks a more general conclusion about the place of grand narratives. The relationship between the anxieties of the present and the hopes of the past allows him to make his point about grand narratives in a focused way, even if it is overgeneralized. As he explains it in 1989:

> The presumption of the moderns, of Christianity, Enlightenment, Marxism, has always been that another voice is stifled in the discourse of 'reality' and that it is a question of putting a true hero (the creature of God, the reasonable citizen, or the enfranchised proletarian) back in his position as subject, wrongfully usurped by the impostor. What we called 'depoliticization' twenty-five years ago was in fact the announcement of the erasure of this great figure of the alternative, and at the same time, that of the great founding legitimacies. That is more or less what I have tried to designate, clumsily, by the term 'postmodern'. (Lyotard, 1992b: 169)

As far as Lyotard is concerned, this leaves social theory with a different kind of task, namely 'to work out a conception and a practice completely different from the ones that inspired "classical" modernity'. At the very least this seems to mean that we cannot retain our focus on the realm of social and political struggles. Classical forms of social theory influenced by Marx, Weber, and Durkheim have shared an assumption that injustice and oppression are only 'real' when they take place within the public realm of politics. In their different ways they were dismissive of the private, personal, and intimate realms which were deemed 'subjective' and so beyond the concerns of a social theory which sought to be 'objective' and 'scientific'. We have to explore new forms of social theory, but Lyotard seems confident that we should still be concerned with giving voice to the intractable. As he expresses it: 'Certainly, something of the intractable persists in the present system, but it is not possible to locate and support its expressions or signs in the same area of the community and with the same means as those of half a century ago' (Lyotard, 1993b: 169).

As Lyotard makes clear in *The Differend* which he wrote in 1982, society is inhabited by differends. This crucial notion was explained by Lyotard in this piece. 'I would say that there is a differend between two parties when the "settlement" of the conflict that opposes them appears in the idiom of one of them while the tort from which the other suffers cannot signify itself in this idiom' (Lyotard, 1993b: 9). The wage contract does not prevent but in fact presupposes that workers or their trade union representatives will have to speak of their labour as if it were a commodity of which they were the owners. Marxism refuses to do so. As Lyotard continues to insist:

> With the logic of *capital*, the aspect of Marxism that remains alive is, at least, this sense of differend, which forbids any reconciliation of the parties in the idiom of either one of them. Something like this occurred in 1968, and has occurred in the women's movement for ten years, and the differend underlies the question of the immigrant workers. There are other cases. (Lyotard, 1993b: 10)

In insisting on the differend, Lyotard is refusing the authority which would seek a reconciliation between different voices at the expense of silencing them. He would question philosophers and social theorists who present themselves as authorities and who would encourage people to believe that there can be competence and authority in matters of justice, in matters of beauty, of happiness, and perhaps even of truth. As Lyotard argued in a piece on television entitled 'A Podium without a Podium'

> If philosophers agree to help their fellow citizens to believe in authority in matters where there isn't any, to legitimate this authority, then they cease to ponder in the sense in which I spoke of thinking, and they thereby cease to be philosophers ... They become what one calls intellectuals, that is, persons who legitimate a claimed competence ... their own, but persons who above all legitimate the very idea that there ought to be competence in everything. (Lyotard, 1993b: 95)

Lyotard wanted to be part of the small minority of philosophers since Plato who does not succumb to this temptation. This is something we have to keep in mind if we are to do justice to him in a collection of social theorists.

When Lyotard is thinking about the postmodern in his piece on 'A Svelte Appendix to the Postmodern Question' (1982: 27), he thinks that our role 'as thinkers is to deepen what language there is, to critique the shallow notion of information, to reveal an irremediable opacity within language itself'. It is through the notion of irreconcilability in language that he seems to be developing his notion of the differend. He thinks that when Habermas gives lessons in progressive thought to Derrida and Foucault and when he speaks of the neoirrationalism of French thought in the name of the project of modernity, he is seriously mistaken about what is at issue in modernity. As Lyotard seeks to explain it:

> The issue was not and is not (for modernity has not come to an end), the Enlightenment pure and simple, it was an is the insinuation of will into reason. Kant spoke of a drive of reason to go beyond experience, and he understood philosophy anthropologically as a Drang, an impulse to fight, to create differends (*Streiten*). (p. 26)

Even if we are left unclear about this closing terse phrase, it gives us some feeling for Lyotard's turn towards Kant and his notion of the sublime.

Lyotard confronts Habermas when he draws upon his particular reading of Wittgenstein and his notion of language games to say that 'Language is not an "instrument of communication", it is a highly complex archipelago formed of domains of phrases, phrases from such different regimes that one cannot translate a phrase from one regime (a descriptive, for example) into a phrase from another (an evaluation, a prescriptive)' (p. 28). It was as if Lyotard hoped to be able to somehow capture the political insights into the differends through his exploration of the incommensurability of the phrase regimes between the scientific, literary, and artistic avant-gardes. And connecting to more recent moments:

> As for what you call French philosophy of recent years, if it has been postmodern in some way, this is because it has also stressed incommensurability, through its reflections on the deconstruction of writing (Derrida), on the disorder of discourse (Foucault), on the epistemological paradox (Serres), on alterity (Levinas), on the effect of meaning by nomadic encounter (Deleuze). (Lyotard, 1983b: 28)

Eruptions

No historical forces or even an indomitable popular will can account for the inexplicable mass demonstrations in Algeria or the events in Paris in May 1968. These events took the world by surprise and it seemed impossible to predict them. '1968' functions as a name that refuses a sense of temporality which connects to a regulated succession of events. The meaning of these events are yet to be determined because they serve to defy the established political criteria through which we seek to order them. Rather, as Bill Readings has it 'these names indicate referents whose meanings is yet to be determined, that evoke a work of political discussion in order to invent the criteria by which they may be judged' (Lyotard, 1983b: xiv).

Lyotard was very aware of the weight of the capitalist economy and institutions of the modern state. He had also learnt that any politics which seeks to organize resistance through political parties and trade unions only serves to strengthen the state. In an advanced capitalist democracy, capitalism does not so much suffer from contradictions so much as profit from them. Resistance comes to be co-opted as it becomes mediated by a representational system. The workers' strength is no longer their own but rather is returned to them as illusory representation, whether it be through the wage contract or through the integration of the unions into a 'communist' state. Lyotard had long become sceptical of the claims of different political systems but knew that despite the capacity of systems of political representation to absorb and channel resistance, unpredictable events happened. Lyotard was concerned to listen, to hear an emerging politics which could not speak the language of the political. He was concerned to be a minoritarian thinker, helping to nurture a politics which is devoid of all totalitarian traces.

Lyotard was concerned to discover ways of thinking, speaking, and acting politically without presuming an authority. The notion of authority presumes a capacity to legislate for others, to say what is 'right' and 'wrong'. He no longer believed that we could establish prescriptions as to the nature of justice, as if there were neutral and determinate criteria. As far as he was concerned this was the first step toward totalitarianism and terror, since difference is precluded right from the start. He was not concerned with establishing an alternative authority which would stand opposed to that legitimated within capitalist democracies. He was suspicious about authorities which would claim to legislate for others and so he questioned a modernity which had assumed a universal and impartial conception of reason which could legislate what was 'good' and 'right' for others. He was concerned to establish a vision of the postmodern which would give space for others who had been silenced and shamed through the arrogance of a dominant reason which presumed to be able to speak on behalf of others.

So Lyotard questions the claims to representation that are encoded within an Enlightenment vision of modernity. We had to learn how to listen to others. He could have learnt congruent insights from feminism. Women had been silenced with the institutions of democratic representations and had to develop their own practices of consciousness-raising in which they could discover their different voices and so explore their own desires for themselves, rather than evaluate their lives according to criteria provided by a dominant masculinity. They could not say in advance 'what they wanted' for they had to explore who they could become as women. They rejected the idea that this meant they were 'irrational' because they refused to say, but insisted on taking time and space for themselves. This resonates with Lyotard's vision of politics as an uncertain process of indeterminate judgment. But it was difficult for men to learn how to listen if they already assumed a reason which could legislate for others. Rather we needed a different vision of justice which did not seek to be justified once and for all. Ready to listen to others, justice would no longer seek to be authoritative but would involve listening to different voices. Rather than attempting to determine the identity of the political, Lyotard insists on a politics of difference.

These are ideas which Lyotard learnt through the events of May 1968 and the politics of refusal which students voiced. They refused to understand their intellectual activity as a process of training that would assign them to pregiven positions within the State. They insisted that learning was an open process of exploration and that they did not know what kind of people they may become through critically engaging with the culture they inherited. They insisted upon questioning traditions handed down to them as they learnt to think and desire for themselves, refusing what authorities had prepared for them. They readily questioned the representational claims of democracy, that society can reflect itself to itself. Rather students felt they had to speak for themselves as they questioned the right of traditional authorities to legislate for them. Through this eruption which people could not have anticipated, theory and action seemed to have become one. May 1968 was to remain a potent memory for Lyotard, a moment of boundless intensity which seemed to allow the sudden transformation of political into libidinal economy. As Lyotard wrote in *Derive a Partir de Marx et Freud* (1973: 10), his writing is 'an effort to raise theory to the same degree of intensity as had been attained by practice in May 68'.

In his work *Libidinal Economy*, Lyotard is concerned to announce a desire revolution. He is concerned to escape from the deceptive authority of meaning and as he makes clear at this time:

> What is important in a text is not its meaning, what it is trying to say, but what it does and causes to be done. What it does: the affective charge it contains and communicates; what it causes to be done: the transformation of these potential energies into something else – other texts, but also paintings, photos, film sequences, political actions, inspirations to love, refusals to obey, economic initiatives. (*Derive a Partir de Marx and Freud*, 1973: 6)

This emphasis on the energies and intensities produced by a text, rather than its meaning remain a crucial theme for Deleuze. For Lyotard at this time it has to do with his suspicion of a reason which is so closely allied with power. As he has it: 'Reason is already in power in capital. And it is not because it is not rational that we want to destroy capital, but because it is. Reason and power are one and the same' (pp. 12–13).

Lyotard wants to break with a tradition of critique because he thinks of it is as merely a negative activity. Insofar as it is rational, he thinks it is basically dependent upon the system it is criticizing. It is the exercise of another form of authority which claims to know best. As far as he is concerned,

> The critic remains within the sphere of what is criticized . . . And [this activity] is profoundly hierarchical: from where does the critic derive his power over the object of his criticism ? Does he *know* better ? Is he the teacher, the educator ? Is he then universality, the university, the State . . . The confessor and God helping the sinner to save himself ? This staying-within-the-same-sphere reformism sits very well with the maintenance of authoritarian structures . . . one must drift beyond criticism. But more than this, drifting is itself the end of criticism. (Rudiments Paiens, Paris UGE, 1977, pp. 14–15)

Minority Affirmations

Rather than critique, Lyotard is concerned with what he calls minority affirmations. Following Nietzsche he is also pursuing a 'new way to say "yes"'. They occur, like art, unheeded by theory, as barely noticed microscopic changes in everyday life. 'They are refined and delicate, long before their expression or appearance on the public stage: thousands of muffled grumblings among housewives long before the Women's Liberation Movement; thousands of jokes told and retold in Prague before the "Spring"' (1977: 117). He sees similar movements taking place within the sphere of production for:

> within the body of capital, there exists another form of socio-economic life, another noncentred 'domain' made up from a host of individual or anarchic acts of exchange, which have nothing to do with the 'rationality' of production. And it cannot be said that that form of life is a contestation or critique of capitalism (it is not even certain that it bears a relation to the decadent idea of work). (Lyotard, 1977: 137)

As Christa Burger (1992: 76) notes, whilst fighting 'against such phenomena being interpreted, since interpretation, like critique, remains caught in the dichotomous categories of the dominant rationality' which would rob these affirmations of their specific power, Lyotard provides his own virtually classical interpretation. This tendency gets only stronger in his later writings drawing on Kant's aesthetic writings. In this instance he sees these minority affirmations as a reversal of the 'ruse of reason' which no longer reveals itself in the course of world history, but '*la petite vie*', gradually transforming it into 'a sort of "civil society" which has little to do with Hegel's, but is simultaneously informal and active, and continually eludes the instances of power' (1977: 138).

Since the late 1970s narrative has been a key concept in Lyotard's work. It seems as if a reading of Solzhenitsyn's *Gulag Archiplego* produced a kind of awakening that forced a rethinking of his intellectual work. For a period at least he seems to forsake his earlier work. As Burger (1992: 77) has it: 'The canonical narrative, the evil in history, appears in two almost equally sinister guises: in Marxist and capitalist variants. Both are totalitarian; both demand belief'. People have to accept their silence as they are spoken for within these dominant narratives in which they are no longer listened too. Whatever resistance they make has already been accounted for. Either it is a sign of their 'false consciousness' or else in the money-narrative which is capitalism's canonical story it 'tells us that we can tell any stories we like but it also tells us that authors must reap the profits on their narratives ... So there is an element of religion in capitalism: the exclusive worship of the narrative entrepreneur.' (Benjamin, 1989).

We cannot put our faith in theory to question these master-narratives because theory is just another form of master-narrative. Lyotard puts more hope in the spread of 'unbelief' and the destruction of the narrative monopolies by a politics of 'little narratives'. Lyotard dates an erosion of master-narratives by 'thousands of uncomfortable little stories' (Benjamin, 1989: 127) from events like May 1968 or the *Gulag Archipelago*, which he describes as a 'narrative explosion' in which 'the dignity of narration' was saved.

But Lyotard is also suspicious of theory on account of its piety of remembering and because of its need to struggle against oblivion. At times it is important to forget so that we can break with the grip of the ways in which the past is remembered by those who have the power to remember in the present. But as Burger (1992: 79) also appreciates:

> As with everything in Lyotard's work, the polemic against memory also has its political point: because capitalism is a system which makes use of anything, it also pulls memory into its circle of operations, setting in train an endless movement of museification of culture. Only the radical destruction of memory can stop this movement.

This also connects to his challenge to representation, which inevitably for

Lyotard involves a hierarchical referring back of a sign to its meaning. Again this is something we need to be able to escape from.

Involved in Lyotard's thinking the postmodern is a break with designations which he takes to be a metaphysical or 'theological' procedure which serves to negate what is 'present' in favour of a level which lies above or beneath it. Lyotard's intention here is to break with metanarratives which implicitly depend upon a two-stage schema of the appropriation of reality. This is characteristic both of a Hegel–Marx tradition and of previous conservative cultural critique. Lyotard follows Nietzsche in preferring to accept what is present as it is. As Nietzsche writes in *The Will To Power*:

> It is of cardinal importance that one should abolish the 'true world' (that is, the distinction between true and apparent world, and thus a two-dimensional thinking). It is the great inspirer of doubt and devaluator in respect of the world 'we are': it has been our most dangerous attempt yet to assassinate life. (Nietzsche, 1968: 314)

Lyotard's affirmation means precisely the renunciation of a metaphysical level from which the present-at-hand can be criticized as imperfect, defective, and somehow falling short for not corresponding with its object. In his terms both morality and critique presuppose two distinct levels, one being the level of what is present-at-hand and the other a level of 'reality' with which the existent can be confronted. In contrast Lyotard prefers an affirmative position toward social reality even if it means we should somehow think the 'pious' Marxist concept of alienation positively/affirmatively, that is without the idea of loss. He thinks that we must stop conceiving of alienation as the 'loss' of something. It is supposedly a strength of the libidinal economy he calls for that it dispenses with representation. This is partly because he does not bemoan the destruction of the subject by capitalism as a loss. Rather he seeks to discover within the dynamics of capitalism forces which eliminate all hierarchies at the same time as it eliminates the subject.

APPRAISAL OF KEY ADVANCES AND CONTROVERSIES

Critics of Lyotard have argued that his affirmative aesthetics can at any point go over into a 'saying-yes to the world just as it is, without deviation, exception and selection' (Nietzsche). This could involve a saying yes to power, which he is supposed to be combating. If this is a danger it is one which Lyotard is usually careful to avoid. But it did seem in his exhibition commissioned by France's socialist government, to which he gave the title *Les Immateriaux*, as if he was uncritical of the new technologies and wary of the 'apocalyptic' visions expressed by the Greens. As with Foucault, he welcomed the disappearance of the concept of 'man' as a short-lived product of the process of evolution. As far as he was concerned the 'human', as substantivized adjective, refers to an old domain of knowledges which the techno-sciences have recently made their own.

The ideas associated in Lyotard's mind with the concept of the 'material', which fuel the immediate sense that the human being possesses a particular identity, have grown weaker with the new techno-sciences. This has worked to undermine ideas we inherit of experience, memory, work, autonomy, and generally the radical distinction of the human from the non-human. At the same time the ideas of general interaction which have, for instance, allowed us to 'read' the human cerebral cortex as one reads an electronic field, have grown stronger. Always searching for new formulations which help avoid confusions that have settled around the notion of the postmodern, Lyotard in the mid-1980s is concerned to counterpose modernity, which he now associates with the concepts of the material, subject, and project, to postmodernity, in which *les immateriaux*, the disappearance of the subject and interaction, become critical terms.

Changes in the sphere of production, which are working to transform our ideas of human beings and work as well as our forms of perception, help Lyotard think of the present as indeed a postmodern period of transition. In his text of the period *Le Differend*, he introduces an epoch of philosophizing which is to supersede that of the grand metanarratives. What seems to be crucial is the ways different areas of art have become reflexive. But as Burger (1992: 85) notes, 'it is quite evident that in the aesthetic field Lyotard is clearly concerned precisely not to define the postmodern in opposition to the modern, but to connect it to it. It is only thus that he can bring his *own* aesthetic position into play'. According to Lyotard, it is the shift in the reception of art from sense perception to reflection that characterizes the postmodern.

Since theorists of art and architecture have turned postmodernism into a battlecry of a thoroughly aggressive antimodernism, Lyotard has felt that he had to distance himself from the aesthetic postmodern. He is more interested in exploring whether modern art can be explicated in the terms of Kant's analytic of the sublime. To do this he draws less on Kant's argumentation and more on individual concepts like formlessness and nonrepresentability. But as Burger points out, Kant's theory is formulated from the perspective of the experiencing subject whereas Lyotard, by contrast, discusses the problem of nonrepresentability from the perspective of the producer. Lyotard is describing an artistic project.

For Lyotard, his loss of faith in a politics of redemption and his turn to aesthetics have to do with his resistance to the kind of modernist universalism that could be associated with Habermas. He no longer understood politics as the ordering of the political through an impartial and universal conception of reason. When he talks about 'depoliticization' or 'antipolitics' he is breaking with an Enlightenment project which proclaims the capacity of rational thought to make 'man' the master of his world and so realize 'mankind's' essential freedom. He takes a distance from the Enlightenment model of politics whether in its liberal or Marxist forms as the site of a secular redemption. Postmodernism marks a loss of faith in the modernist idea of emancipation that believes that history will save us through political action by producing a transcendent, liberated, and empowered subject.

The loss of faith in traditional political resistance is linked to the rise of the modern bureaucratic state as an essentially unipolar society, as Bill Readings has characterized it. As he puts it:

> the unipolar Western state, by presuming the intertranslatability of political forces, turns almost all resistance into a source of energy. All dissidence can be expressed, provided that it allows itself to be represented. Politics ends once the state becomes the sole site where the political is managed, an end in itself. (Lyotard, 1993b: xx)

So it is that as capitalism becomes a global system, power appears as administration rather than as coercion, managerial rather than as directly oppressive. Managerial discourses present themselves as neutral, bringing 'efficiency' into every sphere. The transformation in the public sphere, including the universities, has proved difficult to resist. Lyotard's work is consistently engaged in an attempt to rethink the terms of resistance, to find ways 'to think against a state that has no outside, that seeks always to realise itself as the state of things.' (Lyotard, 1993b: xx)

Lyotard argues against the pretensions to speak in the name of others. He identifies this as a crucial injustice, be it liberal or totalitarian. To pretend to speak for the oppressed is to objectify them once more. He sees this as part of a general complicity of radical organizations with the systems they claim to oppose. They simply reinforce the political structures of representation, as do trade unions when they treat workers they claim to represent as nothing but the mute references of their own discourse. But Lyotard's attack on the politics of representation is more than a plea for autonomy, for letting people speak for themselves. Bill Readings appreciates that it is more radically an argument against discursive legitimation as such, as against the kind of modernist politics defended by Habermas. As Lyotard points out in 'The Grip' (*Mainmise*), the dream of discursive autonomy is itself founded on a forgetting of debt and obligation to the other. It raises for Lyotard the crucial question of the presumption of authority. As Readings frames it: 'To presume that all people can in principle speak for themselves is a double victimization: it assumes the speaker's access to discourse and it assumes that the speaker is inherently a potential modern subject' (Lyotard, 1993b: xxi).

Lyotard's early appeal to spontaneous popular resistance comes to be replaced by a focus on judgment and witness. In the writings on May 1968, it seems that desire can still breach the dominant mode of discursive representation, erupt in a way that cannot be controlled by the state. Resistance becomes a form of attention which can listen for intractable differend with representation, 'which forbids any reconciliation of the parties in the idiom of either one of them' ('The Differend'). The turn to the differend is connected with a turn to Judaism and a decisive rejection of an alternative ground for political critique. As Readings puts it 'Politics becomes a matter of justice, of handling differences, rather than of establishing truth or even countertruth.' (Lyotard, 1993b: xxiv) As Lyotard explores in *Just Gaming* there is a clear philosophical rejection of models of the perfect society which have haunted the West. His discussions on the postmodern which are often pulled in different directions, share a sense that the time of 'big politics' is over, the idea of the political as the site where humanity struggles to define its destiny and realize its meanings, may well have passed.

Paradoxically this means a refusal to think that politics will ever come to an end. As politics ceases to be the sphere in which human beings explore the meanings of their lives, so as Readings has it 'politics ceases to be the search for an identity, a redemptive significance that might lie behind or beyond the activities of everyday life. Rather, politics is the attempt to handle conflicts that admit to no resolution, to think justice in relation to conflict and difference' (Lyotard, 1993b: xxiv). In his argument with Habermas Lyotard is thinking against attempts to render the predicament of modernity as the locus of a determinate historical project for the realization of a universal subject. Testifying to difference does not mean overcoming it by achieving communication between them, but rather a respectful acknowledgement as Readings puts it 'of the impossibility and necessity of exchange, around a differend that is sensed but cannot be expressed in a shared idiom, over which no final agreement can be reached' (Lyotard, 1993b: xxvi).

Lyotard insists that these differences are not accidentally but structurally repressed by an Enlightenment vision of modernity which seeks transparency in representation, communication, and accounting. A minoritarian politics does not seek to take its place in 'big politics', to gain representation. They do not want to include everyone in a larger consensus but rather testify to their differend with the Western discourse of a universal humanity. Paradoxically it is Lyotard's sense of debt and obligation to tradition that works to undermine the Enlightenment claim to freedom through knowledge.

This sense of a debt which cannot be repaid underpins Lyotard's writings on Judaism and 'the jews'. Judaism clings to a tradition founded on respect for the unrepresentable learning that they cannot make images of the divine. Auschwitz names a debt from which European humanity cannot be freed, an obligation towards atonement that must not be historically rationalized as one event among others. It names the injustice of understanding history as a project of liberating humanity from the past, from tradition, from obligation to the other, as Levinas has it. Social theories have failed to come to terms with Auschwitz because it shows the horrors that waited unrecognized within modernity.

In 1990, in the shadow of the profanation of the Jewish cemetery of Carpentras in France, where Jews had lived for more than a millennium, Lyotard wrote a piece on 'Europe, the Jews and the Book', where he makes the claim

> that the Jews represent 'something that Europe does not want to or cannot know anything about'. Even when they are dead, it abolishes their memory and refuses them burial in its land. All this takes place in the unconscious and has no right to speak. When the deed is done in full daylight, Europe is seized for an instant by the horror and the terror of 'confronting its own desire'. (Lyotard, 1993b: 159)

As Lyotard understands it, in the West since the French Revolution extended the Christian motif of fraternity, 'We are brothers, not as sons of God but as free and equal citizens. It is not an Other who gives us the law. It is our civic community that does, that obliges, prohibits, permits. That is called emancipation from the Other, and autonomy.' (p. 163) Integration or extermination were the options offered to 'the jews' by the modern enlightened state. They are revealed in the full horror by the event named 'Auschwitz'.

Lyotard wrote *Heidegger and 'the jews'* as part of his conviction that we have to bear witness to the 'Forgotten' in thought, writing, art and public practice. The negative lesson that the 'forgetting' of the Shoah by Heidegger, who was the great thinker of being, 'is that this Forgotten is not primarily Being, but the obligation of justice' (Heidegger and the 'the jews', in Lyotard, 1993b: 147). In reminding us of this obligation he explains that he uses the expression 'the jews' in a more general sense, possibly as a reminder of a more general obligation towards judgment and an awareness of difference when he says

> the expression 'the jews' refers to all those who, wherever they are, seek to remember and to bear witness to something that is constitutively *forgotten*, not only in each individual mind, but in the very thought of the West. And it refers to all those who assume this anamnesis and this witnessing as an obligation, a responsibility, or a debt, not only toward thought, but towards justice. (Lyotard, 1993b: p. 141)

LYOTARD'S MAJOR WORKS

Lyotard, J.-F. (1984a) *The Postmodern Condition*. Manchester: Manchester University Press.

Lyotard, J.-F. (1984b) *Driftworks*. New York: Semiotext(e).

Lyotard, J.-F. (1985) *Just Gaming*. Manchester: Manchester University Press.

Lyotard, J.-F. (1988a) *Peregrinations: Law, Form, Event*. New York: Columbia University Press.

Lyotard, J.-F. (1988b) *The Differend*. Minneapolis: University of Minnesota Press.

Lyotard, J.-F. (1990) *Heidegger and 'the jews'*. Minneapolis: University of Minnesota Press.

Lyotard, J.-F. (1991a) *The Inhuman*. Cambridge: Polity Press.

Lyotard, J.-F. (1991b) *Phenomenology*. New York: State University of New York Press.

Lyotard, J.-F. (1992) *The Postmodern Explained to Children*. London: Turnaround.

Lyotard, J.-F. (1993a) *Libidinal Economy*. London: Athlone Press.

Lyotard, J.-F. (1993b) *Jean-François Lyotard: Political Writings* (Ed. B. Readings.) London: UCL Press.

Lyotard, J.-F. (1995) *Toward the Postmodern*. Manchester: New Jersey Humanities Press.

SECONDARY REFERENCES

Bauman, Z. (1993) *Postmodern Ethics*. Oxford: Blackwell.

Benjamin, A. (ed.) (1989) *The Lyotard Reader*. Oxford: Blackwell.

Benjamin, A. (ed.) (1992) *Judging Lyotard*. London: Routledge.

Bennington, G. (1988) *Lyotard: Writing the Event*. Manchester: Manchester University Press.

Bernstein, R. (1991) *The New Constellation*. Cambridge: Polity Press.

Best, S. and Kellner, D. (1991) *Postmodern Theory: Critical Interrogations*. London: Macmillan.

Burger, C. (1992) 'Modernity and postmodernity: Jean-François Lyotard', in S. Lash and J. Friedman (eds) *Modernity and Identity*. Oxford: Blackwell.

Connor, S. (1992) *Theory and Cultural Value*. Oxford: Blackwell.

Dews, P. (1987) *Logics of Disintegration*. London: Verso.

Foster, H. (ed.) (1983) *Postmodern Culture*. London: Pluto Press.

Heller, A. (1987) *Beyond Justice*. Oxford: Blackwell.
Heller, A. and Feher, F. (1988) *The Postmodern Political Condition*. Cambridge: Polity.
Lash, S. and Friedman, J. (eds) (1992) *Modernity and Identity*. Oxford: Blackwell.
Nicholson, L. (ed.) (1990) *Feminism/Postmodernism*. New York: Routledge.
Nietzsche, F. (1968) *The Will to Power*. (Trans. Walter Kaufman and R.J Hollingdale.) London: Weidenfeld and Nicolson.
Readings, B. (1991) *Introducing Lyotard: Art and Politics*. London: Routledge.
Rojek C. and Turner, B. (eds) (1998) *The Politics of Jean-François Lyotard*. London: Routledge.
Rorty, R. (1991) *Essays on Heidegger and Others* Cambridge: Cambridge University Press.
Sim, S. (1996) *Jean-François Lyotard*. London: Harvester Wheatsheaf.

12

Jacques Lacan

ANTHONY ELLIOTT

BIOGRAPHICAL DETAILS AND THEORETICAL CONTEXT

Jacques Lacan was born in 1901 in France, the year after Sigmund Freud's foundational *The Interpretation of Dreams* was published. Lacan was educated at the Collège Stanislas, and, after completing his secondary education, he studied medicine in Paris. He went on to do his clinical training in psychiatry under the supervision of Gaetan Gatian de Clérambault. He published his first articles while he trained as a psychiatrist, and these were mostly on psychiatric and neurological topics. In 1932, Lacan published his doctoral thesis 'Paranoid psychosis and its relation to the personality', a copy of which he sent to Freud. As a psychoanalyst, Lacan was highly unconventional; his fascination with Freud and psychoanalysis was matched by his passion for philosophy, literature, and the arts. His public seminars at the Hospital Sainte-Anne were a mixture of psychoanalytic theory, continental philosophy, and surrealism; the seminars were increasingly well attended, mostly by an eclectic mix of students and professionals. In the 1960s, Lacan moved his seminar to the Ecole Normale Supérieure, as well as founded his own psychoanalytic organization, the Ecole Freudienne de Paris. In addition to his work as a practising psychoanalyst, Lacan wrote many papers on a range of theoretical issues. As the influence of his ideas spread, he travelled to the United States to give lectures at John Hopkins University, Yale University, and the Massachusetts Institute of Technology. He died in Paris in 1981, at the age of 80.

Believing himself to be following in Freud's footsteps, Lacan sought to revolutionize the temperate Freudianism of his time, to rescue psychoanalysis from its institutionalized conservative and conformist tendencies, and to reinscribe and resituate psychic meanings and processes within broader social systems and historical structures. Universally acclaimed for his philosophical interpretation of Freud, Lacan, along with his structuralist and post-structuralist contemporaries such as Lévi-Strauss, Foucault, Barthes, and Derrida, was unquestionably one of the major French theorists of the post-war era. His writings, principally his magisterial 900 page *Ecrits*, which was published in France in 1966, as well as his published seminars, are notorious for their complexity and difficulty. Indeed Lacan's style is often infuriatingly obscure, cryptic, and elusive. Important intellectual reasons can be offered for the complexity of Lacan's language, however. For one thing, in fashioning a difficult form of thought or discourse, Lacan wanted to be true to his object of study: namely, the psyche and its relation to human subjectivity. For another, he sought to fashion a psychoanalytic language which would not submit easily to normalization (which he thought had been Freud's fate at the hands of American psychoanalysis); he sought a method that could not easily be flattened.

Lacan's work is thus quite different in scope from that of other psychoanalytic innovators, such as Melanie Klein, D.W. Winnicott, or Wilfred Bion. While he kept abreast of developments in mainstream psychoanalysis (he borrowed from Klein's account of the paranoid–schizoid position, for instance, in formulating his idea of the ego as an agent of misrecognition), Lacan primarily developed a 'return to Freud' that sought to exceed the confines of psychology and a reductive clinical understanding of psychoanalysis. In widening the frontiers of Freudian theory, Lacan drew from many varied sources: first, from his encounter with the surrealists; second from his friendships with George Bataille, Alexandre Koyré, and Alexandre Kojeve, which introduced him to European philosophy, so that in turn he borrowed, and reworked, philosophical notions from Hegel, Husserl, Nietzsche, and Heidegger; third, his reading of the linguistic approaches of Ferdinand de Saussure and Roman Jakobson led to the privileging of structures and the decentring of the subject; and finally his encounter with the structural anthropology of Lévi-Strauss added to his enlarged conception of the Oedipus complex and the triangular structure of the individual's relation to society and history.

The importance of Lacan's thought for contemporary social theory is considerable and varied, and requires some comment before proceeding further. Lacan was a psychoanalyst, not a social theorist. To some, therefore, it might seem odd that a profile is devoted to him in a book that is primarily concerned with modern social theory. And yet I shall propose in what follows that Lacan should indeed be considered a major social theorist, a theorist who developed a systematic approach to the study of the relation between self and society. Lacan's importance consists in certain key themes and problematics which he has helped to bring to prominence in social theory – including the status of the imaginary in personal and social life, the symbolic ordering of social relations, the fracturing effects of the unconscious upon social order, and the phallocentric structuring of sexual subjectivity in contemporary culture.

SOCIAL THEORY AND CONTRIBUTIONS

Lacan's 'Return to Freud'

Perhaps the most central preoccupation of Lacan's interpretation of Freudian psychoanalysis is the primacy accorded to the unconscious in the human subject's relations with others. Freud's discovery of the repressed unconscious, which contradicted the unitary rational subject, and hence the belief that the ego was master in its own house, was of great importance to Lacan, as indicated by his sceptical and mostly negative comments about American ego-psychology and its negation of the spirit of subversion of psychoanalysis. The theoretical downgrading of the unconscious at the hands of the American ego-psychologists and of Anna Freud's followers was, according to Lacan, an attempt to adapt psychoanalysis to the cultural conformism of the present epoch. By translating Freud's maxim on the task of psychoanalysis, *'Wo Es war, soll Ich werden'*, in conformity with the ideals of enlightenment reason – that is, that the unconscious is to be made conscious – the American model presented an idealistic and deceptive view that patients might free themselves from all constraint. In contrast, Lacan showed little interest in issues of adaptation, nor in debates about mental health. He instead challenged the defenders of adaptational psychoanalysis by translating Freud's sentence as 'Where it was, there I must be', thus granting primacy to the unconscious. The unconscious, Lacan argued, precedes 'I'.

Informing this reading of Freud was Lacan's structural recasting of the psyche, consisting of three terms or orders – the *imaginary*, the *symbolic*, and the *real*. Lacan included in the category of the imaginary the paradoxes, illusions, and deceptions of the optical image; narcissism and its connection with doubles; as well as the death drive and anxieties of fragmentation and disintegration. The category of the symbolic included all the reworking of theory he had undertaken through an engagement with structural linguistics, including language and its founding of the unconscious, symbolic spacing through difference, and the primacy of the signifier. The order of the real was derived from Freud's discussion of psychical reality, and, while redefined several times throughout Lacan's career, was equated with that which resists mirror-play and all attempts at symbolization. Let us now turn to consider Lacan's structural account of the psyche in more detail.

The mirror stage and misrecognition

There are two, essentially contrasting, conceptions of the genesis of the ego in Freud's writings. The first conception equates the ego as a representative of reality-testing, making it responsible for the control of unconscious drives and passion. Freud elaborated this conception in the early part of his career, and in it the ego is understood as a product of the gradual differentiation of the unconscious-preconscious-conscious system. The second conception, elaborated by Freud after his introduction of the concept of narcissism in the metapsychological papers of 1915, locates the genesis of the ego in terms of projection and identification. It is this second conception of the ego that Lacan adopts, focusing on the ego's structuring by means of representations derived from the other. In his 1949 paper 'The mirror stage as formative of the function of the I', Lacan advances the thesis of the self-deception of the ego by considering the infant identifying with a mirror image of a complete unified body. Following closely Freud's proposition that the ego is fundamentally narcissistic in character, as well as his insight that a period of self-love precedes the object-love of the Oedipus complex, Lacan notes that the infant is initially unable to differentiate between its own body and the outside world. The key moment of this pre-Oedipal state of being is that of fragmentation, of an endless array of part objects, all of which collide with multiplex drives and passions. The infant's drafting of a distinction between itself and the outside between the age of six and 18 months, says Lacan, takes place within the paradoxes and illusions of the visual field, or what he calls the mirror stage. As a metaphorical and structural concept, the mirror provides the subject with relief from the experience of fragmentation, by granting an illusory sense of bodily unity through its reflecting surface. As Lacan (1977: 1–2) develops this:

> unable as yet to walk, or even to stand up, and held tightly as he is by some support, human or artificial ... he nevertheless overcomes in a flutter of jubilant activity, the obstruction of his support and, fixing his attitude in a slightly leaning-forward position, in order to hold it in his gaze, brings back an instantaneous aspect of the image.

Note that Lacan stresses that the image is cast within the field of optics: it is in and through a *reflecting surface* that the subject narcissistically invests its self-image. This contrasts radically with other psychoanalytic conceptions of mirroring, such as the work of D.W. Winnicott, who views early interchanges between self and others as crucial to the founding of a 'true' self. It also contrasts with other social theorists of intersubjectivity, such as Cooley, who wrote of a 'looking glass self' that exists in relation to the gaze of others.

Lacan situates the constitution of the ego in a line of fiction. The ego is created as defensive armour to support the psyche against its otherwise terrifying experiences of fragmentation and dread. The capture of the self or 'I' by the subject's reflection in the mirror is inseparable from what Lacan terms misrecognition of its own truth (*meconnaissance*). The mirror stage is profoundly imaginary in character, argues Lacan, because the consoling image of self-unity presented in the mirror is diametrically opposed to the multiplicity of drives and desires experienced by the child. In a word, the mirror *lies*. This process of misrecognition, Lacan writes,

> situates the agency of the ego, before its social determination, in a fictional direction, which will always remain irreducible for the individual alone, or rather, which will only rejoin the coming-into-being of the subject asymptotically, whatever the success of the dialectical syntheses by which he must resolve his discordance with his own reality. (Lacan, 1977: 2)

Language, Symbolic Order and the Unconscious

Having argued that the ego is a paranoid structure, an agent of misconstruction and misrecognition, Lacan set out to show that the subject is also divided through its insertion into a symbolic order of positions in relation to other subjects. Through an engagement with Ferdinand de Saussure's *Course in General Linguistics* and Claude Lévi-Strauss's *The Elementary Structures of Kinship*, Lacan arrived at a structuralist theory of the subject in which the concepts of signifier, system, otherness and difference figure prominently. The central texts in which he elaborates this antihumanist or structural-scientific conception of psychoanalysis are 'The field and function of speech and language in psychoanalysis' (1953) and 'The agency of the letter in the unconscious, or reason since Freud' (1957), both published in *Ecrits* (1977).

In setting out his idea that the human subject, and hence by implication culture and society, is dominated by the primacy of language, Lacan drew from and refashioned Saussure's theory of the arbitrary nature of the linguistic sign. The importance that Saussure placed upon the status of oppositions – upon not things themselves but on the relationship between things – appealed to Lacan's psychoanalytic and structuralist sensibilities. Saussure, as well as the analysis of language developed by Roman Jacobson, provided Lacan with the means to bridge his theoretical concerns with both symbolic production and the formal organization of desire. He argued in his seminar, following Saussure, that the linguistic sign comprises two parts: the signifier (the acoustic component or linguistic mark) and the signified (the conceptual element). In line with structuralist thought, Lacan argued that the relationship between signifiers and signifieds is arbitrary. The meaning of signifiers – 'man', for example – is defined by difference, in this case by the signifier 'woman'. However, where Saussure placed the signified over the signifier, Lacan inverts the formula, putting the signified under the signifier, to which he ascribed primacy in the life of the psyche, subject, and society. All is determined for Lacan by the movement of signifiers. In fact, the position of each of us as individual subjects is determined by our place in the system of signifiers, our lives are negotiated through the plane of enunciation. The signifier represents the subject for Lacan; the primacy of the signifier in the constitution of the subject indicates the rooting of the unconscious in language.

The idea that language might be a product of the unconscious was widespread among many analysts, and indeed Lacan continually affirmed in his writings and seminars that the importance he placed upon language was in keeping with the spirit of Freud's corpus. However, Lacan's structuralist elaboration of Saussure is, in fact, a radical conceptual departure from the Freudian conception of the unconscious. Whereas Freud sees connections between the psychic systems of unconscious representation (fantasy) and conscious thought (language), Lacan views subjectivity itself as constituted to its roots in language. This linguistification of the unconscious has important ramifications, making of this psychic strata not something which is internal to the subject (as with, say, a bodily heart or kidney), but rather an intersubjective space of communication, with language constantly sinking or fading into the gaps which separate signifier from signifier. The unconscious, writes Lacan, represents 'the sum of the effects of the parole on a subject, at the level where the subject constitutes itself from the effects of the signifier' (Lacan quoted in Ragland-Sullivan, 1986: 106) Or, in Lacan's infamous slogan: 'The unconscious is structured like a language'.

If the unconscious is structured like a language, as a chain of signifiers, the apparent stability of the mirror image of the subject is alienated twice over. First, the subject is alienated through the mirrored deceptions of the imaginary order, in which the ego is organized into a paranoid structure; secondly, the person is constituted as an *I* in the symbolic order, an order or law indifferent to the desires and emotions of individual subjects. Language is thus the vehicle of speech for the subject and a function of the symbolic order, an order in which the individual is *subjected* to received social meanings, logic, and differentiation. It is this conception of the function of the symbol which paves the way for Lacan's incorporation of Lévi-Strauss's structural anthropology. Drawing upon Lévi-Strauss's conception of the unconscious as a symbolic system of underlying relations which order social life, Lacan argues that the rules of matrimonial exchange are founded by a preferential order of kinship which is constitutive of the social system:

> The marriage tie is governed by an order of preference whose law concerning the kinship names is, like language, imperative for the group in its forms, but unconscious in its structure ... The primordial Law is therefore that which in regulating marriage ties superimposes the kingdom of culture on that of a nature abandoned to the law of mating. . . This law, then, is revealed clearly enough as identical with an order of language. For without kinship nominations, no power is capable of instituting the order of preferences and taboos that bind and weave the yarn of lineage through succeeding generations. (Lacan, 1977: 66)

This primordial Law to which Lacan refers is the Freudian Oedipus complex, now rewritten in linguistic terms. What Lacan terms *nom-du-pére* (name-of-the-father) is the cornerstone of his structural revision of the Oedipus complex. For Lacan, as for Freud, the father intrudes into the imaginary, blissful union of the child–mother dyad in a symbolic capacity, as the representative of the wider cultural network and the social taboo on incest. It is, above all, the *exteriority* of this process which Lacan underlines. Broadly speaking, Lacan is not arguing that each individual father forbids the mother–infant unity. Rather he suggests the 'paternal metaphor' intrudes into the child's narcissistically structured ego to refer the child to what is outside, to what has the force of the law – namely, language.

APPRAISAL OF KEY ADVANCES AND CONTROVERSIES

The political pessimism of Lacan's doctrines – the distorting traps of the imaginary, the symbolic determination of the subject, the lack or failure of desire – has proved attractive to many social theorists and cultural analysts. His portrayal of the ego as a paranoid structure has served as a balance against conservative and liberal theories that construct the self at the centre of rational psychological functioning. Lacan, by contrast, stresses that the self is always alienated from its own history, is constituted in and through otherness, and is inserted into a symbolic order as a decentred subject. The theme of otherness in particular is something that runs deep in contemporary social thought, and Lacan's reflections on the strangeness that mediates subjectivity and culture has been highly influential across the social sciences and the humanities. However, Lacan's 'return to Freud' has also come under fire by many social theorists and cultural commentators. In this section, I shall consider the case for and against Lacan in social theory (see also Macey, 1988; Elliott, 1994; Elliott and Spezzano, 2000).

Lacanian and Post-Lacanian Social Theory

In the early 1930s, two maidservants of humble origins viciously murdered their wealthy employers in the town of Le Mans in northwestern France. The celebrated crime of the Papin sisters both shocked and gripped the French public and press: it was reported as a tale of class hatred, of social tension, of hysteria and madness. On the day of the crime, a power failure had prevented Christine Papin from carrying out her household duties, for which she was firmly rebuked by her employer, Mme Lancelin. The sisters thereupon lashed out and attacked the Lancelins, gouging out their victims' eyes and cutting up their bodies. Jacques Lacan, fascinated by the case of the Papin sisters, suggested that while the crime was undertaken against a backdrop of rising social, economic, racial, and national hatreds, another – more structural – psychic force was at work: that of paranoid delusion and alienation. Elizabeth Roudinesco, in her biography of the French psychoanalyst, writes that Lacan

> set out to show that only paranoia could explain the mystery of the sisters' act. The episode of insanity seemed to arise out of a seemingly everyday incident: a power failure. But this incident might well have had an unconscious significance for the Papin sisters. Lacan suggested it stood for the silence that had long existed between the mistresses and the maids: no current could flow between the employers and their servants because they didn't speak to one another. Thus the crime triggered by the power failure was a violent acting out of a *non-dit*: something unspoken, of whose meaning the chief actors in the drama were unaware. (Roudinesco, 1997: 63–4)

Although many years prior to the formalization of his psychoanalytical account of the imaginary, symbolic, and real orders, Lacan presents the crime of the Papin sisters primarily in terms of an interweaving of language, symbolism, the unconscious and paranoid alienation.

Lacan, as his reflections on the case of the Papin sisters illustrates, was profoundly interested in the links between the individual and society. Yet however deeply engaged by the connections between psychoanalysis, philosophy, and contemporary theory, Lacan failed to develop an account of the relevance of his theories to social life in any detailed fashion. As a psychoanalyst, he was preoccupied by other (clinical and institutional) issues. On the other hand, he was aware of (and followed with great interest) the many attempts by others to bring Lacanian theory to bear upon issues of pressing social, cultural, and political importance. The Marxist Louis Althusser, a friend of Lacan's, was among the first social theorists to argue for the importance of Lacanian theory to the development of a theory of ideology. By bridging Marxist and Lacanian theory, Althusser sought to challenge traditional conceptions of ideology as a set of false beliefs or illusions. For Althusser, the view that social practices are real, while the ideas and beliefs which sustain them are simply false illusions, mistakenly assumes that ideology is imaginary in only a passive sense, as a weak copy of the structures of our social practice. In breaking from the imaginary/real opposition of traditional Marxism, where the former stands as a sort of ethereal medium which veils real political and economic structures, Althusser argues that the imaginary is embodied in the relations to the real that are organized and sustained through ideology. Ideology is the *imaginary relation* of individuals to their real conditions of social existence. This imaginary dimension of ideology, which Althusser develops from Lacan's Freud, is not understood as some kind of private space internal to individuals. Rather, Althusser emphasizes that the imaginary dimensions of ideology exist on the 'outside', but are continually woven through us as an effect of subjective positioning. He defines this process as follows:

> All ideology represents in its necessarily imaginary distortion is not the existing relations of production (and the other relations that derive from them), but above all the (imaginary) relationship of individuals to the relations of production and the relations that derive from them. What is represented in ideology is therefore not the system of real relations which govern the existence of individuals, but the imaginary relation of these individuals to the real relations in which they live. (Althusser, 1984: 38–9)

On this view, then, ideology is the social cement of human society. It positions human subjects at a place where ideological meanings are constituted, and thereby structures the real organization of social relations. It establishes, in sum, the unconscious dimensions by which subjects come to 'live out' their real relation to society.

Althusser, commonly regarded as the founder of applied Lacanian doctrine, promoted a structuralist approach to issues of subjectivity, agency, and ideology in the social sciences. Consideration of the status of subjectivity, and especially the notion of the decentring of the subject, became widespread across disciplines concerned with the study of human activity. In the writings of Pierre Machery, Etienne Balibar, Stuart Hall, Fredric Jameson, Paul Hirst, and Barry Hindess, to name only a few, the Lacanian/ Althusserian framework figured prominently in addressing key political issues such as nationalism, race, ethnicity, and class. Debate over the specular structure of ideology raised important issues concerning the creative capabilities of human subjects. To what extent Lacanian theory dissolved the subject in social analysis generated considerable controversy in social theory. Some argued that the decentring of the subject is formally equivalent to its disappearance, a conceptual move that mirrors the decline of the individual brought about by contemporary social change (see, for example, Giddens, 1979). Others argued that the subject is not desubjectivized in Lacanian theory in such a thoroughgoing manner.

Lacan's influence is also strongly evident in the study of culture, especially popular culture. Cultural and media studies throughout the 1980s and 1990s has indicated a considerable Lacanian debt, specifically in the field of cinema studies. The writings of Stephen Heath, Christian Metz, Laura Mulvey and Teresa De Lauretis, among others, have drawn from Lacanian theory to analyse the complex, contradictory ways in which spectator–subject positions are constituted, as well as rearticulated, in relation to symbolic systems. Perhaps the most vibrant deployment of Lacanian theory for the analysis of popular culture can be found in the writings of the Slovenian critic Slavoj Zizek (1989, 1991). Seeking to extend Lacanian criticism beyond such notions as the symbolic positioning of the subject, Zizek relates the imaginary and symbolic fields to Lacan's order of the real to produce a highly original account of the traumatic and disruptive aspects of human subjectivity. In Zizek, the real is portrayed as that which erupts at the edge of the mirror, as a leftover of the symbolic order, a leftover which returns to derail intersubjective draftings of identity construction and cultural forms.

The most fruitful area of engagement with Lacan's Freud, however, has occurred in feminist studies. Many feminists have turned to Lacanian theory to advance political debate on issues of subjectivity, gender, and sexual difference. Here there is a key stress on the role of symbolic forms in the constitution of the self and thus of gender. The symbolic order, language, the Name-of-the-Father, the phallus as transcendental signifier: these are the signature concepts through which Lacanian and post-Lacanian feminists analyse asymmetrical power relations of gender and sexuality. 'There is no woman', says Lacan (1975), 'but excluded from the value of words'. What Lacan means by this pessimistic reading of gender relationships is that, in patriarchal societies, femininity always remains on the outside of language and power. In contemporary culture, the phallus comes to be identified with the penis and hence with male power. Woman functions in the symbolic order of language as excluded Other, lack, negativity. Lurking within this apparently rigid, phallocentric organization of sexual difference, however, Lacan discerns something more fluid and ambivalent. Since human subjects are split at the core, radically divided between the narcissistic traps of the imaginary and the unconscious ruptures of the symbolic order, so too gender determination is always open to displacement. In short, if femininity is constituted in relation to otherness, this is an otherness that threatens to outstrip the foundations of sexual difference.

It will be apparent that there are two dominant, and competing, strands in Lacan's psychoanalytic interpretation of sexual difference. The first stresses the symbolic determination of the subject; the second highlights the fracturing effects of the unconscious upon phallic organizations of language and culture. Not surprisingly, it is also possible to discern these different emphases of Lacan's approach to sexual difference in much feminist social theory. An emphasis upon the symbolic determination of the subject, for example, is strongly evident in Juliet Mitchell's pathbreaking book, *Psychoanalysis and Feminism* (1974). Arguing that feminism must found its utopic vision upon a full examination of the most distressing and painful elements of gender relations, Mitchell deftly situates the relevance of Lacan's Freud in relation to social theory. 'If psychoanalysis is phallocentric', writes Mitchell (1984: 274) in a subsequent book of essays, *Women: The Longest Revolution*, 'it is because the human social order that it perceives refracted through the individual human subject is patrocentric. To date, the father stands in the position of the third term that must break the asocial dyadic unit of mother and child'. Of course, everything hangs on the projected time-frame of 'to date'; certainly, Mitchell's work has been sharply criticized for its deterministic and ahistorical approach to issues of gender power. By contrast, in the writings of Julia Kristeva, Luce Irigaray, and Hélene Cixous it is possible to discern a more critical stance towards Lacan's deterministic account of the symbolic positioning of gendered subjectivity. Indeed, this brand of feminism might be described as 'neo-Lacanian' or 'post-Lacanian', primarily because a more positive image of femininity is evoked. As Cixous (1980: 262) takes aim at Lacan, 'What's a desire originating from lack? A pretty meagre desire'. By contrast, the vital feminist task is to explore and valorize women's difference from men in order to go beyond the repressive confines of phallocentric culture. In the work of Irigaray and Cixous, this has involved a reconsideration of the affective dimensions of female sexual pleasure – in which Lacan's writings and seminars have figured as both inspiration and limitation. In the writings of Kristeva, the importance of Lacan's thought consists primarily in certain major themes which she draws from and reworks: themes including the narcissistic lures of the imaginary, the centrality of language to gender spacing through difference, and the mutations of the symbolic order.

Critique of Lacan

Notwithstanding Lacan's considerable contributions to contemporary social theory, his rereading of Freud has failed to generate the revolution in philosophical understanding to problems of subjectivity, intersubjectivity, and culture which once was routinely asserted by Lacanian-orientated social theorists. There are three core respects, I argue, in which Lacan's psychoanalytic thought is particularly deficient, especially when considered in the light of the typical preoccupations of social theory with the relations between self and society.

First, while Lacan's conception of the imaginary is of great interest to social theory, it is associated too closely with the logic of the specular (see Elliott, 1992: chapter 4); the idea that the imaginary is only constituted when the self is reflected as an object fails to grasp the point that it is the psyche which elaborates and invests this specular image. How, after all, does the small infant come to (mis)recognize itself in the mirror? How, exactly, does the individual subject cash in on this conferring of an ideal self, however brittle or illusory? These difficulties are especially well illuminated in Cornelius Castoriadis's critique of Lacan. Rejecting the standpoint that the imaginary is born from a specular image which is somehow 'already there', Castoriadis rather contends that the production of images and forms actually *is* the work of the imaginary. In his words:

> The imaginary does not come from the image in the mirror or from the gaze of the other. Instead, the 'mirror' itself and its possibility, and the other as mirror, are the works of the imaginary, which is creation *ex nihilo*. Those who speak of the 'imaginary', understanding by this the 'specular', the reflection of the 'fictive', do no more than repeat, usually without realizing it, the affirmation which has for all time chained them to the underground of the famous cave: it is necessary that this world be an image *of* something. (Castoriadis, 1987: 3)

For Castoriadis, the argument that the ego is constituted through a misrecognition of its reflected image fundamentally ignores the point that it is the psyche which *invests* the 'mirror' with desire. The problem with Lacan's position is that surely for an individual to begin to recognize its reflected image in the 'mirror' it must *already* possess the imaginary capacities for identification and representation, or what Freud named psychical reality. In the end, Castoriadis argues, Lacan's theory palpably cannot account for the psychical processes by which mirror images are *created* and *formed*. That is to say, Lacan's account of specular identity fails to address how it comes about that the other as mirror is perceived as real – how the reflected object is rendered intelligible to the subject.

Secondly, there are major substantive and political problems with Lacan's contention that the unconscious/conscious dualism should be conceptualized as a linguistic relation. Many critics, including Paul Ricoeur, Jean-François Lyotard, and Jean Laplanche, have argued the Freudian point against Lacan that the unconscious is resistant to ordered syntax. Against this linguistification of the psyche, we need to return to Freud's account of the unconscious, a realm of the psyche which, he notes,

> is not simply more careless, more irrational, more forgetful and more incomplete than waking thought; it is completely different from it qualitatively and for that reason not immediately comparable with it. It [the unconscious] does not think, calculate or judge in any way at all; it restricts itself to giving things a new form. (Freud, [1900] 1935–74: 507)

This 'new form' of which Freud speaks, and explicitly contrasts with waking thought and language, concerns representation: the flux of desires and fantasies in which things strange and unknown make themselves felt at the level of psychic functioning.

Thirdly, the politics of Lacanianism has often been criticized for its determinism and pessimism (see Castoriadis, 1984; Frosh, 1987; Elliott, 1994). Certainly, Lacan's structuralist leanings led him to underscore the symbolic determination of the subject. 'Symbols', he writes (1977: 68), 'envelop the life of man in a network so total that they join together, before he comes into the world, those who are going to engender him "by flesh and blood"; so total that they will bring to his birth ... the shape of his destiny'. Lacan's view that the subject enters a symbolic order which is prestructured linguistically, and in which the law appears terroristic, creates immense difficulties for theorizing human agency and the creative dimensions of subjective and intersubjective life. Whereas Freud, in his own decentring of the ego, at least posits the subject's prospects for critical self-reflection and autonomy, Lacan sees the self as a complete distortion, a defensive structure.

According to Lacan, the structure of human knowledge is delusional through and through, with the imaginary order offering a misleading promise of self-unity on the one side, and the symbolic and real orders operating antagonistically on the other. As has been noted by Castoriadis and others, however, there are major epistemological difficulties with Lacan's account, including the central issue of paranoid delusion and its infinite regress. For if the imaginary is a specular trap, the law omnipotent, and the symbolic order a mask for lack and loss, how exactly is the subject to know when something of value or substance has ever been found? How is a meaningful relationship with the outside world to be forged, let alone transformed (as with the practice of psychoanalysis)? And what of the theorist or social scientist? Are all claims to knowledge punctured by the illusory traps of the imaginary and its hall of mirrors? What of Lacan's discourse? If truth is inconceivable, communication paradoxical and endlessly problematic, and general social theories authoritarian, how to assess the master's pronouncements? Of course, this is precisely why Lacan formulated his theorems in such cryptic and elusive terms: in order to give full vent to the skidding signifiers of the unconscious. But there must be serious reservations about such claims, primarily because issues of self-actualization and critical self-reflection remain unaddressed in Lacan's work.

LACAN'S MAJOR WORKS

Lacan, J. ([1970] 1966) 'Of structure as an inmixing of an otherness prerequisite to any subject whatever', in R. Macksey and E. Donato (eds), *The Structuralist Controversy.* Baltimore: Johns Hopkins University Press.

Lacan, J. (1975) *Le Séminaire: Livre XX. Encore, 1962–63.* (Ed. J.-A. Miller.) Paris: Seuil.

Lacan, J. (1977) *Ecrits: A selection.* London: Tavistock Press.

Lacan, J. (1979) *The Four Fundamental Concepts of Psychoanalysis.* Harmondsworth: Penguin.

Lacan, J. (1988a) *The Seminar of Jacques Lacan, Vol. 1: Freud's Papers on Technique 1953–54.* Cambridge: Cambridge University Press.

Lacan, J. (1988b) *The Seminar of Jacques Lacan, Vol. 2: The Ego in Freud's Theory and in the Technique of Psychoanalysis 1954–5.* Cambridge: Cambridge University Press.

Lacan, J. (1990) *Television: A Challenge to the Psychoanalytic Establishment.* (Ed. J. Copjec.) New York: Norton.

Lacan, J. (1991) *Le Séminaire: Livre XVII. L'envers de la psychanalyse, 1969–70.* (Ed. J.-A. Miller.) Paris: Seuil.

Lacan, J. (1992) *The Ethics of Psychoanalysis 1959–60: The Seminar of Jacques Lacan.* London: Routledge.

Lacan, J. (1993) *The Psychoses, 1955–56: The Seminar of Jacques Lacan.* London: Routledge.

SECONDARY REFERENCES

Althusser, L. (1984): 'Ideological and ideological state apparatuses' and 'Freud and Lacan', in *Essays on Ideology.* London: Verso.

Benvenuto, B. and Kennedy, R. (eds) (1986) *The Works of Jacques Lacan.* London: Free Association Books.

Borch-Jacobsen, M. (1991) *Lacan: The Absolute Master.* Stanford, CA: Stanford University Press.

Bowie, M. (1991) *Lacan.* London: Fontana.

Bracher, M., Alcorn, M., Corthell, R., and Massardier-Kenney, F (eds) (1994) *Lacanian Theory of Discourse: Subject, Structure and Society.* New York: New York University Press.

Castoriadis, C. (1984) *Crossroads in the Labyrinth.* Cambridge, MA: MIT Press.

Castoriadis, C. (1987) *The Imaginary Institution of Society.* Cambridge: Polity.

Cixous, H. (1980) 'The laugh of the Medusa' in E. Marks and I. de Courtivron (eds), *New French Feminisms.* Brighton: Harvester.

Dews, P. (1987) *Logics of Disintegration.* London: Verso.

Elliott, A. (1992) *Social Theory and Psychoanalysis in Transition: Self and Society from Freud to Kristeva.* Oxford: Blackwell.

Elliott, A. (1994) *Psychoanalytic Theory: An Introduction.* Oxford: Blackwell.

Elliott, A. (1996) *Subject to Ourselves: Social Theory, Psychoanalysis and Postmodernity.* Oxford: Polity.

Elliott, A. and Spezzano, C. (eds) (2000) *Psychoanalysis at its Limits: Navigating the Postmodern Turn.* London and New York: Free Association Books.

Evans, D. (1996) *An Introductory Dictionary of Lacanian Psychoanalysis.* London: Routledge.

Felman, S. (1987) *Jacques Lacan and the Adventures of Insight: Psychoanalysis in Contemporary Culture.* Cambridge, MA: Harvard University Press.

Freud, S. (1935–74) *The Standard Edition of the Complete Psychological Works of Sigmund Freud*. London: Hogarth Press.

Frosh, S. (1987) *The Politics of Psychoanalysis*. London: Macmillan.

Gallop, J. (1982) *Reading Lacan*. Ithaca, NY: Cornell University Press.

Giddens, A. (1979) *Central Problems in Social Theory*. London: Macmillan.

Grosz, E. (1990) *Jacques Lacan: A Feminist Introduction*. London: Routledge.

Forrester, J. (1990) *The Seductions of Psychoanalysis: On Freud, Lacan and Derrida*. Cambridge: Cambridge University Press.

Kristeva, J. (1984) *Revolution in Poetic Language*. New York: Columbia University Press.

Laplanche, J. and Lecaire, S. (1972) 'The Unconscious', *Yale French Studies*, 48.

Lemaire, A. (1970) *Jacques Lacan*. London: Routledge.

Lyotard, J.-F. (1990) 'The dream-work does not think', in A. Benjamin (ed.), *The Lyotard Reader*. Oxford: Blackwell.

MacCannell, J. F. (1986) *Figuring Lacan: Criticism and the Cultural Unconscious*. London: Croom Helm.

Macey, D. (1988) *Lacan in Contexts*. London: Verso.

Macey, D. (1995) 'On the subject of Lacan', in A. Elliott and S. Frosh (eds), *Psychoanalysis in Contexts*. London: Routledge.

Metz, C. (1982) *Psychoanalysis and Cinema*. London: Macmillan.

Mitchell, J. (1974) *Psychoanalysis and Feminism*. Harmondsworth: Penguin.

Mitchell, J. (1984) *Women: The Longest Revolution*. London: Virago.

Mitchell, J. and Rose, J. (eds) (1982) *Feminine Sexuality: Jacques Lacan and the Ecole Freudienne*. London: Macmillan.

Ricoeur, P. (1970) *Freud and Philosophy: An Essay on Interpretation*. New Haven, CT: Yale University Press.

Ragland-Sullivan, E.-R. (1986) *Jacques Lacan and the Philosophy of Psychoanalysis*. Chicago: University of Illinois Press.

Roudinesco, E. (1997) *Jacques Lacan*. Oxford: Polity.

Schneiderman, S. (1980) *Jacques Lacan: The Death of an Intellectual Hero*. Cambridge, MA: Harvard University Press.

Turkle, S. (1978) *Psychoanalytic Politics: Freud's French Revolution*. New York: Basic Books.

Wilden, A. (ed.) (1968) *The Language of the Self: The Function of Language in Psychoanalysis*. Baltimore, MD: Johns Hopkins University Press.

Zizek, S. (1989) *The Sublime Object of Ideology*. London: Verso.

Zizek, S. (1991) *Looking Awry: An Introduction to Jacques Lacan through Popular Culture*. Cambridge, MA: MIT Press.

13

Jacques Derrida

CHRISTINA HOWELLS

BIOGRAPHICAL DETAILS AND THEORETICAL CONTEXT

Jacques Derrida was born in Algeria in July 1930. His education was severely disrupted in the early 1940s by the draconian measures taken during the Second World War to exclude Jews from schools dedicated to Aryans, but in 1949 he left Algeria for Paris, and studied at the Lycée Louis le Grand until 1952, when he entered the Ecole Normale Supérieure (ENS) of the rue d'Ulm as a philosophy student. There he met his future wife, Marguerite Aucouturier, whom he married in 1957, and Louis Althusser, also from Algiers, who was already a tutor at the Ecole, and with whom he formed a life-long friendship. In the same year he passed the Agrégation, and won a scholarship to Harvard, to work on unpublished writings by Husserl. But his emergent philosophical career was to be further interrupted by two years military service back in Algeria as a teacher of French and English to children of the forces in Koléa. His return to France in 1959, and most especially the now famous conference paper on genesis and structure in Husserl, delivered in Cerisy-la-Salle, marks the moment at which the career of Jacques Derrida, certainly one of the most original and influential philosophers of his generation, seems to come into focus and enter the public domain, leaving behind the intimacy of a colonial childhood and a complicated and fragmented education. This is not the place to speculate on the role played by Derrida's early years in his later political, ethical, and philosophical choices, but his position as part of both French colonial rule and a racially persecuted minority cannot but have contributed to his radical questioning of identity and, more recently, to his passionate concern for democracy and justice.

In fact, Derrida's philosophical career was to soar quickly to impressive heights. Four years' teaching in the Sorbonne (1960–4), trips to Prague, the Jean-Cavaillés 'epistemology' prize for his first book – the translation of and introduction to Husserl's *Origin of Geometry*, publications in *Critique* and *Tel Quel*, and in 1964 a teaching post at the ENS, all give clear indications of Derrida's early success. And 1966 marked the start of his extraordinary celebrity, with the now notorious conference on 'The Ends of Man' in Johns Hopkins, Baltimore, the paper on 'La différance' in the Sorbonne, and the simultaneous publication in 1967 of three major texts: *De la Grammatologie*, *L'Ecriture et la différence*, and *La Voix et le Phénomène*.

Derrida's philosophical approach is particularly hard to categorize, for a variety of reasons, not least because much of his best work constitutes a critique of other texts, philosophical, political, literary, or psychoanalytic. The term most readily associated with his writings, 'deconstruction', was, he explains (1987b: 388), chosen by him from Littré to translate Heidegger's *Destruktion* and *Abbau*, both of which imply a dismantling but not a destruction of the traditional organizing concepts of Western ontology and metaphysics. When he chose the term he can have had little idea of the importance it would later assume for his later thinking. Derrida's early work was primarily concerned with a critique of Husserl and phenomenology. Soon Heidegger, Hegel, Nietzsche, Plato, Freud, Levinas, Rousseau, Foucault, Lévi-Strauss, Mallarmé, amongst many others, were to become objects of his deconstructive analysis. Deconstruction has been described as a form of 'close reading', and to an extent the description is correct, if inadequate. Deconstruction does indeed read closely and minutely: it disentangles the knots and conflations of hasty or specious argumentation, it uncovers what may have been concealed, it focuses on marginalia and footnotes, in the expectation that what has been relegated to the margins may prove paradoxically central to a less parochial understanding of the text. Deconstruction reads between the lines and against the grain; it joins in the play in the linguistic mechanism, but not in the sense of the 'free-play' sometimes attributed to deconstruction by Derrida's opponents, or indeed his less rigorous followers. It involves especially the demonstration of textual self-contradiction, again not merely in the traditional philosophical sense of finding flaws in the logic of an opponent's argument, but rather in the sense of teasing out the underlying incompatibility between what writers believe themselves to be arguing and what the text actually says. This gap between authorial intention and textual meanings is a key focus of deconstruction, and gives the lie most forcibly to those who try to argue that Derrida is not interested in authorial intention. On the contrary, it is one of his prime fascinations, along with all the tricks of language, logic, and metaphysics that interfere with the expression of that intention, distort it and deviate it, and sometimes cause writers to say precisely the opposite of what they (thought they) intended.

Derrida's early work is, then, devoted primarily to a reconsideration of phenomenology. This is closely followed by a critique of structuralism, especially through Lévi-Strauss, and of structural linguistics through Saussure. Other linguistic threads are followed with (and sometimes against) Jakobson, Benveniste, Ricoeur, Austin, and Searle. Derrida's fascination with language is probably at its most evident, and perhaps its most playful, in the essays of the 1970s devoted to literary writers who are themselves ludic rather than logical: Genet, Sollers, Artaud, Joyce, and poet-wordsmiths such as Mallarmé, Baudelaire, or Ponge. The latest phase of Derrida's development is his concern with psychoanalysis, ethics, and politics, foregrounded since the 1980s, but in fact already apparent in his earliest essays of the 1960s, such as those on Freud, Bataille, and Levinas. This is the aspect of Derrida's thought which is of most immediate relevance to social theory, though his studies of phenomenology, structuralism, language, and literature are all part of the deconstructive enterprise, and have an essential contribution to make in the theoretical domain, in particular in their problematization of identity, expression, intention, and meaning.

SOCIAL THEORY AND CONTRIBUTIONS

Derrida is clearly a philosopher rather than a social theorist, but his philosophy, like any major epistemological shift, has radical implications for theories of the social. From the outset, in his earliest work on phenomenology, Derrida's conception of consciousness implied a view of human subjectivity as radical as that of structuralism, while being so well-grounded and so finely argued philosophically that it could not be easily dismissed or overlooked. Phenomenology was, in the first half of the twentieth century, a force to be reckoned with: its ambitions were radical, it set out to revolutionize epistemology, psychology, and ultimately science, and Derrida's engagement with it is serious and tenacious. Phenomenology is a philosophy of consciousness which sets out to avoid both empiricism and idealism by rethinking the fundamental distinction between subject and object. Consciousness, according to phenomenology, is always directed outside itself to the world in a relationship of intentionality. Phenomenology, Husserl argued, involves a rejection of the 'natural attitude of experience and thought' (1967: 43) and an attempt to purify consciousness of the contingencies of psychology and empiricism in order ultimately to observe the essences of 'transcendental' (i.e. not individual) consciousness.

Derrida studied phenomenology in Paris with Levinas and Ricoeur. He considers Husserl to have been one of the major influences on his thinking, and much of his philosophical work seems to spring from his critique of and engagement with phenomenology. The major problem with phenomenology, in Derrida's view, comes from its attempt to ground knowledge in experience, evidence and self-presence. Its failure is due not to the inadequacy of its execution, but rather to the fact that it is based on false and misguided premises. Derrida's MA dissertation in 1954 and his first two published books all deal with Husserl: the translation and study of *The Origin of Geometry* in 1962, and in 1967, *Speech and Phenomena: Introduction to the problem of the sign in the philosophy of Husserl*. Phenomenology, in Derrida's view of it, is both a critique of metaphysics and a participant in the metaphysical enterprise. It cannot avoid entrapment in the system it is setting out to criticize. Husserl's attempt most notably to preserve the purity of the self-presence of consciousness in the face of its apparent contamination by external elements such as indication or communication is undermined, in Derrida's view, by its own arguments. Husserl deludes himself when he imagines that consciousness is pure, unmediated self-presence without need of representation. Derrida's argument proceeds via an analysis of the implications of the phenomenological conception of temporality which he shows to be self-contradictory and self-destructive. In a fine analysis, too closely textual to be susceptible of easy summary, Derrida reveals the fissuring inherent in the present moment, and the concomitant fissuring of self-presence in consciousness itself.

Abstract though it may perhaps seem, this question of the self-division of consciousness is probably the single most important argument for Derrida's whole deconstructive endeavour, since its far-reaching implications undermine so many of the assumptions of philosophy, and not only of phenomenology. The self-identity of the human subject, for example, cannot survive the fissuring of its mainstay, consciousness. What else can guarantee subjective identity if consciousness itself is not self-identical? And so much else will necessarily follow the fall of the subject, in a tumbling house-of-cards where language, communication, intersubjectivity of course, the subject–object division, and ultimately all representation and knowledge of the world that supposes a knowing subject will lose their foundation in the post-nuclear landscape of deconstruction (1967c: 13).

Derrida's reflections on language also start in his study of Husserl; first in the work on *The Origin of Geometry* where Derrida takes Husserl to task for the contradictions enshrined in his theory of the historicity of ideal objects. For Husserl, ideal objects such as the concepts of geometry have their origin in human thought rather than in nature, but they are not located in space or time and do not depend on any particular human subject. They emerge rather from a process of idealization and imagination which marks a form of nonpersonalized intellectual progress. It will already be clear that Husserl is on treacherous terrain, and Derrida focuses in particular on his conception of the role of language in the understanding and transmission of the concepts of mathematics and science. For Husserl, linguistic objectivation and mathematical symbolization are an occasion for alienation and degradation. In other words, the language of mathematics to some extent masks its truth in its purest form; even apparently fundamental axioms are surrounded by a 'sedimentation of meaning' that separates them from their 'origin' (1962: 44). But of course, Derrida argues, it is language and in particular writing, that creates an autonomous transcendental field in the first place, an ideal objective meaning, independent of any singular subject. Husserl describes failure, misunderstanding, and noncommunication as merely contingent and dependent on empirical weakness; for Derrida they constitute part of the very conditions of possibility of objectivity. What Husserl wants to relativize as nonessential is for Derrida fundamental to the nature of the historical transmission of ideas and may be radical. Failure is part of a finitude which can never be entirely overcome.

This debate over the status of language in mathematics is, like Derrida's critique of Husserl's conception of temporality, highly technical. But its consequences are radical. If language is not extraneous to the concepts it conveys, but rather an inalienable part of them, if it is not merely the husk of ideas which transcend it, then the view of language as a mere transmitter of pre-existing thought becomes untenable. Husserl's conception of language is one of the major subjects of Derrida's attention in *Speech and Phenomena*, devoted to Husserl's theory of the sign, and the work may be seen in some respects as a generalization of the ideas previously explored in the domain of mathematics and geometry. Husserl's position as a phenomenologist is that in the innermost self-presence of consciousness language is inessential and, if present, as for example in interior monologue, it will necessarily teach nothing to the subject who is engaged in it. Derrida disagrees and, as so often, uses Husserl's own ideas to refute him. The nature of the sign, in Husserl's account of it, is to be repeatable and representative. It is these very features that Derrida uses to undermine the vital distinctions Husserl needs to maintain between ideal and real, fictive and effective, exterior and interior. Husserl's argument is that consciousness is deluded when it imagines it can communicate with itself. Derrida reverses this, as we have seen, to argue that it is Husserl who is deluded when he imagines that consciousness is pure, unmediated self-presence and that it has no need of any kind of representation.

The impossibility of pure self-presence and the problematization of attempts to argue for uncontaminated originality in domains as apparently diverse as consciousness and geometry are probably amongst the best-known features of Derrida's thinking, especially in their relationship to language, speech and writing. Derrida's refutation, most famously in *Of Grammatology*, of the priority of speech over writing has been widely publicized, and frequently dismissed and misunderstood, at least by those too impatient to read any more than second-hand accounts of his ideas. Derrida, of course, does not claim that humankind developed writing, in the usual sense of the term, before it developed speech. Such a claim would be particularly difficult to sustain, though we might note, with Derrida, that the linguist Hjelmslev himself reminds us that the discovery of alphabetic language is hidden in prehistory, citing a remark of Bertrand Russell, not noted for his contribution to deconstruction, to the effect that it is impossible to know for certain whether the oldest form of human expression was spoken or written (1967b). Be that as it may, Derrida's claim is rather that all the features most commonly associated with writing, that is inscription, repeatability, conventionality, are equally to be found in speech. Derrida's term 'archi-écriture' refers to all these features common to both speech and writing, but which are denied and repressed in theories that have an investment in maintaining the natural and unmediated nature of the spoken word. Moreover, speech and writing are too different for writing to be deemed a mere transcription of speech, as is more immediately evident when nonphonetic writing systems such as ideograms and hieroglyphs are considered.

Derrida argues, then, that the enshrined common-sense view that writing represents speech, and that speech represents thought; and its corollary, that such representation necessarily involves a degree of alienation of the original thought, is mistaken. For Derrida, I never express exactly what I intend, not because language or writing deviates my intention, but rather because there never was a pure, original intention, or thought, present to my consciousness, pre-existing its linguistic expression, and progressively distorted in its successive representations. On the contrary, the apparent self-presence of consciousness is not so much a mark of self-identity, but rather of self-division, and even at its most archaic level thought is 'impure' and, to use Artaud's terms, 'stolen' from me by others (Derrida, 1967c). Such a view of consciousness, subjectivity, thought, and language clearly has immense implications for any theory of communication and, necessarily, for any theory of the social. If we are not self-identical, self-present subjects, and if we do not ever fully communicate what we think we intend, then there is no way in which many of the great social aims could ever be fully realized. Common projects will necessarily founder if they presume self-identical subjects working together with self-understanding and self-transparency, not merely because of human weakness and failure to achieve the aims set in their purity, but because the 'subjects' themselves do not correspond to their presumed identity. One conclusion that could be drawn from this is deeply pessimistic: divided subjects, unable to know or understand the world fully, lacking even the possibility of achieving self-knowledge, will not, a fortiori, be able to construct a better society. Such is, indeed, the nihilistic position attributed to Derrida, or allegedly derived from his thinking, by many of his self-styled humanist critics. However, it is the exact antithesis of Derrida's own position.

On the contrary, in Derrida's view, it is precisely our lack of self-identity as subjects that makes ethics, and consequently ethical politics, possible at all. Responsibility, for Derrida, and the taking of responsible decisions, would not be possible, or even thinkable, for a self-identical subject, for such self-identity would preclude substantial change and predetermine all outcomes (1994a: 45, 53). Much of Derrida's most explicit thinking on these issues is to be found in his publications of the last dozen years such as *De l'esprit: Heidegger et la question* (1987), *Force de loi* (1994a), *Politiques de l'amitié* (1994b), *Spectres de Marx* (1993a), *Adieu* (1997a) and *Cosmopolites de tous les pays, encore un effort!* (1997b), but its foundations are laid far earlier in texts such as the 1964 essay on Levinas, 'Violence and metaphysics', or *Of Grammatology* (1967b). One of the key terms Derrida uses in this context is that of the 'promise'. The promise has a very special structure, that of futurity, and also of commitment to the future. The promise will never come about as a future state, but that does not invalidate it; on the contrary, like nonself-identity, it is what frees us from essence, hypostasis, and stagnation. The promise is what enables us to conceive, perhaps even to tolerate, but also importantly to narrow, the gap, for example, between law and justice. Law aims at justice but is never identical with it; nor could it be, given that law is precisely the attempt to understand and enshrine what is just, but its very enshrining necessarily comes between the ideal and the real by subjecting the ideal to the laws of empirical cases. The promise is also, Derrida maintains, the structure of democracy, for democracy too is an ideal which, in all attempts to enact it, encounters perpetual internal contradictions and conflicts which will always impede its full realization. The danger, Derrida argues, lies not in the recognition that full democracy will never be achieved in any state, or perfect justice in any legal system, but rather in the illusion that either is possible, or worse, already achieved. Such illusions are not merely mistaken, they encourage a counterproductive social and historical complacency and a potentially pernicious misunderstanding of other political or juridical models.

APPRAISAL OF KEY ADVANCES AND CONTROVERSIES

Derrida's work is nothing if not controversial. The controversies include the well-known debate (which may appear more like a *dialogue de sourds*) with Searle over Austin and his theory of performatives, the violent conflict surrounding the pro-Nazi sympathies of Heidegger and the alleged anti-Semitism of Paul de Man, but also less transparently political questions associated with some of Derrida's more gnomic pronouncements such as *'il n'y a pas de hors-texte'* ('there is nothing outside the text') or even his theory of metaphor. We will look at some of these issues briefly, but a general point needs to be made first: in so far as deconstruction sets out to question prevailing orthodoxy in philosophy, theories of language, psychoanalysis, ethics, or politics it will necessarily disturb and sometimes distress. Derrida enjoys writing, he relishes the stunning effect his more radical statements may have on his conservative critics, he takes visible pleasure in the cut-and-thrust of debate, but, like the most solemn of his critics, he tries to say what he means and he means what he says. His writing is not generally difficult or obscure just for the sake of it. Like Lacan, Derrida does not want to be read *'en oblique'*, that is to say with a hasty glance down the page, his writing requires time for reflection, and it does not always receive it. Hence the vast number of misrepresentations of his ideas which may seem bewildering to anyone who has genuinely read his writings in their original, nonsimplified form.

A case in point is his skirmish with Habermas. Habermas takes Searle's side in the disagreement over Austin and performatives. The debate starts in 1971 when Derrida gave a paper entitled *Signature Evénement Contexte* devoted to Austin's speech-act theory. This has been discussed many times elsewhere (see, for example, Howells, 1998: 64–71), and I will not give the details again here. What matters in this context is that Derrida discusses Austin's way of dealing with apparent exceptions to the rules of his theory, and argues, as we have seen him do for Husserl, and indeed as he will do on many other occasions, that it is paradoxically the excluded exceptions which provide a way in to a better understanding of the apparent 'rules', in this case of performatives. The paper seems to have enraged one of the best-known followers of Austin, the philosopher John Searle, who retaliated in 1977 in an article entitled 'Reiterating the differences: A Reply to Derrida', which accuses Derrida of misrepresenting Austin. Searle is direct and patronizing: Derrida says things 'that are obviously false'; Searle lists 'his major misunderstandings and mistakes' and claims that 'Derrida's Austin is unrecognizable' (Searle, 1977: 83). But bizarrely, however much right he may or may not have on his side over Austin, Searle is clearly deeply mistaken over Derrida, for he attributes to him, almost systematically, views which are the exact opposite of those he in fact holds or argues. The most straightforward and evident of these concerns the distinction between speech and writing. As we have seen, Derrida is concerned to problematize the simple speech–writing opposition, and to contest the prioritizing of speech. Searle, however, seems to have contrived to read otherwise, for he contemptuously dismisses Derrida's alleged attempt to distinguish between speech and writing using the criteria of iterability and absence, which Searle rejects as grounds for discrimation. We have, then, the strange situation of Searle attributing to Derrida the opposite of the views he actually holds and using his own arguments to challenge him. What seems to have happened is that Searle has failed to distinguish between Derrida's initial exposition of the ideas he intends to challenge, and the views he is himself proposing. Be this as it may, in *The Philosophical Discourse of Modernity,* Habermas takes Searle's side in the debate, explicitly basing his argument not on any text by Derrida but rather on Jonathan Culler's lively but necessarily simplifying account of deconstruction, which Habermas prefers as being easier than Derrida's own writings. Such intellectual laziness draws an uncharacteristically curt retort from Derrida: '*Cela est faux*' (1990c: 245).

This kind of dependence on secondary sources may be woefully unscholarly, but it is typical of a debonair attitude towards deconstruction on the part of certain thinkers who righteously proclaim the necessity of a classical kind of proof, while not bothering to read, or read closely, the texts they are attacking (see Ricoeur, 1975; I discuss this briefly in Howells, 1998: 61–2). Other controversies are, however, based on differences of more substance, such as that surrounding Derrida's apparently idealist claim that '*il n'y a pas de hors-texte*' ('There is nothing outside the text') (1967b: 227; 1972a: 364). It is true that Derrida later adds 'il n'y a pas de hors contexte' ('there is nothing outside the context') (1990c: 252), which he says means much the same, but rather than being mutually illuminating the further paradox may merely muddy the waters. In this case, perhaps, Derrida's statements cannot be defended on the grounds that they are limpidly clear if carefully read. However, the fact remains that in context neither statement is particularly difficult to understand. In the first place, the 'text' itself has a very special meaning for Derrida: it is what in modern literature has replaced the 'book' and its connotations of totality and full meaning. The 'text' evokes rather fragmentation, its woven texture implying heterogeneity and, Derrida suggests, 'a tissue of traces' (1967c: 429). The text does not refer to or reflect a pre-existing world (its referent, or the 'real'), but rather forms part of a vast nexus of meaning and reference. '*Il n'y a pas de hors-texte*' is far from indicating a kind of idealism of the text: on the contrary, Derrida's position is more subtle and more complex. Since, as he showed in his work on Husserl, there is no presence pre-existing the sign, similarly 'there is nothing before the text, there is no pretext that is not already a text... If there is no "*hors-texte*", this is because generalized graphics has always already begun' (1972a: 364). In other words, the written text is neither a closed totality nor a reflection of a more real external world, it is necessarily open to the broader text of which it is part:

> What is happening in the current upheaval is a revaluation of the relationship between the general text and what used to be considered, in the form of reality (historical, political, economic, sexual etc.), the simple, referable exterior of language or writing, whether that exterior was envisaged as cause or simply as accident. (Derrida, 1972c: 126)

And indeed, this is similar to the view Derrida attributes to Baudrillard when an interviewer mentions Baudrillard's claim that the Gulf War did not take place. It is not a matter of denying the reality of death or suffering, Derrida argues, but rather of recognizing the role played by the media, and especially television, in the manipulation of information and the construction of simulacra (1996: 88–9). To an extent, and certainly in the imaginations of many avid TV watchers, reporting the war took over from and replaced the events themselves, substituting for the thousands of Iraqi deaths an image of defined and memorable visual sequences. Derrida concludes firmly, however, by affirming against Baudrillard's *boutade* that the war *did* take place, *'cette guerre a eu lieu'*, not because he imagines Baudrillard really thinks otherwise, but because he believes that the consequences of Baudrillard's apparent evacuation of the real are more noxious than those of the simplifications involved in any flat, polemical, 'realistic' statement of fact.

And this preference for clarity over finesse has increasingly become Derrida's hallmark in recent years, as he demonstrates the confidence to choose political good above philosophical sophistication. It is as if the philosophical battles have, to an extent, been already fought, and in some cases won, and the current task is for Derrida to use his extraordinary powers of analysis in more urgent practical domains, political, social, and juridical. The ethics and politics of deconstruction are, of course, a matter of considerable controversy, and notoriously hard to determine. Accused by the right of iconoclasm and irresponsibility and by the left of encouraging inactivity by rendering political action unjustifiable, Derrida's work finds no favour either with the militant anti-obscurantism – and arguably anti-intellectualism – of centrist liberal thinkers. However, Derrida's work is increasingly explicit in its ethical and political positions, and far from simply eschewing dogmatism and prescription, as might be expected from any self-respecting deconstructionist, Derrida in fact makes a series of philosophical interventions in issues as diverse and as practical as the legacy of Marxism, the question of Judaism and the State of Israel, the military use of scientific research, abortion, euthanasia, AIDS, the politics of drug-trafficking, and the status accorded to animals. Derrida's own political positions have become, then, in recent years, increasingly public, but always within the context of a finely argued and frequently impressive deconstructive analysis of the issues.

In the late 1980s Derrida faced the difficult and delicate task of responding to the violent political controversy surrounding one of the most influential precursors of deconstruction, Martin Heidegger, and one of its best-known exponents outside France, Paul de Man, who was a personal friend of Derrida's. Both Heidegger and de Man were accused of fascist/Nazi sympathies, though their cases were very different in degree, and unlike Heidegger, de Man had made clear during his lifetime his abhorrence of fascism and totalitarianism, and was not able to answer for (or indeed abjure) his early, anti-Semitic newspaper writings, since they were only discovered posthumously. The episode is itself well-known, certainly in France, since it was used by Derrida's opponents as an occasion to discredit deconstruction by associating it with the shady politics of its friends and ancestors. Derrida's response was to attempt to dissociate himself from the taint of fascist politics without betraying either Heidegger or de Man by an overhasty dismissal of them. In the case of Heidegger, which arose first, Derrida approached the issue through an examination of what the German philosopher calls the *Geist*, or spirit, and showed how the fortunes of that term, studiously avoided in early and late Heidegger, but present in the infamous Rectorial Address in the mid-1930s, mirrored Heidegger's own fluctuating attitude to the most fundamental questions concerning the status of the human. In the case of Paul de Man, Derrida's approach was somewhat different as he tried to understand how de Man could have entertained ideas which seem, 50 years later, so collusive with fascist ideology. The main argument concerns the ambiguity and complexity of de Man's political positions during the war, but despite his concessions to de Man's youthful *insouciance*, Derrida's conclusions are sombre as he forcefully dissociates himself and deconstruction, as well as the de Man he knew so well, from the offensive anti-Semitism of the juvenilia in question. He is, however, at pains to stress his own refusal to condemn a man who is now dead, and whose mature political life was irreproachable. Moralistic condemnation of someone no longer in a position to defend himself seems to Derrida to participate in the very logic it is condemning (1988: 221), and the same criticisms may be made of the confused attempt to tar deconstruction with the brush of fascism. Derrida takes the opportunity to pose the very fundamental question of what underlies the apparently widespread determination to discredit deconstruction. Why, Derrida asks, do we witness such hostility to a mode of analysis which attempts precisely to 'deconstruct the foundations of obscurantism, totalitarianism or nazism, of racism and of authoritarian hierarchies in general?' (1988: 224):

> Why do people not understand that the exercise of responsibility (theoretical and ethico-political) demands that nothing should be excluded *a priori* from deconstructive questioning? For deconstruction is, in my view, the very implementation of that responsibility, especially when it analyses the traditional or dogmatic axioms of the concept of responsibility. Why do people feign not to see that deconstruction is anything but a nihilism or a scepticism, as is still frequently claimed despite so many texts which demonstrate the opposite *explicitly, thematically, and for more than twenty years?* Why the accusation of irrationalism as soon as someone asks a question concerning reason, its forms, its history, its mutations? Of anti-humanism as soon as a question is raised concerning the essence of man and the construction of the concept 'man'? I could multiply examples of this sort, be it a matter of language, of literature, of philosophy, of technique, of democracy, of all institutions in general etc. In short, what are they afraid of? Who are they trying to frighten? (Derrida, 1988: 141)

Derrida's main contribution to social theory may ultimately be the way he forces us to reflect on these questions which strike at the heart of some of our most cherished and disavowed prejudices.

DERRIDA'S MAJOR WORKS

References in the chapter are to the French texts. Translations are my own. Biographical information is drawn from Derrida and Bennington (1991).

Derrida, J. (1962) Introduction and translation of E. Husserl *L'Origine de la géometrie*. Paris: PUF; *Origin of Geometry* (Husserl): Introduction. (Trans. John P Leavey, Jr.) Lincoln and London: University of Nebraska Press (Bison Books), 1989.

Derrida, J. (1967a) *La Voix et le phénomène*. Paris: PUF; *Speech and Phenomena, and Other Essays on Husserl's Theory of Signs*. (Trans. David B Allison.) Evanston, IL: Northwestern University Press, 1973.

Derrida, J. (1967b) *De la grammatologie*. Paris: Editions de Minuit; *Of Grammatology*. (Trans. Gayatri Chakravorty Spivak,) Baltimore, MD: Johns Hopkins University Press, 1976; 6th printing, 1984.

Derrida, J. (1967c) *L'Ecriture et la différence*. Paris: Editions du Seuil; *Writing and Difference*. (Trans. Alan Bass.) London and Henley: Routledge and Kegan Paul, 1978; repr. 1981.

Derrida, J. (1972a): *La Dissémination*. Paris: Editions du Seuil; *Dissemination*. (Trans. Barbara Johnson.) Chicago: University of Chicago Press, and London: Athlone Press, 1981.

Derrida, J. (1972b) *Marges: de la Philosophy*. Paris: Editions de Minuit; *Margins: Of Philosophy*. (Trans. Alan Bass.) Brighton: Harvester Press, 1982.

Derrida, J. (1972c) *Positions*. Paris: Editions de Minuit; *Positions*. (Trans. Alan Bass.) London: Athlone Press, 1987.

Derrida, J. (1973): *L'Archéologie du frivole: lire Condillac*. Paris: Galilée. *The Archeology of the Frivolous: Reading Condillac*. (Trans. P Leavey, Jr.) Lincoln and London: University of Nebraska Press (Bison Books), 1987.

Derrida, J. (1974) *Glas*. Paris: *Galilée; Glas*. (Trans. John P Leavey, Jr and Richard Rand.) Lincoln: University of Nebraska Press, 1986.

Derrida, J. (1976) *Éperons. Les styles de Nietzsche*. Venice: Corbo e Fiori, (quadrilingual edition); Paris: Flammarion, 1978; *Spurs: Nietzsche's Styles*. (Trans. Barbara Harlow.) Chicago, University of Chicago Press, 1979 (bilingual edition).

Derrida, J. (1980a) *La Carte postale: de Socrate à Freud et au-delà*. Paris: Aubier-Flammarion; *The Post Card: From Socrates to Freud and Beyond*. (Trans. Alan Bass.) Chicago: University of Chicago Press, 1993.

Derrida, J. (1980b) 'En ce moment même dans cet ouvrage me voici', in François Laruelle (ed.), *Textes pour Emmanuel Lévinas*. Paris: Editions Jean-Michel Place; repr. in *Psyché: inventions de l'autre*. Paris, Galilée, 1987.

Derrida, J. (1983) 'The time of a thesis: Punctuations' (Trans. Kathleen McLaughlin), in Alan Montefiore (ed.), *Philosophy in France Today*. Cambridge: Cambridge University Press.

Derrida, J. et al. (1985) *La Faculté de juger*. Paris: Editions de Minuit.

Derrida, J. (1987a) *De l'esprit: Heidegger et la question*. Paris: Galilée; *Of Spirit: Heidegger and the Question*. (Trans. Geoffrey Bennington and Rachel Bowlby). Chicago: University of Chicago Press, 1989.

Derrida, J. (1987b) 'Lettre à un ami japonais', in *Psyché: inventions de l'autre*. Paris: Galilée; 'Letter to a Japanese friend' (Trans. David Wood and Andrew Benjamin), in Peggy Kamuf (ed.), *A Derrida Reader: Between the Blinds*. London and New York: Harvester, 1991.

Derrida, J. (1987c) *Psyché: inventions de l'autre*. Paris: Galilée.

Derrida, J. (1988) *Mémoires: pour Paul de Man*. Paris: Galilée. *Mémoires: for Paul de Man*. (Rev. edn, Trans. Cecile Linsay, Jonathan Culler, Eduardo Cadava and Peggy Kamuf.) New York: Columbia University Press, 1989.

Derrida, J. (1989) '"Il faut bien manger" ou le calcul du sujet', *Confrontations. Après le sujet QUI VIENT*, 20: p. 91–114.

Derrida, J. (1990a) *Mémoires d'aveugle: l'autoportrait et autres ruines*. Paris: Louvre, Réunion des Musées Nationaux; *Memoirs of the Blind: The Self-Portrait and Other Ruins*. (Trans. Pascale-Anne Brault and Michael Naas.) Chicago and London: University of Chicago Press, 1993.

Derrida, J. (1990b) *Du droit à la philosophie*. Paris: Galilée.

Derrida, J. (1990c) *Limited Inc*. (Introductions and Trans. Elisabeth Weber.) Paris: Galilée. 'Limited Inc. abc...', *Glyph*, 2 (1977). Baltimore and London: Johns Hopkins University Press, pp. 162–254. Reprinted in *Limited Inc*., trans. Samuel Weber and Jeffrey Mehlman. Evanston, IL: Northwestern University Press, 1988; repr. 1990.

Derrida, J. (1990d) 'Donner la mort', in *L'Ethique du don. Jacques Derrida et la pensée du don*, Colloque de Royaumont, December 1990. (Ed. J-M Rabaté and M. Wetzel). Paris: Metailie-Transition, 1992.

Derrida, J. (1991a) *Donner le temps 1: la fausse monnaie*. Paris: Galilée; *Given Time 1: Counterfeit Money*. (Trans. Peggy Kamuf.) Chicago and London: University of Chicago Press, 1992.

Derrida, J. (1991b) *L'Autre Cap; suivi de la démocratie ajournée*. Paris: editions de Minuit.

Derrida, J. and Bennington, Geoffrey (1991c) *Jacques Derrida*. Paris: editions du Seuil.

Derrida, J. (1992) *Points de suspension. Entretiens*. Paris: Galilée. *Points...: Interviews 1974–1994*. (Ed. Elisabeth Weber, Trans. Peggy Kamuf.) Stanford, CA: Stanford University Press, 1995.

Derrida, J. (1993a) *Spectres de Marx: l'état de la dette, le travail du deuil et la nouvelle Internationale*. Paris: Galilée. *Specters of Marx: The State of the Debt, the Work of the Mourning and the New International*. (Trans. Peggy Kamuf, Introduction by Bernd Magnus and Stephen Cullenberg.) London and New York: Routledge, 1994.

Derrida, J. (1993b) *Passions. Paris:* Galilée.

Derrida, J. (1994a) *Force de loi: le 'fondement mystique de l'autorité'*. Paris: Galilée. 'Force of law: the "Mystical Foundation of Authority"'. (Trans. Mary Quaintance), in Drucilla Cornell, Michel Rosenfeld and David Gray Carlson (eds.), *Deconstruction and the Possibility of Justice*. New York and London: Routledge, 1992.

Derrida, J. (1994b) *Politiques de l'amitié; suivi de l'oreille de Heidegger*. Paris: Galilée; *Politics of Friendship*. (Trans. George Collins.) London: Verso, 1997.

Derrida, J. (1995a) *Mal d'archive: une impression freudienne*. Paris: Galilée. *Archive Fever: A Freudian Impression*. (Trans. Eric Prenowitz) Chicago and London: University of Chicago Press, 1996.

Derrida, J., Avtonomova, N. S., Podoroza, V. A. and Ryklin, M. (1995b) *Moscou aller-retour*. Paris: Éditions de l'Aube.

Derrida, J. (1996a) '"Il courait mort": salut, salut. Notes pour un courrier aux *Temps Modernes*', *Les Temps Modernes*, 587: 91–114.

Derrida, J. (1996b) *La Religion*, Séminaire de Capri sous la direction de Jacques Derrida et Gianni Vattimo. Paris: Éditions du Seuil.

Derrida, J. (1996c) 'Remarks on deconstruction and pragmatism', in Chantal Mouffe (ed.), *Deconstruction and pragmatism*. London and New York: Routledge.

Derrida, J. (1996d) *Résistances: de la psychanalyse*. Paris: Galilée.

Derrida, J. and Steigler, B. (1996e) *Echographies: de la télévision*. Paris. Galilée.

Derrida, J. (1997a) *Adieu: à Emmanuel Levinas*. Paris: Galilée.

Derrida, J. (1997b) *Cosmopolites de tous les pays, encore un effort!* Paris: Galilée.

Derrida, J. and Cixous, H. (1998) *Voiles*. Paris: Galilée.

Derrida, J. (1999) *Sur Parole: instantanées philosophiques*. Paris: éditions de l'Aube.

Derrida, J. and Fathy, S. (2000a) *Tourner le mots*. Paris: Galilée.

Derrida, J. (2000b) *Le Toucher: Jean-Luc Nancy*. Paris: Galilée.

SECONDARY LITERATURE

Baudrillard, Jean (1970) *Pour une critique de l'économie politique du signe*, Paris: Gallimard.

Beardsworth, Richard (1996) *Derrida and the Political*. London: Routledge.

Critchley, Simon (1992). *The Ethics of Deconstruction*. Oxford: Blackwell.

Culler, Jonathan (1983) *On Deconstruction: Theory and Criticism after Structuralism*. London: Routledge and Kegan Paul.

de Man, Paul (1971) *Blindness and Insight: Essays in the Rhetoric of Contemporary Criticism*. New York: Oxford University Press.

Ellis, John, M. (1989) *Deconstruction*. Princeton, NJ: Princeton University Press.

Giovannangeli, Daniel (1992) 'La Phénoménologie partagée: remarques sur Sartre et Derrida', *Les Études Philosophiques*, 2: 246–56.

Habermas, Jürgen (1987) *The Philosophical Discourse of Modernity: Twelve Lectures.* (Trans. Frederick Lawrence.) Cambridge, MA: MIT Press.

Hartman, Geoffrey (ed.) (1981) *Saving the Text: Literature/Derrida/Philosophy.* Baltimore, MD: Johns Hopkins University Press.

Heidegger, Martin (1967) *Being and Time.* (Trans. John Macquarrie and Edward Robinson.) Oxford: Blackwell.

Heidegger, Martin (1990) 'The Rectorial Address', in Gunther Neske and Emil Kettering (eds.), *Martin Heidegger and National Socialism.* New York: Paragon House.

Heidegger, Martin (2000) *Introduction to Metaphysics.* (Trans. Ralph Manheim.) New Haven, CT and London: Yale University Press.

Hobson, Marian (1998) *Jacques Derrida: Opening Lines.* London and New York: Routledge.

Howells, Christina (1998) *Derrida: Deconstruction from Phenomenology to Ethics.* Cambridge: Polity Press.

Husserl, Edmund (1962) *L'Origine de la géometrie.* (Introduction and Trans.) Paris: PUF.

Husserl, Edmund ([1931] 1967) *Ideas: General Introduction to Pure Phenomenology.* (Trans. W R Boyce-Gibson.) London and New York: Allen and Unwin.

Husserl, Edmund ([1891] 1970a) *Philosophie der Arithmetik: mit ergänzenden Texten (1890–1901).* The Hague: Martinus Nijhoff. 1970.

Husserl, Edmund (1970b) *Logical Investigations,* 2 vols. (Trans. J.N. Findlay.) New York: Humanities Press.

Johnson, Christopher (1993) *System and Writing in the Philosophy of Jacques Derrida.* Cambridge: Cambridge University Press.

Kearney, Richard (1986) *Modern Movements in European Philosophy.* Manchester: Manchester University Press.

Kofman, Sarah (1984) *Lectures de Derrida.* Paris: Galilée.

Levinas, Emmanuel (1961) *Totalité et infini: essai sur l'extériorité.* The Hague: Martinus Nijhoff.

Levinas, Emmanuel (1973) 'Tout autrement', *L'Arc,* special issue on Derrida; repr. in *Noms propres* (Livre de Poche). Montpellier: Fata Morgana, 1976.

Levinas, Emmanuel ([1930] 1984) *La Théorie de l'intuition dans la phénoménologie de Husserl.* Paris: Vrin.

Lévi-Strauss, Claude (1955) *Tristes tropiques.* Paris: Plon.

Lévi-Strauss, Claude (1962) *La Pensée sauvage.* Paris: Plon.

Lévi-Strauss, Claude (1964) *Le Cru et le cuit (Mythologiques, vol. 1).* Paris: Plon.

Montefiore, Alan (ed.) 1983 *Philosophy in France Today.* Cambridge: Cambridge University Press.

Mouffe, Chantal (ed.) (1996) *Deconstruction and pragmatism.* London and New York: Routledge.

Norris, Christopher (1982) *Deconstruction: Theory and Practice,* New Accents series. London and New York: Methuen.

Ricoeur, Paul (1975) *La Métaphore vive.* Paris: Editions du Seuil.

Searle, John (1977) 'Reiterating the Differences: A Reply to Derrida', *Glyph,* 1: 198–208.

14

Roland Barthes

CHRIS ROJEK

BIOGRAPHICAL DETAILS AND THEORETICAL CONTEXT

Roland Barthes (1915–80) was the most celebrated post-structuralist stylist of his generation. It was a status he attained only after a lengthy association with structuralism. For a decade and a half, Barthes was pivotal in the project of trying to situate literary and cultural criticism upon a quasi-scientific footing. In works like *Writing Degree Zero* (1965), *Mythologies* (1957), *Elements of Semiology* (1965) and *The Fashion System* (1967) he laid out the formal principles of semiology, the science of signs. Semiology was, perhaps, the high-water mark of structuralist rhetoric. It was an approach which promised nothing less than the demystification of culture and communication. It was a noble but, with hindsight, giddy, turn in the history of ideas.

From the first, Barthes was wary of the possibility of being confined by the project of academic system-building. Indeed, throughout his life he was more attracted to the practice of writing and teaching, than academic life *per se*. As he observed on several occasions, his academic career was, in fact, somewhat unusual. To begin with, his first publications appeared as monthly newspaper columns in *Lettres Nouvelles*, rather than through the conventional medium of academic journals and conference proceedings. These brief essays were on subjects that scarcely figured in the academic core curriculum of the day: washing powder ads, wrestling, striptease, the Tour de France, the Abbé Pierre, Poujade, the face of Greta Garbo, Elia Kazan's *On the Waterfront*, the Dominici affair (an unsolved murder in rural France), and the evangelist Billy Graham. Eventually, they formed the basis for his influential book *Mythologies* (1957). Barthes added a longer theoretical essay, 'Myth Today,' to the volume, partly to 'academize' a publication which might otherwise have seemed an amorphous concoction. *Mythologies* was not a dry academic text replete with references and a detailed biography. Instead, Barthes maintained a pithy, uncluttered style which was, and remains, quite atypical of orthodox academic writing. It contributed to the *succès de scandale* of the book. *Mythologies* captured a wide audience who saw in it a powerful representative of the Nouvelle Critique developing in social and cultural study.

Barthes was also unusual in devoting himself to semiology when the subject was scarely recognized by academics. Throughout the 1950s linguistics was dominated by functionalist models of language in which questions of the signification and play of meaning in everyday communication were secondary to the causal relations between elements in the language system. Initially, there was scant interest in Barthes arguments from these quarters. Indeed the orthodox functionalist Raymond Picard (1969) produced a famously hostile attack on Barthes and the Nouvelle Critique, accusing both of triviality and irresponsibility.

As for sociology, the subject of popular culture was practically a blank sheet when Barthes started to write about myth and consumer culture. Restrospectively, he has been acknowledged as one of the first postwar writers to take popular culture seriously. Storey (1993: 77) describes *Mythologies* as a 'founding text' of cultural studies. However, in the 1950s, cultural studies had not yet been born, and most academic departments of sociology turned a deaf ear to Barthes's analysis.

Another example of his unorthodox career route is that he was elected to a prestige appointment at the elite College de France in 1976 without holding a PhD. The election was prompted by Michel Foucault, with whom Barthes had a strained personal friendship. Foucault proposed Barthes for the specially created chair of 'literary semiology'. Barthes was habitually diffident about his achievements in public. To be sure, he was a famously private man in Parisian life, who coveted solitude and orderly habits. Yet, surely, as he mounted the podium to give his inaugural lecture, he must have been tempted to say more than the polite platitudes he actually delivered, about the unorthodox path that had led him to this exalted position.

Barthes was born in 1915, and his father was killed in a naval battle one year later. He was raised by his mother. A half brother was born out of wedlock in 1927, which tragically led to the estrangement of Madame Barthes from her family. Barthes grew up in poverty. At the age of 19 he contracted pulmonary tuberculosis. For the next 12 years he was in and out of sanatoria, an experience which he understandably found to be depressing and isolating. Barthes spent much of his twenties either alone or physically debilitated. The experience made him unusually watchful and reflective. Later critics complained of an 'overinterpretative attitude' in his work (Merquior, 1986: 139). By this is meant a tendency to see the human world as chronically coded or riddled with sign systems. Barthes was no Freudian, at least not in a consistent sense. Nonetheless, he fully shared Freud's suspicion of transparency in personal and cultural life. Both men were besotted with the idea of hidden meanings underneath surface appearances. Beyond all doubt, in his youth and early adulthood, as a patient at the mercy of powerful others, Barthes had ample time to ponder the grammar of power in human relations and the 'naturalization' of reality through the manipulation of representation and meaning.

Although he held two brief school teaching appointments during these years, his health was never certain enough to sustain a career. It was during a period of convalesence in Paris in 1946–7 that he began to contemplate writing two books: first, a commentary on the historian Jules Michelet, and second, a work of theory on the nature of writing in what he took to be the stifling environment of petit bourgeois culture.

The second project eventually became his first book, *Writing Degree Zero*. Barthes's illness, and the genteel poverty into which he and his family were plunged after the birth of his half brother, must have impressed upon him the gap between appearance and reality. His life-long interest in how 'normality' is constructed through sign-systems was rooted in these experiences.

In 1947, at the age of 32, Barthes left Paris to work in his first full-time job as a librarian, and then as a teacher, at the French Institute in Bucharest. In a crackdown on Western influence, the Romanian communist government expelled all Institute staff in 1949. Barthes left for Egypt where he taught at the University of Alexandria and was introduced to the ideas on advanced linguistics of A.J. Greimas, who was also a lecturer at the university.

He returned to Paris one year later to work as an assistant in the education office of the General Cultural Department in Paris and a lexicographer at CNRS (Centre national de la recherche scientifique). In 1952 he began his regular 'Mythologies' columns for *Lettres Nouvelles*. In 1955 he transferred to the sociology section of CNRS and moved on to become first chairman of the economic and social science section of the Ecole des Hautes Etudes. The death of his grandmother in 1956 endowed him with a substantial legacy. In 1962 he was appointed director of study in the sociology of signs, symbols, and representations at the same institution. In 1976 he was elected to his chair at the College de France. Four years later, soon after the publication of his exquisite book on photography, *Camera Lucida*, (1920) Roland Barthes died, after being knocked down by a van in Paris.

SOCIAL THEORY AND CONTRIBUTIONS

Barthes's Method

His biographer, Louis-Jean Calvet (1994) suggests that Barthes made a virtue out of eclecticism. His early work was influenced by the writings of Sartre, Marx, Hjelmslev, and Saussure. But he never become a disciple of any of them. Instead, he practised a kind of intellectual *flânerie*, roaming widely across the fields of linguistics, sociology, literature, and popular culture, plucking ideas from the terrain and re-arranging them to suit his purposes.

His method of writing was a literal extension of this. Barthes habitually made notes on index cards, filed them, and periodically shuffled them until a structure emerged. It was not structuralism by design. Barthes did not impose structuralist logic upon his material. Rather, he allowed structures to emerge through accretion.

The practice resembles the cut-up technique developed by the novelist William Burroughs during the same period. Burroughs cut up sentences and rearranged the material to develop new meanings which propelled his writing in unanticipated directions. David Bowie adopted the same practice in writing song lyrics. The most singular feature of this method is the faith it places in the liberating effect of chance.

Barthes's method also embraced chance and contingency. His research was rarely exhaustive. With the exception of *Elements of Semiology*, which might be thought of as a callow book in Barthes's *oeuvre*, he never sought to situate himself in relation to existing paradigms or schools of thought. His structuralism was generally practised rather than theoretically elucidated. Sometimes he enjoyed great analytical success. His book *On Racine* (1963) is widely regarded as a landmark of structuralist method in literary criticism. In contrast, The *Fashion System* (1967), which Barthes struggled to perfect over several years, is generally regarded to be a failure. Barthes's elaborate analysis of 'the vestimentary code' is seen as laboured and unconvincing. It fails to grasp, let alone account for, the two main characteristics of fashion, namely the appeal of individuality and the pressure for constant change.

What is structuralism, and what was Barthes's relation to structuralist method? Structuralism posits a systematic and exhaustive interrogation of language and culture. It derived from Saussure's proposition that articulation is informed, and ultimately governed, by the structural system upon which it is based. Saussure presented this system in linguistic terms. He distinguished three dichotomies: *langue* (language) and *parole* (speech), *synchrony* and *diachrony*, and *signifier* and *signfied*. *Langue* is the underlying system upon which communication is founded, and *parole* is articulation itself. *Synchrony* refers to the system of language at any given moment, and *diachrony* to changes in the development of the system. The *signifier* refers to the acoustic or graphic element of articulation, and the *signified*, is the mental concept typically associated with it.

Structuralism posed a radical challenge to both common sense and analytic philosophy. It dismissed essentialist notions of truth and reality. Indeed, Saussure proposed that the individual units of language are arbitrary in the sense that they derive from custom. Meanings are to be understood as effects of the host sign system in which articulation occurs.

Classical structuralism exhibits none of the concern with individuality and style that marks all of Barthes's work. For example, one of the most famous examples of the application of structuralist method in the social sciences is the anthropological work of Claude Lévi-Strauss. Lévi-Strauss (1966) dedicated himself to uncovering the generative grammar of mythical thought. He believed that an underlying structure unites the myths, rituals, oral traditions, kinship systems, and modes of symbolic representation between outwardly different cultures. His method therefore seeks to reveal the shallowness of form and the depth and unity of structure.

Interestingly, as early as *Writing Degree Zero*, Barthes advocated *individuality* as the defining mark of the author. He comprehended this in somatic terms, as deriving from the biological body of the author, the unique corpus of opinions and attitudes. To consolidate the point, he distinguished between language, style, and writing. Language, he proposed, is simply the natural order of meanings unified by habit. It is the 'boundary' or the 'horizon' which literature and criticism must transcend if it is to be 'noticed'. Style, he continued, is the imagery and vocabulary which ultimately spring from the body. They are the representations of the writer's personal experience and the matrix of the events which have shaped him or her. Crucial to the argument is the proposition that writers have no choice in the style of their body of knowledge and attitudes. These matters emerge from the matrix of culture in which the writer is implicated by virtue of birth. In this sense it is correct to posit a fatalistic structure in writing, since no writer can choose the origins or circumstances of his or her birth. However, Barthes refuses to allow what classical structuralism would propose, which is that writers are devoid of choice, since they merely reflect the values of the structural matrix in which they are rooted. His notion of writing emphasizes the 'individuality' and 'commitment' of the writer.

Yet at the same time, Barthes is concerned to deny the inference that writers are free spirits. He contends that they have no power over the effects of their writing on society. There are traces here of a neo-Durkheimian comprehension of society as the ultimate 'social fact', which possesses priority, externality, and constraint over individual intentionality and behaviour. Barthes's discussion of writing appears to reinforce the Leavisite argument that the writer occupies a heroic role in challenging the conventions of language and style. However, his insistence on the pre-eminence of the social structure repudiates the inference. There is an undoubted tension here, which recurs throughout all of his writing.

During his schooldays and terms of illness, Barthes's friends and fellow patients predicted that he would become a novelist. His literary and cultural writing reveal him struggling to find a voice through criticism. It is not a natural voice. He showed no remorse for discarding it after the poetic turn to post-structuralism in the 1970s. Yet this most *prima facie* confident of critics was ill at ease with the prospect of finally revealing himself through an imagined work of fiction. *A Lover's Discourse* (1977a) and *Camera Lucida* (1982) adopt fictional and poetic techniques yet remain anchored in the tradition of criticism. While Barthes speculated about writing a work of fiction, and shared with friends this intention, he died before the ambition could be realized.

With *S/Z* (1970), Barthes appeared to recognize that his affair with structuralism had run its course. Henceforward, the subjects of his publications switch track freely. *S/Z* is itself an apocalyptic reading of Balzac's short story 'Sazzarine'. Barthes divided the 30-page novella into 561 elements (or 'lexia'). He distinguished five codes to facilitate understanding the story: *hermeneutic* refers to questions of interpretation; *seme* refers to the system of allusions, metaphors and connotation; *symbolic*, refers to the network of symbolic oppositions, such as light and shade, hot and cold; *action* refers to the details of the narrative content; *reference* refers to the network of cultural codes relating to places, events, personalities, stereotypes, and so on. All of the hydraulics of orthodox structuralist analysis seem to be here. Indeed, Barthes's identification of the plurality of codes may be interpreted as constituting a refinement of structuralist literary criticism.

However, no sooner does Barthes set out his stall, than he destabilizes the expectations of the reader. For example, he disarms structuralist rhetoric by noting that the semic code is uneven and untrustworthy (1970: 19). He describes the lexias, which are initially adduced as the principal critical organizing principle in the study, as devices to 'interrupt' the text so as to deny cohesion (1970: 13, 15). He suggests that the structuralist principle of uniformity should be replaced by a new principle of *différence* which represents the fecundity and play of language. Narrative itself is attacked as a seductive code which lulls the reader into docile submission. Barthes rounds upon the act of reading and calls upon readers to become creative agents in elucidating the text.

Perhaps Barthes was influenced by the *auteur* school of French cinema. In an essay written in the same year that *S/Z* was published, Barthes (1970, reprinted in Barthes, 1986) describes the method used to analyse 'Sarrasine' as reading the book in 'slow-motion'. At about the same time, the leading *auteur* Jean Luc Godard insisted that films needed to have a beginning, a middle, and an end, but not necessarily in that order. *S/Z* is the equivalent in literary and cultural criticism of this argument. Barthes seeks to break with the received, bourgeois style of reading which presupposes the primacy of the author, a linear narrative, and symmetry between character and plot. In his hands the text becomes a maze of meaning: dazzling, seductive, unstable, unravelling in unforeseen perspectives. Above all, Barthes celebrates the 'play' of meaning and the 'joy' of reading as a creative agent.

Following *S/Z*, he embarked, consecutively, upon discussions of the sign-world of Japan, the almost erotic joys of language and interpretation, the mentality of the lover, the qualities of the writer Sollers, and the magic of photography. In each case, his work followed an *idée fixe* which he explores for pleasure rather than for the sake of academic integrity. Textual hedonism is the main thread linking Barthes's writing in this period. For all the weight he placed upon the corporeal body of the writer he writes almost exclusively about words and their role in representing and refracting meaning. He never shows the slightest interest in testing his ideas through empirical or comparative analysis. Surprisingly, although he contends that the function of myth is to render what is in fact a historically specific construction into an unalterable, taken-for-granted, natural 'given' of life, he never seriously tries to assemble an historical perspective to demonstrate the origins and evolution of the process. To be sure, he scorns 'the reality effect' of history, pointing to the 'imperious warrant' of historical science (1986: 127). For Barthes, the 'rational' exposition of history is merely an 'imaginary narration', the principles of which are no different from the epic, the novel, or drama. In a passage which both thrillingly reveals the exhaustion he now felt with orthodox structuralism, and conveys his sense of liberation with post-structuralist method, Barthes writes:

> The critical aspect of the old system is *interpretation*, i.e. the operation by which one assigns to a set of confused or even contradictory appearances a unitary structure, a deep meaning, a 'veritable' explanation. Hence, interpretation must gradually give way to a new discourse, whose goal is not the revelation of unique or 'true' structure but the establishment of an interplay of multiple structures: an establishment itself *written*, i.e. uncoupled from the truth of speech; more precisely, it is the relations which organize these concomitant structures, subject to still unknown rules, which must constitute the object of a new theory. (Barthes, 1986: 154)

Interestingly, Barthes hardly ever refers back to his earlier work. Even in the pronounced structuralist phase of his early writing, there is little sense of the intrinsic properties of an entire system of thought evolving. After *S/Z* (1970), each book is a new adventure.

S/Z is generally interpreted as the start of the post-structuralist phase in Barthes's thought. In it he abandoned the quest for a quasi-scientific understanding of literature and culture. Under the influence of Jakobson, Benveniste, Lacan, Kristeva, and the *Tel Quel* group, he now explored the 'happy Babel' of intertextuality (1975). As against Saussure, he reconceptualized language as an 'open network' where meanings are structured but do not obey laws of closure (1977b: 126–7). The very commitment to this principle can be interpreted as playful, for it is a blatant contradiction. Structure without closure is reminiscent of Stuart Hall's (1986) advocacy of 'Marxism without guarantees' . It attempts to retain the authority of structuralist reasoning while simultaneously denying the *sine qua non* of structuralist thought.

Concomitant with it was a new, consuming passion for the play of meaning, the 'incessant sliding of the signified under the signifier' (Lacan, 1977: 154) and the plurality of the text. Gradually, Barthes (1977b) abandoned the notion that the authorial voice or the sign system possessed pre-eminence over articulation. He maintained that the reader plays a creative part in re-aestheticizing and redefining texts. Following Foucault (1970) whose antihumanism now announced 'the death of man', Barthes (1977b) referred to 'the death of the author'. *A Lover's Discourse* (1977a) is organized alphabetically, so as to overcome both the implication of a pre-eminent authorial voice and to deny the base/superstructure dichotomy of structuralism. The effect is to radically decentre the relationship between the author and text as the focus of literary and cultural criticism. The reader and consumer emerge as fertile agents, husbanding meaning out of the cultural object in ways which are unforseen by the author. The text itself becomes a seed-bed of exploding meaning. Every reading is a reinvention, no reading is ever final. The act of reading becomes an act of conception. The idea of an endlessly conceiving text perhaps came from Bakhtin's (1981) dialogic method which sought to express the 'polyphonic' character of the text. In Barthes's hands it became a crusade against structuralist and scientific rhetoric.

True to the basically random, hedonistic form of post-structuralist analysis, the subjects of Barthes's writing in this period were seldom chosen for reasons of topicality or strategy. He continued to see himself as a socialist, but his work was never overtly political. Calvet (1994: 165) records that he regarded the student-worker-led protests and occupations in Paris during the revolutionary 'moment' of May 1968 as 'vulgar' and 'pointless'. Similarly, he displayed no interest in ethnic struggles in Morocco during his year as visiting professor at the University of Rabat (1969–70). Indeed, throughout his life his political involvement was concentrated at a textual rather than a grounded (material) level. Despite the antibourgeois tone of his criticism in *Mythologies*, Barthes himself exemplified solid bourgeois values, notably in his dislike of 'hysteria', his love of calm, and his respect for good manners and propriety.

An obsession with style is the dominant motif of both his structuralist and post-structuralist thought. Eventually, he distinguished between two kinds of writing: the *écrivain*, which is the instrumental, densely conditioned prose typical of orthodox academic and research writing; and the *écrivant* which is the more personal, idiosyncratic prose associated with the creative writer. From the early 1970s, the latter became Barthes's trademark.

Barthes died with an unwritten novel in mind. Following the commercial success of *A Lover's Discourse*, and his oft-stated dislike of the conventions of academic life, it is conceivable that, had he recovered from his injuries, he would have turned to full time fiction. At all events, Calvet's biography implies that in the months prior to his untimely death, Barthes was oppressed with the thought that his life of criticism had run its course (Calvet, 1994: 242–7). This, and the *volte face* towards post-structuralism in the 1970s, has prompted some observers to be sceptical about the depth of his former attachment to structuralism.

Denotation and Connotation

Barthes's status as a founding father of cultural studies and cultural sociology resides in his application of the signifier/signified dichotomy in the study of popular culture. Barthes took over this tool from Saussure, but he massively elaborated it by examining the nature of sign systems in advertising, cinema, television, sport, travel guides, agony columns, science fiction, celebrity, race, food, and many other elements of popular culture. From Barthes came the dual message that nothing in culture was what it seemed to be, and that all of popular culture could be decoded. Not a little of the appeal of this argument lay in its reflexivity. Barthes's method stood the test of being turned upon itself to reveal that even the author symptomizes 'naturalized' codes of communication. It was as if Barthes had dropped a spoon of liver salts into social and cultural analysis, and unleashed a ferment of dissolving hierarchies and melting presuppositions. It was hugely, endlessly exciting.

Yet all indeed was not as it seemed. Barthes himself became distressed when his students in May 1968 taunted him with the slogan that 'structures do not take to the streets' (Calvet, 1968: 164–70). Barthes had not yet broken with his structuralist moorings. The students' understanding of transcendent agency fell foul of his somewhat prosaic belief in the necessity of limits, imposed by the priority, externality, and constraint of the social order. They wanted the world, and they wanted it now.

Similarly, despite the implication that meaning is simply a link in the great chain of decoding, Barthes's left-wing sentiments pointed to bourgeois class rule as an ultimate limit in popular culture. For Barthes it was the bourgeois power structure that naturalized distortion in culture and everyday life. The purpose of distortion was to perpetuate bourgeois domination. The roots of this standpoint probably lie in his early reading of Marx. Be that as it may, the attempt to fuse Marxist structuralism with Saussure's structuralism was rather forced.

Mounin (1977) was one of the first critics to observe that Barthes's application of Saussure's dichotomy was idiosyncratic. It will be remembered that Saussure posited that meaning is arbitrary. For him, the meaning of a word derives from its position in the language chain of which it is a part. In contrast, Barthes attributed symbolic meaning to elements in sign systems. That is, he read signs as carrying an ideological payload. The classical example is the famous analysis in *Mythologies* of a *Paris Match* cover showing a picture of a young Negro soldier in a French uniform saluting, presumably the French flag. Barthes writes:

> Whether naively or not, I see very well what it signifes to me: that France is a great Empire, that all her sons, without colour discrimination, faithfully serve under her flag, and that there is no better answer to detractors of an alleged colonialism then the zeal shown by this Negro in serving

> his so-called oppressors. I am therefore faced with a greater semiological system: there is a signifier, itself already formed with a previous system (*a black soldier is giving the French salute*); there is a signified (it is a purposeful mixture of Frenchness and militariness); and finally there is a presence of the signified through the signifier. (Barthes, 1957: 126–7, emphasis in original)

A remarkable feature of this famous example is the inexactitude which underpins its apparent precision. Barthes *infers* that the French soldier is saluting 'with eyes uplifted' to the fold of the tricolour (p. 126). It is an indispensable move in his argument, because it supports his contention that the subconscious effect of the photograph is to reinforce nationalism and the merit of colonialism. Yet is it not also an additional example of his eclecticism and intellectual *flanerie* for it is asserted and not demonstrated through empirical research?

Leaving that aside, one reason why the example is frequently cited is that it neatly encapsulates the distinction between denotation and connotation which is at the heart of Barthes's analysis of myth. The distinction was originally made by the Danish linguist, Louis Hjelmslev (1961). Denotation refers to the factual articulation of an idea or graphic image. Connotation refers to the chain of representations that the idea or graphic image signifies. In the hands of Barthes, connotation becomes the instrument of ideology. The implicit meaning of the signified becomes the happy hunting ground of the semiologist.

Again, it is worth noting that Barthes's understanding of the effect of ideology focuses upon style rather than content. To refer back to the *Paris Match* cover of the Negro soldier for a moment, what interests Barthes is the lighting of the shot, the 'buttonholing' arrangement of body and representation, the cropping of the picture and, of course, the ideological function performed in the selection of the image as a feature cover for the magazine. As to the roles of the photographer, editor, and publisher, it is merely assumed that they are ideological labourers, salaried by the bourgeoisie, intent on presenting language as truth. There is a critical political economy implicit in this reading, but it is unelaborated and untested. Barthes leaves it to the reader to infer the necessary connections. The whole process by which bourgeois class rule is posited to naturalize distortion in popular culture is undertheorized.

Today, many of Barthes's mythologies read like sophisticated, self-reflexive versions of the radical nineteenth century *feuilletons* of the *Latin Quartier* broadsheets. They are designed to disaggregate what are taken to be the taken-for-granted assumptions of bourgeois thought. They do not situate themselves into a general historical context, nor do they seek to replace bourgeois categories. Their function is esentially critical.

Beyond all doubt, they fulfilled this function in the late 1950s and early 1960s. Anglo-American readers encountered Barthes apparently slashing through myths at a moment in which the homespun platitudes of the Macmillan–Eisenhower governments seemed increasingly indigestible. Barthes's method seemed to promise liberation from the sanctimonious cold moralism of the age.

Revealingly, when Barthes attempted to reprise the style of *Mythologies* in a weekly newspaper column for *Le Nouvel Observateur* in 1978–9, the exercise ran for only three and a half months. Barthes's criticism of consumer society in the 1950s benefited from a clear target (the values of petit bourgeois culture) and affiliation to a clear alternative (socialism).

By the time that Barthes took up his pen again, the position of intellectuals and society was less clear cut. In the time of *Mythologies* it was safe to assume that culture and character were orientated to the models forged under war of liberation from the Nazi threat. Heterosexuality was posited as the dominant and 'natural' form of sexual identity; nationalism was the dominant collective ideology; people felt bound by their relation to class, ethnicity, subculture and so on.

By the late 1970s none of these assumptions was self-evident. Culture and character were now recognized as polyvalent and unfixed. In his later work, Barthes (1977b) himself proposed that it is inadmissible to read any single code of identity, association or practice as paramount. On the contrary, culture and character are composed of a variety of codes which blend and clash in constant interplay.

This seemed radical and liberating in the 1950s and 1960s, when the governance of everyday life seemed to be dominated by uniform codes of behaviour. But by the late 1970s, the question of the theoretical formations emerging from the attack on dominant codes was already rising to the top of the agenda. By 1978, the empire had already struck back, and the turn in cultural criticism was leading to the postcolonial, postfeminist, postsociety positions that gained ascendancy in the 1980s and 1990s. Compared with these developments, Barthes in the 1970s seemed to be beating a hollow drum.

APPRAISAL OF KEY ADVANCES AND CONTROVERSIES

Barthes's application of Saussure's signifier/signified dichotomy was immensely influential. Traces of it are apparent in Derrida's method of deconstruction; Bhabha's (1994), Said's (1978, 1993), and Spivak's (1988, 1990) postcolonialism; the postmodernism of Baudrillard (1983, 1987) and Jameson (1991) and Stuart Hall's (1986, 1988) interest in hybridity and diaspora. In addition, Barthes's application of the signifier/signified dichotomy established the principle that culture is structured like a language. This has been an important foundational element in the development of cultural studies. Without doubt, Barthes is a seminal figure in modern semiology and cultural studies. His assured prose style, and work on codes of signification, became a role model for a widely practised form of cultural analysis.

But his work is also open to basic objections. Two are of note here. First, Barthes failed to counterbalance his advocacy of the plurality of the text with a tenable epistemology. After *S/Z*, his thought progressively exhibited symptoms of solipsism. Because this became more pronounced in his post-structuralist phase, he grew increasingly divorced from conceptualizing categories in terms of transpersonal experience. In his College de France inaugural lecture he surprised, and dismayed, many in his audience, by announcing bluntly that *language is fascist* (Merquior, 1986: 159; Calvet, 1994: 217). Barthes meant that language is ideologically impregnated and therefore, at the subconscious level, compelled subjective capitulation. The implication was stark: communication could not be taken on trust. The very categories we use to make sense of the world are shaped by the suffocating hand of ideology.

The best that can be said about this is that it was a precipitate declaration. The only pre-emptive measure Barthes identified is to develop a writerly refusal to accept boundaries. Transcendence is therefore restricted to episodic interludes of 'ecstacy' achieved by penetrating the veil of received language. But this prejudged that 'belonging' and 'co-operation' are exiled from the realm of human achievement. It discounted the sociability of human nature, and concomitant relations of trust and respect that make social agency possible. Instead it fell back upon a neo-Kantian view of the individual and knowledge. History itself was reduced to a text. Causal explanation, in the Weberian sense of the term, is invalidated.

Although there are obvious analytical advantages in treating history and culture in textual terms, it is not satisfactory to treat readings as equivalent. Napoleon may have believed that he defeated Wellington and Blucher at the Battle of Waterloo in 1815, but if he did, he was deluded. Historical events are not merely 'referential illusions' as Barthes (1986: 148) alleges. They alter the course of common experience. Yet without an epistemological framework, Barthes supplied no way of differentiating between interpretations. His work yielded a cacophony of interpretation, but advanced no conclusions or stable programme of research.

Secondly, what emerges most powerfully from Barthes's work is an approach to culture which emphasized the aestheticization of everyday life. For an author who first made his name as a literary critic, his concentration on the visual codes of reference is remarkable. In successive publications in the 1970s, he transformed Japan into an 'empire of signs'; the lover's body became a monitor of flickering data; and his last full-length published work was a book about photographs.

To some extent, this interest in visual codes is the natural response to the media explosion that occurred in Barthes's own lifetime. By the mid-1950s, wartime austerity in the West had been replaced with rampant consumer culture. Advertising, magazines, and above all, television, deluged consumers with a tidal wave of visual data. Style and visual stimulation became omnipresent, prompting some sociologists to speculate that the human character type in industrial societies was becoming more 'other-directed'. Lowenthal (1968) anticipated the trend in an article published towards the end of the war. His content analysis of a sample of popular magazines in the USA concluded that the popular role models of American society were shifting from work-centred personalities to consumption-centred personalities. The role-model of desirable achievement was switching from nineteenth century figures like Thomas Edison, towards the icons of 1950s consumer culture, Marlon Brando, Marilyn Monroe, and James Dean. Seen in this light, Barthes's interest in mythologies is the natural expression of the enlargement of the visual codes in popular culture which occurred in the decade following the end of the war.

Yet if this development was eye-catching in Barthes's thought, it never produced a satisfactory corresponding theory of visual culture. Barthes's semiology is largely descriptive. It speculates on the implicit meanings connoted by signifieds. When the discussion moves towards questions of political economy, the analysis becomes woolly and clichéd. For example, although he consistently targets the bourgeoisie, his analysis is under-theorized. It amounts to little more than a version of the discredited dominant ideology thesis, in which the operation of class rule is taken for granted, but never historicized, or elucidated, through empirical analysis (Abercombie et al., 1980).

Perhaps one reason why Barthes's discussion of dominant class rule is so unconvincing, is that he realized that the consistent application of the signifier/signified dichotomy problematized authority *per se*. After semiology, critical analysis could no longer be oriented to the goal of replacing one class with another, or contrasting the values of one power formation with those of an alternative. This is because the connotation of all denoted value was elevated to the centre of investigation. Barthes takes an important insight, namely that meaning is interpretive, and runs with it like a hare to the invalid postulate that collective meaning is impossible. Transcendence necessarily becomes an accomplishment of the individual. Moreover, since semiology teaches that signs are unstable, transcendence must be conditional and temporary.

Barthes explored the implications of this in his post-structuralist writing. While there are passages of resounding insight in this work, there is, in general, an absurdist quality to the work. Because no final interpretation is possible, literary and cultural analysis is transformed into a sort of relay event, in which writers operate like track-runners who pass on the baton of interpretation, but never reach the finishing line. Moreover, because language is posited as impregnated with ideological connotations, the shared task of struggling to make sense of the world is violated.

Barthes took over and reinforced the polarity between the individual and society which classical sociology did so much to try and transcend. In his early work there was no need to posit language as a structure possessing priority, externality, and constraint over articulation. As the Chomskyan tradition makes clear, language is a condition of human *embodiment*. As social beings we are equipped with semiotic consciousness and we have the capacity to isolate ideology and co-operate to resist its effect. The reasons why this consciousness is distorted are to be found in the political economy of society. The codes of communication are a symptom of power, not the source of power.

The work of the later Barthes regarded culture as a play form, albeit a deadly one, since it controlled personality and behaviour through semiotic manipulation. In some respects, his position recalls aspects of the Frankfurt School thesis that capitalist culture is 'one dimensional'. However, Barthes never follows Marcuse (1964) in declaring that one dimensional society is 'without opposition'. On the contrary, he recognizes resistance, but he defines it primarily in aesthetic terms. For Barthes, resistance is individual pleasure. He speaks of the 'scandalous pleasure' of what he calls *atopic* reading (1975: 23). Reading here is used in the widest sense to refer to the interpretation of cultural codes, whether they be graphic, visual, aural, electronic or spiritual. By 'atopic', Barthes means aesthetic interventions which create a surplus of meaning over the bourgeois codes which control culture. Through creating surplus meaning, individuals problematize petit bourgeois codes of cultural regulation because they expose *limits*. This is why Barthes described atopic reading as scandalous: it offends petit bourgeois proprieties and reveals cultural order to be a construct of class rule.

Barthes never lost the desire to shock. In the structuralist phase of his work he argued that structure, not self, is the seat of meaning. This was a calculated affront to the petit bourgeois faith in the freedom of the individual and the power of rational communication to solve problems. In the post-structuralist phase of his work, he denies that meaning is possible, except in momentary episodes of aestheticized bliss. The very language that petit bourgeois culture uses to make sense of itself is condemned as 'fascist'. His post-structuralist work is unsatisfactory because it fails to reveal the connections between aesthetics and political economy.

In his last book, Barthes confessed to a lifelong 'desperate resistance to any reductive system' (1982: 8). The paradox is that the dichotomy between individual and society was the reductive system that underpinned all of his writing. By the end of his life, Barthes could conceive of no revolt higher, or more complete, than the revolt into style. His mistrust of collective formations and rational co-operative strategies left him with no place to go except aesthetics. The conviction that this is sufficient to explain culture and society is the perhaps the biggest mythology of all.

BARTHES'S MAJOR WORKS

Barthes, R. (1957) *Mythologies*. St Albans: Paladin.
Barthes, R. (1963) *On Racine*. New York: Octagon.
Barthes, R. (1965) *Writing Degree Zero* and *Elements of Semiology*. Boston: Beacon Press.
Barthes, R. (1967) *The Fashion System*. London: Cape.
Barthes, R. (1970) *S/Z*. New York: Hill & Wang.
Barthes, R. (1975) *The Pleasure of the Text*. London: Jonathan Cape.
Barthes, R. (1977a) *A Lover's Discourse*. New York: Hill & Wang.
Barthes, R. (1977b) *Image-Music-Text*. London: Fontana.
Barthes, R. (1982) *Camera Lucida*. New York: Hillewang.
Barthes, R. (1986) *The Rustle of Language*. Oxford: Blackwell.

SECONDARY REFERENCES

Abercombie. N., Hill, S. and Turner, B.S. (1980) *The Dominant Ideology Thesis*. London: Allen & Unwin.
Bakhtin, M. (1981) *The Dialogic Imagination*, Austin, University of Texas Press.
Baudrillard, J. (1983) *Simulations*. New York: Semiotext.

Baudrillard, J. (1987) *The Ecstacy of Communication*. New York: Semiotext.

Bhabha, H. (1994) *The Location of Culture*. London: Routledge.

Calvet, L.-J. (1994) *Roland Barthes: A Biography*. Cambridge: Polity.

Foucault, M. (1970) *The Order of Things*. London: Tavistock.

Hall, S. (1986) 'The problem of ideology: Marxism without guarantees,' *Journal of Communication Inquiry*, 10 (2): 28–44.

Hall, S. (1988) 'New ethnicities', in K. Mercer (ed.), *Black Film. British Cinema*. London: BFI/ICA Documents. 20–27.

Hjelmslev, L (1961) *Prolegomena to a Theory of Language*. Madison: University of Wisconsin Press.

Jameson, F. (1991) *Postmodernism, or, The Cultural Logic of Late Capitalism*. Durham, NC: Duke University Press.

Lacan, J. (1977) *Ecrits*. London: Tavistock.

Lévi-Strauss, C. (1966) *The Savage Mind*. London: Weidenfeld & Nicolson.

Lowenthal, L. (1968) 'Biographies in popular magazines'; reprinted as 'The Triumph of Mass Idols' in *Literature, Popular Culture & Society*. Palo Alto: Pacific Books, 1961.

Marcuse, H. (1964) *One-Dimensional Man*. London: Abacus.

Merquior, J. (1986) *From Prague to Paris*. London: Verso.

Mounin, G. (1977) *Semiologies Des Textes Litteraires*. Athlone: London

Picard, R. (1969) *New Criticism or New Fraud?* Pullman: Washington State University Press.

Riesman, D. (1950) *The Lonely Crowd*. New York: Basic.

Rylance, R. (1994) *Roland Barthes*. Hemel Hempstead: Harvester-Wheatsheaf.

Said, E. (1978) *Orientalism*. London: RKP.

Said, E. (1993) *Cultural and Imperialism*. London: Chatto & Windus.

Spivak, G. (1988) *In Other Worlds*. London: Routledge.

Spivak, G. (1990) *The Post-Colonial Critic*. London: Routledge.

Storey, J. (1993) *An Introductory Guide to Cultural Theory and Popular Culture*. Hemel Hempstead: Harvester-Wheatsheaf.

15

Julia Kristeva

KELLY OLIVER

BIOGRAPHICAL DETAILS AND THEORETICAL CONTEXT

Julia Kristeva was born in 1941 in Bulgaria. She was educated by French nuns, studied literature and worked as a journalist before going to Paris in 1966 to do graduate work with Lucien Goldmann and Roland Barthes. While in Paris she finished her doctorate in French literature, became involved in the influential journal *Tel Quel*, and began psychoanalytic training. In 1979 she finished her training as a psychoanalyst. Currently, Kristeva is a professor of linguistics at the University of Paris VII and a regular visiting professor at Columbia University. In addition to her work as a practising psychoanalyst and her theoretical writings, Kristeva is a novelist.

Kristeva's work reflects her diverse background. Her writing is an intersection between philosophy, psychoanalysis, linguistics, and cultural and literary theory. She developed the science of what she calls 'semanalysis', which is a combination of Freud's psychoanalysis and Saussure's and Peirce's semiology. With this new science Kristeva challenges traditional psychoanalytic theory, linguistic theory, and philosophy.

Kristeva's goal is to bring the speaking body, complete with drives, back into philosophy and linguistics. In one of her most influential books, *Revolution in Poetic Language*, she criticizes both Husserlian Phenomenology and Saussurean linguistics for formulating theories of the subject and language that cannot account for the processes through which a subject speaks. There are two ways in which Kristeva brings the speaking body back into theories of language. First, she proposes that bodily drives are discharged through language. Second, she maintains that the structure or logic of signification is already operating in the material body. On Kristeva's analysis language is in the body and the body is in language.

Kristeva's most influential contribution to philosophy of language has been her distinction between the semiotic and the symbolic elements of signification. All signification is made up of these two elements in varying proportions. The semiotic element is the organization of drives in signifying practices. It is associated with rhythms and tones that are meaningful parts of language and yet do not represent or signify something. Rhythms and tones do not represent bodily drives; rather bodily drives are discharged through rhythms and tones. The symbolic element of language, on the other hand, is the domain of position and judgment. It is associated with the grammar or structure of language that enables it to signify something. This symbolic element of language should not, however, be confused with Lacan's notion of the Symbolic. Lacan's notion of the Symbolic includes the entire realm of signification, while Kristeva's symbolic is one element of that realm.

The dialectical oscillation between the semiotic and the symbolic is what makes signification possible. Without the symbolic, we have only sounds or delirious babble. But without the semiotic, signification would be empty and we would not speak. The semiotic provides the motivation for engaging in signifying processes; we have a bodily need to communicate. The symbolic provides the structure necessary to communicate. Both elements are essential to signification. And it is the tension between them that makes signification dynamic. The semiotic both motivates signification and threatens the symbolic element. The semiotic provides the negativity and the symbolic provides the stasis or stability that keeps signification both dynamic and structured. The semiotic makes change, even structural change, possible.

In addition to proposing that bodily drives make their way into language, Kristeva maintains that the logic of signification is already present in the material of the body. Once again combining psychoanalytic theory and linguistics, Kristeva relies on both Lacan's account of the infant's entrance into language and Saussure's account of the play of signifiers. Following Freud, Lacan maintains that the entrance into language requires separation, particularly from the maternal body. Saussure maintains that signifiers signify in relation to one another through their differences. Combining these two theses, it seems that language operates according to principles of separation and difference, as well as identification. Kristeva argues that the principles or structures of separation, difference, and identification are operating in the body even before the infant begins to use language.

She calls the bodily structures of separation the 'logic of rejection'. For Kristeva the body, like signification, operates according to an oscillation between instability and stability, or negativity and stases. For example, the process of metabolization is a process that oscillates between instability and stability, between incorporation/identity and separation/differentiation: food is taken into the body and metabolized and expelled from the body. From the time of birth the infant's body is engaging in processes of separation; anality is the prime example. Birth itself is also an experience of separation, one body violently separated from another. The bodily operations of separation and incorporation prepare the way for differentiation and identification necessary for signification.

Part of Kristeva's motivation for emphasizing these bodily separations and privations is to provide an alternative to the Lacanian model of language acquisition. Lacan's account of signification and self-consciousness begins with the mirror stage and the paternal metaphor's substitution of the law of the father for the desire of the mother. On the traditional psychoanalytic model of both Freud and Lacan the child enters the social or language out of fear of castration threats. The child experiences its separation from the maternal body as a tragic loss and consoles itself with words instead. Paternal threats make words the only, if inadequate, alternative to psychosis. Kristeva insists, however, that separation begins prior to the mirror stage or Oedipal situation and that this separation is not only painful but also pleasurable. She insists that the child enters the social and language not just because of paternal threats but also because of paternal love.

Kristeva criticizes the traditional account because it cannot adequately explain the child's move to signification. If the only thing that motivates the move to signification is threats and the pain of separation, then why would anyone make this move? Why not remain in the safe haven of the maternal body and refuse the social and signification with its threats? Kristeva suggests that if the accounts of Freud and Lacan were correct, then more people would be psychotic. She maintains that separation also must be pleasurable and this explains the move away from the maternal body and into signification. Just as the separations inherent in the material of the body are pleasurable, even if they are also sometimes painful, so too the separations that make signification possible are pleasurable. The logic of signification is already operating in the body and therefore the transition to language is not as dramatic and mysterious as traditional psychoanalytic theory makes it out to be.

SOCIAL THEORY AND CONTRIBUTIONS

Kristeva's alternative account of the infant's entrance into the social and signification complicates both the traditional psychoanalytic accounts of the paternal function and of the maternal function. In addition to the Freudian or Lacanian father of the law, Kristeva develops what she calls the 'imaginary father'. The imaginary father provides the loving support necessary for the child to leave behind the maternal body. Kristeva argues that the paternal threats are not enough to encourage the infant to leave the maternal body. Moreover, paternal threats cannot work as a counterbalance or compensation for the abjection of the maternal body necessary in order to enter the social. Kristeva maintains that individuation requires what she calls 'abjection'. The most powerful location of abjection in the development of any individual is the maternal body. In *Powers of Horror,* Kristeva describes the abject as that which calls borders into questions; and in an individual's development the maternal body poses the greatest threat to the border of the subject.

For Kristeva, before the mother can become an object for the infant, she becomes an abject. Through this process of abjection the infant finds the maternal body disgusting, if still fascinating, and is able to leave it behind provided that it has support from a loving imaginary father. It is only by leaving the maternal body that the infant can enter the realm of signification through which they can subsequently take the mother as an object. Still within the phase of abjection, prior to the distinction between subject and object, the infant struggles with separation. Abjection is the process through which the infant overcomes its identification with the mother. The male child can later eroticize the abject maternal body in order to love a woman by splitting the disgusting abject body from the fascinating abject body. The female child, on the other hand, too closely identifies with the maternal female body to split the object and instead splits herself by identifying with the abject maternal body. This is why in *Black Sun* Kristeva calls feminine sexuality a melancholy sexuality. Within heterosexist culture a woman can neither eroticize the abject maternal body nor leave it behind. Kristeva maintains that instead the maternal body becomes a 'Thing' locked in the crypt of her psyche.

Unlike Freud and Lacan, who attribute language acquisition and socialization to the paternal function and ignore the function of the mother as anything other than the primary object or part object, Kristeva emphasizes the importance of the maternal function in the social development of individuals. She insists that there is regulation and structure in the maternal body and the child's relationship to that body. Before the paternal law is in place the infant is subject to maternal regulations, what Kristeva calls 'the law before the law'. While in the womb the foetus is engaged in processes of exchange with the maternal body that are regulated by that body. After birth, there are further exchanges between the maternal body and the infant. The mother monitors and regulates what goes into, and what comes out of, the infant's body. Language acquisition and socialization, insofar as they develop out of regulations and law, have their foundations in the maternal function prior to the Law of the Father of traditional psychoanalysis.

In addition to revolutionizing the position and importance of the maternal function in psychoanalytic theory, Kristeva revolutionizes the paternal function. In *Tales of Love* she suggests that the paternal function does not just include threats and law. The father is not merely the stern father of the law. Rather, she proposes a loving father, 'the imaginary father'. The imaginary father provides the loving support that enables the child to abject its mother and enter the social. Kristeva describes the imaginary father as a mother–father conglomerate. In her scenario the imaginary father performs the function of love. It is the child's feeling that it is loved that allows the child to separate from both the safe haven of the maternal body and the abjected maternal body; threats and laws alone do not provide this necessary support.

In *Powers of Horror*, Kristeva argues that collective identity formation is analogous to individual identity formation. She claims that abjection is co-extensive in both individual and collective identity, which operate according to the same logic of abjection. Whereas individuals marks their difference from the maternal body through a process of abjection, society marks off its difference from animals through a process of abjection. On her analysis, however, the animal realm has been associated with the maternal, which ultimately represents the realm of nature from which human culture must separate to assert its humanity. Kristeva's analysis of the process of abjecting the maternal as inherent in social formation is an elaboration of Freud's thesis that the social is founded on the murder of the father and the incest taboo. Kristeva's provocative reading of the incest taboo as the operations of abjection through which we attempt to guarantee the separation of culture from nature is useful to cultural theorists interested in the dynamics of marginalization and exclusion, especially insofar as Kristeva continually elaborates various ways that the repressed abject returns. The process of abjection is never completed. Rather, like everything repressed, it is bound to return.

Although Kristeva maintains that all language and culture set up separations and order by repressing maternal authority, she also insists that this repressed maternal authority returns in religious rituals, literature, and art. In fact, some of her work suggests that all art is the result of a sublimation of the repressed maternal relation, in other words a form of incest. While in *Powers of Horror* Kristeva does not address sexual difference in relation to abjection, in interviews and later work, including *Black Sun*, Kristeva indicates some of the ways in which the process of abjection works differently for males and females. We could say that the incest taboo affects men and women differently and therefore the repressed maternal returns differently in relation to men and women. Given that men can separate from the maternal body and enter the social, they can also return to it through art and literature without threatening their position within the social order. Art and literature that expresses what Kristeva identifies as the semiotic maternal or abject element of signification is revolutionary insofar as it brings the repressed maternal back into signification and the social order. While the male artist can access this repressed maternal semiotic and still maintain his position within the social order, the female artist's return to the maternal semiotic threatens her social position, which is always more precarious because of her identification with the abjected maternal body. In other words, it is more dangerous for a woman to articulate the excluded or repressed maternal body in her work because as a woman within a patriarchal culture she is already marginal. If a woman identifies with the semiotic in her work, she risks not being taken seriously by the social order. In terms of everyday experience, this means that men can be more experimental than women can be in their work and still be taken seriously.

On the other hand, women can take up the law in revolutionary ways. Kristeva suggests that from her marginal position within the social order, a woman can challenge the symbolic element of signification merely by embracing the law or reason as a woman. When a marginal person inserts herself into the subject position at the centre of culture, she changes the effect of that position. This is why in 'From One Identity to an Other' Kristeva (1980a) claims that perhaps it takes a woman or another marginal figure to propel theoretical reason into infinite analysis of its own subject position as always a subject-in-process (1975: 146). Women also have a privileged access to the maternal body through childbirth. In 'Stabat Mater' in Kristeva, 1983) and 'Motherhood According to Bellini' (in Kristeva, 1980a) Kristeva makes the provocative claim that the desire to have children is a sublimated incestuous desire for reunion with the maternal body. While artists gain access to the repressed maternal body through their work, the mother gains access to the repressed maternal body through childbirth, which is a type of reunion with her own mother.

The repressed maternal within culture is the luminal figure in Kristeva's analysis of the foreigner in *Strangers to Ourselves*. Ultimately it is the maternal body that exiles leave behind and the maternal body that as foreigners they conjure in the imagination of the new culture. On Kristeva's analysis, the body itself is always a screen for the repressed maternal body. So, any uncanniness associated with the body points to the return of the repressed maternal, both familiar and unfamiliar to us. Just as she brings the speaking body back into language by putting language into the body, she brings the subject into the place of the other by putting the other into the subject. Just as the pattern and logic of language is already found within the body, the pattern and logic of otherness is already found within the subject. This is why the subject is never stable but always in process/on trail.

Kristeva suggests that if we can learn to live with the return of the repressed other within our own psyches, then we can learn to live with others. On the one hand, living with others confronts us with our own otherness, the stranger within our own identity. On the other hand, familiarizing ourselves with the stranger within helps us deal with the strangers in our midst. Otherness and strangeness are the products of repression and abjection, which set up the border of our own proper identity both as individuals and as social collectives. For Kristeva, there is an intimate connection between our relations to our own psychic economies and our relations to strangers or foreigners. In *Strangers to Ourselves,* she says 'to worry or to smile, such is the choice when we are assailed by the strange; our decision depends on how familiar we are with our own ghosts' (p. 289). This is because being with others necessitates being with our own otherness.

Xenophobia, then, is the collective analogue to individual phobia in which the abject is excluded as threatening and dangerous in order to justify shutting it out or killing it. Just as individuals need some counterbalance to support abjection so that it does not become phobia, collectivities also need some cultural counterbalance as a 'rebirth with and against abjection'. On the individual level the counterbalance for abjection is the loving imaginary father; on the collective level the counterbalance seems to involve the imagination engaged through interpretation and self-reflective analysis. Kristeva suggests that if we could acknowledge the death drive, there would be fewer deaths.

The acknowledgment of drives is possible only through an elaborative interpretation supported by imagination. Kristeva argues throughout her work that while religion, art, and literature provide important counterbalances to abjection through catharsis, only psychoanalysis or self-reflective analysis provide the elaboration necessary to address the cause and not just abate the symptoms of abjection or repression. Because analytic discourse both discharges and interprets semiotic forces, it can work not only as a safety valve for repressed drives but also a tool for altering the place of those drives within the psychic structure. Interpretation is crucial to changing our relation to otherness and enabling an embrace of the return of the repressed. Interpretation is possible only through imagination, which Kristeva believes has suffered in the twentieth century.

In *New Maladies of the Soul*, Kristeva suggests that contemporary Western culture is facing a flattening of the psyche, which corresponds to a lack of imagination. Our imaginations have been taken over by two-dimensional media images or drugs (prescription and illicit). By substituting surface images for psychic depth, drugs and media images close psychic space, which is the space between the biological and the social, the space in which affects materialize between bodily organs and social customs. Meaning is constituted in this space between the body and culture. The meaning of words (in the narrow sense of the symbolic element of language) is charged with affective meaning (in the broader sense of the semiotic element of language) through the movement of drive energy within psychic space.

In her latest work, the two volumes on the powers and limits of psychoanalysis (1996b, 1997), and *L'avenir d'une révolte*, Kristeva develops a connection between imagination and revolt. Reminiscent of her suggestion in *Revolution in Poetic Language* that poetic revolution is analogous to political revolution, in her recent work Kristeva relates the revolt necessary for creativity and imagination to earlier notions of political revolution. She argues that revolutions take a different form in contemporary Western culture; rather than political revolutions we have moral revolutions, both of which rely on revolts against authority that Kristeva associates with imagination.

APPRAISAL OF KEY ADVANCES AND CONTROVERSIES

Kristeva's theory of abjection has had a significant impact on some social and cultural theorists. The theory of abjection is promising in that it describes a relationship with what is not recognizable as myself. It is limiting, however, in that it describes that relationship as one of exclusion, which can be overcome only through a proper recognition and assimilation – if always only tentative – of abjection through psychoanalytic elaboration. At one extreme, the problem with Kristeva's notion of abjection is that it can be interpreted to suggest that otherness is always assimilated or incorporated into the subject or self-same. At the other extreme, the problem with Kristeva's notion of abjection is that it can be interpreted to suggest that exclusion and antagonism are the only possible relations to otherness.

For example, abjection is a central concept in Judith Butler's *Gender Trouble*. Judith Butler extends Kristeva's theory of abjection when she analyses the dynamics of exclusion inherent in identification. In *Gender Trouble*, Butler maintains that:

> The 'abject' designates that which has been expelled from the body, discharged as excrement, literally rendered 'Other'. This appears as an expulsion of alien elements, but the alien is effectively established through this expulsion. The construction of the 'not-me' as abject establishes the boundaries of the body which are also the first contours of the subject. (Butler, 1990: 133)

Like Kristeva's own use of abjection, Butler's use of abjection seems at times to make violence and exclusion a necessary part of identification and subjectivity.

If taken as standards for identification, however, theories of abjection normalize the most hateful and threatening kinds of discrimination, exclusion, and oppression.

If our identities are necessarily formed by rejecting and excluding what is different, then discrimination is inherent in the process of identification. On the level of individual identification, if self-identity is formed by rejecting what is different, in the first instance, the infant rejects its mother. If abjection of the mother or maternal body is described as a normal or natural part of child development, then one consequence is that without some antidote to this abjection, all of our images of mothers and maternal bodies are at some level abject because we all necessarily rejected our own mothers in order to become individuals. In addition, as Kristeva says in *Black Sun*, matricide becomes our vital necessity.

Part of my own project has been to suggest alternatives to the traditional philosophical and psychoanalytic views of individuation and self-identity that are built around the exclusion of otherness and difference. In particular, as an alternative to models of the mother–infant relationship that view the mother as an obstacle that must be overcome in order for the infant to become a social subject, I endorse a model of the mother–infant relationship that views the mother as the first co-operative partner in a social relationship that makes subjectivity possible.

On the level of social identification, if group identity is formed by rejecting what is different, then war, hatred, and oppression are inevitable and unavoidable parts of social development. If overcoming oppression or living together as persons is possible, we must reject normative notions of abjection. We can endorse theories of abjection as descriptions of the dynamics of oppression and exclusion without accepting that abjection is necessary to self-identity. If, following Kristeva, we carry the analysis of identity on the individual level to the group level, we can suppose that there are ways for groups to identify, for people to come together, without necessarily excluding others as hostile threats. Groups don't need to be at war with each other in order to constitute themselves as groups.

Even with its problems, Kristeva's notion of abjection has been useful for social and cultural theorists. Feminist theorists in particular have used the notion of abjection to help explain the dynamics of women's oppression. Although Kristeva has an ambivalent, sometimes hostile, relation to feminism and some aspects of the feminist movement in France, her theories provide some innovative approaches for feminist theory. One of her central contributions to feminist theory is her call for a new discourse of maternity. In 'Stabat Mater' she criticizes some of the traditional discourses of maternity in Western culture, specifically the myth of the Virgin Mary, because they do not present the mother as primarily a speaking being.

Without a new discourse of maternity we cannot begin to conceive of ethics. If ethics is the philosophy of our obligations to each other, then in order to do ethics we need to analyse the structure of our relations to each other. And if, as Freudian psychoanalytic theory maintains, our relation with our mothers is the model for all subsequent relations, then we need to analyse our relation with our mothers. In Western culture, however, this relation has been figured as a relation to nature, a relation that threatens the social and any possibility of ethical relations. On this view the relation with the mother is not a social relation and therefore not a model for an ethical relation. In order to conceive of an ethical relation, we need to conceive of a relation with the mother as a social relation with a speaking social being. At this point Kristeva's theory is similar to Luce Irigaray's . But whereas Irigaray maintains that we need a new discourse of maternity that allows us to imagine an identification with the maternal body as a social relation rather than an antisocial relation, Kristeva maintains that we need to complicate our notion of maternity in order to separate out the maternal body – which she insists must be abjected – from the mother's other functions as woman or feminine or possibly even as mother.

Kristeva suggests that women's oppression can be at least partially explained as a misplaced abjection. It is necessary to abject the maternal body *qua* the fulfiller of needs. But in Western culture woman, the feminine, and the mother have all been reduced to the reproductive function of the maternal body. The result is that when we abject the maternal body we also abject woman, the feminine, and the mother. We need a new discourse of maternity that can delineate between these various aspects and functions of women. Kristeva has set the stage by highlighting and complicating the maternal function. To view the mother's relation to the developing infant as a *function* uncouples the activities performed by the caretaker from the sex of the caretaker. Although Kristeva may believe that the maternal function should be performed by women, she does use the language of functions to separate care-taking functions from other activities performed by women. Woman, the female, the feminine and the mother cannot be reduced to the maternal function. Women and mothers are primarily speaking social beings.

In 'Women's Time' Kristeva (1993b) identifies two generations of feminism, both of which she accuses of using 'woman' as a religious ideal. The first (pre-1968) feminism is the feminism of suffragettes and existentialists. It is a struggle over the identity of woman as rational citizen, deserving of the 'rights of man'. The ideal 'woman' contains the same characteristics of the ideal 'man' and the struggle is to insert her in man's linear history. The second (post-1968) feminism is the feminism of psychoanalysts and artists. It is a struggle against reducing the identity of woman to the identity of man by inserting her into his linear time. These feminists assert a unique essence of woman or the feminine that falls outside of phallic time and phallic discourse. Kristeva argues that this strategy not only makes feminism into a religion, but also it traps women in an inferior and marginal position with regard to society. She embraces a radical individualism beyond the first two phases of feminism wherein each individual is considered unique to the extreme that there are as many sexualities and 'maladies of the soul' as there are individuals.

Like many intellectuals after May 1968, Kristeva became disillusioned with practical politics. Kristeva's political views and her views on politics are controversial. She maintains that political interpretation, like religion, is a search for one transcendent Meaning. Insofar as they fix an ideal, even political interpretations with emancipatory goals can become totalitarian. This is Kristeva's complaint with contemporary feminist movements. In order for political movements to be emancipatory, they must acknowledge that their fixed ideals are built on exclusions and persecutions. They must admit that their ideals are illusions created in the contexts of particular psychic struggles. Kristeva claims that psychoanalysis cuts through the illusions of political interpretation. She argues that she can do more with psychoanalysis in order to help people and enact change than she can with practical politics. Psychoanalysis makes the ultimate meanings and final causes provided by political ideals and interpretations analysable. Psychoanalysis can disclose other meanings and nonmeanings within the one Meaning of political interpretation. Kristeva suggests that in this way, psychoanalytic discourses can mobilize resistance to totalitarian discourse.

Kristeva's suggestion that psychoanalysis is the appropriate discourse to engage and diffuse social problems is controversial. How can a practice that is aimed at individuals solve social problems? The interpretation and self-analysis that Kristeva claims are necessary to change signifying structures are traditionally put into practice on a personal and individual level in psychoanalytic practice, a practice available to a small minority of the world's population. Even if Kristeva is not suggesting that everyone enter analysis, the use of psychoanalysis to diagnose social problems may be limited. How can a psychoanalytic interpretative diagnosis of social problems contribute to social change? While this question raises the general question of the relation of theory to practice, which is not unique to psychoanalytic theory, it also raises the more specific question of how to bring discussions of the unconscious into the realm of public policy and social change.

One of the central tenents of psychoanalytic theory is that revealing or interpreting unconscious dynamics in itself affects changes in behaviour. Couple this thesis with Kristeva's belief that the dynamics of society operate in ways analogous to the dynamics of individuals and we are lead to believe that psychoanalytic interpretations alone can affect social change. While her analysis might suggest that there is some kind of social or collective unconscious, Kristeva never explicitly addresses this issue. In spite of her own applications of psychoanalytic theory to particular social situations, there remain many unanswered questions about how to apply psychoanalytic theory, formulated in relation to individual and personal problems, to social situations and culture.

Ultimately all of Kristeva's writing challenges traditional social theories that presuppose an autonomous unitary subject. All of her models suggest an alternative model of ethics and politics based on the revised split subject of psychoanalysis that she calls the subject in process. Ethical obligations do not originate in laws of reason or universal principles that transcend the subject. Rather, ethical obligations are inherent in the process through which we become subjects, a process that is the constant negotiation with an other – language as other, the unconscious other within, or the other out of whom we were born. This ethics of psychoanalysis implies a politics. In *Strangers to Ourselves* Kristeva describes this implied politics as far from the patriarchal call to brotherhood. She says that 'it would involve a cosmopolitanism of a new sort that, cutting across governments, economies, and markets, might work for a mankind whose solidarity is founded on the consciousness of its unconscious – desiring, destructive, fearful, empty, impossible' (p. 290).

KRISTEVA'S MAJOR WORKS

Kristeva, J. (1969) *Semeiotiké, Recherches pour une sémanalyse.* Paris: Editions du Seuil.

Kristeva, J. (1970) *Le Texte du Roman.* The Hague: Mouton).

Kristeva, J. (1974a) *La Révolution du langage poétique.* Paris: Seuil, 1974; *Revolution in Poetic Language.* (Trans. Margaret Waller.) New York: Columbia University Press, 1984.

Kristeva, J. (1974b) *Des Chinoises.* Paris: Editions des Femmes; *About Chinese Women.* (Trans. Anita Barrows.) New York: Marion Boyars, 1977.

Kristeva, J. (ed.) (1975) *La traversée des signes.* Paris: Editions du Seuil.

Kristeva, J. (1977) *Polylogue.* Paris: Editions du Seuil.

Kristeva, J. (ed.) (1979) *Folle Vérité.* Paris: Editions du Seuil.

Kristeva, J. (1980a) *Desire in Language.* (Translated Thomas Gora, Alice Jardine, and Leon Roudiez, ed. Leon Roudiez.) New York: Columbia University Press.

Kristeva, J. (1980b) *Pouvoirs de l'horreur.* Paris: Editions du Seuil; *Powers of Horror.* (Trans. Leon Roudiez.) New York: Columbia University Press, 1982.

Kristeva, J. (1981) *Le langage, cet inconnu.* Paris: Editions du Seuil. *Language, the Unknown.* (Trans. Anne Menke.) New York: Columbia University Press, 1989).

Kristeva, J. (1983) *Histoires d'amour.* Paris: Editions Deno(ee)l; *Tales of Love.* (Trans. Leon Roudiez.) New York: Columbia University Press, 1987.

Kristeva, J. (1986) *The Kristeva Reader.* (ed. Toril Moi.) New York: Columbia Press.

Kristeva, J. (1987a) *Au commencement etait l'amour.* Paris: Hachette; *In the Beginning Was Love: Psychoanalysis and Faith.* (Trans. Arthur Goldhammer.) New York: Columbia Press, 1988.

Kristeva, J. (1987b) *Soleil Noir: Depression et Melancolie.* Paris: Gallimard; *Black Sun: Depression and Melancholy.* (Trans. Leon Roudiez.) New York: Columbia University Press, 1989.

Kristeva, J. (1989) *Etrangers à nous-mêmes.* Paris: Fayard; *Strangers to Ourselves.* (Trans. Leon Rousiez.) New York: Columbia University Press, 1991.

Kristeva, J. (1990a) *Lettre ouverte à Harlem Désir.* Paris: Editions Rivages.

Kristeva, J. (1990b) *Les Samoura(ii)s*. Paris: Fayard; *The Samurai*. (Trans. Barbara Bray.) New York: Columbia University Press, 1992.

Kristeva, J. (1991) *Le vieil homme et les loups*. Paris: Fayard; *The old Man and the Wolves*. (Trans. Barbara Bray.) New York: Columbia University Press, 1994.

Kristeva, J. (1993a) *Nations Without Nationalisms*. (Trans. Leon Roudiez.) New York: Columbia University Press.

Kristeva, J. (1993b). *Les Nouvelles maladies de l'ame. Paris: Libraire Artheme Fayard; New Maladies of the Soul* (Trans. Ross Guberman.) New York: Columbia University Press, 1995.

Kristeva, J. (1993c) *Proust and the Sense of Time*. (Trans. Stephen Bann.) New York: Columbia University Press.

Kristeva, J. (1994) *Le temps sensible: Proust et l'expérience littéraire*. Paris: Gallimard. *Time and Sense: Proust and the Experience of Literature*. (Trans. Ross Guberman.) New York: Columbia University Press, 1996.

Kristeva, J. (1996a) *Julia Kristeva Interviews*. (Ed. Ross Guberman.) New York: Columbia University Press.

Kristeva, J. (1996b) *Sens et non-sens de la révolte: Pouvoirs et limites de la psychanalyse I*. Paris: Fayard.

Kristeva, J. (1996c) *Possessions*. Paris: Fayard.

Kristeva, J. (1997) *La révolte intime: Pouvoirs et limites de la psychanalyse II*. Paris: Fayard.

Kristeva, J. (1998a) *L'avenir d'une révolte*. Paris: Calmann-Lévy.

Kristeva, J. (1998b) *Contre la dépression nationale: entretien avec Philippe Petit*. Paris: Les éditions Textuel.

Kristeva, J. and Clément, C. (1998c) *Le Féminin et le Sacré*. Paris: Stock.

Kristeva, J. (1998d) *The Portable Kristeva*. (Ed. Kelly Oliver.) New York: Columbia University Press.

SECONDARY REFERENCES

Allen, Jeffries and Young, Iris (eds) (1989) *The Thinking Muse. Feminism and Modern French Philosophy*. Bloomington: Indiana University Press.

Benjamin, Andrew and Fletcher, John (eds) (1990) *Abjection, Melancholia and Love: The Work of Julia Kristeva*. London and New York: Routledge.

Butler, Judith (1989) 'The body politics of Julia Kristeva', *Hypatia. A Journal of Feminist Philosophy*, 3 (3): 104–18.

Butler, Judith, (1990) *Gender Trouble*. New York: Routledge.

Crownfield, David (ed.) (1992) *Body/text in Julia Kristeva: Religion, Women and Psychoanalysis*. Albany, NY: SUNY Press.

Gallop, Jane (1982) *Feminism and Psychoanalysis: the Daughter's Seduction*. London: Macmillan.

Grosz, Elizabeth (1989) *Sexual Subversions: Three French Feminists*. Sydney, London, and Boston: Allen & Unwin.

Lechte, John (1990) *Julia Kristeva*. London and New York: Routledge.

Moi, Toril (1985) *Sexual/Textual Politics: Feminist Literary Theory*. London and New York: Methuen.

de Nooy, Julia and Hart, Jonathan (1998) *Derrida, Kristeva and the Dividing Line*. New York: Garland Publishing.

Jardine, Alice (1986) 'Opaque texts and transparent contexts: the political difference of Julia Kristeva', in Nancy K. Miller (ed.), *The Poetics of Gender*. New York: Columbia University Press.

Jones, Ann Rosalind (1984) 'Julia Kristeva on femininity: the limits of a semiotic politics', *Feminist Review*, 18: 56–73.

Nye, Andrea (1987) 'Woman clothed with the sun: Julia Kristeva and the escape from/to language', *Signs: Journal of Women in Culture and Society*, 12 (4): 664–6.

Oliver, Kelly (1991) 'Kristeva's imaginary father and the crisis in the paternal function', *Diacritics*, 2-3: 43–63.

Oliver, Kelly, (1993a) *Reading Kristeva: Unraveling the Double-bind*. Bloomington, IN: Indiana: Indiana University Press.

Oliver, Kelly (1993b) 'Julia Kristeva's feminist revolution', *Hypatia: a Journal of Feminist Philosophy*, 8 (3): 94–114.

Oliver, Kelly (ed.) (1993c) *Ethics, Politics and Difference in Julia Kristeva's Writings*. New York: Routledge.

Oliver, Kelly (1998a) *Subjectivity Without Subjects*. New York: Rowman & Littlefield.

Oliver, Kelly (1998b) 'Tracing the signifier behind the scenes of desire', in H. Silverman (ed.) *Cultural Semiosis*, Sydney: Routledge Press.

Oliver, Kelly (1998c) The crisis of meaning: Kristeva's solution to the mind–body problem', in M. Zournazi & J. Lechte (eds.) *After the Revolution: On Kristeva*. New York: Artspace Press.

Rose, Jacqueline (1986) 'Julia Kristeva: take two', in *Sexuality in the Field of Vision*. London: NLB/ Verso.

Smith, Anna (1996) *Julia Kristeva: Readings of Exile and Estrangement*. New York: St Martins Press.

Smith, Anna-Marie (1998) *Julia Kristeva: Speaking the Unspeakable*. New York: Stylus Press.

Smith, Paul (1989) 'Julia Kristeva et al., or, take three or more', in R. Feldstein and J. Roof (eds) *Feminism and Psychoanalysis*. Ithaca, NY: Cornell University Press.

Ziarek, Ewa (1992) 'At the limits of discourse: heterogeneity, alterity, and the maternal body in Kristeva's thought', *Hypatia, a Journal for Feminist Philosophy*, 7 (2): 91–108.

16

Luce Irigaray

CAROLINE BAINBRIDGE

BIOGRAPHICAL DETAILS AND THEORETICAL CONTEXT

Luce Irigaray was born in Belgium in 1930 and emigrated to Paris in the early 1960s. During her time in Belgium, she gained a Masters degree in philosophy and literature from the University of Louvain (1955) and worked as a high school teacher (1956–9). Subsequently, she took up the post of assistant researcher at the Fondation Nationale de la Recherche Scientifique where she worked until she left for France. Once in Paris, Irigaray completed a further Masters degree in psychology (1961) and also gained a Diploma in Psychopathology from the Institut de Psychologie de Paris (1962). Her first doctoral thesis in linguistics, entitled 'The Language of the Demented', was completed at the University of Paris X at Nanterre in 1968 and subsequently published by Mouton (1973).

Between 1970 and 1974, Irigaray taught at the University of Paris VIII at Vincennes and studied psychoanalytic theory at the Ecole Freudienne. She completed her second doctorate in philosophy at the University of Paris VIII in 1974. This was to become her first major work and constituted the source of her infamous ejection from the Parisian academic scene upon its publication in 1974 as *Speculum de l'autre femme*/*Speculum of the Other Woman* (1985a). Irigaray presented this thesis at the Ecole Freudienne where she had been taught by Jacques Lacan. Her critique of Western ideas incorporated theoretical attacks on the key positions outlined in the work of Freud and Lacan and was consequently deemed heretical. Irigaray was immediately alienated from Parisian intellectual circles and her university course proposal for the subsequent year was rejected.

It was not until the 1980s that she began to be recognized as an important theorist by her compatriots. In the meantime, Irigaray continued in her post as Director of Research at the Centre Nationale de la Recherche Scientifique in Paris, working as part of a multidisciplinary team constituted by linguists, neurologists, psychiatrists, and philosophers. She continued also to develop her psychoanalytic practice. In 1982, she was appointed to the Chaire Internationale de Philosophie at Erasmus University in Rotterdam. During the mid- to late-1980s, she taught at the Ecole des Hautes Etudes en Sciences Sociales, the Collège Internationale de

Philosophie and the Centre Américain d'Etudes Critiques in Paris. She has spoken at a number of women's groups and conferences throughout Europe and North America and has been actively involved with the Women's Movement in France, participating in pro-choice campaigns and in efforts to legalize contraception. Her work has been particularly well received in Italy: the Milan Women's Bookstore Collective draws heavily on Irigaray's thought, and Irigaray herself is a regular contributor to the newspaper of the Italian Communist Party. In recent years, her research has concerned itself with sexual order of language and culture. She continues to write and to give papers on her theoretical ideas.

The breadth of Irigaray's work attests to a number of influences and sources for her ideas. However, her refusal of the academic convention of acknowledging sources by using references and providing bibliographies makes it rather difficult to be sure of the origins of her thought. Despite this, it is possible to trace some of her key influences. A former student of Jacques Lacan, Irigaray is strongly influenced by psychoanalytic theories. Her deconstructionist approach to the key philosophical texts of Western thought also reveals the influence of Jacques Derrida. Indeed, the full scope of her engagement with philosophy encompasses a diverse range of European thinkers including Plato, Hegel, Kant, Nietzsche, Heidegger, Marx, and Levinas. Irigaray has described herself as 'having a fling with the philosophers' (1985b: 150). Her reading and critique of philosophy is 'amorous' in the sense that she does not reject the premises of the thought she is analysing. Rather, she attempts to use them, to manipulate textual practices and to seduce the texts themselves into showing the extent to which they are underpinned by a fundamental disavowal of the feminine. In keeping with Lacanian ideas about the locus of the speaking subject within the symbolic order, Irigaray is aware that it would be impossible to begin afresh, attempting to articulate that which remains hidden in symbolic practice without making use of symbolic modes of discourse and representation. To attempt to do so would negate the very possibility of a feminine mode of representation because the subject would be alienated, outside language and incapable of enunciating her position outside symbolic law. The amorous mode of Irigaray's textuality is often seductive and compelling and enables the reader of her thought to perceive the gaps within the theories that subtend culture. Irigaray uses this discursive style repeatedly throughout her work and it is most clearly apparent in those texts which engage with one named philosopher (1991, 1999). More recently, however, Irigaray has moved away from a focus on figures within the occidental intellectual scene and has begun to examine oriental ideas such as Buddhism. This shift in perspective reveals the developmental aspect of Irigaray's thought and also marks a split in the process of her interrogation of ideas. Whereas the great body of the early texts engages in (often scathing) critique, the later texts show a marked interest in a more constructive approach to the question of the feminine and the ways in which it may be able to speak something of its own specificity.

The fundamental idea underpinning Irigaray's work is the notion of the feminine as that which is disavowed within the symbolic order of discourse and theory. The feminine has always been little more than the 'dark continent of psychoanalysis', to paraphrase Freud in his work on femininity. Irigaray makes clear throughout her writings that the debt owed to the maternal by *all* sociosymbolic signifying practices and patterns of representation is repressed and unacknowledged. The feminine becomes buried alive in the symbolic order in this context and thus constitutes the bedrock of symbolic systems, a hidden and repressed support structure. For Irigaray, this repression or disavowal of the feminine amounts to a denial of sexual difference.

For Irigaray, symbolic patterns of representation deny the relevance of sexual difference to the ways in which human subjects relate to issues surrounding corporeality and (re)production. She claims that phallocentrism has a vested interest in subverting difference and denying its existence insofar as it maintains a logic that is rooted in an *a priori* of the same. Subjectivity and meaning are affected by this denial of difference which accounts for the hierarchical nature of many social relations and for the privileging of the masculine term in the binaries that structure such hierarchies.

Irigaray's style is highly complex and allusive. The extreme style of her writing may be interpreted as an attempt to represent the excess of the feminine that goes beyond the boundaries of representation. She makes few references to sources for her 'citations' and she writes in a very slippery manner. Many of her texts are richly poetic in style and depend upon a manipulation of typographical conventions to disrupt the traditional flow of reading and engagement with the text. This has led numerous commentators to contextualize Irigaray's thought, along with that of Hélène Cixous and Julia Kristeva, in terms of *écriture féminine*. To align the work of these thinkers, however, is to miss the very pertinent differences between their ideas. Irigaray is not directly concerned with the question of writing the body, as the scope of her engagement with philosophical ideas reveals.

SOCIAL THEORY AND CONTRIBUTIONS

In her early work, such as *Speculum Of The Other Woman* and *This Sex Which Is Not One*, Irigaray employs a disruptive and highly critical style to engage with the theories that structure symbolic notions of sex and gender. Latterly, her work takes on a simpler style and has come to focus more centrally on the need to implement mechanisms to ensure access to a programme of civil and legal rights for women (and men) that is rooted in the recognition of sexual difference. The developmental aspect of Irigaray's work makes it is impossible to read the recent, apparently more accessible volumes of her *oeuvre* without referring back to readings of her earliest work.

Throughout her work, Irigaray avoids prescriptive measures. Instead, she attempts to evoke the feminine, to make the gaps of what she is able to articulate resonate with meaning for the readers engaging with her thought. Despite the change of style in her more recent publications, Irigaray's work remains highly complex and deeply inscribed with the processes of critique and disruption that characterize the earlier writings. Irigaray has stated that what she wants 'is not to create a theory of woman, but to secure a place for the feminine within sexual difference' (1985b: 159). Throughout her work, sexual difference functions as the yardstick for the analysis of sociocultural relations. Irigaray gives no consideration to modes of difference based on class or race, for example. For Irigaray, woman is specularized and commodified by symbolic patterns of discourse and representation. In what follows, I shall outline Irigaray's critique of symbolic practices before highlighting some of the ways in which her more recent writings strive to offer more constructive theories of what the feminine is and how it may be articulated.

The Critique of Phallogocentrism

Irigaray's critique of the phallogocentric symbolic order centres on the mechanisms employed by psychoanalytic and philosophical theories to exclude a notion of the feminine. *Speculum Of The Other Woman* and *This Sex Which Is Not One* lay out a resounding critique of the psychoanalytic account of the acquisition of gender in which Irigaray shows how Western philosophy has structured its account of the subject in terms of the masculine alone. She uses the tools of deconstruction and psychoanalysis to turn these monolithic theories inside out and to demonstrate the ways in which the feminine is permanently excluded from the symbolic processes which are at play in traditional systems of discourse and representation.

The main consequence of this exclusion of the feminine from symbolic discourse is that the representation of feminine subjectivity becomes impossible. By setting out to disrupt the symbolic practices employed within phallocentrism, Irigaray's linguistic play allows for a perception of the feminine that goes beyond its definition in relation to masculine notions of subjectivity. Such an interrogation of the gaps within dominant discourse opens up the possibility of articulating something of the feminine on its own terms. Let us now move on to consider some of the central ideas in Irigaray's writing.

Specula(riza)tion

Irigaray uses the term 'specula(riza)tion' to describe how the feminine is trapped in a mirroring function in phallocentrism. Woman represents a reflection of the masculine to the masculine subject so that the feminine is defined, not in its own terms, but in relation to specifically masculine attributes such as the phallus. For Irigaray, a logic of sameness upholds symbolic modes of discourse and ensures that masculinity remains dominant.

Irigaray draws a parallel between this mirroring function and Lévi-Strauss's formulation of woman as commodity (Lévi-Strauss, 1969: 36). Here, she draws on the idea that the masculine subject is constructed to produce and exchange while commodities and patterns of exchange confirm the status of the masculine within the symbolic order. As commodities, women function to maintain systems of exchange by participating *unquestioningly* in the processes involved. In this sense, the feminine, becomes a 'specular' other used to speculate, a kind of gold standard for the masculine subject.

The consequence of 'specula(riza)tion' is that women are prohibited from being agents of exchange and are limited to acting as objects of exchange. Under these terms there can be no exchange between men and women because men make commerce *of* women not *with* them. Women are circulated as signs and serve to differentiate meaning without having any meaning of their own. The dominant 'specular' economy is thus punningly described by Irigaray as 'hom(m)osexual': it is homosexual because of the logic of the same that perpetuates it and Irigaray calls it 'hom(m)osexual' in order to make a pun in French on the word *homme* (man).

Locating the Feminine

Throughout the early texts, Irigaray uses playful linguistic mechanisms to show how the feminine is constituted as excess and plurality. She uses the textuality of her work as a mode of enactment of both the feminine and its impossibility. Her efforts to recuperate the feminine from symbolic practices centre on her reworking of notions of masquerade and mimesis.

Arguing that femininity is defined as masquerade and is therefore little more than a construct of masculine desire, Irigaray sets out to show that mimesis of this position allows women to take the masquerade to its extreme. Mimesis reveals the ways in which masquerade exploits women. In mimicry, woman deliberately takes on the feminine style and posture attributed to her within dominant discourse in order to reveal the mechanisms by which she is oppressed and exploited. Mimesis disrupts discursive coherence by deliberately taking on the role ascribed to the feminine in order to draw attention to the flimsiness of its construction, and thus to seduce dominant discourse into revealing its repressed foundation.

Mimesis, then, is a form of deliberate hysteria which offers women a form of representation on their own terms. Through mimesis, women constitute themselves in a way that is impossible in masquerade. Irigaray's use of (hysterical) mimicry in her analysis of philosophy and psychoanalysis thus amounts to an attempt to represent discursively something of those repressed elements of the feminine that are concealed within the gaps of discourse.

Language and the Question of Enunciation

Irigaray's work is intricately bound up with post-structuralist linguistic theories. As in the work of Jacques Lacan, the role of language in the formation of subjectivity is central to Irigaray's thought and its focus on the ways in which the feminine is written out of language. By drawing on psychoanalytic ideas about the constitution of the subject at the moment of recognition of the Law of the Father (which comes with the revelation of castration), Irigaray shows how the specificity of the female body is consistently disavowed in theories of subjectivity. For Irigaray, the most important area in which to begin to renegotiate feminine subjectivity is in relation to the question of enunciation. She elaborates the notion of *parler-femme* (later called 'the sexuation of discourse') in an effort to construct a feminine position of enunciation. *Parler-femme* is one of the most controversial aspects of Irigaray's work. She writes:

> what a feminine syntax might be is not simple or easy to state, because in that 'syntax' there would no longer be either subject or object, 'oneness' would no longer be privileged, there would be no proper meanings, proper names, 'proper' attributes... Instead, that 'syntax' would involve nearness, proximity, but in such an extreme form that it would preclude any distinction of identities, any establishment of ownership, thus any form of appropriation. (Irigaray, 1985b: 134)

This remark seems almost to undo all notions of what syntax *is*. However, in many ways, this is precisely the point: Irigaray is neither setting out to define a language of the feminine nor, indeed, to create one. Her work is an attempt to show how language (in the Saussurean sense of *langage*) delimits and manipulates what is understood as femininity. *Parler-femme* draws attention to the fact that women need to address their exclusion from language. Irigaray does not prescribe a mode of feminine language. Instead, she tries to show how *parler-femme* enables women to articulate their sexed identities in and on their own terms (*par les femmes*). The apparent utopianism of Irigaray's attempts to evoke the conditions necessary for *parler-femme* to become possible serves the familiar dual purpose of effecting both a critique of, and a (possible/utopian) way out of, the restraining boundaries of symbolic practices.

Another apparently utopian 'technique' used by Irigaray to evoke the feminine relates to her attempts to formulate a female genealogy. Closely imbricated in the process of *parler-femme*, the notion of female genealogy helps to locate the feminine in its own terms rather than within the constricted and constricting discursive accounts of histories that predominate under the rule of the phallic signifier. The disavowal of the feminine has a devastating impact on mother–daughter or woman-to-woman relations, according to Irigaray. With no means of autonomous self-definition, the mother is consumed by the maternal role. Little girls have no image of the feminine with which to identify. The mother is subjected to the Law of the Father and to patterns of exchange; she gives up her father's name in order to take her husband's name: she has no name/identity of her own. Her role and function within culture and society becomes little more than reproductive. For Irigaray, the repercussion of this is that women have no access to a history of their own.

More recently, the focus of Irigaray's work has tended to relate more to the ethical relationship and status of the couple than to issues of individual subjectivity. Yet it remains the case that, for Irigaray, a truly ethical relationship depends on the 'recognition' (her term from *I Love To You*) of the repressed nature of the feminine within phallocentric representational and discursive practices, and on the renegotiation of female subjectivity in these terms.

An Ethics of Sexual Difference

Irigaray delineates an ethics of sexual difference which envisions a world inhabited by at least two sexed identities, each of which would respect the radical alterity of the other/Other and each of which would admire the irreducible difference that such an other would embody. For Irigaray, an ethical relationship between the sexes would affect symbolic practice, not only at the level of morality, but also in terms of the ways in which civil rights are codified and implemented. Hence the very large degree of emphasis in the more recent texts on the place of women in legal and civil terms (1993b, 1993c). Related to these ideas is the notion of space-time. For Irigaray, woman is little more than a space by reference to which and in which man is able to locate himself as a subject. Once again, woman is trapped into the realm of the maternal in this respect. She embodies the place of origin for the masculine subject and, consequently, has no access to her own space of origin, nor indeed to any space of her own outside the maternal realm. Irigaray's thoughts on gendered space-time are closely related to her highly theoretical forays into the realm of the divine, which is made accessible by reference to figures of mediation.

Mediation

In Irigaray's most recent work, the trope of mediation is extremely important. In her work since *An Ethics of Sexual Difference*, Irigaray has consistently alluded to the importance of mediation for the construction of an interval or between space in which it may be possible to situate the other as subject in its own right. For Irigaray, mediation, in the form of angels, or thresholds, or love, or the placenta, is the necessary foundation upon which to build an ethical relation between the sexes. The mediating forces she refers to help to undo dualistic systems and attempt to posit a new modality of subjectivity that is grounded in the recognition of (sexual) difference.

Irigaray's work on mediation, and especially on angels, is closely related to her conceptualization of the divine. Irigaray argues that women need access to a divine form of their own creation in order to have access to a sense of their own finitude and mortality. In order to become a subject in her own right, woman needs to create a divine image that allows her to relate to a mode of otherness and (in)finitude that does not reside within her own body. Moreover, Irigaray's recent turn to the importance of love for the renegotiation of symbolic subjectivities highlights the way in which her work has begun to move away from an emphasis on critique and disruption toward an attempt to engage otherwise with the systems she formerly found so problematic.

APPRAISAL OF KEY ADVANCES AND CONTROVERSIES

Irigaray's project to elaborate a philosophy of the feminine in terms which celebrate the specificity of the female body and woman's experience of desire and subjectivity, is couched in terms which centralize the question of sexual difference. Whilst much of what Irigaray has to say is underpinned by a fundamental critique of the phallogocentrism of psychoanalytic and philosophical accounts of sexual difference, there is also a utopian gesture implicit in her work, which offers feminism a quite unique vision of the future of the feminine. Irigaray's use of psychoanalysis and philosophy as a starting point for her critique of Western ontology has provided a focal point for the reception of her work, especially during the 1970s and 1980s. Much of the early analysis and critique of Irigaray's work was premised on a relatively small portion of her work which was available internationally (essays from *Speculum* and *This Sex*). The framework of this critique is discussed below. More recently, however, there has been a resurgent interest in Irigaray's work led by feminist cultural and theoretical practitioners who argue for the need to engage with Irigaray's texts (Whitford, 1991; Burke et al., 1994).

There are three positions that are commonly held in relation to Irigaray's work. First, certain feminists have challenged Irigaray's work as (biologically) essentialist (Moi, 1985; Plaza, 1978; Sayers, 1982; Segal, 1987). Such critics argue that Irigaray's work is ultimately essentialist as it is based on a notion of feminine specificity that is somehow grounded in the psychic or material female body. However, one could argue that the critique of essentialism in Irigaray's work does not take account of the radical attempts made throughout her work to posit a critique of patriarchy that makes possible a mode of change that has ramifications for notions of gendered subjectivity. Moreover, in claiming that Irigaray's work is ahistorical and nonmaterialist, such accounts reveal the extent to which Irigaray's work has been dismissed on the basis of misreadings of her earliest texts. As Naomi Schor has pointed out, Irigaray is not interested in *defining* 'woman', but is, rather, committed to *theorizing* feminine specificity in terms which consider the importance of sexual difference (Burke et al., 1994: 66).

Secondly, further studies have attempted to locate Irigaray's work as impossible and antifeminist because of her insistence on the alterity of the feminine within symbolic practice (Ragland-Sullivan, 1986). The Lacanian critique of Irigaray as a theorist who fails to appreciate the *gravitas* of positing a feminine psyche to oppose the masculine one described by Lacan, situates Irigaray as attempting to misrepresent Lacan's teachings. Such a critique focuses upon the apparently imaginary-centred perspective of Irigaray's theory of the feminine. Taking Lacanian ideas about the non-existence of '(~~the~~) woman' at face value, such accounts disavow the ironically critical engagement with Lacanian thought that dominates Irigaray's work on psychoanalysis.

Thirdly, some feminist commentators have sought to engage with the deconstructionist element of Irigaray's work in order to expose something of the repressive mechanisms used within sociosymbolic praxis to disavow the feminine and its position within the symbolic order (Braidotti, 1991; Burke et al., 1994; Connor, 1992; Fuss, 1989; Gallop, 1982; Grosz, 1989; Schwab, 1991; Whitford, 1991a). These critics advocate the necessity to engage with Irigaray's thought and discursive style in order to locate her work as a 'philosophy of change'. Most notably, in this respect, feminists such as Elizabeth Grosz and Margaret Whitford have made important arguments in favour of reading Irigaray on her own terms. In particular, Margaret Whitford has suggested that:

> she is proposing her work as a sort of intermediary between women, as that indispensable third party in any symbolic relationship (which is therefore precisely not a dual imaginary relationship), as an object of exchange, especially between women, which we can use to avoid one of the common impasses of attempts at a woman's sociality: unmediated (because unsymbolized) affects. In Irigarayan terms, it might create the *espacement* or the 'space between' that is difficult to women who are required to constitute a space for men. Her work is offered as an object, a discourse, for women to exchange among themselves, a sort of commodity, so that women themselves do not have to function as the commodity, or as the *sacrifice* on which sociality is built. (Whitford, 1991a: 51–2)

Many of Irigaray's critics have wrestled with her often difficult and challenging work in an attempt to produce an understanding of her objectives that is accessible to feminists struggling for women's rights and for female subjectivity. The ways in which this has been done are myriad and complex. A number of textual theoreticians have sought to use Irigaray for textual/political purposes (Apter, 1990; Jones, 1981, 1985; Simpson-Zinn, 1985; Worsham, 1991). The large majority of this work situates Irigaray (often alongside

Julia Kristeva and Hélène Cixous) in the context of *écriture féminine*. Many of the critics who label Irigaray as a proponent of *écriture féminine* do so for two reasons. Firstly, they highlight the very complex stylistic processes at play in Irigaray's work as an example of 'writing the body'. Secondly, there is a tendency to seize upon her focus on the question of language and the way in which it pervades her work as a whole.

It is clear from Irigaray's work that her interest lies not so much in the logocentric or writing-focused elements of language, but rather in the process of speech itself, of *énonciation* in the sense elaborated by Emile Benveniste (1971). This emphasis on questions of *énonciation* highlights the view that Irigaray does not set out to elaborate a technique of female or feminine writing. Her project does not attempt to address the question of feminine desire through the written text, but rather focuses on the importance of seeking out ways of insinuating the feminine into language as a speaking subject-position.

Despite Joy Simpson-Zinn's claim that 'past and present struggles in the social sphere are not ignored by French feminists, Hélène Cixous and Luce Irigaray, but the first step toward social change is, in their opinion, a new language, a new text, a new vision' (1985: 78), it seems rather more appropriate to highlight the fact that, for Irigaray at least, written language traps the feminine in a system of phallogocentrism and prohibits the representation of the feminine as anything other than virgin/mother/whore or 'the dark continent', the unseen and unspeakable buried aspect of symbolic practice (Irigaray, 1985a, 1985b). As Margaret Whitford has pointed out, aligning Irigaray with Cixous and Kristeva as a proponent of *écriture féminine* 'blurs the differences, both theoretical and political, between the three women. But it also reduces the complexity of Irigaray's work to the simplicity of a formula – "writing the body", and conveniently ignores that Irigaray's brief comments on women and writing in *This Sex Which Is Not One* have been made to represent more or less the totality of her work' (Whitford, 1991b: 2–3).

Recently, feminists engaging with Irigaray's work have shown that it consists of much more than an attempt to 'write the body' or merely to inscribe feminine desire onto the discursive body. The implication of this is that Irigaray's insistence upon the need to formulate a means of speaking (as) woman, reflects a desire to rework traditional patterns of sexed subjectivity in order to facilitate the production of the feminine in language and other symbolic systems. Feminists have seized upon this and have sought to demonstrate that Irigaray's thought can be used as a resource in relation to a number of disciplines and arenas including feminist philosophy, textual practice and criticism, psychoanalytic practice, history, law, ethics, gender studies, and sexual politics. Current work on Irigaray's thought sets out to examine the roots of her ideas, tracing her debt to theorists such as Derrida, Foucault, and Heidegger (Burke et al., 1994). This shift in the way that feminists now choose to draw on Irigaray's thought marks the acknowledgement of her struggle to highlight 'the necessity or inevitability of radical social or symbolic transformation' (Whitford, 1994: 29). Largely, this shift in perspective on Irigaray's work has been facilitated by the widespread availability of her texts in translation, which has enabled feminists to undertake a more detailed reading of Irigaray's influences and origins. The wealth of material being produced in this context indicates a depth of potential in this return to Irigaray's work as text and the scene of writing surrounding her work will inevitably shift and evolve. The extent of the debate around Irigaray's thought is yet to be fully realized, yet it is undoubtedly the case that her work will continue to influence the directions forged by feminist interrogations of culture.

IRIGARAY'S MAJOR WORKS

Irigaray, Luce (1985a) *Speculum of the Other Woman*. (Trans. Gillian C. Gill.) Ithaca, NY: Cornell University Press.

Irigaray, Luce (1985b) *This Sex Which Is Not One*. (Trans. Catherine Porter.) Ithaca, NY: Cornell University Press.

Irigaray, Luce (1991) *Marine Lover of Friedrich Nietzsche*. (Trans. Gillian C. Gill.) New York: Columbia University Press.

Irigaray, Luce (1992) *Elemental Passions*. (Trans. Joanne Collie and Judith Still.) London: Athlone Press.

Irigaray, Luce (1993a) *An Ethics of Sexual Difference*. (Trans. Carolyn Burke and Gillian C. Gill.) London: Athlone Press.

Irigaray, Luce (1993b) *Je, tu, nous: Toward a Culture of Difference*. (Trans. Alison Martin.) New York and London: Routledge.

Irigaray, Luce (1993c) *Sexes and Genealogies*. (Trans. Gillian C. Gill.) New York: Columbia University Press.

Irigaray, Luce (1994) *Thinking The Difference: For a Peaceful Revolution*. (Trans. Karin Montin.) London: Athlone Press.

Irigaray, Luce (1995) *Speech Is Never Neuter*. (Trans. Gail Schwab.) London: Athlone Press.

Irigaray, Luce (1996) *I Love To You: Sketch for a Possible Felicity in History*. (Trans. Alison Martin.) London and New York: Routledge.

Irigaray, Luce (1999) *The Forgetting of Air in Martin Heidegger*. (Trans. Mary Beth Mader.) London: Athlone Press.

Irigaray, Luce (1999) *To Be Two*. (Trans. Monique Rhodes and Marco F. Cocito-Monoc.) London: Athlone Press.

Articles

Irigaray, Luce (1975) 'Schizophrenia and the question of the sign', *Semiotext(e)*, 2 (1): 31–42.

Irigaray, Luce (1980) 'When the goods get together', in E. Marks and I. de Courtivron (eds) *New French Feminisms*. Amherst: University of Massachusetts Press.

Irigaray, Luce (1985) 'Is the subject of science sexed?', *Cultural Critique*, 1: 73–88. (Trans. Edith Oberle.)

Irigaray, Luce (1994) 'Ecce Mulier? Fragments', in P.J. Burgard (ed.), *Nietzsche and The Feminine*. Charlottesville and London: University Press of Virginia.

Irigaray, Luce (1995) 'The question of the other', *Yale French Studies*, 87: 7–19.

SECONDARY REFERENCES

Apter, Emily (1990) 'The story of I; Luce Irigaray's theoretical masochism', *NWSA Journal (A Publication of the National Women's Association)*, 2 (2): 186–98.

Benveniste, Emile (1971) *Problems in General Linguistics*. (Trans. Mary Elizabeth Meek.) Coral Gables, FL: University of Miami Press.

Braidotti, Rosi (1991) *Patterns of Dissonance: A study of women in contemporary philosophy*. (Trans. Elizabeth Guild.) Cambridge: Polity Press.

Burke, Carolyn, Schor, Naomi and Whitford, Margaret (eds) (1994) *Engaging With Irigaray*. New York: Columbia University Press.

Chanter, Tina (1995) *Ethics of Eros: Irigaray's Rewriting of the Philosophers*. New York and London: Routledge.

Connor, Stephen (1992) *Theory and Cultural Value*. Oxford: Blackwell.

Deutscher, Penelope (1996) 'Irigaray anxiety: Luce Irigaray and her ethics for improper selves', *Radical Philosophy*, 80 (Nov/Dec): 6–15.

Fuss, Diana (1989) *Essentially Speaking: Feminism, Nature, Difference*. London; Routledge.

Gallop, Jane (1982) *Feminism and Psychoanalysis: The Daughter's Seduction*. London: Macmillan.

Grosz, Elizabeth (1989) *Sexual Subversions: Three French Feminists*. Sydney and London: Allen and Unwin.

Holmlund, Christine (1989) 'I love Luce: the lesbian, mimesis and masquerade in Irigaray, Freud and mainstream film', *New Formations*, 9: 105–23.

Jones, Ann Rosalind (1981) 'Writing the body: toward an understanding of *L'écriture féminine*', *Feminist Studies*, 2: 247–63.

Jones, Ann Rosalind (1985) 'Inscribing femininity: French theories of the feminine' in Gayle Green and Coppelia Khan (eds) *Making A Difference: Feminist Literary Criticism*. London and New York: Methuen.

Kim, C. W. Maggie, St. Ville, Susan M. and Simonaitis, Susan M. (1993) *Transfigurations: Theology and the French Feminists*. Minneapolis, MN: Fortress Press.

Lévi-Strauss, Claude (1969) *The Elementary Structures of Kinship*. (Trans. James Harle Bell, John Richard von Sturmer and Rodney Needham.) London: Eyre and Spottiswoode.

Moi, Toril (1985) *Sexual/Textual Politics: Feminist Literary Theory*. London and New York: Routledge.

Morris, Meaghan (1988) *The Pirate's Fiancée: Feminism, Reading, Postmodernism*. London and New York: Verso.

Nordquist, Joan (1996) *French Feminist Theory (III): Luce Irigaray and Hélène Cixous: A Bibliography*. Santa Cruz: Reference and Research Services.

Oppel, Frances (1993) '"Speaking Immemorial Waters": Irigaray with Nietzsche', in P. Patton (ed.) *Nietzsche, Feminism and Political Theory*. London and New York: Routledge.

Perez, Emma (1994) 'Irigaray's female symbolic in the making of Chicana lesbian sitios y lenguas (Sites and Discourses)', in L. Doan and R.

Wiegman (eds) *The Lesbian Postmodern*. New York: Columbia University Press.

Plaza, Monique (1978) '"Phallomorphic power" and the psychology of "woman"', *Ideology and Consciousness*, 4: 4–36.

Ragland-Sullivan, Ellie (1986) *Jacques Lacan and the Philosophy of Psychoanalysis*. London: Croom Helm.

Sayers, Janet (1982) *Biological Politics: Feminist and Anti-Feminist Perspectives*. London and New York: Tavistock Publications.

Schwab, Gail (1991) 'Irigarayan dialogism: play and power play', in D. M. Bauer and McKinstrey (eds) *Feminism, Bakhtin and the Dialogic*. New York: SUNY Press.

Segal, Lynne (1987) *Is The Future Female? Troubled Thoughts on Contemporary Feminism*. London: Virago.

Shepherdson, Charles (1992) 'Biology and history: some psychoanalytical aspects of the writing of Luce Irigaray', *Textual Politics*, 6 (1): 47–86.

Silverman, Kaja (1988) *The Acoustic Mirror: the Female Voice in Psychoanalysis and Cinema*. Bloomington: Indiana University Press.

Simpson-Zinn, Joy (1985) 'The *différance* of *l'écriture féminine*', *Chimeress: A Journal of French and Italian Literature*, 18 (1): 77–93.

Stockton, Kathryn Bond (1994) *God Between their Lips: Desire Between Women in Irigaray, Brontë and Eliot*. Stanford, CA: Stanford University Press.

Tavor Bannet, Eve (1993) 'There have to be at least two', *Diacritics*, 23 (1): 84–98.

van Buren, Jane (1995) 'Postmodernism – feminism and the deconstruction of the feminine: Kristeva and Irigaray', *The American Journal of Psychoanalysis*, 55 (3): 231–43.

Whitford, Margaret (1991a) *Luce Irigaray: Philosophy in the Feminine*. London: Routledge.

Whitford, Margaret (ed.) (1991b) *The Irigaray Reader*. Oxford: Blackwell.

Worsham, Lynn (1991) 'Writing against writing: the predicament of *ecriture féminine* in composition studies', in Patricia Harkin and John Schilb (eds) *Contending With Words: Composition and Rhetoric in A Postmodern Age*. New York: Modern Language Association of America.

Wright, Elizabeth (ed.) (1992) *Feminism and Psychoanalysis: A Critical Dictionary*. Oxford: Blackwell.

17

Jean Baudrillard

MIKE GANE

BIOGRAPHICAL DETAILS AND THEORETICAL CONTEXT

Jean Baudrillard, born in July 1929, is still very actively engaged in writing. His book *L'Echange Impossible* was published in September 1999, following his book of photographs called *Car l'Illusion ne s'oppose pas à la Realité* which was published at the end of 1998. He was born in Reims but little in fact is known about Baudrillard's early life other than that he specialized in languages and taught German at a lycée for about 10 years. His earlier academic career had not been smooth; he has referred somewhat obscurely to his 'Rimbaud period' when he abandoned his studies for a time. He failed to get into the Ecole Normale Supérieur, and failed the important gateway examination, the *agrégation*. In the 1966 he finally got into University teaching at the age of 37 'by an indirect route' (1993a: 19). In the 1960s he became known as a brilliant and prolific translator, German to French, translating the major works of Peter Weiss, Brecht, Marx and Engels, and the anthropologist Wilhelm Muhlmann.

Baudrillard's first published essays were written for *Les Temps Modernes* in 1962–3 on literary themes. Leaving German literature, Baudrillard moved towards sociology under the teaching first of Henri Lefebvre and then the decisive influence of Roland Barthes. From 1967 Baudrillard was associated with the journal *Utopie* which was close to, though without organizational ties with, the situationist movement. From 1969–73 he taught sociology at Nanterre and was attached to the Centre d'Etudes des Communications de Masse, at this critical time of the confrontation with McLuhan in media theory. From 1975 he worked with Virilio for about 15 years on the journal *Traverses*. From the same year he began to teach regularly in America. The journals he edited were not associated with any political organization but were engaged in radical and critical cultural theory on the radical left. Later he was to say that the years 'at Nanterre in the sixties and seventies were some of the best years. Once these were over we mourned' (1993a: 20). He presented his doctoral *habilitation* at the Sorbonne in February 1986. He retired from the University in 1987.

Baudrillard's formation was therefore decisively influenced by his wide reading of German literature, philosophy, and social theory in a meeting of Marxist and

Nietzschean traditions. But clearly the influence of French themes can be seen in the importance of Rimbaud and the Situationists and structuralism (Durkheim and Mauss to Barthes). This marks out the distinctive character of Baudrillard's engagement which in the 1960s and early 1970s was essentially an engagement from within Marxism, with the radical emergence of the system of objects and the consumer society. He then made a radical shift towards an anthropological position against modernism (including Marxism, psychoanalysis, and structuralism). It was from this perspective that he launched his famous confrontations with writers such as Michel Foucault (Baudrillard, 1987), and cultural critiques such as his famous attack on the architecture of the Pompidou Centre ('Beaubourg Effect', in 1994b), political critiques of the French Socialist and Communist Parties (1985), and in the end an attack on the continued viability of the social sciences themselves with his thesis of the 'end of the social' (1983). Some of these essays made a considerable impact when they became available in English in the Foreign Accents series edited by Lotringer, who also published a long interview with Baudrillard called 'Forget Baudrillard' in 1987. His challenge to modernism led him in this period to be identified as the father of a theory of postmodernity and a new postmodernist style, and even baptized 'pimp of postmodernism' (Moore, 1988). Baudrillard's relation to postmodernism has, however, always been critical and nuanced, and only in the 1990s has his position finally become clear. But one further strand in Baudrillard's work should be noted. From his earliest writings it has been evident that he always had time and space to write on politics and political ideas. The collection entitled *La Gauche Divine: Chronique des Années 1977–1984* (1985) contains Baudrillard's analysis of the failure of the Socialist and Communist Parties to confront the problems of the post-1968 political conditions, and *Ecran Total* (1997b) collects Baudrillard's writing for the left-wing newspaper *Liberation* over the decade from 1987, including his provocative analysis of the Gulf War (1995). Two theses dominate these political analyses. The first is that proletarian revolutionary transition is no longer on the agenda in Western societies, and secondly this new situation is one of involution within the boundaries of the West with real 'events' occurring only on the fault line (e.g. Bosnia) of this culture (see Cushman and Mestrovic, 1996).

Baudrillard's work draws on a large number of sources. He himself has identified Nietzsche as the most important and long lasting. It is evident that there is a continuing engagement with and use of modern literature, from Kafka to Ballard, as well as those key theorists he identified in texts of the 1970s: Marx, Mauss and Bataille, Saussure, Freud, Benjamin, and McLuhan. Because his work has entailed the development of a theory of mass communications he is today often linked with the work of Paul Virilio with whom he worked closely for many years on the journal *Traverses*. However, Baudrillard's writings in the 1990s were no longer aimed at providing a 'critical analysis' of modern and postmodern culture. Critiques such as Virilio's, like Marxism itself, remained trapped, he argues, within enlightenment rationalist traditions. Baudrillard, in an ultimate challenge, tried in various ways to develop 'fatal theory': philosophers have always interpreted a disenchanted world, the point is to make it even more enigmatic. Some of his interests here have led him to adopt some of the paradoxical formulations of recent science with the result that he has been identified as one of the contemporary 'intellectual impostures' – a description he has, with usual wit, embraced enthusiastically.

Thus Baudrillard seems particularly sensitive to alterations of the current cultural and political conjuncture. His writing is reflexive to a high degree, not only with respect to the changing effectiveness of concepts and ideas, but also to the forms of the interventions themselves. Facing the defeat of the May 1968 revolutionary movement, his writing has sought to rework radical theory in a way which comes to terms with the cultural, technological, and political forms of the 'advanced' societies. For many radicals of the 1960s the option has been either to retrench into a fundamentalist Marxism, or to adopt the framework of the consumer society with qualifications (to make it more democratic, more ecologically aware, and to promote within it a postmodern form of multicultural tolerance). In this context Baudrillard provides an alternative which regards these variations as disastrously involuted forms of a *ressentiment* culture in which a secret *stratégie du pire* holds sway. He is therefore an outsider whose ideas are profoundly at odds with contemporary progressive opinion, be it socialist, liberal, or feminist.

SOCIAL THEORY AND CONTRIBUTIONS

Baudrillard is probably best known for his association with postmodern consumer culture, and his theses on simulation and hyperreality, yet these ideas have been widely misunderstood and misinterpreted. A key document must therefore be Baudrillard's own summing up of his work available in his *Habilitation* presentation called *L'Autre par Lui-même* (published in English as *The Ecstasy of Communication*, 1988b). This text is crucial for a reading of Baudrillard's work up to the mid-1980s although his thinking has gone through further important developments. In his own account he refers to his first major set of writings, on the object and consumer society, as critical structuralism. By the mid-1970s and especially with the book *Symbolic Exchange and Death* (1993b) he had worked through a critique of structuralism and Marxism to a position based on symbolic exchange theory. Yet by the early 1980s he had redefined his position as one based on the force of pure seduction: 'there is no longer any symbolic referent to the challenge of signs and to the challenge through signs ... The object itself takes the initiative or reversibility... Another succession is determinant' (1988b: 80). In the mid 1990s he was to move further in this trajectory to one based not on symbolic but impossible exchange.

One way of reading these positional changes can be made by adopting the image used by Baudrillard in his *habilitation presentation*, that of the double spiral of the symbol and the sign. His first set of writings on the object and consumer cultures can be seen therefore as an analysis of the semiotic cultures of Western societies for which, in his writings in the 1970s, he produced a famous genealogy of their simulacral forms (1994b). Over the last 15 years he has been working on a 'fourth order' of this genealogy which corresponds to a theory of postmodernity. There is, however, little if any direct critical commentary on this phase of Baudrillard's work, for most discussion has concerned the theory of the 'third order' concerning mass media, mass society, and hyperreal phenomena (mistaken as postmodernity). But Baudrillard's writings in the period 1975–90 were focused on the other side of the spiral, that of the symbol, with essays on symbolic exchange, seduction, fatal strategies, and evil. In the 1990s he has been writing on what he has termed 'the perfect crime', the vast transformation of Western cultures under the impact of communication technology towards the virtualization of the world.

Thus Baudrillard's writing is made up of a number of projects which are coherently articulated within the idea of the double spiral (on one side the symbol, the other the sign). This makes it possible to identify four sets of theoretical writing. The first concerns the quasi-Marxist analysis of the commodity-object, sign-exchange, and consumer society. The second concerns the theory of symbolic orders and symbolic exchange and has a strong anthropological character entailing a radicalization of the notion of the gift and death. The third set comes back to focus on contemporary culture but is no longer framed in a base-superstructure model. The new analysis relies on the concepts of seduction, fate, and evil drawn from anthropological perspectives and employing them, even methodologically, alongside a surprising survival from French sociology, the concept of pathology (1993c). The fourth set concerns the transition of cultures from third to fourth order simulacral forms from a position identified as that of impossible exchange. There is a movement in Baudrillard's work from that of critical structuralism and with Marxism with its desire to expose the alienated workings of the modern social system and its culture, to a theory of the object as pure sign and to a mode of writing which is more poetic, 'fatal', enigmatic, fragmented, embracing the paradoxes produced in the advanced sciences. In Baudrillard's terms, then, the very evolution of the sign in Western cultures through the genealogy of its various simulacral forms produces its own ironic self-destruction. This situation provides new opportunities and calls for a metamorphosis in the form of radical theory.

A key element of Baudrillard's work has therefore been a crucial contribution to the theory of the symbolic order (with notable studies of fate, evil, seduction, and death) which has required a refusal to make a discipline boundary between anthropology and social theory, indeed to confront sociology with radical anthropology (Genosko, 1998). In Baudrillard's early writing the simple ambivalence of the symbol was contrasted with the univocality of the sign. The radicalization of his theory became clear in his view that the symbolic order is not simply primordial, but is the superior form, even as it is destroyed by modern rationalities. It is characterized in Baudrillard's view by four significant features. First, as opposed to the sign it does not organize itself on the reality principle, since the world is apprehended as fable and narrative. Secondly the apprehension of time is nonlinear, nonaccumulative, nonprogressive, since the narrative and the gift are both fatal and reversible. Thirdly, other cultures are not apprehended as belonging to a homogeneous world system of differences but in the order of radical otherness, since the symbolic order (based on the rule) is not parallel to the culture of human rights (based on law). Fourthly, the relation to the order of things is not possessive, the symbolic order is articulated on metamorphosis in ritual time and space. What is new in Baudrillard's version of the symbolic order is that it is active, dynamic, strategic, based on challenge of radical illusion.

It is clear that this view of 'primitive culture' reverses many of the assumptions found in the work of sociologists like Max Weber who sometimes refer to these cultures as superstitious, passive, conservative, and traditional. It is one of the many 'banal' illusions of the semiotic cultures that they are progressive, active, accumulative. Baudrillard gives Weber's analysis of rationalization a radical Nietzschean reading through an analysis of simulacral forms. With the emergence of the idea of the real world, and the ideology of the real (Majastre, 1996: 209), there emerges the cultures of the sign (in the Saussurean manner: signifier/signified/referent-real). This introduces a split in the semiotic cultures between the representation of the meaning, say of death and the idea of real biological death. This split becomes a generalized premise of the existence of all phenomena subject to objective and scientific investigation. It introduces the dimension of the difference between the true and the false, but also disturbs illusion by introducing the opposition between the real and the simulacrum. According to Baudrillard's genealogy, a first order of simulacra can be seen in the representations of the body and the world in the Renaissance period: in the model of the human automaton, in *trompe l'oeil* forms, and represented in media like stucco. With the explosive Industrial Revolution and the beginnings of mass production, a second order of simulacral forms comes into existence as mass reproduction: the human is represented in crude mechanical robotics, and mass (re)production of commodities in new media like plastic. But this second order is still based on the principle of utility where production and reproduction arise from an original hand-crafted object. This gives way with the implosive advent of the consumer society to sign-exchange and the emergence of the 'system of objects' – a society dominated by computerized mass media images. Baudrillard's challenging theory is that this affects all domains: relation to the order of things is not only subject to mass media, particularly televisual, mediation (which shifts cultural phenomena into the hyperreal), but also with the matrix revolution (which shifts simulacra into simulational forms). The transition from this third order to fourth order simulacral forms arrives with the full long-term impact of the information revolution, which leads to the greatest rupture of all, an apocalpyse which occurs without protagonist or victim, neither explosive nor implosive: the postmodernization and the virtualization of the world.

It is important to note that the genealogy of simulacral forms is not a simple historical procession. It is clear that Baudrillard thinks in terms of variations in the way each culture evolves in relation to his theoretical genealogy. In the case of America for example, it is important that Baudrillard insists on its specificity. First Baudrillard situates his own analysis as an ironic recasting of what he calls de Tocqueville's paradox, that is, the way the American world tends both to absolute insignificance, and to absolute originality, a 'genius in its irrepressible development of equality, banality, and indifference' (1988a: 89). And, secondly, he adopts McLuhan's thesis, which suggests that American culture is characterized by the absence of second order simulacra. In other words it has a completely different form of modernity from that of Europe. It is evident from the *Cool Memories* series more generally that even within Europe Baudrillard's analyses do not homogenize. The cultures of France, Italy, Spain, Germany, for example, are all treated as individualities in their own right. Given that Baudrillard has become one of the most travelled theorists, and not only maintains the practice of the journal but also the camera (his photographs also maintain this view of cultural individuality, 1998c), any reading of Baudrillard's contribution must come to terms with the great diversity of the forms of his work (which includes a volume of poetry, 1978) and the vast range and detail of his analyses.

APPRAISAL OF KEY ADVANCES AND CONTROVERSIES

It seems clear that there are three or four major themes in Baudrillard's work which have had considerable theoretical impact. The first is a consequence of his early writings on the object and sign-exchange. These ideas have been taken up principally by those wishing to develop a line of Marxism in opposition to structural and particularly Althusserian theory, which continues to stress the importance of modes of economic production and Marx's theory of capitalism. Baudrillard, along with many others of course, suggested that the evolution of consumer society was a crucial development rendering orthodox Marxism obsolete. Baudrillard's attempt to theorize sign-exchange as an evolution of commodity exchange received considerable critical attention. The notion of hyperreality, particularly in relation to American culture, however was bitterly contested by Marxists in particular because it suggested that successful political class struggle and dialectical progression was no longer possible. Baudrillard's second theme, that of the superiority of symbolic exchange as a revolutionary principle, led him into an opposition to vitually all the major critical theorists. His third theme, that of the analysis of seduction, fatal strategies, and evil, as secret forms within the semiotic cultures themselves, gave rise to great misunderstanding and further notoriety. He now became the object of praise or vilification as 'high priest of postmodernism'. The theory of the fourth order simulacral forms has fallen on deaf ears. Even among the sympathetic recent commentaries and discussion of Genosko, and Butler, there is great resistance to accepting that any such transition has occurred in Baudrillard's analyses, or if it has it does not deserve to be taken seriously. For these writers Baudrillard remains above all a theorist of third order forms.

The first theme, that of the theory of the object system, has been the subject of an important and continuing debate. Baudrillard's fusion of critical structuralism (Baudrillard's *System of Objects* and Roland Barthes's *The Fashion System* were contemporaneous), with a situationist perspective on the society of the spectacle (Debord), was nevertheless conceived in a problematic in which Baudrillard could still refer to capitalism and class struggle. His debt to Lukacs and Marcuse is clear in his critique of that form of Marxism which insisted on the universality of the concept of mode of production and the principle of overdetermined contradiction. The most important aspects of Baudrillard's position lay in the fact that it contested the ahistorical analysis of capitalist society and at the same time confronted the economic reductionism of much of orthodox Marxism. Baudrillard's critical discussion of Marxism also picked up the point that its major thinkers had already pointed to radical shifts in the nature of capitalist organization. He pointed particularly to Lenin's notion of the importance of the transition from market to monopoly capitalism. Baudrillard gave this transition an extremely radical interpretation: it initiated the determination of social relation by the semiotic code (1975). Others have argued that Baudrillard's work makes possible a theory of the mode of information (Poster, 1990), or the mode of consumption (Ritzer, 1999).

But the theory of the object as a relation of sign-exchange pushed Baudrillard's theorizing towards aesthetics. At one point (1981: 185) he argued that the 'object' emerged specifically with the work of the Bauhaus. In other words the transition from the commodity form proper towards the object was essentially a coupling of function (use value) with aesthetic value. This development of the analysis of the commodity evidently departed from the theory of reification and fetishism in important ways. The key development was certainly the attempt to apply semiotics rather than phenomenology to the analysis of exchange. Clearly implicit in Baudrillard's interpretation is a reliance on Saussure's definition of the sign, but Baudrillard was already theorizing the sign and sign-exchange as historically associated with a particular stage of the development of capitalism when it was discovered that Saussure had also worked on but not completed a study of anagrams in classical literature of antiquity (Starobinski's, 1979, book on this was first published in 1971). With this clear opposition between the anagram and the sign Baudrillard was able to provide content to his previously somewhat gestural notion of the ambivalence of the symbol (Genosko, 1994, 1998).

Certainly the more orthodox Marxists, particularly the Althusserians, rejected both the structuralist methodology of this style of analysis and the general theory of consumer society. Baudrillard's analysis was a contribution to a form of analysis which had much wider resonance (parallels are to be found in writers as far apart as Marcuse, Debord, Barthes, and Lyotard), an analysis which suggested the moment of proletarian revolution had passed and that with mass consumerism a new form of social integration had been evolved within the capitalist order. Althusserian Marxism posed the question in terms of ideological state apparatuses and the new crisis of capitalist legitimation in the universities in conditions of a world-wide crisis of capitalism, but still held to the view that the determinant and revolutionary contradiction was that between capital and labour. Baudrillard's reply to this idea was to suggest that reinforcing the economic and political organization of the proletariat in the new conditions of mass consumerism actually facilitated the neutralization of the proletariat as a class within late capitalist forms, since the principal site of integration was then not confronted (1985).

Baudrillard's second thematic, which was a logical development of the theory of the symbol, led to a radicalization of the notion of the symbolic order (Genosko, 1998). It seems that the preparation of this line of analysis was to some extent inspired by the work of Foucault on madness. Baudrillard's genealogy of forms of relations to the dead parallel's Foucault's analysis of the role of sequestration and asylums in the genealogy of madness. For Baudrillard, death is a fundamental symbolic form. His analysis follows closely its genealogy as revealed in relation to the body. He charts carefully the movement from early forms in which the dead body is retained in the group to those in which there is a hierarchy of those who pass, under the control of priests, to heavenly immortality. His analysis of the cemeteries or the necropolis charts the social distance between the living and the dead body. After this period of sequestration, the dead, like the mad, are subject to the vicissitudes of civilization.

When Foucault published his famous *Discipline and Punish*, with its theory of modern forms of power and surveillance, Baudrillard regarded this as a major turning point in Foucault's work. He wrote a stunning review of it, published as *Forget Foucault*, in which he argued that Foucault's thought itself had been ensnared in the system of micro power and control he seemed to be analysing (1987). It became evident from this moment on that Baudrillard was to regard structuralism, post-structuralism, and deconstructionism as complicit with the code of modern consumer culture and unable to confront it. Baudrillard also lamented Saussure's own failure to develop the opposition to the sign in an adequate theory of the symbol, just as he lamented Freud's and Lacan's universalization of a particular form of the Oedipal complex, and Lévi-Strauss's failure to develop a symbolic theory of the savage mind (1993b). Lyotard retorted that Baudrillard had produced yet another myth of the primitive.

Baudrillard, however, did not stay within the ambit of the theory of symbolic exchange for very long, at least according to the *habilitation* presentation. In the three works of the next period, that is *Seduction*, *Fatal Strategies*, and *The Transparency of Evil*, Baudrillard tried to demonstrate the power of fatal over critical theory. The logic of this change of position seems determined by the very loss of revolutionary agency by social forces. No longer aligned with the active alienated subject, Baudrillard concluded that power of agency had passed to the side of the object. What was strikingly effective in Baudrillard's return to the analysis of current cultures in the 1980s was his general proposition that social checks and balances (the ideal of liberal containment of power) and the framework of dialectical progressive development (the ideal of revolutionary sublation) were outmoded logics, and as he himself expressed it 'our societies have passed beyond this limit point' (1988b: 82; see Bauman, 1992).

The new situation, he claimed, was not principally one of unremitting mass homogenization, though this was occurring in the exemplary logic of cloning and replication, and what he identified as the culture of indifference and impatience (homogenization entailed the disappearance of the historical event: even war could no longer take place, 1995). The dominant logic was, however, exponential, a logic driven by the liberation of energies. Baudrillard began to identify the emergence of extreme phenomena against the background of indifference. Two linked propositions were developed at this point. First, the fatal strategy of the object could be seen as a form of intensification: the world was in the grip of the delirious passion of the object. Hyperreal phenomena were just one form of this ecstatic movement of things – more than sexual in the *stratégie du pire*: pornography; more than fat: obesity. But secondly, with the liberation of energies and the deregulation of balances, Baudrillard also identified the disintegration of boundaries. This led to the emergence of what he called transpolitical phenomena. This process concerned not the intensification of logics, but the intensification of indistinctions. Thus more than sexual: transsexual; more than historical: transhistorical; more than aesthetic: transaesthetic; more than genetic: transgenetic. Baudrillard had already noted that objects were no longer made from traditional materials but new homogenized media like plastics. At this juncture even the boundaries of objects (including those of species) were in the process of dissolution.

Some of Baudrillard's brilliant analyses of these transitions were picked up at the time in a somewhat bizarre way. From at least three quite different points of view he became identified as proposing a postmodern genre of theorizing about a postmodern condition. The first interpretation was developed by Jameson whose work was decisively influenced by Baudrillard at this time. Jameson (1991) simply argued that by maintaining a Marxist framework, Baudrillard's analysis could really be seen as accounting for the culture of late capitalism. Kellner also presented Baudrillard as the theorist of postmodern culture and suggested that Baudrillard was in complete complicity with this logic as revealed by the new fatal styles of analysis adopted (1989). Feminists such as Meagan Morris (1988) and Suzanne Moore (1988) saw Baudrillard's analysis of the sexual object as deeply conservative, patriarchal, and reactionary.

The final theme in Baudrillard's work is the theory of the fourth order simulacral forms. Central to this theory is the continuation of the analysis of the fate of reality, objects, and exchange. If the world has indeed escaped the frameworks of regulating balances, then events and phenomena follow a delirious course in a radically new space. Here Baudrillard draws increasingly on the language of the advanced sciences, particularly where the relation of subject and object have become problematic. The structures of time and space are no longer Euclidean, subject and object no longer independent. It is as if, he suggests, for a period in the history of the sciences, the object was caught unawares by theory (1988b: 87). Today the object is no longer content to remain passive in relation to the subject. From a world of rigorous structural determinations, the current situation is one of radical indeterminacy of fundamental principles and knowledge. Baudrillard's most recent essay (1999) concerns the aspect of exchange. In this new, 'postmodern' situation, exchange itself become increasingly difficult. In consequence he argues, analysis must be made from a position of 'impossible exchange', recognizing the full force of the requirement for a new kind of theory appropriate to a world in radical uncertainty beyond the matrix, one which deals with unique objects, singularities.

It is now becoming clear that Baudrillard has been trying to analyse and theorize the fourth order since the mid 1980s, while most commentaries have remained stubbornly within his concept of hyperreality and the code. It is also becoming more evident that if Baudrillard does have a concept of postmodernity it does not have the third order as its object. Indeed it might well be that the break between third and fourth order phenomena is for Baudrillard the most significant one and the one which marks the rupture with hypermodernity. Yet Baudrillard's analysis suggests this most fundamental transition is not marked by any visible revolutionary event, and as it becomes accomplished it therefore becomes the 'perfect crime'. Unlike Virilio, for example for whom the apocalypse in the real may arrive with a 'general accident', for Baudrillard in the 'third' order the last judgment had already occurred but the messiah (or the revolution), missed the appointment (1987), but in the fourth order there is not even an appointment: 'for mutants there can no longer be any 'Last Judgement: for what body will one resurrect?' (1988: 51).

Critique

Because Baudrillard has adopted a large variety of ways of developing his ideas it has been very common for critiques to suggest that his work is not as coherent as he has claimed or that it lacks a solid evidential base. His attack on the reality principle has alienated him from rationalists and theorists in the materialist tradition, while his uncompromising critiques of democracies and Western hegemony has alienated him from liberals and the human rights movement. Many of those who supported his writings on consumer society and hyperreality have found it difficult to follow, let alone accept, his theory of fourth order simulacra as a theory of postmodernity. One strand of opposition has suggested that his theorizing is still a reductive technological determinism which refuses the complexity of current societies. The genealogies he has evolved, it is claimed, oversimplify by submerging many conflicting tendencies within the frame of a single 'order' of simulacra. Baudrillard does not even attempt to analyse how these orders may combine or collide. Indeed it is not altogether clear how they relate to the evolution of individual cultures, or how they are constructed as concepts (how they relate to ideologies for example). But more fundamental is the criticism that Baudrillard has reintroduced primitive premodern forms of superstition, and prejudice, into the social sciences, thereby abandoning the idea that there can be advances in rational knowledge and discoveries about the real world. In other words his theory has become simply a mirror of commodity fetishism (Callinicos, 1989). Finally there is criticism of his own presentation of his apparently relentless pessimism about Western cultures. Whereas with writers like Nietzsche there remained the promise of transcendence and affirmation, Baudrillard suggests this is regarded an outdated utopian vision. Critics have suggested, however, that despite himself Baudrillard remains surprisingly modernist and affirmative (Zurbrugg, 1993, 1997; Mestrovic, 1998).

It is difficult to estimate the lasting effects of Baudrillard's work, but they are likely to be profound. It is already apparent, as Ritzer (1997, 1999) has noted, that in retrospect, Baudrillard was remarkably perceptive in picking up the precise details of the emerging consumer society in the 1960s (in Baudrillard, 1998b: 17). Others have pointed to the way he identified the major implications of the information revolution, and the importance of simulation modelling. He became notorious by identifying at the same time the death of the social and the emergence of hyperreal culture. All of these developments were situated, in the first instance, in his theory of a modified capitalism. But his work in the 1990s has suggested that a further and even more radical transition has occurred, what he has called the shift into fourth order simulacra. This is perhaps for Baudrillard the decisive shift, but one which is unprecedented in its form, for it is a revolution without agent, 'without victim and without motive', without therefore any resistance, indeed if experienced at all it is with complete indifference (1996b: 1). It is a transition, however, which throws down the greatest of challenges to theory, which, Baudrillard argues, must be transformed radically if it is to grasp what is happening. Theory itself must reverse its basic terms. A conventional frame which analyses the distinction of things within a given homogeneous time and space must be replaced by one which analyses the way in which things are 'inseparable' from each other and yet which no longer 'interact in a homogeneous space' (1996b: 54). Thus, in retrospect it may be, and this will be contested for some time of course, that Baudrillard's legacy will be that his studies of consumer society and hyperreal simulacra only chart the way to an analysis of the way extreme phenomena act once they have passed into the fourth order void.

BAUDRILLARD'S MAJOR WORKS

Baudrillard, J. (1975) *The Mirror of Production.* St Louis, MO: Telos.

Baudrillard, J. (1978) *L'Ange de Stuc.* Paris: Galilee.

Baudrillard, J. (1981) *For a Critique of the Political Economy of the Sign.* St Louis, MO: Telos.

Baudrillard, J. (1983) *In the Shadow of the Silent Majorities.* New York: Semiotext(e).

Baudrillard, J. (1985) *La Gauche Divine.* Paris: Grasset.

Baudrillard, J. (1987) *Forget Foucault.* New York: Semiotext(e).

Baudrillard, J. (1988a) *America.* London: Verso.

Baudrillard, J. (1988b) *The Ecstasy of Communication.* New York: Semiotext(e).

Baudrillard, J. (1990a) *Seduction.* London: Macmillan.

Baudrillard, J. (1990b) *Fatal Strategies.* London: Pluto.

Baudrillard, J. (1990c) *Cool Memories.* London Verso.

Baudrillard, J. (1993a) *Baudrillard Live: Selected Interviews.* London: Routledge.

Baudrillard, J. (1993b) *Symbolic Exchange and Death.* London: Sage.

Baudrillard, J. (1993c) *The Transparency of Evil.* London: Verso.

Baudrillard, J. (1994a) *The Illusion of the End.* Cambridge: Polity.

Baudrillard, J. (1994b) *Simulacra and Simulation.* Ann Arbor: University of Michigan Press.

Baudrillard, J. (1995) *The Gulf War Did Not Take Place.* Sydney: Power.

Baudrillard, J. (1996a) *Cool Memories II.* Cambridge: Polity.

Baudrillard, J. (1996b) *The Perfect Crime.* London: Verso.

Baudrillard, J. (1996c) *The System of Objects.* London: Verso.

Baudrillard, J. (1997a) *Fragments. Cool Memories III.* London: Verso.

Baudrillard, J. (1997b) *Ecran Total.* Paris: Galilee.

Baudrillard, J. (1998a) *Paroxsym: Interviews with Phillipe Petit.* London: Verso.

Baudrillard, J. (1998b) *The Consumer Society: Myths and Structures.* London: Sage.

Baudrillard, J. (1998c) *Car l'Illusion ne s'oppose pas à la Realité.* Paris: Descartes.

Baudrillard, J. (1999) *L'Echange Impossible.* Paris: Galilee.

SECONDARY REFERENCES

Abbas, A. (ed.) (1990) *The Provocation of Jean Baudrillard.* Hong Kong: Twilight.

Bauman, Z, (1992) *Intimations of Postmodernism.* London: Routledge.

Best, S. (1989) 'The commodification of reality and the reality of commodification', *Critical Perspectives in Social Theory,* 19 (3): 32–51.

Butler, R. (1999) *Jean Baudrillard: The Defence of the Real.* London: Sage.

Callinicos, A. (1989) *Against Postmodernism: A Marxist Critique.* Cambridge: Polity.

Cushman, T. and Mestrovic, S. (eds) (1996) *This Time We Knew.* New York: New York University Press.

Denzin, N. (1991) *Images of Postmodern Society: Social Theory and Contemporary Cinema.* London: Sage.

Frankovits, A. (ed.) (1984) *Seduced and Abandoned: The Baudrillard Scene.* Glebe: Stonemoss.

Gane, M. (1991a) *Baudrillard: Critical and Fatal Theory.* London: Routledge.

Gane, M. (1991b) *Baudrillard's Bestiary: Baudrillard and Culture.* London: Routledge.

Gane, M. (2000a) *Jean Baudrillard: in Radical Uncertainty.* London: Pluto.

Gane, M. (ed.) (2000b) *Jean Baudrillard: Masters of Social Theory. 4 Vols.* London: Sage.

Genosko, G. (1994) *Baudrillard and Signs: Signification Ablaze.* London: Routledge.

Genosko, G. (1998) *Undisciplined Theory.* London: Sage.

Genosko, G. (1999) *McLuhan and Baudrillard: The Masters of Implosion.* London: Routledge.

Gottdiener, M. (1995) *Postmodern Semiotics: Material Culture and the Forms of Modern Life.* Oxford: Blackwell.

Horrocks, C. (1999) *Baudrillard and the Millenium.* Cambridge: Icon.

Jameson, F. (1991) *Postmodernism, or, the Cultural Logic of Late Capitalism.* Durham N.C. Duke University Press.

Kellner, D. (1989) *Jean Baudrillard: From Marxism to Postmodernity and Beyond.* Cambridge: Polity.

Kellner, D. (1989) 'Boundaries and borderlines: reflections on Baudrillard and critical theory', *Current Perspectives in Social Theory,* 19: 5–22.

Kellner, D. (ed.) (1994) *Baudrillard: A Critical Reader.* Oxford: Blackwell.

Kroker, A. (1985) 'Baudrillard's Marx', *Theory Culture and Society,* 2 (3): 69–83.

Kroker, A. (1992) *The Possessed Individual: Technology and Postmodernism.* London: Macmillan.

Levin, C. (1996) *Jean Baudrillard: A Study of Cultural Metaphysics.* London: Prentice Hall.

Luke, T. W. (1991) 'Power and politics in hyperreality – the critical project of Jean Baudrillard', *Social Science Journal,* 28 (3): 347–67.

Majastre, J. O. (ed.) (1996) *Sans Oublier Baudrillard.* Brussels: La Lettre Volee.

Merrin, W. (1994) 'Uncritical criticism? Norris, Baudrillard and the Gulf War', *Economy and Society,* 23 (2): 141–54.

Mestrovic, S. (1998) *Anthony Giddens, The Last Modernist.* London: Routledge.

Moore, S. (1988) 'Baudrillard – a different drummer,' in R. Chapman and Rutherford, J. (eds), *Male Order:*

Unwrapping Masculinity. London: Lawrence and Wishart.
Morris, M. (1988) *The Pirate's Fianceé*. London: Verso.
Norris, C. (1989) 'Lost in the funhouse: Baudrillard and the politics of postmodernism', *Textual Practice*, 3 (3): 360–87.
Norris, C. (1992) *Uncritical Theory: Postmodernism and Society: Intellectuals and the Gulf War*. London: Lawrence and Wishart.
Poster, M. (1990) *The Mode of Information: Poststructuralism and Social Context*. Cambridge: Polity.
Ritzer, G. (1997) *Postmodern Social Theory*. New York: McGraw-Hill.
Ritzer, G. (1999) *Enchanting a Disenchanted World: Revolutionizing the Means of Consumption*. London: Pine Forge.
Rojek, C. and Turner, B. (eds) (1993) *Forget Baudrillard?* London: Routledge.
Starobinski, J. (1979) *Words Upon Words: The Anagrams of Ferdinand Saussure*. New Haven: Yale University Press.
Stearns, W. and Chaloupka, W. (eds) (1992) *Jean Baudrillard: The Disappearance of Art and Politics*. London: Macmillan.
Smart, B. (1990) 'On the disorder of things: sociology, postmodernity, and the "end of the social"', *Sociology*, 24 (3): 397–416.
Wernick, A. (1984) 'Sign and commodity: aspects of the cultural dynamic of advanced capitalism', *Canadian Journal of Political and Social Theory*, 8 (1-2): 17–34.
Zurbrugg, N. (1993) 'Baudrillard, modernism and postmodernism', *Economy and Society*, 22 (4): 482–500.
Zurbrugg, N. (ed.) (1997) *Art and Artefact*. London: Sage.

18

Gilles Deleuze and Félix Guattari

PAUL PATTON

BIOGRAPHICAL DETAILS AND THEORETICAL CONTEXT

Deleuze and Guattari belonged to a generation of French intellectuals whose political consciousness was formed, as Guattari once said, 'in the enthusiasm and naiveté of the Liberation' (Deleuze and Guattari, 1972: 15). Deleuze was born in 1925. He studied philosophy in Paris at the Lycée Carnot and the Sorbonne during the Second World War. Trained in the history of philosophy by professors such as Ferdinand Alquié, Georges Canguilhem, and Jean Hippolyte, he passed the *agrégation* in 1949. He later taught at the University of Lyon. In 1969, at Foucault's invitation, he took up a post at the experimental University of Paris 8 at Vincennes (later St Denis), where he taught until his retirement in 1987. After a long period of respiratory illness, Deleuze committed suicide in 1995.

In addition to short studies of Proust, Hume, Bergson, and Kant, Deleuze wrote influential books on Nietzsche and Spinoza. Foucault acknowledged Deleuze's reconstruction of Nietzsche's theory of the will to power in terms of active and reactive forces as an important influence on his own thinking about power. Deleuze's major work, *Difference and Repetition* ([1969] 1994), outlined a metaphysics of difference which takes its point of departure from the manner in which philosophy hitherto had conceived of repetition. Deleuze argues that a concept of difference 'in itself' must entail a concept of repetition as involving variation and not simply repetition of the same. Elements of this philosophy of difference informed the social and political philosophy subsequently developed in collaboration with Guattari.

Whereas Deleuze first came into contact with political movements and activists during the years after 1968, Guattari had a long career of activism in radical psychotherapy and communist organizations. Born in 1930, he studied pharmacy and philosophy at university and was active in the French Communist Party during the 1950s. He left to work with a dissident left newspaper *La Voie Communiste* from 1958 to 1965, and with various extraparliamentary left groups thereafter. He worked at an experimental psychiatric hospital – the Clinique de la Borde – from 1953. He trained in Lacanian psychoanalysis from 1962 to 1969 when he joined the Ecole

Freudienne de Paris as an analyst. He played an important role in the development of institutional psychotherapy and subseqent 'antipsychiatry' movements. He died of a heart attack in 1992.

Anti-Oedipus brought notoriety to the authors as founders of a new synthesis of Freudian and Marxian thought known as 'the philosophy of desire'. They rejected the idea that the social production of reality was independent of desiring-production, maintaining instead that:

> the social field is immediately invested by desire, that it is the historically determined product of desire, and that libido has no need of any mediation or sublimation, any psychic operation, any transformation, in order to invade and invest the productive forces and the relations of production. There is only desire and the social, and nothing else'. (Deleuze and Guattari, 1977: 28–9)

In the aftermath of May 1968, *Anti-Oedipus* was widely read in the belief that periods of revolutionary ferment saw the emergence of unadulterated desire and a will to change, which was as quickly suppressed by the established organizations of political opposition (such as the communist party and trade unions) as it was by the forces of order. From this period onwards, Deleuze and Guattari both became involved with a variety of groups and causes, including the *Groupe d'Information sur les Prisons* (GIP) begun by Foucault and others in 1972, protests against the treatment of immigrant workers, and support for homosexual rights. Later they took public positions on issues such as the imprisonment of Antonio Negri and other Italian intellectuals on charges of complicity with terrorism. Guattari co-authored a book with Negri in 1985, the French title of which translates as *New Spaces of Freedom* (Guattari and Negri, 1990).

Deleuze and Guattari shared many of the political and theoretical orientations of the post-1968 libertarian left such as the politics of language and signification and a concern for the micro-politics of social life. Nevertheless, in a 1972 interview with Deleuze, Foucault tells the story of a Maoist who once said to him: 'I can easily understand Sartre's purpose in siding with us; I can understand his goals and his involvement in politics; I can partially understand your position, since you've always been concerned with the problem of confinement. But Deleuze is an enigma' (Deleuze and Foucault, 1977: 205). In reply, Deleuze points to the emergence of a new conception of the relationship between theory and practice in his own work with Guattari, one which stands in marked contrast to the idea that the intellectual represents the vanguard of a proletarian movement which embodies the forces of social change. Rather than a determinate and hierarchical relationship, theory and practice are understood to involve'a system of relays within ... a multiplicity of parts that are both theoretical and practical' (Deleuze and Foucault, 1977: 206). In these terms, Deleuze and Guattari's *Anti-Oedipus* can be understood as a theoretical relay of practical resistance to the role of psychoanalysis in the repression of potentially revolutionary expressions of desire. Their 'schizoanalytic' analysis of unconscious desire and its forms of political investment is conceived as a means to the 'liberation' of the creative or 'schizo' processes present in a given social field.

At the same time, Deleuze does not hesitate to describe *Anti-Oedipus* as 'from beginning to end a book of political philosophy' (Deleuze, 1995: 170). As well as the experimental and challenging *A Thousand Plateaus*, Deleuze and Guattari published a study of *Kafka* in 1985 (Deleuze and Guattari, 1986) and in 1991 *What is Philosophy*? (Deleuze and Guattari, 1994). Their final collaborative work outlines a conception of philosophy which reflects the aims as well as the methods of their own practice of conceptual invention. Philosophy, as they understand it, is essentially a critical exercise of thought which, unlike science and art, produces concepts which express pure events in terms of which we can understand everyday events and processes.

SOCIAL THEORY AND CONTRIBUTIONS

Deleuze and Guattari's polemical assault in *Anti-Oedipus* took the form of an external as well as an internal critique of the psychoanalytic theory of desire (Holland, 1999: 24). Their external critique argued that the Oedipal representation of desire expressed the marginalization of familial relations in relation to economic reproduction and the corresponding privatization of reproduction within the nuclear family under capitalism. They suggest that the family has become the ideal locus of subjectivity and the principal agent of containment of desire within capitalist society. Psychoanalysis repeats this operation in theory by making familial relations the basis of its theory of desire and the essential components in its theory of the constitution of human subjectivity:

> Hence, instead of participating in an undertaking that will bring about a genuine liberation, psychoanalysis is taking part in the work of bourgeois repression at its most far-reaching level, that is to say, keeping European humanity harnessed to the yoke of daddy-mummy and making no effort to do away with this problem once and for all. (Deleuze and Guattari, 1977: 50)

Their internal critique of psychoanalysis argues that it misrepresents the fundamentally productive nature and function of the unconscious. Their point is not to deny that unsatisfied desire may give rise to phantasmatic satisfactions but to deny that this reactive phenomena is the essence of desire. On their view, desire incorporates the power of differential reproduction which is the condition of all creativity and change. Their rejection of the psychoanalytic concept of desire is more than just a theoretical disagreement since they see this as a necessary precondition of dismantling the familial codification and containment of desire which serves to maintain the unstable equilibrium of the capitalist social machine.

Deleuze and Guattari's own theory of desire combines elements of Marx's concept of production and Freud's concept of libido. Desire is a complex process of the transformation of libidinal energy which they call a desire-machine. This process has three phases which they define in terms of distinct kinds of synthesis: a connective synthesis of flows and part-objects, a disjunctive synthesis of meanings attached to the elementary machines, and a conjunctive synthesis of resultant differences which give rise to intensities that are consumed by the body in question. Since this process is open to infinite variation, any fixed representation of desire such as the Oedipus complex amounts to a distortion. On this point, Deleuze and Guattari follow Lacan who insisted that the unconscious was structured like a sign system. However, unlike Lacan they argue that we can distinguish between the different kinds of machinic assemblages that determine individual perceptions, attitudes, expectations, and ways of speaking. The final section of *Anti-Oedipus* outlines a pragmatic schizoanalysis, the task of which is to 'undo the expressive oedipal unconscious, always artificial, repressive and repressed, mediated by the family, in order to attain the immediate, productive unconscious' (Deleuze and Guattari, 1977: 98). At the heart of this project lies a distinction between paranoiac or reactionary assemblages of desire and schizoid revolutionary assemblages.

While schizoanalysis 'has strictly no political program to propose' (Deleuze and Guattari, 1977: 380), it does offer a series of conceptual contrasts in terms of which we can evaluate the assemblages in play in a given social field. The evaluative structure outlined in *Anti-Oedipus* reappears in *A Thousand Plateaus*, where the machinic theory of desire is expanded into a theory of social, linguistic, intellectual, and other machinic assemblages. In accordance with the contrast between two poles of desire drawn in *Anti-Oedipus*, molar and molecular lines are contrasted with lines of flight; processes of deterritorialization contrasted with reterritorialization, stratification with destratification, nomadism with capture and so on. *A Thousand Plateaus* outlines a reiterated theory of assemblages in which the concept of assemblage provides formal continuity across the analyses of very different contents in each plateau. The book itself is a conceptual assemblage in which the successive plateaus describe a variety of assemblages in relation to different fields of content: machinic assemblages of desire; collective assemblages of enunciation; nomadic assemblages and apparatuses of capture; ideational, pictorial, and musical assemblages. There are two kinds of assemblage: extensive, molar multiplicities that are divisible, unifiable, totalizable and organizable; and molecular, intensive multiplicities that are not unifiable or totalizable and that do not divide without changing in nature.

In the Introduction to *A Thousand Plateaus*, in a terminology of trees and rhizomes chosen for its broad cultural resonance, Deleuze and Guattari contrast arborescent and rhizomatic assemblages or multiplicities. Arborescent systems are hierarchical and 'unifiable' objects in the sense that their boundaries can be clearly defined and their parts connected according to an invariant principle of unity. They embody the principles of organization found in modern bureaucracies, factories, armies and schools, in other words, in all of the central social mechanisms of power. By contrast, rhizomes lack principles of unity or connection such as central axes or invariant elements. They are fuzzy or indeterminate objects, defined 'by the outside: by the abstract line, the line of flight or deterritorialization according to which they change in nature (metamorphose into something else) and connect with other multiplicities' (Deleuze and Guattari, 1987: 9). Lines of flight or deterritorialization are the determining elements in any given assemblage in the sense that they define the form of creativity specific to that assemblage and the particular ways in which it can effect transformation in other assemblages or in itself.

Assemblages are defined in terms of a quadripartite structure along two axes. On the first axis, assemblages are composed of discursive and nondiscursive components: they are both assemblages of bodies and matter and assemblages of enunciation or utterance. Deleuze and Guattari distinguish between forms of content which involve bodies, their interactions and passions; and forms of expression which involve utterances, speech acts, or statements. In this respect, assemblages are close to what Foucault called *dispositifs* of power and knowledge, such as the modern system of penal imprisonment, or the complex arrangements of discourse and practices which define modern sexuality. On the second axis, assemblages are defined by the nature of the movements that govern their operation. On the one hand, there is the constitution of territories and fields of interiority; on the other hand, there are points of deterritorialization, and lines of flight along which the assemblage breaks down or becomes transformed into something else. Every assemblage has both movements of reterritorialization, which tend to fix and stabilize its elements, and 'cutting edges of deterritorialization which carry it away' (Deleuze and Guattari, 1987: 88). For Deleuze and Guattari, these movements of deterritorialization are constitutive of any assemblage: the articulation of the corporeal and discursive elements of a given assemblage 'is effected by the movements of deterritorialization that quantify their forms. That is why a social field is defined less by its conflicts and contradictions than by the lines of flight running through it' (Deleuze and Guattari, 1987: 90).

While assemblages are more or less concrete arrangements of things, their mode of functioning cannot be understood independently of the virtual or abstract machine which determines their mode of operation. Deleuze and Guattari propose that the constitutive function of the movements of deterritorialization is directed by an abstract machine which inhabits the assemblage like its virtual double.

Abstract machines are ontologically prior to the distinction between content and expression within a given assemblage, existing in 'the aspect or moment at which nothing but functions and matters remain' (Deleuze and Guattari, 1987: 141). The abstract machine immanent in a given assemblage 'presides over' the distinction between forms of content and expression and distributes this across the various strata, domains, and territories. It also 'conjugates' the movements of deterritorialization that affect those forms (Deleuze and Guattari, 1987: 141). Abstract machines are virtual multiplicities which are neither corporeal nor semiotic but 'diagrammatic' entities that do not exist independently of the assemblages in which they are actualized or expressed. They are virtual machines in the same sense as the software program which turns a given assemblage of computer hardware into a certain kind of technical machine (a calculating machine, a drawing machine etc).

Deleuze and Guattari's machinic ontology is an ethics in Spinoza's sense of the term which privileges the processes of mutation and metamorphosis which they call 'deterritorialization'. The concept of deterritorialization derives from Lacan's use of the term 'territorialization' to refer to the imprint of maternal care and nourishment on the child's libido and the resultant formation of part-objects and erogenous zones. In *Anti-Oedipus,* it was also used in the context of their historical account of the emergence of capitalism as a result of the conjugation of deterritorialized flows of labour and money. In the Conclusion to *A Thousand Plateaus,* deterritorialization is defined with deceptive simplicity as the complex movement or process by which something escapes or departs from a given territory (Deleuze and Guattari, 1987: 508). This process always involves at least two elements, namely the territory which is being left behind or reconstituted and the deterritorializing element. A territory of any kind always includes 'vectors of deterritorialization', either because the territory itself is inhabited by dynamic movements or processes or because the assemblage which sustains it is connected to other assemblages. In the case of Marx's account of primitive accumulation, the development of commodity markets is one such vector of deterritorialization in relation to the social and economic space of feudal agriculture, encouraging the shift to large-scale commercial production. The conjugation of the stream of displaced labour with the flow of deterritorialized money capital provided the conditions under which capitalist industry could develop. Second, deterritorialization is always 'inseparable from correlative reterritorializations' (Deleuze and Guattari, 1987: 509). Reterritorialization does not mean returning to the original territory, but rather refers to the ways in which deterritorialized elements recombine and enter into new relations in the constitution of a new assemblage or the modification of the old. In this context, Deleuze and Guattari distinguish between the *connection* of deterritorialized flows, which refers to the ways in which distinct deterritorializations can interact to accelerate one another, and the *conjugation* of distinct flows which refers to the ways in which one may incorporate or 'overcode' another, thereby effecting a relative blockage of its movement (Deleuze and Guattari, 1987: 220).

The normative typology of processes of deterritorialization at the end of *A Thousand Plateaus* distinguishes four types. First, deterritorialization is either relative or absolute. It is relative in so far as it concerns only movements within the actual – as opposed to the virtual – order of things. Elsewhere, they describe absolute deterritorialization as 'the deeper movement... identical to the earth itself' (Deleuze and Guattari, 1987: 143). Secondly, relative deterriorialization can take either a negative or a positive form. It is negative when the deterritorialized element is immediately subjected to forms of reterritorialization which enclose or obstruct its line of flight. It is positive when the line of flight prevails over secondary reterritorializations, even though it may still fail to connect with other deterritorialized elements or enter into a new assemblage with new forces. By contrast, absolute deterritorialization refers to a qualitatively different type of movement which concerns the virtual as opposed to the actual order of things. This is the state in which there are only qualitative multiplicities, the state of 'unformed matter on the plane of consistency' (Deleuze and Guattari, 1987: 55–6). Whereas relative deterritorialization takes place on the molar dimension of individual or collective life, absolute deterritorialization takes place on the molecular plane of social existence. However, absolute deterritorialization is not a further stage or something that comes after relative deterritorialization. On the contrary, it exists only in and through relative deterriorialization: 'There is a perpetual immanence of absolute deterritorialization within relative deterritorialization' (Deleuze and Guattari, 1987: 56). Real transformations in a given field require the recombination of deterritorialized elements in mutually supportive and productive ways. In this sense, social or political assemblages are truly revolutionary only when they involve assemblages of connection rather than conjugation. Under these conditions, absolute deterritorialization 'connects lines of flight, raises them to the power of an abstract vital line or draws a plane of consistency' (Deleuze and Guattari, 1987: 510).

APPRAISAL OF KEY ADVANCES AND CONTROVERSIES

Deleuze and Guattari were not Marxists in any traditional doctrinal sense. Nevertheless, an anticapitalist thematic pervades all their writings, up to and including *What is Philosophy*? In an interview with Antonio Negri, Deleuze reaffirms his sympathy with Marx and describes capitalism as a fantastic system for the fabrication of great wealth and great suffering. He asserts that any philosophy worthy of being called political must take account of the nature and evolution of capitalism (Deleuze, 1995: 171).

In *Anti-Oedipus* (1977) and *A Thousand Plateaus* (1987), he and Guattari develop their own account of capitalism as a unique mode of economic and political capture of the social field. Whereas for Marx, it is the mode of production which explains the nature of society in each epoch, for Deleuze and Guattari, it is the abstract machines of desire and power which define the nature of a given society: 'We define social formations by *machinic processes* and not by modes of production (these on the contrary depend on the processes)' (Deleuze and Guattari, 1987: 435). Previous social machines operate by means of the extrinsic codification of social processes. Social codes determine the quality of particular flows, for example prestige as opposed to consumption goods, thereby establishing indirect relations between flows of different kinds. They also determine the manner in which, within certain limits, a surplus is drawn from the primary flows: in code-governed societies, surplus value invariably takes the form of code surplus. Finally, because they are extrinsic to the processes of production and circulation of goods, systems of codification imply the existence of forms of collective belief, judgment, and evaluation on the part of the agents of these processes. By contrast, capitalism has no need to mark bodies or to constitute a memory for its agents. Since it works by means of an axiomatic intrinsic to the social processes of production, circulation, and consumption it is a profoundly cynical machine: 'the capitalist is merely striking a pose when he bemoans the fact that nowadays no one believes in anything any more' (Deleuze and Guattari, 1977: 250).

The concept of capitalism as an axiomatic system is a distinctive contribution which provides a privileged point of entry into Deleuze and Guattari's political thought. Since their concept of philosophy allows no place for metaphor, their use of the term 'axiomatic' must be regarded as the invention of a new concept by means of the adaptation of the concept of an axiomatic system in mathematical logic. They assert that it is 'the real characteristics of axiomatics that lead us to say that capitalism and present-day politics are an axiomatic in the literal sense' (Deleuze and Guattari, 1987: 461). Chief among these characteristics is the difference between an axiomatic system and a code. Whereas a code establishes a systematic correspondence directly between the elements of different signifying systems, an axiomatic system is defined by purely syntactic rules for the generation of strings of nonsignifying or uninterpreted symbols. The resultant strings of symbols may be given an interpretation by the specification of a model and the assignment of significations to elements of the formal language. In these terms, capital may be supposed to function as 'an axiomatic of abstract quantities' (Deleuze and Guattari, 1977: 228). As a universal equivalent, money is a purely quantitative measure that is indifferent to the qualitative character of flows of different kinds. Commodity production under capitalist conditions generalizes this formal equality of all social goods and relations. Factors of production appear in the balance sheet of an enterprise simply as units of monetary value. Objects produced under noncapitalist regimes of code may also be drawn into the global market, where they are exchanged equally as items of value alongside capitalistically produced goods. To the extent that they are subsumed under the exchange relation, objects produced under the most diverse regimes of code, such as artefacts of indigenous handicraft, and products of fully automated production systems, may be 'formally united' within the capitalist axiomatic.

Deleuze and Guattari speak of the capitalist axiomatic in a restricted and primarily economic sense but also in a broader sense where this refers to a social machine which includes a juridical and a political, as well as a technocratic apparatus. It is as though there were two aspects of capitalism, or a distinction to be drawn between capital understood as a general axiomatic of decoded flows and capitalism understood as a mechanism or set of mechanisms for the maintenance of a relatively stable assemblage of the social factors required to sustain the extraction of flow surplus. Capitalism as an economic system forms an axiomatic but so does capitalist society: 'The true axiomatic is that of the social machine itself, which takes the place of the old codings and organizes all the decoded flows, including the flows of scientific and technical code, for the benefit of the capitalist system and in the service of its ends' (Deleuze and Guattari, 1977: 233). This points to a second distinctive feature of axiomatic systems that justifies this adaptation of the concept. Subject to certain overriding constraints such as consistency or the generation of surplus value, there is considerable scope for variation in the axioms which may be appropriate for a given model. The history of capitalism has involved experimentation and evolution with regard to axioms, its successive crises each provoke a response which may take the form of the addition of new axioms (the incorporation of trade unions, centralized wage fixing, social welfare etc) or the elimination of existing axioms (the elimination of trade unions and currency controls leading to the deregulation of banking, finance, and labour markets). None of these axioms is essential to the continued functioning of capital as such, any more than are the axioms of bourgeois social life. Economic activity is increased when family members dine individually at McDonalds.

As Marx and Engels pointed out in *The Communist Manifesto*, capitalism threatens to sweep away all the values of civilized social existence and replace them with the 'cash nexus'. The circulation of capital through the differential relation between the flows of finance and the flows of personal income, along with the circulation of information through the electronic circuits of mass communication, propels the entire world towards a society in which all the signs of the past are detached from their origins and written over with new signs, and the motley representatives of the present appear as 'paintings of all that has ever been believed' (Deleuze and Guattari, 1977: 34). Capitalism constantly approaches this limit only to displace it further ahead by reconstituting its own immanent relative limits. The capitalist axiomatic generates schizo-flows which are the basis of its restless and cosmopolitan energy while at the same time setting new limits on the socius. In this sense, the capitalist axiomatic is a machine which represses the very social forces and flows of matter and energy which it produces. Deleuze comments in his interview with Negri that what he and Guattari found most useful in Marx was 'his analysis of capitalism as an immanent system that's constantly overcoming its own limitations, and then coming up against them once more in broader form, because its fundamental limit is Capital itself' (Deleuze, 1995: 171). The lesson he and Guattari draw from this is that, at the macro-social level of economic and political institutions, there is a permanent possibility of piecemeal social change. While the capitalist economy may constitute an axiomatic system inseparable from the fabric of modern social life, this does not mean that particular axioms cannot be removed or replaced by others.

In common with Foucault and other post-structuralist political thinkers, Deleuze and Guattari do not envisage global revolutionary change but rather a process of constant experimentation played out in between economic and political institutions and the subinstitutional movements of desire and affect. Deleuze and Guattari provide a conceptual language in which to describe the impact of social movements which impose new political demands upon the qualitative or cultural dimensions of social life. More generally, they contrast the dynamism of such forms of social transformation with the essentially parasitic and reactive character of forms of capture. It is not the control of state power which interests them but rather the forms of social change which take place alongside or beneath any given form of state, and the manner in which these changes react back upon political institutions themselves. For this reason, they insist on the distinction between macro-political and micro-political social analysis and point to the micro-sociology of Gabriel Tarde as an alternative to class analysis which addresses the molecular level of social life. In these terms, for example, in respect of the 1789 revolution 'what one needs to know is which peasants, in which areas of the south of France, stopped greeting the local landowners' (Deleuze and Guattari, 1987: 216). The issue here is not simply a difference in scale but a difference in kind. On the one hand, politics is played out in conflicts between molar social entities such as social classes, sexes, and nations. On the other hand, it is simultaneously played out at the molecular level in terms of social affinities, sexual orientations, and varieties of communal belonging.

Deleuze and Guattari advocate a minoritarian politics based upon a qualitative concept of minority. This is their version of an identity politics based upon a relational understanding of difference, in contrast to the widespread tendency to recognize and evaluate difference only from the standpoint of an implicit standard. They define minority in opposition to majority, but insist that the difference between them is not quantitative since social minorities can be more numerous than the so-called majority. Both concepts involve the relationship of a group to the larger collectivity of which it is a part. Given any socially significant distinction between two groups, the majority is defined as the group which most closely approximates the standard while the minority is defined by the gap which separates its members from that standard. Majority can take many simultaneous forms within society:

Let us suppose that the constant or standard is the average adult-white-heterosexual-European-male speaking a standard language ... It is obvious that 'man' holds the majority, even if he is less numerous than mosquitoes, children, women, blacks, peasants, homosexuals, etc. That is because he appears twice, once in the constant and again in the variable from which the constant is extracted. Majority assumes a state of power and domination, not the other way around.' (Deleuze and Guattari, 1987: 105, 291)

A liberal politics of difference might simply defend the right of the minorities to figure in the majority. In other words, it would seek to broaden the standard so that it becomes male or female, European or non-European, hetero- or homosexual, and so on. Deleuze and Guattari do not deny the importance of such changes to the nature of majority. At the end of Plateau 13 '7000 B.C.: Apparatus of Capture', they assert:

this is not to say that the struggle on the level of the axioms is without importance: on the contrary, it is determining (at the most diverse levels: women's struggle for the vote, for abortion, for jobs; the struggle of the regions for autonomy; the struggle of the Third World; the struggle of the oppressed masses and minorities in the East or West ... (Deleuze and Guattari, 1987: 470–1)

However, they go further and introduce a third term in addition to the pair majority–minority, namely becoming-minor or minoritarian, by which they mean a creative process of becoming-different or divergence from the majority. Becoming-minor involves the subjection of the standard to a process of continuous variation or deterritorialization (Deleuze and Guattari, 1987: 106).

Deleuze and Guattari's third term suggests that social minorities might be conceived in one of two ways: either as outcasts but potentially included among the majority, or as collectivities of an entirely different kind which threaten the very existence of a majority. In contrast to liberal versions of gender neutrality or multiculturalism, Deleuze and Guattari's political perspective is directed not at the installation of new constants or the attainment of majority status, but rather at the minoritarian-becoming of everyone, including the bearers of minority status. They are advocates of the transformative potential of becoming-minor, or becoming-revolutionary, against the normalizing power of the majority. The importance of minority therefore does not reside in the fact of its relative exclusion from the majority but in the political potential of its divergence from the norm. As they define it, minority implies the capacity to deterritorialize the dominant social codes. Conversely, it is the process of deterritorialization which for them constitutes the essence of revolutionary politics: not the incorporation of minority demands by adjustment to the axioms of the social machine, nor the reconstitution of a code, but the process of becoming-minor and enlarging the gap between minor and norm. What is important, in their view, is a 'revolutionary becoming' which is in principle open to anyone (Deleuze and Parnet, 1987: 147).

DELEUZE AND GUATTARI'S MAJOR WORKS

Deleuze

Deleuze, G. (1972) *Proust and Signs*. (Trans. Richard Howard.) New York: George Braziller.

Deleuze, G. (1983) *Nietzsche and Philosophy*. (Trans. Hugh Tomlinson.) London: Athlone Press.

Deleuze, G. (1984) *Kant's Critical Philosophy: The Doctrine of the Faculties*. (Trans. Hugh Tomlinson and Barbara Habberjam.) London: Athlone and Minneapolis: University of Minnesota Press.

Deleuze, G. (1986) *Cinema 1: The Movement-Image*. (Trans. Hugh Tomlinson and Barbara Habberjam.) London: Athlone and Minneapolis: University of Minnesota Press.

Deleuze, G. (1988a) *Bergsonism*. (Trans. Hugh Tomlinson and Barbara Habberjam.) New York: Zone Books.

Deleuze, G. (1988b) *Foucault*. (Trans. Sean Hand; Foreword by Paul Bové.) Minneapolis: University of Minnesota Press.

Deleuze, G. (1988c) *Spinoza: Practical Philosophy*. (Trans. Robert Hurley.) San Francisco: City Lights.

Deleuze, G. and Foucault, M. (1977) 'Conversation between Michel Foucault and Gilles Deleuze', in *Language, Counter-memory, Practice: Selected Essays and Interviews*. (Ed. and trans. D. F. Bouchard and S. Simons.) Ithaca, NY: Cornell University Press.

Deleuze, G. (1989) *Cinema 2: The Time-Image*. (Trans. Hugh Tomlinson and Robert Galeta.) London: Athlone and Minneapolis: University of Minnesota Press.

Deleuze, G. (1990a) *Expressionism in Philosophy: Spinoza*. (Trans. Martin Joughin.) New York: Zone Books.

Deleuze, G. (1990b) *The Logic of Sense*. (Trans. Mark Lester with Charles Stivale; Ed. Constantin Boundas.) New York: Columbia University Press and London: Athlone.

Deleuze, G. (1991) *Empiricism and Subjectivity: an Essay on Hume's Theory of Human Nature*. (Trans. Constantin V. Boundas.) New York: Columbia University Press.

Deleuze, G. (1993) *The Fold: Leibniz and the Baroque*. (Trans. Tom Conley.) Minneapolis and London: University of Minnesota Press.

Deleuze, G. (1994) *Difference and Repetition*. (Trans. Paul Patton.) London: Athlone Press and New York: Columbia University Press.

Deleuze, G. (1995) *Negotiations 1972–1990*. (Trans. Martin Joughin.) New York: Columbia University Press.

Deleuze, G. (1998) 'How do we recognize structuralism?'. (Trans. Melissa McMahon and Charles J. Stivale) in C.J. Stivale, *The Two-fold Thought of Deleuze and Guattari*. New York: Guilford Press.

Deleuze, G. and Parnet, C. (1987) *Dialogues*. (Trans. Hugh Tomlinson and Barbara Habberjam.) London: Athlone Press.

Guattari

Guattari, F. (1984) *Molecular Revolution: Psychiatry and Politics*. (Trans. Rosemary Sheed.) Harmondsworth: Penguin.

Guattari, F. (1995a) *Chaosophy*. (Ed. Sylvère Lotringer.) New York: Semiotext(e).

Guattari, F. (1995b) *Chaosmosis: an Ethico-aesthetic Paradigm*. (Trans. Paul Bains and Julian Pefanis.) Sydney: Power Publications and Bloomington and Indianapolis: Indiana University Press.

Guattari, F. (1996a) *The Guattari Reader*. (Ed. by Gary Genosko.) Oxford and Cambridge, MA: Blackwell.

Guattari, F. (1996b) *Soft Subversions*. (Ed. Sylvère Lotringer.) New York: Semiotext(e).

Guattari, F. (2000) *The Three Ecologies*. (Trans. Ian Pindar and Paul Sutton.) London and New Brunswick, NJ: The Athlone Press.

Guattari, F. and Negri, A. (1990), *Communists Like Us*. (Trans. Michael Ryan.) New York: Semiotext(e).

Deleuze and Guattari

Deleuze, G. and Guattari, F. (1972) 'Deleuze et Guattari s'expliquent..,' *La Quinzaine Littéraire*, 143: 15–19.

Deleuze, G. and Guattari, F. (1977) *Anti-Oedipus: Capitalism and Schizophrenia*. (Trans. Robert Hurley, Mark Seem and Helen R. Lane.) New York: Viking Press.

Deleuze, G. and Guattari, F. (1986) *Kafka: Towards a Minor Literature*. (Trans. Dana Polan.) Minneapolis: University of Minnesota Press.

Deleuze, G. and Guattari, F. (1987) *A Thousand Plateaus: Capitalism and Schizophrenia*. (Trans. Brian Massumi.) Minneapolis: University of Minnesota Press.

Deleuze, G. and Guattari, F. (1994) *What is Philosophy?*. (Trans. Hugh Tomlinson and Graham Burchell.) New York: Columbia University Press.

SECONDARY REFERENCES

Ansell-Pearson, K. (ed.) (1997) *Deleuze and Philosophy: the Difference Engineer*. London and New York: Routledge.

Ansell-Pearson, K. (1999) *Germinal Life: The Difference and Repetition of Deleuze*. London and New York: Routledge.

Bogue, R. (1989) *Deleuze and Guattari*. London and New York: Routledge.

Boundas, C. and Olkowski, D. (eds) (1994) *Deleuze and the Theater of Philosophy*. New York: Routledge.

Braidotti, R. (1994) *Nomadic Subjects*. New York: Columbia University Press.

Dean, K. and Massumi, B. (1992) *First and Last Emperors: The Absolute State and the Body of the Despot*. Brooklyn, NY: Autonomedia.

Goodchild, P. (1996) *Deleuze and Guattari: An Introduction to the Politics of Desire*. London: Sage.

Goodchild, P. (1997) 'Deleuzian ethics', *Theory Culture and Society*, 14 (2): 39–50.

Goulimari, P. (1999) 'A minoritarian feminism? Things to do with Deleuze and Guattari', *Hypatia*, 14 (2): 97–120.

Grosz, E. (1994a) *Volatile Bodies: Towards a Corporeal Feminism*. Bloomington: Indiana University Press and Sydney: Allen and Unwin.

Grosz, E. (1994b) 'A thousand tiny sexes: feminism and rhizomatics', in C. Boundas and D. Olkowski (eds) *Gilles Deleuze and the Theater of Philosophy*. New York: Routledge.

Hardt, M. (1993) *Gilles Deleuze: An Apprenticeship in Philosophy*. Minneapolis: University of Minnesota Press.

Hardt, M. (1998) 'The withering of civil society', in E. Kaufman and K. J. Heller (eds), *Deleuze and Guattari: New Mappings in Politics, Philosophy, and Culture*. Minneapolis: University of Minnesota Press.

Holland, E. W. (1991) 'Deterritorialising "deterritorialisation" – from the *Anti-Oedipus* to *A Thousand Plateaus*', *Substance*, 66 (3): 55–65.

Holland, E. W. (1997) 'Marx and poststructuralist philosophies of difference', *The South Atlantic Quarterly*, 96 (3): 525–41.

Holland, E. W. (1988) 'From schizophrenia to social control', in E. Kaufman and K.J. Heller (eds) *Deleuze and Guattari: New Mappings in Politics, Philosophy, and Culture*. Minneapolis: University of Minnesota Press.

Holland, E. W. (1999) *Deleuze and Guattari's Anti-Oedipus: Introduction to Schizoanalysis*. London and New York: Routledge.

Kaufman, E. and Heller, K.J. (eds) (1998) *Deleuze and Guattari: New Mappings in Politics, Philosophy, and Culture*. Minneapolis and London: University of Minnesota Press.

Lorraine, T. (1999) *Irigaray and Deleuze: Experiments in Visceral Philosophy*. Ithaca, NY and London: Cornell University Press.

Massumi, B. (1992) *A User's Guide to Capitalism and Schizophrenia*. Cambridge, MA: MIT Press.

Massumi, B. (1998) 'Requiem for our prospective dead (toward a participatory critique of capitalist power)' in E. Kaufman and K.J. Heller (eds) *Deleuze and Guattari: New Mappings in Politics, Philosophy, and Culture*. Minneapolis: University of Minnesota Press.

May, T. (1991) 'The politics of life in the thought of Gilles Deleuze', *Substance*, 66 (3): 24–35.

May, T. (1994) *The Political Philosophy of Postructuralist Anarchism*. University Park: Pennsylvania State University Press.

May, T. (1995) *The Moral Theory of Postructuralism*. University Park: Pennsylvania State University Press.

May, T. (1997) *Reconsidering Difference*. University Park: Pennsylvania State University Press.

Miller, C.L. (1993) 'The postidentitarian predicament in the footnotes of *A Thousand Plateaus:* nomadology, anthropology, and authority', *Diacritics*, 23 (3): 6–35.

Patton, P. (1996) (ed.) *Deleuze: A Critical Reader*. Oxford and Cambridge, MA: Blackwell.

Patton, P. (1997) 'Deleuze and political thought', in Andrew Vincent (ed.) *Political Theory: Tradition and Diversity*. Cambridge: Cambridge University Press.

Patton, P. (2000) *Deleuze and the Political*. London and New York: Routledge.

Schrift, A. D. (1995) 'Putting Nietzsche to work: the case of Gilles Deleuze', in P. Sedgewick (ed.) *Nietzsche: A Critical Reader*. Oxford: Blackwell.

Stivale, C. J. (1998) *The Two-Fold Thought of Deleuze and Guattari*. New York: The Guilford Press.

Surin, K. (1991) 'The undecidable and the fugitive; *Mille Plateaux* and the state–form', *Substance*, 66 (3): 102–113.

Surin, K. (1994) '"Reinventing a physiology of collective liberation": going "beyond Marx" in the Marxism(s) of Negri, Guattari and Deleuze', *Rethinking Marxism*, 7: 9–27.

Surin, K. (1997) 'The epochality of Deleuzian thought', *Theory Culture and Society*, 14 (2): 9–21.

Surin, K. (1998) 'The future states of politics' *Culture Machine: The Journal – Taking Risks With the Future*. [http://Culturemachine.tees.ac.uk/frm_f1.htm].

19

Paul Virilio

JOHN ARMITAGE

BIOGRAPHICAL DETAILS AND THEORETICAL CONTEXT

Born in Paris in 1932, Paul Virilio was evacuated in 1939 to the port of Nantes, where he was traumatized by the spectacle of the *Blitzkrieg* during the Second World War. After training at the *Ecole des Métiers d'Art* in Paris, Virilio became an artist in stained glass. However, in 1950, he converted to Christianity and, following military service in the colonial army during the Algerian war of independence (1954–62), he studied phenomenology with Merleau-Ponty at the Sorbonne. Fascinated by the military, spatial, and organizational aspects of urban territory, Virilio's early writings began to appear, while he was acting as a self-styled 'urbanist', in *Architecture Principe*, the group and review of the same name he established with the architect Claude Parent in 1963 (Virilio and Parent, 1996). Virilio produced his first major work, a photographic and philosophical study of the architecture of war, *Bunker Archeology* (1994a), in 1975. Virilio's phenomenologically grounded and controversial social theory, including concepts such as 'deterritorialization', 'dromology' (the logic of speed), and the 'aesthetics of disappearance', draws on the writings of Husserl, Heidegger, and, above all, Merleau-Ponty. After participating in the *événements* of May 1968 in Paris, Virilio was nominated Professor by the students at the école Spéciale d'Architecture, and later helped to found the International College of Philosophy. Being an untrained architect, Virilio has never felt compelled to restrict his concerns to the spatial arts. Indeed, like his philosopher friends, the late Gilles Deleuze and Félix Guattari, Virilio has written numerous texts on a variety of topics; these include *Speed & Politics: An Essay on Dromology* (1986), *The Aesthetics of Disappearance* (1991a), *War and Cinema: The Logistics of Perception* (1989), *Politics of the Very Worst* (1999a), and, most recently, *Polar Inertia* (1999b). Even so, it is only in recent years that the power of Virilio's social theory has begun to be felt in the English-speaking world, a situation that is probably due in no small part to the fact that he rarely leaves Paris and seldom appears in public outside France. Virilio retired in 1998. He currently devotes himself to writing and working with private organizations concerned with housing the homeless in Paris.

The significance of Virilio's theoretical work stems from his claim that, in a society dominated by war, the military-industrial complex is of crucial importance in debates over the creation of the city and the spatial organization of social life. In *Speed & Politics* (1986), for example, Virilio offers a credible 'war model' of the growth of the modern city and the evolution of human society. Thus, according to Virilio, the fortified city of the feudal period was a motionless and generally unassailable war machine coupled to an attempt to modulate the circulation and the momentum of the movements of the urban masses. As a consequence, the fortified city was a political space of habitable inertia, the political configuration, and the physical underpinning of the feudal era. However, for Virilio, the key question is why the fortified city disappeared. His somewhat unconventional answer is that it did so due to the advent of increasingly transportable and accelerated weapons systems. For such innovations not only 'exposed' the fortified city and transformed siege warfare into a war of motion but also undermined the efforts of the authorities to govern the flow of the urban citizenry and therefore heralded the arrival of what Virilio calls the 'habitable circulation' of the masses. Unlike Marx then, Virilio postulates that the transition from feudalism to capitalism was not an economic transformation but a military, spatial, political, and technological metamorphosis. Broadly speaking, where Marx wrote of the materialist conception of history, Virilio writes of the military conception of history.

Commencing in 1958 with a phenomenological investigation of military space and the organization of territory, especially concerning the 'Atlantic Wall' – the 15,000 Nazi bunkers built in the Second World War along the shoreline of France to repel any Allied assault – Virilio deepened his explorations within the *Architecture Principe* group and via a psychologically based *gestalt* theory of the 'oblique function'. This theory culminated in the construction of a 'bunker church' in Nevers in 1966 and the Thomson–Houston aerospace research centre in Villacoublay in 1969 (Johnson, 1996). Later, Virilio broadened his theoretical sweep, arguing in the 1970s, for instance, that the relentless militarization of the contemporary cityscape was prompting the deterritorialization of urban space and the arrival of speed politics. Reviewing the frightening dromological fall-out from the communications technology revolution in information transmission, Virilio enquired into the prospects for 'revolutionary resistance' to 'pure power' and started probing the connections between military technologies and the organization of social space. Consequently, during the 1980s, Virilio cultivated the next important stage of his theoretical work through aesthetically derived notions of 'disappearance', 'fractalization', physical space, war, cinema, logistics, and perception. By contrast, throughout the 1990s, Virilio has critically examined the social repercussions of the use of remote-controlled and cybernetic technologies in the urban environment, and new information and communications technologies such as the Internet. Concentrating on 'polar inertia', the 'third', or, 'transplant revolution', and cybernetic performance art, Virilio's post-Einsteinian social theory is presently focused on 'endo-colonization', 'cyberfeminism', and 'technological fundamentalism'.

Although Virilio has made a significant contribution to 'hypermodern' social theory, it is important to stress that he characterizes himself as a 'critic of the art of technology' and not as a social theorist. In fact, and despite the inclusion of his profile in this book, Virilio abhors social theory.

SOCIAL THEORY AND CONTRIBUTIONS

The Oblique Function, Dromology, and the Integral Accident

Virilio's early essays on the oblique function – a proposed new urban order based on 'the end of the vertical as an axis of elevation, the end of the horizontal as permanent plane, in favour of the oblique axis and the inclined plane' – were published in the mid 1960s in *Architecture Principe* (Virilio and Parent, 1996: v). Today, though, it is the fact that Virilio's essays foreshadowed his military and political critiques of deterritorialization and the revolution in information transmission that surfaced in *Bunker Archeology* (1994a), *L'insécurité du territoire* (1976), and *Speed & Politics* (1986) that makes them of interest to contemporary postmodern social theorists.

Virilio's scepticism concerning the political economy of wealth is sustained by his dromocratic conception of power. Decisively swayed by Sun Tzu's *The Art of War* (1993), and his debate with himself about the 'positive' (Fascist) and 'negative' (anti-Fascist) aspects of Marinetti's artistic theory of Futurism, Virilio argues that political economy cannot be subsumed under the political economy of wealth, with an understanding of the management of the economy of the state being its general aim. On the contrary, the histories of sociopolitical institutions like the military and artistic movements such as Futurism demonstrate that war and the need for speed, rather than commerce and the urge for wealth, were the foundations of society. It is important to state that Virilio is not arguing that the political economy of wealth has been superseded by the political economy of speed; rather, he suggests that in addition to the political economy of wealth, there has to be a political economy of speed. Consequently, in *Popular Defense & Ecological Struggles* (1990) and *Pure War* (1997a), Virilio developed his dromological inquiry to include considerations on pure power – the enforcement of surrender without engagement – and revolutionary resistance – an imaginative case against the militarization of urban space. The 'rationale' of pure war might be encapsulated as the logic of militarized technoscience in the era of 'Infowar', an era in which unspecified civilian 'enemies' are invoked by the state in order to justify increased spending on the 'military weaponry' of new information and communications technologies such as the Internet. Thus, for Virilio, it is the weapons of the military-industrial complex that are responsible for integral accidents like the 1987 world stock market crash, brought about by the failure of automated programme trading.

The Aesthetics of Disappearance and the Crisis of the Physical Dimension

In *The Aesthetics of Disappearance* (1991a) and *The Lost Dimension* (1991b), Virilio, supporting Mandelbrot's (1977) geometry of fractals, demonstrates that social theory must take account of interruptions in the rhythm of human consciousness and 'morphological irruptions' in the physical dimension. Utilizing the concept of 'picnolepsy' (frequent interruption) and Einstein's General Relativity Theory, he argues that modern vision and the modern city are both the products of military power and time-based cinematic technologies of disappearance. Furthermore, although there are political and cinematic aspects to our visual consciousness of the cityscape, what is indispensable to them is their ability to designate the technological disappearance of the grand aesthetic and spatial narratives and the advent of micro-narratives. In Virilio's terms, Mandelbrot's geometry of fractals reveals the appearance of the 'overexposed' city – as when the morphological irruption between space and time splinters into a countless number of visual interpretations, and 'the crisis of whole dimensions' (Virilio, 1991b: 9–28). Significant here is that Virilio's concerns about the aesthetics of disappearance and the crisis of the physical dimension are not exercised by the textual construction of totalizing intellectual 'explanations', but with the strategic positioning of productive interruptions and the creative dynamics of what he calls the 'tendency' (Virilio, 1989: 80). As Virilio argues in *The Lost Dimension* (1991b), the rule in the overexposed city is the disappearance of aesthetics and whole dimensions into a militarized and cinematographic field of retinal persistence, interruption, and 'technological space-time'.

War, Cinema, and The Logistics of Pure Perception

In *War and Cinema* (1989), Virilio applies the concept of 'substitution' when touching on the different classes of reality that have unravelled since the origin of time. Bearing a remarkable likeness to Baudrillard's (1983) concept of 'simulation', Virilio's primary concern is with the link between war, cinematic substitution, and what he calls the logistics of perception – the supplying of cinematic images and information on film to the front line. The idea of the logistics of perception arises because, in the context of postmodern wars like the Persian Gulf War of 1991, not only do settled topographical features disappear in the midst of battle but so too does the architecture of war. For the military high command entombs itself in subterranean bunkers with the chief aim of evading what one of Coppola's helicopters in the film *Apocalypse Now* announced as 'Death from Above'. Consequently, Virilio (1989: 66) conceptualizes a logistics of perception where 'the world disappears in war, and war as a phenomenon disappears from the eyes of the world'. Thus, in *L'écran du désert: chroniques de guerre* (1991c), Virilio analyses the relationship between war, substitution, human and synthetic perception. Such interests are fuelled by Virilio's contention that military perception in warfare is comparable to civilian perception and, specifically, to the art of film-making. According to Virilio, therefore, cinematic substitution results in a 'war of images', or, Infowar. Infowar is not traditional war, where the images produced are images of actual battles. Rather, it is a war where the disparity between the images of battles and the actual battles is 'derealized'. Like Baudrillard's (1995) infamous claim that the Gulf War did not take place, Virilio's assertion that war and cinema are virtually indistinguishable is open to dispute. However, Virilio's stance on the appearance of Infowar is consistent with his view that the only way to match social developments in the war machine is to adopt a critical theoretical position with regard to the various parallels that exist between war, cinema, and the logistics of perception; a view he developed in his vehement critique of *The Vision Machine* (1994b).

In Virilio's universe, then, people 'no longer believe their eyes'. Indeed, 'their *faith in perception*' has become 'slave to the faith in the technical *sightline*', a situation in which contemporary substitution has reduced the 'visual field' to the 'line of a sighting device' (1994b: 13; original emphases). Seen from this perspective, *The Vision Machine* (1994b) is a survey of what I have called 'pure perception' (Armitage, 2000a: 10). For, today, the military-industrial complex has developed ominous technological substitutions and potentialities such as virtual reality and the Internet. In Virilio's terms, 'the main aim' of pure perception is '*to register the waning of reality*' as an aesthetics of disappearance arises 'from the unprecedented limits imposed on subjective vision by the instrumental splitting of modes of perception and representation' (1994b: 49, original emphasis). Hence, Virilio conceives of vision machines as the accelerated products of a '*sightless vision*' that 'is itself merely the reproduction of an intense blindness that will become the latest and last form of industrialization: *the industrialization of the non-gaze*' (1994b: 73, original emphases). Virilio further details the far-reaching social relationships between vision and remote-controlled technologies in *Polar Inertia* (1999b).

Polar Inertia, the Third Revolution, Cyberfeminism, and Technological Fundamentalism

In *Polar Inertia* (1999b), Virilio considers pure perception, speed, and human stasis.

In 'Indirect Light', for instance, Virilio examines the difference between the new video screens adopted by the Paris Metro system and 'real' perceptual objects such as mirrors from a theoretical standpoint that broadly conforms to what Foucault (1977) labelled 'surveillance societies' and Deleuze (1995) called 'control societies'. In contrast, other articles note the discrepancy between technologically generated inertia and biologically induced human movement in the context of discussions about the introduction of 'wave machines' in Japanese swimming pools, the effacement of a variety of 'local times' around the world and their gradual replacement by a single 'global time', and the disparity between 'classical optical communication' and 'electro-optical commutation'. In the era of pure perception, though, Virilio argues that it is not the creation of acceleration and deceleration that becomes important but the creation of 'Polar Inertia'. Here, Virilio proposes that in the early modern era of mobility, in his terms the era of emancipation, inertia did not exist. The concept of polar inertia thus excludes what would have been alternate aspects of the speed equation – simple acceleration or deceleration – in the industrial age. But, as Virilio suggests, in the postindustrial age of the absolute speed of light, it is no longer necessary for anyone to make any journey since one has already arrived. In such circumstances, then, the geographical difference between 'here' and 'there' is obliterated by the speed of light. Additionally, in its terminal mode, as exemplified by reclusive billionaires such as the late Howard Hughes, polar inertia becomes a kind of Foucauldian incarceration. Holed up in a single room in the Desert Inn hotel in Las Vegas for 15 years, endlessly watching Sturges' *Ice Station Zebra,* Hughes, Virilio's 'technological monk', was not only polar inertia incarnate but, more importantly, the first inhabitant of an increasingly '*mass situation*, the quest for the progress of speed without the knowledge of the engine's exterminating character' (Virilio, 1997a: 77, original emphasis). So, at the broadest level, Virilio's writings on polar inertia show that physical geographical spaces no longer have significant human content. Consequently, in *The Art of the Motor* (1995), Virilio turned his attention to the relationship between the human body and technology.

On the beginning of the twenty-first century, then, Virilio's social theory is concerned with what he calls the third, or the transplant, revolution – the almost total collapse of the distinction between the human body and technology. Intimately linked to the technological enhancement and substitution of body-parts through the miniaturization of technological objects, the third revolution is a revolution conducted by militarized technoscience against the human body through the promotion of what the Virilio calls 'neo-eugenics'. Such developments are also the foundations of Virilio's (1995: 109–112) criticisms of the work of Stelarc, the Australian cybernetic performance artist. However, it should be stressed that Virilio's criticisms are linked to the development of his notion of endo-colonization – what takes place when a political power like the state turns against its own people, or, as in the case of technoscience, the human body.

For these reasons, in *Open Sky* (1997b), *La bombe informatique* (1998), and *Politics of the Very Worst* (1999a), Virilio has elaborated a critique of cyberfeminism that Plant (1997), following Haraway's (1985) 'manifesto for cyborgs', describes as a revolution on the part of cybernetic technology and feminists against the rule of patriarchy. However, Virilio has little time for cyberfeminism or 'cybersex', notions that he criticizes, likening cybersex, for instance, to the technological replacement of the emotions. For Virilio, it is imperative to reject cybernetic sexuality, refocus theoretical attention on the human subject, and resist the domination of both men and women by technology. In the world according to Virilio, then, cyberfeminism is merely one more form of technological fundamentalism – the religion of all those who believe in the absolute power of technology (Virilio and Kittler, 1999). Having departed from the religious sensibility required in order to understand the ubiquity, instantaneity, and immediacy of new information and communications technologies, cyberfeminists, along with numerous other social groups, have thus capitulated to the raptures of cyberspace.

APPRAISAL OF KEY ADVANCES AND CONTROVERSIES

Appraising the key advances and controversies of Virilio's thought is problematic not simply because it is only recently that it has come to be appreciated by social theorists but because there is very little substantial secondary literature or interpretive commentary specifically on Virilio (although see, for example, the small and often intermittent sections on Virilio in Conley, 1997; Der Derian, 1992; Wark, 1994). Nonetheless, Virilio's writings on military space and the social organization of society have, almost without exception, forecast rather than followed subsequent social and theoretical developments. It is for this reason that contemporary postmodern social theorists like Bauman (1998: 12) are keenly studying Virilio's work. However, Virilio's thought remains much misunderstood. Here, then, I shall evaluate the essential contribution of Virilio's writings by suggesting that they exist *beyond* the terms of postmodernism and that they should be conceived of as a contribution to the emerging debate over 'hypermodernism'. Lastly, I shall consider some objections to Virilio's work before concluding.

From Modernism to Hypermodernism and Beyond

Virilio's exegesis of military space and the social organization of territory is an important contribution to critical social theory because it diverges from the increasingly sterile current debate over the differentiation of modernism and postmodernism. It is, for instance, quite wrong of critical social theorists such as Harvey (1989: 351), Waite (1996: 116), and positivist physicists like Sokal and Bricmont (1998: 159–66) to characterize Virilio's thought as postmodern social theory. Indeed, such characterizations are so far wide of the mark it is difficult to know where to begin.

First, although the concept of postmodernism, like Virilio, came to prominence in architectural criticism in the 1960s, Virilio's thought is neither a reaction against the International Style nor a reaction against modernism. Postmodernism, Virilio proposes, has been a 'catastrophe' in architecture and has nothing to do with his phenomenologically grounded writings (Armitage, 2000a). For Virilio's work draws on the modernist tradition in the arts and sciences. In it, he references modernist writers and artists such as Kafka and Marinetti. His philosophical reference points are Husserl and Merleau-Ponty, phenomenologists and modernists. Furthermore, Virilio cites Einstein's writings on General Relativity Theory, an instance of his commitment to the theory of scientific modernism established in 1915.

Second, Virilio sees no connection between his thought and that of deconstructionist and post-structuralist theorists like Derrida. Virilio has, for example, never shown any interest in de Saussure's structural linguistics, preferring the world of phenomenology and existentialism. As an anti-Marxist (and anti-Sartrean), committed anarchist, and thinker who has 'absolutely no confidence in psychoanalysis', he has little in common with the pioneers of structuralism such as the semiologist Barthes, the Marxist philosopher Althusser, the psychoanalyst Lacan, and the anthropologist Lévi-Strauss (Virilio, 1997a: 39). Virilio's theoretical connections with Foucault's (1977) *Discipline and Punish* and Deleuze and Guattari's (1987) *A Thousand Plateaus* also need to be treated with care. This is because, unlike most post-structuralist theorists, Virilio is a humanist and a practising Christian. His work is opposed to the viewpoint of antihumanism and to the philosophy of Foucault's and Deleuze and Guattari's messiah, Nietzsche. Consequently, there are only indeterminate and convergent relationships between Virilio's thought and Foucault and Deleuze's post-structuralist theories, something that Virilio has pointed out (Virilio, 1997a: 44–5). For Virilio, the crucial pointers on all his social theory have been the Second World War, military strategy, and spatial planning.

Third, in contrast to many postmodern social theorists, Virilio does not wholly condemn modernity. Rather, he views his work as a 'critical analysis of modernity, but through a perception of technology which is largely... catastroph*ic*, not catastroph*ist*'. Arguing that 'we are not out of modernity yet, by far', it is, then, 'the drama of total war' that lies at the core of Virilio's social theory (Armitage, 2000a: 26). Concentrating his thought on the varying speeds of modernity, Virilio's texts thus concern themselves with its key characteristics such as technoscience, surveillance, urbanism, and alienation. Moreover, and despite his reputation as a Cassandra, Virilio often insists that his conception of modernity, as distinct from the theorists of postmodernism, is essentially optimistic (Armitage, 2000a).

Furthermore, Virilio is not wholly antipathetic to reason, even if he is critical of aspects of the 'Enlightenment project'. However, he certainly is inimical to Hegelian and Marxist theories of knowledge and ideology. In this respect, Virilio can be considered as a kind of 'left Heideggerian' (Kellner, 2000). Virilio's critical relationship to modernity is, then, somewhat removed from the description of it given by postmodern social theorists like Waite (1996).

Fourth, Virilio's thought has almost nothing to do with that of advocates of postmodernism like Lyotard (1984) or Baudrillard (1983). Unlike Lyotard's writings, for instance, Virilio's writings remain true to the principle of hope with regard to making sense of history. Actually, nearly the entirety of Virilio's work is a sustained attempt to make sense of his own history and, through it, ours too. Nor does Virilio accept the demise of *all* the 'metanarratives', insisting in interviews, for example, 'that the narrative of justice is beyond deconstruction' (Armitage, 2000a: 39). Likewise, Virilio's hostility to Marxism, semiotics, and Nietzschean 'nihilism' explains his antagonism toward Baudrillard's concept of simulation. Again, unlike many postmodern social theorists, Virilio does not share Baudrillard's admiration for McLuhan's (1994) 'drooling' (Virilio, 1995: 10) over new media technologies. Similarly, Virilio's writings are less concerned with Baudrillard's 'hyperreality' and 'irony' and more concerned with social reality and the celebration of the poor.

For these reasons, it is very difficult to appraise the important advances of Virilio's thought in terms of postmodern social theory. It is also why I believe it is preferable to interpret it as the work of a social theorist whose thinking addresses what might be called the question of hypermodernism; a tentative term and embryonic tendency in contemporary social theory that seeks to move away from the polarized assumptions of modernism and postmodernism and toward an understanding of the 'excessive' intensities and displacements inherent within social thought about the modern world and how it is represented (Armitage, 2000b).

Critique of Virilio

Virilio's social theory and numerous activities have courted controversy since the 1960s. When Virilio and Parent wrote their articles in the *Architecture Principe* review, for example, they demanded that the world abandon horizontal planes and organize itself immediately on inclined planes instead. Not surprisingly, these claims met with infuriated opposition from fellow architects and indifference from the world. Similarly, Virilio's conceptions of the state, technology, and speed have also been subject to critique. Deleuze and Guattari (1987: 351–423), for instance, attempted what Crogan (1999) calls a problematic effort to 'subsume' Virilio's thought into their own post-structuralist approach to social theory. However, as Crogan argues, Deleuze and Guattari's 'static, ahistorical model' of the state and technology cannot be combined with Virilio's writings without undoing 'its own coherency in the process'. In turn, Virilio's *The Aesthetics of Disappearance* (1991a) has outraged the neo-Marxian geographer Harvey (1989: 293, 299, 351). For Harvey, Virilio's 'response' to what the former calls 'time-space compression' 'has been to try and ride the tiger of time-space compression through construction of a language and an imagery that can mirror and hopefully command it'. Harvey places the 'frenetic writings' of Virilio (and Baudrillard) in this category because 'they seem hell-bent on fusing with time-space compression and replicating it in their own flamboyant rhetoric'. Harvey, of course, has 'seen this response before, most specifically in Nietzsche's extraordinary evocations in *The Will To Power*'. Yet, in *The Aesthetics of Disappearance* (1991a), Virilio's unfolding and wholly intentional reactions to the emergence of the dromocratic condition are actually concerned with 'the importance of interruption, of accident, of things that are stopped as *productive*' (1997a: 44, original emphasis). As he told Lotringer: 'It's entirely different from what Gilles Deleuze does in *Milles Plateaux.* He progresses by snatches, whereas I handle breaks and absences. The fact of stopping and saying "let's go somewhere else" is very important for me' (Virilio, 1997a: 45). What Virilio's 'frenetic writings' actually substantiate throughout the 1980s are the material and, crucially, the *immaterial* consequences of dromological changes in aesthetics, military power, space, cinema, politics, and technology. In an era increasingly eclipsed by the technologically produced disappearance of social life, war, matter, and human perception, this is a very significant achievement. In the contemporary era, though, the limitations of Virilio's social theory are likely to rest not – as Harvey suggests – with his similarities but with his *differences* from Nietzsche. As Waite, quoting the American performance artist Laurie Anderson, has argued:

> Virilio still desperately holds on to a modicum of modernist *critique* of postmodern military tactics, strategies, and technologies, whereas Nietzsche basically would have been impatient with mere critique, moving quickly to *appropriate* them for his own *use*, at least conceptually and rhetorically, as metaphors and techniques of persuasion to preserve power for elites over corpses – 'now that the living outnumber the dead'. (Waite, 1996: 381–2, original emphases)

Although there are many controversial questions connected to Virilio's social theory, his hypermodern critique of military tactics, strategies, and technologies is beginning to collide with the thought of a number of other social theorists such as the Krokers' (1997). The reason for such collisions is that Virilio's texts like *The Politics of the Very Worst* (1999a) address some of the most disturbing and significant contemporary social developments of our time, developments often designed to preserve the power of the increasingly virtual global elites over the creation of actual local corpses. A child of Hitler's *Blitzkrieg*, Virilio has theorized the social logic of late militarism and the spatial organization of territory. These are the most important aspects of his thought. Revealing the likely dromological and political conditions of the twenty-first century, Virilio interprets modernity in terms of a military conception of history and the endo-colonization of the human body by technoscience. As I have indicated, the concept of hypermodernism needs to be uppermost in any understanding of Virilio's particular contribution to social theory.

Virilio is, therefore, one of the most important and thought-provoking social theorists on the contemporary intellectual battlefield. However, unlike Lyotard's or Baudrillard's postmodernism, Virilio's hypermodernism does not articulate itself as a divergence from modernism and modernity but as a critical analysis of modernism and modernity through a catastrophic perception of technology. Indeed, Virilio defines his general position as 'a critic of the art of technology' (1997a: 172). Virilio's theoretical position and social sensibilities concerning technology thus remain beyond the realm of even the critical social sciences. He does not depend on intellectual 'explanations' but on 'the obvious quality of the implicit' (Virilio, 1997a: 44). On the one hand, then, Virilio is a social theorist who movingly considers the tendencies of the present period. On the other, he is a social theorist who utterly rejects social theory and especially sociology (Virilio, 1997a: 17).

Consequently, it is debatable whether there is anything to be gained from social theorists attempting to establish the 'truth' or otherwise of Virilio's thought. For Virilio's critical responses to the military, speed politics, cinema, art, and technology are ethical and emotional responses to the arrival of technological society. Moreover, Virilio is aware that his work is 'often dismissed in terms of scandalous charges!' As he has noted, in an unpublished interview with Nicholas Zurbrugg in 1998, in France 'there's no tolerance' for 'irony, for wordplay, for argument that takes things to the limit and to excess'. Hence, to raise the question of Virilio's social theory is to raise the question of whether, outside France, his work should be dismissed in terms of scandalous charges, received in terms suffused with praise, or a mixture of both. In short, it is to raise the question of how much tolerance there is in the English-speaking world for irony, for wordplay, and for arguments that take things to excess. For these and other reasons, Virilio's hypermodern social theory looks set to continue eliciting theoretical argument and social debate for many years to come.

VIRILIO'S MAJOR WORKS

Virilio, P. (1976) *L' insécurité du territoire*. Paris: Stock.

Virilio, P. (1986) *Speed & Politics: An Essay on Dromology*. New York: Semiotext(e).

Virilio, P. (1989) *War and Cinema: The Logistics of Perception*. London and New York: Verso.

Virilio, P. (1990) *Popular Defense & Ecological Struggles*. New York: Semiotext(e).

Virilio, P. (1991a) *The Aesthetics of Disappearance*. New York: Semiotext(e).

Virilio, P. (1991b) *The Lost Dimension*. New York: Semiotext(e).

Virilio, P. (1991c) *L'écran du désert: chroniques de guerre*. Paris: Galilée.

Virilio, P. (1994a) *Bunker Archeology*. Princeton: Princeton, NJ: Princeton Architectural Press.

Virilio, P. (1994b) *The Vision Machine*. Bloomington and London: Indiana University Press and British Film Institute.

Virilio, P. (1995) *The Art of the Motor*. Minneapolis: University of Minnesota Press.

Virilio, P. (1997a) *Pure War: Revised Edition*. New York: Semiotext(e).

Virilio, P. (1997b) *Open Sky*. London: Verso.

Virilio, P. (1998) *La bombe informatique*. Paris: Galilée.

Virilio, P (1999a) *Politics of the Very Worst*. New York: Semiotext(e).

Virilio, P. (1999b) *Polar Inertia*. London: Sage.

Other Works

Virilio, P. and Parent, C. (eds.) (1996) *Architecture Principe, 1966 et 1996*. Besançon: L' imprimeur.

Virilio, P. and Kittler, F. (1999) 'The information bomb: Paul Virilio and Friedrich Kittler in conversation. Edited and Introduced by John Armitage', *Angelaki*, 4 (2): 81–90.

SECONDARY REFERENCES

Armitage, J. (1997) 'Accelerated aesthetics: Paul Virilio's *The Vision Machine*', *Angelaki*, 2 (3): 199–210.

Armitage, J. (ed.) (2000a) *Paul Virilio: From Modernism to Hypermodernism and Beyond*. London: Sage in association with *Theory, Culture & Society*.

Armitage, J. (ed.) (2000b) 'From Modernism to Hypermodernism and Beyond: An Interview with Paul Virilio', in J. Armitage (ed.), *Paul Virilio: From Modernism to Hypermodernism and Beyond*. London: Sage in association with *Theory, Culture & Society*.

Baudrillard, J. (1983) *Simulations*. New York: Semiotext(e).

Baudrillard, J. (1995) *The Gulf War Did Not Take Place.* Bloomington and Indianapolis: Indiana University Press.

Bauman, Z. (1998) *Globalization: The Human Consequences.* Cambridge: Polity Press.

Conley, V.A. (1997) *Ecopolitics: The Environment in Poststructuralist Thought.* London: Routledge.

Crawford, T.H. (1999) 'Conducting Technologies: Virilio's and Latour's Philosophies of the Present State', *Angelaki*, 4 (2): 171–81.

Crogan, P. (1999) 'Theory of State: Deleuze, Guattari and Virilio on the State, Technology, and Speed', *Angelaki*, 4 (2): 137–48.

Deleuze, G. (1995) 'Postscript on control societies', *Negotiations: 1972–1990.* New York: Columbia University Press.

Deleuze, G. and Guattari, F. (1987) *A Thousand Plateaus: Capitalism and Schizophrenia.* Minneapolis: University of Minnesota Press.

Der Derian, J. (1992) *Antidiplomacy: Spies, Terror, Speed and War.* Oxford: Blackwell.

Der Derian, J. (ed.) (1998) *The Virilio Reader.* Oxford: Blackwell.

Foucault, M. (1977) *Discipline and Punish: The Birth of the Prison.* Harmondsworth: Penguin.

Haraway, D. (1985) 'A manifesto for cyborgs: science, technology and socialist feminism in the 1980s', *Socialist Review*, 80 (2): 65–108.

Harvey, D. (1989) *The Condition of Postmodernity: An Enquiry Into the Origins of Cultural Change.* Oxford: Blackwell.

Johnson, P. (ed.) (1996) *The Function of the Oblique: The Architecture of Claude Parent and Paul Virilio.* London: Architectural Association.

Kellner, D. (2000) 'Virilio, war, and technology: some critical reflections', in J. Armitage (ed.) *Paul Virilio: From Modernism to Hypermodernism and beyond.* London: Sage.

Kroker, A. (1992) 'Paul Virilio: The postmodern body as war machine', in *The Possessed Individual: Technology and Postmodernity.* Basingstoke: Macmillan.

Kroker, A. and Kroker, M. (eds) (1997) *Digital Delirium.* Montreal: New World Perspectives.

Lyotard, J-F. (1984) *The Postmodern Condition: A Report on Knowledge.* Minneapolis and Manchester: Minnesota Press and Manchester University Press.

Mandelbrot, B. (1977) *The Fractal Geometry of Nature.* New York: Freeman.

McLuhan, M. (1994) *Understanding Media: The Extensions of Man.* Cambridge, MA: MIT Press.

Plant, S. (1997) *Zeros + Ones: Digital Women + The New Technoculture.* London: Fourth Estate.

Sokal, A. and Bricmont, J. (1998) *Intellectual Impostures: Postmodern Philosophers' Abuse of Science.* London: Profile Books.

Tzu, S. (1993) *The Art of War.* Ware: Wordsworth Editions.

Waite, G. (1996) *Nietzshe's Corps/e: Aesthetics, Politics, Prophecy, or the Spectacular Technoculture of Everyday Life.* Durham, NC and London: Duke University Press.

Wark, M. (1994) *Virtual Geography: Living with Global Media Events.* Bloomington and Indianapolis: Indiana University Press.

Zurbrugg, N. (1995) '"Apocalyptic!" "Negative!" "Pessimistic!": Baudrillard, Virilio, and Technoculture' in S. Koop (ed.), *Post: Photography: Post Photography.* Fitzroy: Centre for Contemporary Photography.

20

Henri Lefebvre

ROB SHIELDS

BIOGRAPHICAL DETAILS AND THEORETICAL CONTEXT

Surveys of French intellectual life in the 1950s and 1960s remark that Henri Lefebvre (1901–91) is a permanent outsider, yet one of the most influential forces in French left-wing humanism. Although an unorthodox writer who was officially excluded from the *Parti Communiste Français* long before the work of thinkers such as Lyotard, Althusser, or Foucault on the French left caught the attention of most Anglophone theorists, Lefebvre figured as the most translated of French writers during the 1950s and 1960s. Thanks to his 1939 paperback on *Dialectical Materialism* (Lefebvre, 1968c) translated into over two dozen languages and printed on a vast scale in over a dozen editions) he ranked as 'The Father of the Dialectic' for at least two generations of students world-wide. By the 1980s he was idolized by American postmodernists and geographers as the pioneer of critiques of the city and the 'spatial turn' in theory.

Henri Lefebvre was a Marxist and existentialist philosopher (see Lefebvre, 1946), a sociologist of urban and rural life, and a theorist of the state, of international flows of capital, and of social space. Born in 1901 in the south of France, he died in his beloved home region of Haut Pyrenees in the ancient town Navarrenx in 1991. During that period, he witnessed the modernization of French everyday life, the industrialization of the economy, and suburbanization of its cities. In the process, the rural way of life of the traditional peasant was destroyed (Ross, 1996). Some of the most important elements in the context in which Lefebvre found himself can be listed in chronological order. After his initial schooling on the West coast of France at Brieuc and in Paris, he was profoundly affected by not only the lack of food and heat in occupied Paris but the widespread post-First World War *malaise* of the French populace who felt alienated from the new industrialized forms of work and bureaucratic institutions of civil society in the early 1920s. This spurred him to focus on alienation and led him to the philosophies and social criticism of Marx and Hegel, which in turn paved the route to joining the *Parti Communiste Français* (PCF). Lefebvre's career was disrupted by the Second World War. His books and manuscripts were burnt by the Vichy regime during the war and he was persecuted for his

Communist writings by the postwar authorities. Pushed out of the centres of intellectual influence, he completed his doctoral thesis on changes in rural France. But when it was published as the *La vallée de Campan* (1963) he was lauded as a founder of the study of rural society.

Still an outsider to the Paris establishment, he finally obtained a formal university position in Strasbourg in the mid 1950s, identifying with the political avant garde and passing the critiques of an earlier generation on to the student movements of the 1960s. He finally moved back to Paris, winning a professorship at the new suburban university in Nanterre where he was an influential figure in the 1968 student occupation of the Sorbonne and Left Bank. Nanterre provided an environment in which he developed his critique of the alienation of modern city life which was obscured by the mystifications of the consumerism and the mythification of Paris by the heritage and tourism industries. These critiques of the city were the basis for Lefebvre's investigation of the cultural construction of stereotypical notions of cities, of nature, and of regions. Accorded international fame he questioned the overspecialization of academic disciplines and their 'parcellization' of urban issues into many disciplines such as planning, geography, surveying, architecture, sociology, and psychology (to name only a few), which dealt with space and other human geography issues. During his international travels from the early 1970s he developed one of the first theories of what came to be referred to as 'globalization'.

The influence of Lefebvre is thus broad and often unrecognized. One telltale sign of his influence is the appearance of some of his signature-concepts in left-intellectual discourse. Although these are not exclusively 'his' of course, Lefebvre contributed so much to certain lines of inquiry that it is difficult to discuss notions such as 'everyday life', 'modernity', 'mystification', 'the social production of space', 'humanistic Marxism', or even 'alienation' from either a left-wing or humanist position without retracing some of his arguments. Of course these terms predate Lefebvre but he was one of the original thinkers who established their importance for understanding behaviour in the context of everyday modern life.

SOCIAL THEORY AND CONTRIBUTIONS

We have already enumerated a range of disciplines in which Lefebvre is an important contributor. The core of his humanism is his critique of the alienating conditions of everyday life which he developed together with Norbert Guterman in the late 1930s and finally published in 1947 as *Critique of Everyday Life* (1991a, see also 1968b). This was the first of what were to be three volumes (1991a, 1961, 1981a respectively). Lefebvre argued a Marxist interpretation of 'Everydayness' (*quotidienneté, Altäglichkeit*), or banality as a soul-destroying feature of modernity, along with Lukàcs and Heidegger, who saw it as a metaphysical, or spiritual, problem. Lefebvre extends Marx's analysis by discovering new forms of alienation, and arguing that capitalism not only organizes relations of production in an exploitive manner (which produces several forms of alienation in workers) but that every aspect of life is emptied of meaning or significance, which is then purchased back in the form of spectacular commodities. Rather than resolving alienation, consumption is part of the misrecognition of their alienated state by modern consumers, in a cycle which Lefebvre and Guterman referred to as the 'mystification' of consciousness. Their early collaboration in *La Conscience mystifiée* (1936) and in the first ever mass publication of the works of the young Karl Marx on alienation and his essays, *The German Ideology* and *Theses on Feuerbach* (see Lefebvre and Guterman, 1934) influenced Walter Benjamin's Marxist analysis of culture (1993). The adopted concept of 'everydayness' originated with Lukàcs. Ironically these works on alienation were not available to him, allowing Lukàcs to develop a distinct concept, 'reification', without the cognitive stress of Lefebvre and Guterman's theory of mystification which is closer to Marx and Engel's positing of the existence of classes' 'false consciousness'. A further irony is that Lefebvre's extension of alienation into the key concept in an entire critique of modern life turns on an oversimplified reading of Marx and Engels' many different types of estrangement and dispossession. The range of ideas are replaced by the French *aliénation* as if they were all synonyms of a social-psychological type alienation. By contrast with this cognitive state, Marx and Engels often give the idea the sense of forceful expropriation of profit or value – an active 'taking away', which is lost in Guterman and Lefebvre's translation.

Against 'mystification', against the banality of the *'metro-bulot-dodo'* life of the suburban commuter, Lefebvre proposes that we seize and act on all 'Moments' of revelation, emotional clarity, and self-presence as the basis for becoming more self-fulfilled (*l'homme totale* – see 1959). This concept of 'Moments' reappears throughout his work as a theory of presence and the foundation of a practice of emancipation. Experiences of revelation, déja-vu sensations, but especially love and committed struggle are examples of Moments. By definition Moments are instances of disalienation. They have no duration but can be relived (see Hess, 1994). Lefebvre argues that these cannot easily be reappropriated by consumer capitalism and commodified; they cannot be codified. They are 'escape-hatches' from the alienated condition of everyday life which can be experienced unexpectedly, anywhere and at any time. Perhaps ironically for someone lately stereotyped as a theorist of space, Lefebvre can be said to have a form of temporal theory of authenticity based in the 'timelessness' and instantaneity of Moments. Moments become the measuring rod by which the quality of life in different societies is evaluated in his later work (see Harvey, 1991).

Even before discovering the work of Hegel and Marx, Lefebvre was influenced by Schopenhauer to develop a romantic humanism which glorified 'adventure', spontaneity, and self-expression. He is called by one German biographer a *'Romantische Revolutionär'* (Meyer, 1973; Lefebvre et al., 1958). In the mix of students and activists in mid-1920s Paris, Lefebvre was part of a group of *Philosophes* (including also Nisan, Friedman, and Mandelbrot) who were loosely connected with Gide, and influenced by surrealists such as Breton (who was the one who introduced Lefebvre to Hegel and Marx) and Dadaists such as Tzara. In turn, the philosophes' protoexistentialist rejection of metaphysical solutions in favour of action influenced Sartre and his circle (see Lefebvre, 1925; Short, 1966, 1979; Trebitsch, 1987).

Apart from his work on the young Marx (with Guterman probably doing most of the translation), Lefebvre and Guterman produced a well-timed *Introduction'* to Hegel (1938) which coincided with Kojéve's influential lectures on his 'anthropological' interpretation of Hegelianism. The first interwar attempt at an anti-Fascist reading of *Nietzsche* (1939) and a rigorous critique of National Socialism and nationalism followed. But it was Lefebvre's Marxist primer on the theory of *Dialectical Materialism* (1968c) which made him internationally famous as a Marxist theorist, despite the disapproval and destruction of a more existentialist manuscript on everyday life by the PCF censor. By the end of the Second World War, despite participating in the Resistance and nearly starving in 1944–5, he had a more sociological critique of everyday life ready for publication.

The spoils and fame from the international media interest in existential philosophy caused a long-running dispute between Lefebvre and Sartre through the 1940s up until a reconciliation in which they both recognized each other's influence on themselves. Lefebvre's attacks on Sartre's *Being and Nothingness* (1958) had been goaded-on by the PCF who feared the latter's influence (Lefebvre, 1950). When Lefebvre acknowledged Sartre's status, and Sartre acknowledged using Lefebvre's dialectical method, Lefebvre himself was attacked and decisively excluded from the PCF (Lefebvre, 1958, 1975b; Poster, 1975).

Perhaps most interesting is the extension of this critique from the arena of everyday life and relations between the household and society at large into a full-blown analysis of urban life (Trebitsch, 1991). Lefebvre does this by drawing on his collaboration with the *Situationniste International* (SI) in the early 1960s. This took the form of reading group discussions on the Paris Commune of 1871 which Lefebvre published as *La Proclamation de la Commune* (1965b). The Commune – an uprising and direct democracy of workers in inner Paris – involved the occupation of key symbolic sites in Paris (Lefebvre, 1969). It took the form of an extended festival, a Mardi Gras that overflowed the bounds of social regulation to the extent that it became a 'revolutionary festival' (Ross, 1988). Lefebvre later examined the work of Bakhtin, but his approach is distinctive in that he focuses on the revolutionary potential of play, in parallel with the ideas of Lyotard (libidinal economy – see Kleinspehn, 1975) and of Deleuze and Guattari (desire as a productive force) (Lefebvre and Régulier, 1978; see Lefebvre, 1988). Lefebvre co-authored work and interviews with Kolakowski on 'Evolution or Revolution' (1974), which awaits comparison with the opposed work of Sorokin on the sociology of revolutions. This unique idea was later put into practice by Lefebvre's seminar students at Nanterre, who led the occupation of the Sorbonne and much of Paris in May 1968. Every person has a 'right to the city' (1968a) – that is, to the city understood as the pre-eminent site of social interaction and exchange, which Lefebvre refers to as 'social centrality'. Lefebvre analysed the impact of changing social relations and economic factors under capitalism upon the quality of access and participation in the urban milieu. This interaction should not degenerate into commodified spectacles or into simply 'shopping' but should be the social form of self-presence in which individuals enjoy the right of association into collectives and self-determination.

His important definition of the city was never properly absorbed by urban theorists. What is 'the urban', he asked? The urban is not a certain population, a geographic size, or a collection of buildings. Nor is it a node, a transhipment point or a centre of production. It is all of these together, and thus any definition must search for the essential quality of all of these aspects. Lefebvre understands the urban from this phenomenological basis as a Hegelian *form* but this is not to say that he is simply phenomenologist. Like social space, the urban is a 'concrete abstraction'.

> It is concrete in having a given substance, and still concrete when it becomes part of our activity, by resisting or obeying it... It is abstract by virtue of its definite, measurable contours, and also because it can enter into a social existence... and become the bearer of a whole series of new relations... (Lefebvre, 1968: 119 [1939b])

The urban *is* social centrality, where the many elements and aspects of capitalism intersect in space despite often merely being part of the place for a short time, as is the case with goods or people in transit. 'Cityness' is the simultaneous gathering and dispersing of goods, information, and people. Some cities achieve this more fully than others – and hence our own perceptions of some as 'great cities' *per se*.

After the first set of works explicitly concerned with urban struggles and the experience of May 1968, *The Production of Space* (1991c, first published 1974) forms the keystone of the all-important 'second phase' of Lefebvre's analysis of the urban which began around 1972 (see Lefebvre, 1996; Kofman and Lebas, 1996). (This may be seen as beginning with his 1972 contribution to the colloquium 'The Institutions of the Post-Industrial Society', sponsored by the Museum of Modern Art in New York. The location is important: Lefebvre noted that he was always inspired by New York from his first visit at the end of the 1930s (1980: 234).) This later phase deals with social space itself and the 'planetary' or global. As argued in *The Production of Space* and restated later in *De l'Etat* (Vol. 4, 1978b) Lefebvre moved his analysis of 'space' from the old synchronic order of discourses 'on' space (archetypically, that of 'social space' as found in sociological texts on 'territoriality' and social ecology) to the manner in which understandings of geographical space, place landscape, and property is cultural and thereby has a history of change. Rather than discussing a particular theory of social space, he examined struggles over the meaning of space and considered how relations across territories were given cultural meaning. In the process, Lefebvre attempted to establish the presence of a 'lived' experience and understanding of geographical space alongside the hegemonic theories of space promulgated by disciplines such as philosophy or geography or urban planning or the everyday attitude which ignored the spatial altogether. Thus a large portion of *The Production of Space* was devoted to developing a radical phenomenology of space as the humanistic basis from which to launch a critique of the denial of individuals' and communities' 'rights to space'. In capitalist societies, for example, geographical space is 'spatialized' as lots. Land is always owned by someone. Hence a privatized notion of space anchors the understanding of property which is a central cultural feature of capitalist societies.

Historical notions of space are analysed on three axes. These three aspects are explained in different ways by Lefebvre – simplified for the purpose of introducing them, we might say that the 'perceived space' (*le perçu*) of everyday social life and commonsensical perception blends popular action and outlook but is often ignored in the professional and theoretical 'conceived space' (*le conçu*) of cartographers, urban planners, or property speculators. Nonetheless, the person who is fully human (*l'homme totale*) also dwells in a 'lived space' (*le vecu*) of the imagination and of Moments which has been kept alive and accessible by the arts and literature. This 'third' space not only transcends but has the power to refigure the balance of popular 'perceived space' and the 'conceived space' of arrogant professionals and greedy capitalists.

This sphere offers complex recoded and even decoded versions of lived spatializations, veiled criticism of dominant social orders and of the categories of social thought often expressed in aesthetic terms as symbolic resistance. Lefebvre cites Dada, the work of the surrealists, and particularly the works of René Magritte as examples of art, literary comment, and fantasy regarding other, possible, spatializations. Also included in this aspect are clandestine and underground spatial practices which suggest and prompt alternative (revolutionary) restructurings of institutionalized discourses of space and new modes of spatial praxis, such as that of squatters, illegal aliens, and Third World slum dwellers, who fashion a spatial presence and practice outside of the norms of the prevailing (enforced) social spatialization. For example, in many countries, inequitable property ownership often privileges absentee landlords over landless peasants. Lefebvre calls this

> space as directly *lived* through its associated images and symbols, and hence the space of 'inhabitants' and 'users' . . . This is the dominated . . . space which the imagination seeks to change and appropriate. It overlays physical space, making symbolic use of its objects. Thus representational spaces may be said . . . to tend towards more of less coherent systems of nonverbal symbols and signs. (Lefebvre, 1991c: 39)

Signs? Donaldson-Smith's English translation (1991c) chooses the odd phrase 'representational spaces' rather than the literal translation, 'spaces of representation'. This translation of the text (and every translation is also an interpretation) brings out the importance of Lefebvre's thinking at this time about the semiotics of metaphor and metonymy and the entire mechanics of representation through a sign system. The text is strewn with the debris of near-forgotten theories of linguistic and semiotics. It would seem more obvious to tie the problem of 'lived space' to spatial practice, rather than the social imaginary. However, referring to his Nietzschean ideal of the 'total person', he is interested here in the 'fully lived', preconscious and authentic shards of spatiality which animate people, providing meaning to the entire assemblage of lives and spatializations.

Lefebvre dictated his books, and avoided editing, leaving inconsistencies which are also clues to a troubling problem which continued to haunt Lefebvre – the paradox of an almost impassable gulf between the sign and any authentic reality. This gulf left even the 'total person' either alienated from their nomothetic world or in a state of inarticulate and incoherent union and bliss, which could not be represented, and thus could hardly be expected to serve as a libidinal, mobilizing force for social change, as he and others had hoped might happen during the occupation of the Sorbonne in May 1968. This paradox would drive Lefebvre back to reassess the work of Nietzsche after the completion of *Production de l'espace* (1991c, 1975a).

Lefebvre's tripartitite division is Christian and originates in Catholic mysticism – a hint that Lefebvre preserved his own 'third' element in a dialectic alongside of Marxist theory and PCF praxis (see Shields, 1999). The division of the popular against the professional echoes Lefebvre's contact with the Popular Front and grassroots Communist activism (often via his spouses, of whom there were several) and the experience of 1960s and 1970s city planning battles as neighbourhood communities faced 'slum clearance' moves by planners and 'redevelopment', for others with the ability to pay, by speculators. The privilege granted to art is consistent with his affiliations with artistic and political avant gardes such as the Surrealists and Situationists. The three axes or aspects of space are the elements of a 'triple dialectic' (*dialectique de triplicité* – the details of which Lefebvre does not sketch). The shifting balance between these forces defines what I have referred to as the historical 'spatialization' of an era (Shields, 1990, 1999).

A triple dialectic short-circuits any tendencies to reduce this along the lines of a base–superstructure dualism (or economy–culture, or production–consumption, or action–thought), making it difficult to think in terms other than a dialectical juxtaposition. The multi-dimensional thesis is in direct contrast to the more customary reduction of space to part of the trinity: production, consumption, and exchange (as in Castells, 1977). In addition to these three, common in political economic analyses of space, Lefebvre argues that space, or spatialization as I have suggested it is best translated, is a fourth and determining realm of social relations in which the production and deployment of wealth and surplus value takes place. The spatial may be seen to be an abiding concept in cultural regimes of socioeconomic hierarchies (implemented through physical spatial division), and an indicator of socioeconomical consistency, compatibility, or continuity of privilege, class, and practice. Furthermore, Lefebvre's three-part dialectic is one in which there seems to be little temporal progression from contradiction to synthesis. It appears to be more spatial, with elements that coexist in a tension which is only broken occasionally by Lefebvre's 'third' element which transfigures, reinterprets, or recodes a historical 'settlement' of forces.

This idea of historical spatializations is the basis for a 'transcoding' of Marx's *Grundrisse* into spatial terms (Jameson, 1991). A history of 'modes of production of space' emerges which completes Marx's vision of successive historical modes of production in urban, environmental, and attitudinal terms. A true Communist revolution must not only change the relationship of labourers to the means of production, but also create a new spatialization – shifting the balance away from the 'conceived space' of which private property, city lots, and the surveyor's grid are artifacts. Embracing the 'lived space' of avant gardes is a device for harnessing its reinvigorating potential and redirecting the 'perceived space' of everyday practice in a new manner. This theory provides an early bridge from Marxist thought to environmentalism. Lefebvre was particularly influential on the formative positions of the German Green Party.

The work on the city and on other scales of space is the reason Lefebvre's work has remained important in the English-speaking world – not his once prominent role as the Father of the Dialectic, nor the lost history of his contributions to passing the idea of a personal, revolution of everyday life from the Dadaist of the 1920s to the student countercultures of the 1960s and the 1980s British punks and anarchists (Home, 1988; Plant, 1992). 'Rediscovered' by geographers such as Ed Soja (1989, 1996) and Neil Smith (1984), sociologists such as Mark Gottdiener (1985), and cultural theorists such as Frederic Jameson (1991), Lefebvre spent part of 1983 in California. During this trip, an enduring connection to contemporary social critics of all stripes was made and a final relay was closed in the extensive circuit of intellectual transfers which Lefebvre effected.

APPRAISAL OF KEY ADVANCES AND CONTROVERSIES

Why is this work important? Lefebvre goes beyond previous philosophical debates on the nature of space, and beyond human geography, planning, and architecture, which considered people and things merely 'in' space, to present a coherent theory of the development of different systems of spatiality in different historical periods, or 'historical spatializations' as we have referred to them above. These 'spatializations' are not just physical arrangements of things, but spatial patterns of social action and routine as well as historical conceptions of space and the world (such as a fear of falling off the edge of a flat world). They add up to an sociospatial imaginary and outlook which manifests itself in our every action.

This system of space operates at all scales. At the most personal, we think of ourselves in spatialized terms, imagining ourselves as an ego contained within an objectified body. People extend themselves – mentally and physically – out into space much as a spider extends its limbs in the form of a web. We become as much a part of these extensions as they are of us. Arrangements of objects, work teams, landscapes, and architecture are the concrete instances of this spatialization. Equally, ideas about regions, media images of cities and perceptions of 'good neighbourhoods' are other aspects of this space which is necessarily produced by each society as it makes its mark on the Earth.

What is the use of such an 'unpacking' of the production of the spatial? Lefebvre uses the changing types of historical space to explain why capitalistic accumulation did not occur earlier, even in those ancient economies which were commodity and money-based, which were committed to reason and science, and which were based in cities (see Merrifield, 1993). One well-known explanation is that slavery stunted the development of wage-labour. He finds this unconvincing. No: it was a secular space, itself commodified as lots and private property, quantified by surveyors and stripped of the old local gods and spirits of place, that was necessary. 'What exactly is the mode of existence of social relationships?' asks Lefebvre in his typically dialectical style.

> The study of space offers an answer according to which the social relations of production have a social existence to the extent that they have a spatial existence; they project themselves into a space, becoming inscribed there, and in the process producing that space itself. Failing this, these relations would remain in the realm of 'pure'

abstraction – that is to say, in the realm of representations and hence of ideology: the realm of verbalism, verbiage and empty words. (Lefebvre, 1991c: 129)

As well as being a product of cultures, space is a *medium* – and the changing way we understand, practise, and live in terms of our space provides clues to how our capitalist world of nation-states is giving way to a unanticipated geopolitics – a new sense of our relation to our bodies, world, and planets as a changing space of distance and difference.

In this analysis, Lefebvre broadened the concept of production to 'social production' (unaware of social constructivist theories that had been developed by non-Francophone writers such as Berger and Luckman or by Garfinkel). Contemporaneously with Poulanzas in the mid 1970s he later refined his analysis with an assessment of the role of the state. This included his interest in the changing historical geography of capitalism and the globalization of socioeconomic relations. It must not be forgotten, however, that this was also a turn to rhythm and to space-time (Lefebvre and Régulier-Lefebvre, 1985). Beyond *The Production of Space* stretched a decade and a half of further publishing, including his posthumous book *Rhythmanalyse* (Lefebvre and Régulier-Lefebvre, 1985, 1992). In addition he attempted a rapprochement of *Marx, Hegel, Nietzsche* (1975a) which would extend Marxism to what he called a 'metaphilosophy' (1965a). However, Lefebvre's spatial dialectic is perhaps his most intriguing contribution.

A theoretical spatialization of the dialectic is not, however, pursued by Lefebvre himself. He remains in the classical Hegelian mode. Nor is it fully clarified in the secondary literature, for example, Soja's work, which draws on some theorists of alterity (1996). Nonetheless, we can grasp *through* Lefebvre a legacy which lies beyond even his own accomplishments. We might attribute this to the dialectical style of his texts – to their excess – to the way they continue to ask pertinent questions which rise above even Lefebvre's answers.

In Hegel's view, 'affirmation' is undifferentiated in itself and thus a homogeneous entity, unknowable because lacking in any difference. In this sense it is a purely spatial concept, similar in all respects to an undifferentiated field in which no single point or element stands out. Dialectical negation introduces time – the negation of space – in the form of the *punctum*, the point or instant (the most elementary of temporal concepts). *Aufhebung*, negation of this negation, must subsume both the spatial field and the point which is pure difference in itself. For Hegel, this takes place by means of the spatialization of the point itself, drawing it into a line, trajectory, or flow, movement and passage. In the Hegelian scheme, we could say that the third term is analogous to historical 'progress'. Even if this oversimplifies Hegel, it allows us to illustrate the distinctiveness of Lefebvre's proposal which introduces a third element – 'the lived', Moments, jokes – which allows the intrusion of a horizon or 'outside', a 'beyond' or otherness. This element is always constitutively distinct from the original binary of field and point, or affirmation and negation. In effect the shift is from '(1) affirmation (2) negation (3) negation of the negation (synthesis)' to a new and little explored formula 'affirmation-negation-otherness-synthesis'.

Soja for example envisions this as not 'an additive combination of its binary antecedents but rather... a disordering, deconstruction, and tentative reconstitution of their presumed totalization producing an open alternative that is both similar and strikingly different'. What he derives from Lefebvre's 'differentialist' position (1971a, 1980, 1981b, 1991b) as 'Thirding', 'decomposes the dialectic through an intrusive disruption that explicitly spatializes dialectical reasoning... [it] produces what might best be called a cumulative *trialectics* that is radically open to additional othernesses, to a continued expansion of spatial knowledge' (Soja, 1996: 61).

> The dialectic thus emerges from time and actualizes itself, operating now, in an unforeseen manner, in space. The contradictions of space, without abolishing the contradictions which arise from historical time, leave history behind and transport these old contradictions, in a worldwide simultaneity, onto a higher level. (Lefebvre, 1991c: 129)

Lefebvre seems to have produced a 'both–and' vision of the dialectic. 'Both–and' could be restated as more precisely 'both' (both affirmation and negation) plus 'and' (the third, otherness). He reintegrates within the structure of the dialectic Nietzsche's concept of an irreducible tension, '*Uberwinden*', which is not simply superceded (an interest of Lefebvre's that dates back to the 1930s). This presents the possibility of fixing the dialectic as a counterposed assemblage of three terms which are mutually supporting and mutually parasitical for their status within the dialectic. Only the synopsis, delivered out of the dialectical analysis – and not a part of the dialectic proper - gives the possibility of an overarching synchronic synthesis. By opening a position for alterity, otherness is brought into the dialectical schema without being reduced to the logic of the 'other' as merely a straightforward 'negation' of self, of thesis – of affirmation.

Critique

Lefebvre did not pursue the opportunity to apply this reconceptualization to either the body or to identities such as nationalism. In the case of the body, he remained within the patriarchal tradition dividing bodies and spaces heterosexually into male and female. These are conceived on the basis of a simple negation (A/not-A; that is, male/not-male) and Lefebvre, like most French theorists, was untouched by Commonwealth and American writers' theories of gay and lesbian 'third' alternative identities (A/not-A/neither) outside of a heterosexual dualism (Blum and Nast, 1996). Late twentieth-century postcolonial writers developed alternative theories of ethnic and race identity without reading Lefebvre (with some exceptions, see Gregory, 1994; Soja suggests links between bell hooks and Lefebvre). Except perhaps for the work of Homi Bhabha, the idea of alterity has not been rigorously compared and contrasted against theories of negation and contradiction such as the dialectic.

Avoiding a simple base–superstructure dualism was Lefebvre's prime concern. After the failure of the student occupations of May 1968, he was eclipsed by Louis Althusser's PCF-sponsored 'Scientific Marxism' in which the base–superstructure division was a privileged element of a structural analysis of the repressive forces and institutions of capitalist states (Zimmerman, 1975). Ironically, Lefebvre first became well known to English-speaking theorists through the critiques of his work by Althusserians, such as Manuel Castells, who, in *The Urban Question,* criticized Lefebvre's urban works for their vagueness and antistructuralist bias (Castells, 1977; Martins, 1983: 166; Gottdiener, 1985; see Lefebvre, 1971b).

By contrast, Lefebvre's 'Humanistic Marxism' emphasized the humanistic understanding of alienation as Marx's motivating concept, explored in the economic sphere using the tools of historical materialism and dialectics. By emphasizing the importance of dialectical materialism, he became the quintessential Marxist methodologist and logician (see Lefebvre, 1947). He argued that Marxism was incomplete as long as it remained applied primarily to the economic rather than to all aspects of social life, and the task of twentieth-century Marxism was to extend this application of dialectical materialism beyond the economic, and also reflexively onto Marxist theory and politics.

It is therefore surprising that, given his interest in nationalism, in urbanism, in the closing ties of the global economy, and his activism in French debates concerning the independence of French Morocco and of Algeria, Lefebvre did not foresee the emerging politics of multiculturalism and the problems of France's ethnic ghettos. Lefebvre has little to say on the question of discrimination, or on 'insiders and outsiders' and the ethics of their relationships. He tends to conceive of the state as a once-authentic instrument of a single people which has been seized by the capitalist class for itself.

There are important parallels between the work of Lefebvre and Lukàcs, Adorno, and Marcuse which have not been extensively explored in the scholarship on twentieth-century neo-Marxisms. If Lefebvre moved beyond the economic, and broadened the notion of production and the dialectic, but Lefebvre remains on the modernist terrain of problems concerning state–society relations. In Lefebvre's late work there is no horizon of ethnic, racial, and sexual Others, relations of colonial domination, and no sustained engagement with the environmental movement. In part this is a result of timing – his active authorship dwindled in the early 1980s. His contribution was to provide a series of open texts, studded with not only insights but unresolved and probing questions, and marked by a faith in peoples' intuition and willingness to act. Lefebvre was a 'conducting wire' of ideas and accumulated experience from generation to generation of the European avant garde (Hess, 1988; Marcus, 1989). Those ideas electrified not one generation, but a century on the Left, and made their mark far and wide outside of France. Even where he is not quoted directly, fading from memory, Henri Lefebvre left a legacy of coherence and radicality to utopian humanism.

LEFEBVRE'S MAJOR WORKS

A complete index of Lefebvre's major works is available in Shields' *Lefebvre: Love and Struggle* (1999) with annotations regarding reprints and editions collecting separate parts of previous publications.

Lefebvre, H. (1925) 'Positions d'attaque et de défense du nouveau mysticisme', *Philosophies*, 5-6: 471–506.

Lefebvre, H. (1937) *Le nationalisme contre les nations.* ('Preface' by Paul Nizan.) Paris: Editions Sociales Internationales; reprinted Paris: Méridiens-Klincksliek 1988.

Lefebvre, H. (1939) *Nietzsche.* Paris: Editions Sociales Internationales.

Lefebvre, H. (1946) *L'Existentialisme.* Paris: Editions du Sagittaire.

Lefebvre, H. (1947) *Logique formelle, logique dialectique* Vol. 1 of *A la lumière du matérialisme dialectique.* Paris: Editions Sociales.

Lefebvre, H. (1950) 'Knowledge and social criticism', in *Philosophic Thought in France and the USA.* Albany NY: State University of New York Press; 2nd ed. 1968.

Lefebvre, H. (1958) *Problémes actuels du marxisme.* Paris: Presses universitaires de France; 4th edition, 1970, Collection 'Initiation philosophique'.

Lefebvre, H. (1961) *Critique de la vie quotidienne II, Fondements d'une sociologie de la quotidienneté,* Paris: L'Arche.

Lefebvre, H. (1963) *La vallée de Campan – Etude de sociologie rurale.* Paris: Presses Universitaires de France.

Lefebvre, H. (1965a) *Métaphilosophie.* (Envoi by Jean Wahl.) Paris: Editions de Minuit, Collection 'Arguments'.

Lefebvre, H. (1965b) *La Proclamation de la Commune.* Paris: Gallimard, Collection 'Trente Journées qui ont fait la France'.

Lefebvre, H. (1968a) *Le droit à la ville.* Paris: Anthropos; 2nd ed. Paris: Ed. du Seuil, Collection 'Points'.

Lefebvre, H. (1968b) *La vie quotidienne dans le monde moderne.* Paris: Gallimard, Collection 'Idées'.

Lefebvre, H. (1968c) *Dialectical Materialism.* (Trans. J. Sturrock.) London: Cape.

Lefebvre, H. (1968d) *Sociology of Marx.* (Trans. N. Guterman.) New York: Pantheon.

Lefebvre, H. (1969) *The Explosion: From Nanterre to the Summit.* Paris: Monthly Review Press.

Lefebvre, H. (1970) *La révolution urbaine.* Paris: Gallimard, Collection 'Idées'.

Lefebvre, H. (1971a) *Le manifeste différentialiste.* Paris: Gallimard, Collection 'Idées'.

Lefebvre, H. (1971b) *Au-delé du structuralisme.* Paris: Anthropos.

Lefebvre, H. (1975a) *Hegel, Marx, Nietzsche, ou le royaume des ombres.* Paris: Tournai, Casterman. Collection 'Synthèses contemporaines'.

Lefebvre, H. (1975b) *Le temps des méprises: Entretiens avec Claude Glayman.* Paris: Stock.

Lefebvre, H. (1978) *de l'État*, Vol. 4, *Les contradictions de l'Etat moderne, La dialectique de l'Etat.* Paris: UGE, Collection '10/18'.

Lefebvre, H. (1980) *La présence et l'absence.* Paris: Casterman.

Lefebvre, H. (1981a) *Critique de la vie quotidienne, III. De la modernité au modernisme (Pour une métaphilosophie du quotidien).* Paris: L'Arche.

Lefebvre, H. (1981b) *De la modernité au modernisme: pour une métaphilosophie du quotidien*. Paris: L'Arche Collection Le sens de la marché'.

Lefebvre, H. (1988) 'Toward a leftist cultural politics: remarks occasioned by the centenary of Marx's Death' (Trans. D. Reifman), in C. Grossberg and L. Nelson (eds) *Marxism and the Interpretation of Culture*. Urbana: University of Illinois Press; New York: Macmillan.

Lefebvre, H. (1991a) *The Critique of Everyday Life, Volume 1*. (trans. John Moore.) London: Verso.

Lefebvre, H. (1991b) *Conversation avec Henri Lefebvre*. (Ed. P. Latour and F. Combes.) Paris: Messidor, Collection 'Libres propos'.

Lefebvre, H. (1991c) *The Production of Space*. (Trans. N. Donaldson-Smith.) Oxford: Blackwell.

Lefebvre, H. (1995) *Introduction to Modernity: Twelve Preludes September 1959-May 1961*. (Trans. J. Moore.) London: Verso.

Lefebvre, H. (1996) *Writings on Cities*. (Trans. E. Kofman and E. Lebas.) Oxford: Blackwell.

Lefebvre, H., Goldmann, L. Roy, C., Tzara, T., (1958) 'Le romantisme révolutionnaire', in *Le romantisme révolutionnaire*. Paris: La Nef.

Lefebvre, H. and Guterman, N. (1934) *Morceaux choisis de Karl Marx*. Paris: NRF.

Lefebvre, H. and Guterman, N. (1936) *La conscience mystifiée*. Paris: Gallimard; Paris: Le Sycomore, 1979.

Lefebvre, H. and Guterman, N. (1938) *Morceaux choisis de Hegel*, Paris: Gallimard; reprinted Collection 'Idées', 2 Vols. 1969.

Lefebvre, H. and Kolakowski, L. (1974) 'Evolution or revolution', in F. Elders (ed.) *Reflexive Water: The Basic Concerns of Mankind*. London: Souvenir.

Lefebvre, H. and Régulier, C. (1978) *La révolution n'est plus ce qu'elle était*. Paris: Editions Libres-Hallier.

Lefebvre, H. and Régulier-Lefebvre, C. (1985). 'Le projet rythmanalytique,' *Communications*, 41: 191–199.

Lefebvre, H. and Regulier-Lefebvre, C. (1992) *Eléments de rythmanalyse: Introduction à la connaissance des rythmes*. Preface by René Lorau.) Paris: Ed. Syllepse, Collection 'Explorations et découvertes'.

SECONDARY REFERENCES

Benjamin, W. (1993) *Paris, capitale du XIXe siècle, le livre des passages*. Paris: Editions du CERF.

Blum, V. and Nast, H. (1996) 'Where's the difference? The heterosexualization of alterity in Henri Lefebvre and Jacques Lacan', *Environment and Planning D: Society and Space*, 14: 559–80.

Castells, M. (1977) *The Urban Question: a Marxist approach*. (Trans. A. Sheridan.) London: Edward Arnold.

Gottdiener, M. (1985) *Social Production of Urban Space*. Austin: University of Texas.

Gregory, D. (1994) *Geographical Imaginations*. Blackwell, Oxford.

Harvey, D. (1991) 'Afterword', in H. Lefebvre *The Production of Space*. (Trans. D. Nicholson-Smith.) Oxford: Blackwell.

Hess, R. (1988) *Henri Lefebvre et l'aventure du siècle*. Paris: Editions A. M. Métailié.

Hess, R. (1994) 'La théorie des moments, ce qu'elle pourrait apporter a un dépassement de l'interactionnisme', in *Traces de futurs. Henri Lefebvre le possible et le quotidien*. Paris: La Société Française.

Home, Stuart (1988) *The Assault on Culture: Utopian Currents from Lettrisme to Class War*. London: Aporia Press and Unpopular Books.

Jameson, F. (1991) *Postmodernism or, the Cultural Logic of Late Capitalism*. London: Verso.

Kleinspehn, Thomas (1975) *Der Verdrängte Alltag: Henri, Lefebvres marxistiscbe Kritik des Alltagslebens*. Giessen: Focus Verlag.

Kofman, E. and Lebas, E. (1996) 'Lost in transposition – time, space and the city', in H. Lefebvre, *Writings on Cities*. (Trans. E. Kofman and E. Lebas.) Oxford: Blackwell.

Marcus, G. (1989) *Lipstick Traces*. (Cambridge, MA: Harvard University Press.

Martins, M. (1983) 'The theory of social space in the work of Henri Lefebvre', in R. Forrest, J. Henderson and P. Williams (eds), *Urban Political Economy and Social Theory: Critical Essays in Urban Studies*. Aldershot: Gower.

Merrifield, A. (1993) 'Space and place: a Lefebvrian reconciliation', *Transactions of the Institute of British Geographers*, 18 (4): 516–31.

Meyer, Kurt (1973) *Henri Lefebvre: ein romantischer Revolutionnär*. Vienna: Europa Verlag.

Plant, S. (1992) *Most Radical Gesture: Situationist International in a Postmodern Age*. London: Routledge.

Poster, Mark (1975) *Existential Marxism in Postwar France: From Sartre to Althusser*. Princeton, NJ: Princeton University Press.

Ross, K. (1988) *The Emergence of Social Space: Rimbaud and the Paris Commune*. New York: Macmillan.

Ross, K. (1996) *Fast Cars, Clean Bodies: Decolonization and the Reordering of French Culture*. Cambridge, MA: MIT Press.

Sartre, J.-P. (1958) *Being and Nothingness*. (Trans. H.E. Barnes.) New York: Methuen/Philosophical Library.

Shields, Rob (1990) *Places on the Margin: Alternate Geographies of Modernity*. London: Routledge.

Shields, Rob (1999) *Lefebvre: Love and Struggle: Spatial Dialectics*. London: Routledge.

Short, Robert S. (1966) 'The politics of surrealism 1920–1936', *Journal of Contemporary History*, 1 (2): 3–26.

Short, Robert S. (1979) 'Paris Dada and surrealism', *Journal of European Studies*, 9 (1-2).

Smith, N. (1984) *Uneven Development; Nature, Capital and the Production of Space*. Oxford: Blackwell.

Soja, E. (1989) *Postmodern Geographies, the Reassertion of Space in Critical Social Theory.* London: Verso.

Soja, E. (1996) *Third Space.* Oxford: Blackwell.

Trebitsch, Michel (1987) 'Le groupe Philosophie, de Max Jacob aux surréalistes', *Les Cahiers de l'Institut de l'Histoire du temps présent*, 6: 29–38.

Trebitsch, Michel (1988) 'Présentation', in Henri Lefebvre, *Le Nationalisme contre les Nations*. Paris: Meridions Klincksieck.

Trebitsch, Michel (1991) 'Preface', in Henri Lefebvre, *Critique of Everyday Life.* (Trans. John Moore.) London: Verso.

Zimmerman, Marc (1975) 'Polarities and contraditions: theoretical bases of the Marxist-structuralist encounter', *New German Critique,* 3 (1): 69–90.

21

Paul Ricoeur

KATHLEEN BLAMEY

BIOGRAPHICAL DETAILS AND THEORETICAL CONTEXT

Paul Ricoeur was born in Valence, France in 1913. He was taken in by his paternal grandparents at the age of two, having lost his mother as an infant and his father in combat at the start of the First World War. Along with his sister, Alice, Paul Ricoeur grew up in the sombre environment of an austere Protestant household in the predominantly Catholic city of Rennes. His youth, characteristic of those orphaned by the war and designated *pupilles de la Nation*, was focused around his studies, and holidays, with little in the way of sports or games, were spent poring over the books assigned for the coming academic year. The final year of secondary school brought Ricoeur into the classroom of Roland Dalbiez, his philosophy teacher, an anti-Cartesian realist, who was among the first to incorporate Freud in his philosophical teaching. Ricoeur then attended the University of Rennes, receiving his undergraduate degree in philosophy in 1933. That same year he began teaching at a local high school, while writing his master's thesis with Léon Brunschvicg on *The Problem of God in Lachelier and Lagneau*. After receiving his master's degree in 1934, Ricoeur was awarded a scholarship to study in Paris and prepare for the *agrégation*, which he passed in 1935, receiving second place. During this year of study in Paris, Ricoeur made two important encounters for the course of his philosophical work: he discovered the writings of Edmund Husserl, beginning with the English translation of *Ideas*, and he made the acquaintance of Gabriel Marcel, attending the Friday evening gatherings at the philosopher's home, where discussions addressed philosophical themes or problems and references to authors were prohibited.

In the summer of 1935 Paul Ricoeur married his childhood sweetheart, Simone Lejas, from the Protestant community in Rennes. They would have five children. After a year in Colmar, Ricoeur returned to Brittany, where he taught until he was conscripted into the army with the outbreak of war in 1939. The defeat of France in the spring of 1940 was the beginning of a five-year captivity for Ricoeur in an *oflag* in Pomerania. Among the more than three thousand prisoners were a number of philosophers, who shared books and gave lectures. With Mikel Dufrenne, Ricoeur read Husserl,

Heidegger, and Jaspers. While in captivity, Ricoeur began his translation of Husserl's *Ideen I* in the margins of his copy and worked out the plan of his *Philosophy of the Will*, the first section of which would be his doctoral dissertation, *The Voluntary and the Involuntary*. The early postwar years bear the fruit of this activity: first, the collaboration with Mikel Dufrenne, *Karl Jaspers and the Philosophy of Existence* (1947); then, *Gabriel Marcel and Karl Jaspers. Philosophy of Mystery and Philosophy of Paradox* (1948); finally, the two works comprising Ricoeur's doctoral dissertations, *Philosophy of the Will I. The Voluntary and the Involuntary* ([1950] 1966), and the translation of Husserl's *Ideas I*, with introduction and notes (1950). The grand project of a philosophy of the will would result in two subsequent volumes under the general heading of *Finitude and Guilt–Fallible Man* ([1960] 1965) and *The Symbolism of Evil* ([1960] 1969). During this time, Ricoeur was appointed professor of the history of philosophy, first at the University of Strasbourg (1948–56) and then at the Sorbonne (1956–66).

The study of cultural expressions of human frailty and culpability led Ricoeur to a reading of Freud and to psychoanalysis as an alternative to phenomenology. His work, *Freud and Philosophy* (1970), published in 1965, presented Freud as a 'master of suspicion', who, along with Marx and Nietzsche, revealed the limits of philosophies of consciousness, based on the transparency and immediacy of the subject. With the publication in 1969 of a collection of articles, *The Conflict of Interpretations* (1974a), Ricoeur confronted not only the challenge that Freudian psychoanalysis presented to reflective philosophy, but also the challenge that structuralism presented to the interpretation of texts in the hermeneutical tradition.

During the 1960s, as the university system in France came under attack for its rigidity and for the lack of contact between faculty and students, Ricoeur opted to leave the Sorbonne in 1967 to participate in the formation of a new, smaller university in Nanterre, a suburb of Paris. The student revolts of 1968 began here, spreading in numbers and, in the eyes of some, bringing French society to the brink of revolution. Head of the philosophy department in 1968, Ricoeur was named Dean of the Faculty of Letters in 1969. However, failing to bring a reconciliation between the demands of students for the elimination of any visible hierarchy in the university institution, and the demands of the government for the establishment of order, he resigned his post in 1970. After a three-year hiatus, during which he taught at the Catholic University of Louvain, Ricoeur returned to Nanterre, which was now designated as Paris-X, where he taught until his retirement in 1980.

Paul Ricoeur's commitment to teaching also includes a long list of appointments abroad from the 1950s to the 1990s at institutions such as the University of Montreal, Yale University, the University of Toronto, and the University of Chicago, where he taught on a regular basis from 1967 to 1992. From the 1970s on, Ricoeur's published works bear the imprint of his familiarity with English-language discussions in the philosophy of language and action (*The Rule of Metaphor*, [1975] 1977/78, takes as its interlocutors Max Black and Fontanier, Mary Hesse and Jacques Derrida). In the 1980s, Ricoeur's analyses of the topics of time and narrative grew to encompass three volumes presenting the philosophical history of the concept of time; the analysis of plot, the weaving of action and temporality from Aristotle to contemporary theorists of the narrative; and a study of historiography and the relation between fiction and history. *Time and Narrative* (first published in 1983, 1984, and in 1985) concludes with a discussion of three aporias of time, and the sketch of narrative identity, a framework that Ricoeur examined and reworked in his 1986 Gifford Lectures and the resulting book, *Oneself as Another*, (1992) published in 1990. A second collection of articles, *From Text to Action. Essays in*

Hermeneutics, II ([1986] 1991), extends the hermeneutical model of textual interpretation to the analysis of action and to problems relating to the methodology of the social sciences. Paul Ricoeur's most recent book deals with memory, personal and collective (*La Mémoire, l'Histoire, l'Oubli* [2000]).

SOCIAL THEORY AND CONTRIBUTIONS

In writings that span more than half a century, Paul Ricoeur's philosophical itinerary has ranged over many questions critical to the course of French philosophy. His earliest writings conjoin two traditions, phenomenology and hermeneutics, which, over time, Ricoeur confronts, critiques, and reworks, shaping more adequate tools of analysis and redefining the relationship between disciplines. Let us begin by examining these two traditions and the manner in which they have been adopted and reworked in the writings of Paul Ricoeur.

The phenomenology of Edmund Husserl proposed 'a return to the things themselves', a call that appealed to a generation of young philosophers who were concerned with the direct apprehension of experience, with the question of existence and its concrete manifestations. Phenomenology presented itself as a philosophy of consciousness, but what distinguished it from its Cartesian model was the theme of intentionality, the notion that consciousness was defined by its object, that it was always directed outside of itself, that all consciousness was consciousness of something. In this way, consciousness was never empty, and the task of the phenomenologist was to describe both the content of consciousness, which was apprehended as a sense, and the mode of consciousness itself as it operates in remembering, perceiving, imagining, willing, and so forth. Jean-Paul Sartre relies on phenomenological descriptions of shame, of bad faith, of the ontological relation to the other in *Being and Nothingness*; Maurice Merleau-Ponty presents the eidetic analysis – the investigation of the fundamental structure – of perception in *The Phenomenology of Perception*; and Paul Ricoeur extends phenomenological analysis to the domain of affection and willing in his work on the *Voluntary and the Involuntary* (1950), published in English under the title *Freedom and Nature* (1996).

At the same time as Ricoeur applies the method of phenomenological description to the operations of the will, he attempts, in the commentary and notes to his translation of Husserl's *Ideas*, to separate the descriptive method proposed by Husserl from its idealist presuppositions. Other phenomenologists, Ricoeur recognizes, including Eugen Fink and Husserl himself, claimed that the phenomenological reduction, by which the existence of that which appears to consciousness is bracketed or placed out of bounds, leaves consciousness as the sole source of all appearing. In contrast, Ricoeur, like Merleau-Ponty, attempts to preserve the descriptive core of phenomenology, while rejecting the Husserlian claims of a self-grounding, presuppositionless science that proceeds on the basis of pure intuitions, with the certainty of Cartesian self-evidence. Instead, Ricoeur focuses on the implications of intentionality, developing the notion that the meaning of consciousness lies beyond itself, in its objects, in the world, that consciousness is '*towards meaning* before meaning is for it and, above all, before consciousness is *for itself*' (1991: 39). Ricoeur emphasizes this detour by way of the mediation of the world – whether the objects of perception, the symbols of culture, or the affective sphere of desire and project. Indeed Ricoeur draws out those elements in Husserl's own work that call for the elaboration (*Auslegung*) of modes of experience. Already, on the level of perception, which Husserl takes to be a model of the intentionality of consciousness, all apprehension is perspectival in relation to a here and a now that changes as I move around the object, viewing it from a range of different angles. The presumed unity of the object requires an intentional synthesis, that always goes beyond what is given in each of the distinct perspectives. This rootedness in a perspective, characteristic of perceptual experience, is then extended to all apprehension. Knowing, imagining, valuing, like perceiving, are *situated*, *viewed from* a given angle, *in light of* certain considerations. Ricoeur takes this property of partiality – in the sense of viewing from a perspective, being situated – to exclude the possibility of Hegelian absolute knowledge, of any claim to totalization.

By emphasizing the work of the later Husserl and his analyses of the *Lebenswelt* – the life-world, the domain of experience that is prior to any subject–object dichotomy – Ricoeur attempts to overcome the idealist and solipsistic tendencies of the phenomenological subject. The nature of the 'subject' that remains is, however, open to question. It is here that Ricoeur suggests grafting the '*hermeneutic problem* onto the *phenomenological method*' (1974a: 3). The hermeneutical tradition is, of course, much older than the practice of phenomenology. It appears in the exegesis of ancient texts, exemplified by the interpretation of biblical writings. Understanding a text requires familiarity with the techniques of analysis, the use of metaphor, simile, analogy, as well as the more complex forms of myth and parable. If we recall that, for Husserl, all intentional objects are meanings and meaning is expressed thematically in language, then the passage by way of the systematic study of signification provides a refinement rather than a rejection of the aims of phenomenology. Although Ricoeur himself has frequently practised biblical exegesis in many published writings, the hermeneutical shoot he grafts onto the stem of phenomenology is the more generalized form of textual interpretation coming out of classical philology and the historical sciences, as developed in the work of Schleiermacher and Dilthey. It is they, in Ricoeur's estimation, who transformed hermeneutics into a philosophical task. Dilthey poses an epistemological problem, attempting 'a critique of historical knowledge as solid as the Kantian critique of the knowledge of nature and of subordinating this critique to the diverse procedures of classical hermeneutics: the laws of internal textual connection, of context, of geographic, ethnic, and social environments' (1974a: 5). The epistemological function of hermeneutics, determining the mode proper to historical knowledge, is linked to an ontological dimension, in which the task of interpreting the past is grounded in the fundamental project of understanding through which the distant or remote is made familiar, and what was other is appropriated, the historian entering by way of the texts of the past into the mental life of another, the writings themselves being viewed as the sedimentations of consciousness. Ricoeur, having passed through the critiques of the masters of the demystification of false consciousness – Freud, Nietzsche, and Marx – does not construe hermeneutics in this way as a psychology nor the text as a reification of consciousness. Instead, the techniques of analysis rely on internal and systematic relations in the organization of the text rather than on a form of introspection aimed at deciphering the presumed intention of the author. The hermeneutics practised by Ricoeur has confronted 'the challenge of semiology' (1974a: 236ff) and incorporated the results of structural analysis coming from Saussurean linguistics.

It is Martin Heidegger, Ricoeur acknowledges, who subordinates the question of the method of the historical sciences to the investigation of a fundamental ontology, not slowly, step-by-step, but through a

> sudden reversal of the question. Instead of asking: On what condition can a knowing subject understand a text or history? one asks: What kind of being is it whose being consists of understanding? The hermeneutic problem thus becomes a problem of the Analytic of this being, Dasein, which exists through understanding. (Ricoeur, 1974a: 6)

Hermeneutics as an ontology of understanding is the starting point for

Heidegger's elaboration of the structure of being characterizing Dasein, which precedes all separation into subject–object, self–world. This ontology grounds the possibility of the human as well as the natural sciences in the essential structures of Dasein: being-in-the-world before the things of the world become the objects of perception and knowledge, the anticipatory nature of fore-having that marks Dasein's understanding as historical. Only a being whose being unfolds the meaning of historicality can, from the viewpoint of this fundamental ontology, develop the historical sciences. Dilthey's hermeneutics proposed a methodology proper to the historical sciences competing on the epistemological level with the methodology of the natural sciences. Heidegger's direct ontology, which dismisses the order of scientific investigation as derivative, may appear to resolve the conflict presented by Dilthey, opposing the techniques of understanding that belong to the historical sciences to the explanatory procedures that characterize the natural sciences, by shifting hermeneutics to the primordial level of ontology. This move does not, in Ricoeur's view, eliminate the conflict but makes it even more difficult to resolve:

> [The aporia] is no longer between two modalities of knowing *within* epistemology but *between* ontology and epistemology taken as a whole. With Heidegger's philosophy, we are always engaged in going back to the foundations, but we are left incapable of beginning the movement of return that would lead from the fundamental ontology to the properly epistemological question of the status of the human sciences. Now a philosophy that breaks the dialogue with the sciences is no longer addressed to anything but itself... For me, the question that remains unresolved in Heidegger's work is this: *how can a question of* critique *in general be accounted for within the framework of a fundamental hermeneutics*? (Ricoeur, 1974a: 69)

And this will remain the question Ricoeur puts to Gadamer.

The shortcoming of Heideggerian philosophical hermeneutics is the result of the short cut he takes in passing directly to the level of ontology, circumventing questions of method and conflicts of interpretation. Ricoeur proposes a detour by way of the structure and practice of language, the level on which understanding operates. This indirect path sets ontology and the question of being as its aim rather than its starting point. This rejection of the immediate, of the original or primordial, recalls the gesture by which Ricoeur stripped Husserlian phenomenology of its idealist claims in the confrontation between 'immediate consciousness' and 'false consciousness', requiring the detour by way of the unconscious and the procedures by which it is constituted and its effects made manifest. In this way, consciousness is not a given but a task, and the starting point is not the transparency of self-consciousness but meaninglessness (in Freud), alienation (in Marx), or the illusion of value (in Nietzsche). The procedures that each establishes for deciphering the meaning of false consciousness are viewed by Ricoeur to be constitutive of the reality each seeks to uncover: 'What all three attempted in different ways was to make their "conscious" methods of decoding coincide with the "unconscious" *work* of establishing a code which they attribute to the will to power, to the social being, or to the unconscious psyche' (1974a: 149). This interplay of procedure, object of investigation, and mode of knowledge, characteristic of all theory formation, continues to contain an ontological dimension – this is the underlying principle of the hermeneutic circle. It can be expressed in a general way: the ontology of understanding is implied in the methodology of interpretation. Ricoeur restates it in terms of his indirect path toward being: '... it is only in a conflict of rival hermeneutics that we perceive something of the being to be interpreted ... each hermeneutics discovers the aspect of existence which founds it as method' (1974a: 49). It is perhaps in his recasting of the hermeneutical circle, traditionally ascribed to the *Geisteswissenschaften* – where the object of investigation is at the same time a subjectivity and its expressions in the institutions of culture – that Ricoeur's contribution to social theory is most clearly visible.

Matters in Dispute: the Dialectic of Hermeneutics and Critique

The oppositions, in our own time, that emerge within the *Geisteswissenschaften* – between hermeneutics and critique, between ontology and epistemology, between the consciousness of belonging to a tradition and the unconscious, systematic distortion of ideology – have formed the framework of the dispute between Gadamer's hermeneutical philosophy and Habermas's critique of ideology. Ricoeur considers both of these positions and derives not a fusion of the two but a dialectical process that includes hermeneutics and critique as separate moments. The conflict arises on several related levels. First, on the level of predecessors, Gadamer borrows from German Romanticism and from Heidegger's preunderstanding to rehabilitate the concept of prejudice, while Habermas's concept of interest comes from Marx and the work of the Frankfurt School. The scope and focus of the *Geisteswissenschaften* is the second level of dispute: 'Gadamer appeals to the *human sciences*, which are concerned with the contemporary reinterpretation of cultural tradition, Habermas makes recourse to the *critical social sciences*, directly aimed against institutional reifications' (1991: 285).

The third level of contention opposes the starting point of misunderstanding in Gadamer – related to Dilthey's view that there is interpretation where there is first misunderstanding – to the condition of systematic distortion that defines ideology in Habermas. The fourth, and final, level of conflict pits past against future, placing Gadamer on the side of tradition and the consensus that precedes and allows the hermeneutic task, while Habermas 'invokes the *regulative ideal* of an unrestricted and unconstrained communication that does not precede us but guides us from a future point' (1991: 286). Ricoeur's contribution to this debate is to recognize the competing requirements, 'not to fuse the hermeneutics of tradition and the critique of ideology in a supersystem that would encompass both' (1991: 294) but to work out the conditions for a critical hermeneutics. On the side of hermeneutical philosophy, Ricoeur shifts the primary focus away from the ontology of understanding, rooted in the authority of tradition, which establishes the dichotomy between truth and method and rejects the 'alienating distanciation' of the social sciences in the name of the primacy of belonging. Ricoeur turns instead to the history of hermeneutics itself, which requires a moment of critical distance as the techniques of exegesis are applied to written texts. The features of inscription, which allow the autonomy of the text to stand out, are at the same time the conditions for interpretation, the reconstruction of what the text signifies, through the mediation of explanatory procedures. Ricoeur's critical hermeneutics replaces Gadamer's dialogical model of understanding, proceeding by question and answer in the face-to-face situation of speech, with the model of written discourse, in which the traits of distantiation are primary. The autonomy of the text produces a kind of objectification that, for Ricoeur, is not reductive but productive with regard to meaning. The text is amenable to the systematic analysis of explanatory models borrowed from semiology and other linguistic sciences. The analysis of structure and form requires moving from the *text* as inscription, as discourse fixed by writing, to the *work* which belongs to the order of praxis. Here, Ricoeur joins Habermas in holding that the path of understanding passes by way of reconstruction:

> So if there is a hermeneutics ... it must be constituted across the mediation rather than against the current of structural explanation. For it is the task of understanding to bring to discourse what is initially given as structure. ... The *matter* of the text is not what a naive reading of the text reveals, but what the formal arrangement of the text mediates. If that is so, then truth and method do not constitute a disjunction but rather a dialectical process. (Ricoeur, 1991: 299)

Although Ricoeur agrees with Habermas on the necessity for a critique of the illusions of the subject, he does not fully embrace Habermas's critique of ideology. The differences that remain can be summarized in these general points: first, Ricoeur maintains the fundamental position of hermeneutics, while Habermas restricts hermeneutics to one area of research – the historical-hermeneutic sciences under the authority of tradition – and to one form of interest – the practical interest in the sphere of communicative action. Second, the interest in emancipation, which Habermas reserves for the critical social sciences, arises, in Ricoeur's view, also out of a tradition, that of the *Aufklärung* and of other cultural figures of liberation. In this way, the regulative idea of emancipation projected as a future goal is constructed on the basis of the re-examination of a tradition which precedes us. In addition, Ricoeur finds that both hermeneutics and the critique of ideology stem from a philosophy of finitude. Each position, he holds, marks the limit of the universalist claims of the other. And each raises its claim from a particular domain, preventing any assimilation of one by the other:

> ... each has a privileged place and different regional preferences: on the one hand, an attention to cultural heritages ... on the other hand, a theory of institutions and phenomena of domination, focused on the analysis of reifications and alienations. ... it is the task of philosophical reflection to eliminate deceptive antinomies that would oppose the interest in the reinterpretation of cultural heritages received from the past and the interest in the futuristic projections of a liberated humanity. (Ricoeur, 1991: 306–7)

APPRAISAL OF KEY ADVANCES AND CONTROVERSIES

The aspects of Paul Ricoeur's thought that have been acknowledged as influencing work in social theory are, perhaps unsurprisingly, also those aspects that have drawn the most criticism. We shall examine in turn: the model of the text, the role of explanation in the social sciences, and the relation of philosophy to the social sciences.

The Model of the Text

Postwar philosophy, literary and social theory in France have to a large extent centred on the notion of the *text*. Ricoeur's approach to the text reflects two distinct starting points: the hermeneutical tradition of textual exegesis, to be sure, but also the recent history of linguistics, in particular, Saussure's structural linguistics, which presents the synchronic analysis of language considered a formal system of differential traits. The basic features of structural linguistics – the formal sets of oppositions, the arbitrary relation of signifier to signified, the internal coherence of a closed system of signification – were applied to the analysis of literary works (Barthes, Greimas) and to symbolic systems like myths and kinship relations (Lévi-Strauss). In anthropology, for example, the structural model represents a culture as a system of binary oppositions, forming a code to be deciphered in abstraction from subject, object, and context. In contrast, other anthropologists, such as Clifford Geertz, consider that a culture is better compared to a social semantics and to the interpretation of a collective text, in which a culture's ethos and sensibility are externalized (Geertz, 1973: 448–53). In early debates with structuralists, Ricoeur expressed his concern regarding the need to integrate the sets of oppositions uncovered by the anthropologist into a dialectic of interpretation, in which the determination of meaning included the dimension of self-understanding.

To the Saussurean model, Ricoeur adds Benveniste's linguistics of discourse. The text, as Ricoeur conceives it, belongs not to the formal order of *system* (*langue*) but to the order of *discourse* (*parole*). It is not an unconscious, formal system but a product, a realization of language – an instance of discourse. However, as *written* discourse, the text attains a kind of objectification, distancing 'what is said' from the 'saying', making it autonomous in relation to the intention of its author and the conditions of its production. This is what, in Ricoeur's view, allows the text to stand as a paradigm for the object of the social sciences:

> In the same way that a text is detached from its author, an action is detached from its agent and develops consequences of its own. This autonomization of human action constitutes the *social* dimension of action. An action is a social phenomenon not only because it is done by several agents in such a way that the role of each of them cannot be distinguished from the role of the others, but also because our deeds escape us and have effects we did not intend. (Ricoeur, 1991: 153)

In writings published in *From Text to Action*, Ricoeur works out the consequences of this analogy, confining the methodology of the social sciences to the same hermeneutical circle as the interpretation of texts. Ricoeur is not unaware of the problem this presents to the objectivity of the social sciences, but holds this circle to be inherent in the knowledge of human affairs.

The model of the text, in which the units are themselves meanings, displays shortcomings when applied to the field of action. As John Thompson has shown, the parallel between the fixation of discourse in writing and the distancing of action from the event of its performance is unclear. 'In opposition to Ricoeur, it must be stressed that meaning is not something inherent in an action ... [rather] the meaning of an action is closely linked to its description, such that the meaning may be specified by the manner in which the action is described' (Thompson, 1981: 126). Further, since 'the meaning of an action is linked to its description ... how one describes an action is deeply affected by circumstantial considerations. This point is particularly important for the theory of interpretation, for it creates the possibility of reinterpreting action in the light of institutional arrangements and structural conditions' (Thompson, 1981: 127).

Ricoeur's reference by means of this analogy to the sedimentation of action in social time, through which human deeds become institutions, is thought-provoking but lacking in methodological definition. The focus on language, even as the inscription of discourse in the text, leaves in the shadows important aspects of social action, such as the exercise of power in social institutions and the conditions of dramatic social change.

The Role of Explanation in the Social Sciences

In the development of his critical hermeneutics, Ricoeur affirms the need to join explanation to understanding in the dialectic of interpretation. Ricoeur has shown himself to be a methodological pluralist in the Aristotelian sense, gauging the clarity and precision appropriate to different areas of investigation. The domain of the *Geisteswissenschaften* – whether designated as human sciences, social sciences, or critical social sciences – requires, in Ricoeur's view, a twofold approach: first, the stage of objectification, the process of definition and formal organization that provides the framework of intelligibility; and second, the work of interpretation by which the theoretical constructions are appropriated as meanings and integrated into a hermeneutic comprehension. Ricoeur's analysis of the disciplines of psychoanalysis and ideology critique provide examples of this twofold approach, and have been the major areas of his work to which criticism has been directed.

When phenomenology was confronted with psychoanalysis in *Freud and Philosophy*, Ricoeur acknowledged the defeat of immediate consciousness and the need to incorporate the empirical realism of the unconscious in an economic model expressed in terms of force and energy. The peculiar status of psychoanalysis in relation to the distinction between the natural and the human sciences was expressed in its 'mixed discourse', a discourse of force coupled with the appropriation of experience in a discourse of meaning. Returning some years later to this conjuncture of meaning and force in a comprehensive theory, Ricoeur writes:

> The pair formed by the investigatory procedure and the method of treatment takes exactly the same place as the operative procedures in the observational sciences which connect the level of theoretical entities to that of observable data. This pair constitutes the specific mediation between theory and fact in psychoanalysis. And this mediation operates in the following manner: by coordinating interpretation and the handling of resistances, analytic praxis calls for a theory in which the psyche will be represented both as a text to be interpreted and as a system of forces to be manipulated. (Ricoeur, 1980: 258)

Ricoeur's support of this mixed discourse integral to psychoanalytic practice has been attacked by adversaries on both sides. On the one hand, he has been harshly rebuked by those who cite Freud's own efforts to construct a theoretical model within the framework of the natural sciences, and for whom the relation of the metapsychology to the clinical practice must establish causal criteria for validation (Grünbaum, 1984). On the other hand, the inclusion of a discourse of cause and effect has been attacked by a range of critics coming from phenomenology, existential analysis, and ordinary language philosophy. For the latter, the language game of action, agency, intention, and motive for acting must be kept separate from the language game involving explanations of natural events in terms of causes (Anscombe, 1979). For existential analysis, the thing-like character of the unconscious is the very definition of Sartrian 'bad faith'; and the vocabulary of censure and repression resolves nothing but only reintroduces the dualism of the in-itself and the for-itself within the psyche. Finally, the phenomenologist seeks ways to extend the power of description to areas of nonthetic consciousness through the mediation of the systems of intentional objects (perception, language, culture) by means of which meaning is constructed, in opposition to the alleged reductivism of scientism and objectivism. While maintaining the necessity for this mixed discourse of meaning and force, Ricoeur's more recent writings focus this requirement less on the level of the theory outlined in Freud's metapsychology, than on the level of practice, on the conduct of the analysis itself.

The critique of ideology also gives rise to dissension with regard to (1) the definition of the phenomenon of ideology and (2) the epistemological status of critique as science. Ricoeur defines ideology broadly: ideology corresponds to 'the necessity for a social group to give itself an image of itself, to represent and to realize itself, in the theatrical sense of the word' (1991: 249). In this way, the bounds of ideology are those of the social world; ideology is a reflection of the codification of the social order and at the same time its justification, through the rationalization of a system of belief. A force of social cohesion and integration, it is also a source of distortion and dissimulation: 'Ideology preserves identity, but it also wants to conserve what exists and is therefore already a resistance. Something becomes ideological – in the more negative meaning of the term – when the integrative function becomes frozen ... when schematization and rationalization prevail' (1986: 266). From this point of view, since all social reality 'has a symbolic constitution and incorporates an interpretation, in images and representations, of the social bond itself', Ricoeur concludes that, 'ideology is an unsurpassable phenomenon of social existence' (1991: 255).

This assertion implies, first, that there is no social institution that could be exempt from the practical functions of representation, justification, and rationalization held to characterize ideology. It also implies that there is no nonideological framework from which social theory characterized by critique could conduct its analysis. '... The fundamental reason why social theory cannot entirely free itself from the ideological condition (is that) it can neither carry out a total reflection nor rise to a point of view capable of expressing the totality, and hence cannot abstract itself from the ideological mediation to which the other members of the social group are subsumed' (1991: 263).

This would appear to deprive the critical social sciences of their ambition to uncover the mechanisms of ideology, which are unrecognizable to the members of any given community. In *Knowledge and Human Interests* (1972), Habermas compared the work of critique, considered the explanatory science of the systematic distortions of ideology, to psychoanalysis, considered the explanatory theory of the psyche's resistance to self-recognition. In both instances, distortions occur within the process of communication, but because these distortions are systematic and related to the repressive forces of an authority, they are not accessible to the ordinary techniques of interpretation. They require instead the detour of a theoretical model and antihermeneutical explanatory procedures. The interest in emancipation corresponds to the ruin of ideology, not in Ricoeur's broad definition, but in the narrower sense of a system of belief that objectifies social reality as a natural process and mistakenly identifies the interests of one part of society with those of society as a whole. Given this definition of ideology and its critique, one can indeed, in opposition to Ricoeur, conceive of its outside (undistorted relations of communication) or its other (social rationality). The independent status of the critical social sciences is the basis for Habermas's ideal speech situation, which permits the free passage from discourse to action in practice and serves as a theoretical tool for measuring situations of systematically distorted communications. The goal of the critical social sciences is then to cast aside the veil of ideology and to establish the basis for a society grounded in reason alone.

The Relation between Philosophy and the Social Sciences

The final controversy concerns the place of philosophy in the work of the social sciences. From the mid-nineteenth century, the disciplines that claimed their autonomy from the tutelage of philosophy (anthropology, demography, economics, history, linguistics, psychology, sociology) have reflected the increasing specialization of intellectual work, a diversification that also attests to the development and application of new methods of empirical investigation. The resulting construction of separate spheres of activity – each with its codification of terms, methodological procedures, and manner of processing results – has increased the internal coherence of each discipline while making them less and less capable of communicating with one another. The fragmentation of disciplines produces competition between them and aggravates the tendency for each to view issues from its own distinct viewpoint. Philosophers have responded to the dispossession of these spheres in a number of different ways. Some have simply confirmed that the history of the rise of the human sciences itself attests to the creation and demise of the concept of 'man' (Foucault); others replace philosophy with critique, whose task is the analysis of the role of the social sciences in the technologies of power (Adorno, Marcuse).

Ricoeur's view of the relation between philosophy and the social sciences is a recognition of the inevitable conflict of interpretations. Philosophy, in the form of Ricoeur's critical hermeneutics, then serves the mediating role of examining the theoretical structures upon which each method of analysis has been constructed. The rigorousness of a given method often depends upon the narrowness of its conceptual framework, but this, in turn, results in conflicting viewpoints across disciplines regarding claims of objectivity and universality. If philosophy enters into the fray,

> it proceeds by the confrontation of hermeneutic styles and by the critique of systems of interpretation, carrying the diversity of hermeneutic methods back to the structure of the corresponding theories. In this way it prepares itself to perform its highest task, which would be a true arbitration among the absolutist claims of each of the interpretations. (Ricoeur, 1974a: 15)

However, philosophy, too, as practised by Paul Ricoeur, has abandoned any former 'absolutist' claims – to objectivity, to universality, to pure rationality.

RICOEUR'S MAJOR WORKS

Ricoeur, P. (1965a) *History and Truth.* (Trans. Charles A. Kelbley.) Evanston, IL: Northwestern University Press.

Ricoeur, P. (1965b) *Fallible Man.* (Trans. Charles A. Kelbley.) Chicago: Henry Regnery.

Ricoeur, P. (1966) *Freedom and Nature: The Voluntary and the Involuntary.* (Trans. E.V. Kohák.) Evanston, IL: Northwestern University Press.

Ricoeur, P. (1967) *Husserl. An Analysis of His Phenomenology.* (Trans E.G. Ballard and Lester E. Embree.) Evanston, IL: Northwestern University Press.

Ricoeur, P. (1969) *The Symbolism of Evil* (Trans. E. Buchanan.) New York: Harper and Row.

Ricoeur, P. (1970) *Freud and Philosophy: An Essay on Interpretation.* (Trans. Denis Savage.) New Haven, CT: Yale University Press.

Ricoeur, P. (1974a) *The Conflict of Interpretations. Essays in Hermeneutics.* (Ed. Don Ihde.) Evanston, IL: Northwestern University Press.

Ricoeur, P. (1977/78) *The Rule of Metaphor. Multidisciplinary Studies of the Creation of Meaning in Language.* (Trans. Robert Czerny, with Kathleen McLaughlin and John Costello.) Toronto: University of Toronto Press; London: Routledge and Kegan Paul.

Ricoeur, P. (1984) *Time and Narrative. Vol. I.* (Trans. Kathleen McLaughlin and David Pellauer.) Chicago: University of Chicago Press.

Ricoeur, P. (1985) *Time and Narrative. Vol. II.* (Trans. Kathleen McLaughlin and David Pellauer.) Chicago: Chicago University Press.

Ricoeur, P. (1988) *Time and Narrative. Vol. III.* (Trans. Kathleen Blamey and David Pellauer.) Chicago: University of Chicago Press.

Ricoeur, P. (1991) *From Text to Action. Essays in Hermeneutics, II.* (Trans. Kathleen Blamey and John B. Thompson.) Evanston, IL: Northwestern University Press.

Ricoeur, P. (1992) *Oneself as Another.* (Trans. Kathleen Blamey.) Chicago: University of Chicago Press.

Ricoeur, P. (1998) *Critique and Conviction. Conversations with François Azouvi and Marc de Launay.* (Trans. Kathleen Blamey.) New York: Columbia University Press.

Collections of Paul Ricoeur's Writings on Social Themes

Ricoeur, P. (1974b) *Political and Social Essays.* (Ed. David Stewart and Joseph Bien.) Athens, OH: Ohio University Press.

Ricoeur, P. (1976) *Interpretation Theory: Discourse and the Surplus of Meaning.* (Ed. T. Klein.) Fort Worth: The Texas Christian University Press.

Ricoeur, P. (1980) *Hermeneutics and the Human Sciences. Essays on Language, Action and Interpretation.* (Ed. and trans. John B. Thompson.) Cambridge: Cambridge University Press.

Ricoeur, P. (1986) *Lectures on Ideology and Utopia.* (Ed. George H. Taylor.) New York: Columbia University Press.

SECONDARY REFERENCES

Anscombe, G.E.M. (1979) *Intention.* London: Blackwell.

Dauenhauer, Bernard P. (1998) *Paul Ricoeur. The Promise and Risk of Politics.* New York: Rowman & Littlefield.

Gadamer, Hans-Georg (1975) *Truth and Method.* London: Sheed & Ward.

Geertz, Clifford (1973) *The Interpretation of Cultures.* New York: Basic Books.

Grünbaum, Adolf (1984) *The Foundations of Psychoanalysis.* Berkeley: University of California Press.

Habermas, Jürgen (1972) *Knowledge and Human Interests.* (Trans. Jeremy J. Shapiro.) London: Heinemann.

Hahn, Lewis E. (ed) (1995) *The Philosophy of Paul Ricoeur.* The Library of Living Philosophers, Vol. XXII, Chicago: Open Court.

Ihde, Don (1971) *Hermeneutic Phenomenology. The Philosophy of Paul Ricoeur.* Evanston, IL: Northwestern University Press.

Klemm, David E. and Schweiker, William (eds) (1993) *Meanings in Texts and Actions: Questioning Paul Ricoeur.* Charlottesville and London: University Press of Virginia.

Reagan, Charles E. (ed) (1979) *Studies in the Philosophy of Paul Ricoeur.* Athens, OH: Ohio University Press.

Thompson, John B. (1981) *Critical Hermeneutics. A Study in the Thought of Paul Ricoeur and Jurgen Habermas.* Cambridge: Cambridge University Press.

Wood, David (1991) *On Paul Ricoeur. Narrative and Interpretation* London and New York: Routledge.

22

Niklas Luhmann

JAKOB ARNOLDI

BIOGRAPHICAL DETAILS AND THEORETICAL CONTEXT

Niklas Luhmann was born in 1927 in Lüneburg, Germany, the son of the local brewer. Towards the end of the Second World War, still in his teens, Luhmann was enlisted and sent to the front where he was soon captured by American troops and imprisoned. His experience of the prison camp and later of life in postwar Germany left Luhmann with a wish to study law, which he saw as instrumental in restoring order to the chaotic postwar society. After graduating from the University of Freiburg, Luhmann took a job as a civil servant in the ministry of culture. He continued, however, to pursue his philosophical interests in his spare time. His particular interests were in the works of Descartes, Kant, and Husserl. Realizing that the job as a civil servant would bring with it more and more political involvement (Luhmann was not, and did not wish to be, politically active), Luhmann took up a scholarship to Harvard where he studied for one year under Talcott Parsons. Upon returning to Germany in 1961, Luhmann resumed his job in the civil service but was soon drawn back to academia. He held posts in Speyer and Dortmund and received his *habilitation* in 1966, taking up a chair in Münster. In 1969, he moved to the newly established university in Bielefeld. His first publications were on organizational theory and sociology of law. The 1971 publication of *Theorie der Gesellschaft oder Sozialtechnologie – was leistet die System-forschung?* (co-authored by Jürgen Habermas) brought Luhmann to a wider academic audience and marked the beginning of an ongoing critical debate between Luhmann's systems-theoretic approach and Habermas's reformulation of critical theory.

Since the publication of his general systems theory, *Soziale Systeme*, in 1984 (*Social Systems*, 1995a), Luhmann's work has enjoyed a broad readership both within and outside Germany. Luhmann published on a variety of subjects (function systems, ecological problems and risk, sociology of knowledge and much more) during his lifetime. Many of these themes and concepts are brought together in his main work, *Die Gesellschaft der Gesellschaft*, published in 1997. Luhmann died in November 1998.

The conception of society Luhmann lays out is that of a society with no centre, with no collective or coordinating unity. Instead, modern society is differentiated into autonomous self-referential 'function systems'. From the very beginning, Luhmann tried to combine a phenomenological notion of *meaning* or *sense* (*sinn*) with systems theory. He originally maintained a notion of action, and developed his theory partly using a structural functionalist paradigm (although he from the beginning abandoned Parsons's four-functional action theory scheme). From around 1980, however, Luhmann replaced the notion of action with that of communication. At approximately the same time, Luhmann introduced the notion of *autopoietic systems* into his theory. This, along with other developments in cybernetic theory, also enabled Luhmann to rethink his notion of meaning from a perspective other than phenomenology. He was in particular able to do this following the introduction of George Spencer Brown's (1979) theory of 'form' into his work from the mid-1980s.

Autopoiesis means 'self-producing' or 'self-constituting' and was initially used to describe the (self-) constitution of a living organism (Maturana, 1975, 1981). Luhmann, on the other hand, incorporates the term in his theory of communicative systems. Communication is always 'about' something (like the phenomenological notion of intentionality). It thus entails a *distinction*, which is at the core of Luhmann's notion of meaning. This distinction at the same time constitutes the system – an autopoietic system is a system that (re)produces itself by its operations. It is, so to speak, its own distinctions. I will outline below these core elements of Luhmann's theory, highlighting its rich variety of functionalism, cybernetics, and phenomenology. Thereafter, I will address the key controversies that surround Luhmann's theory. I will argue that Luhmann's work is far more than just functionalism and contains a variety of interesting theoretical notions especially in the areas of phenomenology and cybernetics.

SOCIAL THEORY AND CONTRIBUTIONS

The Outset – Differentiation

Luhmann builds his theory on the notion of a social system as a system of communication. Society, the all-encompassing communicative system, is differentiated into various 'function systems' such as family, law, economy, and science. These functions systems have structured, or codified, their communication to such a degree that they can only observe (or make sense of) their environment through this code. The legal system thus communicates according to a legal/illegal code, the art system according to aesthetic/unaesthetic, while the political system communicates in terms of power (government) or the lack thereof (opposition). Each system can only observe what its own code renders visible and consequently has a 'blind spot' because it cannot observe that it cannot observe what it cannot observe (Luhmann, 1990d: 52) (paradoxes play an important role in Luhmann's theory). As a result, no system can control or foresee its influences on other systems in its environment and indeed is unable to communicate with these other systems – communication takes place within systems, not in-between. The intrinsic 'centrelessness' of modern society, Luhmann argues, means that sociological analysis needs to find structural similarities among the different autonomous systems in order to come to a general description of society. The main similarity that Luhmann points out is that the function systems operate autopoietically and are operationally closed. Operational closure means that a system, in the continuing autopoietic reproduction, builds upon the structure generated by its previous operations. Put differently, the system builds up structured complexity through a concatenation of operations with reference to the 'structure' generated from the former operations, which leads to a state of operational closure. To elaborate on this, Luhmann turns to his general systems theory.

Autopoiesis and Operational Closure

In terms of general systems theory, the basic assumption is that systems exist (Luhmann, 1995a: 12). These can be categorized into machines, organisms, social systems, and psychic systems. Social systems are constituted autopoietically through the meaning (distinction) created in communication, since any such event at the same time constitutes the system. Luhmann's notion of 'system' is therefore not founded upon a notion of a set of elements that are integrated into a whole, for example through shared symbolic values. Rather, every system emerges through difference. Luhmann's general systems theory is concerned with those types of systems that operate via meaning, namely psychic and social systems. However, although both types of systems are meaning-processing, they are radically different since the operational events (and operational events are the system's elements) differ. For social systems the mode of operation is communication (for psychic systems it is cognition). This means that psychic systems, not to mention human beings, do not belong to the social system but are instead one of the more problematic parts of the environment of the social system (Luhmann, 1971: 37, 1997: 30). Communication is thus the absolute 'limit' or border of society.

The point of departure for Luhmann's development of the theory of social systems is Parsons's concept of double contingency. The psychic systems (Luhmann names them Alter and Ego) are 'black boxes' to each other, which is to say that they are reciprocally non-transparent. Ego cannot be sure that Alter means what Alter says and vice versa. The question Luhmann asks is how anything 'meaningful' or 'sensible' can emerge out of this contingent or chaotic encounter. Between the two systems his answer is that it happens by the emergence of a third system – a social system (Luhmann, 1975: 73, 1995a: 100). In other (cybernetic) words: the double-contingent encounter of Alter and Ego is the noise out of which (a third) order emerges, namely the social system. Luhmann therefore rejects the notion of intersubjectivity (Luhmann, 1986b), simply replacing it with the notion of a social system. Communication cannot, of course, take place without psychic and biological systems, that is, human beings, but Luhmann's point is that the communication that is generated is a continuous process of *distinctions*, of 'sense-making', that must be described as communication's own (self-reference), especially since the continuation of the communication relies on the already-generated meaning in (earlier) communication. It thus cannot be attributed to the participating psychic systems. What Luhmann constructs is, in other words, a theory of a 'third' system that also observes, that also makes sense of, the environment through internal operations – he creates, if one likes, a phenomenology of communication (Teubner, forthcoming).

Having established the dislocation of the social system from psychic systems, Luhmann can then elaborate on an analysis of the basic *modus vivendi* of such social systems. The autopoietic operation of drawing a distinction is an actualization of 'something'. Husserl's phenomenology contains a notion of intentionality as an act (noetic event) that 'structures' raw sensuous data (*hylé*) into meaningful phenomena. Husserl furthermore argues that the meaning, or sense, that comes out of this act always implies a *horizon*, of other possible (potential) intentional acts or meaning (Husserl, 1995: 23, 1973: 32). This notion of meaning and intentionality is recast by Luhmann into a notion of observation, which entails the drawing of a *distinction* (Luhmann, 1992: 98–99; Maturana, 1975: 325). Any such observation is an autopoietic operation entailing the 'singling out' of something – or, as George Spencer Brown has formulated it, the drawing of a distinction between the marked and unmarked state, obtained through what he calls *form* (Brown, 1979). The 'noise' or, as an abstract analogy the *hylé*, of the double-contingent encounter is thus structured into meaning, into form, through each operational event (communication) of the social system. As mentioned above, the operational event, the observation, is also what constitutes an autopoietic system. The distinction appears 'twice' as a re-entry: as a distinction between the marked and the unmarked, but also, at the same time, as the event that constitutes the system, thus creating a distinction between the system and environment (Brown, 1979: 76; Luhmann, 1996: 26, 1997: 45).

Any operational event (distinction) must furthermore be linked to a notion of *time*, since any operation is temporal (Luhmann, 1995a: 47). The continuing autopoiesis demands a continuing production of new operations. The 'next' event, however, can rely on already-generated meaning. In general, any phenomenon observed through meaning, for instance an object, can be given an identity; a table can be defined as a table and this identification, or *symbolic generalization* (Luhmann, 1995a: 92), can later be used again for further communication (see also Husserl, 1983: 41). Thus, the continuing autopoietic operations build upon the system's previous operations, which over time lead to operational closure, defined by Luhmann as recursive rendering possible own operations through the result of own operations (Luhmann, 1997: 94). Any meaning generating system is thus 'closed'. Such closure does not mean indifference to the environment. On the contrary, any observation, any event that creates information from the noise of the environment, can only happen through the continuing reproduction of the (re-entering) distinction between system and environment (Luhmann, 1994: 49).

Luhmann's notion of communication means that it cannot be regarded as merely a transferring of information from one subject to another. Instead, Luhmann views communication as a threefold process consisting of utterance or impartation (*mitteilung*), information, and understanding. All three things must take place for communication to happen. At the moment this happens, the social system emerges as a third system. It is at this moment that communication *itself* has processed meaning, an operation that then forms the basis for further communication (operational closure). The dislocating of communication and cognition does not mean, however, that one form of autopoiesis (for example communication) could take place without the other. Even though they are different types of autopoietic systems, the two types of systems have co-evolved. The co-evolution is only rendered possible through a continuing exchange of energy between the two different types of systems, an exchange Luhmann calls interpenetration or, in more recent terminology, structural coupling (Jönhill, 1997: 35).

Semantic Codification of Communication

Society, as the all-encompassing operationally closed communicative system, is further differentiated into subsystems. In other words, the system-environment distinction is replicated inside the social system with new autopoietic distinctions created out of environmental noise. Luhmann divides the (development of) internal differentiation of the social system into four historical stages:

1 The segmented society – an archaic society with a division between various tribes or clans.
2 The core/periphery differentiated society – with differentiation between a central concentration of power and a less privileged periphery.
3 The stratified society – differentiated into socially immobile strata.
4 The functionally differentiated society – differentiated into function systems.

Luhmann's thesis is that in the seventeenth and eighteenth centuries a transition took place from stratified to functionally differentiated society. Functional differentiation is differentiation into function-specific systems, each operating (observing) autonomously through their own binary codes. The function systems that Luhmann mentions in his writings are: economy, politics, law, art, religion, science, education, family, mass media, health. Functional differentiation is a result of communicating systems that observe through a basic semantic difference that determines what the system 'reacts' to as information, and what is left out as noise (Luhmann, 1986a: 85, 1997: 68) What is meant by code is, in other words, a form of semantic 'structure' that serves as a 'guiding difference' (Luhmann, 1987: 16) for the continuing autopoiesis. The consequence of the codification of the autopoiesis is that function systems can only observe through the code (for this paradoxical aspect of self-reference see below).

In terms of the evolution of social systems, both the medium of language, and other media play a key role. Language, as a system of audible signs, enables a clear distinction to be made between information and utterance, and makes 'effective' shared symbolic generalizations possible. Language, therefore, facilitates the operational closure of communication. Luhmann then distinguishes between two types of media, namely *media of dissemination* and *symbolic generalized media*. Regarding media of dissemination, Luhmann includes writing, the printing press, and electronic forms of communication ranging from the telegraph to the Internet. Functional differentiation, however, takes place through a differentiation of symbolic generalized media. Symbolic generalized media are media that can stabilize highly contingent or improbable forms of communication. These media, such as love, money/property, power/law, truth, art/aesthetics, and 'basic values' are semantic devices that have sufficient symbolic value to motivate acceptance of the imparted information and make response relevant. Symbolic generalized media can therefore be termed media precisely because they facilitate and motivate otherwise improbable communication – when one says 'I love you' the other not only understands this information but also finds it relevant enough to think that one at least is entitled to an answer. These media also 'guide' the production of meaning and are thus so closely related to codes that they can be referred to simply as media codes (see Luhmann, 1997: 748–9). Luhmann claims that earlier functional correlates to these media were morals, rhetoric, and shared values. From the seventeenth century, however, a differentiation of symbolic generalized media and subsequent codification of meaning took place. This can, to some extent, be traced historically, since new forms of meaning-processing leave historical traces in the (preserved) form of written material; words take on new meanings or appear in different contexts. Luhmann has reserved the term *semantics* for such symbolic generalizations that are stored over time (Luhmann, 1980: 19, 1995a: 163, 1997: 200). The notion of media codes is, to sum up, quite central in Luhmann's argument which is simply that 'old' forms of communication, mediated by shared values, norms, religion, and so on, are gradually replaced by self-referential codified forms of communication, that is, different forms of communication that are mediated by their own symbolic generalizations and guided by their own meaningful distinctions.

An example of this process is the differentiation of the media code of love or intimacy which started in the seventeenth century. Love is not held, by Luhmann, to be a feeling but rather a (media) code of communication. When one expresses one's love, one talks about 'something' that the Alter Ego can identify and respond to. As for all other symbolically generalized media, it reduces the contingency and complexity of the encounter and makes it asymmetric – Ego expresses something and Alter can respond (Luhmann, 1997: 336). Luhmann has traced the evolution of this semantic code through the study of historical love letters, novels, and poems. In medieval times, the semantics of love mainly consisted of idealizations of persons, where the gallantry of the manner of expression of these feelings was more important than reciprocation of the feelings, not to mention actual fulfilment. In the seventeenth century, however, the semantics of love changed into passionate love where an actual (and mutual) love relationship was sought. Instead of emphasizing the importance of gallantry, the new code of passionate love is built on a notion of freedom and *plaisir*; each person has the right to choose in affairs of the heart and can, when the *plaisir* ceases, choose to terminate the affair. These new semantics of intimacy were in the beginning a strictly extramarital (and thus post-marital) form of communication. Marriage was still a core foundation for the reproduction of stratified differentiation. Still, this emerging media code of love had the ability to codify the individualized and contingent forms of interaction within higher social strata in the period. Such a codification was only possible through new media of dissemination, in this case the printing press. Only when both Ego and Alter knew the code, for instance through romantic novels, could the communication begin (Luhmann, 1986a: 31).

The codification of passionate love changed decisively around 1800 when a new codification of love – romantic love – began to unify marriage, love, and sexuality. One consequence of this development of the semantic code is that it became a code of communication for everybody, not just nobility, leading to the constitution of a function system. Love, as codified symbolic medium that leads to the autopoiesis of a function system, is thus part of a theory of how contingency and complexity are absorbed through semantic codification of communication. This should not lead the reader of Luhmann to assume that function systems have the a priori function of absorbing contingency. For what or whom would this be a function? All function systems operate through references to themselves, and the various function systems are not in any way mutually coordinated. Luhmann's way of theorizing is not through ascribing function to a system but instead by observing how systems create distinctions (meaning) out of the complexity or noise of the environment, thereby securing their autopoiesis. For all function systems, a key feature of the evolution of the code is the increase of the self-reference 'within' it. The code of love, for example, has developed into a state of self-reference where love is increasingly justified as being simply love (Luhmann, 1986a: 30, 44). This increase in self-reference strengthens the autopoiesis and also the autonomy of the system. Yet the system of intimacy is still faced with 'environmental challenges' as are other systems. Can a code of lifelong love, for instance, leave sufficient space for Alter and Ego's demands for individual fulfilment in contemporary culture?

APPRAISAL OF KEY ADVANCES AND CONTROVERSIES

Ecological Problems and the Contingency of Steering

The problems that occur in a centreless and highly complex society where 'the whole is less than its parts' (Luhmann, 1982: 238) is a key theme in Luhmann's work. An example of this problem is ecological risks (risk, naturally, is not related only to ecology – see next section). Luhmann's notion of social systems means that it is questionable to what extent society is able to observe, let alone adapt to, ecological problems. Luhmann sees the autopoiesis of society to be 'disturbed' by ecological problems but is rather pessimistic as to whether this irritation can generate resonance, that is, actually restructure the autopoietic operations. The question is in which function systems resonance can be generated and if so, how resulting responses can be coordinated with other function systems. The 'autopoietic imperative' of the function systems works against this. They must continue their operations and can only do so with reference to the structure of their past operations – function systems thus proceed 'backwards into the future' (Luhmann, 1993: 35) – just as they operate according to their own code, so that they tend to make sense of the environment in accordance with this. The only possible solution that Luhmann sees is an increase in each function system's ability to incorporate its own distinction between system and environment into its operations (Luhmann, 1990d: 257). A second obstacle is the 'steering', or coordination of a differentiated society. The 'gain' of functional differentiation is that each function system is able to tolerate higher degrees of complexity, as long as other function systems in the environment are sensitive to problems to which it is indifferent (Luhmann, 1982: 237, 1997: 761). However, as mentioned earlier, the differentiation also creates unpredictability and contingency since each function system is faced with an increasingly complex and unpredictable environment consisting of the output from other function systems. If, for instance, resonance is created regarding ecological problems within the political system, this system is still confronted with the immense complexity of 'steering' the environment, which consists of the operations of the other systems (for other examples of such political 'contingency' see Jessop, 1997; Luhmann, 1971, 1990d; Wilke, 1992).

Luhmann again and again argues that the codification of communication evolves towards states of self-reference. Law thus becomes its own sole argument as does love, economy, aesthetics in other self-referential systems. This paradoxical state of society has perhaps been best demonstrated in relation to law. The semantic codification of law leads to a development from natural (God-given or religiously founded) law to positive law. Law, in other words, has changed from merely reflecting general (often religiously founded) values to defining by itself, or through itself, what is legal or illegal. This leads, as in the case of other media-codes, to self-referential development where there is nothing 'behind' legality. Can the law, for example, be illegal? The legal system's form is the ultimate border, outside of which (to repeat the paradox) there is no legal communication (Teubner, 1993: 2). The evolved self-reference of the function codes also has the effect that function systems become highly sensitive to the environment. As more environmental 'noise' can be transformed into information through the code, anything can thus be traded or speculated in, or anything can, at least since Marcel Duchamp, be an object of art. In similar fashion the range of possible political issues increases, leaving the political system faced with a much wider range of political issues than before (Luhmann, 1990b: 36, 1997: 764).

Critique

One particular, and often voiced, criticism deals with Luhmann's relationship to Parsonian structural functionalism. It should be made clear that Luhmann's work differs significantly from Parsonian structural functionalism. Luhmann shifts the emphasis from action to communication; he starts out with a notion of difference as opposed to a notion of integration; and, most importantly, Luhmann, unlike Parsons, does not see social change as a process of 'modernization' moving towards a harmonious integration of different function systems (Luhmann, 1997: 568). However, there is little doubt that there are similarities, not least of which is the much criticized lack of a notion of social power or inequality. Terms like class, gender, or race are either toned down to the point of insignificance or are simply nonexistent in most of Luhmann's work. The main reason for this omission is Luhmann's emphasis on the transition from stratified differentiation to functional differentiation. The 'tipping over' of social strata (as the main form of differentiation) into functional differentiation leads, it is claimed, to a democratization of status and power as positions within each system tend to be allocated independently from other systems (Luhmann, 1995c: 246, 1997: 625, 734, 742). Political power, for example, is thus achieved independently of economic wealth, and the education system, which increasingly functions as the distributor of careers and social status, operates (or should operate) independently of social class background (Luhmann, 1987: 188; Luhmann and Schorr, 1979: 317).

This notion of democratization can be (and has been) criticized. Luhmann's argument is based on the claim that the emergence of autonomous media codes makes the communication accessible without influence from other function systems. It is arguable if this really had the effect that Luhmann postulates. That is, whether such a historical shift in mobility patterns actually did occur (Schwinn, 1998). One reason for this, still argued in a Luhmannian vocabulary, may be that social class and status is determined by access to organizations, not just access to self-referentially codified communication (Nassehi and Nollmann, 1997). Furthermore, Luhmann's dislocation of social systems from psychic systems means that it is left unexplainable why some persons, for reasons of class or status, might face a particular risk of exclusion from the function systems or not have any prospects of a high status in any of them (Arnoldi, 1998; Kronauer, 1998). These objections are examples of how Luhmann's emphasis on a fundamental historical shift from one main form of differentiation to another leads to claims of democratization which fail to take into account various forms of power. The notion of functional differentiation remains, however, an innovative explanation of differentiation through differences in the mode of creating information out of environmental noise. One disadvantage, however, is that the level of abstraction in Luhmann's theory makes empirical verification, in particular through micro-sociological research, impossible (Knorr-Cetina, 1992).

Another significant break away from functionalism is due to the fact that Luhmann's phenomenological account of communication results in a turning away from positivism. Anything observed, including scientific 'truth', is a product of meaning-processing through a (contingent) distinction made by the observer. By creating a social system in analogy to Husserl's transcendental ego, Luhmann creates a fascinating and powerful response to the lack of emphasis of the social in Husserl's philosophy. Luhmann combines this with notions of complexity and self-referential codification. Function systems react to the environment with operational closure exactly because of the complexity of the environment – complexity meaning that there is more environmental noise than the system can (have time to) make sense of. Because no system has the 'requisite variety' to process all noise into meaning, they are left having to rely on their own operational closed mode of operation. This in turn leads to increased mutual complexity as other systems in the environment do the same (which again forces the first system to operate even more self-referentially). Luhmann does indeed end up with a deterministic view of the form of operation of function systems, partly because function systems can observe only with reference to their own structured complexity generated by their past operations (see also Husserl, 1973: 122), partly because of their need to rely on symbolically generalized media. However, this same point provides a compelling insight into society's inability to adapt swiftly to environmental challenges and why, even in cases where a function system does react, the form of change is unpredictable. And it is from this position that Luhmann calls for more 'reflexive' forms of operation from the function systems, that is, the need for systems to incorporate their own system-environment distinctions in their operations.

The key weakness of Luhmann's phenomenology of communication comes from the distinction between psychic and social systems. Luhmann does emphasize the structural coupling or interpenetration between these two different types of systems because they supply each other with energy and complexity (noise). Nevertheless, they remain mutually distinct as each other's environment since the autopoietic meaning-processing is held to be separate. Jürgen Habermas argues that this separation of subject from life-world, of consciousness from communication, displaces exactly the unity which is 'constitutive for linguistically constituted forms of life' (Habermas, 1990: 383). It must, for example, be argued that socialization is more than 'self-socialization' (Luhmann's claim based on his notion of closure, see 1995a: 241) and that the social environment influences the autopoiesis of psychic system and vice versa to a degree that structural couplings consist of more than just exchange of energy and complexity, that is, that it also influences the sense-making itself (Arnoldi, 1998). However, the phenomenological aspects of Luhmann's theory at the same time offer a whole new way of using phenomenology in the social sciences, the potential of which has yet to be fully explored. It may suggest, for example, how changes appear in the general forms of the social system's sense-making. Luhmann, in fact, builds his notion of risk on this. Any meaning-processing in a complex environment is faced with the necessity of actualizing something and letting all other possible operations remain as merely a potential horizon. The future is thus a horizon containing the possible acts that are, in the present, denied actualization, which makes the future risky. Luhmann argues that often the only adequate form of *protention* available to contemporary complex societies is in the form of risk (see Luhmann, 1992, 1993; Nassehi, 1993).

Finally, Luhmann has formulated his theory with reference not only to autopoiesis, but also to a range of cybernetic themes (self-organization, dissipative structures, nonlinearity etc.) that currently are spreading, under the label of 'complexity theory', into a range of diverse disciplines, including the social sciences (Thrift, 1999), with the aim of explicating highly unpredictable, mathematically nonlinear, self-organizing 'patterns' (Coveney and Highfield, 1996; Eve et al., 1997; Khalil and Boulding, 1996; Prigogine and Stengers, 1984). Luhmann (in addition perhaps to Edgar Morin) is one of the few that have actually succeeded in implementing these notions into substantial social theory.

I have identified and discussed some main threads in Luhmann's work and pointed out that several elements of Luhmann's work must be regarded with scepticism. In must also be stressed that it is necessary to approach such highly abstract 'grand theory' as Luhmann's with a certain sense of irony. The idea of constructing such big theoretical systems is held by many to be rather old-fashioned. In fact, Luhmann's own theory tells us that all observations have a blind spot – that they cannot see their own distinctions. So however 'grand' this theory might be, it of course also excludes that which it cannot observe. None the less, it also makes many other things observable and is therefore worth engaging with.

LUHMANN'S MAJOR WORKS

Luhmann, Niklas (1971) *Politische Planung*. Opladen: Westdeutscher Verlag.

Luhmann, Niklas (1975) *Sociologische Aufklärungen 2*. Stuttgart: Vestdeutscher Verlag.

Luhmann, Niklas (1979) *Trust and Power*. Chichester: Wiley.

Luhmann, Niklas (1980) *Gesellschaftstruktur und Semantik*, Vol. 1. Frankfurt: Suhrkamp.

Luhmann, Niklas (1981) *Gesellschaftstruktur und Semantik*, Vol. 2. Frankfurt: Suhrkamp.

Luhmann, Niklas (1982) *The Differentiation of Society*. New York: Columbia University Press.

Luhmann, Niklas (1985) *A Sociological Theory of Law*. London: Routledge.

Luhmann, Niklas (1986a) *Love as Passion*. Cambridge: Polity Press.

Luhmann, Niklas (1986b) 'Die Lebenswelt – Nach ruchsprachen mit phenomenologen', *Archiv für Rechts- und Sozialphilosophie*, 72: 176–94.

Luhmann, Niklas (1987) *Soziologische Aufklärung*, Vol. 4. Opladen: Westdeutcher Verlag.

Luhmann, Niklas (1989a) *Ecological Communication*. Cambridge: Polity Press.

Luhmann, Niklas (1989b) *Gesellschaftstruktur und Semantik*, Vol. 3. Frankfurt: Suhrkamp.

Luhmann, Niklas (1990a) *Essays on Self-reference*. New York: Columbia University Press.

Luhmann, Niklas (1990b) *Political Theory in the Welfare State*. New York: de Gruyter.

Luhmann, Niklas (1990c) *Die Wissenschaft der Gesellschaft*. Frankfurt: Suhrkamp.

Luhmann, Niklas (1990d) *Ökologische Kommunikation*. Opladen: Westdeutscher Verlag.

Luhmann, Niklas (1992) *Beobachtungen der Moderne*. Opladen: Vestdeutscher Verlag.

Luhmann, Niklas (1993) *Risk – a Sociological Theory*. New York: De Gruyter.

Luhmann, Niklas (1993) *Das Recht der Gesellschaft*. Frankfurt: Suhrkamp.

Luhmann, Niklas (1994) *Die Wirtschaft der Gesellschaft*. Frankfurt: Suhrkamp.

Luhmann, Niklas (1995a) *Social Systems*. Stanford: Stanford University Press.

Luhmann, Niklas (1995b) *Die Kunst der Gesellschaft*. Frankfurt: Suhrkamp.

Luhmann, Niklas (1995c) *Soziologische Auflkärung*, Vol. 6. Opladen: Westdeutscher Verlag.

Luhmann, Niklas (1996) *Die Realität der Massenmedien*. Opladen: Westdeutscher Verlag.

Luhmann, Niklas (1997) *Die Gesellschaft der Gesellschaft*. Frankfurt: Suhrkamp.

Luhmann, Niklas (1998) *Observations of Modernity*, Stanford, CA: Stanford University Press.

Luhmann, Niklas, and Schorr, Karl-Eberhard (1979) *Reflexionsprobleme im Erziehungssystem*. Stuttgart: Klett-Cotta.

SECONDARY REFERENCES

Arnoldi, Jakob (1998) 'Modernisering, social mobilitet og systemteori – en diskussion af Niklas Luhmanns systemsteori', *Dansk Sociologi*, 9 (2): 7–20.

Brown, George Spencer (1979) *Laws of Form*. New York: E.P. Dutton.

Coveney, Peter and Highfield, Roger (1996) *Frontiers of Complexity – The Search for Order in a Chaotic World*. London: Faber and Faber.

Eve, Raymond A., Hornsfall, Sara and Lee, Mary E. (eds) (1997) *Chaos, Complexity and Sociology* Thousand Oaks, CA: Sage.

Foerster, Heinz von (1984) *Observing Systems*. Seaside, OR: Intersystems Publications.

Habermas, Jürgen (1990) *The Philosophical Discourse of Modernity*. Cambridge: Polity Press.

Husserl, Edmund (1973) *Experience and Judgment*. Evanston, IL: Northwestern University Press.

Husserl, Edmund (1983) *Ideas Pertaining to a Pure Phenomenology and to a Phenomenological Philosophy, Part 1*. Dordrecht: Kluwer.

Husserl, Edmund ([1950] 1995) *Cartesian Meditations*. Dordrecht: Kluwer.

Jessop, Bob (1997) 'The governance of complexity and the complexity of governance', in A. Amin and J. Hausner (eds), *Beyond Markets and Hierarchy: Interactive Governance and Social Complexity*. Aldershot: Edward Elgar.

Jönhill, Jan Inge (1997) *Samhallet som system och dess ekologiska omvarld: En studie i Niklas Luhmannssociologiska systemteori*. Lund: University of Lund.

Khalil, Elias L., and Boulding, Kenneth E. (Eds.) (1996) *Evolution, Order and Complexity*. London: Routledge.

Kneer, Georg, and Nassehi, Armin (1993) *Niklas Luhmanns Theorie sozialer Systeme. Eine Einführung*. Munich: Fink-Verlag.

Knorr-Cetina, Karin (1992) 'Zur Underkomplexität der Differentierungstheorie', *Zeitschrift für Soziologie*, 21: 406–19.

Kronauer, Martin (1998) 'Exklusion in der Armutforschung und der Systemtheorie. Anmerkungen zu einer problematischen Beziehung', Paper presented at conference on Exclusion? Theoretical and Empirical Problems, Bielefeldt.

Maturana, Humberto R. (1975) 'The organizations of the living: a theory of the living organization', *International Journal Man-Machine Studies*, 7: 313–32.

Maturana, Humberto R. (1981) 'Autopoiesis', in M. Zeleny (ed.), *Autopoiesis – A Theory of Living Systems*. New York: North Holland.

Meja, Volker, Misgeld, Dieter, and Stehr, Nico (eds) (1987) *Modern German Sociology*. New York: Columbia University Press.

Miller, Max (1994) 'Intersystemic discourse and coordinated dissent: a critique of Luhmann's concepts ecological communication', *Theory Culture & Society*, 11 (2): 101–21.

Mingers, John (1995) *Self-Producing Systems*. New York: Plenum Press.

Nassehi, Armin (1993) *Die Zeit der Gesellschaft*. Opladen: Westdeutscher Verlag.

Nassehi, Armin and Nollmann, Gerd (1997) 'Inklusionen. Organisationssoziologische Ergänzungen der Inklusions-/Exklusionstheorie', *Soziale Systeme*, 3: 393–411.

Neckel, Sighardt, and Wolf, Jürgen (1994) 'The fascination of amorality: Luhmann's theory of morality and its resonances among German Intellectuals', *Theory, Culture & Society*, 11 (2): 69–99.

Paterson, John (1997) 'An introduction to Luhmann', *Theory, Culture & Society*, 14 (1): 37–39.

Prigogine, Ilya and Stengers, Isabelle (1984) *Order Out of Chaos – Man's New Dialogue with Nature*. London: Heinemann.

Schwinn, Thomas (1998) 'Soziale Ungleich und Soziale Differenzierung', *Zeitschrift für Soziologie*, 27: 3–17.

Sciully, Davis (1994) 'An interview with Niklas Luhmann', *Theory, Culture & Society*, 11 (2): 37–68.

Teubner, Günther (1993) *Law as an Autopoietic System*. Oxford: Blackwell.

Teubner, Günther (Forthcoming) 'Economics of gift – positivity of justice: the mutual paranoia of Jacques Derrida and Niklas Luhmann', *Theory, Culture & Society*.

Thrift, Nigel (1999) 'The place of complexity', *Theory, Culture & Society*, 16 (3): 31–69.

Wilke, Helmut (1992) *Ironie des Staates – Grundlinien einer Staatstheorie polyzentrischer Gesellschaft*. Frankfurt: Suhrkamp.

Viskovatoff, Alex (1999) 'Foundations of Niklas Luhmann's theory of social systems', *Philosophy of the Social Sciences*, 29: 481–516.

Zeleny, Milan (ed.) (1981) *Autopoiesis*. New York: North Holland.

23

Charles Taylor

MARCOS ANCELOVICI AND FRANCIS DUPUIS-DÉRI

BIOGRAPHICAL DETAILS AND THEORETICAL CONTEXT

Charles Taylor was born in 1931 in Montreal. He grew up in a French–English bilingual family and in a divided society. He witnessed the French Canadians' struggle for recognition, in the Canadian province of Quebec, at the time mainly controlled culturally and economically by English Canadians and Americans. Issues of identity, language, nationalism, and politics of recognition were part of Taylor's everyday life.

In the early 1950s, after completing his BA in History at McGill University, Taylor attended Oxford University as a Rhodes Scholar to study philosophy. He found Anglo-Saxon human sciences dominated by copycats of natural scientists. As Taylor (1996: 209) explained: 'I felt that there was a huge discrepancy between the discourse of science and of political philosophy, on the one hand, and the reality of life and of political passions, on the other'. Taylor was particularly critical of positivism and methodological individualism. He felt more at home with the continental philosophical tradition. His intellectual guides were primarily Aristotle, Herder, and Hegel. While at Oxford, he studied with Elizabeth Anscombe and chose Sir Isaiah Berlin as his doctoral supervisor. According to Taylor (1997a: v), it was Maurice Merleau-Ponty's *Phénoménologie de la Perception* that really showed him the path he wanted to take, especially with regard to the critique of positivism. In his first book, *The Explanation of Behaviour* (1964), Taylor already condemned positivism and advocated an understanding of a situated and self-interpreting self.

Taylor taught at several universities, including Princeton University, UC-Berkeley, and Université de Montréal. His passion for politics also led him to join the Canadian social-democratic New Democratic Party (NDP) in 1961 and to run as an NDP candidate in four federal elections between 1962 and 1968. However, Taylor never got elected, partly because at that time the Canadian federal political system was dominated by the Liberal and Conservative parties.

During the 1970s, Taylor focused mainly on his academic work. While a professor of philosophy and political science at McGill University, he published *Hegel* (1975), a widely acclaimed work. He then moved to Oxford University, where he was Chichele Professor of Social and Political Theory from 1976 to 1979. Nevertheless, Taylor left the prestigious Chichele Chair for Canadian politics in order to join the supporters of Canadian federalism during the 1980 referendum campaign on the independence of Quebec. Organized by the Parti Québécois (PQ), in power in Quebec since 1976, this referendum was to seal the fate of Quebec as a Canadian province or as a sovereign state. A vast majority of Quebeckers (almost 60%) chose to remain in the Canadian federation. Such a result pleased Taylor, for he believes that Canadian federalism can accommodate cultural differences, and therefore fulfil Quebec's demands, if only English Canadians were ready to grant collective rights to French Canadians and Natives. In the 1980s and 1990s, however, several failures to amend the Canadian constitution by introducing a reference to the 'nation québécoise' or at least to Quebec as a 'distinct society' fuelled Quebeckers' frustration with the federal system.

During the 1990s, Charles Taylor participated in several Quebec provincial commissions trying to find a way out of this political deadlock. His official report was published in *Reconciling the Solitudes* (1993), a collection of essays on Canadian federalism. This work allowed Taylor to articulate his advocacy of federalism. In 1995, a new referendum on Quebec's independence was held and once again Taylor did not hesitate to appear on television and participate in public debates to defend the federalist option. The dramatic results of the referendum revealed the depth of the identity crisis that was affecting Quebec: 49.6 per cent in favour of Quebec's sovereignty and 50.4 per cent against it.

Although he assumed the responsibilities of a public intellectual, Taylor continued to teach political science and philosophy at McGill University. In 1989, he published *Sources of the Self: The Making of the Modern Identity*, in which he analysed the development of the modern self through the works of great philosophers and writers. With this book and other shorter essays – in particular 'The Politics of Recognition' (1995a) – Taylor emerged as one of the leading 'communitarian' thinkers (along with Alasdair McIntyre, Michael Sandel, and Michael Walzer) in opposition to 'liberals' (such as John Rawls and Jürgen Habermas). Nonetheless, Taylor rejects the communitarian label and tries to find a middle ground. He does not praise nor criticize modernity as a whole. He identifies three major problems with modernity: individualism (atomization of society and a life boiled down to little and silly pleasures); hegemony of instrumental reason (technology and quest for efficiency); and a low political participation.

Moreover, Taylor argues that we ought not to reduce modernity to rationality, utilitarianism, and individual rights. It is important to also consider other sources or phenomena such as the Romantic Movement. 'Modern society', claims Taylor (1979: 71), 'is Romantic in its private and imaginative life and utilitarian or instrumentalist in its public, effective life.' Thus, even if autonomy and procedural justice matter a great deal for the modern self, identity, culture, morality, and transcendence are not archaic issues but constitutive elements of the modern tradition. Another facet of modernity on which Taylor has been working recently is the rise of secular civilization. A Catholic thinker, who has participated in seminars on contemporary thought with Pope John Paul II, Taylor is convinced that many of the standard accounts of the rise of secularism are distorted or too simple, and is thus trying to develop an alternative view of this historical development.

SOCIAL THEORY AND CONTRIBUTIONS

Charles Taylor's consistent emphasis on the analysis of the self as situated – what he calls 'philosophical anthropology' – brings him to put forward theories that are more sociologically grounded than those of most philosophers. Taylor believes that human beings, including philosophers, have to be understood as embedded in a historical, social, and cultural context. Such a perspective requires us to look at the background distinctions that enable us to grasp directions and follow rules. The latter must be approached through practices, for a rule 'exists only in the practices it animates, and does not require and may not have any express formulation' (Taylor, 1995c: 178). Drawing upon phenomenology, Taylor (1995c: 170) goes further and contends that 'Our body is not just the executant of the goals we frame, nor just the locus of causal factors shaping our representations. Our understanding itself is embodied. That is, our bodily know-how, and the way we act and move, can encode components of our understanding of self and world'. As Taylor (1995c: 171) acknowledges, one of the concepts that best captures this phenomenon is Pierre Bourdieu's concept of habitus.

On the grounds of his philosophical anthropology, Taylor made significant contributions to social theory and philosophy. We can regroup them around three themes: hermeneutics and language, the inescapability of moral frameworks, and the dialogic construction of modern identity and the politics of recognition.

Hermeneutics and Language

From its very beginning Taylor's endeavour was developed in reaction to positivism. His first target was behaviourism (Taylor, 1964, 1985a) and advocates of a mechanistic psychology founded on neurophysiology, chemistry, and physics, according to whom it is better to talk of 'movement' rather than 'action'. Such an approach rules out 'intentions' as mere illusions and depicts every movement of the body as being some sort of 'reflex' having nothing to do with individual will. In contrast, Taylor argues that human behaviour is so complex that even a self-proclaimed scientific theory of behaviour would have to use subjective concepts such as 'intention,' 'desire', 'good', 'wrong'. While Taylor acknowledges that 'intentions' do not explain pure reflexes, he claims that neurophysiology is helpless to explain culturally situated actions. He argues that 'man is a cultural animal' (1985a: 178) and that the study of social action requires considering the common words actors use to make sense of their actions. Taylor's approach is in this respect similar to that of anthropologist Clifford Geertz. As Geertz (1973: 6–7) explains when drawing upon Gilbert Ryle's discussion of 'thick description', rapidly contracting one's eyelids can mean very different things. It can be a twitch, a wink, a fake-wink, and so on. The only way to understand what someone is actually doing when they rapidly contract their eyelids is to ask what their intention is. And that, in turn, implies interpreting the intersubjective meanings sustaining that intention.

Interpretation and self-interpretation are indeed at the core of Taylor's approach. 'The interpretation aims to bring to light an underlying coherence or sense' of a text or a text-analogue of behaviour (Taylor, 1985g: 15). It follows that Taylor rejects a science based on verification and advocates a hermeneutical science. The latter proposes to study intersubjective meanings embedded in social reality. These meanings exist in a field, that is, in relation to the meanings of other things. As Taylor (1985g: 36) stresses, intersubjective meanings are different from subjective meanings; they are 'constitutive of the social matrix in which individuals find themselves and act'. In contrast to studies like Gabriel Almond and Sidney Verba's *The Civic Culture*, Taylor (1985g: 36) argues that:

> It is not just that the people in our society all or mostly have a given set of ideas in their heads and subscribe to a given set of goals. The meanings and norms implicit in these practices are not just in the minds of the actors but are out there in the practices themselves, practices which cannot be

> conceived as a set of individual actions, but which are essentially modes of social relation, of mutual action.

Moreover, intersubjective meanings are partially constituted by self-definitions, for according to Taylor human beings are self-interpreting animals. Therefore, what hermeneutical science aims to interpret is itself an interpretation (1985g: 26). Put differently, it aims to interpret a preinterpreted world. Although Giddens (1993) coined this expression with a different purpose in mind, one could say that there is a 'double hermeneutics' at work.

Language is important for understanding individuals' intentions and actions since it is through words that individuals develop and express their intentions. Moreover, action also happens through words. As Austin (1962) has argued, speaking is necessarily performative. Thus, one should not see words as a purely neutral tool of communication. Taylor distinguishes two ways of understanding the nature of language: designative and expressive. The designative approach (Skinner, Quine, Davidson) claims that words are neutral instruments used to describe an object or an idea. On the other hand, the expressive approach claims that it is through language that individuals are able to express not only their authenticity, but also the authenticity of the world. Words do not simply designate, they express things and feelings, they make things and ideas manifest by making them appear to us.

Language is also by its very nature a common good shared by its users. It is the property of a collectivity or a community. It cannot belong to a single individual. Here, Taylor draws upon the Romantic philosophy of language developed by Hamann, Herder, and Humboldt, the social psychology of Mead, and Bakhtin's notion of dialogism to explain the formation of the self-interpretations which constitute the individual. For Taylor, we become capable of understanding ourselves and of defining our identity through the acquisition of languages (words, but also gestures, arts, love, etc.). These languages are learned through our relations with others, specifically these 'others' who matter to us (i.e., George Herbert Mead's 'significant others'). And even when our significant others disappear from our lives, the dialogue with them – and thereby their contribution to our self – continues. Since learning a language always implies entering an already started conversation, a self exists only within 'webs of interlocutions' (Taylor, 1989: 36).

Following Herder, Taylor argues that language is the embodiment of the collective experience of a community. It registers the sentiments and emotions of the community's history. It is 'a pattern of activity by which we express/realize a certain way of being in the world' (Taylor, 1995b: 97). It is a singular resource without which we could not experience certain ways of being, feeling, and relating to each other. Moreover, it provides us with distinctions and categories that constitute the backbone of our moral universe.

Moral Frameworks

Our moral universe is organized around moral frameworks. We relate to other human beings, conceive a 'good life', develop an understanding of our own worth, build life plans, and give meaning to our lives, on the basis of moral frameworks. According to Taylor (1989: 19), a moral framework 'incorporates a crucial set of qualitative distinctions. To think, feel, judge within such a framework is to function with the sense that some action, or mode of life, or mode of feeling is incomparably higher that the others which are more readily available to us'. Moral frameworks enable us to draw distinctions and give priority to certain goods and thereby to certain goals. They are frameworks of 'strong evaluations', that is, 'discriminations of right or wrong, better or worse, higher or lower, which are not rendered valid by our own desires, inclinations, or choices, but rather stand independent of these and offer standards by which they can be judged' (Taylor, 1989: 4). These strong evaluations themselves presuppose the existence of 'hypergoods', that is, 'goods which are not only incomparably more important than others but provide the standpoint from which these must be weighed, judged, decided about' (Taylor, 1989: 63).

We cannot pretend to live by seizing whatever option presents itself to us. The very act of choosing is meaningful only insofar as it leans against a hierarchy of goods. Therefore, moral frameworks are inescapable, even if they are not always articulated. A person lacking moral frameworks would be deeply disturbed, not able to distinguish trivial matters from fundamental ones. Such a case would be seen as pathological (Taylor, 1989: 31; Ancelovici and Dupuis-Déri, 1998: 255). Taylor goes even further: moral frameworks are actually constitutive of our identity, our sense of the good being inseparable from our sense of self.

Taylor criticizes utilitarianism, postmodernism, and liberal rationalism for being unable to provide the moral orientation that individuals need to make sense of their life-narratives. To distinguish between two goods, utilitarians would say that the best good is the one that offers the greatest happiness to more people; postmodernists would simply dismiss the question, claiming that all goods are equal or that it is a purely subjective issue; and liberal rationalists or advocates of procedural justice (Kant, Rawls, Habermas) would argue that through communication and reasonable deliberation, autonomous individuals would be able to rationally identify the best good. In contrast, Taylor stresses the importance of the context in order to identify the best good. Moreover, individuals evaluate different goods on the basis of what they want their life to be and to mean. Similarly, people's individuality is constructed and makes sense only within a relation to a past, a present, and a future. Following Hegel, Taylor (1979) gives priority to *Sittlichkeit* (that is, an ethical community) at the expense of *Moralität* (that is, a universalistic moral point of view). Thus, he emphasizes the embeddedness of the self and relates it to Aristotle's concept of *phronesis* or practical reason, which refers to the idea of being reasonable in respect to a specific situation rather than being rational according to universal standards.

Identity and Recognition

Taylor rules out the naturalist conception of the self as free from moral frameworks and endowed with the ability to recreate itself indefinitely through rational mastery and self-discipline. This is what he calls Locke's 'punctual self' (1989: 159–76). In contrast to Locke, Taylor claims that the self cannot be studied objectively, that is, independently of its self-interpretations and of the other's gaze. We are *living beings* independently of our self-understanding, but we are *selves* only insofar as we evolve in a moral space and interpret our situation in that space through a language of articulation that we accept as valid. Put differently, defining one's identity requires 'a definition of where I am speaking from and to whom' (Taylor, 1989: 36).

Consequently, the less we know where we stand, the less we know who we are. The result is an identity crisis, that is, 'an acute form of disorientation' that people experience when they lack a moral framework 'within which things can take on a stable significance, within which some life possibilities can be seen as good or meaningful, others as bad or trivial' (Taylor, 1989: 27–8). According to Taylor, this is a modern problem. Although people always have had an identity, the answer to the question 'Who am I?' became problematic with the collapse of rigid social hierarchies and the questioning of the honour system's inequality. As Peter Berger (1973: 92) points out, there is a 'built-in identity crisis' in modern societies because of the unstable social contexts and deep uncertainty that characterize them. Moreover, modern identities are progressively defined in terms of categories (citizenship, ethnicity, profession, age, etc.) rather than networks (family, locality, etc.). Thus, one's sense of one's worth has become dependent upon categorical identities.

The instability of modern identities makes our interactions with others even more important. Not only because the social dynamics underlying the construction of identity has changed, but also because human beings have become more sensitive to the other's gaze. The other is no longer a simple reference that allows us to develop a definition of what we are not and thereby to distinguish ourselves. He or she now plays an explicit, active role in the construction of our identity. For according to Taylor, in the modern world we need the other's *recognition* to be confident of our identity: 'Our identity is partly shaped by recognition or its absence, often by the *mis*recognition of others (...) Nonrecognition or misrecognition can inflict harm, can be a form of oppression, imprisoning someone in a false, distorted, and reduced mode of being' (Taylor, 1995a: 225). In this sense, recognition is not an issue of manners. It is a vital human need and thereby arguably a right. Drawing upon Herder's romanticism, Taylor goes even further and claims that both individual and collective authenticity must be cherished, for both specific individuals and communities have something unique to say about themselves and about the world.

Recognition should not be treated as a formal right. Although Taylor advocates cultural rights for minorities, what he has in mind is rather a moral claim demanding society to truly recognize difference. The longing for such a recognition can be a powerful force in history, because it is experienced existentially as a challenge and because its satisfaction is a condition of dignity. For example, according to Taylor (1997b: 45), 'This is what gives nationalism its emotive power. This is what places it so frequently in the register of pride and humiliation'. The need for recognition is thus one of the factors explaining the rise of nationalism. Following Ernest Gellner and Benedict Anderson, Taylor presents nationalism as a quintessentially modern phenomenon. But in addition to Gellner's functional account and to Anderson's emphasis on the particular kind of social imaginary that characterizes the nation, Taylor stresses the psychological foundations of nationalism. He aims to grasp the sources of its moral thrust. Hence the importance of his notion of recognition. The latter bridges the gap between identity and dignity, and eventually between psychological and political emancipation.

APPRAISAL OF KEY ADVANCES AND CONTROVERSIES

Charles Taylor's thinking has received significant attention from American sociologists in the last decade. In 1985, Robert Bellah and his colleagues noted that Taylor had helped them 'to see the illusions of a private expressiveness and the emptiness of formal freedom' (1985: 331 n.12). More recently, Alan Wolfe (1990: 627) argued that for sociologists, 'there is no more important philosopher writing in the world today than Charles Taylor'. In the same vein, Craig Calhoun wrote that 'Taylor's work would enrich enormously the scholarship of any sociologist' (1991: 262). The importance of Taylor's work has also been acknowledged by several of today's most respected scholars, such as Isaiah Berlin, Raymond Boudon, Jacques Bouveresse, Clifford Geertz, Jürgen Habermas, Paul Ricoeur, and Richard Rorty (see Tully, 1994; Laforest and de Lara, 1998).

One of Taylor's most influential concepts, particularly for contemporary debates on multiculturalism and cultural rights, is perhaps the 'politics of recognition'. At first glance, it seems that this concept is almost a natural outgrowth of Taylor's reflection on the modern self. However, Taylor (1996: 214–15) stresses that his conceptualization of the politics of recognition was inspired by the French Canadian nationalism that he witnessed in Quebec during his youth. According to him, nationalist politics and identity politics belong to the same species: 'national struggles are the site from which the model comes to be applied to feminism, to the struggles of cultural minorities, to the gay movement, et cetera' (Taylor, 1997: 46). Although movements making recognition-claims have been active for a long time now, Taylor remarks that we lacked the appropriate philosophical language to make sense of them. Hence the 'epistemic gain' (Taylor, 1989: 57–8, 72) realized by the concept of recognition. Among other neo-Hegelian scholars stressing the usefulness of that concept, we should note the work of Axel Honneth. But while Taylor insists on cultural rights and focuses on multiculturalism, Honneth (1996) puts forward a more encompassing framework that aims at making sense of the 'moral grammar of social conflicts'.

The concept of recognition is both an analytical and a political tool. It can be used to explain certain claims as well as to define their content and justify them. In fact, the politics of recognition seems to be emerging as the meta-discourse of the 'postsocialist' condition (see Fraser, 1997). According to Taylor, social and political movements began to openly acknowledge their need for recognition only recently. Previously, they expressed their claims in economic terms or asked for formal equality. Thus, 'What is new ... is that the demand for recognition is now explicit. And it has been made explicit ... by the spread of the idea that we are formed by recognition' (Taylor, 1995a: 251).

Taylor's concept is also significant in the light of contemporary debates regarding the curriculum in the education system. There is a clear relationship between demands for multiculturalism in secondary schools and university humanities departments, on the one hand, and the emergence of struggles for a changed self-image, on the other. While, say, Allan Bloom (1987) is appalled by such a situation, scholars like Charles Taylor, Amy Gutmann (1992), and Susan Wolf (1992), among others, believe that it is necessary for the sake of members of 'minority' cultures as well as of the 'majority' culture. For encountering new cultures results in the development of new vocabularies that allow us to articulate new contrasts. Drawing upon Gadamer's idea of 'fusion of horizons', Taylor contends that through this process, 'We learn to move in a broader horizon, where what we once took for granted as the background to valuation can be situated as one possibility alongside the different background of the unfamiliar culture' (1995a: 252). Consequently, judgments, positions, or tastes are relativized and become, thereby, more reflexive.

Taylor does not only offer a new meta-discourse based on the politics of recognition. Writing in the context of the liberal–communitarian debate, he also argues that in spite of the Bill of Rights, liberalism has failed to properly accommodate difference: 'the supposedly fair and difference-blind society is not only inhuman (because suppressing identities) but also, in a subtle and unconscious way, itself highly discriminatory' (1995a: 237). Taylor claims that liberalism is unable to legitimize measures that should 'ensure survival in indefinite future generations. For the populations concerned, however, that's what is at stake. We need only think of the historical resonance of "la survivance" among French Canadians' (1995a: 306 n.16) Indeed, Native peoples and French Canadians care about individual rights but also want their respective cultures to survive. That is the reason why Taylor supports laws protecting the French language in Quebec. Such laws, although articulated in terms of collective rights, are necessary for the self-realization of individuals. Moreover, without them individuals belonging to minority cultures are condemned to face discrimination and thereby to being marginalized.

Critique of Taylor

Although Taylor's account of modern identity has the merit of pinpointing the moral space as one of the fundamental fields within which the self defines itself, his concept of politics of recognition suffers from some limitations and flaws. Susan Wolf (1992) argues for instance that several elements of Taylor's theory do not apply to women and feminism. As she points out, even though the notion of 'survival' expresses genuine concerns among Natives, Quebeckers, and Jews, it is not as relevant for women (see also Halley, 1999 and Tamir, 1999). For the problem of women is not that patriarchal societies do not recognize their culture, but rather that they hold in contempt roles traditionally associated with women.

Another problem of Taylor's theory stems from its implicit static conception of identity (Ancelovici, 1998). Admittedly, Taylor recognizes that the 'issue of our condition can never be exhausted for us by what we *are*, because we are always also changing and *becoming*. ... So the issue for us has to be not only where we *are*, but where we're *going*' (1989: 47). Nevertheless, accepting the possibility of evolution and change is quite different from conceptualizing and theorizing this actual change. Considering the instability of modern identities and their propensity to go through crises, a dynamic approach focusing on change and flux rather than permanence and consistency would seem more appropriate. A dynamic conception of identity would thus aim at understanding these impure and hybrid spheres of our selves which result from our increasing encounters with otherness.

Alas, Taylor overlooks processes of hybridization. As Homi K. Bhabha (1996: 57) point out, Taylor's emphasis on 'whole societies over some considerable stretch of time' in order to 'exclude partial cultural milieux within a society as well as short phases of a major culture' introduces 'a temporal criterion of cultural worth' which presents immigrant minorities as foreign bodies. Thus, Taylor draws upon Bakhtin's dialogism but rules out the possible hybridizing result of such process. He does not develop his own argument in order to see to what extent the fusion of horizons can translate into new self-interpretations and moral frameworks, and eventually beget a transformation of individual identity. The dialogical process seems to be confined within cultures, that is, for Taylor, within relatively distinct and closed communities. Here Taylor faces the limitation of his holistic ontology since grasping hybridity implies precisely apprehending cultural identity not within one culture and in isolation from others, but rather at the crossroads of interpenetrating symbolic structures or cultural continuums. This is the dynamic usually underlying the identity construction of migrants. In fact, Taylor sacrifices the potential implications of dialogism so as to justify the cultural and political claims put forward by minority groups (Ancelovici, 1998). He is then faced with a paradox commonly afflicting identity politics. As Seyla Benhabib (1998: 89) puts it, 'Identity/difference claims are inherently unstable, contestable, revisable and negotiable. Yet to found a politics, they must be presented as if they were not so'.

Moreover, in some cases, the politics of recognition can lead to a zero-sum game. Since identity is relational and cultures are interwoven, recognizing the specificity of the 'other' often entails redefining one's identity. Such a redefinition can have dramatic implications. For example, according to Philip Resnick: 'a majority of English-speaking Canadians have come to accept the French fact as a crucial feature of the Canadian mosaic, as something which makes us indisputably different from the United States. ... It has become part of the identity of Canada, domestically and internationally (one thinks of la francophonie)' (1990: vii; see also Meisel et al., 1999: chap. 3) It follows that for English Canadians, recognizing the 'French fact' as something alien to them would jeopardize their identity.

Taylor's concept of politics of recognition also suffers from its underlying myth of total liberation. Although recognition undeniably plays a role in the construction of identity and answers 'a profound and universal craving for status and understanding' (Berlin, 1969: 158), its relationship to freedom may be more problematic than Taylor generally suggests. As Isaiah Berlin (1969: 157) points out, the outcome of recognition is not necessarily freedom:

> I may, in my bitter longing for status, prefer to be bullied and misgoverned by some member of my own race or social class, by whom I am, nevertheless, recognized as a man and rival – that is as an equal – to being well and tolerantly treated by someone from some higher and remote group, who does not recognize me for what I wish to feel myself to be.

In this respect, Nancy Fraser's reconceptualization of recognition as an issue of justice rather than self-realization opens a promising theoretical path. Indeed, in her effort to reconcile distribution with recognition, Fraser (1999) stresses the necessity of granting to individuals and groups the status of full partners in social interaction. The locus of recognition is not so much individual psychology (i.e., a changed self-image) but social relations (i.e., the transformation of social arrangements impeding some people to fully participate in society). Such a change of emphasis allows us to avoid the pitfall of trying to restore an allegedly 'pure', that is, not distorted, self-image that would enable people to be 'really' free.

TAYLOR'S MAJOR WORKS

Taylor, C. (1964) *The Explanation of Behaviour*. London: Routledge & Kegan Paul.

Taylor, C. (1975) *Hegel*. Cambridge: Cambridge University Press.

Taylor, C. (1979) *Hegel and Modern Society*. Cambridge: Cambridge University Press.

Taylor, C. (1985a) 'How is mechanism conceivable?', in *Human Agency and Language: Philosophical Papers 1*. Cambridge: Cambridge University Press; first published in M. Grene (ed.), *Interpretations of Life and Mind: Essays around the Problem of Reduction*. London: Routledge and Kegan Paul. 1971.

Taylor, C. (1985b) 'Introduction', in *Philosophy and the Human Sciences: Philosophical Papers 2*. Cambridge: Cambridge University Press.

Taylor, C. (1985c) 'Atomism', in *Philosophy and the Human Sciences: Philosophical Papers 2*. Cambridge: Cambridge University Press, first published in A. Kontos (ed.), *Powers, Possessions and Freedom*. Toronto: Toronto University Press. 1979.

Taylor, C. (1985d) 'What's wrong with negative liberty', in *Philosophy and the Human Sciences: Philosophical Papers 2*. Cambridge: Cambridge University Press; first published in A. Ryan (ed.), *The Idea of Freedom*. Oxford: Oxford University Press. 1979.

Taylor, C. (1985e) 'Language and human nature', in *Human Agency and Language: Philosophical Papers 1*. Cambridge: Cambridge University Press; shorter version first published as 'Theories of Meaning', *Man and World* 13 (3–4): 281–302, 1980.

Taylor, C. (1985f) 'Understanding and ethnocentricity', in *Philosophy and the Human Sciences: Philosophical Papers 2*. Cambridge: Cambridge University Press; first published in C. Taylor, *Social Theory as Practice*. Oxford: Oxford University Press. 1983.

Taylor, C. (1985g) 'Interpretation and the sciences of man', in *Philosophy and the Human Sciences: Philosophical Papers 2*. Cambridge: Cambridge University Press; first published in *The Review of Metaphysics* Vol. 25 (1) 3–51, September 1971.

Taylor, C. (1989) *Sources of the Self: The Making of the Modern Identity*. Cambridge, MA: Harvard University Press.

Taylor, C. (1991) *The Malaise of Modernity*. Concord, ON: Anansi; also published under the title *The Ethics of Authenticity*. Cambridge, MA: Harvard University Press. 1992.

Taylor, C. (1993) *Reconciling the Solitudes: Essays on Canadian Federalism and Nationalism*. Montreal: McGill-Queens University Press.

Taylor, C. (1995a) 'The politics of recognition', in *Philosophical Arguments*. Cambridge, MA: Harvard University Press; first published in A. Gutmann (ed.), *Multiculturalism and 'The Politics of Recognition'*. Princeton, NJ: Princeton University Press. 1992.

Taylor, C. (1995b) 'The importance of Herder', in *Philosophical Arguments*. Cambridge, MA: Harvard University Press.

Taylor, C. (1995c) 'To follow a rule', in *Philosophical Arguments*. Cambridge, MA: Harvard University Press.

Taylor, C. (1996) 'De l'anthropologie philosophie à la politique de la reconnaissance', Interview by P. de Lara in *Le Débat*, 89: 208–23.

Taylor, C. (1997a) 'Avant-propos', in *La Liberté des Modernes*. Paris: Presses Universitaires de France.

Taylor, C. (1997b) 'Nationalism and modernity', in R. McKim and J. McMahan (eds), *The Morality of Nationalism*. Oxford: Oxford University Press.

Taylor, C. (1999) 'Une place pour la transcendance?' Unpublished lecture delivered in Quebec City.

SECONDARY REFERENCES

Ancelovici, M. (1998) *I Belong Therefore I Am: Charles Taylor's Conception of Identity and Community in Question*. Presented at the 93rd Annual Meeting of the American Sociological Association in San Francisco, CA.

Ancelovici, M. and Dupuis-Déri, F. (1998) 'Interview with Professor Charles Taylor', *Citizenship Studies*, 2 (2): 247–56.

Avineri, S. and de-Shalit, A. (eds) (1992) *Communitarianism and Individualism*. Oxford: Oxford University Press.

Austin, J.L. (1962) *How to Do Things with Words*. Cambridge, MA: Harvard University Press.

Bellah, R.N., Madsen, R., Sullivan, W.N., Swilder, A. and Tipton, S.N. (1985) *Habits of the Heart: Individualism and Commitment in American Life*. Berkeley, CA: University of California Press/ Perennial Library.

Benhabib, S. (1992) *Situating the Self: Gender, Community and Postmodernism in Contemporary Ethics*. New York: Routledge.

Benhabib, S. (1998) 'Democracy and identity: in search of the civic polity', *Philosophy & Social Criticism*. 24 (2/3): 85–100.

Berlin, I. (1969) *Four Essays on Liberty*. Oxford: Oxford UP.

Berger, P. (1973) 'On the obsolescence of the concept of honor', in P.L. Berger, B. Berger, and H. Kellner. *The Homeless Mind. Modernization and Consciousness*. New York, NY: Vintage.

Bhabha, H.K. (1996) 'Culture's in-between', in S. Hall and P. du Gay (eds), *Questions of Cultural Identity*. London: Sage.

Birnbaum, P. (1996) 'From multiculturalism to nationalism', *Political Theory*, 24 (1): 33–45.

Bloom, A. (1987) *The Closing of the American Mind*. New York: Simon & Schuster.

Calhoun, C. (1991) 'Morality, identity, and historical explanation: Charles Taylor on the source of the self'. *Sociological Theory*, 9 (2): 232–63.

Fraser, N. (1997) *Justice Interrupts: Critical Reflections on the 'Postsocialist' Condition*. New York and London: Routledge.

Fraser, N. (1999) *Social Justice in the Age of Identity Politics: Redistribution, Recognition, and Participation*. London: Centre for Theoretical Studies.

Geertz, C. (1973) 'Thick description: toward an interpretative theory of culture', in *The Interpretation of Cultures*. New York, NY: BasicBooks.

Giddens, A. (1993) *New Rules of Sociological Method*. Stanford, CA: Stanford University Press.

Gutmann, A. (1992) *Multiculturalism and 'The Politics of Recognition'*. Princeton, MJ: Princeton University Press.

Habermas, J. (1998) *The Inclusion of the Other: Studies in Political Theory*. Cambridge, MA: MIT Press.

Halley, J.E. (1999) 'Culture constrains', in S. Moller Okin (ed.), *Is Multiculturalism Bad for Women?* Princeton, NJ: Princeton University Press.

Holmes, S. (1993) *The Anatomy of Antiliberalism*. Cambridge, MA: Harvard University Press.

Honneth, A. (1996) *The Struggle for Recognition: The Moral Grammar of Social Conflicts*. Cambridge, MA: MIT Press.

Kymlicka, W. (1989) *Liberalism, Community, and Culture*. Oxford: Clarendon Press.

Laforest, G. (1994) 'Philosophy and political judgment in a multinational federation', in J. Tully (ed.), *Philosophy in an Age of Pluralism: The Philosophy of Charles Taylor in Question*. Cambridge: Cambridge University Press.

Laforest, G. and de Lara, P. (eds) (1998) *Charles Taylor et l'interprétation de l'identité moderne*. Québec: Centre culturel international de Cerisy-la-Salle/ Cerf/Presses de l'Université Laval.

Mead, G. H. (1934) *Mind, Self, and Society*. Chicago, IL: University of Chicago Press.

Meisel, J., Rocher, G. and Silver, A. (eds) (1999) *As I Recall - Si Je Me Souviens Bien: Historical Prespectives*. Montreal: Institute for Research on Public Policy.

Miller, D. (1995) *On Nationality*. Oxford: Clarendon Press.

Mulhall, S. and Swift, A. (1992) *Liberals and Communitarians*. Oxford: Blackwell.

Resnick, P. (1990) *Letters to a Quebecois Friend*. Montreal: McGill-Queens University Press.

Sandel, M. (1982) *Liberalism and the Limits of Justice*. Cambridge: Cambridge University Press.

Somers, M.R. (1994) 'The narrative constitution of identity: a relational and network approach', *Theory and Society*, 23 (5): 605–49.

Tamir, Y. (1993) *Liberal Nationalism*. Princeton, NJ: Princeton University Press.

Tamir, Y. (1999) 'Siding with the underdogs', in S. Moller Okin (ed.), *Is Multiculturalism Bad for Women?* Princeton, NJ: Princeton University Press.

Tully, J. (ed.) (1994) *Philosophy in an Age of Pluralism: The Philosophy of Charles Taylor in Question*. Cambridge: Cambridge University Press.

Tully, J. (1996) *Strange Multiplicity: Constitutionalism in the Age of Pluralism*. Cambridge: Cambridge University Press.

Tully, J. (Forthcoming) 'Freedom and disclosure in multinational states', in A. G. Gagnon and J. Tully (eds) *Struggles for Recognition*. Cambridge: Cambridge University Press.

Walzer, M. (1990) 'The communitarian critique of liberalism', *Political Theory*, 18 (1): 627–28.

Wolf, S. (1992) 'Comment', in A. Gutmann (ed.), *Multiculturalism and 'The Politics of Recognition'*. Princeton, NJ : Princeton University Press.

Wolfe, A. (1990) 'Review of Charles Taylor's *Sources of the Self*', *Contemporary Sociology*, 19 (4).

24

Richard Rorty

BRYAN S. TURNER

BIOGRAPHICAL DETAILS AND THEORETICAL CONTEXT

Richard Rorty was born in New York in 1931 and was the University Professor of Humanities at the University of Virginia. Rorty is a controversial figure in (professional) philosophy, mainly because in works like *The Linguistic Turn* (1967) he has suggested that the entire Western philosophical tradition is on the defensive. Philosophy can no longer give an adequate account of the grounds upon which its view of unitary Truth could be confirmed, and hence it is likely that we have moved into a 'post-philosophical' world. The role of philosophy, he argues in *The Consequences of Pragmatism* (1982), is not to provide eternal foundations of Truth, but rather to be a voice alongside literature and art in the edification of humankind. The measure of philosophical progress is not demonstrated by philosophy 'becoming more rigorous but by becoming more imaginative' (Rorty, 1998a: 9). Rorty as a result is just as likely to write 'philosophical' commentaries on Nabokov, Orwell, or Proust in *Contingency, Irony and Solidarity* (1989) as he is to write 'professional' pieces on John Dewey, Donald Davidson, or Michael Dummett in *Objectivity, Relativism and Truth* (1991). Because Rorty has been concerned to establish the proper limitations of philosophical knowledge in a world which is unstable, changeable, and insecure, his philosophical critique has much in common with postmodernism. Whereas J.-F. Lyotard defined postmodernism as 'incredulity toward metanarratives' (1984: xxiv), Rorty in one of his most influential essays ('Private irony and liberal hope') defines an ironist as somebody who has 'radical and continuing doubts about the final vocabulary she currently uses' (Rorty, 1989: 73). Elsewhere (Rorty, 1991b: 199) he has defended the relevance of the oxymoronic title 'postmodern bourgeois liberalism' as a broad description of his own agenda in contemporary philosophy. Rorty's philosophy and social theory can be seen as an application of, and debate with, the legacy of John Dewey (1859–1952). Rorty's postphilosophical philosophy attempts to reconcile the pragmatism of Dewey with the deconstructive intentions of continental philosophy (Diggins, 1994; Hickman, 1998). Rorty identifies his pragmatic position with 'polytheism' in the sense that a polytheist does not believe that there is an object of knowledge that would permit one to commensurate and to rank human needs (Rorty, 1998b). As Rorty attempts to show in *Achieving our Country* (1998c), the Deweyan legacy is still highly relevant to progressive attempts to realize the emancipatory spirit of 'the American Creed'.

Rorty's reputation in modern philosophy was originally built on the foundations of his philosophy of science, namely *Philosophy and the Mirror of Nature* (1979). One aspect of his argument is to claim that philosophers should give up the fantasy that philosophical truths could be a mirror of (or to) nature. If there are any philosophical truths, they are not representations (mirrors) of an objective reality. Because Rorty holds that all observations of nature are theory-dependent and that a correspondence theory of truth is untenable, he rejects realism as a plausible position. In many respects, his criticisms of representational theories of truth remain his principal contribution to what we might regard as mainstream or professional philosophy. His philosophy of science has been widely debated and reviewed (Malachowski, 1990; Margolis, 1986) and much of that debate lies outside the scope of this chapter. In this profile, my aim is to focus on his contributions to social and political theory rather than to philosophy as such. This attempt to separate his philosophy of science from his social theory is admittedly somewhat arbitrary. The pragmatism that drives his view of the limited nature of philosophy is the same pragmatism that drives his view of political theory and politics. Thus, his criticisms of representational theories of truth in *Philosophy and The Mirror of Nature* form the basis of his social philosophy in which the attack on representational or correspondence theory is necessarily combined with his (somewhat idiosyncratic) version of liberalism. The notion that social values and beliefs must remain tentative (because they cannot find a final or ultimate justification) is derived from the prior critique of the correspondence theory of truth in the arena of natural science.

In general, Rorty's criticisms of conventional philosophy of science are highly compatible with the sociology of knowledge. First, Rorty has argued that traditional philosophy has ignored the relevance of history to an understanding of philosophical concepts, mainly because philosophers have rejected the idea that concepts are context-dependent. From Descartes onwards, philosophers have wanted to treat their ideas as eternal and universal, and to assume that these universal ideas disclose the Truth. For Rorty, the task of philosophers is more properly to help their readers abandon outdated ideas and to find more appropriate ways of thinking about society and their lives. As such, philosophy is a product of specific times and places rather than a grand narrative. Rorty's approach to truth claims owes a great deal to Dewey and Wittgenstein for whom the assertibility of truth claims is a function of language, and language is a set of social practices. The result of Dewey's pragmatism for Rorty is that it demolishes the Cartesian tradition that Truth can be grasped by a 'Mind Apart' and it introduces the social into the heart of any debate about truth and reality. In fact, it brings Rorty very close to ethnomethodology, because the social practices that interest Rorty are not the practices of humanity but what you and I do when we try to make sense of our everyday world. One reason for including Rorty in this profile of contemporary social thought is because we believe that his philosophical work should be more widely discussed and appreciated by sociologists and anthropologists.

One additional point should be made in this introduction as a guide for reading Rorty. Through much of the 1980s and 1990s, Rorty explicated his philosophy and social theory through the medium of the academic essay or review article. Generally speaking, Rorty is not a thinker who feels particularly comfortable with the book-length explication of his ideas.

The virtue of the essay form is its accessibility and its modesty, but the negative aspect of this mode of communication is that Rorty's work is repetitious. Rorty's basic argument is relatively simple and therefore powerful. There can be no final and watertight verification of Truth, and therefore we must be suspicious of philosophers or politicians who claim to have found the Truth or attempt to run society as if social policy could be based upon a big Truth. Because life is contingent and essentially messy, we should pay attention to those poets or philosophers who can provide modest but practical guides to action. Reading Dickens may prove to be a better guide to action through the sentiments than a large dose of Kant or Hegel. What we need is edification and moral suasion, not a demonstration of the unfolding of the Spirit in History. The essay form rather than the Big Book perhaps better suits Rorty's philosophical views on the contingent nature of truth and the basically problematic and uncertain nature of society and politics. His work is also repetitious for the additional reason that his philosophical contributions to social theory have been brought together in three volumes of essays: *Contingency, Irony and Solidarity* (1989), *Essays on Heidegger and Others* (1991a), and *Truth and Progress* (1998a). Given the necessary limitations of this profile of Rorty, I shall concentrate primarily on his contributions to social and political theory, namely his essays on human rights, liberalism, and his critique of political dogmatism.

SOCIAL THEORY AND CONTRIBUTIONS

Historicism and Relativism

In this discussion, I shall be particularly concerned to discuss the importance of Rorty's pragmatism for the analysis of rights, tolerance, and justice. Rorty's pragmatism is not unlike the sociology of knowledge in that for both positions the justification of a scientific claim requires an audience and an audience is *par excellence* a sociological concept. Like sociology, Rorty's pragmatism is seen to be relativistic , but he wants to reject the naive view that relativism means that one belief is as good as any other. He feels somewhat disconcerted by accusations that his type of relativism will result in a corruption of youth, and in his recent work he has constantly returned to the problem of relativism (Rorty, 1999). His understanding of relativism is, to my mind, well within mainstream sociology of knowledge. For example, he argues that foundationalists insist that truths are found, where relativists argue that they are made or invented (Rorty, 1999: xvii). In short, knowledge is socially constructed.

He has, however, attacked the notion of incommensurability as irrational (Rorty, 1980). Translation between languages is a practical problem, but its very existence suggests that incommensurability is not tenable as an overarching view of human cultures. Rorty's interest in human rights can be construed as a criticism of a strong relativist programme. While Rorty frequently appeals to anthropological and occasionally sociological case studies to illustrate a philosophical point, generally speaking, the study of human rights has been neglected by sociology and anthropology. In more recent years, this lack of interest has been reinforced by the intervention of postmodern theories of difference, otherness, and justice. Critics of postmodern theory have typically claimed that, because of its radical inclination towards relativism and its lack of serious ethical vision, postmodern theory cannot provide any genuine guidance for political belief or, more significantly, for political action. Postmodern theorists provide an ironic and paradoxical reflection upon the political reality of our times which leads to radical philosophical doubt and scepticism towards political commitment rather than any unidimensional political engagement. For some critics of the positivism in the social sciences such as Leo Strauss (1950), this relativism has of course a much longer history and can be, for example, located in the nineteenth-century debate over historicism. Max Weber's philosophy of the social sciences with its cautious attempt to resolve the fact–value distinction is a direct product of historicism. In this context it is interesting to consider Rorty's essays on human rights and politics, because on the one hand he wants to reject any Grand Theory solution to politics and ethics, and on the other he is not wholly comfortable with ironic relativism if it precludes possibilities of solidarity and commitment.

It is worth dwelling briefly on the historical issue of relativism in German sociology, because it can be claimed plausibly that many of the issues of pragmatism, truth, and relativism in Rorty's philosophy were at least anticipated by the famous debate over historicism in the late nineteenth century. Carlo Antoni's influential *From History to Sociology* (1998), which first appeared in Italian in 1940, remains the definitive discussion. The problem about cultural relativism was experienced acutely with respect to interpretation. From a sociological point of view, the meaning of any social action or cultural institution is deeply embedded in its social and historical context, and hence the meaning of actions are quite simply particular to a given context. How is any general knowledge of society as such possible? In *From History to Sociology,* Antoni referred to this issue in terms of the problem of historicism, namely the view that the meaning and importance of culture can only be understood historically within its specific setting, that is contextually. This historical problem was particularly critical in the case of Western Christianity. If the faith which has been inherited by the Christian churches is a specific historical phenomenon, how can Christian theology claim any universal authority and relevance for the prophetic message of Jesus Christ? The crisis of the authority of values and morality in German culture had been first experienced in debates about the character of the authority of the texts of Christianity, which had occurred through the evolution of biblical criticism. Biblical scholarship had raised profound problems in confidence in the authority and authenticity of the biblical foundations of authority. The problem for Protestant theology was that biblical criticism through the eighteenth and nineteenth centuries had made the biblical text into a historical document. In short, Protestantism, through its rational inquiry into the Bible, had exposed theological truth to historicism. Similar problems about authenticity and authority are faced in the analysis of art and culture, where claims about aesthetics may simply appear as opinions rather than truths about cultural objects. For Antoni, these specific debates in theology, history, politics, and sociology in fact constituted a general and profound crisis of authority and certainty, not only in Germany but in Europe as a whole, a crisis which spanned the entire nineteenth and early twentieth centuries.

Within Antoni's account of historical relativism, one can detect three forms of historicism: naturalistic, metaphysical, and aesthetic. One solution to relativism attempted to develop the positivistic methods of the natural sciences as a basis for certainty in social inquiry. This solution tended to collapse history into positivistic sociology. By contrast, metaphysical historicism developed into idealism, which attempted to find some certainty outside time in the realm of pure thought such as post-Kantian idealism or pure faith such as German theology. Aesthetic historicism concentrated on the experience of the historian as a point of common agreement, namely the aesthetic experience of reality could produce a form of certainty in the context of chaotic values.

This historicist issue underpinned Weber's attempt to develop a specific methodology for sociology, but it also coloured his substantive sociology of capitalism. For Weber, industrial capitalism through the application of rational science technology has transformed the relationship between human beings and their environment; it has undermined the authenticity of the life-world through the commodification of culture. For Weber, rational capitalism has demystified the everyday world and incorporated the sphere of *Erlebnis* (direct personal experience) into the system of rational economic exchange. In Weber's pessimistic view of 'the iron cage', there is no escape from the process of rationalization which, through the application of science, has embraced all spheres of life including the spiritual domain. It is the 'fate' of the modern world to suffer the routinization of life through bureaucracy, science, and discipline in which the magical and charismatic aura of social existence is slowly but surely effaced.

While Rorty perceives the current crisis in philosophy as a product of internal criticism (the linguistic turn and pragmatism) and external changes (postmodernism), we can argue forcefully that the contemporary crisis of the authority of values is in fact a long-term consequence of historicism. Rorty's plea that philosophy stops trying to 'escape from history' (that is, recognize the contextualization of its claims) is pure historicism. Although there are few direct references to Weber in Rorty's major essays, there is a close proximity between them. The question facing Weber was how to reconcile liberalism with political leadership. The question for Rorty is how to reconcile liberal hope with solidarity. The principal difficulty for Rorty, who still wants edification from philosophy, is how to avoid nihilism, that is how to avoid the iron cage.

Rorty, Rights and Relativism

While modernist critics have rejected postmodernism as a serious political position, Steven Shute's and Susan Hurley's *On Human Rights* (1993) is important because it contains articles by Lyotard and Rorty presenting arguments on the question of human rights. Lyotard has been particularly engaged with the issue of otherness and the other with respect to rights and obligations concerning the Jewish community in contemporary society (Boyne, 1990). As we have seen, Rorty has become closely associated with postmodern theory because he denies that any philosophical or ideological position can have any ultimate authority or justification. We live in a contingent world of competing stories where no particular narrative has general consent or legitimizing force. For Rorty, belief in the validity of a position or the justification of a perspective is a matter of ongoing argumentation from different vantage points and perspectives. The result is that our beliefs about the world and social reality are necessarily ad hoc, contingent, provisional, and local. Our beliefs about the world rather like scientists' claims about nature have to be prefaced by phrases such as 'For the time being ...' and 'From this vantage point...'. It is this persistent denial that there could be any permanent and unitary justification for belief which has given Rorty the title of a postmodern philosopher. The crucial essay in this regard is 'Private Irony and Liberal Hope' (Rorty, 1989).

Although Rorty feels relatively comfortable with the title 'postmodern bourgeois liberal', he derives his position, not from mainstream postmodern thought such as Baudrillard, Bauman, and Lyotard, but rather from the pragmatism of the American philosophers Dewey and Peirce. Rorty's theories about democracy, philosophy, and solidarity are taken from the work of American pragmatists rather than from European forms of postmodern theory. However, Rorty is clearly influenced by the radical work of Nietzsche and Heidegger which is illustrated in his article 'Self-Creation and Affiliation' (Rorty, 1989). On this broad basis, Rorty makes a profound distinction between metaphysicians who believe that an ultimate or general justification for belief of a unified form is possible and ironists who believe that no such general justification is either possible or desirable. Rorty is critical of the whole legacy of Kant with its emphasis on rationalism, individualism, and certainty.

Rorty combines this critical attitude towards professional philosophy with a profound sympathy for contemporary feminist social thought. Rorty believes, along with feminism theorists, that the Western account of reason and rationality is significantly dominated by a gender perspective that is partial and biased rather than neutral and universal. Feminists have been particularly concerned with the role of emotions and symbolism in analytical thought and Rorty draws upon this critical attitude in developing his own theory of rights. In his recent work on rights, Rorty identifies himself with the empiricism of David Hume against the rationalist and universalistic tradition of Kant and Hegel. The down-to-earth common sense tradition of Scottish philosophy appears to have some similarity with Rorty's often rather homespun approach to philosophizing. Certainly in his treatment of Hume, Rorty has been influenced by the feminist theories of Annette C. Baier, particularly in her analysis of Hume's moral philosophy in her *A Progress of Sentiments: Reflections of Hume's treatise* (1991). Whereas Kant attempted to treat moral judgments as a branch of rational inquiry, and interpreted aesthetic appreciation of beauty as a disinterested neutral judgment, Hume gave a central place to sentiment and affect in moral debate and aesthetic inquiry. Critical social thought, following Nietzsche's rejection of the Kantian approach to aesthetics, has argued that aesthetic judgment is essentially bound up with an emotional orientation to reality and cannot be divorced from sentiment. It is partly for this reason that there has been in recent years a particular interest in the notion of the sublime and in Burke's analysis of the sublime in relation to judgments about beauty. Insofar as Rorty derives considerable intellectual stimulation from Nietzsche, we may assume that he is solidly within this anti-Kantian paradigm.

What then does Rorty have to say about rights? Rorty begins his philosophical account of rights by rejecting all foundationalist attempts to argue that human rights can be derived from some general or universal characteristic of human beings as such, for example, their rationality or their humanity. This position is, of course, completely in line with his criticism in the philosophy of science of the mirror metaphor in notions of correspondence. For Rorty, any attempt to identify or discover some essential feature of human beings is, philosophically speaking, a cul-de-sac. He is completely contemptuous of all such universalistic approaches to rights from a foundationalist standpoint, because it clashes with his basic relativism. For Rorty, the recent horrors of ethnic cleansing in Kosova make any attempt to discover some rational foundation to human behaviour totally pointless, indeed offensive. Similarly the Holocaust makes any attempt to find a moral or rational foundation to human behaviour, whereby we could appeal to the reasonableness of human beings to live together in harmony and peace, a moral offence. Rorty argues that we should stop asking why we differ from animals and merely say that 'we can *feel for each* other to a much greater extent than they can' (Rorty, 1998a: 176). It is better to give up on transcendental categories like God or Natural Law or History and start pinning our hopes on one another.

Following from this rejection of foundationalism, there are two major features to Rorty's account of rights. As we have already noticed, he starts by putting considerable emphasis on the importance of sympathy and affective attachment to other human beings. It is the sentimental attachment of human beings through emotion and everyday companionship that provides the possibility for an argument about rights rather than some abstract claim about rationality. Human beings are primarily sentimental creatures, not rational philosophers. The next stage of his argument is the most significant, namely that we should attempt to improve the world through various forms of sentimental education. It is for this reason that the tradition of Rousseau in educational theory is particularly significant for Rorty. It is through a system of education which would make people identify with other human beings rather than dismissing them as not truly human, that we have an opportunity of identifying an appropriate framework within which to discuss rights at all. Rorty's optimistic belief is that we can make the world a better place by training our children into sympathy and concern for other human beings as themselves sentimental creatures rather than rational actors. It is here of course that Rorty's dependence on the legacy of Dewey's pragmatism is particularly obvious. Rather than bother with debates about rational foundations to morality, we should simply get on with the business of trying to improve society through educational mechanisms. The classics of literature are crucial to a sentimental education, not the empty pursuits of rationalist philosophers. We can raise and enhance intersubjective sentiment through exposing our children and young people to the great traditions of literature and drama, wherein genuine moral dilemmas are explored systematically and sympathetically. The tragedy of Yugoslavia is more likely to be resolved by training children into a sympathetic appreciation of other people's problems and tragedies rather than instructing children in the tradition of Kantian philosophy. The issue behind human rights is an issue of recognition – how to get human beings to recognize other human beings as creatures worthy of their concern and care.

On Human Frailty

In this chapter I want to suggest that Rorty's argument could be reformulated to make it compatible with one version of foundationalism (Turner, 1993). While I am profoundly sympathetic to Rorty's argument about sentiments and moral behaviour, there is an alternative to relativism, which avoids some aspects of the charge against Rorty that his work is unable to cope with the problem of cruelty. It provides a possible response to the very reasonable question 'is cruelty something about which liberals can be ironic?' (Critchley, 1998: 812) Arguments about cultural relativism can be, and have been, manipulated and abused by authoritarian governments to justify various forms of state violence under the banner of cultural authenticity and difference (Woodiwiss, 1998). It is all too easy to justify abuses against children and women on the one hand, or devastation of the natural environment on the other, by an appeal to local cultural difference and diversity. Philosophical and sociological arguments against relativism are therefore an important part of the political programme to protect and defend human rights traditions.

There is therefore a strong argument in favour of at least a general theory of human rights, even if it is difficult to sustain the idea of universal rights. The argument is briefly that the frailty of the human body provides at least one place for starting an account of a foundation for human rights discourse. Because of this frailty and the precarious nature of social reality, human beings require the protective security of general human rights. Although not all rights assume this form of protective security, a large element of human rights legal tradition is to provide some general security for human beings. The notion of the frailty of the human body, namely our disposition towards disease, disability, and death, can be derived from a sociology of the body influenced by writers such as Arnold Gehlen and Peter L. Berger. This notion of frailty can be supported by various feminist views of the importance of caring and nurturing. One might also note here that Rorty has a particular sympathy for the work of Heidegger from which moral philosophers have developed the importance of concern and caring (Rorty, 1991a). The question of human vulnerability of course is particularly prominent in the area of debates about torture and political brutality, an issue dealt with supremely well in *The Body in Pain* (Scarry, 1985).

In addition to the human body being fragile and frail, we live in a social environment which is essentially contingent and precarious and this precariousness is an inevitable consequence of the nature of power and its investment in the state. This argument is a variation on the theme in social contract theory derived from the work of Thomas Hobbes. Powerful institutions such as the state, which are set up according to social contract theory to protect the interests of rational actors, can of course function to terrorize and dominate civil society. While strong states may protect society from civil wars, they can, for that very reason, be a danger to the very existence of citizens. By precariousness I also mean that institutions which are rationally designed to serve certain specific purposes may evolve in ways which contradict these original charters. Social life is essentially contingent and risky; individuals, even when they collect together for concerted action, cannot necessarily protect themselves against the uncertainties and vagaries of social reality. Such a view of social reality would sit very easily with Rorty's own sense of the contingency of selfhood and a liberal community (Rorty, 1989).

While social theorists might grant that social reality is precarious, the argument that human beings are universally frail may appear to be controversial and contentious. There are a number of problems here. If human beings are frail by definition, then frailty is variable and my argument could easily be converted into a Darwinistic theory of the survival of the fittest. In a patriarchal regime, those that are least frail may combine to dominate and subordinate the vulnerable and fragile. Hobbes's *Leviathan* was written in a society with precisely these Darwinistic tendencies as the English Civil War was to illustrate dramatically. The disposition of the strong to support and protect the weak must be based consequently upon some collectively shared sympathy or empathy for human beings in their collective frailty and weakness. Following Rorty, we can derive a theory of human rights from certain aspects of feminist theory, from a critical view of the limitations of utilitarian accounts of reason and from the notions of sympathy, sentiment, and emotionality. Insofar as the strong protect the weak, it is through a recognition of likeness which is itself a product of affective attachment and sentiment. Rational human beings want their rights to be recognized because they see in the plight of others their own (potential) misery. If ageing is an inevitable process, we can all anticipate our own frailty, and in this context sympathy is crucial in deciding to whom our moral concern might be directed (Turner, 1994). From a sociological perspective, sympathy derives from the fundamental experiences of social reciprocity in everyday life, particularly from the relationship between mother and child.

If this argument is to be sustained, we will require a more elaborate notion of human frailty. For example, the argument could be made more sophisticated by developing a distinction between pain and suffering. Human beings can suffer without an experience of pain and conversely they can have an experience of pain without suffering. Suffering is essentially a situation where the self is threatened or destroyed from outside, for example through humiliation. We can suffer the loss of a loved one without physical pain, whereas toothache may give us extreme physical pain without a sense of loss of self or humiliation. While suffering is variable, pain might be regarded as universal. This argument is closely related to a position adopted by Rorty in his essay on 'Private Irony and Liberal Hope' (Rorty, 1989) where he argues that

> the idea that we have an overriding obligation to diminish cruelty, to make human beings equal in respect of their liability to suffering, seems to take for granted that there is something within human beings which deserves respect and protection quite independently of the language they speak. It suggests that a non-linguistic ability, the ability to feel pain, is what is important, and the differences in the vocabulary are much less important. (Rorty, 1989: 88)

This argument about human frailty, dependence, and suffering can provide an argument to support the notion of a universalistic foundation for human rights. In short, it is possible to argue that frailty is a universal condition of the human species because pain is a fundamental experience of all organic life. While Rorty may be able to argue that suffering is local and variable, the concept of the frailty of the human body could be defended through the concept of human pain. It would as a consequence be possible to adopt all of Rorty's philosophical arguments about irony, cultural variation, the absence of authoritative justification and so forth, while also adhering to a universalistic view of human nature and human embodiment as the underlying criterion of all humanity, and this is the foundation of any theory of human rights. It would also be possible to accept that this foundationalist view of human rights is theory-dependent, and argue that ontological insecurity provides a rights discourse that promotes rather than precludes cross-cultural agreements about dignity. One could therefore embrace postmodern irony while also advocating a universalistic notion of human rights as a protective screen to limit the contingencies of embodiment and social relations.

APPRAISAL OF KEY ADVANCES AND CONTROVERSIES

In this critical evaluation of Rorty, I shall ignore the question of whether Rorty has developed an adequate comprehension of philosophers like Heidegger, Foucault, and Derrida. This type of criticism can often become a fruitless exercise in textual exegesis. I am also not directly interested in criticism of his philosophy of science. My principal concern is to examine the value of Rorty's postmodern philosophy for social and political theory.

Rorty's political theory as a platform for political action is minimalistic. He recommends that young people should be exposed to literature that will educate them in sympathy so they may better understand the suffering of others. These recommendations may be perfectly appropriate as a method of improving the education of young rich Americans, but it does nothing necessarily for the dispossessed and downtrodden of the Third World. Rorty could be accused of being a modern day Leibniz, namely, believing that we live in the best of all possible worlds and further more liberal capitalist democracy is about the best world that the working class could aspire to. Rorty's version of postmodernism certainly rules out what we might call Big Picture Politics – it rules out visionary aspiration and a theology of hope. His interpretation of pragmatism may in fact end up as political passivity. Critics like Critchley have therefore accused Rorty of complacency, because his postmodern bourgeois ethic appears to be an unambiguous defence of modern America.

Rorty has attempted to defend himself from his critics in his *Achieving Our Country* (1998c). The book is a defence of his own political liberalism through a criticism of the decline of the left. The decline of socialist intellectuals in America is signalled by their growing concern for culture and their lack of interest in 'real' politics. The cultural left has assumed that the reform of the literary canon is equivalent to a transformation of society. The cultural left is 'a spectatorial, disgusted, mocking Left rather than a Left which dreams of achieving our country' (Rorty, 1998c: 35). The basic argument of his recent study is that, without an emotional attachment to one's country, politics cannot be creative and imaginative. The weakness of contemporary America is the absence of a civic religion (of the sort that inspired Whitman and Dewey) as the moral force behind citizenship.

The central difficulty with Rorty's political philosophy is how to reconcile his postmodernism with his notion of solidarity. One somewhat odd feature of Rorty's prose style is the use of the pronoun 'we'. The following examples are taken more or less at random – 'we rich North American bourgeois' (Rorty, 1991b: 201); 'we shall have to give up our fear of being called "'bourgeois reformers"' (Rorty, 1998c: 239); and 'For we intellectuals, who are mostly academics, are ourselves quite well insulated, at least in the short run, from the effects of globalization' (Rorty, 1998c: 89). In a similar fashion, the title of his recent book speaks confidently about 'our country'. Now in part Rorty could be defended from complacency by arguing that this 'we' is ironic. Nevertheless it betrays a failure to grasp the real issue of postmodern politics, that the polity is made up of many 'we' categories, all of whom are competing for a voice in the public arena and who claim, especially in America, that their voices – the voices of black communities, aboriginal peoples, the unemployed, and the culturally excluded – are not recognized, not heard and not considered. To whose We-category does Rorty belong, and why should that voice be privileged? I take it that this is the gist of Nancy Fraser's criticism of Rorty when she asks rhetorically whether the interests of poets and workers can really coincide? (Fraser, 1989). The problem which remains unresolved in Rorty's liberalism is how to reconcile conflicting views of citizenship within a liberal democracy, especially in the United States where the history of civic ideals has been fractured around open and inclusive, as well as ascriptive and exclusionary traditions (Smith, 1997). To reconcile those claims , it is necessary to develop a discourse that is not local and relativistic.

RORTY'S MAJOR WORKS

Rorty, R. (ed.) (1967) *The Linguistic Turn*. Chicago: University of Chicago Press.

Rorty, R. (1979) *Philosophy and the Mirror of Nature*. Princeton, NJ: Princeton University Press.

Rorty, R. (1980) 'Pragmatism, relativism and irrationalism', *Proceedings and Addresses of the American Philosophical Association*, 53: 727–30.

Rorty, R. (1982) *The Consequences of Pragmatism*. Minneapolis: University of Minnesota Press.

Rorty, R. (1989) *Contingency, Irony and Solidarity*. Cambridge: Cambridge University Press.

Rorty, R. (1991a) *Essays on Heidegger and Others*. Cambridge: Cambridge University Press.

Rorty, R. (1991b) *Objectivity, Relativism and Truth*. Cambridge: Cambridge University Press.

Rorty, R. (1998a) *Truth and Progress. Philosophical Papers*. Cambridge: Cambridge University Press.

Rorty, R. (1998b) 'Pragmatism as romantic polytheism', in M. Dickstein (ed.) *The Revival of Pragmatism. New Essays on Social Thought, Law and Culture*. Durham, NC and London: Duke University Press.

Rorty, R. (1998c) *Achieving Our Country. Leftist Thought in Twentieth-Century America*. Cambridge, MA: Harvard University Press.

Rorty, R. (1999) *Philosophy and Social Hope*. London: Penguin Books.

SECONDARY REFERENCES

Antoni, C. (1998) *From History to Sociology*. London and New York: Routledge.

Baier, A. (1991) *A Progress of Sentiments: Reflections on Hume's Treatise*. Cambridge, MA: Harvard University Press.

Boyne, R. (1990) *Foucault and Derrida: The Other Side of Reason*. London: Unwin Hyman.

Critchley, S. (1998) 'Metaphysics in the dark. A response to Richard Rorty and Ernesto Laclau', *Political Theory*, 26 (6): 803–17.

Diggins, J. P. (1994) *The Promise of Pragmatism. Modernism and the Crisis of Knowledge and Authority*. Chicago: University of Chicago Press.

Fraser. N. (1989) *Unruly Practices. Power, Discourse and Gender in Contemporary Social Theory*. Minneapolis: University of Minnesota Press.

Gellner, E. (1992) *Postmodernism, Reason and Religion*. London: Routledge.

Hickman, L.A. (ed.) (1998) *Reading Dewey. Interpretations for a Postmodern Generation*. Bloomington and Indianapolis: Indiana University Press.

Lyotard, J.-F. (1984) *The Postmodern Condition: A Report on Knowledge*. Manchester: University of Manchester Press.

Malachowski, A.R. (ed.) (1990) *Reading Rorty. Critical Responses to Philosophy and the Mirror of Nature (and Beyond)* Oxford: Basil Blackwell.

Margolis, J. (1986) *Pragmatism without Foundations. Reconciling Realism and Relativism*. Oxford: Basil Blackwell.

Scarry, E. (1985) *The Body in Pain: The making and unmaking of the world*. Oxford: Oxford University Press.

Shute, S., and Hurley, S. (1993) *On Human Rights: The Oxford Amnesty Lectures*. New York: Basic Books.

Smith, R.M. (1997) *Civic Ideals. Conflicting Visions of Citizenship in U.S History* New Haven, CT and London: Yale University Press.

Strauss, L. (1950) *Natural Right and History*. Chicago: University of Chicago Press.

Turner, B.S. (ed.) (1993) *Citizenship and Social Theory*. London: Sage.

Turner, B.S. (1994) 'Outline of theory of human rights', *Sociology*, 27 (3): 489–512.

Woodiwiss, A. (1998) *Globalisation, Human Rights and Labour Law in Pacific Asia*. Cambridge: Cambridge University Press.

25

Nancy Chodorow

GEOFFREY GERSHENSON AND MICHELLE WILLIAMS

BIOGRAPHICAL DETAILS AND THEORETICAL CONTEXT

Born in 1944, Nancy Julia Chodorow is of the generation that came of age in the 1960s with the New Left and the rise of feminism. As an undergraduate at Radcliffe College (BA in social anthropology, 1966), Chodorow was educated in a cross-disciplinary curriculum in social relations and influenced by the anthropologists Beatrice and John W.M. Whiting. She went on to graduate studies at Brandeis University (PhD in sociology, 1974), where she attended Philip Slater's seminar on the sociology of family interaction and participated in an extracurricular, student-led 'Mother–Daughter Group' inspired by Slater's work on mother–son relationships (Slater, [1968] 1992). As a graduate student at Brandeis and subsequently as a professor of sociology at the University of California, Santa Cruz (1974–86) and the University of California, Berkeley (1986–present), Chodorow has worked in intellectual environments particularly hos-pitable to feminist scholarship, interdisciplinary research, and radical theory. In 1974 she published 'Family Structure and Feminine Personality', an essay that anticipated the argument of her landmark *The Reproduction of Mothering: Psychoanalysis and the Sociology of Gender* ([1978] 1999a). The book was influential from the beginning, establishing Chodorow as a prominent voice in feminism and psychoanalytic sociology. From 1985 to 1993, while continuing as a professor of sociology, Chodorow undertook training at the San Francisco Psychoana-lytic Institute; she is now a practising clinical psychoanalyst and psychotherapist as well as a sociologist. Since *The Reproduction of Mothering*, Chodorow has written numerous articles and three books: *Feminism and Psychoanalytic Theory* (1989), *Femininities, Masculinities, Sexualities: Freud and Beyond* (1994), and *The Power of Feelings: Personal Meaning in Psychoanalysis, Gender, and Culture* (1999b). In each of these works Chodorow operates at the intersection of psychoanalytic and social theory, focusing primarily on questions of feminism, gender, and subjectivity.

Chodorow's work can be placed in the intertwining theoretical contexts of feminism and psychoanalysis. When she began her sociological career, the culture of feminism was largely hostile to psychoanalysis. Prominent feminists were agreed in viewing the Freudian tradition as patriarchal, wedded to biologically deterministic accounts of human subjectivity, aligned with the politics of the Cold War, and generally antithetical to the feminist project (Buhle, 1998). In the mid-1970s, when Chodorow began to incorporate psychoanalysis into her work on gender, she was located at the margins of academic feminism along with Juliet Mitchell, Dorothy Dinnerstein, Jean Baker Miller, Gayle Rubin, Jessica Benjamin, Jane Flax, and a few others. When *The Reproduction of Mothering* appeared in 1978, it challenged the anti-Freudian orthodoxy of radical feminism and helped to overturn it. Its influence is suggested by its 1996 selection in *Contemporary Sociology* as one of the 10 most influential books in sociology of the previous 25 years. Against biologistic accounts of gender personality, *The Reproduction of Mothering* emphasized cultural determinants, and against prevailing sociological accounts emphasizing role theory, it enlisted psychoanalytic theory to explore the earliest sources of selfhood and personality. Analytical in tone and content, and arriving at a time when the academic world was ready to receive its message, the book succeeded in giving a persuasive account of the way in which gender is constituted. Chodorow subtly and accessibly organized her argument around a compelling theme: difference in the 'relational' character of male and female selfhood. In her analysis, female personalities tend to be constituted on the basis of a more permeable 'self-in-relation', facilitating empathy and community but complicating the project of self-differentiation. Male personalities, by contrast, tend to be constituted on the basis of a self in denial of relation, facilitating individuation but also grounding it in a fragile ego that requires rigid and potentially destructive forms of boundary-setting to shore up the self. Chodorow's theory of gender personality, further elaborated in her subsequent writings, continues to be influential across disciplines in the social sciences and humanities.

As a social theorist interested in questions of human subjectivity, Chodorow stands out for her persistent and probing engagement with the thought and legacy of Freud. Her negotiation of the Freudian tradition has been guided by a two-fold concern: to bring the analytic lens to the story of female development – a story relatively neglected by a psychoanalytic tradition richer in its analysis of male development – and to give due attention to the powerful role of the mother in the formation of personality. Bringing daughters and mothers into a psychoanalytic tradition historically more concerned with fathers and sons, Chodorow has since the mid-1970s written from within the clinical, British-based object-relations tradition associated with Melanie Klein and D.W. Winnicott, which emphasizes the importance to personality of transferences between internal and external 'object-worlds' through processes of introjection and projection. In Chodorow's earlier writing, including *The Reproduction of Mothering*, she relies heavily on the approaches of Fairbairn and Balint. In her later work she deepens and broadens her engagement with psychoanalysis, entering into sustained dialogue with Freud, Klein, and Winnicott. Today she is perhaps best described as a heterodox, synthetic Kleinian; her work incorporates insights not just from within object-relations theory but from imaginative ego-psychologists such as Erik Erikson and Hans Loewald. In her dual capacities as sociologist and psychoanalyst, Chodorow is interested in dissolving the boundaries separating the two disciplines within which she works, advocating an understanding of the self as a construction of both culture and psyche.

SOCIAL THEORY AND CONTRIBUTIONS

The Gendered Self

The Reproduction of Mothering is the obvious place from which to begin a summary of

Chodorow's contribution to social thought. For our purposes the book can be divided into two parts. The first part, which takes up most of the analysis and is the key to the book's influence, posits that a typical kind of patriarchal family structure tends to produce differential outcomes in gender personality. More precisely, Chodorow argues that in families in which the primary parental caregiver is the woman and not the man – in which the woman primarily 'mothers' and the man primarily pursues work outside the family – early childhood experiences are likely to differ for boys and girls, producing differently constituted kinds of personalities. The female personality generated by such a family structure, Chodorow suggests, will tend to be constituted as a self that is fundamentally in relation to, rather than detached from, others, a self that is connected to others and world. The male personality, by contrast, will tend to be constituted as a self that is fundamentally in denial of attachment to others, that is differentiated and detached from others and the world. After establishing in the first part of the book that a typical kind of family structure tends to beget gendered personalities, Chodorow goes on in the less influential and less closely elaborated second part to give an explanation of how gendered personality tends to reproduce the family structure that first generated it. Here Chodorow builds on the work of Parsons, Slater, and the Frankfurt School, loosely situating her account in a Marxian framework. Gender personality reproduces patriarchal family structure (and thereby helps to reproduce patriarchal forms of capitalism) by inclining men to prefer work that takes them outside the home in pursuit of achievement in the rule-bound, less affect-laden milieu of the capitalist workplace, and by inclining women to prefer the more affect-laden and relational work of caregiving within the family. The gendering of occupational preferences thus contributes to the reproduction of a sexist division of labour and, in the case of women, the reproduction of mothering.

The step-by-step developmental account of gender personality in *The Reproduction of Mothering* remains the cornerstone of Chodorow's psychoanalytic feminist contribution to social thought. Chodorow organizes her analysis around three broadly defined and overlapping phases in early childhood development. In the first, pre-Oedipal phase, dominated by the dyadic relationship between mother and child, the infant begins from a condition of oneness with mother and world, unable to differentiate between the 'me' and the 'not-me'. In Chodorow's conception, and against the traditional psychoanalytic view that the gendering of the psyche begins in the later Oedipal phase, it is in the pre-Oedipal phase that the psyche begins to be constituted as male and female. The key agent in this process is the mother, who tends (in families in which the woman is the primary caregiver) to identify narcissistically with her daughter, experiencing her as an extension or double of herself. As a consequence daughters typically experience the powerful pre-Oedipal bond between mother and child more intensely and for a longer period of time than do sons. This prolonged and intensified sense of oneness with the mother serves to complicate the daughter's ability to separate and individuate. By contrast, Chodorow sees the mother as tending to relate 'anaclitically' to her son, experiencing him as an other. Over time this serves to weaken the intensity and shorten the duration of the pre-Oedipal symbiosis between mother and son. This hastening of the son's loss of a fundamental sense of oneness with the mother serves to hurry him toward separation and individuation.

Development in the Oedipal period, during which the child's attachments to parents are eroticized, builds on the differential experiences of the pre-Oedipal phase. Two differences are key in Chodorow's account of Oedipal development: girls tend to come into the

Oedipal phase with a more powerfully felt pre-Oedipal bond to the mother, and, unlike boys, they are required by norms of heterosexuality to move from primary love for the mother to eroticized love for the father. These differences, Chodorow argues, result in a male love that tends to be exclusive and dyadic in its orientation, a female love that tends to be more diffuse in orientation. The boy's primary concern in the Oedipal phase continues to be with the mother, though the nature of his attachment to her shifts from pre-Oedipal symbiosis to eroticized feelings for her as an other. The girl, by contrast, balances the pre-Oedipal bond to the mother with an eroticized, Oedipal love for the father. In Freud's account, the girl's Oedipal experience is conceived as symmetrical to that of the boy; love for the father is taken to be exclusive and dyadic, accompanied by rivalry with the mother. In Chodorow's revisionist account, while the girl partly experiences her mother as a rival, even more she remains attached to her. Love for the father supplements rather than replaces love for the mother. While boys learn to experience love as a dyadic experience that adds eroticized Oedipal love for the mother to the overwhelming power (both frightening and attracting) of pre-Oedipal feelings toward her, girls learn to experience love as a triadic experience that is typically less overwhelming in its power but also more conflictual in nature, requiring negotiation between the demands of two different attachments. Chodorow's influential account of the Oedipal experience thus suggests that the female self generated by a typical kind of patriarchal family structure tends to be endowed with relatively greater 'relational complexity'.

The third and final important moment in Chodorow's story of early childhood development centres on the differential manner in which girls and boys resolve the Oedipus complex, repressing erotic attachments to mother and father. For boys, both the intensity and exclusivity of the love for the mother requires a particularly severe act of repression. Girls, whose love for the father typically is less intense (partly because he is experienced as a more remote, secondary figure and partly because love for him is tempered by love for the mother), tend to repress their Oedipal feelings in a milder, less severe way. As such, while the typical boy must forcefully and rigidly detach himself from pre-Oedipal and Oedipal feelings, the typical girl is less threatened by those feelings and can afford to stay in more continuous connection to them.

The outcome of these different developmental paths is the gendering of personality. Most importantly for Chodorow, family structures in which women are primary caregivers are likely to result in a female self that is fundamentally a self-in-relation and a male self that is fundamentally a self in denial of relation. Girls, beginning with the greater intensity and duration of their pre-Oedipal attachments, tend to acquire a stronger sense of being connected to others and to the world; their Oedipal and post-Oedipal experience is such that they do not sever this sense of connectedness. Girls are thus more likely, relative to boys, to go on to be more attentive to relationships with others; endowed with stronger capacities for empathy, nurturance, and care-taking; troubled by difficulties with individuation and the setting of boundaries between self and others; and more open to the emotional origins of their preferences and actions, as well as to the persuasion and judgments of others. Boys, on the other hand, having typically been forced out of pre-Oedipal unity at an earlier age, are likely to have a stronger sense of being individuated selves, detached and detachable from others and the world. The severe character of the typical boy's post-Oedipal repression further requires of him a more substantial detachment from inner feelings. Relative to the typical female personality, the male personality makes choices less on the basis of the emotional origins of preferences and more on the basis of rules, general categories, and abstract principles. Finally, for boys, the construction of gender identity – of their sense of being masculine rather than feminine – tends to be more fragile, since it is defined against a feminine and maternal other to which they paradoxically feel (unconsciously if not consciously) deeply attached. To cope with the dreaded (but also idealized) feminine that threatens without and within, boys and men resort to a range of defensive measures to demarcate and defend clear boundaries between masculine and feminine.

In her later work on gender personality, Chodorow offers two important amendments to *The Reproduction of Mothering*. First, she moderates the causal claim that family structure and the gendering of personality, which again was the focus of the first part of the book, produces male domination in society as a whole, which was the contention of the second part of the book. As she puts it in the introduction to *Feminism and Psychoanalytic Theory*, 'I no longer think that one factor, or one dynamic, can explain male dominance' (1989: 5). Whereas *The Reproduction of Mothering* 'implied that women's mothering was the cause or prime mover of male dominance', the later Chodorow takes it to be but 'one extremely important' factor among many (1989: 6). Second, whereas *The Reproduction of Mothering* gives an account of *general* tendencies in gender personality, in her later work Chodorow is interested to explore particularity and variation within and across gender. In *Femininities, Masculinities, Sexualities*, Chodorow writes against 'universalizing gender theories of psychoanalysis' (1994: ix). While still seeing value in the generalizations on gender established in *The Reproduction of Mothering*, the later Chodorow is equally if not more interested to counter the 'tendency to turn generalizations into universal claims and polarizations' (1994: 90). Reflecting her psychoanalytic training, her 'clinical observation of the extraordinary uniqueness, complexity, and particularity of any individual psyche', and her 'increasing certainty about the importance of context, specificity, and personal individuality' (1994: ix–x), *Femininities, Masculinities, Sexualities* explores difference and variation in Freud's conceptions of femininity, in alternative sexualities, and in female and male modes of love.

Relational Individualism

Since *The Reproduction of Mothering* Chodorow has written extensively not only on the gendering of subjectivity but on human subjectivity at large. Perhaps the key concept linking both sets of writings is the central attention she gives to the relationality of the self. While important to the argument of *The Reproduction of Mothering*, the relationality of the self becomes the focus of Chodorow's analysis in several of the essays that compose *Feminism and Psychoanalytic Theory*, beginning with 'Gender Relation and Difference', a widely read essay originally published as a journal article in 1980. Moving from gender to subjectivity in general, *Feminism and Psychoanalytic Theory* calls for a social and psychoanalytic theory and practice that abandons radically individualistic notions of subjectivity that makes the shift 'Toward a Relational Individualism', to use the title of her 1986 essay. Chodorow's thinking about relational selfhood is importantly indebted to Winnicott's foundational accounts on the processes by which selves come to relate creatively to others as subjects rather than objects (see Winnicott, [1971] 1993, 1965). In Chodorow's Winnicottian understanding, human freedom must be conceptualized in relational terms – that is, as a condition experienced by selves acting in creative and 'intersubjective' relation to other selves. In 'Beyond Drive Theory' (originally published in 1985), Chodorow brings this relational, intersubjective understanding of the self into conversation with the left Freudian social theories of Herbert Marcuse and Norman O. Brown, both of whose emancipatory visions, she contends, are undermined by radically individualist notions of the self. Building on Freudian drive theory, both Marcuse and Brown define freedom as instinctual liberation; both then experience theoretical difficulties in getting from the radically individualist self to the construction of community that each recognizes to be essential to human freedom. Writing as a psychoanalytic feminist against the masculinist biases in both of these left Freudian interpretations of subjectivity, Chodorow urges theorists to put a relational understanding of self and freedom at 'the core of . . . social and political vision' (1989: 135).

Leaving others to engage in the construction of that vision, Chodorow's latest book, *The Power of Feelings*, offers what is undoubtedly her most ambitious and comprehensive statement to date on the question of human subjectivity. Aligning herself with 1950s theorists such as Erikson, Loewald, Winnicott, and Schachtel who used psychoanalysis to inquire into broader questions of personal fulfilment and cultural life, Chodorow organizes her argument around the core contention that personal meaning is constructed at the nexus of psyche and culture, 'neither reducible to the other, both operating together as one intertwined process' (1999b: 9). Throughout the text she attempts to enact a series of theoretical reconciliations, synthesizing competing orientations toward questions of the self and tending to opt for, as she puts it, 'both–and' rather than 'either–or' solutions to theoretical problems (1999b: 3). The starting point for Chodorow's analysis is the notion that personal meaning is created through processes of transference, introjection, projection, and fantasy. Conceived spatially, meaning originates neither entirely from an 'internal' nor entirely from an 'external' reality, but rather from the intertwining of the two. Conceived temporally, meaning originates neither wholly in the present nor wholly from the past, but rather from the intertwining of both; while 'psychological agency is always in the present', one's current transferences are typically 'imbued with the subjective past' – a past that generates psychological patterns and places 'limits on the possible' (1999b: 63, 41). In *The Power of Feelings* Chodorow places herself in a middle position between, on the one hand, psychoanalysts who tend to occlude the role of ('external') culture in the construction of personal meaning, and on the other hand, cultural theorists and social scientists who tend to occlude the role of the ('internal') psyche in the construction of personal meaning. She works to heal the split between a narrow psychologism and an equally narrow cultural determinism, first in a section on gender (writing against both psychoanalytic conceptions that neglect culture and contemporary feminist conceptions that neglect the psyche) and then in a section on subjectivity in general (using the discipline of cultural anthropology as her site of exploration).

APPRAISAL OF KEY ADVANCES AND CONTROVERSIES

In considering Chodorow's influence on intellectual discourse and academic scholarship, it is perhaps best to begin with the general point that her work has been important in the larger effort to bring the psyche into social and cultural analysis, a move that largely has been resisted by the social scientific mainstream of the American academy. The trajectory of her writings in the last two decades reflects the general intellectual shift from structuralist metanarrative to poststructuralist sensitivity to the local and the particular, Chodorow has remained consistent in opposing a point of commonality shared by most American social scientists across the structuralist/post-structuralist divide: a reluctance to draw on the richness of Freud's thought and legacy. In Chodorow's Freudian and feminist perspective, one cannot theorize about social life without taking into account the way in which society is constituted by (gendered) psyches. Focusing on the object-relations strand of psychoanalysis and in particular on the role of the pre-Oedipal mother, her writings have helped to popularize a view of psychoanalysis that moves beyond vulgar interpretations of Freud. And by providing an influential account of female development that integrates psychoanalytic theory without incorporating its patriarchal orthodoxies, Chodorow has played an especially important role in establishing a place for psychoanalysis within the mainstream of feminist theory and practice.

Looking to the specific bodies of scholarship influenced by Chodorow, one might divide them into two overlapping groups. The first and perhaps most important emanates from Chodorow's work on gender, which has introduced a particular kind of feminist perspective into disciplines across the social sciences and humanities. That perspective is interested to explore, problematize, and to a certain extent revalue the historically undervalued feminine voice and standpoint, taking it to be distinctive for its relationality and connectedness to self, others, and world. It is also interested to explore, problematize, and to a certain extent devalue the historically overvalued masculine voice and standpoint, taking it to be distinctive for its detachedness from self, others, and world, for its rootedness in a relatively fragile ego and a relatively insecure gender identity, and for its resulting propensity to shore up self and masculinity through aggressive and misogynistic boundary-setting (personal and social, material and symbolic). Among these studies, Carol Gilligan's influential *In a Different Voice* ([1982] 1996) deserves special mention. Gilligan draws on Chodorow in arguing for characteristically male and female patterns of moral decision-making, with men tending toward an 'ethic of justice' grounded in abstract, general moral principles, and with women tending toward an 'ethic of care' grounded in concrete, particular relationships and consequences. Also influential has been Evelyn Fox Keller's *Reflections on Gender and Science* (1985), which incorporates Chodorow in examining the abstracting and instrumental character of male subjectivity in relation to the history of science. In sociology, Chodorow's conception of gender personality has contributed to scholarship in the sociology of gender, work, emotions, and family; her influence can be seen in the work of Christine Williams, Karin Martin, Jennifer Pierce, Michael Messner, Miriam Johnson, and Lillian Rubin among others. Examples of her influence in anthropology and classics include the work of Gilbert Herdt and Helene Foley respectively. In political science, her work has influenced students of political theory and political culture, including Nancy Hartsock, Michael Rogin, Hanna Pitkin, Christine Di Stefano, Susan Moller Okin, and Seyla Benhabib among others. In literature and literary criticism, Chodorow's account of gender has inspired new ways of thinking about authors, texts, and readers; examples include studies by Elizabeth Abel, Janet Adelman, Marianne Hirsch, Coppélia Kahn, and Janice Radway.

A second body of scholarship has been influenced by Chodorow's work on the relational character of subjectivity. Here Chodorow has contributed to the rise of relational thinking in psychoanalysis and psychoanalytic feminist social thought. Within psychoanalysis her work has been important not only for its conception of female development and gender personality but for its influence on American relational psychoanalysis and more generally for its role in popularizing and clarifying object-relations and Kleinian theory. Within psychoanalytic feminist social thought, Chodorow's work has informed an emerging body of theory seeking to ground social thought in a relational conception of the subject and an intersubjective definition of human emancipation. Other participants in this theoretical enterprise include: Jessica Benjamin, who in *The Bonds of Love* (1988) and elsewhere brings object-relations feminism into dialogue with the Hegelian–Marxist concerns of the Frankfurt School; Jane Flax, who in *Thinking Fragments* (1990) builds bridges between object-relations feminism and postmodernism; and Madelon Sprengnether, who in *The Spectral Mother* (1990) explores the history of Freudian and post-Freudian confusion on, and occlusion of, the pre-Oedipal mother.

Controversies

With the wide influence enjoyed by Chodorow have come a variety of criticisms. These criticisms aim at three broad and overlapping target areas: the cultural and social, the psychoanalytic, and the political content of Chodorow's thought. Culturalist or sociological critiques of Chodorow have persisted from the publication of *The Reproduction of Mothering* to the present. Issuing from a range of theoretical perspectives, these criticisms share in a dissatisfaction with the thinness – empirical and theoretical – of Chodorow's treatments of social and cultural phenomena. To begin, critics of *The Reproduction of Mothering* from both structuralist and post-structuralist perspectives have challenged what they see to be the reductionist character of each of its central contentions. Her analysis of gendering, they maintain, reduces the determination of personality to the single cause of family structure, while her analysis of social reproduction reduces gender personality (e.g. Lorber et al., 1981; Young, 1989). Both of these reductionisms, the critics allege, neglect the wide range of social factors, material and symbolic, shaping personality and facilitating social reproduction. Relatedly, *The Reproduction of Mothering* has been criticized for generalizing about gender personality across lines of class, race, ethnicity, and nationality, for insufficiently attending to the fact that different personality configurations are also influenced by different social locations. The book relies on the clinical literature of psychoanalysis – which draws predominantly from white, European and North American, middle-class patients – yet makes claims about female and male personality in general (Fraser and Nicholson, 1990; Lorber et al., 1981).

Since the writing of *The Reproduction of Mothering*, Chodorow has acknowledged the force of some of these criticisms. She continues to see the generalizations on gender personality as valid and useful insofar as they suggest tendencies that continue to be culturally important, but as we have noted above, she has also become more attentive to the variable contextual factors that make gender identity a highly particular and complicated construction (Chodorow, 1994, 1999a, 1999b). As we have also suggested, the later Chodorow does grant that *The Reproduction of Mothering* implied more causal importance than it should have to family structure and gender personality in explaining larger social patterns of patriarchal capitalism, effectively minimizing the importance of a wide range of social and familial factors that constitute personality and culture (Chodorow, 1989: 5–7). Though Chodorow was criticized from the beginning for the thinness of her treatment of the social, the general trajectory of her writing has nonetheless moved still further from engaging in the more historically-informed kind of social analysis her sociological and culturalist critics would like to see. Eschewing the Marx–Freud commitments of her early writings, the later Chodorow takes an inward turn insofar as she becomes less preoccupied with the complexities of the social, more preoccupied with the complexities of the psychological. As a general proposition Chodorow accepts the centra-lity of particular social histories to cultural and personal meaning, but as a whole her work as a social theorist is relatively inattentive to social and cultural history (Gottlieb, 1984; Laslett, 1996; MacCannell, 1991). The later Chodorow tends to theorize about subjectivity and meaning for the sake of making general rather than historically rooted, culturally contextualized statements about them. Her concerns with subjectivity do not seem to be grounded in a closely elaborated conception of the history of modern, Western, or North American culture. She argues in *The Power of Feelings* for the general idea that meaning is created in the intertwining of a particular, historical psyche and a particular, historical culture; her theoretical imagination, however, is more interested to tease out the complexities of the former than of the latter.

A second set of critical concerns, also issuing from a variety of theoretical perspectives, revolves around Chodorow's interpretations of the psyche. Clinical psychoanalysts have criticized Chodorow for neglecting the role of drives and the body (e.g. Person, 1995). In recent writings she has modified her position and begun to integrate drives and the centrality of body into her object-relations perspective, a change she attributes to her experience as a clinical psychoanalyst (Chodorow, 1999a). Lacanian and post-structuralist critics have typically criticized Chodorow and object-relations theory generally for believing that there exists such a thing as a centred, integrated self-constructed by and through gender identification (Butler, 1990; Rose, 1982; Seidman, 1994). Chodorow, in turn, has denied the charge, tending to see such claims as philosophically advanced but clinically naive about the fundamental need for self-identity in nonpsychotic human functioning (Chodorow, 1999b). More specifically, critics have challenged particular moments in her account of gendering, with some questioning the assumptions about maternal agency in her analysis (which, to recall, puts emphasis on narcissistic identification with daughters and anaclitic relations to sons) (Elliot, 1991; Golden, 1992; Sprengnether, 1990), and with others wishing for a more elaborated account of the role of the father in gendering and development (Moi, 1989; Young, 1989).

A third set of concerns, overlapping with and building on the first two, involve the perceived political implications and connotations of Chodorow's scholarship. Though Chodorow's work is primarily explanatory and descriptive rather than normative and prescriptive in orientation, controversy has surrounded what her critics argue are the normative and political implications of Chodorow's analyses. First, a number of critics, often writing from post-structuralist and Lacanian perspectives, have taken Chodorow's work to serve in the name of a conservative politics of identity (Elliot, 1991; Fraser and Nicholson, 1990; Moi, 1989). Chodorow's account of differential gender personality, in this view, effectively serves to reproduce some of the gender stereotypes against which she writes. In depicting femininity as characteristically relational, empathetic and caring, these critics contend, Chodorow normalizes a representation of the feminine that is itself a social and political construction, embodying the values of the (disappearing) white, two-parent, middle-class, postwar American nuclear family. In this view, Chodorow's work has the political effect of pathologizing practices and representations of womanhood that depart from the norms of femininity reified by her scholarship. It is partly in response to these criticisms that Chodorow has sought in her more recent work to explore, and in the process normalize, alternative conceptions of gender and sexuality (Chodorow, 1994).

Second, a number of critics have found inadequate what one might label Chodorow's politics of transformation, seeing in it a failure to take account of the panoply of social determinants, material and symbolic, shaping gender identity and personality (Elliott, 1994; Gottlieb, 1984; Lorber et al., 1981). In *The Reproduction of Mothering*, Chodorow pinned her hopes on transformation through changes in the family structure – specifically, through practices of shared parenting. Criticized for a rather limited politics that remained within the confines of family structure, Chodorow has preferred not to advance a broader political position. In the preface to the recently published second edition of *The Reproduction of Mothering*, her critics will find reason to complain that she further dilutes an already minimalist feminist politics, for Chodorow backs away even from her earlier advocacy of shared parenting, now finding problematic any attempt to prescribe on the basis of a larger moral or political view. In Chodorow's latest view, if you take seriously 'psychological subjectivity from within – feelings, fantasy, psychical meaning – [as] central to a meaningful life, then you cannot also legislate subjectivity from without, or advocate a solution based on a theory of political equality and a conception of women's and children's best interests that ignores this very subjectivity' (1999a: xv).

The diversity and disparity of these criticisms point not just to gaps and weaknesses in Chodorow's work but perhaps also to a quality of her thought that makes it susceptible to misinterpretation: its multidimensionality and complexity. Indeed, as a social thinker Chodorow stands out not so much for the originality of her contribution, though her work has been both original and pathbreaking, but for the ingenious and penetrating ways in which she synthesizes a wide range of perspectives and insights. Her scholarship connects ideas derived from a diversity of traditions within feminism, psychoanalysis, sociology, and anthropology, joining them together in a manner that allows us to view familiar social facts in altogether new and different ways.

CHODOROW'S MAJOR WORKS

Chodorow, N. (1984) 'An exchange: mothering and the reproduction of power', *Socialist Review*, 78: 121–24.

Chodorow, N. (1989) *Feminism and Psychoanalytic Theory.* Cambridge: Polity Press, and New Haven, CT: Yale University Press.

Chodorow, N. (1994) *Femininities, Masculinities, Sexualities: Freud and Beyond*. Lexington: The University Press of Kentucky, and London: Free Association Books.

Chodorow, N. ([1978] 1999a) *The Reproduction of Mothering*, 2nd edition, updated with a new preface. Berkeley: University of California Press.

Chodorow, N. (1999b) *The Power of Feelings: Personal Meaning in Psychoanalysis, Gender, and Culture*. New Haven, CT: Yale University Press.

SECONDARY REFERENCES

Abel, E. (1989) *Virginia Woolf and the Fictions of Psychoanalysis*. Chicago, IL: University of Chicago Press.

Adelman, J.(1992) *Suffocating Mothers*. London and New York: Routledge.

Benjamin, J. (1988) *The Bonds of Love: Psychoanalysis, Feminism, and the Problem of Domination*. New York: Pantheon Books.

Buhle, M.J. (1998) *Feminism and its Discontents: A Century of Struggle with Psychoanalysis*. Cambridge, MA: Harvard University Press.

Butler, J. (1990) 'Gender trouble, feminist theory, and psychoanalytic discourse', in L. Nicholson (ed.), *Feminism/Postmodernism*. New York: Routledge.

Elliot, P. (1991) *From Mastery to Analysis: Theories of Gender in Psychoanalytic Feminism*. Ithaca, NY: Cornell University Press.

Elliott, A. (1994) *Psychoanalytic Theory: An Introduction*. Oxford and Cambridge, MA: Blackwell.

Flax, J. (1990) *Thinking Fragments: Psychoanalysis, Feminism, and Postmodernism in the Contemporary West*. Berkeley: University of California Press.

Fraser, N. and Nicholson, L.J. (1990) 'Social criticism without philosophy', in L. Nicholson (ed.), *Feminism/Postmodernism*. New York: Routledge.

Frosh, S. (1987) *The Politics of Psychoanalysis*. London: Macmillan.

Gilligan, C. ([1982] 1996) *In a Different Voice: Psychological Theory and Women's Development*. Cambridge, MA: Harvard University Press.

Golden, C. (1992) 'Book review of feminism and psychoanalytic theory', *Women and Therapy*, 12 (3): 103–8.

Gottlieb, R. (1984) 'Mothering and the reproduction of power: Chodorow, Dinnerstein, and social theory', *Socialist Review*, 77: 93–119.

Goldner, V. (1991) 'Toward a critical relational theory of gender', *Psychoanalytic Dialogues*, 1: 249–72.

Hartsock, N. (1983) 'The feminist standpoint: developing a grounding for a specifically feminist historical materialism', in S. Harding and M. Hintikka (eds), *Discovering Reality*. Boston: D. Reidel.

Keller, E.F. (1985) *Reflections on Gender and Science*. New Haven, CT: Yale University Press.

Klein, M. (1975a) *Love, Guilt, and Reparation, and Other Works, 1921–1945*. New York: Delta.

Klein, M. (1975b) *Envy and Gratitude and Other Works, 1946–1963*. New York: Delta.

Laslett, B. (1996) 'The gendering of social theory: sociology and its discontents', in *Contemporary Sociology*, 25 (3): 305-9.

Lorber, J., Coser, R. L., Rossi, A. S. and Chodorow, N. (1981) 'On *The Reproduction of Mothering*: a methodological debate', *Signs*, 6 (3): 482–514.

MacCannell, J.F. (1991) 'Mothers of necessity: psychoanalysis for feminism', *American Literary History*, 3(3): 623–46.

Martin, K. (1996) *Puberty, Sexuality and the Self: Boys and Girls at Adolescence*. New York: Routledge.

Meyers, D. T. (ed.) (1997) *Feminist Social Thought: A Reader*. New York and London: Routledge.

Mitchell, S. and Black, M. (1995) *Freud and Beyond: A History of Modern Psychoanalytic Thought*. New York: Basic Books.

Moi, T. (1989) 'Patriarchal thought and the drive for knowledge', in T. Brennan (ed.), *Between Feminism and Psychoanalysis*. London: Routledge.

Person, E.S. (1995) 'Book review of *Feminities, Masculinities, Sexualities: Freud and Beyond* by N. Chodorow, *International Journal of Psychoanalysis*, 76: 1276–9.

Pierce, J. (1995) *Gender Trials: Emotional Lives in Contemporary Law Firms*. Berkeley: University of California Press.

Pitkin, H. (1984) *Fortune is a Woman: Gender and Politics in the Thought of Niccolò Machiavelli*. Berkeley: University of California Press.

Rose, J. (1982) 'Introduction', in J. Mitchell and J. Rose (eds), *Feminine Sexuality: Jacques Lacan and the Ecole Freudienne*. London: MacMillan.

Rose, J. (1986) *Sexuality in the Field of Vision*. London: Verso.

Seidman, S. (1994) *Contested Knowledge: Social Theory in the Postmodern Era*. Oxford and Cambridge, MA: Blackwell.

Slater, P. ([1968] 1992) *Glory of Hera*. Princeton, NJ: Princeton University Press.

Sprengnether, M. (1990) *The Spectral Mother*. Ithaca, NY: Cornell University Press.

Thorne, B. (1996) 'Brandeis as a generative institution: critical perspectives, marginality and feminism', *Theory and Society*, 25, special issue on *Gender, Agency, and the Development of Feminist Sociology*.

Williams, C. (1989) *Gender Differences at Work*. Berkeley: University of California Press.

Winnicott, D.W. (1965) *The Maturational Processes and the Facilitating Environment*. New York: International Universities Press.

Winnicott, D.W. ([1971] 1993) *Playing and Reality*. New York: Routledge.

Young, I.M. (1989) 'Is male gender identity the cause of male domination?' in J. Treibilcot (ed.), *Mothering*. New Jersey: Rowman and Allanheld.

26

Anthony Giddens

ANTHONY ELLIOTT

BIOGRAPHICAL DETAILS AND THEORETICAL CONTEXT

Anthony Giddens stands out as one of the most significant British social theorists of the postwar era. His writings on the classical sociological tradition, as well as his interpretations of contemporary social theory, have had a profound impact on conceptual debates in the social sciences over recent decades. Especially in social and political theory, Giddens has expanded the terrain of debate by interpreting, deconstructing, and reconstructing such traditions as structural-functionalism, interpretative sociology, critical theory, ethnomethodology, systems theory, psychoanalysis, structuralism, and post-structuralism. However, the contribution of Giddens to social theory rests on more than his capabilities as a first-rate hermeneuticist. For, above all, he is a 'grand theorist', a sociologist whose contributions rank in importance alongside the writings of theorists including Parsons, Habermas, and Foucault. Giddens's structuration theory is a richly textured analysis of the late modern world, with particular emphasis upon processes of social reproduction and political transformation. The extensive breadth of Giddens's social theory has been employed to illuminate social, cultural and political research, although the precise relationship between structuration theory and empirical sociological research is contested (see Clark et al., 1990). Certainly Giddens's own research concerns, like his theoretical interests, are very wide-ranging – stretching from his work on modernization and modernity to his analysis of sexuality and intimacy to his more recent work on the development of a 'Third Way' or 'radical centre' as a means of managing global capitalism with greater equity and freedom.

Giddens was born on 18 January 1938 in Edmonton, north London. His father was a clerical worker at London Transport, and his mother a housewife who raised her son in a typically working-class community in the postwar era. Giddens attended a local grammar school; the first in his family to pursue higher education, he subsequently gained admission to the University of Hull, where he studied psychology and sociology. After completing his BA at Hull, he commenced an MA at the London School of Economics. The title of his Master's thesis was 'Sport and Society in Contemporary England'. He was supervised by David Lockwood and Asher Tropp, and an emerging interest in the sociology of sport reflected much about his own background, primarily his long-standing commitment to the Spurs football team. In the thesis Giddens attempted to demonstrate, following the work of Max Weber, that sport had become rationalized and codified, as well as permeated by class divisions. The topic of sport was a very marginal concern in mainstream sociology when Giddens started to write about it, and he subsequently commented that he felt that his supervisors did not take his work at the LSE all that seriously.

After completing his studies at the LSE, Giddens was appointed Lecturer in Sociology at the University of Leicester, where he worked alongside Norbert Elias and Ilya Neustadt. It was at Leicester that Giddens's interest in social theory developed, and the theme of ordinary or practical knowledge – the idea that the world holds subjective meaning for its members, and that such meaning stands in a reflexive relation to the subject matter of sociology, namely human social practices – emerged as one of his central sociological concerns. In 1968 and 1969, he taught at Simon Fraser University in Vancouver and the University of California, Los Angeles. At this time, his principal research concerned the history of sociological thought, primarily the work of Marx, Weber, and Durkheim. Concentrating on the connections and divergences between the founding fathers of the discipline, Giddens started drawing up plans for his first book.

Returning to England, Giddens resigned his position at Leicester in order to take up a post at Cambridge University, where he remained until the mid-1990s. His first book, *Capitalism and Modern Social Theory*, appeared in 1971, and remains to this day one of the most referenced sociological textbooks on Marx, Weber, and Durkheim. In examining the origins of classical sociology, Giddens signalled his emerging ambition to reinterpret the theoretical foundations of the social sciences – a project developed from his Durkheimian-titled *New Rules of Sociological Method* (1976) to *Politics, Sociology and Social Theory* (1995). *Capitalism and Modern Social Theory* established an international reputation for Giddens as one of the foremost interpreters of classical social thought, and it was at Cambridge University that he continued this appropriation of European social theory in order to criticize orthodox American sociology.

Giddens's most ambitious work, *The Constitution of Society* (1984), proposed a vast, dramatic restructuring of the methodological and substantive concerns of social theory in the light of current problems of the social sciences. Regarded as one of the most important books since the grand sociological theorizing of Talcott Parsons, *The Constitution of Society* presented a whole new vocabulary for grasping the age of modernization: 'structuration', 'reflexivity', 'time–space distantiation', 'double hermeneutic', and 'ontological security' – just to name a few terms Giddens introduced. Subsequent to *The Constitution of Society*, Giddens produced an astonishing range of books. His analysis of warfare, its new technologies and globalization, as developed in *The Nation-State and Violence* (1985), has been highly influential in political science and international relations. *The Consequences of Modernity* (1990) was Giddens's response to postmodernism, in which he argued that the West and the developed industrial societies were entering conditions of 'reflexive modernization'. And in *Modernity and Self-Identity* (1991) and *The Transformation of Intimacy* (1992b), he addressed issues of the self, identity, intimacy and sexuality in the context of social transformations sweeping the globe.

In 1996, Giddens left Cambridge University to take up the post of Director of the London School of Economics and Political Science. As Director of the LSE, Giddens has not only been much more directly involved with the shaping of higher education in Britain, but his writings have also become more politically focused. Before taking up the directorship, Giddens had tried, in his book *Beyond Left and Right* (1994), to reconnect sociology to public policy and to outline a radical political agenda beyond orthodox divisions of left and right. He continued this project in his bestseller *The Third Way* (1998). In 1999, Giddens gave the Reith Lectures on globalization and its political consequences, subsequently published as *Runaway World* (1999).

My aim in this profile is to provide a brief overview of Giddens's writings in social and political theory. Given the broad sweep of his interests as well as his exceptional productivity, I have decided to concentrate on specific aspects of Giddens's work, namely structuration theory, modernity and modernization, and his critique of radical politics. After examining Giddens's more substantive contributions to social theory, I shall turn to consider some of the issues raised by his critics.

SOCIAL THEORY AND CONTRIBUTIONS

The Theory of Structuration

In a series of books, principally *New Rules of Sociological Method* (1976), *Central Problems in Social Theory* (1979), and *The Constitution of Society* (1984), Giddens sets out a highly original conceptualization of the relation between action and structure, agent and system, individual and society. The problem of the relation between action and social structure is one that lies at the heart of social theory and the philosophy of social science, and most social theorists have tended to stress one term at the expense of the other. In deterministic approaches, for example, social structure is accorded priority over action, as is evident in varieties of structuralism, post-structuralism, systems theory, and structural sociology. In voluntaristic approaches, by contrast, attention is focused on individuals and the meanings attached to human action, of which the traditions of hermeneutics, phenomenology, and ordinary language philosophy are exemplary. Each of these contrasting approaches has their admirers and critics. However, Giddens argues that it is not possible to resolve the question of how the action of individual agents is related to the structural features of society by merely supplementing or augmenting one approach through reference to the other. In an attempt to move beyond such dualism, Giddens borrowed the term 'structuration' from French. The starting point of his analysis is not society as fixed and given, but rather the active flow of social life. In contrast to approaches that downgrade agency, Giddens argues that people are knowledgeable about the social structures they produce and reproduce in their conduct. Society, he argues, can be understood as a complex of recurrent practices which form institutions. For Giddens, the central task of social theory is to grasp how action is structured in everyday contexts of social practices, while simultaneously recognizing that the structural elements of action are reproduced by the performance of action. Giddens thus proposes that the dualism of agency and structure should instead be understood as complementary terms of a duality, the 'duality of structure'. 'By the duality of structure', writes Giddens, 'I mean that social structures are both constituted by human agency, and yet at the same time are the very medium of this constitution'.

Perhaps the most useful way to gain a purchase on the radical aspects of Giddens's social theory is by contrasting his conception of structure with the mainstream sociological literature. Sociologists have tended to conceptualize structure in terms of institutional constraint, often in a quasi-hydraulical or mechanical fashion, such that structure is likened to the biological workings of the body or the girders of a building. Giddens strongly rejects functionalist, biological, and empiricist analyses of structure. Following the 'linguistic turn' in twentieth century social theory, Giddens critically draws upon structuralist and post-structuralist theory, specifically the relationship posited between language and speech in linguistics. He does this, not because society is structured like a language (as structuralists have argued), but because he believes that language can be taken as exemplifying core aspects of social life. Language, according to Giddens, has a virtual existence; it 'exists' outside of time and space, and is only present in its instantiations as speech or writing. By contrast, speech presupposes a subject and exists in time/space intersections. In Giddens's reading of structural linguistics, the subject draws from the rules of language in order to produce a phrase or sentence, and in so doing contributes to the reproduction of that language as a whole. Giddens draws extensively from such a conception of the structures of language in order to account for structures of action. His theorem is that agents draw from structures in order to perform and carry out social interactions, and in so doing contribute to the reproduction of institutions and structures. This analysis leads to a very specific conception of structure and social systems. 'Structure', writes Giddens (1984: 26), 'has no existence independent of the knowledge that agents have about what they do in their day-to-day activity'.

Giddens's theoretical approach emphasizes that structures should be conceptualized as 'rules and resources': the application of rules which comprise structure may be regarded as generating differential access to social, economic, cultural, and political resources. In *The Constitution of Society* Giddens argues that the sense of 'rule' most relevant to understanding social life is that which pertains to a mathematical formula – for instance, if the sequence is 2,4,6,8, the formula is $x=n+2$. Understanding a formula, says Giddens, enables an agent to carry on in social life in a routine manner, to apply the rule in a range of different contexts. The same is true of bureaucratic rules, traffic rules, rules of football, rules of grammar, rules of social etiquette: to know a rule does not necessarily mean that one is able explicitly to formulate the principle, but it does mean that one can use the rule 'to go on' in social life. 'The rules and resources of social action', writes Giddens, 'are at the same time the means of systems reproduction' (1984: 19). Systems reproduction, as Giddens conceives it, is complex and contradictory, involving structures, systems, and institutions. Social systems, for Giddens, are not equivalent with structures. Social systems are regularized patterns of interaction; such systems are in turn structured by rules and resources. Institutions are understood by Giddens as involving different modalities in and through which structuration occurs. Political institutions, for example, involve the generation of commands over people in relation to issues of authorization, signification, and legitimation; economic institutions, by contrast, involve the allocation of resources through processes of signification and legitimation.

To understand this recursive quality of social life it is necessary also to consider Giddens's discussion of human agency and individual subjectivity. Action, according to Giddens, must be analytically distinguished from the 'acts' of an individual. Whereas acts are discrete segments of individual doing, action refers to the continuous flow of people's social practices. On a general plane, Giddens advances a 'stratification model' of the human subject comprising three levels of knowledge or motivation: discursive consciousness, practical consciousness, and the unconscious. *Discursive consciousness* refers to what agents are able to say, both to themselves and to others, about their own action; as Giddens repeatedly emphasizes, agents are knowledgeable about what they are doing, and this awareness often has a highly discursive component. *Practical consciousness* also refers to what actors know about their own actions, beliefs, and motivations, but it is practical in the sense that it cannot be expressed discursively; what cannot be put into words, Giddens says following Wittgenstein, is what has to be done. Human beings know about their activities and the world in a sense that cannot be readily articulated; such practical stocks of knowledge are central, according to Giddens, to the project of social scientific research. Finally, the *unconscious*, says Giddens, is also a crucial feature of human motivation, and is differentiated from discursive and practical consciousness by the barrier of repression.

While Giddens accords the unconscious a residual role in the reproduction of social life (as something that 'erupts' at moments of stress or crisis), he nonetheless makes considerable use of psychoanalytical theory in order to theorize the routine patterning of social relations. Drawing from Freud, Lacan, and Erikson, Giddens argues that the emotional presence and absence of the primary caretaker (most usually, the mother) provides the foundation for a sense of what he terms 'ontological security', as well as trust in the taken-for-granted, routine nature of social life. Indeed the routine is accorded a central place in Giddens's social theory, both for grasping the production and maintenance of ontological security, and comprehending the modes of socialization by which actors learn the implicit rules of how to go on in social life. To do this, Giddens draws from a vast array of sociological micro-theorists, including Goffman and Garfinkel. His debt to ethnomethodology and phenomenology is reflected in much of the language of structuration theory, as is evident from his references to 'skilled performances', 'copresence', 'seriality', 'contextuality', 'knowledgeability', and 'mutual knowledge'.

In the last few paragraphs I have noted how Giddens approaches issues of human action, agency, and subjectivity. It is important to link these more subjective aspects of his social theory back to issues of social practices and structures in order to grasp his emphasis upon duality in structuration theory. Agents, according to Giddens, draw on the rules and resources of structures, and in so doing contribute to the systemic reproduction of institutions, systems, and structures. In studying social life, says Giddens, it is important to recognize the role of 'methodological bracketing'. Giddens argues that the social sciences simultaneously pursue *institutional analysis*, in which the structural features of society are analysed, and the *analysis of strategic conduct*, in which the manner in which actors carry on social interaction is studied. These different levels of analysis are central to social scientific research, and both are crucial to structuration theory. Connected to this, Giddens argues that the subjects of study of the social sciences are concept-using agents, individuals whose concepts enter into the manner in which their actions are constituted. He calls this intersection of the social world as constituted by lay actors on the one hand, and the metalanguages created by social scientists on the other, the 'double hermeneutic'.

Modernity and the Late Modern Age

In *The Consequences of Modernity* (1990) and *Modernity and Self-Identity* (1991), Giddens develops a comprehensive analysis of the complex relation between self and society in the late modern age. Rejecting Marx's equation of modernity with capitalism, and wary of Weber's portrait of the iron cage of bureaucracy, Giddens instead presents an image of modernity as a juggernaut. As with structuration theory, Giddens's approach to modernity involves considerable terminological innovation: 'embedding and disembedding mechanisms', 'symbolic tokens', 'expert systems', 'the dialectic of trust and risk', and, crucially, 'reflexivity'. Reflexivity, according to Giddens, should be conceived as a continuous flow of individual and collective 'self-monitoring'. 'The reflexivity of modern social life', writes Giddens, 'consists in the fact that social practices are constantly examined and reformed in the light of incoming information about those very practices, thus constitutively altering their character' (1990: 38). Elsewhere Giddens (1991: 28) writes: 'To live in the "world" produced by high modernity has the feeling of riding a juggernaut. It is not just that more or less continuous and profound processes of change occur; rather, change does not consistently conform either to human expectation or to human control'.

The experiential character of contemporary daily life is well grasped by two of Giddens's key concepts: *trust* and *risk* as interwoven with *abstract systems*. For Giddens, the relation between individual subjectivity and social contexts of action is a highly mobile one; and it is something that we make sense of and utilize through 'abstract systems'. Abstract systems are institutional domains of technical and social knowledge: they include systems of expertise of all kinds, from local forms of knowledge to science, technology, and mass communications. Giddens is underscoring much more than simply the impact of expertise on people's lives, far-reaching though that is. Rather, Giddens extends the notion of expertise to cover 'trust relations' – the personal and collective investment of active trust in social life. The psychological investment of trust contributes to the power of specialized, expert knowledge – indeed it lies at the bedrock of our Age of Experts – and also plays a key role in the forging of a sense of security in day-to-day social life.

Trust and security are thus both a condition and outcome of social reflexivity. Giddens sees the reflexive appropriation of expert knowledge as fundamental in a globalizing, culturally cosmopolitan society. While a key aim may be the regularization of stability and order in our identities and in society, reflexive modernity is radically experimental however, and is constantly producing new types of incalculable risk and insecurity. This means that, whether we like it or not, we must recognize the ambivalence of a social universe of expanded reflexivity: there are no clear paths of individual or social development in the late modern age. On the contrary, human attempts at control of the social world are undertaken against a reflexive backdrop of a variety of other ways of doing things. Giddens offers the following overview, for example, in relation to global warming:

> Many experts consider that global warming is occurring and they may be right. The hypothesis is disputed by some, however, and it has even been suggested that the real trend, if there is one at all, is in the opposite direction, towards the cooling of the global climate. Probably the most that can be said with some surety is that we cannot be certain that global warming is *not* occurring. Yet such a conditional conclusion will yield not a precise calculation of risks but rather an array of 'scenarios' – whose plausibility will be influenced, among other things, by how many people become convinced of the thesis of global warming and take action on that basis. In the social world, where institutional reflexivity has become a central constituent, the complexity of 'scenarios' is even more marked. (Giddens, 1994: 59)

The complexity of 'scenarios' is thus central to our engagement with the wider social world. Reflexivity, according to Giddens, influences the way in which these scenarios are constructed, perceived, coped with, and reacted to.

In *The Transformation of Intimacy* (1992b), Giddens connects the notion of reflexivity to sexuality, gender, and intimate relationships. With modernization and the decline of tradition, says Giddens, the sexual life of the human subject becomes a 'project' that has to be managed and defined against the backdrop of new opportunities and risks – including, for example, artificial insemination, experiments in ectogenesis (the creation of human life without pregnancy), AIDS, sexual harassment, and the like. Linking gender to new technologies, Giddens argues we live in an era of 'plastic sexuality'. 'Plastic sexuality' (1992b: 2), writes Giddens, 'is decentred sexuality, freed from the needs of reproduction ... and from the rule of the phallus, from the overweening importance of male sexual experience'. Sexuality thus becomes open-ended, elaborated not through pregiven roles, but through reflexively forged relationships. The self today, as the rise of therapy testifies, is faced with profound dilemmas in respect of sexuality: Who am I?, What do I desire?, What satisfactions do I want from sexual relations? – these are core issues for the self according to Giddens. This does not mean that sexual experience occurs without institutional constraint, however. Giddens contends that the development of modern institutions produce a 'sequestration of experience' – sexual, existential, and moral – which squeeze to the sidelines core problems relating to sexuality, intimacy, mortality and death (see Elliott, 1992).

The Third Way

In *Beyond Left and Right: The Future of Radical Politics* (1994), Giddens asserts that we live today in a radically damaged world, for which radical political remedies are required beyond the neoliberalism offered by the right or reformist socialism offered by the left. To this end, Giddens provides a detailed framework for the rethinking of radical politics. This framework touches on issues of tradition and social solidarity, of social movements, of the restructuring of democratic processes and the welfare state, and of the location of violence in world politics. Giddens's interpretation of the rise of radical politics can perhaps best be grasped by contrasting dominant discussions in the fields of critical theory and postmodernism. Theorists of the self-endangerment of modern politics, from Daniel Bell to Jürgen Habermas, characteristically focus upon the loss of community produced by the invasion of personal and cultural life by the global capitalist system. Postmodernist social and political theorists, from Michel Foucault to Jean-François Lyotard, alternatively focus on the contemporary plurality of knowledge claims, and conclude that there are no ordered paths to political development. Giddens's approach, by contrast, takes a radically different tack. He develops neither a lament nor celebration of the ambivalences of contemporary political processes. Instead, Giddens asks: What happens when politics begins to reflect on itself? What happens when political activity, understanding its own successes and excesses, begins to reflect on its own institutional conditions?

At issue, says Giddens, are reflexivity and risk, both of which he isolates as central to transformations in society, culture, and politics. By reflexivity, as noted, Giddens refers to that circularity of knowledge and information promoted by mass communications in a globalizing, cosmopolitan world. Reflexivity functions as a means of regularly reordering and redefining what political activity is. Of central importance in this respect is the impact of globalization. Globalizing processes, says Giddens, radically intensify our personal and social awareness of risk, transforming local contexts into global consequences. Thus the panic selling of shares on the Dow Jones has implications for the entire global economy, from local retail trade to the international division of labour. At the beginning of the twenty-first century, a world of intensified reflexivity is a world of people reflecting upon the political consequences of human action, from the desolation of the rain forests to the widespread manufacture of weapons of mass destruction. In such social conditions, politics becomes radically experimental in character. People are increasingly aware of new types of incalculable risk and insecurity, and must attempt to navigate the troubled waters of modern political culture. This means that, whether we like it or not, we are all engaged in a kind of continual reinvention of identity and politics, with no clear paths of development from one state of risk to another.

It is against this backdrop of transformations in risk, reflexivity and globalization that Giddens develops a new framework for radical politics. The core dimensions of Giddens's blueprint for the restructuring of radical political thought include the following claims:

1 We live today in a post-traditional social order. This does not mean, as many cultural critics and post-modernists claim, that tradition disappears. On the contrary, in a globalizing, culturally cosmopolitan society, traditions are forced into the open for public discussion and debate. Reasons or explanations are increasingly required for the preservation of tradition, and this should be understood as one of the key elements in the reinvention of social solidarity. The new social movements, such as those concerned with ecology, peace, or human rights, are examples of groups refashioning tradition (the call to conserve and protect 'nature') in the building of social solidarities. The opposite of this can be seen, says Giddens, in the rise of fundamentalism, which forecloses questions of public debate and is 'nothing other than tradition defended in the traditional way'.

2 Radical forms of democratization, fuelled by reflexivity, are at work in politics, from the interpersonal to the global levels. But the issue of democratization cannot be confined only to the formal political sphere, since these processes also expose the limits of liberal political democracy itself. As the American sociologist Daniel Bell put this some years ago, the nation-state has become too small to tackle global problems and too large to handle local ones. Instead, Giddens speaks of a 'democratizing of democracy', by which he means that all areas of personal and political life are increasingly ordered through dialogue rather than pre-established power relations. The mechanisms of such dialogic democracy are already set in process, from the transformation of gender and parent–child relations through to the development of social movements and self-help groups. The rise of psychotherapy and psychoanalysis is also cast in a favourable political light by Giddens. Democratizing influences such as these also influence the more traditional sphere of institutional politics as well.

3 The welfare state requires further radical forms of restructuring, and this needs to be done in relation to wider issues of global poverty. Here Giddens urges the reconstruction of welfare away from the traditional 'top down dispensation of benefits' in favour of what he terms 'positive welfare'. Welfare that is positive is primarily concerned with promoting autonomy in relation to personal and collective responsibilities, and focuses centrally on gender imbalances as much as class deprivations.

4 The prospects for global justice begin to emerge in relation to a 'post-scarcity order'. This is a complex idea, but it is central to Giddens's political theory. Giddens is not suggesting that politics has entered an age in which scarcity has been eliminated. On the contrary, he argues that there will always be scarcities of goods and resources. Rather, a post-scarcity society is a society in which 'scarcity' itself comes under close reflexive scrutiny. Coping with the negative consequences of industrialism, says Giddens, has led to a radical reappraisal of the capitalistic drive for continuous accumulation. This broadening of political goals beyond the narrowly economic is reflected today in the pursuit of 'responsible growth'. Several key social transformations are central here. The entry of women into the paid labour force, the restructuring of gender and intimacy, the rise of individualization as opposed to egoism, and the ecological crisis: these developments have all contributed to a shift away from secularized Puritanism towards social solidarity and obligation.

APPRAISAL OF KEY ADVANCES AND CONTROVERSIES

Having briefly discussed Giddens's principal contributions to social theory, I can now note some of the major criticisms of his work. For some critics, Giddens's social-theoretical project is cast so wide that his books can be viewed as a kind of theoretical supermarket, in which a variety of unusual commodities (Merleau-Ponty, Gadamer, Hagerstrand, Garfinkel) are stocked beside better known brand names (Marx, Freud, Weber, Durkheim). Some commentators see Giddens's theoretical eclecticism as unhelpful, while others criticize his appropriation of particular traditions of thought. Roy Boyne (1991), for instance, sharply criticizes Giddens's appropriation of structuralist and post-structuralist theory, claiming that he 'systematically misrepresents' French social theory. In what follows, I shall leave to one side this type of criticism, since I think that hermeneutic issues about Giddens's interpretation of theorists like Foucault, Lacan, and Derrida are largely beside the point. The more interesting questions about Giddens's work are those that concentrate on his project of formulating a general social theory; and what perhaps is especially interesting is that – notwithstanding Giddens's claim to have inaugurated a 'duality' for the subject/object binary – most critiques of his work tend to concentrate on either the subjective or social-institutional shortcomings of his analysis.

In several celebrated critiques, Margaret Archer (1982, 1990) argues not only that it is undesirable to amalgamate agency with structure, but that it is necessary to treat structure and agency as analytically distinct in order to deal with core methodological and substantive problems in the social sciences. At the core of Archer's critique of Giddens is an anxiety about his claim that structures have no existence independent of the knowledge that human subjects have about what they do in their daily lives. She argues that Giddens's structuration theory fails to accord sufficient ontological status to the pre-existence of social forms, specifically the impact of social distributions of populations upon human action. Archer juxtaposes to Giddens a morphogenetic theory which focuses on the dialectical interplay between agency and the emergent properties of social systems. Similarly Nicos Mouzelis (1989) argues that, while the notion of structuration is appropriate to routine social practices where agents carry out their actions without undue levels of reflection, there are other forms of social life which require that structure and agency be kept apart. Theoretical reflection upon the social world, for example, involves dualism in Mouzelis's eyes since there is a shift from the individual to the collective level, and this necessarily depends upon a distancing of our immediate, everyday lives from broader social structures.

In an especially sharp critique of Giddens's structuration theory, John B. Thompson (1989) questions the analytical value of (a) the notion of rules and resources for grasping social structure, and (b) conceiving of structural constraint as modelled upon certain linguistic and grammatical forms. According to Thompson, Giddens's account of rules and resources is vague and misleading. Linguistic and grammatical rules, says Thompson, are important forms of constraint upon human action; however, they are not the only forms of constraint in social life, and indeed when considering social constraint the core issue is to understand how an agent's range of alternatives is limited. Thompson acknowledges that Giddens goes some distance in accounting for this by distinguishing between structure, system, and institutions. But again he questions Giddens's account of the transformational properties of structures, and suggests there is confusion here between structural and institutional constraint. A worker at the Ford Motor Company, notes Thompson, can be said to contribute to the reproduction of the institution, and thus also said to contribute to the reproduction of capitalism as a structure, to the extent that the worker pursues their everyday employment activities. However it is also possible that the worker might undertake activities that threaten or transform the institution, but without similarly transforming their structural conditions. 'Every act of production and reproduction', writes Thompson (1989: 70), 'may also be a potential act of transformation, as Giddens rightly insists; but the extent to which an action transforms an institution does not coincide with the extent to which social structure is thereby transformed'.

Other critics have likewise targeted Giddens's conceptualization of subjectivity, agency and the agent. Bryan S. Turner, for example, finds Giddens's theory of the human agent lacking a sufficient account of embodiment (Turner, 1992). Alan Sica has suggested that, notwithstanding his commitment to macrosocial theory, Giddens's borrowings from Garfinkel, Goffman, Erikson and others indicates an awareness that a theory of the subject and its complex darkness has been central to the project of contemporary social theory. Sica writes:

> Giddens reinvolves himself with 'the subjective' because he knows that a general theory of action will surely fail that does not come to terms with it. But he fondly thinks, it seems, that by inventing a new vocabulary, by bringing in the ubiquitous 'duality of structure' or 'reflexive rationalization of conduct', he can make good his escape from both the calcified Marxism with-out a subject (Althusser) or sloppy-hearted Parsonism, which is all norms, values and wishes. (Sica, 1989: 48)

Sica, in short, questions Giddens's emphasis upon the taken-for-granted rules of daily actions as a basis for explicating subjectivity, suggesting that in the process he downgrades not only the subterranean, unconscious forces of the subject but also the discomfort between self and society.

Extending these points, Ian Craib (1992: 171) argues that Giddens's model of the subject is experientially and psychodynamically reductive, the core of which he attributes to Giddens's 'misuse or misinterpretation of psychoanalysis'. Craib notes that Giddens limits the reach of Freud in an attempt to bring conceptual clarity to his dialectical model of consciousness, preconsciousness, and the unconscious; Giddens argues, for instance, that regressive psychic functioning is generally initiated only in moments of societal stress. The result is that Giddens's conception of the person lacks complexity of desires, contradictions of experience, and a sense of internal division. This argument is interesting, but it carries wider implications than Craib perhaps realizes. The issue is not how well or badly Giddens reads Freud; my point is that Giddens's circumscription of the functioning of the unconscious carries substantive implications for his theorem of the duality of structure. Giddens adopts the novel view that structural rules and resources have no existence independent of the memory traces of subjects. If this argument is to be sustained, what is required is a much more detailed account of the unconscious representations and affects that underpin and condition practical and discursive consciousness as these relate to, and draw from, structure (see Elliott, 1994, 1996).

Giddens has sought to defend his writings from his critics in various places (see Giddens in Held and Thompson, 1989, in Clark et al., 1990, and in Bryant and Jary, 1991). Giddens's confidence in his theoretical project, and the tone of his authorial voice, is such that he rarely concedes many points to his critics. However, what his more recent writings make clear is that structuration theory has much broader scope – ranging from issues of intimacy to politics, sexuality to public policy – than many working in the social sciences previously realized. Giddens's work has undoubtedly provided a comprehensive social theory for the analysis of social reproduction and political domination, a powerful interpretation of the complex ways in which action and structure intersect, and a vision of modernity and modernization that is richer and more detailed than other versions of critical social theory, especially versions of postmodernist theory.

GIDDENS'S MAJOR WORKS

Giddens, A. (1971) *Capitalism and Modern Social Theory.* Cambridge and New York: Cambridge University Press.

Giddens, A. (1972a) *Politics and Sociology in the Thought of Max Weber.* London, Macmillan and New York: Pall Mall.

Giddens, A. (ed.) (1972b) *Emile Durkheim: Selected Writings.* Cambridge and New York: Cambridge University Press.

Giddens, A. (1973a) *The Class Structure of the Advanced Societies.* London: Hutchinson University Library and New York: Harper & Row.

Giddens, A. (ed.) (1973b) *Positivism and Sociology.* London: Heinemann and New York: Basic Books.

Giddens, A. (1976) *New Rules of Sociological Method.* London: Hutchinson and New York: Basic Books.

Giddens, A. (1977) *Studies in Social and Political Theory.* London: Hutchinson and New York: Basic Books.

Giddens, A. (1978) *Emile Durkheim.* London: Fontana and New York: Penguin.

Giddens, A. (1979) *Central Problems in Social Theory.* London: Macmillan and Berkeley: University of California Press.

Giddens, A. (1981) *A Contemporary Critique of Historical Materialism.* London: Macmillan and Berkeley: University of California Press.

Giddens, A. (1982) *Sociology: A Brief but Critical Introduction.* London: Macmillan and New York: Harcourt, Brace, Jovanowitch.

Giddens, A. (1983) *Profiles and Critiques in Social Theory.* London: Macmillan and Berkeley: University of California Press.

Giddens, A. (1984) *The Constitution of Society. Outline of the Theory of Structuration.* Cambridge: Polity Press and Berkeley: University of California Press.

Giddens, A. (1985) *The Nation-State and Violence.* Cambridge: Polity Press and Berkeley: University of California Press.

Giddens, A. (1986) *Durkheim on Politics and the State.* Cambridge: Polity Press and Palo Alto, CA: Stanford University Press.

Giddens, A. (1987) *Social Theory and Modern Sociology.* Cambridge: Polity Press and Palo Alto, CA: Stanford University Press.

Giddens, A. (1988) *Sociology.* Cambridge: Polity Press and New York: Norton.

Giddens, A. (1990) *The Consequences of Modernity.* Cambridge: Polity Press and Palo Alto, CA: Stanford University Press.

Giddens, A. (1991) *Modernity and Self-Identity.* Cambridge: Polity Press and Palo Alto, CA: Stanford University Press.

Giddens, A. (1992a) *Human Societies.* Cambridge: Polity Press.

Giddens, A. (1992b) *The Transformation of Intimacy.* Cambridge: Polity Press and Palo Alto, CA: Stanford University Press.

Giddens, A. (1994) *Beyond Left and Right.* Cambridge: Polity Press and Palo Alto, CA: Stanford University Press.

Giddens, A. (1995) *Politics, Sociology and Social Theory.* Cambridge: Polity Press and Palo Alto, CA: Stanford University Press.

Giddens, A. (1996) *In Defence of Sociology.* Cambridge: Polity Press and Palo Alto, CA: Stanford University Press.

Giddens, A. (1998) *The Third Way.* Cambridge: Polity Press.

Giddens, A. (1999) *Runaway World: How Globalization is Reshaping our Lives.* London: Profile Books.

Giddens, A., Beck, U. and Lash, S. (1994) *Reflexive Modernisation.* Cambridge: Polity Press and Palo Alto, CA: Stanford University Press.

Giddens, A. and Held, D. (1982) *Classes, Conflict and Power.* London: Macmillan and Berkeley: University of California Press.

Giddens, A. and Mackenzie, G. (1982) *Classes and the Division of Labour.* Cambridge and New York: Cambridge University Press.

Giddens, A. and Stanworth, P.H. (1974) *Elites and Power In British Society.* Cambridge and New York: Cambridge University Press.

Giddens, A. and Pierson, C. (1998) *Conversations with Anthony Giddens.* Cambridge: Polity Press.

Giddens, A. and Turner, J. (1988) *Social Theory Today.* Cambridge: Polity Press and Palo Alto, CA: Stanford University Press.

SECONDARY REFERENCES

Archer, M. (1982) 'Morphogenesis vs. structuration', *British Journal of Sociology,* 33: 455–83.

Archer, M. (1990) 'Human agency and social structure', in J. Clark, C. Modgil, and S. Modgil (eds) *Anthony Giddens.* New York: Falmer Press.

Boyne, R. (1991) 'Giddens' misreading of French sociology' in C.G.A. Bryant and D. Jary (eds) *Giddens' Theory of Structuration.* London: Routledge.

Bryant, C.G.A. and Jary, D. (1991) *Giddens' Theory of Structuration.* London: Routledge.

Bryant, C.G.A. and Jary, D. (1997) *Anthony Giddens: Critical Assessments.* London: Routledge.

Cohen, I. (1991) *Structuration Theory: Anthony Giddens and the Constitution of Social Life.* London: Macmillan.

Clark, J., Modgil, C. and Modgil, S. (1990) *Anthony Giddens: Consensus and Controversy.* New York: Falmer Press.

Craib, I. (1992) *Anthony Giddens.* London: Routledge.

Elliott, A. (1992) 'Looking at sex and love in the modern age', *The Times Higher Education Supplement,* September 11: 18–9.

Elliott, A. (1994) *Psychoanalytic Theory: An Introduction.* Oxford: Blackwell.

Elliott, A. (1996) *Subject To Ourselves*. Cambridge: Polity Press.

Held, D. and Thompson, J.B. (1989) *Social Theory of Modern Societies: Giddens and his Critics*. Cambridge: Cambridge University Press.

Mestrovic, S. (1998) *Anthony Giddens: The Last Modernist*. London: Routledge.

O'Brien, M. and Penna, S. (1998) *Theorising Modernity: Reflexivity, Environment and Identity in Giddens's Social Theory*. Longman and New York: Longman.

Thompson, J.B. (1989) 'The theory of structuration', in D. Held, and J.B. Thompson (eds) *Social Theory of Modern Societies*. Cambridge: Cambridge University Press.

Tucker, K. (1998) *Anthony Giddens and Modern Social Theory*. London: Sage.

Turner, B.S. (1992) *Regulating Bodies*. London: Routledge

27

Ulrich Beck

NICK STEVENSON

> The same loneliness that closes us opens us again.
>
> (Anne Michaels)

BIOGRAPHICAL DETAILS AND THEORETICAL CONTEXT

Ulrich Beck was born in Pomern (which was to become a part of the German Republic in 1944) although he grew up in Hanover in what was then West Germany. He began his academic career in Munich, eventually becoming a sociology professor in the mid-1980s in the small provincial town of Bamberg. Beck is currently Professor of Sociology at the University of Munich and the *British Journal of Sociology* Professor at the London School of Economics and Political Science. Previously, Beck served on the Future Commission for the German Government (1995–7), received an honorary degree in social science from Jyvaskyla University, and was Distinguished Research Professor at the University of Cardiff (1995–8). He is also a fellow of several scientific institutions, including the Institute for Advanced Study in Berlin (1990–1).

The growing literature on notions of risk and society within the sociological canon is largely due to the profound influence of Ulrich Beck. The publication in the former West Germany of his book *Risk Society; Towards a New Modernity* in 1986 quickly became a best-selling work. Its appearance in the wake of the nuclear accident at Chernobyl brought Beck to national, and now to international, prominence amongst sociologists as well as political activists and lay communities. This all too rare event in social theory gives us an initial clue as to Beck's particular genius. What Beck did that was so exciting was to take a seeming disconnected set of social phenomena including the ecological crisis, AIDs, feminism, the development of the media of mass communication, consumerism, the ethic of self-development and the decline of overt forms of class antagonism in the context of welfare democracies and bring them under the umbrella of the 'risk society'. In the space between varieties of Marxism that predicted new phases of unbridled exploitation, the rebirth of liberalism promised by the 'end of history' thesis and postmodernism's concentration on the fragmentation of the subject came a fresh new voice. More recently, with the end of the Cold War and the demise of state socialism, Beck's call to rethink established social and political categories has found a wide audience. Beck provides a comprehensive assault on many of the existing paradigms within social theory, while pointing to a number of neglected connections and concerns, the most prominent of these being the reconnection of society and nature ushered in by the ecological crisis of industrial modernity.

While Beck has constantly revised his notion of a risk society it has not changed greatly since its initial appearance. Why then does Beck think that notions of risk are so important in the modern age? Beck makes an initial distinction between ideas of risk assessment that came along with modernity and preindustrial notions of fate. Risks that are defined as fate place them beyond human control. The plagues, famines, and natural disasters that characterized the preindustrial world were under this rubric to be endured by humanity. Conversely, along with industrial society, come notions of risk in that they were explicitly based upon calculable decisions made within the context of a technological civilization. This set up a calculus of risks involving legal definitions, insurance companies, and protection against the hazards of the industrial society. The welfare state was a way of insuring against the risks of industrialism associated with illness, old age, and unemployment. However, since the middle of the twentieth century, industrial society has been confronted with questions of uninsurable risk. The potential destruction of the planet in a nuclear and chemical age has meant that humans are now living with risks they can not be insured against. Who is to say how safe our food is after BSE? How do we know there will not be another Chernobyl? What are the long-term consequences of global warming? Can we be sure that networked capitalism will not lead to global financial collapse? These features, Beck argues, can not, as they have been traditionally, be perceived as minority interests for social theory, but have come resolutely centre stage.

SOCIAL THEORY AND CONTRIBUTIONS

Ulrich Beck (1992, 1995) has most forcefully brought notions of risk to bear through a discussion of the hazards that have become associated with the development of industrial society. Beck argues that the development of scientific rationality and economic progress have produced a range of ecological risks from the pollution of the seas to the poisoning of the population. These risks can no longer be dismissed as the side effects of industrialism. Instead they have become central to the definition of society at the end of the twentieth century. The risk society evolves through two phases: the first is where the evident dangers of self-destruction are dealt with through the legal and political institutions of industrial society. These might include reliance upon scientific experts, the belief that new laws and political policies can effectively deal with pollution, and the idea that ecological questions are secondary to notions of economic distribution. In the contemporary risk society none of these features and claims can be sustained. The emergence of a post-traditional society has seen the axis of the family, gender, occupation, and belief in science and economic progress become radically undermined. The 'second modernity' therefore involves an increasingly reflexive questioning of areas of social experience that the enlightenment failed to problematize. We become ever aware of the fallibility of expert opinion, the 'invisible' destruction of nature and the incalculability of environmental hazards.

Beck brings these questions together through what he calls 'reflexive' modernization, which he contrasts with the idea that modernity has become more reflective. Simple reflection theory holds that the modernization of society leads to the increasing capacity of subjects to ask questions about the society they are living within. Such optimism can be traced back to the enlightenment (more science, public-sphere and experts equals more self-criticism), and contrasted with the pessimist's view that such developments only result in more domination and control. Instead, 'reflexive' modernization can lead to reflection on the forces that are threatening to plunge modernity into self-dissolution, but this is not necessarily the case. Hence Beck is clear that this is not a theory of progress or decline, but one that takes up the ambivalence of modernity by focusing upon 'deep-seated institutional crises in late industrial society' (Beck, 1994: 178). Reflexive modernization is about unintended self-confrontation rather than reflection. What makes Beck's claims so novel within traditions of sociological and cultural theory is that the unintended consequences and side-effects of industrialism rather than the class struggle or instrumental reason is the motor of history.

Living in the contemporary world means learning to live with the possibility of large-scale hazards that throw into question attempts at bureaucratic normalization, the imperatives of the economic system, and the assurances of scientific experts. Not only are we learning to live in a post-traditional society, but one which is haunted by the possibility of large-scale hazards like Chernobyl. We are, despite the end of the Cold War, currently living within the shadow of our own annihilation. No one really knows what the long-term consequences of the ecological destruction of nature will be and what level of risk in connection with the environment is sustainable. Politics and economics in such a society can no longer be conceptualized as a struggle over resources, and environmental degradation is not easily dismissed as a partial side-effect. The international production of harmful substances, the pollution of the seas, and the dangers of nuclear power all call into question the mechanisms of national governance and our relations of trust with societies' central institutions.

In Beck's terms, then, what are the consequences of these arguments for questions of ecological politics and citizenship? First, the risks produced by industrial society are global rather than national in character. That is, they point towards a new kind of politics beyond the relatively stable antipathies of the Cold War. This both introduces the possibilities of the emergence of 'mobile enemies' and of new forms of consensus where states have no permanent enemies or 'others' (Beck, 1998). Secondly, principles like 'the polluter pays' or 'individual culpability' actually allow pollution levels to rise. This is because it is often difficult to attribute pollution to any one source, as such a causal relation may evade scientific demonstration and there is often a struggle over who is actually to blame. The consequence of 'definition struggles' which seek a primary 'cause' often end up hiding the pervasive ways in which modern society has become a scientific laboratory. Beck writes on the escalating risks of the modern era:

> The more pollutants are put in circulation, the more acceptable levels related to individual substances are set, the more liberally this occurs, the more insane the entire hocus-pocus becomes, because the overall toxic threat to the population grows – presuming the simple equation that the total volume of various toxic substances means a higher degree of overall toxicity. (Beck, 1992: 66)

The risk society is predicated on the ambivalence that science has both produced and legitimized these risks, while being the primary force, other than popular protest, through which these dimensions can be made visible. In this respect, the ecological movement can not afford to be antiscientific, but rather has to turn science back upon itself. Scientific rationality and judgment need to be open to the community as a whole as modernity is revealed to be a more uncertain and fragile construction than was previously assumed to be the case. Further, the pervasive power of technical reason has given birth to a new form of politics that Beck (1996) calls 'subpolitics'. The humanity-wide project of saving the environment has actually been brought about through the destruction of nature as well as the accompanying culture of risk and uncertainty that have become wrapped around human conceptions of well being. The politicization of science and technology is rapidly introducing a reflexive culture whereby politics and morality is gaining the upper hand over scientific experts. Thus a shared environment of global risk enables the formation of an ecological politics that seeks to recover democratic exchange. Whereas struggles for citizenship have historically been organized in material settings like the workplace, subpolitics is much more likely to be symbolically shaped through the domains of consumption, television media and the repoliticization of science.

If the ecological movement asks us to attend to the obligations we have to the earth, it also raises the question of the regeneration of public spaces and democratic dialogue. Beck (1995) exhibits an awareness of these dimensions through the possible emergence of an 'authoritarian technocracy'. Here he argues that industrial society (as we have seen) responded to the problem of ecological risk through the formal development of certain laws, belief in 'cleaner' technology, and more informed experts. What is required is a placing of the burden of proof on the agents of money and power that new products and ways of generating electricity are 'nonhazardous'. Democratic dialogue needs to introduce into its repertoires the principles of doubt and uncertainty. Only when we become aware of the limitations and dangers of technological reason and proceed from worst case scenarios can we begin to have an 'informed' debate. The democratic imperative behind such recommendations is that we need to have such a conversation before the introduction of new hazards into the community. As Beck (1995: 179) argues 'caution would be the mother in the kitchen of toxins'. Such a move would break the cycle whereby state bureaucracies seek to legalize and legitimate public risks, circumventing open forms of democratic dialogue.

Beck (1992) then arguably outlines a more ambivalent relation between politics, culture, and questions of social exclusion than is available in an account that simply stresses the ways in which consumer culture undermines our shared capacity to seek just solutions to social problems. For example, Beck is clear that ecological consciousness is most likely to make itself felt within prosperous classes, given their investments in health and lifestyle more generally. Indeed, Beck argues that many ecological risks contain a social *boomerang effect* in that everything that threatens life on earth ultimately threatens to destroy those who profit from the commodification of nature. However, Beck does not seek to deny that risk politics and class politics may indeed overlap, with hazardous industries being transferred to the Third World and the poor being those most likely to be affected by environmental pollution. The logic of risk society is such that it is capable of turning 'capital against capital' and 'workers against workers' as there are no fixed boundaries to 'winners' and 'losers' in the risk society.

Again, however, Beck (1997) has consistently sought to argue that the 'age of side effects' or the 'break up of industrial society' does not necessarily lead in one direction rather than another. Giving up faith in industrial progress does not guarantee that we will ask the 'right' questions and that modernity will not continue to propagate a 'dark side'. Eighteenth and nineteenth century Europe and America saw the development of democracy and universal principles as well as the persistence and development of the oppression of women, nationalism, racism, and other features which culminated in the concentration camps. That is, 'reflexive' modernization may not lead to a reflection upon modernization and its consequences, but onto forms of counter-modernization. Whereas 'reflexive' modernization dissolves the boundaries of class, gender and nation, counter-modernity seeks to renaturalize these questions by recreating boundaries and repressing critical questions. Counter-modernity then represents the partial repression of doubt, ambiguity, and ethical complexity. However, this is not the same thing as tradition, as counter-modernity is a reactive response to the radical questioning of tradition.

These processes are given additional weight through what Beck terms as processes of individualization. By this Beck means that life is increasingly lived as an individual project. The decline of class loyalties and bonds (along with growing income inequalities) means that individuals are increasingly thrown back on their own biographies, with human relations increasingly becoming susceptible to individual choice. For Beck the classic plea of industrial society 'I am hungry', becomes replaced with 'I am afraid'. These developments mean that our cultural perceptions become more attuned to what Milan Kundera called the 'lightness of being', and ethical questions as to how you should live your life. What Beck does not mean is that the self is being increasingly determined by market individualism or by social isolation more generally. Individualization means the disembedding of the ways of industrial society and the reinvention of new communal ties and biographies. As more areas of social life are less defined by tradition the more our biographies require choice and planning. We are then living in the age of DIY biographies. Beck's views contrast with communitarian ideas that suggest that communities need to be remade through the imposition of shared moral rules. That is, it is not the case that individuals are becoming trapped within empty forms of consumer narcissism or a retreat away from politics into the private sphere. Under the conditions of welfare industrialism 'people are invited to constitute themselves as individuals: to plan, understand, design themselves as individuals and, should they fail, to blame themselves' (Beck, 1999: 9). Thus, individuals are 'condemned' to become authors of their own lives. The disintegration of the nuclear family and rigid class hierarchies means we are all released from the structures of industrial society into the uncertainties of a world risk society.

Beck illustrates many of these features by commenting upon some of the profound changes taking place within our personal lives. Industrial society was based upon a strict separation between public and private, with women largely excluded from the public worlds and their identities being shaped by a rigid gender system. However, with women entering into the workforce after the end of the Second World War we are beginning to witness the break-up of the gender system. This also releases men from being the sole supporter of the family, and thereby unties the previous connections between work, family and gender. The partial deconstruction of public and private worlds inevitably means that love becomes a more contingent social arrangement. Love, no longer colonized by economic necessity, becomes an empty sign that has to be filled in by the participants within the relationship. In this, argue Beck and Beck-Gernsheim (1995), love has taken the place of religion in that it is the central way in which modern subjects attribute their lives with meaning. Love relationships are the places where we can be ourselves, gain intimate contact with others, and find a place where we can belong. However, affective relations, due to the decline of overt class antagonisms, are also the places where individuals are most likely to experience intense conflict. This is largely because more equal relationships imply more freedom for women, but for men it implies more competition, more housework, less 'control', and more time with their children.

Hence, to return to the dialectic Beck unravels between modernity and counter-modernity, arguably individualization processes have no necessary political trajectory. For example, counterforms of modernity can respond to a more chaotic world emerging within interpersonal relations between the sexes by renaturalizing the roles and identities of men and women. Indeed this is a key instance of subpolitics in that 'the political constellation of industrial society is becoming *un*political, while what was unpolitical in industrialism is becoming political' (Beck 1997: 99). Such a dynamic means that we often look for politics in the wrong place. In this respect then, Beck represents the key antagonism within 'reflexive' modernity between a politics that builds upon individualized forms of reflexivity and the re-inscription of fundamentalist certitude. Such a politics asks us to think again about widespread assumptions in respect of the colonization of economic reason, the decline of values or postmodern forms of fragmentation. That is modernity has given birth to both 'freedom's children' who have learnt that fun, mobile phones, and opposition to mainstream politics can be a force for change, and 'ugly citizens' and moralizers who seek to reaffirm modernity's perceived loss of security (Beck, 1998). The main political dividing line in the struggles that mark the future will be between those who seek to remake civil society and community out of freedom and those who seek to introduce new forms of discipline and compulsion. Indeed it is the ethic of individualization when joined with globalization that is most likely to lead politics in a cosmopolitan direction. The decline of national industrialism is increasingly giving rise to a global cosmopolitan ethic, which realizes that the key problems raised by common citizenship can no longer be thought and experienced in national terms (Beck 1999).

APPRAISAL OF KEY ADVANCES AND CONTROVERSIES

Beck's critical assessment of mainstream sociology has brought its fair share of criticism. The risk society thesis, as it has been developed by Beck, suggests that the canons of social and political theory are currently ill equipped to deal with the key questions asked by the 'second modernity'. From the founding works of Marx and Weber to the later contributions of Habermas and Foucault, Beck suggests that all are in need of substantial revision. Here I will only be able to deal with some of the questions Beck's writing raises in the context of contemporary currents within social and political theory. In what follows, I want to look at four key controversies in respect of Beck's views before going on to suggest what a potential reply might look like. These issues have been left as open as possible so that readers might make up their own minds.

Capitalist Modernity

A number of Marxist-inspired critics have argued that capitalism rather than 'side effects' remains the main driving force behind modernity. In such a view it is commodification rather than the unintended consequences of industrialism which is transforming the world. The privatization of public utilities, the concentration of economic and political power into the hands of a few multinationals, and the imperative of capital accumulation all point towards a social theory with capitalism rather than industrialism at its centre. The risks of unemployment, poverty, social exclusion, and ill health are all ultimately tied into the relations of production and distribution of wealth in society (McGuigan, 1999; Rustin, 1994; Soper, 1995). What these critics are arguing is that we are witnessing the intensification of modernity rather than the arrival of a postmodern or a risk society. For example, Alex Callinicos (1999) charges that Beck considerably overstates the democratizing force of modernity. That is, while Beck points to the considerable opportunities to be had in the diminishing power of experts, the unpredictable flow of public opinion, and more democratic households, many of the inegalitarian features of the capitalist economy remain triumphant due to the collapse of state socialism, the weakening of the nation-state, and globalization. These developments have led to the redistribution of economic and political power away from the people (in particular nation-states) and into the hands of large-scale multinationals. This more traditional political economy approach would argue that the traditional social sciences continue to serve us well despite Beck's arguments to the contrary.

Beck could respond to these charges by arguing that he is well aware of the negative potential of modernity. The dialectic he opens in his writing is fully appreciative of the destructive effects of unbridled capitalism. In particular he emphasizes the growing gaps between rich and poor, global poverty, the mobility of capital, and the shrinking supply of work in capitalist economies. However, these features need to be connected more forcibly to the ecologically destructive power of industrialism. In Beck's view we have moved beyond the binary politics of left and right into a more uncertain and risky world than many of his critics seem to be aware. The impetus for social change is no longer to be found within the political establishment, but increasingly new ideas like ecological security, gender equality, and campaigns to end Third World debt which have built upon the new individualism and are global in orientation. Further, Beck's analysis in this and in other respects, comes close to that of Anthony Giddens (1990), in that capitalism is just one feature of modernity that includes industrialism, surveillance, and the control of the means of violence. More precisely, Beck would need to argue that capitalism is now itself embedded within the frameworks of the risk society rather than the other way round. That is, it is the production of risk through the changing relations between men and women, global nuclear threats, ecological hazards, and so on – all of which are the unintended product of industrialism – that deserves our political attentions, rather than a narrower focus on capitalism. Whereas his critics remain trapped in the binaries of Cold War thinking (communism vs. capitalism) the more uncertain features of globalized risk opens many new features.

The Project of Modernity

Beck has also attracted a sceptical response from those who argue that he is overoptimistic in respect of the rational inheritance of the enlightenment. In this his arguments come close (although there are substantial differences) to those of Jurgen Habermas (1985) who reminds us of the continued relevance of the moral and ethical resources of the enlightenment. Both Habermas and Beck argue that there needs to be a redemptive and critical attempt to recover the public significance of reasoned discussion. He differs from Habermas in the view that everyday life is being reshaped by 'side effects' rather than instrumental reason, and that modernity is currently a more contested domain (given the contradictory imperatives of subpolitics) than Habermas's arguments in respect of the colonization of the life-world.

While these questions deserve a more detailed analysis, both Bauman (1993) and Smart (1999) have argued that the 'revival of reason' offered by reflexive modernization will do little to offer a future more riven by doubt and ethical complexity. That is, as Beck defines it in his early work, the recovery of reason is just as likely to foster rather than undermine what Bauman (1993: 204) calls 'the suicidal tendency of technological rule'. Beck's analysis remains dependent upon the continued domination of scientific reason, rather than engaging in a more ethical politics. Bauman expands this point by arguing that the most likely response to public expressions of risk is the systematic privatization of risk, not the remoralization of public space. For Bauman, Beck seems to presume that 'more not less modernity' would necessarily undermine attempts by 'private' consumers to avoid public risks. Bauman points out that privatized 'risk-fighting', from attempts to lose weight to taking vitamin tablets, are all big business. In a consumer society there is a strong temptation to buy oneself out of the debate privately rather than publicly engaging in the construction of shared moral and ethical norms. There is therefore no direct connection between the public acceptance of risk and the political action necessary to deal with these questions. In their different ways both Bauman and Smart point to the need of a wider ethical recovery, which is not addressed but undermined by the new individualism and scientific reason.

Again these remarks pose serious questions to Beck's position. However, I think it is possible to argue, certainly within Beck's later analysis (and here he seems to have learnt from Bauman), that we might draw different conclusions. The humanity-wide attempt to reconnect nature and humanity and reverse the de struction of the environment is a political-ethical movement. Undoubtedly there will be private attempts to shirk responsibility and to 'privately' protect ourselves from many of the negative consequences of environmental degradation. However, Beck could point out that these attempts in respect of global warming, the poisoning of food, and the nuclear threat are almost bound to fail: ecological problems are everyone's problems. The ecological movement, feminism, and other social movements are already providing a different ethical basis for personal life that brings responsibility right down to the level of the individual. The globalization of everyday life both serves to ask new questions as well as entrapping us in other logics. Further, Beck could go on to argue, whether these new movements are able to combat the side effects of industrialism and save the planet in the process is not for him to decide. As we have already seen, Beck is clear that cosmopolitan politics has no guarantees of success in a global risk society.

Rationalization of Modernity

Beck could also be criticized for arguing that modernity is more marked by risk and reflexivity than it is by bureaucratic control and order. Returning to traditions within social theory that would include Weber, Adorno, and Foucault we might argue that the modern world is becoming more bureaucratized and ordered, not chaotic and reflexive. The most recent defender of this particular thesis has been George Ritzer (1993) in respect of McDonaldization. For Ritzer, society has become standardized and normalized by processes of efficiency, calculability, predictability, and control. In other words, these features of 'formal rationality' produce a risk-free environment for the production of fast food. Ritzer's (1999a) most recent writing has expanded the thesis of MacDonaldization to take account of what he calls the 'cathedrals of consumption' (from shopping on the Internet to the rise of shopping malls) which also embody these features. Seemingly whether we are out shopping or going to the 'movies' we are caught up in processes of cultural standardization. Further, new sites of consumption are utilizing processes of 'enchantment' through simulation and themeing to hide these aspects from their consumers. While Ritzer agrees with Weber that these rational processes have irrational and dehumanizing effects (such as the replacement of human labour with technology) these are unlikely to seriously undermine the wider features of the system. Indeed, when challenged by Bryan Turner (1999) that he fails to account for many of the questions that can be associated with the risk society, Ritzer (1999b: 241) replies that 'the risks that Beck emphasises will decline with increasing rationalisation'.

These claims point to some of the weakest aspects of contemporary sociology and partially account for Beck's current popularity. While a number of points could be made in response, from the political neutrality of Ritzer's remarks to his overwhelming 'faith' in the formal aspects of rationality, these will not be pursued here. Beck's case seriously undermines claims like those of Ritzer who argue that modernity can be explained through the triumph of instrumental reason. Instead Beck points out how such processes have rebounded back upon themselves and sought to undermine many of the aspects Ritzer takes for granted. In this respect, Beck could claim that organizations like McDonalds are having to operate within an increasingly reflexive environment where claims and counterclaims abound in respect of the amount they pay their workers, questions about animal rights, the ethics of eating meat, and issues related to the medical effects of using antibiotics in the raising of animals. That McDonalds seek to present themselves as a predictable and risk-free environment (a picture Ritzer takes at face value) is an attempt to repress the ethical questions Beck has sought to open. McDonaldization in Beck's analysis is representative of many of the forces that are representative of ecological forms of irresponsibility which can no longer hide behind claims to 'formal rationality'.

The Hermeneutic Deficit

A number of Beck's other critics have accused him of ignoring the different ways in which notions of risk are translated into more popular forms of understanding. In short, the concern is that Beck's theories remain connected to an instrumental and technocratic agenda that seeks to 'manage' an environmental crisis. That is, while Beck describes the risk society as a social crisis, there is little concern with the way different populations, cultures, and political movements might decide to reinterpret and interrupt dominant conceptions of the natural. According to Lash (1994) and Wynne (1996), Beck's analysis stays on the side of the technocratic professionals (including politicians, scientists, and government bureaucrats) by failing to connect with the different frames and projections that are currently available to more grass-root organizations. As Mary Douglas (1992: 48) has argued, 'there is no intrinsic reason why the analysis of risk perception should not engage in comparisons of culture'. By failing to make this move Beck is accused of unintentionally reinforcing the divide between experts and lay opinion. Thus Beck ends up producing a view of the subject that is not far from a calculative-rationalist approach in that he fails to problematize the complexity and cultural variability of different risk cultures within and between diverse social groups and societies. Rather than developing notions of reflexivity through an explicitly aesthetic set of concerns like Lash, or seeking to treat seriously many of the reservations and resistances that 'ordinary people' might have to the agendas and cultures of scientists, he is arguably more concerned to introduce the principle of responsibility into elite discussions.

However, while Lash (1994) and Wynne (1996) claim that Beck is insufficiently concerned with the ways in which the environment becomes socially constructed others might equally claim that the risk society is insufficiently philosophically realist in its conception. For example, Soper (1995) argues that while we need to attend to the ways in which nature is culturally constructed we equally need to maintain a more overtly realist discourse that attends to evidence of environmental degradation. Recently, Beck (1999) has sought to answer these criticisms by arguing that there is no need to choose between realism and constructivism. First, he argues, there is a need to address institutional dimensions and questions of power within the risk society in such a way that takes us beyond merely cultural questions related to meaning. Secondly, and building on some perceptive criticisms made by Adam (1998), Beck argues that risks are simultaneously real and constructed. By this he means that while many ecological risks are invisible or are stored up over time we are dependent upon different discourses and knowledges to make them visible. Further, that these knowledges (or manufactured uncertainties) might help define new risks of which we were previously unaware, and that the definition of risk can be said to have a double reference. However, the complexity of risk cultures and struggles over the definition of risk does not make them any less real. In this sense a constructivist framework is unable to define or declare what really 'is' or 'is not' (Beck 1999: 133).

While these debates are ongoing, Beck has undoubtedly made a lasting contribution to social and political theory. In helping define the contours of what he calls a second modernity his critique is simultaneously dependent upon the possible emergence of other modernities that are more responsible in respect of public dialogue and societies dominant institutions. Beck provocatively asks us to dispense with the illusion that the central categories of nineteenth century sociology are adequate to understand the increasingly fluid and fragile 'nature' of a global risk society. This does not herald a return to the logics of order and control, but the public development of genuinely self-critical societies.

BECK'S MAJOR WORKS

Beck, U. (1992) *Risk Society: Towards a New Modernity.* London: Sage.

Beck, U. (1995) *Ecological Politics in the Age of Risk.* Cambridge: Polity Press.

Beck, U. (1997) *The Reinvention of Politics: Rethinking Modernity in the Global Social Order.* Cambridge: Polity Press.

Beck, U. (1998) *Democracy Without Enemies.* Cambridge: Polity Press.

Beck, U. (1999) *World Risk Society.* Cambridge: Polity Press.

Beck, U. and Beck-Gernsheim, E. (1995) *The Normal Chaos of Love.* Cambridge: Polity Press.

Beck, U. Giddens, A. and Lash, S. (1994) *Reflexive Modernisation: Politics, Tradition and Aesthetics in the Modern Social Order.* Cambridge: Polity Press.

Other Works

Beck, U. (1994) 'Replies and critiques', in Beck, U., Giddens, A. and Lash, S. *Reflexive Modernisation: Politics, Tradition and Aesthetics in the Modern Social Order.* Cambridge: Polity Press.

Beck. U. (1996) 'World risk society as cosmopolitan society?', *Theory, Culture and Society,* 13 (4): 1–32.

SECONDARY REFERENCES

Adam, B. (1998) *Timescapes of Modernity: The Environment and Invisible Hazards.* London: Routledge.

Alexander, J. (1995) *Fin de Siècle Social Theory: Relativism, Reduction, and the Problem of Reason.* London: Verso.

Albrow, G. (1986) *The Global Age.* Cambridge: Polity Press.

Bauman, Z. (1993) *Postmodern Ethics.* Oxford: Blackwell.

Benton, T. (1994) (eds) *Social Theory and the Global Environment.* London: Routledge.

Callinicos, A. (1999) *Social Theory: A Historical Introduction.* Cambridge: Polity Press.

Douglas, M. (1992) *Risk and Blame: Essays in Cultural Theory.* London: Routledge.

Elliott, A. (1994) *Subject to Ourselves: Social Theory, Psychoanalysis and Postmodernity.* Cambridge: Polity Press.

Goldblatt, D. (1996) *Social Theory and the Environment.* Cambridge: Polity.

Giddens, A. (1990) *The Consequences of Modernity.* Cambridge: Polity Press.

Giddens, A. (1994) *Beyond Left and Right.* Cambridge: Polity Press.

Franklin, J. (1998) *The Politics of the Risk Society.* Cambridge, Polity Press.

Habermas, J. (1985) *The Philosophical Discourse of Modernity.* Cambridge: Polity Press.

Lash, S. (1994) 'Reflexivity and its doubles: structure, aesthetics, community', in Beck, U. Giddens, A. Lash, S. *Reflexive Modernisation: Politics, Tradition and Aesthetics in the Modern Social Order.* Cambridge: Polity Press.

Lash, S. Szerszynski, B. and Wynne, B. (eds) *Risk, Environment and Modernity.* London: Sage.

Lash, S. and Urry, J. (1994) *Economy of Time and Space.* London: Sage.

Luhmann, N. (1993) *Risk: A Sociological Theory.* New York: Aldine de Gruyter.

Nowotyn, H. (1992) 'Reputation at risk', *The Times Higher Education Supplement,* November 20.

MacNaughten, P. and Urry, J. (1998) *Contested Natures.* London: Sage.

McGuigan, J. (1999) *Modernity and Postmodern Culture.* Buckingham: Open University Press.

Ritzer, G. (1993) *The McDonaldisation of Society: an Investigation into the Changing Character of Contemporary Social Life.* London: Sage.

Ritzer, G. (1999a) *Enchanting A Disenchanted World: Revolutionising the Means of Consumption*. London: Sage.

Ritzer, G. (1999b) 'Assessing the Resistance', in B. Smart (ed.) *Resisting McDonaldisation*. London: Sage.

Rustin, M. (1994) 'Incomplete modernity – Ulrich Beck's risk society', *Radical Philosophy*, 67 (summer): 3–12.

Smart, B. (1999) *Facing Modernity: Ambivalence, Reflexivity and Morality*. London: Sage.

Soper, K. (1995) *What is Nature*? Oxford: Blackwell.

Stevenson, N. (1999) *The Transformation of the Media: Globalisation, Morality and Ethics*. London and New York: Pearson.

Turner, B.S. (1994) *Orientalism, Postmodernism and Globalism*. London: Routledge.

Turner, B.S. (1999) 'McCitizens: risk, coolness and irony in contemporary politics', in B. Smart (ed.) *Resisting McDonaldisation*. London: Sage.

Wynne, B. (1996) 'May the sheep safely graze? A reflexive view of the expert–lay knowledge divide', in S. Lash, B. Szerszynski and B. Wynne (eds) *Risk, Environment and Modernity*. London: Sage.

28

Pierre Bourdieu

BRIDGET FOWLER

BIOGRAPHICAL DETAILS AND THEORETICAL CONTEXT

Bourdieu has taught us to beware the false impression of continuity implicit in the 'biographical illusion' (1994: 81–8), so that it is with some trepidation that I offer a view of his life. He was born in 1930, in a small market town in the Béarn agricultural region of the Pyrenees, where his father was a postman: a man who would have moved between two worlds, part of a modern communication system within a traditional agricultural area.

Pierre Bourdieu owed his subsequent 'belle carrière académique' (as he has entitled others' achievements) to the local lycée, where he was taught classics. From there, as a promising pupil, he was moved to the famous Parisian lycée of Louis-le-Grand. He then entered the route he describes so vividly in *The State Nobility*, the arduous preparatory classes for the examination to the grandes écoles and, in his case, acceptance by the École Normale Supérieure (ENS). Once there, Bourdieu was confronted with the strong postwar influence of Sartre, who had responded to the repressive form of French Stalinist Marxism by initiating a neo-Hegelian phenomenology, derived from Husserl and Heidegger. Negotiating Sartre's voluntaristic existentialism became a key issue for the new generation at the École, Althusser, Foucault and Bourdieu, all of whom were trained in philosophy. One ENS professor was particularly influential: Canguilhem, who extended Bachelard's 'applied rationalism' ([1949] 1986), with its concept of *coupures* (ruptures), into a new 'genetic structuralism' (Bourdieu, 1998b).

From Canguilhem, Bourdieu discovered a historical epistemology applied to science, marked by ruptures and shaped by its social context (Canguilhem, 1988). In this epistemology science appeared as the arena for intellectual discourses, some of which had a 'doxic' or taken-for-granted power, as in the Greek account of humours or the early germ theory of disease. Canguilhem further outlined a struggle between science (itself sometimes 'doxic', hence later to be shown to be mistaken) and scientific ideology – examples of which were the works of Herbert Spencer and Mendel. Such ideas were to have a profound impact on the whole ENS generation, leading in Bourdieu's case to a historical sociogenesis of scholarly myths, such as the genesis of pure aesthetics (1993c) and the genesis of the nation-state (1998a).

From this meditative, ascetic period Bourdieu was swept into the Algerian War, pitchforked into work in Kabylia, the mountainous area of the South, which possessed many similarities with the Béarn of his birth. Here he was to get his fieldwork training as an anthropologist, with the help of native Algerians. From this period came Bourdieu's key formulations of the difference between a commodity-based society in which economic concerns were pre-eminent and one in which material interests took their place alongside other social imperatives, making for a dignified, collective culture and a leisurely art of life. Works such as *The Algerians, Outline of a Theory of Practice* and *The Logic of Practice* portray this division (compare Bourdieu 1998a: 92–109), while they can also be read as stages in Bourdieu's break in the 1970s with Lévi-Strauss and the 'blissful structuralism' of his Algerian stay. In contrast, to the sociologist, Bourdieu's work is perhaps most striking for its interweaving of ethnographic observation alongside theoretical interpretations from Marx, Durkheim and Weber.

When he returned to France, he was to work in lycées and at the University of Lille. Bourdieu subsequently returned to Paris in 1964, to organize research at the L'École Pratique des Hautes Études, under the aegis of Raymond Aron. Here he developed a team studying education, which produced a series of books on students and the school. When, in 1968, the May events had student as well as factory demonstrations at their centre, the account in *Reproduction* of the role of education as a distinctive modern legitimating myth became one of the powerful catalysts for change.

Throughout his career, Bourdieu has undertaken studies of issues marginalized by sociology – taste, photography (Bourdieu et al., 1990), haute couture, academic life – so as to raise the most profound questions in the philosophy of action (1990a; Pinto, 1998: 113). His distinctive method is to break with the abstract or 'theoreticist' approach to questions of social reality (freedom, necessity, law, etc.). Instead, he resorts to social science, deploying a technology of probability statements in order to show the objective structures within contemporary French society (the greater likelihood, for example, of social science academics being women, ethnic minorities or from the subordinate class relative to other disciplines, 1988a). Armed also with studies of agents' *subjective interpretation*, Bourdieu's distinctive approach shows how structures are meaningfully incorporated into agents' most deep-rooted dispositions in the form of anticipated outcomes over time. Perceived outcomes direct psychological investments and govern expenditures of energy in the broadest sense - in turn reinforcing or further weakening existing structures. Bourdieu's writings are thus preoccupied with the unconscious, the passions and reason: the body and the mind. His writings consequently challenge two professions: sociology and philosophy; his latest theoretical work, *Méditations Pascaliennes* (1997b), returns as much to Pascal or Wittgenstein as to sociology's classical theorists.

Bourdieu has now become indisputably recognized or 'consecrated'. His academic success has been amplified through the media, which has pronounced him France's foremost intellectual. Yet he is also deeply embattled. He has taken up the view that neoliberalism is a distinctive ideological form, generated by economists and administrators, not least the *'énarques'* who graduated from the prestigious École Normale d'Administration (1996a, 1998c). He has also alerted attention to the danger for scientific thought represented by a fast-reading soundbite culture (1997a). In these later years of his career we see him choosing political action, compelled by the threat that 'civilization' is itself at risk. When specialized intellectuals such as Bourdieu intervene directly in the field of power and speak outside the scientific city (1975), they often provoke a purely political assessment of their entire works. The time for a leisurely and serious scientific analysis of his theory may be passing.

SOCIAL THEORY AND CONTRIBUTIONS

When Bourdieu lived amongst the Berber Kabylians, an ancient form of life was being gripped by a form of 'social vivisection', imposed simultaneously by the proximity of capitalism and the war. Nevertheless, in their household living and agriculture, he was able to outline an entirely different form of experience, marked by a cyclical sense of time. Kabylians, in turn, highlighted the historical nature of the forms of Western society since for them calculative economic activity was largely the preserve of women ('For the Kabyle, the economic economy as we practise it is a women's economy', 1998a: 99). The economistic ethos of the West's 'harried leisure classes' was replaced in Kabylian practices by a pleasure in sociability (1977: 195) and by the 'peasant ethos' of painstaking trouble with nature, often where this would bring no direct material advantage. Bourdieu stressed that the whole inheritance of the peasant required that they attend to the long-term needs of the soil: the property 'inherits' the owner (1990a: 152). Kabylian practices were further orchestrated through certain 'primitive' classifications of thought and perception: male/female, honourable/dishonourable, dry/wet and so forth (1990a: 97). Contemporary non-scientific Western classifications substituted alternative binary oppositions for such divisions of perception, especially those between noble/common and refined/popular. Both classificatory patterns served to provide a practical sense for coping with everyday dilemmas of action.

Here there are two important points to make. The first is the break with structuralism and with an objectivating anthropological form of the 'sovereign gaze', which disregards actors' subjective meanings. For example, Bourdieu notes that only 3 per cent of marriages are in accordance with the rules demanding that the choice be of parallel-cousins (1990a, 1998a: 141–2). Thus agents are *not* Lévi-Straussian bearers of structures but rather pay lip-service to them, often acting differently. If their interests lie in conformity to the rules, all well and good, otherwise Bourdieu sees transgressive tactics as common. He uses an image that later becomes a symbol of people's 'practical logic' more generally: Kabyleans *improvise* like jazz trumpeters.

Kabyle society is based on a subsistence economy, which is collectively structured around gifts: gifts of labour-services at harvest-time, presents and meals at wedding-feasts, women for marriages. Here Bourdieu follows Mauss in his basic view of gift-giving as acting to bind actors in solidarity within precapitalist societies, so that they may have not just their material needs satisfied but also any collective needs met, such as military defences. Gift-exchange should not be opposed to Western economic rationality in idealized terms. Gift-exchange is neither profit-dominated, nor is it totally disinterested. Each agent possesses an interest in his or her gift being returned after an undefined period. However, Bourdieu argues further, following Lacan, that 'misrecognition' of interest due to the time gap is crucial, as is the misrecognition that the greatest symbolic capital, or prestige, goes to those who can afford to give most. Both these patterns of giving tend to reproduce great families, in what he will later call the paternalistic 'illusio'. Thus the social order is perpetuated through 'practical euphemisms' and 'collective repression' (1998a: 96–99).

Gift-giving favours dominant families, but it is still founded on a logic of reciprocity. Gift-giving is not, therefore, the primordial form of economic competition. The rough equality in gift-exchange is also facilitated by the absence in

Kabylia, of any exclusive literary culture, and its accompanying degradation of popular language (1961, 1991; Guillory, 1993). Kabyleans, like the laity of feudal societies, possess a common culture.

Common up to a point: for Bourdieu has turned recently to the nature of masculine domination and the origins of phallocratic doxa with Kabylean society as his case-study (1990b, 1998d). Such doxa operate beyond the sphere of ideology, by using an appeal to paternalism, viz., women's need of protection from men. Bourdieu analyses the resilience of such gender inequalities, not least in more differentiated societies (1998d: 97–115). But whereas in Kabylia, opposition by women was at the most individual and confined to magical solutions, in our own period there has emerged, from the ranks of the excluded, a lucid but alienated view of the masculine game of power. A transformation of oppression is most likely to occur when cultural capital can be mustered against it, as in the case of modern feminism and gay rights (Bourdieu, 1990b, 1998d: 96, 129–34).

Education

Bourdieu's first books on education, coauthored with J-C. Passeron, revealed the contradictions within French society, such that the Republican School, which should have been *'L'école émancipatrice'* became *'L'école conservatrice'*. The consequence was the low level of entry of the children of peasants and workers into higher education: only 6 per cent in the early 1960s at the time of Bourdieu's research. The reason lay in the nature of the teachers or pedagogic authority itself: the 'symbolic arbitrary' (the culture transmitted within the school) in fact resembled very closely the home culture of the haute bourgeoisie and was remote from that of the subordinate class. Hence the principles for academic knowledge were instilled as part of domestic culture, not least through the museum visits of family leisure, which provided the building blocks to academic high culture. Given the symbolic violence to other groups implicit in educational selections of a specific cultural arbitrary, Bourdieu regards the postwar meritocratic ideology as a new mode of legitimating power.

This is a powerful blend of Marx and Weber but it has, in my mind, certain problems. It fails to explain why the 'natives' (the subordinate class, with their distinctive culture) do not become restless: the answer, I think has to do with full employment and with the mission of salvation for all held by a minority of 'prophetic' teachers, a group that Bourdieu and Passeron themselves describe but without close study. Such teachers see their work as channelling bright working-class children to realize themselves through the school. Indeed, the occasional 'miraculous survivor' testifies to their good faith. Widespread collusion with such cultural hopes on the part of the respectable working-class pupils is a response to the alluring images of an open bourgeoisie, evoked daily through acts of cultural goodwill on the part of exemplary teachers (Snyders, 1976: 165, 181).

The State Nobility develops Bourdieu's arguments about social class reproduction through education. Bourdieu dissects the peculiarly French institution of the *'grandes écoles'* which cater for the best national candidates. In virtuoso manner, he deploys a battery of probing instruments to lay bare their underlying relational significance. He is thus able to construct and tests a theoretical homology between the hierarchies of academic 'space' and those of the field of power, showing how the 'independent culture' of those from the dominant classes are converted into intellectual 'brilliance'.

This research reveals that the most academically-prestigious (grande porte) schools acquire 60 per cent of their intake from the dominant class. Bourdieu proceeds to apply an anthropological model of power, contending that the student body of each grande école (such as HEC, Polytechnique, ENA, and ENS) is constituted through a *Hegelian spirit* or *esprit de corps* into a distinctive social essence, as naturalized as gender. The more elevated their discipline within the academic hierarchy – philosophy outranking geography, for instance – the more often the initiates mistake their success for the power of extraordinary gifts.

The 'state nobility' is Bourdieu's concept for that section of the dominant class which enters the highest level of the French administrative system, manages finance capital and the great companies, and attains distinguished positions within the political, legal and medical professions. As a *bourgeois* class, its legitimation requires that its bureaucratic recruitment be impersonal and based on the free exchangeability of educational distinctions. Yet its *nobility* derives from its exclusive possession of (cultural) capital. Like the *noblesse de robe*, the State nobility is distinguished by its possession of the 'magic' of state-certified academic titles:

> We thus must make a radical break with... Weber... and restore to analysis the profound ambiguity of institutions that conceal behind a mask of 'modernity' and rationality the efficiency of social mechanisms ordinarily associated with the most archaic societies. The academic title is indeed the manifestation *par excellence* of... *state magic*. (Bourdieu, 1996a: 376, author's emphasis)

The Academic Field

Among the most illuminating of Bourdieu's studies is *The Ontology of Martin Heidegger*, which should be read alongside *Homo Academicus* as an extended elaboration of the strategies and structures of one such academic model, the world of Heideggerian philosophy.

The first stage for Bourdieu is to go beyond Adorno's historical materialism, which, as in an electrical short-circuit, simply links up Heidegger's philosophy with his Black Forest origins and his petty bourgeois class background. Using structuralist techniques, Bourdieu notes a direct homology between the ideas of Heidegger and those of 'the conservative revolution' (Schmitt, Bruck, Muller, and Junger). Their 'third way' aimed to go beyond the opposites of capitalism and socialism, mechanistic atomism and *gemeinschaft*, positivism and organicism, in a new conservative revolution. There is a 'polyphonic' affinity between Heidegger's style as an 'emissary prophet' and these 'plebeian intellectuals' camped outside academia.

Bourdieu's next move is more original. Heidegger, he argues, could only offer this programme his support in disguised form, by converting their critiques and yearnings into struggles within the fields of academic philosophy itself (1988b: 36). Consequently Heidegger's unique position-taking must be delineated contextually: against Cassirer's pre-eminent neo-Kantianism, against Cohen and against Husserl. In particular, Heidegger must obey the censorships of the field (1988b: 72, 1991: ch. 6) by deploying an elevated language, which euphemizes the social meanings of the plebeian conservatives. Heidegger's 'aristocratic populism' becomes, for these reasons, both unfalsifiable and formalist. What is ultimately at stake in Bourdieu's subtle hermeneutic analysis is to explain how such a philosophical rhetoric might seize the field from more impressive candidates. Against Heidegger's eternalizing of certain states of being, Husserl, earlier, had adopted a rigorous approach to the subjective experience of time, alongside a historical approach to reason. It is *his* heritage that Bourdieu uses to enrich historical materialism with a deeper consciousness of time (1998a: 80–2).

Cultural Theory

Bourdieu seeks to question revered myths by showing the interests lurking behind disinterestedness. Thus he breaks again with the Frankfurt problematic which had distinguished modernists from other cultural producers in terms of their two-dimensional ways of seeing. He stresses modernists' contribution to a pure aesthetic which guarantees them, as artists, 'profits of distinction' and serves to differentiate their enlightened public from the 'barbarous' people.

The field of literature and art possesses some characteristics in common with the Kabylean world of symbolic exchange: they are both universes in which there are taboos on reducing things to their monetary price. But within this world we can still interpret artists' beliefs as profoundly connected to their experience within the material world and especially to the capital or skills they possess: their artistic and intellectual capital, or the social circle within which their family moves. Thus Bourdieu's decisive move was to take terms like 'prophet' and 'priest', which Weber had introduced as generic types, and apply them to artists and writers (1987). In the process he has indisputably added to our understanding of the *mechanisms of consecration* which set apart the established avant-garde from the prophet-like emergent avant-garde of a new generation. Bourdieu's concerns are: how does an oppositional, disenchanted way of seeing – the vision of the world that characterizes so much of modern visual art and writing – come to be the mark of the 'spiritual honour' of the haute bourgeoisie? Paradoxically, a new situation has emerged in the twentieth century, in which culture has become 'capital' in forms of educational knowledge and qualifications.

Bourdieu's two most dazzling contributions to the sociology of culture are his books on cultural consumption (*Distinction*) and production (*The Rules of Art*). *Distinction* links art anthropologically to the profane world of everyday consumption. Within the various forms of cultural consumption, Bourdieu could place certain pure types into relief, such as the 'legitimate' (high art) taste for Mondrian or for photographs of cabbages. These choices emerged from the operation of the principles of classification outlined in Durkheim and Mauss (in this case – high rather than low, refined over vulgar, coruscating over bland). Preferences for each alternative could only be explained by the agents' social position so that those most remote from material urgencies and most well-endowed with a high volume of cultural capital, were the most likely to choose aesthetically legitimate activities.

Distinction's questions sometimes mistakenly imply that certain tastes are mutually exclusive and are occasionally badly phrased so as to 'lead' the respondent (e.g. qu. 22, 1984: 516). But the book also possesses great insights into clashing aesthetic worlds and exemplary boldness in explaining them. Through his method of homologies, Bourdieu demystifies the profound structuring of taste by education, and education, in turn, by the material trajectories of families. He proffers a powerful redefinition of modern class experience on the model of the exclusion of the colonized race. At a deeper phenomenological level, the lower class, lacking cultural route-maps, feels intimidated by its ignorance. What he later identified as 'the racism of intelligence' (1996a: 36) was shown to extend even to the representations of the body (1984).

Distinction could be seen – mistakenly – as the return of the repressed: a lower-class expression of Nietszchean *ressentiment*. It brilliantly exposes Kantian aesthetics as a historically limited judgment which proposes its professorial high seriousness as a measure of all taste. But *Distinction* also refuses the aesthetic populism implicit in simply valorizing lower-class taste wholesale. In brief, here historical materialism comes of age. *Distinction* offers a richness and complexity of analysis of class, time and space which has been absent for many years.

The Rules of Art

To understand the singularity of the artist, the sociologist will link him or her to their class of origin, family trajectory, and their ontological security. But this is radically insufficient. Bourdieu explores the literary/artistic field or cultural institution itself, especially the struggles between rival movements within modernity. In 1850s' France a massive redirection was taking place as artists and writers created a direct response to the market ideology that the most important works were those that sold the most. They founded the 'realist bohemia' within which Flaubert's, Baudelaire's, and Manet's modernism had its roots. In so doing, they indirectly initiated mechanisms that culturally dispossessed the people.

The first 'objectivist' task of the sociologist is to bring to light the political doctrines of different avant-gardes and their assumptions about style. By assessing the writer's text, and his or her total life project into the context of all other authors writing at the time, the sociologist will be able to show the distinctiveness of the author. But the writer's work is reduced neither to a mechanical expression of an artistic group nor to class experience. For the sociological task is not complete until it reveals the subjective understanding of the artists themselves, for example, Flaubert's break with both the bourgeoisie and the people. The complete sociological act juxtaposes an objective, historical account of the author with an interpretative account of their subjective views. It provides a 'piquant sauce' for literature, intensifying literary experience (1996b: xvii).

APPRAISAL OF KEY ADVANCES AND CONTROVERSIES

Bourdieu's major stake in his claim to have advanced social science is his 'theory of practice'. This view of action is a subtle blend of experience and cultural unconscious. Aiming to do justice both to the coercive power of social structures and to human rationality, Bourdieu's model is of a strategic agent who resembles well-trained player of American football or a mature painter. As is the case for them, practice requires incorporating a deep knowledge of the game into economical gestures.

Practice tends – but never invariably – to lead to the reproduction of structures and interests, for two main reasons. First, due to the nature of social recognition, the accumulation of material and cultural capital usually enhances ambition and liberates self-confidence (1996a: 410). Second, dominants tend to be members of great families. They can complement their individual competencies within a specialized field by well-placed family members in other key fields (1998a: 70).

This theory, which is all too often reduced to a 'Holy Trinity' of habitus, capital, and field, is developed throughout Bourdieu's studies. In my view, this is a crucial development in historical materialism, and one that has powerfully blended a theory of socialization from ethnography with a Marxist/Weberian theory of social domination. While it is not without problematic elements, it effectively outranks the claims of any serious living contenders as the most mature and sustained synthesis of our period.

In the critical fallout from Bourdieu's efforts, we can see a certain clustering of divergent concerns. These approach his 'realist constructivism' (see 1993b: 915) in terms of the problem of his concept of capital, the artistic status of popular culture, the alleged overdeterminist, oversocialized character of his theory of practice, and finally the connection of his sociology with postmodernism.

Theory of Cultural Capital

Bourdieu has attempted to explain the position of the liberal professions, politicians and bureaucrats in terms of a highly controversial theory of cultural capital. This has extended Marxism by regarding the dominated fraction of the dominant class as using their educational assets in a competitive game of power. In the process, Bourdieu risks losing the specificity of economic capital (Calhoun, 1993: 68–9). While this is true, however, it would not be difficult for Bourdieu to supplement his account of economic capital. He could elaborate on his view of the regulated body and time in connection with labour, spelling out the distinctive instrumental rationality occurring when those richest in material capital attempt to rule for themselves – indeed *La Misère du monde* and *Acts of Resistance* are vital steps towards such a goal.

Cultural capital is analytically more complex than Bourdieu's earliest formulations (but see 1996a: 373–89). It is like economic capital in the sense that its accumulation is at the cost of a competition with others, in a zero-sum game. Its scarcity means cultural capital can easily be converted into high economic rewards. But it still lacks the precise dependence on surplus-extraction required for economic capital. For this reason, those 'theoretical classes' high in cultural capital may not have such a strong potential for conflict, despite coming from different regions of social space from the subordinate classes (1998a: 10–11). Conceptual models such as cultural capital are simultaneously metaphors and may lead to confusion. Bourdieu has also noted more recently that those with cultural capital are often found in autonomous universes (art, science, social work). Such universes are committed to disinterestedness in profit-seeking terms (1998a: 75–123) although this is no guarantee against aristocratic elitism.

Is There Popular Art?

Various critics have noted the clash between Bourdieu's sympathies with working-class people and his failure to accept that there is such a thing as popular art (Shusterman, 1992: 172; Alexander, 1995: 178; Fowler, 1997; Frith, 1996: 9, 251). Bourdieu is adamant that his earlier work suffered from *illusions* of cultural communism (1993a: 2). Indeed, he has justifiably identified a form of populism in which the working class only acquire dignity if they read and write like intellectuals. But his response overall is not entirely convincing.

Admittedly, such defences of rap or other forms of popular music are insufficiently aware of why Bourdieu proposes his view. Shusterman, for example, argues that the Brooklyn-based hip hop group Stetsasonic encompasses many of the defining characteristics of art in its consecrated modernist form, not least the self-conscious awareness of being artistic (see his analysis of their rap 'Talking all that Jazz' in Shusterman, 1992: 212–35). Frith argues that fans make a complex distinction as to whether or not the music possesses value on aesthetic grounds and that these critical rationales are elaborated in detail in the specialized music press (1996: 66–7). A similar view is put by Grignon and Passeron (1989). They argue that the use of Bourdieu's theory has become over-routinized or formulaic, especially with regard to the concepts of 'capital, field, and habitus'. In particular, popular culture encodes some recognition of the hegemonic character of dominant culture but also develops in a more autonomous manner than Bourdieu's depictions of it would suggest: a view which I share. A more nuanced view than that of Frith concerning the struggles in opening up the canon are provided by Guillory (1993). This poses admirably the significance of the canon as cultural capital but interprets the present canon wars in terms of the challenge from fractions of the dominants (for example, in management schools) who no longer need that baggage (Guillory, 1993: 46–7).

Shusterman and Frith have applied something like a Kantian judgment about aesthetic value to the rock music which Bourdieu would regard as irredeemably part of the commercial field. But Bourdieu would regard this as neither here nor there. His thesis is part of the institutional theory of art in which certain critics are 'socially mandated' to state what is and is not art. Their judgments are the only ones that matter. The Shusterman/Frith stance is repudiated because it neglects the *hierarchical* ranking of professionals' classifications.

Yet we might still challenge this point. Indeed, in the British cultural space, it is very clear that heterodox critics from the 1940s on (e.g. Leavisites, Priestley, Williams, cultural materialists) have succeeded in acquiring sufficient symbolic power to challenge literary formalism. Of course, Bourdieu's position reminds us of the derisive backstage contempt which is characteristic of the spiritual aristocracy, where knowledge is at stake in a game of distinction and condescension. Illustrating this by drawing on the recuperation of bebop jazz in France in the 1950s, he pithily captures such reforms in his thesis that 'popular art' can become consecrated but only when it is no longer popular! Such a concession is telling but insufficient. Bourdieu's thesis still over-simplifies the wider struggles over popular art. Perhaps it has therefore underestimated the potential for reflexivity within the cultural field.

Feminist Theorists and Overdeterminism

A similar debate has occurred over masculine domination. Butler has made the strong claim that Bourdieu's theory fails to take account of performative statements by lower-class women which provoke transformations (1990 and 1997; see for a critique of both Bourdieu and Butler, Lovell, 2000). Bourdieu's riposte is that Butler puts forward only an 'idealist constructivism', capable only of a narrow, text-based model of critique as the template for social change. Gender change for Butler, he argues, is much like putting on a new set of clothes, since she ignores the way gender is objectified and reified, both through conditioned bodily responses and social institutions. The crux – for Bourdieu – is that gendered structures are not vulnerable to textual criticism precisely because only certain agents, vested with the right to make public statements can expect others to take their (performative) statements seriously.

This critique of Butler's voluntarism undoubtedly has some force and finds Butler's weakest spots. But in his turn, Bourdieu has certain telling gaps. He glosses over occasions when the performatives of the leaders chosen by the subordinate group or class clash historically with the utterances of the powerful. They do so not because they match them in legitimate linguistic or cultural capital (although this may be sometimes so). They do so because they acquire a certain weight and honour in becoming ascetic 'spokespersons' of the oppressed group.

An Affinity with Postmodernism?

Bourdieu's sociology continues the main project of the Enlightenment, which is to identify the sources of mystification or magic persisting into modernity. Bourdieu notes forms of 'fetishism' – linguistic, political, artistic – that are uniquely found from the nineteenth century onwards among the dominant class. He tells us that the mode of reception which identifies painting as 'a reality with no other end than to be contemplated, is very unequally distributed.' (1997b: 293). Bourdieu refers to this mode of appropriation not simply as a fetish (1984: 284), but one in which the whole of bourgeois dignity is invested.

It is also in connection with this theory of magic that Bourdieu describes all those forms of 'spirit' that create group unity. The spirit of the republican *grande école* figures strongly (1996a), not so much because of its austere demands but because of the solidarity it induces amongst former students. Indeed, a variety of 'spirits' are alluded to in Bourdieu's late work: the 'spirit of the family', for example, or 'the spirit of the state' (1998a).

Marx had initially identified as *false eternalization* those modes of human existence that were commonplace after the transition to capitalism but actually stemmed from a particular set of historical conditions, such as the appearance of 'free labour'. Bourdieu's task has similarly been to pinpoint as *false universalizations* the experience of the privileged few, shown most spectacularly in the case of education and art, but also better known in the area of masculine domination.

Such a critical exposure of false universalism leads Bourdieu to challenge the other major theoretician of the Enlightenment project, Jürgen Habermas (see especially Habermas, 1984). For Bourdieu, this project remains too close to the normative philosophical tradition and the scholastic point of view. Recognizing only external coercive domination, Habermas fails to see the forms of *symbolic* violence that have colonized the mind (1997b: 80–1). He cannot understand the role of authorization through job entitlement or other forms of recognized power which allow only a select few to 'do things with words'. He fails to grasp the material conditions for reason, including time for contemplation (see 1997b: chs 1 and 2, 1998a: 127–30).

Yet while critical of Habermas, Bourdieu is neither a nihilist nor a relativist. Various authors have claimed him for postmodernist (Brubaker, 1993: 230–1; Lash, 1990). But this is a label he has never used of himself. Indeed, he wants to avoid both the mistake of a naive idealization (Merton) and that of a *naive cynicism* (the strong programme in the sociology of science) (1997b: 132–6). Certainly, Bourdieu wants to adopt a type of perspectivism: this insists, for example, on describing and situating the sometimes illusory thinking of the oppressed as well as the ideological myths of the dominants (1990b: 28). Indeed we could see his social theory as avant-garde insofar as it sees the same phenomena from several perspectives at once.

Such perspectivism might encourage a radical sense of contingency or nihilism in which truth becomes merely an effect of power and local discourses. But in Bourdieu, as we have seen, perspectivism is woven into a realist social theory where identifiable social structures, exerting a determining power, can be known scientifically. For Bourdieu (unlike postmodernists) such structures can be identified in falsifiable theoretical forms (1991b: 6).

Materially instituted in the ordering of space, objectified in forms of various sorts of capital (economic, political, cultural), social structures are ultimately embodied and encoded in the most basic dispositions of the actor – the habitus. There, as 'structuring structures', they exert an extraordinary force. Yet the force of the habitus can also be resisted as a consequence of reflection (Bourdieu and Wacquant, 1992: 132–3, 139, 210–12; Grenfell et al., 1998: 17–18). Whereas postmodernism may take the form of 'philosophical aestheticism' (Bourdieu and Wacquant, 1992: 155), Bourdieu wants to defend a 'critical and reflexive realism which breaks at once with epistemic absolutism and with irrationalist relativism' (1997b: 133).

It has been claimed recently that it is the *republican tradition* that has most strongly informed Bourdieu's political thought (Verdès-Leroux: 1998). It is true that republicanism has been an important theme within his work in the sense that he has been critical of the absence of rational pedagogy and other rational practices governing access to unequal resources within the public sphere. Moreover he deploys precisely the Machiavellian republican tactic of insisting on interests and *realpolitik* as against 'abstract moralism'. Republicanism is simultaneously defended as an embattled civilizational achievement but is also to be extended, by being disconnected from its seventeenth century link to the genesis of the national state (1998a).

The key to these actions is the insistence on practicable social transformation or a 'realistic utopia', a victory which might possibly be snatched from another 'utopia fast becoming social reality' (neoliberalism). For neoliberalism represents the decline of republican institutions in the sphere of welfare, law, and education, established in the name of the rights of citizens (1998c). Bourdieu has recently identified publicly with new movements that have taken their rational kernel (and legitimacy) from the old forms of republicanism – the États Généraux, for example – which recalls the 1789 popular revolutionary movement for democratic representation and an antimonarchical form of executive power. But Bourdieu's politics are not limited to a narrow national republicanism. For he has publicly backed the emergence of a European Trade Union Federation and the European Works Council in a move decisively beyond the old French tradition, towards a 'new internationalism'. This movement – unlike *ouvriérism* – is not simply to be drawn from those who suffer most: working-class, migrants, unemployed. It is also to be drawn from artists and intellectuals – all those with cultural but little economic capital – whose past progressive actions permit a gamble on their solidarity in the face of the technocrats' social Darwinism.

Conclusion

There is justifiable contention about aspects of Bourdieu's theory. Yet we should remember what has often been missed, especially in accounts of its allegedly ultra-determinist and egoistic synthesis. (We must therefore resist strenuously Alexander's 1995 account of his reductive atomistic universe.) Resources can be found for critical awareness and action in his sociology: not least his non-idealist assessments of reciprocity (for example, in Kabylia), which fit loosely with both his defence of the autonomous universes of science and art (see 1996b) and his perception of neoliberalism as a threat to civilization (1993b; 1998c). Bourdieu's rational utopianism is not a pious nod towards reflexivity. On the contrary, it represents a realistic assessment of the potential for transformation given a better grasp of the many obstacles to reason. The most confusing of these are sham claims to universal openness:

> There is no contradiction, despite appearances, of struggling *at the same time against* the mystifying hypocrisy of abstract universalism and *for* universal access to conditions of access to the universal, the primordial objective of every real humanism which both universalist preaching and the nihilist pseudo-subversion forget. (Bourdieu, 2000: 71 author's emphasis)

BOURDIEU'S MAJOR WORKS

Bourdieu, P. (1961) *The Algerians*. New York: Beacon Press.

Bourdieu, P. (1975) 'The Specificity of the scientific field and the social conditions for the progress of reason', *Social Science Information*, XIV: 19–47.

Bourdieu, P. (1977) *Outline of a Theory of Practice*. Cambridge: Cambridge University press.

Bourdieu, P. (1984) *Distinction*. London: Routledge.

Bourdieu, P. (1987) 'Legitimation and structured interests in Weber's sociology of religion, in S. Lash and S. Whimster (eds) *Max Weber, Rationality and Modernity*. Allen and Unwin.

Bourdieu, P. (1988a) *Homo Academicus*. Cambridge: Polity Press.

Bourdieu, P. (1988b) *The Ontology of Martin Heidegger*. Cambridge: Polity Press.

Bourdieu, P. (1990a) *The Logic of Practice*. Cambridge: Polity Press.

Bourdieu, P. (1990b) 'La domination masculine', *Actes de la Recherche en Sciences Sociales*, 84: 2–31.

Bourdieu, P. (1991) *Language and Symbolic Power*. Cambridge: Polity Press.

Bourdieu, P. (1993a) *Sociology in Question*. London: Sage.

Bourdieu, P. (1993b) *La misère du monde*. Paris, Seuil.

Bourdieu, P. (1993c) *The Field of Cultural Production*. Cambridge: Polity Press.

Bourdieu, P. (1994) *Raisons pratiques*. Paris: Seuil.

Bourdieu, P. (1996a) *The State Nobility*. Cambridge: Polity Press.

Bourdieu, P. (1996b) *The Rules of Art*. Cambridge: Polity Press.

Bourdieu, P. (1997a) *Sur la télévision*. Paris: Liber.

Bourdieu, P (1997b) *Méditations Pascaliennes*. Paris, Seuil.

Bourdieu, P. (1998a) *Practical Reason*. Cambridge: Polity (a partial translation of Bourdieu).

Bourdieu, P. (1998b) 'George Canguilhem: an obituary notice', *Economy and Society*, 27 (2-3): 190–2.

Bourdieu, P. (1998c) *Acts of Resistance*. Cambridge: Polity Press.

Bourdieu, P. (1998d) *La Domination Masculine*. Paris: Seuil.

Bourdieu, P., Boltanski, L., Castel, R. and Chamboredon, J.-C., (1990) *Photography, A Middle-brow Art*. Cambridge: Polity Press.

Bourdieu, P. (2000) Pascalian Meditation. Cambridge: Polity Press.

Bourdieu, P., Chamboredon, J.-C. and Passeron, J.-C. ([1968] 1991) *The Craft of Sociology*. Berlin: de Gruyter.

Bourdieu, P. and Wacquant, L. J. D. (1992) *An Invitation to Reflexive Sociology*. Cambridge: Polity Press.

SECONDARY REFERENCES

Alexander, J.C. (1995) *Fin de Siécle Social Theory: Relativism, Reduction and Reason*. London: Verso.

Bachelard, G. ([1949] 1986) *Le Rationalisme Appliqué*. Paris: Presses Universitaires de Paris.

Brubaker, R. (1993) 'Social heory as habitus', in C. Calhoun, E. Lipuma and M. Postone (eds) *Bourdieu: Critical Perspectives*. Cambridge: Polity.

Butler, J. (1990) *Gender Trouble, Feminism and the Subversion of Identity*. London: Routledge.

Butler, J. (1997) *Excitable Speech*. London: Routledge.

Calhoun, C. (1993) 'Habitus, field and capital: the question of historical specificity', in C. Calhoun, E. Lipuma and M. Postone (eds) *Bourdieu: Critical Perspectives*. Cambridge: Polity.

Canguilhem, G. (1988) *Ideology and Rationality in the History of the Life Sciences*. Cambridge, MA: MIT Press.

Fowler, B. (1997) *Pierre Bourdieu and Cultural Theory*. London: Sage.

Frith, S. (1996) *Performing Rites*. Oxford: Oxford University Press.

Grenfell, M., James, D., Hodkinson, P., Reay, D. and Robbins, D. (1998) *Bourdieu and Education*. London: Falmer.

Grignon, C. and Passeron, J-C. (1989) *Le Savant et Le Populaire*. Paris: Seuil.

Guillory, J. (1993) *Cultural Capital*. Chicago: University of Chicago Press.

Habermas, J. (1984) *The Theory of Communicative Action*. Cambridge: Polity.

Lash, S. (1990) *The Sociology of Postmodernism*. London: Routledge.

Lovell, T. (2000) 'Thinking feminism with and against Bourdieu', *Feminist Theory*, 1 (1): 11-32; reprinted in B. Fowler (ed.) *Reading Bourdieu on Society and Culture, Sociological Review Monographs*. Oxford: Blackwell.

Pinto, L. (1998) *Pierre Bourdieu et la théorie du monde sociale*. Paris: Albin Michel.

Shusterman, R. (1992) *Pragmatist Aesthetics*. Oxford: Blackwell.

Snyders, G. (1976) *Ecole, classe et lutte des classes*. Paris: Presses Universitaire de France.

Verdés-Leroux, J. (1998) *Le savant et la politique: essai sur le terrorisme sociologique de Pierre Bourdieu*. Paris: Grasset.

29

Zygmunt Bauman

BARRY SMART

BIOGRAPHICAL DETAILS AND THEORETICAL CONTEXT

The task of providing a profile of a major social theorist is always challenging, but it is even more daunting when the work is still in process, when it manages to remain analytically sensitive and acutely responsive to a diverse range of complex local and global processes of transformation to which contemporary social life and human experience continues, inevitably under modern conditions, to be subject. The works of Zygmunt Bauman are wide-ranging and include meta-theoretical texts that address important issues central to the practice of social science, and sociology in particular, as well as a series of significant studies that lay bare the complex anatomy of late modern social existence, studies which attempt to provide us with a critical understanding of the dilemmas we confront as we attempt to come to terms with the turbulence of a social world in perpetual motion and to be better equipped to face up to our moral responsibilities. Bauman, particularly in an impressive series of critical analytical explorations of the transformation of modernity, consistently provides new insights into the conditions we encounter, the possibilities we need to confront, the choices we make, and the fact that we cannot avoid making choices, such is the price of our 'freedom', as well as the complex consequences that follow from the same, both the anticipated or intended consequences, those that fit or come close to the designs socially engineered, but more importantly those unanticipated outcomes that Bauman has suggested testify to 'the non-finality of any ordering project' (1991: 230). Amongst contemporary social theorists Zygmunt Bauman has few, if any, peers and his work is widely recognized as providing a key reference point for anyone seeking to achieve a better appreciation and understanding of the complexity of contemporary social life. While Bauman is unable, for good reason, to offer a detailed answer or resolution to the problematic question of 'how to go on', his work does present a convincing case for our capacity to live with, if not make the most of, the forms of ambivalence increasingly acknowledged to be a corollary of modernity, and as such his work is justifiably regarded as providing a realistic outline of 'the chances of saving human dignity' (Morawski, 1998: 36).

In thinking about the task of providing details of biography and the theoretical context in which Bauman's works might be situated or be said to belong, it would be remiss of me not to briefly acknowledge the contentious issue of the 'author function' addressed by Michel Foucault (1971) and clearly central to the current exercise. The figure of the author, as Foucault cautioned, continues to be employed in literature, the humanities, and the social sciences as 'the unifying principle' through which particular writings and texts are selected for analysis and accorded a 'unity'. Foucault's reflections on the authorial figure alert us to the difficult issue of the sources or texts (to be) selected for analysis, and by implication those texts excluded or marginalized in the process; it is important to be aware of the selective character of the 'unity' accorded to the writings of a particular author, of the individual works identified as constitutive of the author's *oeuvre* (Smart, 2000a). In the case of the work of Zygmunt Bauman there are numerous texts from which to select and on which to reflect (Kilminster and Varcoe, 1996); however it is a particular later set of texts dealing with the transformation of modernity (Bauman, 1987, 1989, 1991, 1993) which increasingly have been identified as representative of an important form of 'unity' in his work, indeed as exemplifying the very best of his work. While each of his earlier books might seem 'to be on a different topic' (Varcoe and Kilminster, 1996: 215), with the emergence of the series of works sharing an explicit analytic focus on modernity and the emergence of a condition of postmodernity Bauman has demonstrated the relevance and importance of critical sociological thought for achieving a more effective practical understanding of contemporary social life. As I will show below, the greater effectiveness of such an analysis derives from its disclosure of 'sources of moral power' that Bauman argues have tended to be concealed, if not discredited, within modern ethical philosophy and political practice: it is a disclosure that enhances the chances of a '"moralization" of social life', one indeed that presents an opportunity for a 'renaissance of morality' (1993: 3).

What then are we to make of Bauman's work and what is the appropriate context in which to situate it? Such questions are not easy to answer. Significant relevant details of biography are already relatively well known (Kilminster and Varcoe, 1996, 1998; Morawski, 1998; Beilharz, 1998). Born in 1925 in Poznan, Poland, of Jewish descent, Bauman was forced by the rise of Nazism to leave his homeland in 1939. He subsequently received a university education in Soviet Russia where he embraced 'the Marxist worldview in the light of the utopian belief and hope that the Soviet Union was genuinely a country of justice, equality, freedom; that an ethnic pedigree really did not matter' (Morawski, 1998: 30). Bauman returned to Poland after the Second World War and his early career was spent at the University of Warsaw. However, he was forced to leave Poland for a second time in 1968 after he and a number of other, mainly Jewish, colleagues were victimized (Kilminster and Varcoe, 1998) for their increasingly critical exposure of a regime that had become despotic. Bauman moved via the University of Tel Aviv to the University of Leeds in 1971 where he was awarded the Chair of Sociology. He currently holds the position of Emeritus Professor at Leeds and in the wake of the collapse of communism in Eastern Europe he has been 'reinstated in his chair of sociology at the University of Warsaw' (Kilminster and Varcoe, 1998: 24).

As far as the general question of the broad theoretical context in which Bauman's work might be situated is concerned, a number of issues and influences have already been identified by analysts (Kilminster and Varcoe, 1998; Smith, 1998). One important formative intellectual influence is that of Marxism. As in the case of the works of a number of leading European critical social theorists, in particular other prominent Jewish intellectuals who were also forced into exile, Max Horkheimer, Theodor Adorno, and Herbert Marcuse come to mind (Jay, 1973: 253–280), Marxism clearly assumed an important place in the formation of Bauman's early work. However, the most significant insights appear to have emerged with a leave-taking from the paradigm, with the recognition that it is through a critical analysis of the Enlightenment tradition as a whole, and the associated project of modernity and its consequences, that a more effective understanding of the problems and possibilities encountered in contemporary social life will emerge (Bauman, 1987). In any event Marxism constitutes only one of the intellectual influences that have helped to shape Bauman's thinking and it would be misleading to overstate the paradigm's importance, although it might well be argued that what Derrida has described as a certain 'spirit of Marxism' – '*radical* critique . . . the critical idea or the questioning stance' (1994: 88–9), if not an emancipatory element, continues to inform his work (Kilminster and Varcoe, 1996: 241; Beilharz, 1998: 27–8). Many other notable intellectual influences on Bauman's work have been identified. These are too numerous to list in full but include the formative influence of two key intellectual figures, Stanislaw Ossowski and Julian Hochfeld, teachers who stimulated Bauman (1972b) to reflect on the difficulties of reconciling 'the demands of reason' and 'the demands of ethics', and to respond to the philosophical underpinnings of the Polish sociological tradition, which it is argued turned in his hands 'into a kind of Marxist hermeneutics in the 1970s and early 1980s' (Morawski, 1998: 31); the work of Antonio Gramsci, which Bauman describes as 'the turning point in my intellectual life' (Kilminster and Varcoe, 1992: 208); an affinity with the work of Georg Simmel (Morawski, 1998: 35); and last but by no means least a sociological adaptation of the notion of 'ethics as first philosophy' derived from the writings of the French philosopher Emmanuel Levinas (1989), a key influence in the moral turn taken in Bauman's (1993, 1995, 1997) exploration of the discontents and dilemmas of postmodernity.

Identifying intellectual influences on the work of a major social theorist only clarifies part of the theoretical setting in which the work might be held to belong. There is also a question of the idiosyncratic features of biography, the twists and turns of life-history that may affect the perspective(s) employed, and account for the key concerns which have motivated a life's work, which have provided the stimulus for thinking critically about the modern condition. In respect of Bauman's work the issues of Jewish descent, the experiences of exile, of being an émigré, of living as a stranger, have been identified as providing the vantage point of 'outsider' from which to make sense of different ways of life. Reflecting on Bauman's work, and in particular the place of hermeneutic analysis within it, Dennis Smith argues that it is precisely the experience of being an outsider that leads to the development of a 'privileged insight into the defining boundaries of our world and can help shape a discourse which allows communication across those boundaries' (1998: 41). The experience and perspective of 'outsiderness' has enabled Bauman to produce acute analyses and perceptive understandings of culture and social life and, as a number of analysts have recognized, this quality has contributed significantly to his development of a distinctive style of social theorizing (Beilharz, 2000a).

SOCIAL THEORY AND CONTRIBUTIONS

Bauman's early and perhaps less well-known works, certainly to English speaking readers, are in Polish and their themes seem to reflect the key concerns of Eastern European intellectuals of the time – questions of socialism, democracy, and centralized planning – as well as meta-theoretical concerns intrinsic to the discipline of sociology. Reflecting on this stage in Bauman's career Stefan Morawski argues that 'in his Polish period [he] was striving towards a fully fledged systematic outline of the sociological subject-matter and method of investigation' (1998: 32), but that subsequently he abandoned this particular search for a style of theorizing that ultimately regards sociology as a critical, open-ended commentary on the experience of social life, an interpretative endeavour that 'undermines the trust in the exclusivity and completeness of any interpretation' (Bauman, 1990: 231). However, while such a sociology implicitly confirms the 'endemic relativity of all meaning (its "insidedness" in relation to a given form of life)' it is evident that for Bauman it does not need to result in a 'relativism of interpretation' (1978: 221). At issue here is the problem of how to avoid 'the twin dangers of ethnocentric conceit and relativistic humility' (Bauman, 1978: 222), a matter that subsequently re-appears in a revised form in Bauman's (1992b) critical reflections on the question of postmodern 'interpreting' forms of sociology. In this context Bauman discusses a number of alternative contemporary strategies for the practice of sociology and two are particularly pertinent to the subsequent development of his own work. The first strategy constitutes a critical postmodernized version of an older modern strategy, one in which 'premises are recognized as assumptions' and reference is made to 'values rather than laws; to assumptions instead of foundations; to purposes, and not to "groundings"' and where there has been a significant shift of emphasis away from the provision of knowledge for a centralized modern state engineered design of a better society and towards the generation of forms of knowledge 'which may be used by human individuals in their efforts to enlarge the sphere of autonomy and solidarity. This looks more and more like the last chance of emancipation' (Bauman, 1992b: 110). This particular shift is exemplified by the ethical turn in Bauman's subsequent work to which I will turn below.

Closely connected to this strategy is another advocated by Bauman, notably for sociology to proceed to do what it has, at its best, always sought to do, that is to increase understanding of 'what makes society tick, in order to make it tick, if possible, in a more "emancipating" way' (1992b: 111), an objective that constitutes in many respects a restatement of orientations and analytic interests expressed in earlier works, for example in deliberations on social class, elites, and the labour movement in Britain (*Between Class and Elite*), in reflections on socialism (*Socialism – The Active Utopia*), and in the attempt to lead the discipline of sociology towards a more critical and emancipatory practice (*Towards a Critical Sociology*). To move more effectively towards this particular end Bauman argues that it is now necessary to recognize that we are encountering a new object of investigation, a new society, a society that has relatively little, if any, need for 'mass industrial labour and conscript armies' but does need 'to engage its members in their capacity as consumers' (1998c: 80). In short it is to an analysis of the 'consumer society' and the impact of consumerism that sociological inquiry needs to be directed (Bauman, 1988, 1992b, 1998b) if it is to increase our understanding of contemporary social life.

There is a resonance here between Bauman's analysis of prevailing conditions and the path taken by an earlier generation of critical analysts who recognized that it was inappropriate to simply continue to place work, industry, and production at the centre of analysis to the neglect of culture and consumption. In a manner that bears comparison with Bauman's work, members of the Frankfurt School outlined criticisms of Enlightenment philosophy and the pursuit of domination or mastery, identified as a corollary of the instrumental rationalization of the world, rejected reductionist approaches to the study of cultural phenomena and directed analytic attention to the impact of the culture industry, mass culture and mass consumption on social and political life, acknowledged the absence of any potential agency of radical social transformation, and argued that rationality was unable to provide guidance for political strategy and action (Horkheimer, 1974). However, there are also interesting and important differences that need to be noted. For example, whereas Adorno and Horkheimer conceived modern industrial capitalist society to be an increasingly administered and repressive society, one in which there appeared to be little prospect of overcoming socio-economic contradictions or finally realizing human potential, a diagnosis which ultimately led them to resign themselves to theory as 'the only form of *praxis* still open to honest men' (Jay, 1973: 280) and to distance themselves from the political objectives they had inherited from a Marxist paradigm that exercised a significant influence over their thinking, Bauman argues that it is primarily through processes of seduction rather than forces of repression that contemporary society is constituted. In short, the individual in late-modern or post-modern society is considered to be rather more subject to the seductive forces of the market and somewhat less to the surveillance practices and administrative orders of the state (1992b: 17, 51-2, 101), and by placing emphasis on the degrees of 'freedom' that are a corollary of the ambivalence of modernity Bauman ultimately provides a significantly different, and in many respects potentially more optimistic, analysis of the prospects and possibilities confronting late modern subjects.

Theorizing Modernity and Postmodernity: Ambivalence and the Disorder of Things

A number of prominent intellectual themes and significant social and political concerns run through Bauman's work and various continuities have been identified, perhaps the most notable of which have been an analytic focus on the articulation of culture and power (Kilminster and Varcoe, 1996; Morawski, 1998) and the generation of a critical and emancipatory form of sociology (Smith, 1998). From his study of the working class and the labour movement in Britain published in *Between Class and Elite* (1972a), his identification of the 'critical capacity' of culture in *Culture as Praxis* (1973), and his reflections on both the modern socialist utopia in *Socialism – The Active Utopia* (1976b) and the prospects for a critical sociology based on emancipatory reason outlined in *Towards a Critical Sociology* (1976a), through to his later writings on the post-modern discontents of modernity, an interrelated analytic interest in the articulation of culture and power and a strong commitment to a critical and emancipatory form of sociology has remained a consistent feature of his work. Faced with questions about coherence and continuity in his work Bauman has readily acknowledged the importance of the topic of culture to his work and has remarked that the other main concern running through his writings has been 'the working class, standing for the down-trodden or the underdog, for suffering in general' (Kilminster and Varcoe, 1992: 206; see also Bauman, 1999). In a comparable manner Smith has suggested that two intellectual projects may be found in Bauman's works in the 1970s and 1980s, 'one was to make sense of culture and sociology; the other was to explain socialism, capitalism and class' (1998: 40–1). These two projects lead on to the body of work for which Bauman has been most widely acclaimed and to which I intend to direct most of my attention, notably the series of studies of modernity and the advent of a condition of post-modernity.

It is in *Legislators and Interpreters* that Bauman introduces his distinctive analysis of the 'kind of experience which was articulated in the particular world-view and associated intellectual strategies to be given the name of "modernity"'(1987: 2). In a wide-ranging analysis of modern

Western European intellectual history since the Enlightenment, Bauman outlines the key features of the prevailing modern world-view in the following terms. The world is conceived to be a potentially 'orderly totality', amenable to control, to ordering, through planning, design, and the exercise of mastery achieved via technologies of intervention. The effectiveness of 'ordering action' and the control it continually promises (but ultimately fails to deliver) is closely articulated with the adequacy (or not) of our knowledge of the order(ing) of things. As Bauman remarks, there is an assumption that 'effectivity of control and correctness of knowledge are tightly related (the second explains the first, the first corroborates the second)' (1987: 3). The discussion offered of this particular 'power/knowledge syndrome' reveals the reality of modern existence to be far more complex than the ordering-design project of modernity has anticipated. The legislative modern strategy of intellectual work has been continually undermined and frustrated by the respects in which the quest for order and certainty has produced forms of disorder and uncertainty in its wake. As Georg Simmel was moved to remark in his reflections on the 'intellectual relationship of modern science to the world,... every problem solved throws up more than one new one, and that coming closer to things often only shows us how far away they still are from us' (1990: 475). And through Bauman's work we are now able to appreciate precisely why this is the case, notably that living with ambivalence is an inescapable corollary of the modern project, of the form of life of modernity itself. Recognition of 'the contingency of the modern self, of the contingency of modern society' (Bauman, 1991: 231) made possible by reflexive social inquiry constitutes the condition of postmodernity.

Such a conception of the modern view of the world is made possible by the emergence of an alternative postmodern view, an appropriate vantage-point from which a radically different interpretation and understanding of the contemporary world and intellectual practice can be generated. In his elaboration of such a postmodern viewpoint Bauman makes reference to the way in which the world is conceived in terms of 'an unlimited number of models of order, each one generated by a relatively autonomous set of practices' (1987: 4). From this perspective there exists a pluralism of experience, values, and criteria of truth that does not constitute a temporary aberration awaiting resolution through a projected/promised fulfilment of the modern project. To the contrary, there is a long-standing postmodern 'pluralization of communally and traditionally contexted discourses, which reclaim the localization of truth, judgment and taste which modernity denied and set to overcome in practice' (Bauman, 1987: 127). It is in this context that a rather different intellectual strategy becomes apparent, one designated postmodern by Bauman, an intellectual role equated with interpretation and translation in which the central task is to facilitate the development of communication and understanding between and across different 'communally based traditions' (1987: 5).

Bauman's contribution to the debate over modern and postmodern conditions is not confined to a concern with the identification of differences in the strategies of Western intellectuals, to the contrary his work draws attention to and attempts to capture the distinctiveness of a related range of broader transformations in the experience of contemporary social life. One of the key transformations to which Bauman draws attention in his critical reflections on late modern social life is the way in which political domination is now achieved not so much through 'legitimation' – the establishment of 'universal standards of truth, morality, taste does not seem so important' (1992b: 97) – as through a combination of 'seduction' and 'repression'. It is through the deployment of techniques of seduction and to a lesser extent repression that the attempted cultivation and/or reproduction of orderly forms of social life has been pursued in a consumer society such as ours. Seduction is appropriate and effective for those subjects, a growing number, if not the majority, in Western capitalist societies and beyond, for whom market-dependency is not simply a fact of life but is eagerly embraced as consumption becomes not simply a means to an end but increasingly the end itself towards which all existence is directed. In Bauman's view repression is 'indispensable to reach the areas seduction cannot, and is not meant to, reach' (1992b: 98), notably the marginalized subjects, the excluded, those who are not entirely 'absorbed by market dependency', nonconsumers, or those described as 'flawed consumers' (1988: 84–6, 1997: 41).

The issue of consumption and the conception of our society as a 'consumer society' are important features of Bauman's analysis of prevailing conditions and experiences. Bauman argues that whereas in modern industrial capitalist society production, work and the work ethic – 'that normative pressure to seek the meaning of life, and the identity of the self, in the role one plays in production, and in the excellence of such role-playing as documented by a successful career' (1988: 75) – are central, in our contemporary society consumption, consumer choice, and a consumer ethic, have become pivotal to identity, to our sense of self, and our relationships with others, as well as to the maintenance and reproduction of institutions, groups, and structures. In such a society, 'a society organized around consumer freedom, everybody is defined by his or her consumption. Insiders are wholesome persons because they exercise their market freedom. Outsiders are nothing else but flawed consumers' (Bauman, 1988: 93). Evident here is a development of a set of concerns outlined in an earlier work, *Memories of Class*, in terms of power struggles in industrial society over distribution and consumption and the emergence of a 'new consumer discipline', a consumer orientation which has been 'transformed into a self-sustained and self-perpetuating pattern of life' (1982: 179). It is in these earlier critical reflections on the increasing signs of exhaustion of industrial society and the need to rid ourselves of outmoded notions and to equip ourselves with categories that help us to better understand prevailing conditions, that Bauman identifies 'new contradictions and new victims' that are bound up with the development of consumer society, a thematic thread that is present to varying degrees in subsequent texts but which only receives a more detailed consideration in a later discussion of the 'new poor' (1998b).

Bauman argues that consumption and consumer choice are simultaneously the 'focus and the playground' (1988: 61) for the expression of particular forms of individual freedom, and that it is predominantly through the cultivation of the freedom of the consumer rather than the suppression of individual freedom that the reproduction of contemporary capitalism is realized, although repression remains 'the paramount tool of subordination of the considerable margin of society' (1992b: 98). Elaborating on the new mechanisms of systemic reproduction and social integration Bauman remarks that the market and consumer freedom thrive on variety and that contrary to the thinking of '"mass culture" critics', a veiled reference perhaps to the kind of analysis associated with the Frankfurt School, increasing uniformity has not been the outcome of the development of consumer capitalism, such a view merely represents 'the lament of expropriated gamekeepers' (1992b: 51–2, 101).

APPRAISAL OF KEY ADVANCES AND CONTROVERSIES

If there is one of Bauman's analyses that might be argued to exemplify the distinctiveness and the significance of his work it is his study *Modernity and the Holocaust* (1989). This widely acclaimed study is important on a number of counts. It offers a critical sociological analysis of the events of the Holocaust that took place in

Germany during the Second World War, placing particular emphasis on key features of modern civilization, especially the modern bureaucratic mode of administration and its consequences for social life and individual conduct. At the heart of Bauman's analysis is a critical exposure of the ways in which modern forms of social life routinely produce both moral indifference and moral invisibility, a key objective being to draw attention to the too-frequently neglected 'destructive potential of the civilizing process' by demonstrating that it is 'among other things, a process of divesting the use and deployment of violence from moral calculus, and of emancipating the desiderata of rationality from interference of ethical norms or moral inhibitions' (1989: 28). In this way Bauman offers an account of the Holocaust that places emphasis on the social production of immorality and moral indifference; it is an account which suggests that most people when confronted with a 'situation that does not contain a good choice, or renders such a good choice very costly, argue themselves away from the issue of moral duty... adopting instead the precepts of rational interest and self-preservation' (1989: 206). In consequence the Holocaust is transformed in Bauman's account from a purely German problem to serve as an exemplification of the way in which modern rationality and ethics may lead us in opposing directions (Joas, 1998).

If the primary aim of the study is to offer a critical sociological analysis of the Holocaust it is also evident that discussion of the events and processes involved allows Bauman to take up and develop a radical line of criticism of modernity and its consequences begun by members of the Frankfurt School, most notably Adorno and Horkheimer (1973), but more importantly it provides a suitable context in which to alert us to the neglect of ethical and moral matters in science in general and sociology in particular. What Bauman terms the 'self-imposed moral silence of science' needs to be disturbed, and the sociological relegation of ethical and moral matters to the discourse of philosophy needs to be remedied.

Sociological reasoning, following Durkheim's work, has tended to consider morality in relation to a societal requirement for social integration (Smart, 2000b). Reflecting on the limitations of such a sociological approach, Bauman argues that in so far as the 'will of society' is regarded as the foundation of morality and its sole function is considered to be the maintenance of society, then 'substantive evaluation of specific moral systems is effectively removed from the sociological agenda' (1989: 172). Taking issue with the notion that 'each society has in the main a morality suited to it' and challenging the assumption that 'society... is the source and the end of morality' (Durkheim, 1974: 56, 59), Bauman outlines an alternative to the conception of society as 'essentially an actively moralizing force' (1989: 172), an alternative that places emphasis on the existence of 'presocietal' sources of morality, on the condition of being with other human beings as the intersubjective root of morality. Drawing on the work of Emmanuel Levinas and his notion of 'ethics as first philosophy' in particular, Bauman places emphasis on responsibility as the 'primary and irremovable attribute of human existence' (1989: 182), an attribute that is deemed from the beginning to be synonymous with subjectivity rather than an effect of societal processes (Smart, 1999).

The analytic turn made by Bauman towards a sociological theory of morality in the concluding chapters of the Holocaust study is sustained and elaborated in a series of subsequent texts in which questions of moral responsibility and ethics are placed in the foreground of an analysis of the postmodern dilemmas encountered under late-modern conditions.

Sociology and the Re(dis)covery of Ethical Life

Another way in which the development of Bauman's work might be described is in terms of a relative shift of emphasis from an earlier overriding analytic preoccupation with the hermeneutic task of 'understanding the "other"' (1978: 203) to a later ethical prioritization of the requirement to recall our unconditional responsibility towards the other as constitutive of our being human, as 'the ultimate "given" of human being' (Bauman, 1998a: 15). In a sense this shift of emphasis evident in Bauman's work follows from a process of radical reflection on both the form a critical sociology needs to take if it is to lay any claim, in a late modern context, to being emancipatory, and the transformed – 'postmodernized' – conditions now encountered and the different forms of analysis and understanding they require or demand. Implied here is a radical recasting of an earlier project which sought to outline the possibility of moving 'towards a critical sociology' (Bauman, 1976a) and an associated recognition that 'there is a genuine emancipatory chance in postmodernity' (Bauman, 1997: 33).

To understand and respond responsibly to the complex conditions now encountered it is necessary to think differently about modern institutions and associated processes and consequences. It is necessary to acknowledge and explore the ways in which global or transnational forces are eroding the sovereignty of nation-states and the respects in which market forces shape more and more areas of everyday life and conduct in an increasingly consumer-orientated society. It also means recognizing that moral indifference, if not moral devastation, is a corollary of modern bureaucratic organization and the 'rational' interests intrinsic to modern business. It is in this context, in the absence of any evident alternative to 'the market-centred version of freedom' (Bauman, 1992: 184), living with the failure of socialism, that is after 'modernity's last stand' (Bauman, 1991: 262), but aware that the discrediting of modern utopias need not lead to apathy, despair, or the end of hope, that Bauman turns to the work of Levinas and draws on the notion of ethics as first philosophy. The work of Levinas offers a critical moral-political analytic resource, one that presents a potentially positive alternative to the melancholy lament that in the face of the corruption of reason, or its eclipse (Horkheimer, 1974), theorizing is the only form of praxis open to virtuous individuals. For Bauman there are opportunities as well as risks and threats in current conditions: the late-modern or postmodern human condition is difficult, but not beyond hope. Indeed it is precisely in 'the incurable uncertainty and ambivalence of the human condition laid bare by the postmodern transformations' (Bauman, 1998a: 15) that the prospects for a reinvigoration of morality now lie.

Concluding Remarks: Sociology after Uncertainty

The realization that a modern legislative, social-engineering form of sociological analysis can not fulfil its promise to narrate universality and contribute to the delivery of a designed ordering of social life, because notwithstanding the efforts of various agencies armed with forms of knowledge, possessing skills and deploying technologies directed towards a re-design, manipulation, and management of our existence, ambivalence and contingency remain, and are destined to remain, persistent and prominent features of modern experience, has led to a more sober, realistic, and yet potentially more positive conception of both the conditions and circumstances we encounter and the contribution a more reflexively critical sociology might offer to an improvement of the human condition. It is through its radical exposure of the illusions, realities and practical consequences of modernity and its measured, critical, and ethically sensitive analysis of social life that the magnitude of Bauman's contribution to sociology and to our understanding of the contemporary human condition can be measured. The practice of sociology is now located in a context where uncertainty is recognized to be an inescapable corollary of modern life and the knowledge the discipline is able to provide serves not to reassure, for it cannot provide the 'comfort of certainty', but to make us more aware of where we stand, how we came to be where we are, and what choices are open to us, 'disclosing the consequences and connections of our habitual daily conduct which are all but invisible within the narrow perspective of our "private" individual experience' (Bauman, 1988: 90). Such a sociology is not only temporally located *after* a recognition of the inescapable uncertainty of contemporary social life, it is in an ethical and political sense *after uncertainty*, pursuing it, identifying, cultivating, and nurturing open-endedness as a necessary condition of the freedom to choose what to do, or how to act. Such a sociology is emancipatory in the sense that it allows us to recognize that there are other possibilities to prevailing forms of life, that we can be other than we are, for 'the self is not given to us' as Foucault (1986: 351) remarks, and that there are 'alternatives to our customary way of life' as Bauman (1988: 90) emphasizes. Such a sociology, one to which Bauman's work makes a major contribution, does not provide quiet comfort, security, or certainty, but it does offer us the possibility of acting with a greater understanding of the conditions in which we find ourselves, and most importantly this includes a more acute appreciation of our moral responsibilities towards others.

BAUMAN'S MAJOR WORKS

Bauman, Z. (1972a) *Between Class and Elite*. Manchester: Manchester University Press.

Bauman, Z. (1972b) 'Culture, values and science of society', *The University of Leeds Review*, 15 (2): 185–203.

Bauman, Z. (1973) *Culture as Praxis*. London: Routledge & Kegan Paul.

Bauman, Z. (1976a) *Towards a Critical Sociology – An Essay on Commonsense and Emancipation*. London: Routledge.

Bauman, Z. (1976b) *Socialism – The Active Utopia*. London: Allen & Unwin.

Bauman, Z. (1978) *Hermeneutics and Social Science – Approaches to Understanding*. London: Hutchinson.

Bauman, Z. (1982) *Memories of Class – The Prehistory and After-life of Class*. London: Routledge.

Bauman, Z. (1987) *Legislators and Interpreters – On Modernity, Post-modernity and Intellectuals*. Cambridge: Polity Press.

Bauman, Z. (1988) *Freedom*. Milton Keynes: Open University Press.

Bauman, Z. (1989) *Modernity and the Holocaust*. Cambridge: Polity Press.

Bauman, Z. (1990) *Thinking Sociologically*. Oxford: Blackwell.

Bauman, Z. (1991) *Modernity and Ambivalence*. Cambridge: Polity Press.

Bauman, Z. (1992a) *Mortality, Immortality & Other Life Strategies*. Cambridge: Polity Press.

Bauman, Z. (1992b) *Intimations of Postmodernity*. London: Routledge.

Bauman, Z. (1993) *Postmodern Ethics*. Oxford: Blackwell.

Bauman, Z. (1995) *Life in Fragments – Essays in Postmodern Morality*. Oxford: Blackwell.

Bauman, Z. (1997) *Postmodernity and its Discontents*. New York: New York University Press.

Bauman, Z. (1998a) 'What prospects of morality in times of uncertainty?', *Theory, Culture & Society*, 15 (1): 11–22.

Bauman, Z. (1998b) *Work, Consumerism and the New Poor*. Buckingham: Open University Press.

Bauman, Z. (1998c) *Globalization – The Human Consequences*. Cambridge: Polity Press.

Bauman, Z. (1999) 'Introduction' to new edition of *Culture as Praxis*. London: Sage.

SECONDARY REFERENCES

Adorno, M. and Horkheimer, M. (1973) *The Dialectic of Enlightenment*. London: Allen Lane.

Beilharz, P. (1998) 'Reading Zygmunt Bauman: looking for clues', *Thesis Eleven*, 54: 25–36.

Beilharz, P. (2000a) *Zygmunt Bauman – Modernity as Ambivalence*. London: Sage.

Beilharz, P. (2000b) *The Bauman Reader*. Oxford: Blackwell.

Derrida, J. (1994) *Specters of Marx – The State of the Debt, the Work of Mourning, & the New International*. London: Routledge.

Durkheim, E. (1974) *Sociology and Philosophy*. New York: The Free Press.

Foucault, M. (1971) 'Orders of discourse', *Social Science Information*, 10 (2): 7–30.

Foucault, M. (1986) *The Foucault Reader*. (Ed. by Paul Rabinow.) Harmondsworth: Penguin.

Horkheimer, M. (1974) *The Eclipse of Reason*. New York: Seabury Press.

Jay, M. (1973) *The Dialectical Imagination – A History of the Frankfurt School and the Institute of Social Research*. London: Heinemann.

Joas, H. (1998) 'Bauman in Germany – modern violence and the problems of German self-understanding', *Theory, Culture & Society*, 15 (1): 47–56.

Kellner, D. (1998) 'Zygmunt Bauman's postmodern turn', *Theory, Culture & Society*, 15 (1): 73–86.

Kilminster, R. and Varcoe, I. (1992) 'Sociology, post-modernity and exile: an interview with Zygmunt Bauman', Appendix to Z. Bauman. *Intimations of Postmodernity*. London: Routledge.

Kilminster, R. and Varcoe, I. (1996) *Culture, Modernity and Revolution: Essays in Honour of Zygmunt Bauman*. London: Routledge.

Kilminster, R. and Varcoe, I. (1998) 'Three appreciations of Zygmunt Bauman', *Theory, Culture & Society*, 15, 1: 23–8.

Levinas, E. (1989) *The Levinas Reader*. (Ed. Sean Hand.) Oxford: Blackwell.

Morawski, S. (1998) 'Bauman's ways of seeing the world', *Theory, Culture & Society*, 15 (1): 29–38.

Nijhoff, P. (1998) 'The right to inconsistency', *Theory, Culture & Society*, 15 (1): 87–112.

Simmel, G. (1990) *The Philosophy of Money*. (Ed. David Frisby) London: Routledge.

Smart, B. (1999) *Facing Modernity – Ambivalence, Reflexivity and Morality*. London: Sage.

Smart, B. (2000a) 'Michel Foucault (1926–84)', in George Ritzer (ed.) *The Blackwell Companion to Major Social Theorists*. Oxford: Blackwell.

Smart, B. (2000b) 'Morality and ethics', in *The Handbook of Social Theory*. (Eds. George Ritzer and Barry Smart.) London: Sage.

Smith, D. (1998) 'Zygmunt Bauman – how to be a successful outsider', *Theory, Culture & Society*, 15 (1): 39–46.

Varcoe, I. and Kilminster, R. (1996) 'Addendum: culture and power in the writings of Zygmunt Bauman', in R. Kilminster and I. Varcoe (eds) *Culture, Modernity and Revolution – Essays in Honour of Zygmunt Bauman*. London: Routledge.

30

Donna J. Haraway

PATRICIA TICINETO CLOUGH AND JOSEPH SCHNEIDER

BIOGRAPHICAL DETAILS AND THEORETICAL CONTEXT

Since 1980 Donna J. Haraway has been a defining figure in the Program in the History of Consciousness at the University of California, Santa Cruz. Haraway's academic path to Santa Cruz and the 'Hist Con' programme, which she credits as having been an extraordinarily enabling and provocative place for her work, began in familiar disciplinary spaces at the small, liberal arts Colorado College not far from her home town of Denver, where she was born in 1944.

Haraway early on had begun to mix things that academic convention separates: she took a triple undergraduate major in zoology, philosophy, and English. After graduating in 1966, she spent the next year (and what a year it must have been, given French politics of the time) on a Fulbright at the *Faculté des Sciences, Université de Paris*, and *Fondation Teilhard de Chardin*. Drawing on and expanding a growing sense of political activism that was fuelled in Paris but that had its roots in her Irish Catholic background and family, Haraway joined the anti-Vietnam war and civil rights movements upon returning to the United States and as she began a PhD programme in biology at Yale University.

Turning away from initial plans to pursue experimental work, and under the supervision of G. Evelyn Hutchinson, Haraway became interested in the historical and philosophical study of biology as a practice of knowledge and as a set of rich metaphors through which to see and critically examine myriad forms of social life, some of which were human. Her dissertation took up Thomas Kuhn's (1970) famous notion of paradigm and how it might help understand the development of organicism in late nineteenth- and twentieth-century biology. Clearly, Haraway's shift away from doing biology to studying it as a way of knowing and seeing the world would be profoundly important for the shape and content of her future study, work, and life.

Finishing her course work in biology at Yale in 1972, Haraway and Jaye Miller – a historian, fellow graduate student, and political activist – moved to the University of Hawaii, where Haraway completed her dissertation and taught general science and women's studies courses. Two years and a finished thesis later, she was hired in the Department of the History of Science at Johns Hopkins University. Her revised dissertation was published in 1976 as *Crystals, Fabrics, and Fields: Metaphors of Organicism in 20th Century Developmental Biology.* During this time at Hopkins, Haraway and Miller separated as husband and wife as Miller became increasingly involved in gay activist politics, although it would be wrong to say that he and Haraway became estranged. At about this same time, Haraway met Rusten Hogness, a graduate student in the history of science, and began a relationship that continues today.

After six years at Johns Hopkins, Haraway's life and career took what was to become another consequential turn. She was hired in 1979 for a position in feminist studies and science studies by Hayden White and James Clifford, who were building the new Program in the History of Consciousness at Santa Cruz. This turn westward was perhaps foreshadowed in 1977 when Haraway, Hogness, and Miller bought a piece of property with a restorable house on it north of San Francisco. The particular mix of things in Haraway's life in northern California proved to be rich and intellectually productive.

After arriving in Santa Cruz, Haraway began and continued work on a series of papers that would become signature pieces of a distinctive style and voice that cuts across the disciplinary boundaries of biology, primate studies, feminism, the history of science, postmodern criticism, and cultural studies (to name a few) that are used to define her work, or, perhaps equally often, to say what her work is not. Haraway authored two major papers that appeared in 1978 in *Signs*, the then still new journal of feminist studies, in which she began her critical examination of primatology. A series of other papers published in the early 1980s set the stage for the widely-cited 1984 'Teddy Bear Patriarchy: Taxidermy in the Garden of Eden, New York City, 1908–36', which offered a stunning deconstructive reading of the Ackley African Hall in the Museum of Natural History in New York. Next came an essay that was to define and anchor a new field of study: 'Manifesto for Cyborgs: Science, Technology, and Socialist Feminism in the 1980s', published in 1985, that again boldly disrespected carefully policed boundaries of thought and knowledge dealing with science, technology, and gender. Three years later Haraway published an equally profound commentary on a series of disputes that had electrified the intersection of feminism and the study of science: 'Situated Knowledges: The Science Question in Feminism as a Site of Discourse on the Privilege of Partial Perspective'. Engaging feminist colleagues and philosophers of science alike, Haraway critically deconstructed scientific objectivity but proposed what she saw as a better version. The next year, 1989, she published 'The Biopolitics of Postmodern Bodies: Determinations of Self in Immune System Discourse', in which she uses the human immune system as a metaphor for postmodernity; and her second book, the acclaimed *Primate Visions: Gender, Race, and Nature in the World of Modern Science* also came out. Three years later in 1991 *Simians, Cyborgs, and Women: The Reinvention of Nature* was published. These two books collected revisions of these and other previously published essays along with other material written during the 1980s.

During her two decades at Santa Cruz, Haraway has regularly taught graduate courses in science and politics, feminist theory, science fiction, and, more recently, in theories of race, colonialism, identity, and technology. She has maintained an active community presence on the UCSC campus, serving on and chairing various important committees. In 1997 Haraway continued her bold and creative thought with publication of *Modest_Witness@Second_Millennium. FemaleMan©_Meets_Oncomouse.™ Feminism and Technoscience.* In this same year she was named winner of the Excellence in Teaching Award at UCSC. Her most recent book, an extended set of interviews with former graduate student Thyrza Nichols Goodeve, has been published as *How Like A Leaf* (1999), a phrase she uses quite seriously therein to characterize her body/self and its connections to 'nature'.

As a biologist and cultural critic of science, Haraway has produced a widely read body of work aimed at reconfiguring the relationship of nature, culture, and technology. While her criticism of primatology set forth in *Primate Visions* deconstructs the opposition of nature and culture, human and animal, a critical engagement with cybertechnologies found in her later work deconstructs the opposition of nature and technology, human and machine. Taken together, Haraway's writings historically and socially situate recent developments in biotechnology and technoscience while suggesting some of their future implications, even their promise.

Haraway's work reminds social theorists that there are 'actants' and 'agencies' other than human. For her, human and nonhuman agencies are mixed in 'material-semiotic entities'; these are technoscientific knowledge objects, such as the gene, the database, the chip, the foetus, the immune system, the neural net, the ecosystem. Given their dynamism, material-semiotic entities are social processes, embedded in or productive of social contexts that traditionally have not been the subject of social theorizing. Haraway's work urges sociologists to rethink social theory in terms of a considerably more complex sociality, that is, to address sociality on different scales, from the microphysical to the macrophysical. She urges us to imagine ways to jump, even skip, from one scale of sociality to another. Haraway thus promotes a 'risky interdisciplinarity' in order critically to engage the dynamism of various contexts at various scales of sociality and to pursue in each and every context a criticism of domination within categories of sex, gender, race, class, ethnicity, and nation. In her reconfigured relationship of nature, culture, and technology, she challenges the familiar epistemologies and ontologies on which most social theory rests.

SOCIAL THEORY AND CONTRIBUTIONS

Epistemological Revisions from Primatology to Cybertechnologies

Like a number of cultural critics of the late twentieth-century, Haraway focused her early criticism on the epistemological assumptions that ground, and are taken for granted in, various disciplinary discourses established at the end of the nineteenth century. Her aim is to rethink disciplinarity by showing how certain rhetorics function to create boundaries, making an inside and outside of the discipline and only authorizing what is inside. Haraway is especially concerned to highlight rhetorics that install and sustain oppositions within categories of race, class, gender, sexuality, and nation. She aims to show how these oppositions depend on the more inclusive oppositions of culture and nature, nature and technology.

In her essay 'Teddy Bear Patriarchy', Haraway subjects the discipline of primatology to cultural criticism. While her intention is to raise the larger question of what counts as 'nature' in primate studies, she does this through particular strategies of cultural criticism that have come to characterize her work: they are feminist, antiracist, and multicultural, all moving together in a Marxism revised for the new millennium. In that essay she discusses Carl Akeley, the man who designed the dioramas of African Hall in the Museum of Natural History in New York City. She retraces Akeley's career from big game hunting in Africa to photographing the animals of Africa, to developing the craft of taxidermy in order that he might turn into scientific method what he had learned from stuffing Jumbo for P.T. Barnum. Haraway points to the ways the methods of gun, camera, and taxidermy became interimplicated technologies of realist narrativity. Realist narrativity, Haraway suggests, is a formula for authorizing empirical data in that it grounds scientific authority in immediate vision as observation, a requirement of what Haraway calls 'naked-eye' science. The realist narrative does this by dramatizing scientists' efforts to obtain data – that is, travelling to the field or natural habitat, suffering the trials of staging first hand vision and obtaining observations, and finally returning home with tales about what was seen and experienced.

In the case of the diorama, the realist narrative is deployed especially to materialize or embody a *primate vision*. Presented through the eye of the hunter/photographer/scientist, the dioramas dramatize culture's separation from nature, the human's separation from animal existence. They offer an origin story of human development. Presenting the animals often in family groupings, Akeley's dioramas urge the viewer to see in the animal a reminder of what the human is or has become – the most developed member of family and culture. Just as the father is privileged over the mother and child, the human is privileged over the animal. Haraway argues that the dioramas do several things at once: link a biological organicism with the patriarchal ideology of the family; ground a certain kind of evolutionary theorizing; strengthen the opposition of nature and culture, human and animal; and enforce disciplinary boundaries between the sciences and the humanities, the natural sciences and the social sciences.

Focusing on the implied masculinism of this organicist/realist narration, Haraway elaborates a feminist cultural criticism of science that is necessarily interdisciplinary. She draws together feminist history, feminist film criticism, and feminist literary criticism in order to engage in the deconstruction of rhetorics, discourses, and narrative logics – or what might be called disciplinary writing technologies. But Haraway's emphasis on writing technologies in the discursive analysis of scientific authority is not meant to reduce science to fiction in any narrow sense of the term; nor is it meant to suggest that the animal, the natural, or the human are only or merely cultural productions. Rather, for Haraway, discursive analysis opens up to a treatment of 'material-semiotic entities', where there is an absolute simultaneity of materiality and semiosis, that is, where nature and culture cannot be separated from or reduced to each other. While her treatment of material-semiotic entities has implications for ontology, Haraway focuses, at least at first, on epistemology due, at least in part, to her engagement in the debates over what Sandra Harding first named 'the science question in feminism'.

In a ground-breaking text, Harding (1986) brought together the works of a number of feminist theorists who were engaged in criticisms of positivistic, empiricist practices of science. Harding also firmly set in place a desire and a hope for a feminist 'successor science', an empirical science which, she maintained, would be characterized by a 'strong objectivity' only when the standpoint of the scientist or researcher is made evident. Standpoint epistemologies, as they came to be known, were elaborated, often focusing on the identity and the experience of the knower. They were developed for the most part by those who had been excluded from the authority of science and who would offer their experience and vision as a way to understand the world from the positions of the marginalized, the oppressed, and the exploited. 'Subjugated knowledges' were written and spoken by nonwhite people, neocolonial subjects, and the subjects of marginalized sexualities.

But standpoint epistemology also has been used to characterize the subject positions realized in the production of what has been called 'knowledge itself', abstract disciplinary knowledge. For example, Dorothy Smith (1987) has elaborated a standpoint epistemology that is grounded in what she names 'the relations of ruling', where abstract knowledge is central and highly valued. She argues that, usually, women free men to engage in abstract knowledge production, so that it is women's work as mothers, wives, and daughters that is exploited. Translating Marx's treatment of working-class consciousness to women's consciousness, Smith argues that women can have a more objective perspective of the way the relations of ruling are produced and reproduced; women's position thus offers a standpoint in relationship to their erased and devalued contribution to the production of abstract knowledge.

Haraway's contribution to debates over standpoint epistemology comes in what she calls 'the partial perspectives of situated knowledges'. In her much anthologized essay 'Situated Knowledges', Haraway would surprise readers who had found in her earlier work a strong resistance to realism and to the technologies of vision central to enlightenment positivist, empirical science. Haraway insists that a deployment of visual technologies cannot be avoided by feminist researchers unless they plan to give up on science altogether. Unwilling to do that, Haraway insists that along with exposing the historical and ideological specificity of scientific practices – thereby deconstructing their absolute authority – feminists must also aim to give a *better* account of the world. This better account, however, comes with the recognition of the irreducible difference and radical multiplicity of local knowledges. Haraway thus accepts a version of realism, but one that is to be expressed in partial visions or partial perspectives. The familiar scientific term 'objectivity' is rescued but with a profoundly and consequentially altered meaning.

Partial Perspectives and Material-Semiotic Entities: The Ontological Implications

Partial perspectives are epistemologically demanding. While it is understood that the marginalized, the oppressed, and the exploited might not easily be taken in by what Haraway calls the 'god trick' – that is, seeing everything, everywhere, from nowhere – nonetheless, partial perspectives are not themselves innocent. They are ideological, and they are historically specific, but they are recognized as such in their practice. Partial perspectives have, therefore – and provocatively so – a 'strong objectivity'; they are not reducible to the truth about the world through a truer self-knowing; the self-presence implied in that familiar move is what Haraway calls a 'bad visual system'. Instead, she argues, all vision is always mediated by techniques or technologies; vision is never 'naked' or direct. Situated knowledges make their technological mediation explicit and thus are shown to be 'techno-scientific'. In this sense, every object of study should be seen as an event, a technoscientific production. The object of study becomes then inextricable from the apparatus or the technology of both its production and further elaboration. For example, when light is made to be seen as either a particle or a wave, each instance of 'light' unfolds as such through a particular inscription device and becomes then part of differing applications in the world. For Haraway, knowledge objects such as the gene, the computer program, the chip, the foetus, the immune system, and the neural net are more productively seen as events than as objects. As such, they are dynamic and generative. Each object/event is like a temporary knot in a field of moving forces.

Material-semiotic entities require a form of criticism that is different from a scientist's self-reflection or reflexivity. Grasped as event, including human and nonhuman agencies, material-semiotic entities require a criticism that engages the social contexts or social processes that these entities bring into being as they themselves unfold. Haraway argues that to engage these social processes or contexts, to intervene in them, more than a practice of human self-reflexivity is needed. Instead, Haraway promotes criticism by 'diffraction'. While retaining a place for vision, diffraction is more about registering movement (as when light passes through the slits of a prism and the diffracted rays are registered on something like a screen). Diffraction is about registering histories of movement in a field of moving forces such that the movement or dynamism of forces (contexts and processes) can be reoriented or redirected, that is, disturbed and changed.

Diffraction implies a collapse of the opposition of epistemology and ontology and is thus more characteristic of the nonhumanistic poststructural criticism of the late twentieth century. Yet, Haraway does not draw on the nonhumanism of post-structuralism; and it is perhaps surprising that she makes no connections to Jacques Derrida's treatment of writing as technology or to Gilles Deleuze's elaboration of biophilosophy. Her work, nonetheless, is ontologically bold; and like most post-structuralist critics, Haraway refuses to accept the negativity of either Heidegger's treatment of modern technology (*ge-stell*) or the many Marxist reductions of teletechnology to a mere effect of transnational capital. For Haraway, technology, theory, science, and rationality cannot be separated; a revised ontology of technology is needed. From her early 'Manifesto for Cyborgs' essay to her decade-later book, *Modest_Witness@Second_Millennium*, Haraway has rethought the border between human and nonhuman, between human and machine, in the figure of the cyborg.

The cyborg is a historically specific material-semiotic entity, organism, and communication technology, a post-Second World War knowledge object which, as Haraway sees it, belongs to the 'telos of the West's escalating domination', offering the possibility of a 'final imposition of a grid of control over the planet' (Haraway, 1991: 154). But the cyborg also promises future freedoms and attracts Haraway because it evokes partiality, perversity, and necessitates the reworking of the oppositions of private and public, nature and culture, machine and organism, the living and the inert. It demands a criticism which is not merely for or against late twentieth century technology but is instead more nuanced. This is when criticism by diffraction becomes more desirable, if not necessary; when intervention becomes essential, sometimes to stop, but more often to interrupt, redirect, or reorient the process of technological elaboration. Indeed, Haraway's most sustained treatment of diffraction appears in *Modest Witness* in relationship to 'Oncomouse'.

Oncomouse is a patented research organism, grown to the specifications of biomedical research, such as that on cancer or AIDS. As a transgenic organism, standing at the doorway of cross-species cloning, Oncomouse opens up to an understanding of biology as biotechnology, as 'biology always already rewriting itself' as Vicki Kirby (1991: 91) puts it. For Haraway, Oncomouse also is a narrative figure, for which she wants to compose a counternarrative, a fiction to live by in the age of genetic engineering. Since one of the central issues of genetic engineering is the patenting process that makes the genome a commodity from which surplus value can be extracted, Oncomouse is a figure in a story about the changes realized in late twentieth-century capitalism.

In her treatment of Oncomouse, Haraway's focus on the intermix of transnational capital and knowledge objects is, however, in no way remarkable. In all her work, Haraway traces the transformation of capitalism – from when the extraction of surplus value from human labour is central to production to when technoscience becomes central to production and to the extraction of surplus value. In all her work, Haraway is always concerned with the effects of the transformation of capitalist production on bodies, women's bodies but also on what she calls 'postmodern bodies' – from the labouring bodies of women working in the integrated circuit of transnational capital, which Haraway treats in 'Manifesto', to the technoscientifically produced bodies discussed in 'The Biopolitics of Postmodern Bodies'. Haraway has focused on the contentious relationship between labour and the ownership of the means of production in a global context; she has raised questions such as: who should own genetic material extracted from local areas? What labour counts, and do local labourers have a claim to surplus value or to determining further applications of genetic material? Who should have access to information technologies and how shall the capacity to use them, itself, be communicated? Finally, questions are raised about race, gender, ethnicity, age, sexuality, and nation in order to guard against practices of technoscience and genetic engineering guided only by commercial gains.

APPRAISAL OF KEY ADVANCES AND CONTROVERSIES

Donna Haraway's cultural criticism of science presumes that technoscience is a primary agent of power relations in contemporary societies around the globe, albeit with varying local effects. As such, she points to the inextricability of science and relations of power. In this understanding, she is one of a number of critics of science, including sociologists, who have insisted that relations of power are internal to science rather than external to it. In the 1970s, these sociologists began to rethink the sociology of science established beginning in the mid-1940s by Robert K. Merton and continued by his students. Merton had proposed to study science in terms of the patterned social relationships between knowledge practitioners, the effects of science on society, and the institutional development of science, including the political dynamics of funding. The next generation of sociologists doing science studies, however, shifted their focus to the content of science, that is, to the social production of scientific knowledge itself. They proposed that relations of power are part of the production of scientific knowledge and that this knowledge, like all cultural practice, is thoroughly ideological.

Michael Lynch and Steve Woolgar (1990) have suggested that while poststructuralism is to be counted as an influence on the new sociology of science, perhaps even more important, at least at first, were philosophers and historians of science, such as Thomas Kuhn, Ludwig Fleck, Michael Polanyi, Imre Lakatos, and Paul Feyerabend. Their work opened up the possibility of treating scientific knowledge as itself socially produced. With the development of the Edinburgh 'strong programme' of science studies, science no longer would be studied only in terms of its 'truth'-fulness or its mimetic relationship to 'reality' or 'nature'. Instead, scientific knowledge was to be treated in terms of the local processes of its production. The contents of scientific knowledge would be treated as an accomplishment, as a doing. Researchers were to question how scientists actually produce models or do experiments or even 'discover' facts; how various technologies are central to the production of scientific knowledge, and how scientists use and then recreate the authority of scientific knowledge.

In the context of these changes in science studies, no one has been more influential than Donna Haraway in developing a cultural criticism of science and scientific knowledge that interrogates dominations of class, race, gender, sexuality, age, and nation (although many sociologists who study science interrogate the production of scientific knowledge in terms of differences of race, class, gender and/or sexuality; see, for example, Aronowitz, 1988; Clarke and Olesen, 1999; and Star, 1991; other sociologists of science, perhaps most famously, Latour, 1987, 1993, rarely do). No other cultural critic has had more influence than Haraway in bringing forward difficult questions that point to the ways scientific work and knowledge are interimplicated with a wide range of global and local practices of exploitation and domination. In this work she has established links between cultural studies and science studies that benefit both lines of work. Indeed, although Haraway has insistently pressed her colleagues in science studies to consider questions of sexuality, gender, race, and class, she also has oriented her cultural studies colleagues to think about science, especially technoscience. Her own work here has given form to a cultural criticism of the body that necessarily denaturalizes the body so as to include technonatures, technobodies, and cyborgs. Haraway's figure of the cyborg, although not original with her, has spawned countless clones and there is yet no end to its productivity.

But the excitement over the cultural studies of science during the 1980s and early 1990s was followed by a strong negative reaction. By the end of the 1990s, science studies, along with all cultural criticism that focuses primarily on rhetorics, narrative logics, or discursive constructions of disciplinary authority, had become the object of a sharp criticism. Perhaps the most perverse instance of this was that by Alan Sokal involving *Social Text*, a journal of Marxist cultural studies. In an essay appearing in a special issue on science studies, Sokal (1996a) drew connections between the field of modern physics and Derridean deconstruction, feminist theory, and marxist cultural studies. Later, Sokal (1996b) claimed that his essay had purposely offered insupportable arguments and had drawn illogical conclusions, which nonetheless had gone unrecognized as such by the journal's editors. This had occurred, Sokal argued, because of the editors' unquestioned presumption of the political correctness of the cultural criticism of science, which Sokal claimed was embedded in his essay. Sokal maintained that his aim in perpetrating the hoax was to teach those 'leftists' involved in science studies that they know neither science nor politics, not if they meant to turn the latter against the former and break with what he described as 'the two century-old identification' of the left with science aimed at laying bare 'the mystifications promoted by the powerful' (1996b: 64).

Haraway's work was not directly addressed in the so-called 'Sokal Affair', although it was implicated. In fact, it is Haraway's work that stands as a strong response to the kind of trivializing criticism made by Sokal, who also claimed, with seeming amazement, that the cultural critics of science and disciplinary discourses think that 'there is no reality', 'no materiality'. More than other feminist cultural critics who have been subjected to severe criticism on these grounds, such as Judith Butler (1993) and Gayatri Chakravorty Spivak (1999), Haraway makes clear that matter and materiality have not been ignored in the cultural criticism of science or in the discursive analysis of disciplinary authority. Rather, she argues, matter and materiality must be conceived differently under the regime of transnational capital, global telecommunications, and technoscience. Haraway, who respectfully recognizes Butler and Spivak in her own work, argues, as they do, that the changes in the conception of matter and materiality also require that we rethink family, nations, bodies, machines, nature, technology, and the disciplines. Her work makes clear that it is in fact *for* leftist politics that a different kind of self-criticism of science is necessary.

Against Sokal's claim that the cultural studies of science make leftist politics impossible, Haraway seems always to draw out the implications of her work for political action. Indeed, the practice of diffraction is nothing less than political activism, although conceived specifically for the domain of technoscience. Diffraction, after all, requires intervention, both individual and collective, in the domain of technoscience, which had become the primary agency of global/local power relations at millennium's end. But with Butler and Spivak, Haraway also explores a certain feminist sensibility in relationship to leftist politics – a leaning towards partiality, difference, and the necessary reconfiguring of the arrangement of social spaces presumed in Western discourse, that is, the idealized arrangement of the public and private spheres, the state and civil society, family and national ideologies.

Haraway's work proposes that in the context of neocolonial societies and late capitalist postmodern societies, social spaces are being reconfigured in various ways under the pressure of the transnationalization of capital and the globalization of teletechnology. With Spivak and Butler, she argues for a new sense of relatedness, one that includes nonhuman agencies. She calls for an 'unfamiliar unconscious, a different primal scene where everything does not stem from the dramas of identity and reproduction' (Haraway, 1997a: 265). While valuing the nonknowingness of the unconscious as well as its movement of desire, Haraway nonetheless wants to disconnect the unconscious from the familiar Oedipal narrative. She argues that 'perhaps the most promising monsters in cyborg worlds are embodied in non-oedipal narratives with a different logic of repression, which we need to understand for our survival' (1985: 66). Haraway reminds leftists that feminist politics more than ever demands a rethinking of 'bonding through kinship and "the family"' and that there is a need to imagine different 'models of solidarity'.

When Haraway criticizes the (Oedipal) logic of realist narrativity deployed typically to authorize scientific texts, as she first did in 'Teddy Bear Patriarchy', her aim is not only to invite experimental writing in the narrow sense of that term. It is, rather, to seek new ways of bonding and connecting across difference, that is, new ways to organize social spaces – including the private and public spheres, the state and the civil society, the nation and the family both in late capitalist postmodern societies and neocolonial societies under the regime of transnationalized capital and globalized teletechnology.

Haraway promotes experimentation in writing as a way to help reconfigure social spaces. These experimental writing forms hold the promise of an intervention consistent with her figure of diffraction. It is in these terms that Haraway's work has influenced some of the experiments in sociology, and especially those in recent ethnographic writing linked to the critique of the colonial heritage in anthropology that has emerged over the last two decades. On one hand, an autoethnographic form has been developed in which accounts of diasporic experience have been offered by those who have lived them; on the other, there are social scientists who have turned the reporting of comparative, cross-cultural data to an exploration of forms of dialogue between ethnographer and subjects of study, or between Western and non-Western social scientists. Here too, autoethnography is used as a form for treating the experience of doing fieldwork and the writing linked to it. In both cases, autoethnographic experimentation points to demands made by subjects who expect to tell their own stories, or, at least, to present their stories in dialogue with the ethnographer.

There are also autoethnographic experiments that point to the reconfiguration of the private and public spheres, especially in postmodern, late-capitalist societies (see, for example, Ellis, 1995 and Richardson, 1997). But this attempt at reconfiguration, although highlighting the play of emotions in social life, easily can be recuperated in and by quite familiar forms. Often focusing on the traumas of domestic or family life – for example, sickness and death, incest and physical abuse, addictions and psychosomatic disorders – autoethnography has a kinship with the confessional and melodramatic culture of talk television. Yet these writers often do not recognize this kinship, and the writing is presented as both an autoreferential and a realist account of experience without problematizing the technoscientific apparatus of its own production. This kind of autoethnography, then, disappoints the promise of diffraction and is a form of hyper self-reflection, as Haraway might put it; not yet the kind of 'swerve' away from reflection that she imagines.

Other sociologists have combined autobiographical forms of writing with cultural criticism of technoscience in more promising ways. Often meant to be performed in order to engage various media or information technologies, these writing experiments engage the larger sense of writing as technology. They put the autoreferential treatment of experience on the same plane as the technoscientific apparatuses through and by which such experience is produced. That is, the writing/performance becomes something like a collage, in which each element is intended not to fit seamlessly with the others and, indeed, intended perhaps not to 'fit' at all. Rather, the elements are free to interfere with each other, often in ways that cannot be anticipated in advance (see, for example, Pfohl, 1992; Gordon, 1997; Orr, 1999; Denzin, 1997; Clough, 1998, 2000; Schneider and Wang, 2000).

While social theorists seem not to have considered these forms of experimental writing, they may well be a rich resource with which to think and act toward the transformations to which Donna Haraway's work points.

HARAWAY'S MAJOR WORKS

Books

Haraway, D.J. (1976) *Crystals, Fabrics, and Fields: Metaphors of Organicism in 20th Century Developmental Biology*. New Haven, CT: Yale University Press.

Haraway, D.J. (1989a) *Primate Visions: Gender, Race, and Nature in the World of Modern Science*. New York: Routledge.

Haraway, D.J. (1991) *Simians, Cyborgs, and Women: The Reinvention of Nature*. New York: Routledge.

Haraway, D.J. (1997a) *Modest_Witness@Second_Millennium.FemaleMan_Meets_Oncomouse.*™ *Feminism and Technoscience*. New York: Routledge.

Haraway, D.J. (1999a): *How Like A Leaf. An Interview with Thyrza Nichols Goodeve*. New York: Routledge.

Articles

Haraway, D.J. (1978a) 'Animal sociology and a natural economy of the body politic, Part I. A political physiology of dominance', *Signs*, 4: 21–36.

Haraway, D.J. (1978b) 'Animal sociology. Part II. The past is the contested zone: human nature and theories of production and reproduction in primate behavior studies', *Signs*, 4: 37–60.

Haraway, D.J. (1979): 'The biological enterprise: sex, mind, and profit from human engineering to sociobiology', *Radical History Review*, 20: 206–37.

Haraway, D.J. (1981) 'In the beginning was the word: the genesis of biological theory', *Signs, 6: 469–81.*

Haraway, D.J. (1981–82) 'The high cost of information in post World War II evolutionary biology: ergonomics, semiotics, and the sociobiology of communications systems', *Philosophical Forum*, 13: 244–78.

Haraway, D.J. (1983) 'The contest for primate nature: daughters of man the hunter in the field, 1960–80', in Mark Kaun (ed.) *The Future of American Democracy: Views from the Left*. Philadelphia, PA: Temple University Press.

Haraway, D.J. (1984) 'Class, race, sex, scientific objects of knowledge: a socialist-feminist perspective on the social construction of productive nature and some political consequences', in Violet Haas and Carolyn Perrucci (eds), *Women in Scientific and Engineering Professions*. Ann Arbor, MI: University of Michigan Press.

Haraway, D.J. (1984/85) 'Teddy bear patriarchy: taxidermy in the Garden of Eden, New York City, 1908–1936', *Social Text*, 11: 19–64.

Haraway, D.J. (1985) 'Manifesto for cyborgs: science, technology, and socialist feminism in the 1980s', *Socialist Review*, 80: 65–108.

Haraway, D.J. (1986) 'Primatology is politics by other means: women's place is in the jungle', in Ruth Bleier (ed.) *Feminist Approaches to Science*. Oxford: Pergamon.

Haraway, D.J. (1988) 'Situated knowledges: the science question in feminism as a site of discourse on the privilege of partial perspective', *Feminist Studies*, 14: 575–99.

Haraway, D.J. (1989) 'The biopolitics of postmodern bodies: determinations of self in immune system discourse', *Differences: A Journal of Feminist Cultural Studies*, 1: 3–43.

Haraway, D.J. (1990): 'Cyborg at large'. An interview conducted by Constance Penley and Andrew Ross', *Social Text*, 25/26: 8–23.

Haraway, D.J. (1991) 'The promise of monsters: reproductive politics for inappropriate/d others', in Larry Grossberg, Cary Nelson, and Paula Treichler (eds) *Cultural Studies*. New York: Routledge.

Haraway, D.J. (1992): 'Otherworldly conversations, terran topics, local terms', *Science as Culture*, 3: 59–92.

Haraway, D.J. (1994): 'A game of cat's cradle: science studies, feminist theory, cultural studies', *Configurations: A Journal of Literature and Science*, 1: 59–71.

Haraway, D.J. (1995a): 'Cyborgs and symbionts: living together in the new world order', in Chris Hables Gray, Heidi J. Figueroa-Sarriera, and Steven Mentor (ed.) *The Cyborg Handbook*. New York: Routledge.

Haraway, D.J. (1995b) 'Writing, literacy and technology: toward a cyborg writing', in Gary Olson and Elizabeth Hirsh (eds) *Women Writing Culture*. Albany, NY: State University of New York Press.

Haraway, D.J. (1996): 'Modest witness: feminists diffractions in science studies', in Peter Galison and David Stump (eds), *The Disunity of Sciences: Boundaries, Contexts, and Power.* Stanford, CA: Stanford University Press.

Haraway, D.J. (1997b) 'enlightenment@science_-wars.com: a personal reflection of love and war', *Social Text*, 50: 123–29.

Haraway, D.J. (1999b) 'Virtual speculum in the new world order', Adele E. Clarke and Virginia L. Olesen (eds) *Revisioning Women, Health and Healing: Feminist, Cultural, and Technoscience Perspectives*. New York: Routledge.

SECONDARY REFERENCES

Aronowitz, Stanley (1988) *Science as Power, Discourse, and Ideology in Modern Society*. Minneapolis: University of Minnesota Press.

Butler, Judith (1993) *Bodies that Matter: On the Discursive Limits of 'Sex'*. New York: Routledge.

Clarke, Adele E. and Olesen, Virginia L. (eds) (1999) *Revisioning Women, Health and Healing: Feminist, Cultural, and Technoscience Perspectives*. New York: Routledge.

Clough, Patricia Ticineto (1998) *The End(s) of Ethnography: From Realism to Social Criticism*. New York: Peter Lang.

Clough, Particia Ticineto (2000) *Autoaffection: Unconscious Thought in the Age of Teletechnology*. Minneapolis: University of Minnesota Press.

Denzin, Norman (1997) *Interpretive Ethnography: Ethnographic Practices for the 21st Century*. Newbury Park, CA: Sage.

Ellis, Carolyn (1995) *Final Negotiations: A Story of Love, Loss, and Chronic Illness*. Philadelphia, PA: Temple University Press.

Gordon, Avery (1997) *Ghostly Matters: Haunting and the Sociological Imagination*. Minneapolis: University of Minnesota Press.

Harding, Sandra (1986) *The Science Question in Feminism*. Ithaca, NY: Cornell University Press.

Kirby, Vicki (1991) 'Corpus delicti: the body at the scene of writing', in R. Diprose and R. Ferrell (eds) *Cartographies: Poststructuralism and the Mapping of Bodies and Spaces*. Sydney: Allen and Unwin.

Kuhn, Thomas (1970) *The Structure of Scientific Revolutions*, 2nd ed. Chicago: University of Chicago Press.

Latour, Bruno (1987) *Science in Action*. Cambridge, MA: Harvard University Press.

Latour, Bruno (1993) *We Have Never Been Modern*. Cambridge, MA: Harvard University Press.

Lynch, Michael and Woolgar, Steve (1990) 'Introduction: sociological orientations to representational practice in science', in Michael Lynch and Steve Woolgar (eds) *Representation in Scientific Practice*. Cambridge, MA: MIT Press.

Orr, Jackie (1999) 'Performing methods: history, hysteria, and the new science of psychiatry', in *Pathology and the Postmodern: Mental Illness as Discourse and Experience*. London: Sage.

Pfohl, Stephen (1992) *Death at the Parasite Cafe: Social Science (Fictions) & the Postmodern*. New York: St. Martin's.

Richardson, Laurel (1997) *Fields of Play: Constructing an Academic Life*. New Brunswick, NJ: Rutgers University Press.

Schneider, Joseph W. and Wang, Laihua (2000) *Giving Care, Writing Self: A 'New' Ethnography*. New York: Peter Lang.

Smith, Dorothy (1987) *The Everyday World as Problematic: A Feminist Sociology*. Boston: Northeastern University Press.

Sokal, Alan (1996a) 'Transgressing the boundaries: toward a transformative hermeneutics of quantum gravity', *Social Text*, 46/47: 217–52.

Sokal, Alan (1996b) 'A physicist experiments with cultural studies', *Lingua Franca*, May/June: 64.

Spivak, Gayatri Chakravorty (1999) *A Critique of Postcolonial Reason: Toward A History of the Vanishing Present*. Cambridge, MA: Harvard.

Star, Susan Leigh (1991) 'Power, technology, and the phenomenology of conventions: on being allergic to onions,' in John Law (ed.) *A Sociology of Monsters: Power, Technology and the Modern World*. Oxford: Blackwell.

31

Fredric Jameson

SEAN HOMER

BIOGRAPHICAL DETAILS AND THEORETICAL CONTEXT

Fredric Jameson was born in Cleveland, Ohio in 1934. He completed his BA at Haverford College in 1954 and went on to complete an MA (1956) and PhD (1959) at Yale University. Jameson's doctoral thesis was subsequently published as *Sartre: The Origins of a Style* (1961). While undertaking his doctoral studies, Jameson was awarded a number of research fellowships and studied at the University of Aix-Marseille (1954–5) and the Universities of Munich and Berlin (1956–7). Jameson taught at Harvard University from 1959 to 1967, and moved to the University of California at San Diego in 1967 where he was appointed Professor of French in 1971. From 1976 to 1983 Jameson taught at Yale University and from 1983 to 1985 was Professor of Literature and History of Consciousness at the University of California at Santa Cruz. He moved to Duke University in 1986 where he is currently Distinguished Professor of Comparative Literature and director of the Graduate Program in Literature and the Center for Cultural Theory.

Jameson has been described as 'probably the most important cultural critic writing in English today' (MacCabe, 1992: ix) and he is widely acknowledged as the foremost proponent for that tradition of critical theory variously identified as Hegelian or Western Marxism. Indeed, Perry Anderson has gone so far as to suggest that Jameson's work at once marks the culmination of Western Marxism while, at the same time, significantly exceeding its traditional geographical and cultural limits (1998: 71–4). Through his early critical surveys of the Frankfurt School and the Hegelian tradition of dialectical criticism in *Marxism and Form* (1971) to Russian formalism and French structuralism in *The Prison House of Language* (1972), Jameson has contributed more than any other figure to the renaissance of Marxist literary and cultural criticism in the USA since the early 1970s. These two early books represent key texts in the dissemination of what were at the time the still relatively unknown traditions of continental theory and Western Marxism within the North American academy.

With the publication of *The Political Unconscious* (1981), and his first sustained engagement with post-structuralism and

Althusserian Marxism, Jameson emerged as a major theoretician in his own right. Jameson gained a further international readership with the publication of his seminal essays on postmodernity in the early 1980s, culminating with the monumental study *Postmodernism, or, The Cultural Logic of Late Capitalism* (1991). His analyses of the spatiotemporal dynamics of postmodernity and its cultural logic have provided some of the most influential, as well as the most controversial, ideas produced in this often hyperbolic and always contested field of social and cultural theory. His work in the 1990s on globalization, finance capital, and geopolitical aesthetics has only served to confirm Jameson's status as a singularly unique and audacious critic, as he attempts to map the cultural and political implications of capitalism's universalizing logic. Parallel to his meticulous dissection of the ideological assumptions behind the major schools of continental theory, Jameson's more occasional, single author studies – Sartre ([1961] 1984a), Wyndham Lewis (1979), Adorno (1990a) and Brecht (1998b) – have radically challenged accepted readings of these figures and elaborated a uniquely Jamesonian theory of modernist aesthetic practice. In the later books on Adorno and Brecht in particular, he has sought to restore the properly Marxian context and conceptual framework within which these writers worked and to offer us a reading of Adorno and Brecht which counters the relativism and nominalism of much current postmodern and post-structuralist thinking.

Jameson's formative political and theoretical experience was marked by two interrelated events, the aftermath of McCarthyism and the emergence of the New Left. The central figure in his early political and philosophical development was the French existentialist Jean-Paul Sartre. Jameson's study of Sartre originated in a period when New Criticism was still hegemonic in the United States. The principal contender to this politically conservative group of critics was the phenomenologically informed work of George Poulet and J. Hillis Miller. The first works of what we now call 'theory', specifically the early Roland Barthes and some of Adorno's work, were only slowly becoming known and had as yet to make a strong intellectual impact. In the light of Jameson's subsequent commitment, the Sartre book is remarkable for the absence of reference to either Marxism or History. This essentially phenomenological study, however, can be seen in the context of a wider attempt within the academy to radically break with the dominant critical paradigm of the conservative New Criticism.

Reflecting on his own 'conversion' to 'Sartreanism', Jameson suggests that it was 'always rather different from more conventional modernist conversions of either the aesthetic or the philosophical type' (1985: v). Unlike Kantianism, Heideggerianism, or more recently Derrida's deconstruction, a commitment to Sartreanism was 'more a matter of a general problematic than of agreement with Sartre's own positions' (1985: v). In relation to his later understanding of Marxism, Jameson has described Sartre as a role model of the politically engaged intellectual.

Douglas Kellner notes that in the 1950s Sartre was received in the United States as an exemplary figure of the 'individualist radical intellectual' and a 'rebel against convention of all sorts' (1989: 8). Reading Jameson contextually, writes Kellner, one 'encounters a young literary critic radicalized by study in Europe during the 1950s and by the political movements of the 1960s, turning to Marxism as the solution to his own theoretical and political dilemmas' (1989: 9). Sartre, perhaps more than any other figure on the left, came to symbolize the figure of the *intellectual engagé*, the committed intellectual who sought to intervene politically but from outside of any mass political organization or traditional Party structure. This search for a viable form of Marxism, both politically and theoretically relevant to one's own historical moment and situation, at the same time divorced from the dogmatism and orthodoxy of the communist party and the Soviet Union, has always strongly informed Jameson's own view of Marxism.

In the 'Preface' to *Marxism and Form* Jameson articulated the specific dilemmas faced by the Marxist critic in North America in the late 1960s. When North American students thought of Marxism, he wrote, they only had recourse to the struggles and polemics of the 1930s, which bore little relation to their contemporary needs and aspirations. The few familiar Marxist critics still readily accessible, Christopher Caudwell or Ernst Fischer, no longer seemed adequate or applicable to current critical requirements, particularly with the shift of critical emphasis since the 1930s from content-based criticisms to more formally based methods. What was required, he suggested, was a form of Marxism specific to the demands of postindustrial monopoly capitalism, with its intensification of commodification, the occultation of social class, and increasing fragmentation of existential experience. In other words, Marxism is not a rigid system one applies to any given state of affairs but a situated discourse, an open and flexible body of thought that develops according to the specific historical circumstances. It is perfectly consistent, writes Jameson, 'with the spirit of Marxism – with the principle that thought reflects its concrete social situation – that there should exist several different Marxisms in the world today, each answering the specific needs and problems of its own socio-economic system' (1971: xviii). For Jameson, the unique questions raised by monopoly capitalism could only be adequately addressed by that tradition of Hegelian Marxism from Lukács through to Sartre and Adorno.

SOCIAL THEORY AND CONTRIBUTIONS

Jameson is first and foremost a cultural theorist and critic. His relevance for contemporary social theory rests primarily on the extraordinary defence of Marxism's emancipatory narrative and critique of post-structuralism in *The Political Unconscious* (1981) and, above all, through his theorization of postmodernity as the cultural logic of late capitalism. The publication of *The Political Unconscious* established Jameson, in the words of Terry Eagleton, 'as without question the foremost American Marxist critic, and one of the leading literary theorists of the Anglophone world' (1986). In the United States *The Political Unconscious* was extremely influential and generated enormous interest, with special issues of *Diacritics* (1982), *Critical Exchange* (1983) and *New Orleans Review* (1984) all devoted to Jameson's work. In the UK and Continental Europe, however, its reception was rather more muted. Robert Young (1990) identified three principal reasons for the extreme variance in the North American and British receptions of the text. First, *The Political Unconscious* appeared at a time when the tide of deconstruction seemed virtually unstoppable, yet Jameson's Marxism seemed at once able to appropriate Derrida's insights and at the same time supersede deconstruction itself. Secondly, Jameson's Marxism seemed to offer a return to a kind of ethical criticism which structuralism and deconstruction had effectively ruled out of debate. As Young writes, 'this appealed to a traditional understanding of criticism's value, as well as to male critics who felt increasingly upstaged by the forceful politics that feminism had made available to women' (1990: 91). Finally, and perhaps most significantly for the text's reception in Britain and Europe, *The Political Unconscious* was seen to herald what Jameson called the 'Althusserian Revolution', and yet the text was appearing in Britain in a post-Althusserian context. Jameson's British readership was already familiar with Althusser's work, and more specifically the Althusserian influence on literary theory through the work of Eagleton and Macherey. Jameson thus appeared to be heralding a theoretical revolution that had already passed by and for which the critique was now firmly established within British Marxism.

Jameson's appropriation of Althusserian antihistoricism within his own stridently historicist project represented an outstanding *tour de force* of dialectical thinking and prose. In a long and densely argued opening chapter entitled 'On Interpretation' Jameson subjected Althusser's three forms of historical causality or *effectivity* – mechanical, expressive, and structural – to a thorough re-examination, arguing not only that Marxism is a historicism but, moreover, that as an absolute historicism it can accommodate the Althusserian critique. Jameson's title also signals the polemical thrust of his work against post-structuralist critiques of interpretation. Marxism's primacy as a theoretical and political discourse, he argued, rests on the very density of its semantic yield. It is not merely one more theory of interpretation but 'the absolute horizon of all reading and interpretation' (1981: 17). Furthermore, Marxism's holistic and totalizing character means that it is not just one more theory of history or form of sociological study but the final untranscendable horizon of History (with a capital H) itself.

Marxism and Historicism

The force of Jameson's argument has always, in part, rested on his ability to accommodate potential critiques within his own dialectical framework. Thus in *The Political Unconscious* Jameson conceded to post-structuralism many of its insights into difference, otherness, and alterity while at the same time arguing for the priority of Marxism's totalizing historical narrative. According to Jameson, Derrida's conception of *differance*, Foucault's privileging of micropolitics, or Deleuze and Gauttari's identification of the schizophrenic nature of capitalism and desire all retain a certain explanatory force and local validity, but only when they are placed in the context of the larger historical narrative or conception of the social whole. In short, post-structuralist notions of difference and particularism very accurately describe the symptoms of the current historical moment but they cannot account for the conditions of possibility for those symptoms. For Jameson, therefore, we must situate the *ideologies* of post-structuralism within the broader Marxian understanding of History.

Jameson proposes to do this through a series of three dialectically expanding horizons of interpretation, which he identifies as the political, the social, and the historical. The first horizon coincides with the individual text itself which, following Lévi-Strauss' work on myth, Jameson suggests we read as a symbolic act, or as an imaginary attempt to resolve a real social contradiction. The second horizon transcends the text itself to locate it in relation to the social and the broader conflict of class discourse. The final horizon in turn locates the ideologies of class discourse in relation to the untranscendable horizon of History. The difficulty with Jameson's notion of dialectically expanding semantic horizons is precisely how each is related to the others and how one moves one's analysis from one level to the next. The fact that Jameson's own text demonstrates each level of analysis in relation to discrete examples may suggest that he himself had not fully resolved this dilemma.

The Marxian view of history as teleological, a predetermined narrative leading inevitably to a classless society, has been widely criticized in social and political theory (see Giddens, 1982; Castoriadis, 1987). Indeed, the very notion that Marxism is itself a historicism, or theory of history, had received its most stringent critique in the 1960s from within Marxism itself, through the work of the structuralist Marxist Louis Althusser. While Althusser himself remained a committed Marxist, his critique of historicism pathed the way for a sustained Foucauldian and post-structuralist critique of Marxism's conception of the social totality and its teleological historical narrative of human emancipation. If in the early 1980s, therefore, Jameson was to reassert an essentially Hegelian conception of History, then an encounter with Althusserianism was unavoidable.

In brief, Althusser argued that the inevitable outcome of reading Marxism as a historicism is that it conflates the various distinct levels of society (the economic, the political, the ideological etc.), reducing and flattening the social totality into a version of the Hegelian conception of totality, thus eliding their real differences. The full weight of Althusser's critique of historicism is directed against the notion of 'expressive causality', which he identifies with the Hegelian conception of history. The two essential characteristics, or errors, of Hegel's conception of history, argued Althusser, are its positing of a *homogenous continuity* of time and its *contemporaneity*. In other words, history is reduced to the mere succession of one event, or period, after another which always co-exist in one and the same time. The most serious misconception deriving from Hegel's view of history, observes Althusser, is its formulation of the social whole, or totality, as an *expressive whole*, in the sense that 'it presupposes in principle that the whole in question be reducible to an *inner essence*, of which the elements of the whole are then no more than phenomenal forms of expression, the inner principle of the essence being present at each point in the whole' (Althusser and Balibar, 1970: 186). This reduces the heterogeneity of historical time to an homogeneous continuum and the specificity and relative autonomy of the distinct levels of the social totality to a contemporaneous or homogeneous present.

Jameson concedes that on its own terms the Althusserian critique is 'quite unanswerable' (1981: 27), but in a characteristic rhetorical gesture suggests that this is to miss Althusser's point. Althusser is not attacking historicism as such but rather the notion of periodization and the question of the representation of History, that is, the notion that history is just 'one damn thing after another' and reductive forms of allegorical interpretation which seek to rewrite given sequences or periods in terms of a hidden master-narrative. If, on the other hand, we understand allegory not as the reduction of the heterogeneity of historical sequences to a predetermined narrative but as an opening up of multiple horizons, in the sense outlined above, then the concept of a historical narrative can be rehabilitated. History, writes Jameson, 'is *not* a text, not a narrative, master or otherwise, but that, as an absent cause, it is inaccessible to us except in textual form, and that our approach to it and to the Real itself necessarily passes through its prior textualization, its narrativization in the political unconscious' (1981: 35). As with the Althusserian conception of structure, History is not immediately present, not knowable in-itself but is something we know through its effects or textualizations.

Utopia and Ideology

Seeing History as an inaccessible absent cause facilitates one of Jameson's most provocative and polemical rhetorical gestures, that is, his insistence on the necessity of utopian thought. Marxism's conception of ideology as 'false consciousness' or as 'structural limitation', argues Jameson, represents the historic originality of its negative dialectic, or, its negative demystifying hermeneutic. Marxism, however, also has a tradition of a positive or redemptive hermeneutic and it is within this arena that 'some noninstrumental conception of culture may be tested' (1981: 286). Following Ernst Bloch, Jameson argues that all ideology must be grasped at one and the same time as utopian in the sense that it projects a 'collective' representation. At its simplest this collective dialectic operates as a form of 'compensatory exchange'. For example, theories of the manipulatory aspects of the media, and of 'mass' culture in general, must account for the addressee's acquiescence if they are not to posit an entirely passive spectator. Audiences are not simply duped into consuming reactionary culture but derive pleasure from it, and therefore, the addresser must be providing some form of compensatory gratification in return for the spectators' acquiescence. For Jameson, ideological manipulation and utopian gratification are inseparable aspects of *all* cultural texts. The notion that all cultural texts contain a utopian dimension is for Jameson the logical extension of 'the proposition that *all* class consciousness – or in other words, all ideology in the strongest sense, including the most exclusive forms of ruling-class consciousness just as much as that of oppositional or oppressed classes – is in its very nature Utopian' (1981: 289).

Class consciousness emerges from the struggle between various groups or classes and therefore is always defined in relation to another class. In this sense class consciousness, of whatever class, is utopian to the extent that it expresses the unity of a collectivity and the projection of a classless society. Even the most reactionary forms of ruling-class culture and ideology are utopian to the extent that they affirm collective solidarity. Eagleton argues that 'Jameson's startling claim to discern a proleptic image of utopia in any human collectivity whatsoever, which would presumably encompass racist rallies' (1990: 404) is ridiculously gullible or faintly perverse. Whilst Jameson would insist that a racist rally is indeed utopian to the extent that it projects a 'white' collectivity, this must be seen as a compensatory projection rather than an 'anticipatory' one. In other words, racism could be said to offer forms of compensation and gratification for present social problems – unemployment, bad housing, lack of services and so on – but insofar as it does not project a fully classless society it is not a positive anticipation of utopia. The question of distinguishing between compensatory and anticipatory projections is problematic and one can clearly envisage a situation whereby Jameson may interpret a racist rally as compensatory, while the racists themselves would see it as anticipatory, in which case the heuristic value of the concept would appear to be seriously compromised.

Critique of Jameson

Jameson's appraisal and reformulation of Althusserian Marxism is nothing less than a virtuoso performance of dialectical subtlety and rhetorical ingenuity. His reassertion of Marxism's historicizing project, of the essential role narrative plays in relation to historical understanding and of the inevitability of interpretation were all welcome correctives to post-structuralist axioms. Yet, at the same time, there remained in Jameson's work a tendency to overhastily assimilate cultural and historical diversity to a single unified narrative. Thus, in a series of contentious essays on 'Third World' literature, Jameson advanced the astonishing proposition that all Third World texts 'necessarily project a political dimension in the form of national allegory: *the story of the private individual destiny is always an allegory of the embattled situation of the public third-world culture and society*' (1986: 69, italics in original). To substantiate this claim Jameson offers a reading of a work by the Chinese writer Lu Xun and *Xala* by the Senegalese writer Ousmane Sembsne. Jameson's readings are, as always, illuminating and provocative, but can we really reduce the diversity and heterogeneity of 'all' Third World literature to the examples of two writers and on the basis of such a reduction can we seriously argue that third-world literature *always* constitutes national allegories? Reflecting on his increasing discomfort upon reading Jameson's essay Aijaz Ahmad observes that, 'the further I read the more I realized, with no little chagrin, that the man whom I had for so long, so affectionately, even though from a physical distance, taken as a comrade was, in his own opinion, my civilizational Other' (1987: 3–4). Jameson's totalizing logic treats the whole 'Third World', a problematic concept in itself, as a homogenous entity in which the Other is constituted as the same. In Jameson's text the Third World is defined solely in terms of its experience of colonialism and simply reduplicates the history of European colonialism. 'History itself', therefore, appears to be nothing less than the history of the West, that is, of modernization and the rise of capitalism, and the question of other histories has been ruled out of account. Jameson would not appear to have accommodated the Althusserian notion of structural causality within his own conception of structural historicism so much as to have annulled the former through a revamped Hegelianism in the shape of the latter (see Homer, 1998: 62–9).

APPRAISAL OF KEY ADVANCES AND CONTROVERSIES

Until the early 1980s Jameson's work centred on literary modernism, and the call that he had made in the opening pages of *Marxism and Form* (1971) for an analysis of the contemporary conjuncture had yet to emerge. This situation was to change radically with a series of studies of postmodernism culminating in Jameson's seminal 1984 article 'Postmodernism, or, The Cultural Logic of Late Capitalism', which, in the words of Perry Anderson, 'redrew the whole map of the postmodern at one stroke – a prodigious inaugural gesture that has commanded the field ever since' (1998: 54). The significance of Jameson's work on postmodernism remains his attempt to ground this most fluid and slippery of concepts in concrete transformations in the social and economic field. Above all he has sought to theorize the relations between the transformations taking place at the level of culture and everyday experience and the consolidation of a global economic system.

Jameson's work hinges on the question of whether or not a transition and/or break from modernity to postmodernity has taken place. First, Jameson contends that there has been a radical transformation of our experience of time and space in the postmodern era. Postmodernism marks the ascendance of the category of space over time and hence our experience of history, narrative and memory have all waned in the postmodern world. As a correlative to this our subjective experience has also undergone a significant transformation, whereby traditional notions of a centred autonomous subject have been replaced by decentred, fragmented subjects. Following Baudrillard (1968), Jameson argued that the realm of human needs had now been transcended in the pervasive culture of the image, cybernetic space, and schizoid intensity. Second, the cultural logic essay dramatically expanded the term postmodernism beyond the narrow confines of the architectural and literary debates it was then largely concerned with to cover virtually the whole field of contemporary arts and theoretical discourse. In short, Jameson transformed the debate from one of architectural or literary styles to address much broader issues of social and cultural change. Third, he insisted that postmodernism did not represent an epochal break with capitalism, as theorists such as Jean-François Lyotard (1984) argued, but rather that it represented a restructuration of capitalism itself. Drawing on the work of the economist Ernest Mandel, Jameson argued that Mandel's identification of 'late capitalism' provided the social base for the emergence of postmodern culture. Fourth, Jameson refused to resort to moral judgments on whether or not postmodernism was good or bad, progressive or reactionary, insisting on the need to historically situate and analyse the phenomenon of postmodernism itself. Finally, in opposition to notions of a culture of hyperreality and virtuality proposed by Baudrillard, Jameson sought to anchor postmodern culture within the objective alterations of the economic order of capital, arguing that the realm of culture has expanded to such an extent that it is now virtually co-extensive with the economy. The commodity form, he argued, has now penetrated cultural artefacts to such a degree that any aspiration to resist commodification through art, a quintessentially modernist gesture in Adorno's aesthetic theory, is simply futile. All culture today is always-already commodified, or, if it attempts to resist its status as a commodity it is rapidly and effortlessly recuperated. At the same time, the dialectical contrary of the commodification of culture has been the acculturation of the commodity and the aestheticization of politics. In short, we are now faced with an entirely new mode of living the quotidian, or what Jameson has called an 'acculturation of everyday life'.

The Aporias of Postmodernity

At the time Jameson's achievement was breathtaking: in a characteristically bravura performance he confronted postmodernism on its own terms, acknowledging and granting many of its insights into contemporary experience, whilst simultaneously subsuming it within the very historical paradigm, Marxism, that it had so ostentatiously discredited. The cultural logic essay, however, raised a number of critical issues that it failed to adequately address – economically, culturally, historically, and above all politically. Utilizing Raymond Williams' distinction between 'dominant, residual and emergent' cultures (1977: 121–7) Jameson argued that postmodernism represented the first truly global cultural dominant. Fred Pfeil, on the other hand, has pointed out that postmodernism appears to be a great deal more culturally specific than Jameson suggests, that is to say, the cultural expression of the North American 'Professional Managerial Class' (1990: 97–125). Postcolonial and feminist critics have also pointed to the geographical, racial, and gender specificity of much postmodern theory and culture.

The cultural logic thesis was arguably achieved at too great a level of abstraction. Jameson presents, on the one hand, a highly persuasive account of the isolated subject's experience within the disorientating world of globalized capitalism, while, on the other, a very generalized theory of the structural transformations of capital itself. What this work lacked and the monumental *Postmodernism, or, The Cultural Logic of Late Capitalism* (1991) conspicuously failed to deliver was any systematic account of the mediations between individual subjects and the world system itself. The key categories of mediation employed here, as with Jameson's previous work, were commodification and reification. Postmodernity was seen to mark a further intensification of reification whereby the commodity form had now penetrated the last enclaves of resistance to capital, that is to say, the aesthetic, the Third World and the Psyche. If this is the case, however, it would appear to rule out the possibility for any form of resistance to the new global market and hence the possibility of historical change. This dilemma was starkly presented in Jameson's notion of a new postmodern political aesthetic of 'cognitive mapping'. Developing the notion from the urban studies of Kevin Lynch in the 1960s, Jameson deployed it to account for a subject's inability to mentally represent or locate themselves in the transnational, globalized world of late capitalism. What this dialectic of immediate perception and inconceivable totality lacked was any indication or analysis of the intermediate forms of mediation between individuals and the global economy – that is to say, forms of mediation, be they group, institutional, regional, or national, that at once shape our identity or subjectivity and, at the same time, provide the space for political resistance to the otherwise relentless logic of reification. There was always a sense, therefore, in which Jameson's perception of postmodern culture represents a specifically North American perspective on global change, a situation that is hardly surprising when for many globalization has itself become synonymous with 'Americanization'.

Finance Capital and Cultural Abstraction

Jameson's work on postmodernism exhibits a remarkable consistency since his initial surveys of the debate in 1982. There is one key area, however, in which his work has undergone a significant revision. In his more recent writings on postmodernity Jameson has sought to substantiate the economic basis of postmodernity through an analysis of the preeminent role of finance capital in the global economy. In the 1984 essay Jameson drew upon Mandel's theory of 'long waves' of capital expansion to account for the restructuration of capitalist relations in the era of postmodernity. Adopting Mandel's ternary schema of market, monopoly, and late capitalism, Jameson correlated this with his own aesthetic schema of realism, modernism, and postmodernism. What was always left unclear was precisely how one mapped onto the other or what the nature of the relationship between the two might be.

There also appeared to be a marked discrepancy between Jameson's own periodization of postmodernism and Mandel's periodization of late capitalism. Turning to Giovanni Arrighi's (1994) *The Long Twentieth Century*, Jameson finds the answer to this in the structural role played by speculative finance in the global economy. Arrighi's elaboration of the nature and operation of finance capital, contends Jameson, serves to crystallize all the problems and questions that have arisen from the early 1980s onwards and especially in the relationship between economics and culture. The advantage of Arrighi's work is that it forestalls the unfortunate teleological implications of the market, monopoly, and late capitalism model whilst retaining a conception of capitalist development as discontinuous and expansive. Furthermore, Arrighi's dialectic of money, capital, and speculative finance is a process that is 'internal' to capital, a spiralling process of decline and renewal at every 'higher' stage of capitalism. This account of the internal logic of capital and its free-floating status within the world economy provides us with one of the keys to understanding the recent transformations in culture. Essentially Arrighi offers us an account of the *abstraction* inherent in capital from its status as money through investment capital to finance capital. In other words, it provides us with a theory of abstraction that closely follows Jameson's own earlier odyssey of the image or sign from realism (where the image is still tied to its referent and can be said to be self-validating, the image quite simply is what is represented) – to modernism (when the image becomes severed from its referent and achieves a degree of semiautonomy) – to postmodernism (where reification penetrates the image itself and rends signifier and signified asunder, the image appears to be free-floating). As this process of abstraction is both internal to capital itself and can be rendered at a systemic level in terms of successive modes of production, or the operation of particular financial markets, Jameson is able to deploy this notion of abstraction at a systemic level – as with his dialectic of realism, modernism, postmodernism – and within specific cultural forms, that is to say, in the analysis of rock music or specific film and literary genres.

Jameson's conceptualization of aesthetic abstraction derived from the logic of speculative finance provides his most sustained attempt to date to define the nature of the relationship between the new cultural forms and practices of postmodernism and the economic transformations of postmodernity or globalization. There are a number of problems with Jameson's account, however, not least his continuing desire to elaborate ternary dialectical schema which always fall just a little bit too neatly into place and appear to elide fundamental differences and discrepancies. At a systemic level, there is also a question mark over just how 'seamless' and co-extensive the relations between the economy and culture are. To quote Jameson:

> any comprehensive new theory of finance capitalism will need to reach out into the expanded realm of cultural production to map its effects:

> indeed mass cultural production and consumption themselves – at one with globalization and the new information technology – are as profoundly economic as the other productive areas of late capitalism, and as fully integrated into the latter's generalized commodity system. (Jameson, 1998a: 142–3)

Mass cultural production is at 'one' with globalization and is 'fully' integrated in to the commodity system; but is this the case? Globalization is surely a more differentiated, contradictory and conflictual process than this. Arrighi's work has also been criticized for operating at too high a level of abstraction to provide anything other than a most general guide to current concerns over finance capital (Pollin, 1996). Finally, Arrighi's theorization of the role of finance capital was formulated against Mandel's thesis of long waves and it remains unclear where this leaves Jameson's periodization of postmodernity and the status of Mandel's ideas within his overall account.

Conclusion

Jameson has produced a body of work that is remarkable for its breadth, insight, and intellectual integrity, as well as its political commitment. In an ostensibly postindustrial, postideological age Jameson's unremitting commitment to restating the central tenents of Marxism has provided a welcome antidote to some of the more excessive claims of post-structuralism and postmodernism. Perhaps more than any other figure in contemporary cultural theory, he has articulated an open, nondoctrinaire, Marxism to meet the challenges of the philosophically sophisticated and esoteric languages of formalism, structuralism, post-structuralism, and postmodernism. He has steered a difficult path through the contemporary critique of Marxism whilst seeking to retain its central tenets of political emancipation. He has rigorously and persuasively argued for the theoretical and political necessity of such 'traditional' categories as commodification, reification, class struggle, ideology, and class consciousness, social totality and mode of production, for any adequate understanding of the contemporary historical moment. The acceptance of Marxism's analysis of history and society as fundamentally correct, as given, presents both the challenge of Jameson's work and its problematic nature, as it is precisely the 'self-evident' nature of many of Marxism's 'truths' that have been thrown into doubt today. Jameson's response to this is what is often referred to as his eclecticism, that is, his method of subsuming other theoretical perspectives within an overarching Marxian framework. This at once allows him to appropriate the insights of post-structuralist and postmodernist theory and at the same time neutralize their critique of Marxism through historicizing those specific discourses. Thus, Jameson appears to present the best of both worlds, at once traditional Marxist with the certainties of history on his side and at the same time radical contemporary theorist sensitive to the critique of orthodoxy.

For many Marxist critics of Jameson's work the overriding difficulty remains the question of the political. As Anderson observes, the one name that is conspicuously missing from Jameson's extensive appropriation of Western Marxism is Gramsci:

> Gramsci's work, the product of a communist leader in prison, reflecting on the defeat of one revolution and the ways to possible victory of another, does not fit the bifurcation of the aesthetic and economic. It was eminently political, as a theory of the state and civil society, and a strategy for their qualitative transformation. This body of thought is by-passed in Jameson's extraordinary resumption of Western Marxism. (Anderson, 1998: 130–1)

Jameson's theorization is often achieved at such a high level of abstraction that the undeniably political impulse behind his work is itself occluded or erased. Without a clear elaboration of the different forms of mediation between subjective experience and a globalized economy, be they group, institutional, regional, national, or transnational, it remains difficult to see where new forms of resistance to the universalizing logic of late capitalism will arise from. And this requires a more differentiated and conflictual view of globalization than Jameson himself presents.

JAMESON'S MAJOR WORKS

Jameson, F. (1971) *Marxism and Form: Twentieth-Century Dialectical Theories of Literature.* Princeton, NJ: Princeton University Press.

Jameson, F. (1972) *The Prison House of Language: A Critical Account of Structuralism and Russian Formalism.* Princeton, NJ: Princeton University Press.

Jameson, F. (1979) *Fables of Aggression: Wyndham Lewis, the Modernist as Fascist.* Berkeley: University of California Press.

Jameson, F. (1981) *The Political Unconscious: Narrative as a Socially Symbolic Act.* London: Routledge.

Jameson, F. (1982) 'On Aronson's Sartre', *Minnesota Review,* 18: 116–27.

Jameson, F. ([1961] 1984a) *Sartre: The Origins of a Style* 2nd edn. New York: Columbia University Press.

Jameson, F. (1984b) 'Postmodernism, or, the cultural logic of late capitalism', *New Left Review,* 146: 53–92.

Jameson, F. (1985) 'Introduction' to *Sartre After Sartre. Yale French Studies,* 65: iii-xi.

Jameson, F. (1986) 'Third World literature in the era of multinational capitalism', *Social Text,* 15: 65–88.

Jameson, F. (1988a) *The Ideologies of Theory, Essays 1971–1986, Vol. 1: Situations of Theory.* London: Routledge.

Jameson, F. (1988b) *The Ideologies of Theory, Essays 1971–1986, Vol. 2: The Syntax of History.* London: Routledge.

Jameson, F. (1990a) *Late Marxism: Adorno, or, The Persistence of the Dialectic.* London: Verso.

Jameson, F. (1990b) *Signatures of the Visible.* London: Routledge.

Jameson, F. (1991) *Postmodernism, or, The Cultural Logic of Late Capitalism.* London: Verso.

Jameson, F. (1992) *The Geopolitical Aesthetic: Cinema and Space in the World System.* London: British Film Institute.

Jameson, F. (1994) *The Seeds of Time.* New York: Columbia University Press.

Jameson, F. (1998a) *The Cultural Turn: Selected Writings on the Postmodern, 1983–1998.* London: Verso.

Jameson, F. (1988b) *Brecht and Method.* London: Verso.

SECONDARY REFERENCES

Ahmad, A. (1987) 'Jameson's rhetoric of otherness and the national allegory', *Social Text,* 17: 3–25.

Althusser, L. and Balibar, E. (1970) *Reading Capital.* London: Verso.

Anderson, P. (1998) *The Origins of Postmodernity.* London: Verso.

Arrighi, G. (1994) *The Long Twentieth Century.* London: Verso.

Baudrillard, J. (1968) *Le Systéme des objets.* Paris: Gallimard.

Burnham, C. (1995) *The Jamesonian Unconscious: The Aesthetics of Marxist Theory.* Durham, NC: Duke University Press.

Castoriadis, C. (1987) *The Imaginary Institution of Society.* Cambridge: Polity Press.

Dowling, William C. (1984) *Jameson, Althusser, Marx: An Introduction to 'The Political Unconscious'.* London: Methuen.

Eagleton, T. (1986) 'Fredric Jameson: the politics of style', in *Against the Grain: Selected Essays, 1975–1985.* London: Verso.

Eagleton, T. (1990) *The Ideology of the Aesthetic.* Oxford: Blackwell.

Giddens, A. (1982) *A Contemporary Critique of Historical Materialism.* London.

Hardt, Michael and Weeks, Kathi (eds) (2000) *The Jameson Reader.* Oxford: Blackwell.

Homer, S. (1998) *Fredric Jameson: Marxism, Hermeneutics, Postmodernism.* Cambridge: Polity Press.

Kellner, D. (ed) (1989) *Postmodernism, Jameson, Critique.* Washington, DC: Maisonneuve Press.

Kellner, D. and Homer, S. (eds) (forthcoming) *Fredric Jameson: A Critical Reader.* Oxford: Blackwell.

Lyotard, J-F. (1984) *The Postmodern Condition: A Report on Knowledge.* Minneapolis: University of Minnesota Press.

MacCabe, C. (1992) 'Preface' to Jameson, F. *The Geopolitical Aesthetic: Cinema and Space in the World System.* London: British Film Institute.

Pfeil, F. (1990) 'Making flippy-floppy: postmodernism and the baby-boom PMC', in *Another Tale to Tell: Politics & Narrative in Postmodern Culture.* London: Verso.

Pollin, R. (1996) 'Contemporary economic stagnation in world historical perspective', *New Left Review,* 129: 109–18.

Williams, R. (1977) *Marxism and Literature.* Oxford: Oxford University Press.

Young, R. (1990) *White Mythologies: Writing History and the West.* London: Routledge.

32

Stuart Hall

CHRIS ROJEK

BIOGRAPHICAL DETAILS AND THEORETICAL CONTEXT

What are the chief theoretical achievements of Stuart Hall? He manoeuvred 'culture' to the head of the agenda in the academic study of society; he brokered a synthesis between the Gramscian and Althusserian traditions which has been immensely influential in cultural studies and cultural sociology; he cultivated and refined Gramsci's concept of the 'organic intellectual' and provided an important role-model for public intellectuals; and he persuaded the left to reassess its relationship with the history and politics of class by declaring 'new times' and the rise of 'the politics of difference'.

The verbs 'to manoeuvre', 'to cultivate', 'to broker' and 'to persuade', suggest a political creature. No assessment of Hall will suffice unless it mentions his quality as a charismatic leader. Between 1964, when Richard Hoggart brought him to the newly formed Centre for Contemporary Cultural Studies in Birmingham, and 1997, when he retired as Professor of Sociology at the Open University, Hall was not simply a spokesman for left-wing cultural criticism in England, he was one of its principal touchstones and talismans. A black scholar, born in Jamaica in 1932, who left the Caribbean as a Rhodes student in the early 1950s, Hall symbolized the poverty of white culture. His interest in social exclusion and the character of class rule are the tangible result of his expatriate experience. Similarly, the fascination, in his recent work, with diasporic culture and hybrid formations, reveal an abiding interest in the politics of difference and the shifting balance of power between established and outsiders. Hall's outsider status has been carefully preserved, despite enjoying a successful career in the British academic system and occupying a prominent position in public life.

SOCIAL THEORY AND CONTRIBUTIONS

Revisionist Marxism

Hall's work is best understood as an exercise in revisionist Marxism. However, his relationship to the Marxist tradition is not simple. He (1996: 499) describes himself as 'formed in critical relation to Marxist traditions'. The ambivalence has been lifelong, culminating in his 'new times' thesis which many on the left saw as a betrayal of Marxist principles. Hall is perhaps most accurately seen as a reluctant Marxist. He understood class oppression and resistance but was never fully persuaded by the logic of class revolution. His postgraduate work at Oxford was on the theme of America versus Europe in the novels of Henry James. It is revealing that Hall was interested in literature before social science. A common criticism of his later academic work is that it is overreliant on the method of reading culture as a text. I shall return to take up these points in more detail later.

In 1957 Hall moved to London where he worked as a supply teacher in secondary schools and joined the *New Left Review*, which he eventually edited between 1959 and 1961. Long before encountering Gramsci's notion of the 'organic intellectual', Hall recognized the dissemination of advanced ideas and political commentary as the *per diem* duty of serious intellectual labour. This had both good and bad consequences for the development of his theoretical work. Throughout there is a tension between a gregarious, and enormously generous, attitude to other traditions of thought and a priggish tendency to proselytize. Morley and Chen (1996) provide abundant evidence of Hall's intellectual and personal generosity. In contrast, Brundson (1996) writes ruefully of his strained relationship with feminism at the Birmingham Centre. More generally, his stereotyping of the model of 'traditional intellectuals' as inferior to that of 'organic intellectuals' is terribly glib. In fact much of Hall's writing, and the cultural studies tradition which he represents, contains the blase presumption of moral superiority.

One cause of this is the concept of the 'organic intellectual' which Hall borrowed from Gramsci. Hall believes that the function of the organic intellectual is to be, at one and the same time, at the vanguard of intellectual theoretical work and to act as a conduit for ideas to those who do not belong professionally to the intelligentsia. This contrasts with the traditional intellectual, who is presented as cultivating detached, objectivist standards of scholarship. Hall (1996: 501) cites personal worries that the 'hothouse' academic environment at the Birmingham Centre was separating him from 'ordinary people', as one factor behind his decision to accept the Chair of Sociology at the Open University. He was attracted to the nonelitist environment in which student access for study is maximized. He saw it as the perfect setting to operationalize Gramsci's notion of the organic intellectual. As he (reprinted in 1996: 268) puts it:

> It is the job of the organic intellectual to know more than traditional intellectuals do: really know, not just pretend to know, not just have the facility of knowledge, but to know deeply and profoundly... If you are in the game of hegemony you have to be smarter than 'them'.

The passage confirms the earlier interpretation of Hall as someone who sees himself as an outsider. It also perhaps, reveals Hall's prejudices. In fact, set against the broad canvas of social theory there is a surprising narrowness of perspective in his work. For example, given Hall's entreaty that organic intellectuals should be fully conversant with their field, and that Hall's field is the culture of everyday life, it is astonishing that phenomenological traditions hardly figure at all in his writings. The body is almost an absent category in his social theory.

It is also remarkable that Hall never situates the concept of culture against that of civilization. The exercise would have corrected the parochial overconcentration on English culture and English questions in his publications. Other concurrent traditions, notably the figurational sociology associated with the work of Norbert Elias and his circle, developed a sophisticated analysis of the dynamics between culture and civilization. A reading of Elias's (1978: 3–50) discussion of the differences between *kultur* and *zivilization* in the German tradition, and the meaning of the *homme civilisé* in French thought, sharply exposes the paucity of Hall's neo-Gramscian perspective which tends to lump questions of culture together with questions of class.

Another serious gap in Hall's *oeuvre* is the neglect of Bourdieu's sociology. Like Hall, Bourdieu uses a class-based approach to study culture. However, he eschews Hall's tendency to drift towards populism about the working class and 'new ethnicities' (Hall, 1992). Instead Bourdieu's sociology seeks to apply an objectivist perspective to class and culture. The cost of this is the absence of a clear set of political conclusions about the requirements of social transformation. The gain is a more reflexive and less partisan reading of culture than Hall accomplishes in his own work.

In 1961 Hall left the *New Left Review* to teach media, film, and popular culture at Chelsea College, University of London. In the same period he embarked on research work for the British Film Institute with Paddy Whannel. This was eventually published as *The Popular Arts* (1964), in the same year that Hall joined the Birmingham Centre.

This was the decisive move in Hall's intellectual development. The Birmingham Centre was a unique intervention in British academic and cultural life. Hall (1996: 500) himself describes it as an 'alternative university'. Conventional pedagogic distinctions between teacher and student were partially suspended, and the 'curriculum' that members of the Centre followed examined the cultural forms which the dominant, postwar Leavisite tradition had either ignored or marginalized. Not surprisingly, working-class culture emerged as the focal point of study and research. Perhaps more surprisingly, in the light of Hall's later preoccupations, questions of race and ethnicity were not prominent on the Birmingham agenda until the late 1970s. Instead the main fronts of research were class and the mass media; the influence of schooling and education in reproducing class inequalities; the character of youth subcultures; policing and social control, and the operation of ideology in grounded relations of culture. Richard Hoggart decided to leave for UNESCO in 1968, and Hall took over as acting director of the Centre before becoming full-time Director in 1972.

The substantive work conducted by Hall and other members of the Centre was informed by a close reading of Gramsci, Althusser, and, to a lesser extent, Raymond Williams. Little distinction was made between theory and applied work. Instead, empirical study was pursued as a form of practical theorizing, in which theoretical propositions were interrogated through fieldwork. This contrasted sharply with the dominant pragmatic tradition in English social science. The work of Mill, T.H. Green, the Webbs, Beveridge, and Ginsberg, tended to support a contract-view of society and a rational-meliorist view of culture. While not openly antitheoretical, its practitioners were happiest developing social and economic policies for tangible, empirical issues while leaving theoretical questions of metaphysics and hermeneutics to continental traditions. In contrast, from the start of his tenure in Birmingham, Hall emphasized the importance of theory and politics in studying cultural life.

Hall's revisionism is evident in his criticisms of Marxist dogma. Hall agreed with Gramsci that the Marxist tradition was flawed by the drift towards economic reductionism. Williams (1963) also criticized Marxism for theorizing culture as the reflection of the economic substructure. Williams emphasized that culture referred to 'a whole way of life' and that 'structures of feeling' could not be mechanically extrapolated from the economic base. Hall was sympathetic to this argument. However, he quickly developed misgivings about the ethnocentric and sentimental character of Williams's work. These misgivings were reinforced by Hall's growing interest in the Althusserian tradition in France. By 1973, Althusserian Marxism had joined Gramscianism as the pre-eminent intellectual influences in the Birmingham School.

Culturalism and Structuralism

Hall's generosity and personal sense of honour is partly expressed in his reluctance to criticize those who influenced and helped him. So Hall's retreat from the ideas of Hoggart, Williams, and E.P. Thompson was never acrimonious or absolute. He genuinely found, and continues to find, much in their work to be useful and important. However, by 1980 he was openly distinguishing 'two paradigms' in cultural studies. *Culturalism* refers to the work of Williams, Hoggart, and Thompson. It regards culture as the terrain of experience through which meaning, belonging, and identity are forged. This tradition recognizes the effect of material inequality in shaping personal and class orientations, but it values consciousness as the central and indispensable agent of change. *Structuralism* refers to the work of Althusser and to a lesser extent, Gramsci. This tradition regards consciousness and experience as mediated through the material conditions and representational schemata of culture. The context in which agency takes place emerges as the decisive point of cultural study. Thus, personal and class consciousness is redefined as the outcome of the economy, ideology, religion, and other structural components of society.

The research that Hall and his associates in the Birmingham Centre conducted between 1973 and 1979 on television and the mass media, youth subcultures, schooling and policing, clearly pursues a structuralist paradigm in the study of culture. Important and enduring conceptual refinements in cultural studies have their origins in this period. For example, the concepts of hegemony and interpellation, borrowed respectively from Gramsci and Althusser, were extended to correct the perceived limitations of the Marxist concept of ideology. In Marx's work, ideology is a key mechanism for achieving class domination. According to Marx, the ruling ideas in society govern the general pattern of relations. The mouthpiece and guarantor of these ideas is the ruling class. Thus, ideology operates to transform historically and socially specific class-bound ideas into the universal moral and cultural categories of human existence, at least within a given territory such as the nation-state or 'the West'. It is, in short, a highly efficient type of social control and the Birmingham School was understandably interested in it as they probed the texture of class consciousness and cultural relations.

However, following Gramsci (1971, 1985), Hall and his associates were critical of the Marxist view of ideology because it polarized dominant and subordinate classes and presented class unity as a pregiven of analysis. They wanted to convey the schisms and contradictions within human agents and structures of social control. In practice, this implied developing a perspective on rule which avoided the suggestion that ideology is external to human subjects so that it stands over them. Hall and his associates also sought to develop a perspective which respects human agency and resists cultural determinism. The incorporation of the concepts of hegemony and interpellation into cultural studies was intended to achieve these goals.

Hegemony means a group-based ruling system of ideas and institutions which establish the general context of cultural life. It therefore posits human agency as occurring within a patterned structure of inequality and manipulation. However, the pattern is theorized as contingent, not closed. Working in a contrasting, semiotic tradition, Eco (1990, 1994) developed the metaphor of 'the open text' to describe culture. This is intended to highlight the unfinished, evolving character of cultural practice and, thus, to deny essentialism. Hall's use of the concept of hegemony springs from the same antiessentialist impulse. Hegemonic rule is acknowledged as being fragmentary and unfinished. Its contradictory nature is recognized in the ordinary accomplishments of cultural practice. In political terms, unlike rule, which derives from ideological domination, hegemonic control is a continuous process of bargaining, negotiation, force, and resistance. Hall favours the analogy of 'shifting power blocs' to capture the contingent nature of hegemonic rule. The alignment of power blocs is not frozen in ice. Rather movement and realignment are built into the very molecules of power.

The concept of interpellation, which Hall takes over from Althusser, is designed to reinforce this reading of power as fluid and contingent. Interpellation means the process by which individuals are organized to become social subjects. Hall and his associates use it to recast the agency/structure debate in social science. Briefly, agency theorists regard the individual as a unified actor possessing freedom, choice, and self-determination. Hall sees this as the standard rhetoric of conservative and liberal thinkers who call upon us to take responsibility for our conditions of life and lecture us that we have no-one but ourselves to blame for our circumstances. They are criticized by the left because they fail to take account of the structures which condition our understanding of 'individuals', 'freedom', 'choice', and 'self-determination'. In its strongest form structuralist theorists argue that human action is determined by structures of power such as class, gender, race, ethnicity, and so on. These structures are 'social facts' in the old Durkheimian sense of the term. That is, they are prior and external to the individual, and exert a constraining influence upon human behaviour. In other versions of structure theory, structures are theorized as 'predisposing' behaviour or 'moulding' choice. Hall wants to transcend this debate because he believes it revolves around a false conceptual polarity. There is no such thing as a 'free' individual. Even the wealthiest person in the world is shaped by family experience, class relations, unconscious forces, and a variety of moral discourses which regulate behaviour. At the same time, there is no zero-sum of power. Every individual has a degree of choice and freedom. The Althusserian concept of interpellation bears directly on the question of how much choice and freedom we have. According to Althusser, capitalism is built around the notion of the independent individual. This is enshrined in the law and is a domain assumption of informal social interaction. Yet cross-cutting this is a variety of emotive collectivist categories that subsume individualism, for example, categories like 'the nation', 'the people', and 'the underclass'. For Althusser, interpellation constantly 'interrupts' the discourse of individualism. It enables the capitalist state to maintain the appearance of open democratic discourse, while manoeuvring people into civil and political processes whose real function is to preserve and expand capitalist domination.

Hall is attracted to the concept because it underlines the proposition that fluidity and plurality in human relations occur in the context of class power. In the 1980s he used it to explore what he called the 'authoritarian populism' of Thatcherism. One of the central issues that interested Hall in the Thatcher period is how at least a substantial section of the working class could voluntarily support a right-wing government which limited their economic, cultural, and political liberty. He argued that the solution is that Thatcherism deployed emotive, populist categories of nationalism and practical moralism which interrupted people's sense of themselves as individuals. For example, during the miner's strike, Thatcher used the term 'the enemy within' to suggest a subversive threat to the state that was intended to mobilize popular sentiment against the individual freedom of workers to withdraw labour in protest against government industrial policy. Similarly, during the Falklands campaign, appeals to patriotism were made to squash dissent. Further, throughout her years in office, Thatcher made regular and approving references to 'Victorian values' as morally superior to the values of the permissive society. Although their provenance and history was actually very elusive, Thatcher presented these categories as if they were self-evident facts of common sense. For Hall, these were all exercises in moral regulation, and their purpose was to coerce people to consent to an authoritarian programme of control which was waged bogusly in the name of protecting and extending personal freedom. It is the clearest example of interpellation in his writing.

Articulation, Encoding/Decoding

Hall's insistence upon acknowledging fluidity, multiplicity, and difference in social and cultural life is a reaction to the perceived inert verities of both orthodox conservatism and vulgar Marxism. The most obvious metaphor to represent the qualities of fluidity, multiplicity, and difference in human life is language. Hall (1986) recognizes the movement towards discursive metaphor in the development of his cultural and social analysis. He connotes it with the liberating realization that human subjects are divided and contradictory, and that cultural forms are ambivalent and incomplete. Several of his key concepts have linguistic origins. Interpellation is one of them. It literally means the verbal interruption of a speaker in a political arena. In Hall's hands, via Althusser, it takes on the meaning of a form of ideological layering which culturally constructs civil subjects out of human beings. Other important examples of the influence of linguistic and discursive metaphors in Hall's thought are articulation and encoding/decoding.

The concept of articulation again has its roots in Gramsci's thought. Hall interprets it as the fusing of ideological, economic, cultural, and political power blocs to impose a decisive generative structure upon the course of human behaviour. The authoritarian populism in Britain of the Thatcher years was one such moment, and more lately the glib 'inclusivism' of Bill Clinton and the New Labour rhetoric of Tony Blair provide further examples (Hall, 1998). Hall's emphasis on articulation as fusion is designed to highlight the continuous copresence of destabilizing and re-energizing tendencies in cultural and social life. Hall wants to avoid fatalism in politics. Articulation suggests that even in the darkest hour of authoritarian rule, the elements of positive, transformative action are in place and that events can spark them into action. The interplay of order and change is of course, at the heart of the concept of hegemony. For Hall, structures of rule are always conditional, and the concept of articulation reinforces this position.

The point is made in another way in the encoding/decoding model which was developed collaboratively at the Centre under the leadership of Hall (1980). This model is concerned with the effect of texts transmitted to audiences, and the active role of audiences in reinterpreting or subverting these messages. The substantive work of the Centre in this area concentrated on television news and current affairs broadcasts. Hall and his associates were interested in discovering how television operates to produce consent by enlisting audience support for a range of narrowly conceived political options. For example, in presenting news about the defects of government policy the typical practice of TV broadcasters is to describe the alternative policies of the opposing parties. Thus, the broadcast complies with the parameters set by the prevailing notion of parliamentary democracy, which, of course, from the vantage point of the left, is too narrow in its constitution and field of political vision. Most importantly, the question of new or oppositional kinds of extraparliamentary politics is left out of account. Thus, a socially and historically specific vision of politics is 'naturally' encoded through the production and transmission of the media text.

The encoding/decoding model also sought to correct what was perceived as a condescending Frankfurt School type reading of the audience. Adorno and Horkheimer (1944) and Marcuse (1964) presented the audience in mass culture as victims of the all-powerful culture industry. Marcuse (1964) even resorted to fatalistic images like the 'one dimensional society' and the 'totally administered society' to underline the putative helplessness of audiences in the face of calculated media indoctrination. Hall and his associates wanted to reverse this fatalism by reclaiming the active, interpretive capacity of the audience. The intellectual influences behind this move were the semiotic turn in continental cultural theory lead by Eco (1987, 1990) and Barthes (1973, 1979). The revival of interest in Volosinov's (1929) theory of the multiaccentuality of the sign was also important. Hall was again straining for an understanding of cultural life which acknowledged the structured character of choice without negating the concept of agency. The humanist emphasis on the open possibility of change was in considerable tension with the Althusserian emphasis on structuralist influences in cultural practice.

Policing the Crisis (Hall et al., 1978), a collaborative project produced by a Birmingham team headed by Hall, was published on the eve of the first Thatcher government. It is an impressive book. It also constitutes the high-water mark of the project to apply Althusserian Marxism to the study of culture. Even then, the book was strongest on discussing the multiple fronts of the British crisis, and the variety of hegemonic strategies for managing consent. In contrast, few commentators judged that a tenable analysis of cultural determination, and the role of the ideological state apparatus as a generative structure in cultural life, had been accomplished (Sparks, 1996: 88). The loosening of Marxist categories and the interest in fluidity and ambiguity, which had always been features of Hall's thinking on culture, were becoming more pronounced.

New Ethnicities and New Times

Between 1958 and 1978 Hall produced only three publications which took race and ethnicity as their lead subject; in the next 20 years over 30 were printed under his name. The conclusion is inescapable: race and ethnicity were supplanting class at the forefront of his intellectual interests. The emergence of postcolonialism in academic life was surely a catalyst. Hall was attracted to the postcolonial debate, not only because concepts like hybridity and diaspora destabilized white power, but because the methods of postcolonial analysis recast the concept of ethnicity. Between the 1950s and 70s the civil rights and black power movements stereotyped 'white power' as being ascendant, and urged black people to find unity in their colour. Hall acknowledges that this released a tremendous amount of creative energy which exposed the limitations of white hegemony. But it also exaggerated the shared historical and cultural experience of the nonwhite diaspora. Afro-Caribbeans, Indians, Pakistanis, and other black ethnic minorities have different self-images and cultural affiliations. New ethnicities, argues Hall (1988) are based first in the recognition of difference, and second in an acceptance of the signifying system as arbitrary. To some extent Hall is here launching yet another sally against reductionism. By drawing attention to the arbitrary character of racial coding, he is denying the essentialist nature of race. In effect, race is analysed as a matter of cultural construction. Hall is also concerned to demonstrate that racial identity is an unstable category and that questions of race always intersect with issues of gender, class, and sexuality. Volosinov's (1929) work had already inured Hall to the multiaccented character of signifying practices. Now, in his (1988) work on new ethnicities, he appropriated Derrida's ([1975] 1992) concept of *différance* to capture the movement of signifiers and the play of difference in culture and communication.

The postcolonialist concept of hybridity accentuates this by obliging analysis to consider the mixed character of social and cultural formations and providing a counterpoint to notions of cultural identity and racial purity. Similarly, the idea of ethnic diaspora suggests the porous character of culture and the permeability of national formations. Hall, is in fact, positing a processual, contingent, relatively open reading of power.

But Hall's interest in postcolonialism was always guarded. He (1986) rejected what he called its 'upward reductionism' which treated power as equivalent to discourse. There is enough of an old fashioned political strategist left in him to insist that progressive change requires political organization, struggle, and the determination of rational goals. However, the politics which Hall now espouses is very different from his *New Left Review* days, or even the moment of *Policing the Crisis*.

In his account of the meaning of 'new times' (Hall and Jacques, 1989) Hall seeks to emphasize continuity with Gramscian analysis. He argues that the twin characteristics of new times are first, the recognition that subjects of power must be conceptualized in pluralist forms and second, the pronounced cultural layering of social, political, and economic struggles. In Hall's mind the new times thesis simply perpetuates the duty of the organic intellectual to be at the vanguard of knowledge and generate debate regarding shifts in the social, cultural, and economic formation of power. However, in its denial of the struggle between capital and labour as the engine of social change, and its espousal of 'the politics of difference' Hall's thesis effectively abandons the central tenets of classical Marxism. Now, in these new times, transformative action is to be studied along a variety of fronts. For example, the struggles of new ethnicities, feminisms, the gay and lesbian movement, ecological protest groups, animal rights groups occupy the fulcrum of the new identity politics. Underlying this is the recognition that consumption and style have closed the gap with production and standardization in the organization of personality and everyday life. Early in his career Hall argued against traditional Marxists that working class affluence would change the meaning of class identity. With the 'new times' thesis Hall signals that classical Marxist political economy is incapable of accurately surveying the expanded cultural and subjective ground of contemporary global capitalism.

Characteristically, he is not interested in discarding Marxism. He is conscious of too many debts and remains determined to fasten cultural analysis onto a materialist understanding of life with others. Again characteristically, his solution is to wrap sticking plaster around components of theory which seem, on the face of it, to be incompatible. Thus, he remains faithful to the Marxist spirit of radical critique and social transcendence, while at the same time noting that a Marxist analysis *per se*, can no longer sustain a convincing picture of the dynamics of present-day society. The conundrum of his position is that the recognition of a flourishing politics of difference seems to pre-empt the possibility of Marxist collectivist transformation. For it points to fragmentation in human subjectivity, and the differentiation of interests in social movements. The recognition of common interests and identity, which Marxist class analysis presents as the indispensable condition of progressive change, appears to be absent.

Appraisal of Key Advances and Controversies

Rendering the incompatible into a popular front of analysis has been Hall's forte as a public intellectual. It is also his main weakness as a social theorist. For much of the 1970s and early 1980s he struggled to combine Althusser's structuralist determinism with Gramsci's more pluralist, action-based approach. *Policing the Crisis* (1978) shows the strain that the project entailed. On an analytical level, it is a book which ultimately works only by falsifying the theoretical premises which inform it. Althusserianism could not be made to fit with Gramscianism. Hall's recognition of the tensions between the two traditions was made transparent in 1983. In that year he published a paper advocating what he called, 'the open horizon' as a principle of theoretical work. He defined this as positing 'determinacy without guaranteed closures', but he also used the phrase 'marxism without guarantees' to describe the change in his outlook. This signals the end of the attempt to solder Althusserianism onto the body of Gramscianism. It is a defining moment in Hall's intellectual development. After it, the attempt to produce a quasi-scientific analysis of culture, which distinguished the Birmingham work in the semiotic/ Althusserian period, was unfussily abandoned.

Henceforward, Hall gravitated to an essayistic style of address which, in the *Marxism Today* period, adopted the serious, journalistic style which, perhaps, is Hall's most effective metier. The switch demonstrates how deeply Hall was influenced by post-structuralism. The ideas of Derrida, Eco, and to some extent, Foucault, marked Hall's writing in the 1980s and 1990s. Post-structuralism eased Hall out of the Marxist strait-jacket of class-bound analysis. Race, ethnicity, and the fragmented subject, emerged as recurring themes in the later work. The new times thesis even celebrated some aspects of postmodernism, notably the emphasis on contingency, dedifferentiation and globalization.

Yet if Hall is a reluctant Marxist, he is a remorseful post-structuralist/postmodernist. The new times/new ethnicities thesis is clearly indebted to Derrida's subversive presentation of the play of *differánce*. Hall clearly admired Derrida's iconoclasm. *Differánce* destablized the metaphysics of presence by acknowledging that the meaning of a positive sign presupposes the suppression of a metonymic chain of negatives. For Derrida the argument exposed the logocentrism of Western thought. Hall took over the argument, but only to suit his own ends. In Hall's hands, somewhere over the rainbow of *differánce*, a viable politics of difference can still be found. The divisions and fragmentations which cross-cut politics and culture today can be resolved in a new unifying principle of action. Characteristically, the nature of the identity in the new political subject capable of articulating the new principle of unity, was substantially undertheorized.

In part, the continued insistence on difference beyond *differánce* is a tribute to Hall's sentimentality. I do not mean this as a pejorative comment. Hall's adult intellect was formed in the extraordinary heat of the left-wing renaissance of the 1960s. The revival of Western Marxism, especially the English publication of Gramsci's writings, galvanized Hall, and left an indelible mark on his theoretical outlook. From this point on, he took it for granted that the responsibility of the intellectual was to foment socialist change. He learned to regard intellectual work which fails to align itself with the struggle of the working class and later, marginal identity groups, as evasive. Politics, and more particularly socialist transformation, became central in Hall's theoretical outlook.

It has become the last redoubt in his later voyage into post-structuralism, postmodernism and postcolonialism. Unlike his contemporary, Andre Gorz (1982), Hall has never been able to 'bid farewell to the working class'. He (1986, reprinted 1996: 146–7) accepts that a linguistic turn has occurred in his later work, but reasserts the materialist verity that inequality is the basis for unity. It is like King Lear refusing to accept that Cordelia is dead.

Marx never made recourse to a linguistic model of social and economic practice because the type of analysis he practised was rooted in a comparative and historical perspective. Hall has eschewed developing such a perspective in any substantial way. Instead he has chosen to theorize in a mobile fashion as events unfold. This has given his work topicality. Never more so than in the 1980s when his analysis of authoritarian populism, through the magazine *Marxism Today*, reached a very wide audience. However, topicality is not the same as relevance. With the wisdom of hindsight, it is odd that Hall spent most of the 1980s pontificating on the significance of authoritarian populism, without once writing seriously about Bill Gates or the rise of network society (Castells, 1996). Throughout this period Hall's analysis was predicated upon transforming the nation-state, when in fact the nation-state was losing its claim to be the prime unit of sociological analysis. Similarly, it is astonishing that a theoretical approach which set such store by 'really knowing, not just pretending to know', utterly failed to predict the collapse of the Berlin wall and, in its wake, the disintegration of Eastern European communism. The lack of historical and comparative detail in Hall's work means that his analysis is forced back into a discursive mode, in which ever new refinements of essentially abstract categories are proferred as a substitute for concrete analysis.

In the end we are left with an enormouosly sympathetic figure, but an ambivalent legacy for social and cultural theory. Within the Anglo-American tradition, Hall has been one of the foremost public intellectuals of the last 30 years. His interventions have frequently been inspiring. *Policing the Crisis* (1978) is a *tour de force*, crystallizing a decade of collaborative work at the Centre and, unintentionally, exposing the limits of the Althusserian tradition of cultural analysis. To be fair, Hall seems to have recognized these limits. After 1978, he showed adroitness in moving the locus of left-wing critical analysis from class to the politics of difference. He has also been courageous in facing post-structuralism and postmodernism squarely. The new times thesis is a qualified acceptance that the world has changed fundamentally. Yet no other figure of equivalent significance on the left made the admission so rapidly and so candidly.

All of this is a tribute to Hall's genuinely questing and reflexive consciousness. After reading Hall, it is impossible for social and cultural analysis to ignore marginal identities, peripheral cultures, and the antinomies of cultural articulation. This cannot have been easy to accomplish. Hall would be the first to point out that he did not work alone. Indeed, throughout Hall's years working in Birmingham the collaborative ethos of the labour was a distinctive feature of the research output from the Centre. Even so, no amount of false modesty can disguise that Hall is the pre-eminent intellectual force in the Birmingham tradition.

Yet in opposing reductionism so ferociously he has diluted the force of cultural and social analysis. The new times/new ethnicities thesis presents so many new actors on the stage that it is impossible to judge which one will change history. The cohesion of these groups is also unclear. Hall drifts towards regarding socialist change in terms of the mobilization of the marginalized. But this glosses over the profound differences within and between Asian, Afro-Caribbean, working class, gay and lesbian cultural formations, and 'hyphenated-identities' in general.

Hall's social and cultural analysis has, in fact, become progressively eclectic to the point where much of it ceases to carry water. What is one to make of a theorist who believes in 'determinacy without guaranteed closures' and 'diversity without homogeneity'? In producing such a nuanced, multiaccented reading of social totality, Hall has dissolved social and economic problems in a sea of cultural relativism. It is the same impasse in which cultural studies is now trapped.

HALL'S MAJOR WORKS

Hall, S. (1980) 'Encoding, decoding', in S. Hall, D. Hobson, A. Lowe and P. Willis (eds), *Culture, Media, Language*. London: Hutchinson.

Hall, S. (1983) 'The problem of ideology: marxism without guarantees', B. (ed.) *Marx: 100 Years On*. London: Lawrence & Wishart.

Hall, S. (1986) 'Postmodernism and articulation: an interview with Stuart Hall', *Journal of Communication Inquiry*, 10 (2): 45–60.

Hall, S. (1988 'New ethnicities' in K. Mercer (ed.) *Black Film, British Cinema*. London: BFI/ICA.

Hall, S. (1992) 'Cultural studies and its theoretical legacies', in L. C. Nelson and P. Treichler (eds) *Cultural Studies*. London: Routledge.

Hall, S. (1996) 'The formation of a diasporic intellectual, an interview with Stuart Hall' in D. Morley and H.K. Cheng (eds) *Stuart Hall: Critical Dialogues in Cultural Studies*. London: Routledge.

Hall, S. (1998) 'The great moving nowhere show', *Marxism Today*, Nov/Dec: 9–15.

Hall, S. and Jacques, M. (1989) *New Times*. London: Lawrence and Wishart.

Hall, S. and Whannel, P. (1964) *The Popular Arts*. London: Hutchinson.

Hall, S., Critcher, C., Jefferson, T., Clarke, J. and Roberts, B. (1978) *Policing The Crisis: 'Mugging', the State, and Law and Order*. London: Macmillan.

SECONDARY REFERENCES

Adorno, T. and Horkheimer, M. (1944) *Dialectic of Enightenment*. London: Verso.

Barthes, R. (1973) *Mythologies*. St Albans: Paladin.

Barthes, R. (1979) *The Eiffel Tower & Other Essays*. New York: Hill and Wang.

Brundson, C. (1996) 'A thief in the night: stories of feminism in the 1970s at CCCS', in D. Morley and H.K. Chen (eds) *Stuart Hall: Critical Dialogues in Cultural Studies*. London: Routledge.

Castells, M. (1996) *The Rise of Network Society*. Oxford: Blackwell.

Derrida, J. ([1975] 1992) '*Differánce*', in A. Easthope and K. McGowan (eds) *A Critical and Cultural Theory Reader*. Buckingham: Open University Press.

Eco, U. (1981) *The Role of the Reader*. London: Hutchinson.

Eco, U. (1987) *Travels in Hyperreality*. London: Picador.

Eco, U. (1990) *The Limits of Interpretation*. Bloomington: Indiana University Press.

Eco, U. (1994) *Apocalypse Postponed*. Bloomington: Indiana University Press.

Elias, N. (1978) *The Civilizing Process, Volume 1: The History of Manners*. Oxford: Blackwell.

Gorz, A. (1982) *Farewell to the Working Class*. London: Pluto.

Gramsci, A. (1971) *Selections From Prison Notebooks*. (Eds G. Nowell Smith and Q. Hoare.) New York: International Publications.

Gramsci, A. (1985) *Selections from Cultural Writings*. (Eds D. Forgcas and G. Nowell Smith.) Cambridge, MA: Harvard University Press.

Jacques, M. (1989) *Politics in the 1990s*. London: Lawrence & Wishart.

Marcuse, H. (1964) *One Dimensional Man*. London: Abacus.

Morley, D. and Chen, H.K. (eds) (1996) *Stuart Hall: Critical Dialogues in Cultural Studies*. London: Routledge.

Sparks, C. (1996) 'Stuart Hall, cultural studies and Marxism', in D. Morley and H.K. Chen (eds) *Stuart Hall: Critical Dialogues in Cultural Studies*. London: Routledge.

Volosinov, V. (1929) *Marxism and the Philosophy of Language*. New York, Seminar Press.

Williams, R. (1963) *Culture and Society 1780–1950*. London: Penguin.

33

Juliet Mitchell

SARAH WRIGHT

BIOGRAPHICAL DETAILS AND THEORETICAL CONTEXT

Juliet Mitchell was born in Christchurch, New Zealand in 1940. In 1944 she left New Zealand on a wartime convoy of ships bound for England. She received a progressive, co-educational schooling at the King Alfred School in London. She was an undergraduate of St Anne's College, Oxford, from 1958–61 where she also began postgraduate studies. Mitchell began her teaching career as assistant lecturer in English at the University of Leeds (1962–3) and from 1965–71 she was full lecturer in the department of English at the University of Reading. It was whilst at Leeds that Juliet Mitchell began to work and write for *New Left Review*, the journal of the British New Left, becoming the only female member of its editorial board in 1963, and it was here that her seminal article, 'Women: The Longest Revolution' was published in 1966. The article, which acknowledges the inflections of both Raymond Williams and Louis Althusser, is a deft, incisive examination of the problems involved in Marxist interpretation of the status of women. It was written in the context of a growing questioning of orthodox Marxism at the start of the 1960s and in particular against the background of a debate within British Marxism between E. P. Thompson and *New Left Review*'s Perry Anderson concerning Althusserian accounts of 'history'. As Julia Swindells and Lisa Jardine have noted (1990: 70), Mitchell's article can be 'traced back to that crucial period of confrontation between "history", "culture" and "Marxism". To which Mitchell added "feminism"'. Second wave feminism would not commence until 1968. Mitchell's article was thus a pioneering account of socialist-feminist materialism. The article provoked an insubstantial, yet 'intemperate and disparaging rebuttal' (Swindells and Jardine, 1990: 71) from *New Left Review*'s managing editor, Quintin Hoare (Hoare, 1967), but quickly established Mitchell as one of the first proponents of the women's liberation movement.

Throughout this period Juliet Mitchell was connected with the antipsychiatry movement and was one of the originators of the Anti-University of London. Here Mitchell established what was one of the first seminar workshops on Women's Studies, and which would later unite with other similar groups to produce the London Women's Liberation Workshop of which Mitchell was a founder and remained a prominent member. In 1971 she gave up her university lecturing post to lecture freelance, in the UK and abroad, on literature and the politics of feminism. In 1972 she published *Women's Estate*, a text which departs from the traditional Marxist-feminist stance which sees woman's position as a function of her relation to capital, to posit a theory which attempts to integrate both status and function, seeing them conjointly determined by women's role in production and reproduction, sexuality, and the socialization of children. Chapter 8 of that book is entitled, 'The Ideology of the Family' and draws on Althusser for an account of ideology influenced partly by Freud and Lacan. Chapter 9 is entitled, 'Psychoanalysis and the Family'. Thus Althusserian ideology may have been 'one strand that led [Juliet Mitchell] to [her] subsequent interest in psychoanalysis' (Mitchell, 1984: 18).

Anglo-American feminism of the 1970s was hostile to psychoanalysis, seeing it as an instrument of patriarchy, and accusing Freud of a biologism which functioned to limit women's social possibilities. Juliet Mitchell's ground-breaking *Psychoanalysis and Feminism* (1974a) takes up Freud through Lacan and with Lévi-Strauss to advocate the implementation of psychoanalysis as an instrument for the theoretical critique of patriarchal society. Mitchell had elucidated the political and social applicability of psychoanalysis, 'its usefulness as interpretative model rather than simply as therapeutic technique' (Grosz, 1990: 20). The mid to late 1970s were to see the passage from structuralism to post-structuralism. Mitchell's book was hugely influential, inspiring a 'vast industry of psychoanalytically inspired texts' (Grosz, 1990: 21) with ramifications for cultural theories at large in an international arena. As Gallop (1989: 27) writes, this book is 'probably the most widely read book in English' that mentions Lacan. Mitchell's interest in Lacan was consolidated in a 1982 book, edited and introduced by Mitchell with Jacqueline Rose, and entitled, *Feminine Sexuality: Jacques Lacan and the 'Ecole Freudienne'*.

After *Psychoanalysis and Feminism*, Mitchell trained as a psychoanalyst, so as to ground her interests in the appropriate field of research. (Pallares-Burke, 2000) From 1974–8 she was a candidate at the Institute of Psychoanalysis in London and in 1978 she became an associate member of the British Psychoanalytical Society and the International Association of Psychoanalysts, gaining full membership in 1988. During the period 1975–8 Mitchell worked as a psychotherapist for the Paddington Centre for Psychotherapy in London and at Camden Council for Social Services. Since 1978 she has worked as a psychoanalyst in her own private practice in London.

Juliet Mitchell's work has enjoyed a large international dimension. Her writing has been translated throughout the world into 20 languages, including Chinese. As Olwen Hufton notes (in an unpublished interview), *Psychoanalysis and Feminism* 'spoke, as it were, to the situation of women multiculturally in a way perhaps not fully known in many countries even in the West'. Besides participating in radio and television discussion programmes in the UK, USA, Australia, Canada, South Africa, and New Zealand, Mitchell has scripted, reported, and presented documentary films, and designed and chaired a UK film and discussion series. She has also delivered numerous inaugural lectures in both the university and clinical environments, and has held visiting professorships and participated in conferences throughout the world. In 1994 a conference, organized by the Freud Institute in London, entitled, 'Psychoanalysis: Twenty Years On', celebrated the wide-reaching implications Mitchell's 1974 text has enjoyed over time. The centre was overwhelmed by the number of applicants. Since 1996 Mitchell has been lecturer in Gender and Society at the University of Cambridge, whilst also occupying the post of A.D. White Distinguished Professor-at-large at Cornell University (1994–9) and Visiting

Professor at Yale University (from 1999). Her latest publication, *Mad Men and Medusas: Reclaiming Hysteria and the Effects of Siblings on the Human Condition* (2000a) questions the 'disappearance' of hysteria from clinical spheres; examines its feminization and provides a radical challenge to other contemporary histories of the 'disease'.

SOCIAL THEORY AND CONTRIBUTIONS

In 'Women: The Longest Revolution' (1966), an article whose title refers to Raymond Williams's *The Long Revolution*, Juliet Mitchell calls for a socialist-materialist feminism to be compatible with accounts of historical materialism. Women occupy a singularly paradoxical position within society: 'they are fundamental to the human condition, yet in their economic, social and political roles, they are marginal' (Mitchell, 1966: 11). For her study of the problems involved in the Marxist interpretation of the status of women, Mitchell returns to the 'classical heritage of the revolutionary movement', the ideas of the great socialist thinkers of the nineteenth century, in which the question of the emancipation of women was afforded recognition. But where Marx, Fourier, Engels, and Bebel by varying degrees reveal the unequal social status of women and programme women's liberation into the socialist revolution, their ideas remain at the level of abstract symbols, or they find it impossible to detach women from the economic sphere, thereby merely increasing women's dependence. The discussion of woman's status is principally economic, emphasizing her subordination within a system of patrilineal inheritance. Her biological status secures her weakness as a producer, in work relations, and her importance as a possession, in reproductive relations. The fullest interpretation of women's status is provided by Simone de Beauvoir. In *The Second Sex* she argues for a fusion of the 'economic' and 'reproductive' explanations of women's subordination by a psychological interpretation of both, but de Beauvoir's theories are atemporal and she ultimately fails to detail a blueprint for the future, beyond asserting that socialism will involve the liberation of women as one of its constituent 'moments'.

Mitchell argues for a radical focus on the specificity of women's condition, to find a place for feminism within socialist theory through a full account of women's social relations. Rejecting the view that women's status can be deduced derivatively from the economy or equated symbolically with society, she maintains that women's position must be seen as a specific structure, which is a unity of different elements. The variations of women's status throughout history will be the result of different combinations of these elements, a structure which Mitchell refers to as 'overdetermined', using the Althusserian notion (advanced in his 'Contradiction and Overdetermination', 1969a) of a complex totality in which each independent sector has its own autonomous reality which can variously reinforce or cancel one another out. The structures affecting women's condition can be divided into the following groups: production, reproduction, sexuality and socialization. These variables must be examined separately to reveal the present unity and possibilities for change.

Taking her dynamic as model, Mitchell analyses each of these four variables in turn to investigate how her theory might have immediate practical use. She concludes that the liberation of women can be achieved only if all four concomitant structures in which they are integrated are transformed. A modification of any one of them could be offset by a reinforcement of another, so that mere permutation of the form of exploitation is achieved. A revolutionary movement must base its analysis on the uneven development of each through time, and attack the weakest link in the configuration. This may then precipitate a general transformation. Mitchell argues for equality in the workplace, with a long-term development in the forces of production. She advocates the separation of sexual pleasure from reproduction to alter the demographic pattern of reproduction in the West, and she also calls for a revision of the socialization of children. Above all, she calls for a re-examination of the workings of ideology, which make notions of the woman and family seem natural.

Woman's Estate (1972c) takes up the question of women's liberation in a more extended form. Here Mitchell examines the history of the women's liberation movement, particularly its background in the mid to late 1960s, and compares it to other resistance groups: ethnic, racial, antiwar, and student movements. Chapters 4 and 7 return to the exposition of ideas set out in 'Women: The Longest Revolution': here too Mitchell advances a repudiation of economic interpretations of Marxism towards a theory which examines the integrating structures of production, reproduction, sexuality, and socialization. However, Mitchell outlines the family as an obstacle to her dynamic of the possibilities for the emancipation of women: 'today women are confined within the family which is a segmentary, monolithic unit, largely separated from production and hence from social human activity ... but the family does more than occupy the woman: it produces her. It is in the family that the psychology of men and women is founded' (Mitchell, 1972c: 151).

Mitchell is increasingly concerned with definitions of the family (as it is here that women reside), but her attention shifts in Chapters 8 and 9 of *Women's Estate* from ideological accounts, to psychoanalytically inspired theories of the family. Mitchell herself attributes this shift in part to Althusser's emphasis on the importance of ideology: 'his definition of it as "the way we live in the world" seemed to me an insistent dimension of any analysis of women' (Mitchell, 1984: 18). Althusser's definition of 'familial ideology', developed in his article, 'Freud and Lacan' (1969b), had therefore '"authorized" a Marxist accommodation of Freud, and in particular of Lacan' (Swindells and Jardine, 1990: 78) as a valuable element of any exploration of the ideology of the family. As Swindells and Jardine have noted (1984: 78), in Chapter 9 of *Women's Estate* (entitled 'Psychoanalysis and the Family') Juliet Mitchell feels more at ease with the issue of the family, which in Chapter 8 (on 'The Ideology of the Family') 'had, for her purposes (explaining the position of women under capitalism via the family) been fraught with "contradiction" and "paradox" – contradictions and paradoxes which are endemic to the classic Marxist account of ideology as it fails to deal with women precisely by relegating them to a "family"'. The 'and' linking 'Psychoanalysis and Feminism', conversely, points up that the 'domain of psychoanalysis is the familial, with women's special need for therapy a consequence of her having been relegated there' (Swindells and Jardine, 1990: 78). Mitchell writes that psychoanalysis works within the framework of the family: 'the borderline between the biological and the social which finds expression in the family is the land that psychoanalysis sets out to chart, it is the land where sexual distinction originates' (Mitchell, 1972c: 167). Freud saw psychoanalysis not in terms of the 'adaptive process prevalent today', but as 'revolutionary, shocking, subversive – a plague that would disrupt society' (Mitchell, 1972c: 167). Psychoanalysis explores the primary relationships between individuals, and examines the production of sexual difference. By its very definition it is an analysis of the most basic social formation – that which finds its expression in the various forms of family. It is therefore psychoanalysis that any analysis of the position and meaning of women must explore. The family serves ideological as well as economic functions. Due to the way society's psychic side has been constituted, women's oppression will persist until the psyches have a revolution equivalent to that of the economic one from capitalism to socialism.

Mitchell's 'Return to Freud'

'The greater part of the feminist movement has identified Freud as the enemy'. writes Juliet Mitchell in the introduction to *Psychoanalysis and Feminism*, and she proceeds, 'but the argument of this book is that a rejection of psychoanalysis and of Freud's works is fatal for feminism' (Mitchell, 1974a: xv). *Psychoanalysis and Feminism* constituted a bold, unprecedented vindication of a feminist vision of Freudian psychoanalysis. It cautioned that Freud's theories had recently been subject to popularization: adulterated or simplistic misinterpretations in feminist texts that were ignorant of his writings. Under a section (Part Two, Section II) entitled 'Feminism and Freud', Mitchell argued that Simone de Beauvoir (*The Second Sex*, originally published in 1949, becoming a major feminist text in the 1960s), Eva Figes (*Patriarchal Attitudes*, 1970), Germaine Greer (*The Female Eunuch*, 1971), Kate Millet (*Sexual Politics*, 1970), Betty Friedan (*The Freudian Mystique*, 1963), Shulamith Firestone (*The Dialectic of Sex*, 1971) and most other Anglo-American feminists mistakenly assume that Freud affirms rather than simply illustrates sexual difference within patriarchy. Extrapolating his ideas about femininity from their context, they accuse him of a biological determinism which restricts women's social potentialities and whose function is to reproduce patriarchal power relations. Mitchell argues that Freud's insights should be read as *descriptive* of the contemporary gender system, not as *prescriptive* of how gendered social relations should function. She writes, 'however it may have been used, psychoanalysis is not a recommendation *for* a patriarchal society, but an analysis *of* one. If we are interested in understanding and challenging this oppression of women, we cannot afford to neglect it' (Mitchell, 1974a: xv).

Mitchell's 'return to Freud' was centred on ideology (coming to Freud alongside Althusser, Lacan and Lévi-Strauss), 'and the access which the unconscious might give to *consciousness* for woman' (Swindells and Jardine, 1990: 82). She sought a feminist theory to run parallel to the Marxist analysis of the differing modes of production: 'so where Marxist theory explains the historical and economic situation, psychoanalysis, in conjunction with the notions of ideology already gained by dialectical materialism, is the way into understanding ideology and sexuality' (Mitchell, 1974a: xxii). Mitchell found in Freud a theory with social and political potential. His was a revolutionary analysis of the unconscious, which functioned to unmask the structures which engender desire and reproduce patriarchal power regimes. Mitchell maintained that this ideological analysis of patriarchal society would lay the ground for its ultimate overthrow.

Part One of *Psychoanalysis and Feminism* is a lucid analysis of Freud's major insights which steers a course through a close and careful reading of Freud's tenets regarding the unconscious and sexuality, the Oedipus and castration complexes, and their particular relevance for femininity.

Part Two examines feminist accusations against, and misinterpretations of, Freud, and clarifies the theories of Reich and Laing. The concluding section takes up Freudian psychoanalysis as a radical project. Mitchell writes that no full understanding of Freud's ideas on femininity and female sexuality is possible without the grasp of two fundamental theories: first, the nature of the unconscious mental life and the laws that govern its behaviour, and secondly, the meaning of sexuality in human life. Hence, 'the way unconscious mental life operates provides the terminology, the fundamental system of thought within which Freud's specific theses have to be understood' (Mitchell, 1974a: 16).

This is significant because Juliet Mitchell wants to rid Freud of his biologism: 'psychoanalysis has nothing to do with biology – except in the sense that our mental life also reflects, in a transformed way, what culture has already done with our biological needs and institutions' (Mitchell, 1974a: 401). Freud's account of the difference between the sexes therefore centres on the psychological characteristics of sexual difference. Using Lacan, Mitchell stresses the symbolic nature of the phallus as the 'transcendental signifier'. As 'the very mark of human desire', the phallus represents 'the very notion of exchange itself' (Mitchell, 1974a: 395). It is patriarchy which defines and designates the penis–phallus equation, not biology, hence revealing the propensity for a transformation of the structures of gender and power. Gendered subjectivity is constituted through loss: that of the primary, dyadic relationship (mother–child): 'the original lack of the object (the mother's breast) evokes the desire for unity and this is the structure upon which identifications will build' (Mitchell, 1974a: 387).

The identifications the child will make are therefore based on recognition of absence or discovery of difference. The child of either sex initially wishes to be the phallus for the mother, but the symbolic father intervenes, effectively taking over the signification of the phallus, with a symbolic threat of castration. The castration complex is understood by the child when the child perceives the anatomical differences in the sexes: assimilated as presence versus castration. The effect of this castration complex is different in the case of each sex. Accordingly, within the Oedipus complex (a premise inflected with anthropological notions of the taboo on incest), the little boy assumes a position as heir to the law of the father (with the mother as love object but with the threat of castration from the father), and the little girl learns her place within that law. The little girl comes to acknowledge her lack, 'recognition of her "castration" is the female infant's entry to girlhood, just as acceptance of the threat and deference to the father in exchange for later possibilities is the boy's debt to future manhood' (Mitchell, 1974a: 96). The girl then shifts from her mother-attachment to a sexual desire for the father, the clitoris is abandoned in favour of the vagina as the source of sexual satisfaction, and in this way the little girl achieves the 'normal', or normative, path to femininity.

As a science which describes patriarchal society, psychoanalysis reveals the ways in which 'the little girl has to acquire, and quickly too, her cultural destiny', which is made to appear 'misleadingly coincident with a biological one' (Mitchell, 1974a: 416). This premise posits males and females within unequal gender relations. Woman is positioned on the side of the sexual object, the lacking Other in deference to man's autonomous agency. Female masochism, penis envy, and women's weak superego are understood as a consequence of the imposition of patriarchal law (the 'Law of the Father') upon women. Crucially, however, although the phallus stands for entry to the symbolic order, in this (Lacanian and significatory) reading of Freud, Mitchell stresses that it is an imaginary object that neither sex can 'have'. Although the phallus is the signifier of sexual difference, Mitchell maintains that it is not necessarily tied to patriarchal social relations. Therefore the phallus as transcendental signifier contains within it the potential for change and, in a nonpatriarchal society, 'some other expression of the entry into culture than the implication for the unconscious exchange of women will have to be found' (Mitchell, 1974a: 415).

APPRAISAL OF KEY ADVANCES AND CONTROVERSIES

Juliet Mitchell's *Psychoanalysis and Feminism* (1974) was a defining moment in the history of feminism, signalling a sudden and extreme departure from all that had gone before, a point illustrated by Elizabeth Grosz (1990):

> arguably, feminist theory has undergone a dramatic turn-about in attitude towards psychoanalysis. If we survey feminist literature on psychoanalysis even superficially over the past twenty years, the re-evaluation of positions – the

> positive affirmation of a theory previously reviled – has never been so stark. For English speakers, this 'moment' of radical rupture in feminist attitudes is marked by the publication of Juliet Mitchell's defence of Freud in *Psychoanalysis and Feminism*. (Grosz, 1990: 19)

Mitchell's text challenged orthodox feminism, signalling the need to interpret Freud differently and to use his work to explain elements of women's oppression. Psychoanalytic theory thus granted feminism an understanding of the ways that patriarchy is reproduced. Using Lacan, Mitchell emphasizes how sexual difference is at the root of ego formation, and how this difference is not an essence but rather the effect of a conflictual process. Her text defied the entrenched conventions of social thought in English speaking countries. Mitchell's work emphasized the importance of an understanding of the unconscious acquisition of the ideas and laws of society and how this acquisition determines psychic structure. This was a case of theory being turned not upside down but inside out, a revision of intellectual thought. As with her earlier feminist work, Mitchell's focus was the political and social applicability of theory for feminism. In 'Women: The Longest Revolution' (1966), Mitchell had been concerned with the 'absence of the question of women within the left' (Mitchell, 1995: 74), where she succeeded in highlighting an aspect of political thought that had previously been invisible. In *Psychoanalysis and Feminism* she addressed the specificity of women across historical epochs and cultures, for, 'there seemed to be some *absolute* difference that was socially or culturally constructed between men and women' (Mitchell, 1995: 75) and integral to patriarchal society. Hence the question for Mitchell in *Psychoanalysis and Feminism* was 'that if patriarchy is so entrenched, there must be historical circumstances which a politics could work on, where that entrenchment could be undermined and eroded' (Mitchell, 1995: 75). It was in highlighting the social and political possibilities for psychoanalysis that the novelty of Mitchell's thesis lay (notably Lacan was uninterested in the social application of his ideas): Mitchell extrapolated a theoretical paradigm from the therapeutic domain.

Juliet Mitchell is credited with spearheading the subsequent fascination with the theories of Jacques Lacan. *Psychoanalysis and Feminism* introduced the English-reading public to the theorist's work, while *Jacques Lacan and the École Freudienne* (1982) edited with Jacqueline Rose, served as a point of departure for many readers of his elliptical writings. *Psychoanalysis and Feminism* had enormous ramifications for social theory at large from the mid-1970s and beyond, spawning a new wave of psychoanalytically influenced criticism. Literary criticism, film studies, feminist texts, and cultural and social theories were affected by Mitchell's hugely influential text. Perhaps no other feminist writer has had such a great impact on intellectual thought outside of feminist critique.

Critique of Mitchell

Juliet Mitchell wrote 'Women: The Longest Revolution' for her *New Left Review* 'friends and colleagues: I remember sitting at a table with all the men of *New Left Review* and ... people saying, ... "I will think about Persia", "I will think about Tanganyika", as they were then, and I said, "Well, I'll think about women" – and there was silence' (Mitchell, 1995: 74). As Swindells and Jardine write in their careful analysis of this period, 'the only acknowledgement of Juliet Mitchell's crucial contribution to Left debate in 1966 by those "friends and colleagues" of NLR was Quintin Hoare's "swipe" at Mitchell' (Swindells and Jardine, 1990: 70–1). Accusing Mitchell of misinterpreting Marx, Hoare takes issue with her reading of history:

> We are warned that the article will not provide an historical narrative of women's position. But what, in fact, happens is that she *excludes* history from her analysis. How can one analyse either the position of women today, or writings on the subject ahistorically? It is this which prevents her

> from realizing that the whole *historical* development of women has been within the family; that women have worked and lived within *its* space and time. (Hoare, 1967: 70).

Hoare's comments reveal his own misunderstanding of Mitchell's application of Althusserian ideology; it is the process of differentiation of the separate structures of the family, through time, which is Mitchell's innovation. Hoare's article, while lacking in substance, highlights the radical nature of Mitchell's project: to create a space for the analysis of women's position within left-wing thought.

More serious accusations are levelled against Mitchell's theoretical framework as developed in *Psychoanalysis and Feminism*. Some have argued that there are theoretical and political difficulties with Mitchell's analysis of gender. Mitchell is accused of universalizing the category of subject, as well as of patriarchal ideology itself: 'these seem universal, cultural categories, in her account, governed by cross-cultural and transhistorical laws' (Grosz, 1990). The law of the father, the prohibition of incest, and the signification of the phallus (and thus women's castration) 'are all, for her, universal a priori conditions'. Elizabeth Grosz (1990) charges Mitchell with accepting Freud wholesale, with regarding Freudian theory as compatible with feminist principles, without any need for modification: 'she remains entirely uncritical of the psychoanalytic tools she uses to develop her account of the construction of femininity' (Grosz, 1990: 197, n.7). Mitchell's position is thus problematic in that it seems to assume that the social reproduction of sexuality and gender is a fixed term, without giving recourse to the contradictions inherent in the acquisition of gendered subjectivity which in turn has political implications. This presumption of what Grosz refers to as 'a pregiven structural grid' which privileges masculinity at the expense of femininity, fixes women symbolically as the lacking Other. Consequently it is unclear why women would ever feel compelled to subvert the gender system. And while Mitchell reaches 'an optimistic, "revolutionary" conclusion' (Wilson, 1981: 70) from *Psychoanalysis and Feminism*, by arguing that, in the conditions of modern production, the family and its associated sexual division of labour was redundant, some critics saw that this Freudian account could do nothing but doom 'as logically impossible the struggles of women to achieve autonomy over men' (Grosz, 1990).

Elizabeth Wilson (1981) rejects the radical potential of Mitchell's project. According to Wilson, Juliet Mitchell, using Lacan, stresses the arbitrary nature of the terms 'masculinity' and 'femininity', which 'only exist by virtue of their difference to one another' (Mitchell, 1980), and 'the differences between men and women completely float away from biology and become purely social constructs' (Wilson, 1981: 69). Wilson accuses Mitchell of psychic determinism. She cites Cora Kaplan's (1979) charge that Freudian theory emphasizes, 'the unalterable distance between gender positions', to claim that Mitchell's paradigm reproduces gender relations within a structure which is universalizing, 'tyrannical' and inescapable: 'the logic of this locks us as securely within the structures of phallic power as does "biologism"' (Wilson, 1981: 69).

Reading Mitchell 'with a cognizance of the problems faced by a more thorough consideration of Lacanian theory' (Gallop, 1982: xiii), Gallop implies that Mitchell's Freud is not sufficiently Lacanian to be of use to feminists. Mitchell privileges the anthropological and sociological dimensions of the phallic order (the law of the Father in patriarchy) whilst neglecting Lacan's emphasis on the importance of language. Feminism, writes Gallop, 'must embrace a psychoanalysis that has been returned to its original audacity through an exchange with linguistic theory' (Gallop, 1982: 14). Mitchell, for Gallop, initiates this project, but at the end of the book, with the proposals for psychoanalysis in the overthrow of patriarchy, Mitchell takes over the position of the writers she has criticized. In her 'incisive analysis' of feminists, Mitchell delineates the trend of 'utopic rationalism' which reveals the inadequacies of previous feminist thinking, yet ultimately embraces their brand of social theory. Gallop questions the significance of a feminism that remains unaltered by psychoanalysis, that 'does not even question its own desire in/for psychoanalysis' and that has not built a political practice out of its understanding of psychoanalysis (Chisholm, 1992: 261). Despite her criticisms, however, Gallop acknowledges Mitchell as her 'point of departure' for this theoretical critique. This point cannot be made too lightly, for whatever the criticisms of her foundational text, Mitchell was responsible for a change in the way that feminism engaged with psychoanalysis. Her understanding of the importance of the ways in which patriarchy affects the acquisition of gendered subjectivity was to have ramifications for social theory at large.

Mitchell's project of supplementing Marx with Freud and Lévi-Strauss was 'quietly abandoned, not least by Mitchell herself as she became immersed in the Lacanian project' (Lovell, 1996: 322). But for all the difficulties acknowledged in the attempt to synthesize Marxism and psychoanalysis, they have often been interlinked in subsequent feminist thought. The Marxist perspective more generally went out of fashion with the move to postmodernism. But many feminists have continued the materialist psychoanalytical understanding of gender. Chodorow, for instance, departs from a dual systems approach to use object-relations in her theory of sexual difference as mediated by the maternal. In France some feminists (Kristeva, Cixous, Irigaray) have gone beyond Lacan's theory in appropriating it for feminism, moving towards a theory of sexed identity which privileges the 'feminine' and 'marginal'. Meanwhile many post-structuralist feminists have moved from Marx to Foucault ('who is particularly attractive to ex-Marxist feminists', Lovell, 1996: 329). Judith Butler (1990) argues that psychoanalytic theory is mistaken in 'forcing a coherence between sex, gender and desire when gender does not "express" sexuality but rather functions culturally as a "regulatory ideal"' (Buhle, 1998: 347): psychoanalysis institutes the very structures it seeks to analyse. Influenced above all by Foucault, queer theory took up sexuality as its theoretical province, largely assigning 'gender' to feminism. However, there is currently something of a shift back to an integration of the two and in a sense a return to the concerns of late 1960s feminists. Butler's 1993 text turns to Althusser's theory of *interpellation* for her discussion of sexuality as a location produced by the force of repetition in language: patriarchal ideologies hail or call out the subject as a sexual identity.

Juliet Mitchell continues to publish widely. Her latest work, *Mad Men and Medusas: Reclaiming Hysteria and the Effects of Siblings on the Human Condition* (2000a), can be seen as the product of her on-going engagement with feminism and psychoanalysis. When she started to work as a clinician, Mitchell became interested not in the construction of femininity and masculinity but in the 'gendering' of the symptom. Why – when the presences and prevalence of male hysteria was a foundation stone of psychoanalysis – does hysteria still fall to women? In the new book, Mitchell traces a genealogy of hysteria from a historical background in Greek and Renaissance medical texts, to witchcraft, spirit possession and other social phenomena, its inception in psychoanalysis with Freud's 'Dora: A Fragment of a Case of Hysteria in a Female' and its later 'disappearance' from clinical spheres. Mitchell writes that hysteria has never disappeared, merely mimetically rehearsed its own disappearance, reappearing under other guises and definitions. She examines the accounts of male hysteria which psychoanalysis, literature, and myth have access to – accounts which have receded at the expense of feminizations of the 'disease'. Mitchell recuperates these and other lost aspects of hysteria, seeing it as a human possibility which a social ordering, not a psychic complex, renders 'feminine'. Crucially, in her latest work, Mitchell questions the prominence of the Oedipus complex as understood by Freud and the castration complex 'returned to' by Lacan, for psychoanalytic accounts of hysteria, and presents siblings or more generally, laterality, as an alternative model to the exclusive theory and practice of intergenerational conflict within the Oedipal dynamic. Mitchell criticizes psychoanalysis for ignoring what it observes: the importance of lateral relations for which siblings are exemplary. She argues that it is from lateral relations – so widely acknowledged as critical in anthropological theories of affinity – that the human subject is thrust back onto the parents who thus become the mother and father of the Oedipus and castration complexes. In a new edition of *Psychoanalysis and Feminism* (2000), she traces how feminism's subsequent use of Lacanian and post-Lacanian psychoanalysis depoliticized the project.

MITCHELL'S MAJOR WORKS

Mitchell, J. (1962) 'Concepts and techniques in the novels of William Golding', *New Left Review*, 15: 63–71.

Mitchell, J. (1966) 'Women: the longest revolution', *New Left Review*, 40: 10–30.

Mitchell, J. (1972a) 'What Maisie Knew: portrait of the artist as a young girl', in J. Goode (ed.) *Air of Reality: New Essays on Henry James*. London: Methuen; reprinted in *Women: The Longest Revolution* (1984).

Mitchell, J. (1972b) 'The Ordeal of Richard Feverel: a sentimental education', in I. Fletcher (ed.) *Meredith Now*. London: Routledge; reprinted in *Women: The Longest Revolution* (1984).

Mitchell, J. (1972c) *Women's Estate*. London: Penguin and New York: Pantheon Books.

Mitchell, J. (1974a) *Psychoanalysis and Feminism*. London: Allen Lane and Penguin Books.

Mitchell, J. (1974b) 'On femininity and the difference between the sexes', in J. Strouse (ed.), *Women and Analysis: Dialogues on Psychoanalytic Views of Femininity*. New York: Dell.

Mitchell, J. (ed.) (1977) 'Introduction', Defoe's *Moll Flanders*. London: Penguin Classics.

Mitchell, J. (1984) *Women: The Longest Revolution: Essays on Feminism, Literature and Psychoanalysis*, London: Virago and New York: Pantheon Books.

Mitchell, J. (1986) *The Selected Melanie Klein*. Harmondsworth: Penguin and New York: Pantheon.

Mitchell, J. (1990) 'Whatever happened to Don Juan?: Don Juan and male hysteria', *Mitos*, 3: 77–84.

Mitchell, J. (1995) 'Psychoanalysis and feminism: twenty years on', *British Journal of Psychotherapy*, 12 (1): 73–77.

Mitchell, J. (1996a) 'Sexuality and psychoanalysis: hysteria', *British Journal of Psychotherapy* 12 (4): 473–9.

Mitchell, J. (1996b) 'Role of recreation in women's oppression', in N.R. Keddie (ed.), *Debating Gender, Debating Sexuality*. New York: New York University Press.

Mitchell, J. (1996c) 'Preface', to J. Raphael-Leff and R. Jozef Perelberg. *Female Experience: Three Generations of British Women Psychoanalysts on Work with Women*. London: Routledge.

Mitchell, J. (1997) 'Sexuality, psychoanalysis and social changes', *International Psychoanalysis* 6 (1): 28–9.

Mitchell, J. (1998a) 'Memory and psychoanalysis', in P. Fara and K. Patterson (eds), *Memory* (Darwin Lectures). Cambridge: Cambridge University Press.

Mitchell, J. (1998b) 'Thinking about emptiness', *Bulletin of the Society for Marital Studies*, 5: 22–28.

Mitchell, J. (1998c) 'Introduction' in J. Philips and L. Stonebridge (eds) *Reading Melanie Klein*. London: Routledge.

Mitchell, J. (1998d) 'Questioning the Oedipus complex', *Replika*, 113–24. (*Replika*: Hungarian Social Science Quarterly. 'Central European *Mysteric*' special issue, 1998.)

Mitchell, J. (1999a) 'Feminism and psychoanalysis at the millennium', *Women: A Cultural Review*, 10 (2): 185–91.

Mitchell, J. (1999b) 'Dora and her doctors', in S. de Mijolla (ed.), *Women in the History of Psychoanalysis*. London: Karnac Books.

Mitchell, J. (1999d) 'Hysteria and the body', in F. Molfino and C. Zanardi (eds), *Symptoms, Body, Femininity: From Hysteria to Bulimia*. Bologna: Clueb Press.

Mitchell, J. (1999e) 'Family or familiarity?', in M. Richards and S. Day Slater (eds), *What is a Parent?* London: Rupert Hart.

Mitchell, J. (2000) 'Psychoanalysis and feminism revisited', in M. Kavna (ed.), *Feminism and Psychoanalysis at the Millennium*. London: Routledge.

Mitchell, J. (2000a) *Mad Men and Medusas: Reclaiming Hysteria and the Effects of Siblings on the Human Condition*. London: Hamish Hamilton and Penguin Books.

Mitchell, J. (2000b) 'The vortex beneath the story', in P. Brooks and A. Woloch (eds), *Whose Freud? The*

Place of Psychoanalysis in Contemporary Culture. London and New Haven, CT: Yale University Press.

Mitchell, J. (in press a) 'Sexuality, psychoanalysis and social changes', *The Institute of Psychoanalysis News.*

Mitchell, J. (in press b) 'Femininity at the Margins', Conference proceedings *In Honour of D. W. Winnicott*, Milan.

Mitchell, J. and Goody, J. (1997) 'Feminism, fatherhood and the family: the case of the CSA', in Mitchell, J. and Oakley, A. (eds) *Who's Afraid of Feminism.* London: Hamish Hamilton and Penguin Books.

Mitchell, J. and Oakley, A. (eds) (1977) *The Rights and Wrongs of Women.* Harmondsworth: Penguin.

Mitchell, J. and Oakley, A. (eds.) (1986) *What Is Feminism?* Oxford: Blackwell.

Mitchell, J. and Oakley, A. (eds) (1997) *Who's Afraid of Feminism?* London: Hamish Hamilton and Penguin Books.

Mitchell, J. and Parsons, M. (1992) *Before I Was I: Psychoanalysis and the Imagination. The Work of Enid Balint.* London: Free Association Books and Guildford Press.

Mitchell, J. and Rose, J. (eds) (1982) *Feminine Sexuality: Jacques Lacan and the Ecole Freudienne.* London: Macmillan.

SECONDARY REFERENCES

Althusser, L. (1969a) 'Contradiction and overdetermination', in *For Marx* (Trans. B. Brewster). London: Verso.

Althusser, L. (1969) 'Freud and Lacan', reprinted in L. Althusser, *Essays on Ideology.* (Trans. B. Brewster.) London: Verso.

Buhle, M. J. (1998) *Feminism and Its Discontents. A Century of Struggle With Psychoanalysis.* Cambridge, MA. and London: Harvard University Press.

Butler, Judith (1990) *Gender Trouble: Feminism and the Subversion of Identity.* London and New York: Routledge.

Butler, Judith (1993) *Bodies That Matter.* London and New York: Routledge.

Chisholm, D. (1992) 'Mitchell, Juliet', in E. Wright (ed.), *Feminism and Psychoanalysis: A Critical Dictionary.* Oxford: Blackwell.

Elliott, A. (1999) ''In the name of Freud and Lacan: Mitchell's account of sexual difference', in *Social Theory and Psychoanalysis in Transition: Self and Society from Freud to Kristeva*, 2nd edn. London: Free Association Books.

Gallop, J. (1982) *Feminism and Psychoanalysis: The Daughter's Seduction.* Basingstoke and London: Macmillan Press.

Gallop, J. (1989) 'Moving backwards or forwards', in T. Brennan T. (ed.) *Between Feminism and Psychoanalysis.* London: Routledge.

Grosz, E. (1990) *Jacques Lacan: A Feminist Introduction.* London: Routledge.

Hoare, Q. (1967) 'On women: ''The longest revolution''', *New Left Review*, 41: 78–81.

Kaplan, C. (1979) 'Radical feminism and literature: rethinking Millett's *Sexual Politics*', *Red Letters* 9: 4–16.

Lovell, T. (1996) 'Feminist social theory', in B. Turner (ed.), *The Blackwell Companion to Social Theory.* Oxford: Blackwell.

Pallares-Burke, M.L. (2000) 'A Luta fermanente', 'Mais', 6–9: *Fohla de S. Paolo.* 15.10.2000.

Swindells, J. and Jardine, L. (1990) *What's Left?: Women in Culture and the Labour Movement.* London: Routledge.

Wilson, E. (1981) 'Psychoanalysis: psychic law and order?', *Feminist Review*, 8: 63–78; reprinted in E. Wilson and A. Weir, *Hidden Agendas.* London: Tavistock, 1986.

34

Edward W. Said

BRYAN S. TURNER

> The man who finds his homeland sweet is still a tender beginner.
>
> (Auerbach)

BIOGRAPHICAL DETAILS AND THEORETICAL CONTEXT

Edward W. Said is the Parr University Professor of English and Comparative Literature at Columbia University. He was born in Jerusalem in 1935, but his family became refugees from Palestine in 1948. His early years have been recorded in his recent autobiography *Out of Place* (Said, 1999a). He grew up in Egypt (where he spent his youth in British schools), Lebanon, Jordan, and the United States. The theme of exile has remained a significant *motif* of both his literary and political theory. Broadly speaking, anybody who takes the calling of an intellectual life seriously cannot be at home in their home. He received his BA from Princeton and his MA and PhD from Harvard where he won the Bowdoin Prize. His doctoral thesis was on Joseph Conrad, a figure who has remained influential in Said's later work on literature and colonialism. At Princeton he came under the influence of Richard Blackmur, one of the leading New Critics. From the 1960s Said became increasingly connected with and involved in Palestinian political struggles. In 1969 and 1970 he visited Amman and Beirut, renewing contacts with relatives like Kamal Nasser, poet and spokesperson for the PLO until 1973. In 1974 Said was Visiting Professor of Comparative Literature at Harvard and during 1975-6 was a fellow at the Center for Advanced Study in the Behavioral Sciences at Stanford, where much of his research on Orientalism was completed. In 1976 his book *Beginnings* won the first annual Lionel Trilling Award and *Orientalism* (1978) was nominated for the National Book Critics Circle Award. In 1977, Said was elected to the Palestine National Council as an independent intellectual and, following the outbreak of the Palestinian Intifada in 1987, Said contributed to the translation into English of the Arabic text of the Palestinian Declaration of Independence in 1988. Throughout the 1990s, Said has remained a critic of American foreign policy, especially the Gulf War, but he has also been a critic of Palestinian corruption and ineptitude. A collection of essays on Edward Said has been edited by Michael Sprinker (1992). Given Said's career as an engaged, cosmopolitan, and public intellectual, it was only fitting that he should give the 1993 Reith Lectures on 'Representations of the Intellectual' (Said, 1994a).

Said has made a number of important contributions to social and literary theory. My argument is that his apparently separate contributions (to literary theory, the history of intellectuals, and to political analysis) converge around a sustained critique of Western assumptions about other cultures, namely around the critique of Orientalism. This profile therefore largely concentrates on his *Orientalism*, the study by which Said's international academic reputation was originally launched. I conclude by suggesting that a major component of Said's discussion of intellectuals and Orientalism has been neglected, namely his tentative moves towards what one may call 'an ethic of cosmopolitan care', which, by a series of examples, attempts to chart a way out of Orientalism.

SOCIAL THEORY AND CONTRIBUTIONS

Said's social theory has broadly three principal components. First, he has made major contributions to contemporary literary studies, especially to the analysis of literature and colonialism. His principal contributions have been *Joseph Conrad and the Fiction of Autobiography* (Said, 1966), *Beginnings: Intention and Method* (Said, 1975), *The World, The Text and the Critic* (Said, 1984a), and *Culture and Imperialism* (Said, 1993a). These works have been critically received, but they are nevertheless an influential aspect of the debate on colonial and postcolonial literature (Fraiman, 1995). Secondly, he has developed a view of the committed and oppositional role of the intellectual in *Representations of the Intellectual* (Said, 1994a). This view of the critical intellectual is thoroughly illustrated in a series of critical analyses of the politics of the Middle East in, for example, *The Question of Palestine* (Said, 1980), *After the Last Sky* (Said, 1986), *Blaming the Victim* (Said, 1988), *The Politics of Dispossession* (Said, 1994b) and *Peace and its Discontents* (Said, 1995). Finally, he has made major contributions to the Orientalist debate in *Orientalism* (Said, 1978), *Covering Islam* (Said, 1981), and *Culture and Imperialism* (Said, 1993a). His work as a whole has given rise to much controversy, but the debate around his views on Orientalism has been particularly robust (Mani and Frankenberg, 1985; Yenenoglu, 1998). His work presupposes a particular engagement between the intellectual, the text, and society. I shall briefly discuss his literary theory and analysis of the intellectual before developing a full exposition of his views on Orientalism.

Intellectuals and Power

In contemporary Western societies, the state no longer assumes direct responsibility for the protection and promotion of high culture and instead relies upon the market to determine what constitutes cultural taste and distinction. Intellectuals no longer have the authority of the state and the elite institutions behind them when they come to pronounce on culture. They have as a result stopped being cultural legislators and are now merely cultural interpreters (Bauman, 1987). With the growth of an information economy, public intellectuals have become increasingly uncoupled from the state. In the eighteenth and nineteenth centuries, with the rise of nationalism, intellectuals had been important in defining national cultures – hence for example the importance of ethnographic studies in defining and shaping core values and standards. The commercialization of culture, the growth of mass culture, the integration of high and low culture in postmodernity, and the transformation of universities by economic rationalism has undermined the traditional role of the public intellectual. The great popularity of cultural studies and the decline of traditional departments of English literature in many British and Commonwealth universities are indicative of these changes in the modern university. Intellectuals no longer have the authority and state support that characterized the intellectuals of the late nineteenth century in the heyday of classical Orientalism.

Said acknowledges some of these changes in intellectual climate in his analysis of Matthew Arnold's *Culture and Anarchy* in *The World, the Text and the Critic* (1984a). Writing of culture as the best that can be thought in a society, Arnold was able to assume the moral authority of English high culture and the role of intellectual as its defender. Arnold could also assume that a strong national culture required a powerful state to impose its hegemonic force at home and abroad. The fragmentation of modern cultures and the growing hybridity of national traditions have reinforced the feeling among public intellectuals, not only that there are no final vocabularies, but that multiculturalism imposes a certain detachment from one's own culture. The intellectual context of contemporary Orientalism has thus changed radically since the publication of *Culture and Anarchy* in 1869.

However, these changes in culture and intellectual authority in North America and Europe have not had the same impact on Said, given his close cultural, as opposed to political, connections with Palestinian national culture. The issue of his involvement in attempting to shape Palestinian politics from a cultural standpoint probably explains many of the tensions and ambiguities in *Representations of the Intellectual*. The Reith lectures were concerned partly to chart the distance between contemporary intellectuals and the world of Julien Benda's *La trahison des clercs*, a cultural distance reinforced by global communication systems and the challenges to national sovereignty. The tension for Said is that on the one hand he recognizes that historically intellectuals have been central to nation-building (through for example the defence of national languages) and on the other that to be critical they have to be, like Said, to some extent homeless. As a result, nostalgia is the main vice of intellectuals.

The role of intellectuals is therefore bound up inevitably with the creation and the critique of boundaries and borders – physical, national and spiritual. Third World intellectuals like Fanon have been influential figures in struggles for national liberation, but then they must become critics of the decolonized new nations. The critical intellectual must go beyond the suffering and restoration of particular nations and cultures to assert and to explore the universal aspects of suffering and oppression, that is 'to universalize the crisis, to give greater scope to what a particular race or nation suffered, to associate that experience with the suffering of others' (Said, 1994a: 33). Often this critical stance will look like (national) disloyalty, but it means ultimately that the radical intellectual is always an exilic intellectual.

Said could be criticized because his view of the intellectual as an outsider precludes the possibility that the intellectual could be either a conservative or close to the seat of power. Said rejects the possibility of the philosopher-king as a combination of power and wisdom. Because it rules out the possibility that intellectuals could ever exercise power and influence from within the administration or government, it could be regarded as a romantic view of intellectual activity whose roots lie inside the Russian nineteenth-century view of the intellectual as anarchist. Said avoids this outcome by recognizing the institutional constraints on intellectuals in the modern world and by bringing a sociological perspective on the ambiguities of intellectual life.

This view of the intellectual as outsider is, as Said recognizes, a somewhat romantic image. In contemporary universities, the academic intellectual is quite likely to be funded by large corporations with little concern for critical public debate. Said takes note of the pressures on contemporary academic intellectuals to become more specialized, more professional and, by implication, more responsive to corporate goals. Said's somewhat modest solution to these difficulties is both to criticize the slide toward subjectivity in which all patterns of behaviour must be regarded as equally important and to defend international or universalistic standards of behaviour as enshrined in human rights legislation. Although certainty about objective moral standards is problematic in the relativistic climate of the world of the modern intellectual, we are not 'completely adrift in self-indulgent subjectivity' (Said, 1994a: 72). The tension for exilic intellectuals is to remain loyal and effective within their own national cultures, especially where those national cultures are under threat, and to remain loyal to international conventions on morality and human rights (Said, 1993a).

This defence of human rights legislation, which for many Third World intellectuals is in fact Western human rights legislation, may look problematic, given Said's apparent commitment to the epistemology of deconstruction in *Orientalism*. More specifically, Said overtly adopts the critical epistemology of Michel Foucault in *Orientalism* to question the notion of 'objective reality' in Orientalist criticism of Eastern cultures. Said has been challenged by various critics who want to argue that Said cannot be a deconstructionist in *Orientalism* and adopt a realist view of epistemology in his challenge to American foreign policy (Clifford, 1988; Turner, 1978; Young, 1990). In this profile of Said, I want to argue that Foucault is not the main influence on *Orientalism* and that Said's epistemology is consistent across his work. If there is any critical evaluation here, it is that Foucault's work is somewhat decorative in Said's writing rather than fundamental, and as a result Said does not embrace a critical postmodern or Rortian epistemology.

Said and Orientalism

The recent philosophical preoccupation with texts is a testimony to the contemporary assumption that any adequate knowledge of social reality must take into account the field of power which constitutes and makes possible such knowledge. The self-referencing of texts can only be understood as an interplay of power, and thus all interpretations of culture are an effect of power relations and power struggles. This principle of power/knowledge, which was central to the philosophy of Michel Foucault (1970), is clearly illustrated by the history of Western understanding of the Orient. While the modern debate about Western views of the Orient was (re)established by Said's *Orientalism* (1978), the anthropological controversy about the character of 'other cultures' can be traced back through the European encounter between Christianity and its antagonists. Said's controversial paradigm had the effect of establishing the notion of 'Orientalism' as a distinctive and pervasive ideology about Islamic Otherness. His critique has laid the contemporary foundation for an extensive inquiry into the problematic relationships between political power, sexual desire, religious identity, and intellectual dominance.

In the social science literature, Said's criticisms of the Orientalist tradition are typically associated with the critical social theory of Foucault. The representations of the Orient are seen to be manifestations of enduring discursive paradigms that constantly reproduce the Orient as an object of knowledge. This emphasis on the legacy of Foucault is mistaken, because it fails to recognize the obvious fact that Said is a professor of comparative literature and not a professor of comparative sociology. One significant influence on Said's approach has been Erich Auerbach's *Mimesis. The Representation of Reality in Western Literature* (1953). Written in Istanbul between 1942 and 1945, the work was published in German in 1946, and is a study of the literary conventions and their transformations whereby the truth of reality is represented by definite conventions of style. The importance of Auerbach, both as literary critic and ethical role model, is recognized explicitly in *The World, The Text and the Critic* (1984a: 5–9) and in *Beginnings* (1975: 68ff). In this perspective, Said's *Orientalism* does for French literary representations of the Orient what *Mimesis* attempted generically for Western literary tradition from the *Odyssey* to Virginia Woolf's *To the Lighthouse*. Furthermore, as I attempt to show in this profile, if Auerbach provided the literary tools of analysis it was Raymond Schwab's *The Oriental Renaissance* (1984) that provided the concept of Orientalism. To show these dependencies in intellectual genealogies are not to present a criticism of Said by showing his work to be derivative. It is in the nature of academic work to derive ideas, and in any case where would one start the story? From whom did Auerbach derive the brilliant idea of a history of representation?

Said's thesis and its criticisms are well known and I shall merely summarize its major components (Turner, 1994). 'The Orient' is constructed in Western ideology as a permanent and enduring object of knowledge in conceptual opposition to the Occident as a negative and alternative pole. The discourse of Orientalism creates a stationary East through the essentialization of the divergent and complex cultural phenomena of other societies into a unitary, integrated and coherent object for the scrutiny of Western literary and scientific discourse. The Orient is reiterated, represented, and interpellated over time and space by these ideological forces; the Orient is both called up and called to account as a subject of Western scholarship. While the Occident is seen to develop historically in terms of various stages of modernization, the unhistorical and stationary Orient exists outside of history. Karl Marx in the so-called 'Asiatic mode of production' contended that India and China had no real history, that is, no historical revolutions which brought about significant changes in the social order, for example through the introduction of private property (Turner, 1978). The Orient is, in Said's perspective, conceptualized through a combination of power/knowledge, and the lineage of Oriental concepts is mapped out by the historical formation of power between Occident and Orient, namely through the history of imperialism and colonial expansion.

The Foucauldian argument is that discursive formations are constructed around both positive and negative contrasts or dichotomies. These polarities constitute knowledge of an object; for example, we understand Islam through a series of contrasts. As a result, Orientalism produces a balance sheet or an audit of negativities between West and East in which the Orient is defined by a series of lacunae: the absence of revolutionary change, the missing middle class, the erosion or denial of active citizenship, the failure of participatory democracy, the absence of autonomous cities, the lack of ascetic disciplines, and the limitations of instrumental rationality as the critical culture of natural science, industrial capitalism and rational government. In the social sciences, this negative accounting sheet found its classical expression in the concept of Oriental despotism, Karl Marx's Asiatic mode of production and Max Weber's analysis of patrimonialism (Turner, 1974). The absolutist tradition of Oriental polities placed decisive limitations on the capacity for such systems to adapt and evolve. Weber sought the cultural origins of capitalism in asceticism, means–ends rationalism, and secularism in *The Protestant Ethic and the Spirit of Capitalism* (Weber, 1930). The Orient lacked the dynamic impact of autonomous cities, rational law, work discipline, and rational administration.

In the geography of the colonial imagination, the Orient is that part of the intellectual map by which the West has historically and negatively oriented itself. The noun 'Orient', which defines a geographical arena, is also a verb 'to orient', that is Orientalism offers a political and psychological positioning which constitutes social identities in a condition of social and sexual antagonism. Orientalism as a mental practice divided the world into friends and strangers whose endless struggles define 'the political'. The Orient has been the negative Other which defines the contested edges and boundaries of the civilized world, and thus regulates the transgressive possibilities of culture. The Occident was part of the ethical cartography of the West which celebrated the puritanical interior of moral responsibility and probity.

It is this geographic Otherness which defines our subjective inwardness; our being is articulated in a terrain of negativities which are oppositional and, according to Said, permanent and ineluctable. In *Culture and Imperialism* Said (1993a) claims that the modern identity of the West has been defined by its colonies, but these colonies are not merely physical places in a political geography; they also organize the boundaries and borders of our consciousness by defining our attitudes towards, for example, sexuality and race. Within the paradigm of Weber's Protestant Ethic, the aboriginal is defined as somebody who is not only poor and traditional, but licentious and lazy. Colonial policy and ideology produced a wide range of national types based on the myth of the lazy native. For example, in the evolution of Orientalism the plays of Shakespeare present a valuable insight into the characterology of such Oriental figures. *The Tempest*, written in 1611, was based on naval records describing shipwrecks from the period. Caliban, who is probably modelled on early encounters with the indigenous peoples of the West Indies and North America, is treacherous and dangerous, contrasting as a negative mirror image of Miranda, who is perfect, naive, and beautiful. Caliban's sexual desire for 'admir'd Miranda' forms part of the moral struggle of the play under the careful scrutiny of the island's patriarch. It is Prospero's rational interventions which master both storms and characters. It is in this respect the foundation of the literary analysis of modern colonialism, because the magical island offered Shakespeare an ideal context for representing the struggles between European reason and its colonial subjects as a confrontation between magic and anarchy on the one hand and reason and statecraft on the other.

APPRAISAL OF KEY ADVANCES AND CONTROVERSIES

The Critical Debate with Said

Having briefly described the principal features of Said's argument in *Orientalism*, I can now indicate some of the major criticisms of Said's perspective (Turner, 1994). He exaggerates the degree of coherence in the Western academic discourse on Islam and he also neglects the range of heterogeneous views which characterized different disciplines within the Oriental sciences. In the twentieth century, it is difficult to classify neatly and unambiguously such diverse figures as Gustave von Grunebaum, Louis Massignon, Wilfred Cantwell Smith, Maxime Rodinson, Montgomery Watt, and Marshall G.S. Hodgson in Said's paradigm as occupying the same location within the Orientalist field. In any case, Said concentrates primarily on literary figures (Conrad and Flaubert) and not on historians and social scientists (Wellhausen, Becker, and Brockelman). Employing the Orient as a mirror of the Occident, many radical writers have often used either 'Asia' or 'Islam' as a device to attack or to question Western culture.

Both Nietzsche and Foucault, who are obviously crucial in Said's own theoretical evolution, looked towards Islam as means of critically attacking aspects of Western culture of which they disapproved. Nietzsche's attitude was itself Orientalist, but nevertheless he praised Islam in *The Anti-Christ* as a strong heroic or manly religion in contrast to Christianity, which he treated as a form of sickness and weakness. Islam is 'noble' because it 'owed its origins to manly instincts, because it said Yes to life' (Nietzsche, 1968: 183). He argued that 'In Christianity neither morality nor religion come into contact with reality at any point' (Nietzsche, 1968: 125). All of its main theological concepts are imaginary. By contrast, Nietzsche praised Buddhism for its realism, its philosophical objectivity, and rationalism; Buddhism had already dispensed with the concept of God long before Christianity appeared on the historical horizon. Nietzsche's studies in comparative religions are ironic comments on the problems of religious truth in an epoch of relativism and perspectivism. Nietzsche's comparative critique of religion as sickness provided a foundational ethic for the analysis of the moral value of modern cultures. In Weber's sociology, this critique was redirected towards an analysis of the religious bases of utilitarian economics. In a similar fashion, Foucault in his journalistic writing on Iran in *Corriere della Sera* treated the Iranian revolution as a significant 'spiritual revolution'. The Iranian revolution provided Foucault with an occasion to express his emotional commitment to the idea of a spiritual revolution as a way of life, which contrasted with the mundane and routine reality of the everyday world. The religious revolution was a triumph of values over the profane world of materialist activity.

If Orientalism expresses a particular combination of power and knowledge, then it must vary and change over time and between different national configurations and traditions. Because Said concentrated primarily on French Orientalism, he neglected important variations between, for example, English or German branches of Orientalism. Furthermore, while there is good reason to believe that classical Orientalism created 'Islam' for example as a changeless essence, Oriental discourse itself changes over time. In the early seventeenth century, Muslim culture ('the Turk') was threatening and dominant, because the Ottoman Empire exercised extensive commercial and military control over the Mediterranean. These attitudes changed profoundly with the growth of European power through the eighteenth and nineteenth centuries;. One can distinguish between classical Orientalism which was dominant in academic circles until the 1930s, and weaker, less strident, and more uncertain forms of Orientalism since 1945. It is important to recognize that there have been significant changes in Orientalism in the second half of the century which reflect changes in state relations with globalization, the changing status of intellectuals in modern society and political changes following the collapse of Soviet communism. In short, globalization has brought about a sense of confusion in the world map, a sense of disorientation in contemporary scholarship.

Said's original theory did not consider the responses to these colonial changes, namely the growth of fundamentalism in many of the 'world religions' as a defensive protest against incorporation and dilution into Western consumerism and Western lifestyles. With the failure of communism, Islamic fundamentalism is one of the few remaining political options in the Third World as a protest against secularization and consumerism. One could also see the movement for the Islamization of science in the same light, namely as an attempt to check secularization and incorporation into a Western model of scientific knowledge (Stenberg, 1996). Islamic fundamentalism challenges the universalistic claims of Western natural and social sciences, and offers an alternative model of understanding and significance. In the context of globalization, many cultural movements have also questioned the dominance of Western literature and arts resulting in a widespread debate on decolonization, subaltern studies, and hybridity.

Because Said has associated Orientalism very closely with Zionism, there is a fundamental political and cultural problem about the relationship between anti-Semitism and Orientalism. If Caliban represents one formative figure in the evolution of European colonial literature, Shylock presents another. *The*

Merchant of Venice, which was written in 1596, has some parallel with Marlowe's *Jew of Malta* and expresses the anti-Semitism of Elizabethan England. There is a general anti-Semitism in Europe, in which antagonism to Jews has often accompanied hostility to Muslims. Generally speaking, the critique of Orientalism has not noticed the ironic connection between two forms of racism, namely against Arabs and against Jews. In his Introduction to *Orientalism* Said writes that:

> In addition, and by an almost inescapable logic, I have found myself writing the history of a strange, secret sharer of Western anti-Semitism. That anti-Semitism and, as I have discussed it in its Islamic branch, Orientalism resemble each other very closely is a historical, cultural and political truth that needs only be mentioned to an Arab Palestinian for its irony to be perfectly understood. (Said, 1978: 27–8)

In a reply to his critics, Said also noted the parallels between what he calls 'Islamophobia' and anti-Semitism. There are thus two discourses of Orientalism for Semites, one relating to Islam and the other to Judaism. Within Orientalism, there are two related discourses for Semites, namely 'the Islamic discourse of gaps and the Judaic discourse of contradictions' (Turner, 1983: 29). While Islam had been defined by its absences (of rationality, cities, asceticism and so forth), Judaism had been defined by the contradictory nature of its religious injunctions where, for example, its dietary laws transferred the quest for personal salvation into a set of ritualistic prescriptions which inhibited the full expression of its monotheistic rationalism according to Weber's analysis in *Ancient Judaism* (Weber, 1952). For Weber, the rationality of Jewish monotheistic prophecy was undermined by a ritualistic dietary scheme. The West oriented its identity between two poles – the lazy sensual Arab and the untrustworthy Jew. Weber criticized the Islamic paradise as merely a sensual reward for warriors; Jewish communities have suffered from the label of a 'pariah status group', because their social and geographical migrations were seen to be politically dangerous.

Throughout the medieval and modern periods, Jews disturbed the consciousness of the Christian West because they were cosmopolitan and strange. The notion of the 'wandering Jew' pinpoints the idea that their commitment to the national polity could not be taken for granted. Hitler's hatred of Viennese Jews arose from his experience of a seething mass of unfriendly and strange faces. While Jews were strange, they were also guilty of religious treachery. Now rejection of these two stereotypes was crucial, if Christianity as the foundation of Western values was to maintain its difference from other Abrahamic faiths. Precisely because Judaism and Islam shared so much in common (monotheism, prophetic and charismatic revelation, the religion of the Book, and a radical eschatology), they had to be separated culturally by a discourse of ethnic and moral difference. Jewish separate identity raised significant questions about the character of civilization processes in Europe.

We can now summarize this discussion by showing that Orientalism can be described in terms of two dimensions. First there is internal and external Orientalism in which attention is focused inwards on ethnic subcommunities or outwards towards an externalized Otherness. Secondly there is a dimension which is divided into positive and negative evaluations. Classical Orientalism involved a negative/external framework of critical rejection of the Other as alien and dangerous. The stereotypes of the 'lazy Arab' and the 'wandering Jew' perfectly express this interpretative option. In the opposite direction, positive/internal Occidentalism identified some communities within the nation-state as a positive expression of identity and consciousness. For example, in Victorian England there was a romantic view of Scottishness in which the heroic Scotsman could safely enter the English consciousness. Queen Victoria did much to legitimize this image of the brave Scottish soldier as the cornerstone of

British colonial power. This position contrasts with internal/negative Occidentalism that treated the Irish as a dangerous, but ultimately pathetic, adversary within the evolving British polity. Finally, there is positive/external Orientalism that converted the native peoples of North America into 'the Noble Savage'. This typology helps us to understand that Orientalism also produced Occidentalism, and that racial stereotypes can be both positive and negative. For Islam, there was a positive view of the manly ethic of Arabic nomadism which was embraced by writers like T.E. Lawrence. There was a strong movement of Orientalism that assumed a positive view of the East as a land of promise, sensuality, and difference which contrasted with the pale grey reality of bourgeois Europe.

Towards a Re-evaluation

The history of Orientalism is in large measure the depressing history of inter-civilizational misunderstanding, antagonism, and racial bigotry. However, Said (1984a) has also been concerned to identify a number of scholars whose work attempted to transcend the narrow limitations of the Orientalist tradition of which they were members. In this respect his observations on Ernest Renan, Louis Massignon, and Raymond Schwab are instructive, because they provide us with a model of what we might call cosmopolitan scholarship. Massignon's principal work was *The Passion of al-Hallaj* (Massignon, 1994), which provides a theological and historical analysis of the religious significance of the mystic Mansur al-Hallaj who became a martyr for peace in Baghdad in 922. For Massignon, al-Hallaj provides a religious figure through whom one can apprehend the mystical truths of both Christianity and Islam. It is through suffering that one can learn compassion, and through compassion a scholar might sympathetically approach and value other cultures. Massignon was, following a shattering religious experience in Iraq in May 1908, converted to Islam, although in his later life he also practised as a Melkite priest. A withdrawn scholar, Massignon became publicly involved in the protests against the Algerian War and in 1961 struggled with friends to drag the bodies of murdered Algerians from the Seine. In Massignon's theology of mysticism, the religious experiences of the divine presence in different traditions provides a common experience of humanity alienation and need for reconciliation.

Raymond Schwab plays an equally important role in Said's vision of intellectual responsibility towards other cultures. While Schwab's intellectual world was quite remote from the Catholicism of Massignon's work, Schwab's task was to understand the impact of the Orient on the West in the period 1770–1850, roughly that is from the French Revolution to the high tide of Western imperialism in the Middle East. In this period, Orientalism became a great adventure of human consciousness in which the polarities between East and West generated a new range of humanistic possibilities, namely a renaissance. This movement is opened up by translation for example in the work of Abraham Anquetil-Duperron, about whom Schwab (1934) wrote an engaging intellectual biography. While the first Renaissance asserted the similarities and commonalities of European cultures, the second Renaissance constructed a culture of differences through its comparative philology, historical studies, and sociology. Orientalism expressed the European need to assimilate and absorb the Other through a set of linguistic strategies, but Schwab's own position was driven by an implicit notion of 'integral humanism', of the need for a dynamic humanism which could transcend these differences.

My contention is that Schwab's monumental history of the first stages of Orientalism, especially the growth of Sanskrit studies, provides the model for Said's own *Orientalism*. Said's appreciative introduction to the English translation of Schwab is reprinted as Chapter 11 in

The World, the Text and the Critic. His discussion of Schwab recognized the scale and importance of Schwab's achievement which was to document the rise of Orientalism as a 'second Renaissance' and its interconnections with romanticism. If the first Renaissance recognized and addressed the internal diversities and divisions of European culture(s), then the second Renaissance recognized the existence of a dense and external world to which Europe had to establish an orientation. Schwab's account implicitly looks at the problem of intellectual responsibility towards other cultures through a detailed analysis of the rise of translation and interpretation. In my view Schwab rather than Foucault set the agenda for Said, which was first to understand Europe's appropriation of Islam and the Middle East alongside the second Renaissance research on India and China, and secondly to begin to probe the problem of intellectual responsibility for and with other cultures.

Said's analysis of writers like Renan, Anquetil-Duperron, Massignon, and Schwab prepared the groundwork for his subsequent reflections on the relationship between intellectuals and borders. In *Orientalism*, the academic Orientalists are condemned, often implicitly, because their relationship to the East–West border was unambiguous. They were committed to the superiority of Western values and religion, but this relationship to other cultures was far more ambiguous in Massignon and Schwab. Even Renan, who criticized traditional Islam for its hostility to rationalism and science, had of course employed textual criticism to write a secular history of Jesus. Said's views on nationalism and human rights can in this light be seen to be consistent with his views on intercivilizational dialogue as illustrated by his commentaries on Massignon and Renan, and by his reading of Schwab. Said, in his own political writing on the Palestinian movement and the Middle East, has maintained his borderland moral position. Said's controversial writing (Said, 1999b) on the political opportunities for Palestinians and Israelis in which he asks Jews and Israelis to cross the 'rhetorical barricades' in the 1990s is directly compatible with the essays in *The World, the Text and the Critic* and with *Orientalism*. The core of this position is not to divide the world into neat dichotomies and to exercise responsibility between the tensions of loyalty to one's culture(s) and to cosmopolitanism. *Representations of the Intellectual* expresses it perfectly – 'cultures are too intermingled, their contents and histories too interdependent and hybrid, for surgical separation into large and mostly ideological oppositions like Orient and Occident' (Said, 1994a: xi).

Conclusion: Intellectuals and Cosmopolitanism

In conclusion, I want to suggest that we could regard Said's moral vision of intellectuality as a defence of cosmopolitanism, which can be defined as the ethical world view of scholars in a global context where cultural hybridity and multiculturalism are beginning to rewrite the traditional Orientalist agenda. Said's sympathetic analysis of the work of Erich Auerbach in *The World, the Text and the Critic* provides a model of the cosmopolitan intellectual and for the concept of intellectual irony which I now wish to sketch in this concluding comment. For a discussion of cosmopolitanism, Auerbach is important for two reasons. First, he argued that the proper topic of philology was human culture as a whole, and secondly that it is not until we have left our (national and metaphorical) home that we can appreciate its true value in the context of a simultaneous appreciation of other cultures. Perhaps it is not too fanciful therefore to believe that, precisely because of their exposure to global concerns and global issues, the cosmopolitan intellectual might, in recognizing the ubiquity of hybridization, reject all claims to cultural superiorty and cultural dominance. This is the central message of *Representations of the Intellectual* that in reality the world is too intermingled to be (mis)represented as divided between Orient and Occident. Precisely because we are exposed to the global forces of postmodernization, the cosmopolitan ironist should welcome a stance which supports the diverse value of postcolonial cultures and celebrates the teaming diversity of human cultures. With an awareness for the tensions between local cultures and global processes, cosmopolitan virtue might come to recognize a stewardship over and for cultures which are fragile and precarious.

Cosmopolitanism can be defended morally, because exclusive national loyalties and ethnic solidarities are more likely to be points of conflict and violence in culturally diverse societies. We need an analysis of cultural membership therefore which will celebrate the uncertainty of belonging, where our 'final vocabularies' (Rorty, 1989) are never final. One can suggest that the components of cosmopolitan virtue are as follows: irony both as a method and as a mentality in order to achieve some emotional distance from our own culture; and reflexivity with respect to other cultural values; scepticism towards the grand narratives of modern ideologies; care for other cultures, especially aboriginal cultures arising from an awareness of their precarious condition and hence acceptance of cultural hybridization; and an ecumenical appreciation of other cultures, especially religious cultures. I believe that these values flow generously from Said's analysis of the pitfalls of traditional Orientalism, his view of the exilic intellectual, and his engagement with the Palestinian national movement.

SAID'S MAJOR WORKS

Said, E.W. (1966) *Joseph Conrad and the Fiction of Autobiography.* Cambridge, MA: Harvard University Press.

Said, E.W. (1975) *Beginnings: Intention and Method.* New York: Columbia University Press.

Said, E.W. (1978) *Orientalism.* New York: Pantheon Books.

Said, E.W. (1980) *The Question of Palestine.* London and New York: Routledge.

Said, E.W. (1981) *Covering Islam. How the Media and the Experts Determine How We See the Rest of the World.* New York: Pantheon Books.

Said, E.W. (1984a) *The World, the Text and the Critic.* London: Faber & Faber.

Said, E.W. (1984b) 'Foreword', in Raymond Schwab (1984) *The Oriental Renaissance. Europe's Discovery of India and the East 1680–1880.* New York: Columbia University Press.

Said, E.W. (1985) 'Orientalism Reconsidered', *Race and Class,* 27(2): 1–15.

Said, E.W. (1986) *After The Last Sky: Palestinian Lives.* New York: Pantheon.

Said, E.W. (1988) *Blaming the Victims.* London: Verso.

Said, E. W. (1993a) *Culture and Imperialism.* New York: Alfred A. Knopf.

Said, E.W. (1993b) 'Nationalism, human rights and interpretation' in B. Johnson (ed.) *Freedom and Interpretation. The Oxford Amnesty Lectures 1992.* New York: Basic Books.

Said, E.W. (1994a) *Representations of the Intellectual.* London: Vintage.

Said, E.W. (1994b) *The Politics of Dispossession. The Struggle for Palestinian Self-Determination 1969–1994.* London: Chatto & Windus.

Said, E.W. (1995) *Peace and its Discontents. Gaza-Jericho 1993–1995.* London:Vintage.

Said, E.W. (1999a) *Out of Place: A Memoir.* London: Granta Books.

Said, E.W. (1999b) 'Unoccupied territory', *London Review of Books,* 7 January: 35–7.

SECONDARY REFERENCES

Auerbach, E. (1953) *Mimesis. The Representation of Reality in Western Literature.* Princeton, NJ: Princeton University Press.

Bauman, Z. (1987) *Legislators and Interpreters. On Modernity, Postmodernity and the Intellectuals.* Cambridge: Polity Press.

Clifford, J. (1988) *The Predicament of Culture: Twentieth-Century Ethnography, Literature and Art.* Cambridge, MA: Harvard University Press.

Foucault, M. (1970) *The Order of Things.* London: Tavistock.

Fraiman, S. (1995) 'Jane Austen and Edward Said: gender, culture and imperialism', *Critical Inquiry,* 21: 805–21.

Mani, L. and Frankenberg, R. (1985) 'The challenge of *Orientalism*', *Economy and Society,* 14(2): 174–92.

Massignon, L. (1994) *The Passion of al Hallaj.* Princeton University Press.

Nietzsche, F. (1968) *The Anti-Christ*. Harmondsworth: Penguin Books.

Rorty, R. (1989) *Contingency, Irony and Solidarity*, Cambridge: Cambridge University Books.

Schwab, R. (1934) *Vie d'Anquetil-Duperron suivie des Usages Civils et religieux des Parses par Anquetil-Duperron*. Paris: E. Leroux.

Schwab, R. ([1950] 1984) *The Oriental Renaissance. Europe's Discovery of India and the East 1680–1880*. New York: Columbia University.

Sprinker, M. (ed.) (1992) *Edward Said. A Critical Reader*. Oxford: Blackwell.

Stenberg, L. (1996) *The Islamization of Science. Four Muslim Positions Developing an Islamic Modernity*. Lund: Novapress.

Turner, B. S. (1974) *Weber and Islam, A Critical Study*. London: Routledge & Kegan Paul.

Turner, B.S. (1978) *Marx and the End of Orientalism*. London: Allen & Unwin.

Turner, B.S. (1983) *Religion and Social Theory*. London: Heinemann.

Turner, B.S. (1994) *Orientalism, Postmodernism and Globalism*. London: Routledge.

Weber, M. (1930) *The Protestant Ethic and the Spirit of Capitalism*. London: George Allen & Unwin.

Weber, M. (1952) *Ancient Judaism*. Glencoe, IL: Free Press.

Yegenoglu, M. (1998) *Colonial Fantasies. Towards a Feminist Reading of Orientalism*. Cambridge: Cambridge University Press.

Young, R. (1990) *White Mythologies. Writing History and the West*. London: Routledge.

Young, R.J.C. (1995) *Colonial Desire. Hybridity in Theory Culture and Race*. London and New York: Routledge.

Index